Annual Editions: Race
and Ethnic Relations, 20/e

John A. Kromkowski

http://create.mheducation.com

ISBN-10: 1259395731   ISBN-13: 9781259395734

Contents

Preface

This 20th Edition of Race and Ethic Relations is designed

- To document contemporary issues in race and ethnicity
- To reveal the origins of race and ethnicity in the American founding and the ongoing construction and production of identities and groups through political, economic, religious, and social regimes and processes
- To address dilemmas traced to European conquests and the American construction of a new order based in the Enlightenment aspiration of universal liberties and freedom and the use of political and legal means to resolve conflict
- To review normative proposals for understanding race and ethnic relations that deepened the search for universals within expressions of diversity and
- To promote ways of acknowledging and celebrating the realities of American racial and ethic pluralism in America.

In America, race and ethnicity are significantly, if not essentially, contextual. They are shaped initially by original encounters with America and then by familial and neighborhood experiences. This volume focuses on ethnic experiences of persons and places that influence identities and communities. Such are the local realities or building blocks from which race and ethnic relations emerge. This volume traces the formation of ethnic and racial distinctions in law, methods of data collection, and policy regimes. Now, we all know that race and ethnicity are neither primordial nor fixed, especially in large immigrant-receiving and mobile countries. Beginning in 1980, the U.S. Census added the Ancestry Question to the Decennial Census and enabled us to measure race and ethnicity. This produced fine grain population profiles and geographical differentiations and a fuller understanding of affinities among long-time residents as well as the various patterns and indicators related to foreign-born persons. By 2010, the Decennial Census was supplemented by the ongoing data collection of the American Community Survey.

Particular ethnicities are covered in this volume. Understanding race and ethnicity based on the self-articulation of meaning and the reliable production of digital, interactive, geographically focused social indicators has become an expected dimension and variable in academic and applied social research and general public discourse. We also explore the dilemmas and contentions of contemporary pluralism. This volume provides examples of normative applications, ways of overcoming legacies structured by the past and embedded in patterns of social continuity, and an invitation to recover a tradition that values diversity because it is a dimension of our common humanity.

Several learning features are included to aid students and expand critical thinking about each article topic. *Learning Outcomes* accompany each article and outline the key concepts that students should focus on as they read the material. *Critical Thinking* questions, located at the end of each article, allow students to test their understanding of key points of the article. A list of recommended *Internet References* at the end of each article guides students to sources of additional information.

Editor

John A. Kromkowski is president of the National Center for Urban Ethnic Affairs (NCUEA) and Associate Professor in the Department of Politics at The Catholic University of America in Washington DC. Kromkowski is the Associate Director of The Council for Research in Values and Philosophy (CRVP) and a fellow of CUA Institute for Policy Research. He is the author and editor of scores of books, convener of a annual international, multiethnic forum and scholarly seminars whose findings are published in the series titled Cultural Heritage and Contemporary Change, accessible at CRVP.Org. Kromkowski has devoted years of public service and advocacy on the Boards of Nonprofit Organizations and advisory panels of local, state and national governments.

Editors/Academic Advisory Board

Members of the Academic Advisory Board are instrumental in the final selection of articles for each edition of Annual Editions: Race and Ethnic Relations. Their review of articles for content, level, and appropriateness provides critical direction to the editors and staff. We think you will find their careful consideration well reflected in this volume.

Unit 1

UNIT

Prepared by: John A. Kromkowski, *The Catholic University of America*

Contemporary Experiences: Persons and Places, Identities, and Communities

Articles in this unit provide a sample of personal and group ethnic experiences with race and ethnicity. Race and ethnicity vary enormously. Senses of identity and lived relationships as well as accounts and reports of group and personal identity shape our understanding of the ethnic and racial factor in America. Experiences related to race and ethnicity are generally derived from local situations and circumstances. This unit is designed to invite empathetic, imaginative engagement with a variety of contexts that constitute race and ethnic relations. This exercise will deepen your ability to ask and to answer various analytical and group specific questions that abound; because America is a large country with a stunning range of racial and ethnic populations.

Close attention to the experiences that constitute personal and group affinities and antipathy affords access to the drama of race and ethnic relations in America. American ethnicities and races are not ancient, primordial forms of human variety. America is among the very young countries of the world. As an immigrant-receiving country, the sense of nationality is fundamentally different and unique. In America race and ethnicity are social constructs: products of social entrepreneurs, responses to immigration, transplanted aspects of cultures and all are ever-changing adaptations to the pluralistic ferment of mobility and change in America. Races and ethnicities are ever intertwined into dense networks that vary from place to place. New ethnic groups are engaged with persons and organizations that have emigrated from the same regions of the world, but settled earlier. The clustering of all ethnic populations many generations removed from immigration constitute sets of local contexts that produce remarkably different patterns of race and ethnic relations. Such localism is a feature of race and ethnic relations that

are experienced in specific lived communities and their bonds of the shared values and traditions that are formative of both personal and group identity.

Newspapers and magazines frequently profile ethnic groups and such research typically presents case studies of local ethnicities. This evidence of ethnic experiences, found in many thousands of weekly profiles of ethnicity, immigrants, and enclave populations, provides accessible sources of information about ethnic organizations and practices. Relying on local newspapers and magazines for access to distinctive locations and their particular qualities are good research strategies. In composite, these findings are the pieces of pluralism that constitute metropolitan areas, states, small towns, and neighborhoods. This approach to exploring our social fabric, our consciousness of human variety and values rooted in American rural traditions, and transplanted cultures of other nations as well as uniquely American urban ethnicities, helps to avoid unfounded generalizations about various rural and national traditions that are becoming part of the racial and ethnic factor in urban America as well as impacting globalization throughout the world.

Reading articles that recount experiences of ethnic populations in specific situations and places is a way of engaging portrayals of unresolved dilemmas related to American pluralism. Ethnic clustering was driven in part by the "creative destructiveness" of economic growth and the bonds of group affinity. The social construction of pluralism includes choices, opportunities, and challenges experienced in both turbulent group relations and the hopeful processes of recovering viable urban communities. The process of forging new relations among communities reveals the development of new strategies and the formation of shared values derived from various traditions and articulated as each group negotiates the pathway from immigrant to ethnic American. Thus "becoming American" occurs in the ongoing process of addressing challenges and opportunities.

Reading articles that address the particular of places rivets our attention on the importance of local knowledge, the qualities of enclave cultures, and the attendant challenges. Such background is foundational for our ability to explore larger scale dimensions of race and ethnic relations and other forces that shaped cultural patterns. The particular social history of a region clearly shapes its self-articulation. A new overarching synthesis founded in the appreciation of American ethnic and religious pluralism must stand the test of social and political realism and

the various crises of the moment. The refashioning of ethnic and racial relationships in support of peaceful resolution of differences and pan-ethnic participation in citizenship require strategies of convergence and inclusion. Christians, Jews, Muslims, and religiously unaffiliated must discover or create pluralistic forms of group relations and use a new politics of values and the appropriation of deeper reasons for convergence among people and traditions. Such a search for order awaits imaginative leaders. New forms of social process are needed to renew religious, ethnic, and cultural modes of conveying meaning to persons who are attentive to various collective legacies without fomenting divisiveness and conflict.

Article   Prepared by: John A. Kromkowski, *The Catholic University of America*

S.C. Rampage Spurs Grief, Concern for Church Safety

Charleston Incident Also Raises Questions about Racism, Gun Policy

SCOTT DANCE AND MICHAEL A. MEMOLI

Learning Outcomes

After reading this article, you will be able to:

- Explain the implication of this murder on the questions of racism and gun policy.

- Summarize the reactions to this act of violence and the notion that churches are traditionally places of peace and sanctuary.

As the nation moved from shock to mourning the six women and three men killed by a white gunman at a black Charleston, S.C., church late Wednesday, chuchgoers gathered across the country Thursday to pray for the victims and for the 21-year-old man arrested for the shootings.

But they—along with leaders of other faiths as well as President Barack Obama—also began to process what the tragedy means for the safety of their parishioners and their communities.

"I think pastors everywhere are going to be on high alert this Sunday and for the next couple of weeks," said the Rev. Jamal Bryant, pastor of Empowerment Temple in Baltimore, an African Methodist Episcopal Church, like the one the shooter targeted. "Everyone all over is trying to get some sense around the insanity that is taking place."

After spending the night glued to their televisions and cellphones as they sought to comprehend what had happened and to pray, Baltimore pastors said Thursday they were focused on mourning. They acknowledged, however, a need for discussions over safety.

"There are a number of policy issues, but right now we need to pray that we turn to each other and not on each other," said the Rev. Frank M. Reid III, pastor of Baltimore's Bethel AME Church. "This is not just a black problem; this is not just a Christian problem; this is a national problem."

Speaking in the White House briefing room, Obama said he and his wife, Michelle, knew several members of the church, including the congregation's pastor, the Rev. Clementa Pinckney, who was killed Wednesday night.

Obama joined church leaders in expressing sorrow and anger over yet another mass shooting during his administration. He said it was "particularly heartbreaking" that the victims were gunned down in a place of worship, and decried the frequency of mass shootings in the United States.

"Now is a time for mourning and for healing, but let's be clear: At some point we as a country will have to reckon with the fact that this type of mass violence does not happen in other countries," Obama warned. "I've had to make statements like this too many times."

He said the moment called for a re-examination of the nation's gun laws, noting that innocent people again were killed "because someone who wanted to inflict harm had no problems getting their hands on a gun."

On Wednesday evening, Baltimore pastor Donte Hickman and 1,000 other black faith leaders at an interdenominational convocation in South Carolina were listening to a sermon when they heard that a gunman had opened fire at Emanuel African Methodist Episcopal Church about 15 miles away, killing nine people.

Fear swept the attendees as police escorted them from a North Charleston church to their vehicles, Hickman said.

Many local pastors said they had met Pinckney and other members of Emanuel through the tight-knit AME community. In addition to Pinckney, the victims were identified as Cynthia Hurd, 54; Tywanza Sanders, 26; the Rev. Sharonda Singleton, 45; Myra Thompson, 59; Ethel Lance, 70; Susie Jackson, 87; the Rev. Daniel Simmons Sr., 74; and DePayne Doctor, 49.

The suspect, Dylann Storm Roof, 21, was captured without resistance Thursday after an all-night manhunt, Charleston's police Chief Greg Mullen said. A citizen spotted his car in Shelby, N.C., nearly four hours from Charleston.

Mullen wouldn't discuss a motive. U.S. Attorney General Loretta E. Lynch said the Justice Department has begun a hate crime investigation.

Roof waived extradition from North Carolina. He also waived his right to counsel, meaning he apparently plans to represent himself or hire his own lawyer.

Joseph Meek Jr., a childhood friend of Roof's, identified him for the FBI after recognizing him in a surveillance camera image. He recognized the stained sweatshirt Roof wore while playing Xbox video games in Meek's home.

In Baltimore, a group gathered Thursday night for a prayer vigil at Bethel AME. Another 200 people were expected to canvass West Baltimore neighborhoods that have been the scene of heightened violence since the death of Freddie Gray in April, urging peace, Bryant said. Gray died of severe spinal cord injuries suffered while in police custody.

Leaders of other faiths joined in the mourning. The Baltimore Jewish Council said it was "deeply saddened by the racially motivated shooting" and condemned it as a "violent and heinous act of discrimination."

Amid the mourning, questions were being raised about the possible effects of the tragedy. Churchgoers were rattled by reports that the suspect sat in the back of a prayer meeting for an hour before opening fire.

Bryant, Reid and leaders of other churches said they already have security staff in place but might have to consider additional training and heightened alert. Pastors said they hoped the shooting wouldn't lead to more congregants' arming themselves before attending services, and that it would not make churches any less welcoming.

"Who do you not open the door to come in to pray or have Bible study?" asked the Rev. Ann Lightner-Fuller, pastor of Mount Calvary AME Church in Towson. "I hope this world doesn't have to come to that, I really do. I can't let that stop me from doing what we do and from loving people and inviting people in."

Hickman, whose church is rebuilding a senior apartments complex that burned amid rioting across the city April 27, said the shooting was a saddening reminder of racism in America.

Roof reportedly supported racial segregation and recently began making racist comments about the riots in Baltimore, Meek said.

"This guy's a kid from a generation that we thought was long gone," Hickman said. "It's just another picture of how far we have not come."

But he said churches should also recognize they will never be able to prevent all tragedies, as the shooting and the fire showed.

"Above all else, we have to practice a modicum of faith," he said. "You will never be able to protect yourself against every harm that can befall you. We should continue to live by faith and know that all things work together for the good, even tragedies like this."

Critical Thinking

1. What do you make of the notion and frequent claim that violent racism could be expected from older generations, but not from younger people?

2. Discuss the sources for the personal and the social consequences of intensely negative and hateful feelings about race and ethnicity.

Internet References

African Methodist Episcopal Church
www.ame-church.com

Centre for the Study of Violence and Reconciliation
www.csvr.org.za

Fellowship of Reconciliation
http://forusa.org

Funeral for Rev. Clementa Pinckney
www.youtube.com

National Crime Prevention Council
www.ncpc.org

Article   Prepared by: John A. Kromkowski, *The Catholic University of America*

Why American Jews Eat Chinese Food on Christmas

A lack of dining options may have started Jewish Christmas, but now it's a full-fledged ritual.

ADAM CHANDLER

Learning Outcomes

After reading this article, you will be able to:

- Describe the cultural history and context that created this curious bonding of Jewish Americans and Chinese Americans.

- Explain what made Chinese food and Chinese restaurants attractive to Jewish Americans.

If there's a single identifiable moment when Jewish Christmas—the annual American tradition where Jews overindulge on Chinese food on December 25—transitioned from kitsch into codified custom, it was during Supreme Court Justice Elena Kagan's 2010 confirmation hearing.

During an otherwise tense series of exchanges, Senator Lindsey Graham paused to ask Kagan where she had spent the previous Christmas. To great laughter, she replied: "You know, like all Jews, I was probably at a Chinese restaurant."

Never willing to let a moment pass without remark, Senator Chuck Schumer jumped in to explain, "If I might, no other restaurants are open."

And so goes the story of Jewish Christmas in a tiny capsule. For many Jewish Americans, the night before Christmas conjures up visions, not of sugar plums, but plum sauce slathered over roast duck or an overstocked plate of beef lo mein, a platter of General Tso's, and (maybe) some hot and sour soup.

But Schumer's declaration that Jews and Chinese food are as much a match of necessity as sweet and sour are, is only half the wonton. The circumstances that birthed Jewish Christmas are also deeply historical, sociological, and religious.

The story begins during the halcyon days of the Lower East Side where, as Jennifer 8. Lee, the producer of *The Search for General Tso,* said, "Jews and Chinese were the two largest non-Christian immigrant groups" at the turn of the century.

So while it's true that Chinese restaurants were notably open on Sundays and during holidays when other restaurants would be closed, the two groups were linked not only by proximity, but by *otherness.* Jewish affinity for Chinese food "reveals a lot about immigration history and what it's like to be outsiders," she explained.

Estimates of the surging Jewish population of New York City run from 400,000 in 1899 to about a million by 1910 (or roughly a quarter of the city's population). And, as some Jews began to assimilate into American life, they not only found acceptance at Chinese restaurants, but also easy passage into the world beyond Kosher food.

"Chinese restaurants were the easiest place to trick yourself into thinking you were eating Kosher food," Ed Schoenfeld, the owner of RedFarm, one of the most laureled Chinese restaurants in New York, said. Indeed, it was something of a perfect match. Jewish law famously prohibits the mixing of milk and meat just as Chinese food traditionally excludes dairy from its dishes. Lee added:

> If you look at the two other main ethnic cuisines in America, which are Italian and Mexican, both of those combine milk and meat to a significant extent. Chinese food allowed Jews to eat foreign cuisines in a safe way.

And so, for Jews, the chop suey palaces and dumpling parlors of the Lower East Side and Chinatown gave the illusion of religious accordance, even if there was still *treif* galore in the form of pork and shellfish. Nevertheless, it's more than a curiosity that a narrow culinary phenomenon that started over a century ago managed to grow into a national ritual that is both specifically American and characteristically Jewish.

"Clearly this whole thing with Chinese food and Jewish people has evolved," Schoenfeld said. "There's no question. Christmas was always a good day for Chinese restaurants, but in recent years, it's become the ultimate day of business."

But there's more to it than that. Ask a food purist about American Chinese food and you'll get a pu-pu platter of hostile rhetoric about its inauthenticity. Driving the point home, earlier this week, CBS reported on two Americans who opened a restaurant in Shanghai that features American-style Chinese dishes like orange chicken, pork egg rolls, and, yes, the beloved General Tso's, all of which don't exist in traditional Chinese cuisine. The restaurant gets it name from another singular upshot of Chinese-American fusion: Fortune Cookie.

Schoenfeld, whose restaurant features an egg roll made with pastrami from Katz's Deli, shrugs off the idea that Americanized Chinese food is somehow an affront to cultural virtue. "Adaptation has been a signature part of the Chinese food experience," he said. "If you went to Italy, you'd see a Chinese restaurant trying to make an Italian customer happy."

That particular mutability has a meaningful link to the Jewish experience, the rituals of which were largely forged in exile. During the First and Second Temple eras, Jewish practice centered around temple life in Jerusalem. Featuring a monarchy and a high priesthood, it bears little resemblance to Jewish life of today with its rabbis and synagogues.

So could it be that Chinese food is a manifestation of Jewish life in America? Lee seems to think so. "I would argue that Chinese food is the ethnic cuisine of American Jews. That, in fact, they identify with it more than they do gefilte fish or all kinds of the Eastern Europe dishes of yore."

Over the centuries, different religious customs have sprung up and new spiritual rituals have taken root, many of which draw on the past. Jewish Christmas, in many ways, could very much be seen as a modern affirmation of faith. After all, there are few days that remind American Jews of their Jewishness more than Christmas in the United States.

Critical Thinking

1. What is the function of food in ethnicity?
2. Does the marketing of ethnic food in restaurants necessarily promote interethnic visibility?
3. Explain the emergence of urban restaurant culture and the dominance of Italian Americans, Mexican Americans, and Chinese Americans in this field.

Internet References

The Anti Defamation League
   www.adl.org
B'nai B'rith International
   www.bnaibrith.org
The Jewish American Committee
   www.ajc.org
The Jewish American Congress
   www.Ajcongress.org

ADAM CHANDLER is a senior associate editor at *The Atlantic*, where he covers global news.

Article   Prepared by: John A. Kromkowski, *The Catholic University of America*

Wedded: Ara Adewole and Yemi Ajayi

Susan Reimer

Learning Outcomes

After reading this article, you will be able to:

- Describe the various components of ethnic marriage and wedding customs.

- Beyond legal certification of marriage and wedding receptions that are community rituals, describe what differentiates this wedding and defines the ethnic substance and ritual described in this article.

Date: November 1

Her story: Ara Adewole, 29, came to Catonsville from Nigeria when she was 14. She works as a registered nurse at Mercy Medical Center. Her parents, Fibi and Olu Adewole, live in Catonsville.

His story: Yemi Ajayi, a 31-year-old doctoral student in biochemical engineering at the University of Maryland, Baltimore County, is also from Nigeria. He moved to Maryland when he was 19. His parents, Grace and David Ajayi, still live in Nigeria.

Their story: Ara and Yemi grew up in neighboring villages in Nigeria. But she has no memory of meeting him at a party while they both were students at UMBC. He would eventually become her friend and confidant when a long-term relationship ended.

"Every time I would discuss a quality I wanted in a guy friend, I realized I was describing him," said Ara.

Yemi said moving from friendship to love with Ara was easy. "I just sort of knew. I saw exactly how kind and loving she was," he said. "The things she would do for me, I had never experienced."

The couple now live in Ellicott City.

The proposal: When Yemi asked Ara to marry him while dropping her off at her parents' home after a date, she said it seemed absolutely right.

Then Ara graduated with her nursing degree and Yemi decided to go to graduate school, and they knew it would be a while before they could have the kind of wedding their families would want. So they married in a courthouse ceremony in May 2011. "We decided we didn't want to wait anymore," said Ara.

She actually didn't get an engagement ring until last year.

The wedding events: When it finally happened, the wedding of Ara and Yemi went on for days. There was a rehearsal dinner on Thursday night. And on Friday night, there was a traditional Nigerian "engagement" ceremony at the Knights of Columbus Beaumont Banquet Facility in Catonsville, where members of the groom's family brought gifts of food and clothing to woo the bride's family.

"Before Christianity, that's how you got married," said Ara. "The groom's family comes to ask for your hand in marriage, and the bride's family welcomes them. There is a lot of back-and-forth between two representatives of the families. It is almost like barter."

There were bags of rice and baskets of fruit, as well as shoes and an umbrella—symbols of how the groom would provide for her and protect her. "You don't come empty-handed," Ara said, laughing.

On Saturday, the couple were married in a religious ceremony officiated by Hezekiah Ilufoye of the Christ Apostolic Church Salvation Center. But midway through the reception, both changed into Nigerian garb and the 300 guests enjoyed traditional Nigerian dancing and music played by the band Akin's Melody. On Sunday morning, there was a service of thanksgiving at the church.

Venue: The Saturday ceremony and reception were held at the Newton White Mansion in Prince George's County. "A family friend attended a wedding there, and Mom and I went to check it out," Ara said. "We were planning a fall wedding, and I could just imagine the colors outside the atrium."

Flowers and decor: Ara knew the atrium would be resplendent with a backdrop of fall foliage, so she chose red, orange and yellow-gold as color scheme to light up the glass-enclosed reception. "Nigerian weddings are very colorful," she said.

Radebaugh Florists in Towson did centerpieces of gerbera daisies, sunflowers and roses. Ara's bouquet was of calla lilies, colorful roses and red berries, while her four bridesmaids and five junior bridesmaids carried roses.

Her dress: Ara wore a Stella York mermaid-style gown from Cameo Bridal Salon in Glen Burnie for the service. "I was looking for something that was flattering and not too fussy. Something I could move well in," she said.

She changed into a traditional Nigerian gown and head wrap for the second part of the reception. Her attendants wore red dresses, also from Cameo. The wedding party also changed into traditional Nigerian garb during the reception.

His attire: Yemi wore a suit from Givenchy that he first spotted on actor Zachary Quinto, who plays Spock in the rebooted "Star Trek" movies. For the traditional part of the reception, he changed into a long tunic, flowing pants and a lavishly embroidered robe called an agbada.

Food: Rice is a favorite Nigerian food, and Ara and Yemi served two kinds: jollof and coconut fried rice. There were also two kinds of salmon—one broiled and the other piled high with seafood—and a meat stew that is common at Nigerian weddings. All the dishes were prepared by Flora's Restaurant in Lanham. Food for the 160 guests at the engagement ceremony—also steeped in Nigerian tradition—was prepared by Justine Catering of Lanham.

Special touches: Yemi's parents traveled from Nigeria for the wedding. "It was very important to me to have traditional aspects to our wedding," he said. "Granted, the bride's family are the ones who own the wedding. The groom's family are guests. But I was really happy that tradition was part of the weekend."

Added Ara: "We don't see it as two people coming together. It is two families merging before God."

Critical Thinking

1. Does continuity and transmission of ethnic tradition depend on the bonds of marriage, family, and community?
2. Explain the sources of culture that promote or diminish the importance of ethnic marriage rituals.
3. Discuss the demographics on interethnic marriage and its relevance to new immigrants.

Internet References

The International Center for Migration, Ethnicity, and Citizenship
www.newschool.edu/icmec/?v=
Library of Congress
www.loc.gov
Social Science Information Gateway
http://www.ariadne.ac.uk/issue2/sosig
Sociosite
www.sociosite.net

Article   Prepared by: John A. Kromkowski, *Catholic University of America*

New African Immigrants

Data gathered from 2010 US Census, American Community Survey and migration policy institute indicate that about two million African-born live in the United States; of which 53 percent are 44 years and under. They are highly educated, very religiously attuned and have strong family orientation. Increasingly, they are making the transition from legal permanent residents and acquiring status as American citizens. Yet this status does not readily translate into a sense of belonging due to constraints that are both external and internal to the African community. Many live in the space between; shuttling between two continents; remaining as sojourners in the American society and the Church, while their American-born or American-raised children struggle to find a niche. They form many national and numerous ethnic-based associations in an effort to maintain an identity within their new environment, and as a forum for addressing issues that confront them. Although these orga- nizations provide members a sense of continuity and belonging within the narrow context, they are a source of dissipation of resources, both human and financial; constituting a hindrance to the African-born quest for visibility within the larger context. The situation calls for a paradigm shift within the African community; for a different pastoral approach to the presence of the African-born and the gifts they bring to the Church. More specifically, it challenges African-born Catholics to see beyond their narrowly defined context of identity, to pull their resources together, and to identify with and engage the broader society so they can better address issues that affect them. Doing so will better position them to transmit their values to their children and provide a forum to inculcate in them a genuine sense of belonging to the Church family in the United States.

ANIEDI OKURE

Learning Outcomes

After reading this article, you will be able to:

- Know what the central challenges are that are faced by immigrants.

- Know what sources of information describe the relationship of new immigrants to others.

The African Born in the United States

Race classification is a complex issue. While this is not a cen- tral concern of this work, it touches on it in relation to the dis- course on the identity of the African born in the United States. The focus however, is to engage the issues of visibility of the African born in the American society and within the Church community, and how the African born find a welcome in both the society and the Church. The reader will notice that the dis- cussion on acculturation of the African born does not engage at length mitigating factors that lie outside the African born community. It mentions them in passing and focuses rather on ways the African born could maintain visibility and belonging to both the Church and the American society.

Characteristics of African-Born in the United States

Data gathered from US Census,[1] American Community Sur- vey, Migration Policy Institute[2] indicate that about two million African-born live in the United States. Figures from African community leaders are much higher.[3] The median age of the all African born is 36.1 years. They are slightly younger compared with the overall foreign-born population with a median age of 37.5 years.[4] In all, 53 percent of the African born in the US are 44 years and under. More than half reside in seven states: New York, California, Texas, Maryland, Virginia, New Jersey and Massachusetts. Between 2000 and 2012, about 600,000 African born gained Legal Permanent Resident status (LPR); of which 94,711 obtained LPR in 2007 alone. Within the same period more than 36,000 were admitted on F-1 (student) and J-1 (pro- fessional) Visas.[5]

Census figures of the African born vary between the offi- cial (census bureau) and other sources. These discrepancies are largely due to who gets counted for what purpose. The first is that many African-born, especially those whose immigration status has expired, generally do not get counted in the official census. The second is that when the census bureau says the African-born, it means just that; namely those who were born in Africa and are now living in the United States legally or are naturalized US citizens. However, many African-born heads of households would generally count their American-born children as African born. We see in this instance that while an African-born couple with four children might think they are six Africans in the household, the census bureau counts two.

The African born are spread out in major metro areas: DC, New York, Atlanta, Houston, Los Angeles, and Boston. They live in inner cities on first arrival and move into the suburbs later as they get better jobs and settle to raise families. They find the suburbs better environments for raising a family. This has consequences for the African community. They are dispersed all around. They are less likely to live in segregated areas so there are no large clusters of African-born communities; a factor contributing to their invisibility.

Other Category of African-Born: Priests and Religious

Presently, there are about 900 priests and 1,200 African sisters in the United States. They too are recent arrivals. A majority arrived since 1990. The number is growing. They are engaged in diverse ministries; in chaplaincies, parish ministry & education. About 5% serve African-born Catholic communities. Most serve the US born Catholic communities in parishes; hospital chaplaincies; prison ministries; military chaplaincy. They are part of the Church in the US; even in rural Midwest in Iowa. There is growing number in ordination classes; including those joining US based religious communities such as the Josephites.

African born sisters are engaged mainly in primary and secondary education, health care ministry and social work. They work for the vulnerable members of the society; they are an integral part of the Church family in the United States.

Compared to other immigrants, the educational status of the African-born in the United States is impressive. Some 48.9% hold a college diploma; about 20% have graduate degrees, 26% have less than college diploma (associate degree, registered nurses, etc.). 7.6% of African born in the 2010 census indicated they were not fluent in English.[6] These statistics show that African-born Catholics have some common denominators that should serve as strong basis for working together and building a strong community: (1) they share the status of foreign born, (2) they have a common language—English/French. Even most French speaking Africans also speak English and more especially (3) they have a common faith and, with the exception of the Ge'ez (Ethiopia & Eritrea), and Coptic (Egypt), they have a common rite—the Latin rite.

Living in Two Homes

The African-born tries to keep home tradition alive in many ways, including food which is used to maintain social relations. Many Africans come to the United States with the hope of returning within a few years to their home country. However, for most, the "few years" turn into 15, 20, 30 years and counting. In the meantime, they have investments here in the form of American-born children, homes they have purchased and are financing, social networks, citizenship and job. They have invested into the US economy for a long time by way of taxes and social security contributions.

In the meantime their long absence from their home country means diminishing connections even when they visit regularly. The visits lasts only a short time. They have less social capital in their country of birth and more social capital in the United States. Yet most have not taken the necessary steps to anchor themselves within the American society and the Church, and take advantage of their social location. Many still see themselves as "immigrants"; a mentality that contributes

to accepting their location on the fringes of the American society and culture. Some of this mentality is also carried into the Church community.

As indicated earlier, there are elements within the American society and in the Church that contribute to this feeling; elements that are beyond the control of the African born. However, the interest here is on factors that are internal to African-born community, things that lie within their control, and, consequently, things that they can change.

Identity Challenge to the African Born

Among the more than 40 million "blacks" in the United States, about 8 percent—3.4 million are foreign born, almost evenly split between Africa and the Caribbean.[7] The way African born and indeed all immigrants define their identities affects how they interact with the larger society and with the Church. Prior to arrival in the United States, the African born was identified by nationality and ethnicity. Upon arrival in the United States, they are categorized within the American mix (Black/African American). The African born ceases to be Nigerian, Tanzanian, Kenyan, Cameroonian, Ethiopian, Congolese, Eritrean, Ghanaian, etc. They ceased to be classified based on native language and ethnicity. They are now black or African American. Feeling somewhat threatened by this new and broad identity category; a category that effectively renders their treasured identity null and void, many African born resort to, and emphasize even their narrower ethnic identity over their broader national identity and seek recognition within this narrower comfort zone. This can be counterproductive especially if such narrowly circumscribed identity reference generates undue in-group sympathies and can slow down if not impede acculturation and integration into the broader society. Social identity theory maintains that strong in-group sympathies can give rise to out-group antipathies which in turn can fuel intolerance and conflict.[8] While intolerance on the part of a minority group can at best be symbolic vis-à-vis the larger group, the adverse effects on the minority in-group can be far reaching. It can fuel isolationist fears of the other's culture and a hindrance to genuine integration. The lesson from the Tutsis and the Hutus in Rwanda highlights this problem in a larger scale.[9]

Regardless of whether or not the African born chose to identify within the broader category of **black/African American,** they are nonetheless identified as such by the American public and the salience of stereotypes associated with blacks continue to impinge on their lives.[10] Like other blacks, the African born is saddled on a daily basis with finding ways to address and negotiate American society's assumptions about them.

Belonging to the American Society

The African born population struggles to belong to the American society. Even naturalized citizens have constant reminders: (a) they cannot be president, although this is applicable to all foreign born (b) their striking intonation makes them distinguished, (c) the constant questions: "Where are you from?" How long are you here for? When are you going back?—Elements that continue to place them outside the inner circle of society, even if mentally. While these are general questions that the foreign born are asked, the foreign born of African descent seem to bear the brunt of it. He or she is asked far more frequently than other foreign born living in the United States. From a cultural standpoint, such questions imply "you are not welcome here" for long.

Response by African-Born

In the light of the "alienating" atmosphere, some African born resurrect and hang onto the home culture and seek out a "welcoming" environment, including other non-catholic Christian churches even if that implies being an occasional participant. They resort to traditional associations. Again, such recourse to reinforce one's identity is not exclusive to the African born; it applies generally to uprooted people. In all, the African born finds that although they are members of the church family, that they are permanent residents and even citizens of the United States, their entitlements and rights can only go so far; there is a glass ceiling.

Reinforcement of Culture

There is no single African born identity. The African born tend to reproduce and reinvent themselves[11] once in the United States. One finds various national and ethnic based organizations across the country, including numerous non-profit organizations started by African born groups or individuals. A consequence of this multiplication is the dissipation of energy and resources among African born. But let us not misread this as advocating for the melting pot theory or the call by some integrationists for the annulment of the immigrant identity and recreating a new one that is fashioned the American way. Even in a true melting pot with a symphony of taste, individual constituting ingredients can still be identified.

Religion and Social Network

The African-born are very religiously attuned. For most, churches are not only religious institutions; they also serve civic centers and forum of socialization.[12] They serve as central networks that provide services such as counseling, shelter, employment resources, financial assistance, health services, real estate tips, etc.[13] These are central to persevering ethnic identity. Some African born have also started to create their own church congregations with loose denominational affiliation. The new trend in African communities includes creating separate churches where African born can worship as African congregation, some with Pan African flavor such as the Bethel Church in Silver Spring, Maryland whose services are rendered in English and French. Others consist only of nationals from the country of origin. This allows for worship in the languages of the ethnic composition of the congregation.[14]

Implications of Identity Re-Enforcement

The energy vested by the African born to create and invest in the micro-identity marker often seems counterproductive. The American society sees and identifies them in the context of black identity and attributes to them the general markers associated with this group. Yet the social arrangements within the African born community tend to ignore this categorization. Instead, one sees a continuous emphasis on, and engagement in the narrower identity circle and consequently in (a) Spreading thin of meager resources which otherwise could have been pulled together for a broader cause, and better service to the community; (b) Group fragmentation by resorting to close-knit organizations which is often limited to a very small geographic region. These close-knit kindred groups serve as important safety anchors, and do give a shot in the arm, in regard to a sense of belonging. However, overconcentration in these groups often isolates the African born from the larger context and slows their integration. The longer they keep together the harder it is to integrate with others. Sometimes, the resistance to integration is driven by concerns among the long standing "officials of the group" and their place in the merger should they occur.

African Born and Church Family in the US

The dynamics described in the context of the general society applies to the African born within the church community. They participate or better, attend church activities but many generally feel as guests. How does this come about? The reasons will be explained later but for now, suffice it to say that the observation is not indictment on the host community or on the African born but a simple acknowledgement the fact.

Church as Family

Most Africans see the Church as a family. The family is the fundamental unit of belonging; a place where every member calls home; a place where one would normally expect an unconditional acceptance and a sense of security. The family is the fundamental unit of identity. Within the family, members stand together shoulder to shoulder, the uniqueness of individuals are acknowledged and each is expected to assume responsibilities unique to his or her place in the family as older members and newer members.

An important aspect of the family is its role as the primary unit of socialization. Older members socialize new members into the family so that they can assume responsibility and carry on the family name and tradition within the larger context of society. The socialization process is crucial for the continuance of the family. It is an important undertaking and requires patience, dedication, commitment of time, and investment of resources; knowing that it will pay off in the long run. The family lives on through the next generation; the generation we leave behind.

Another aspect of the family is that it is the place where we learn the basic process of relationship—that for the family to function properly, we must imbibe the principle of give and take. As new members arrive, older members of the family adjust to accommodate the new ones. An important lesson the new members learn quickly is that the world does not revolve around them. There is a give and take relationship. The family of God is the greatest family one can ever have.

When African Bishops gathered for the 1994 Synod of Bishops, they adopted the theme: *Church* as *God's Family*.[15] For the Bishops, this was the most appropriate guiding principle for evangelization. Just as it is the fundamental unit of society, the Christian family is the primordial unit of the church, or as the Second Vatican Council puts it, the family is the domestic church.[16] The Bishops noted that the image of the Church as family calls attention to the rich concept of solidarity and complementality. It emphasizes warmth in human relationships, acceptance, dialogue, trust, and a helping hand when needed.

The bishops pointed out that *building up the Church as Family* avoids all ethnocentrism and excessive particularism. Seeing the Church as a Family tries instead to encourage reconciliation and true communion between different ethnic groups. It favors solidarity and the sharing of personnel and resources among the particular Churches, without undue ethnic considerations.[17] The Second Vatican Council's Dogmatic Constitution *Lumen Gentium* points out that "the Church is a sign of intimate union with God and of the unity of all mankind."[18]

New Paradigm for Building the Family of God

The US bishops have noted that "The Church of the twenty-first century will be, as it has always been, a Church of many cultures, languages, and traditions, yet simultaneously one, as God is one—Father, Son and Holy Spirit—unity in diversity."[19] The 21st century ushers in an era of world shrinking and calls for a paradigm shift in how we define and operate as a family of God. Today's high-tech media environment imposes on us new sets of challenges. Communication systems and means of transportation have reached an unprecedented height, such that distances that took months to cover a century ago are now covered in hours. In my last trip from Nigeria to the United States, for example, I had dinner in Lagos, breakfast in Paris, and lunch in Washington DC—all within sixteen hours.

Advances in technology, which has accelerated the phenomenon of globalization, spurred the intermingling of peoples, and call into question previously established boundaries and categorization of peoples, particularly nation-state, race, citizenship and nationality. Today the concept of "global citizens" emerging out of the Article 2 of the universal declaration of Human Rights,[20] multi-heritage and multi-racial individuals are part of our common discourse. This fast growing demographic challenges the traditional understanding of race and ethnicity.

Recently I came across a young lady from Mexico who is married to a Nigerian. Her mother is Chinese; her father Mexican. Her paternal grandmother is from Portugal. Their children will have ancestry from Africa, Latin America, Asia and Europe. What will be the racial, ethnic and cultural heritage of these children? While this may not be the norm, the future will certainly be seeing more of such families.

Responding to the signs of the time, multinational corporations have devised new ways of corporate presence and a paradigm shift on how business is conducted. American Express, for example, operates a twenty-four hour customer service. But how are customers attended to? From where are the customers getting their service? If you call American Express customer service department at 10:00 pm Eastern Standard Time in the United States, your customer service will be provided from Asia, most likely from New Delhi, India. Most probably, the customer service consultant in India is not sitting in the office to render the service but in a computer room in the comfort of his or her home.

We see mergers within the corporate world. Unlikely bedfellows get together to maximize their presence or for the sake of survival. It seems that the corporate world is living out the gospel of unity for the sake of the dollar and profit while the family of God, whose vocation is specifically to cultivate oneness in Christ, is falling behind. Jesus prayed that we may be one, just as he and the Father are one (John 17:22). The apostle Paul reminds us that in Christ Jesus, there is no slave or free born, Jew or Greek, male or female (Romans 10:12). How can we live out this vocation within the Church Family in the United States? What new paradigm is needed to bring together persons of different cultural backgrounds in the larger context of the Church family in the United States not as "separate but equal" but truly as a family of God?

The Second Vatican Council proclaims that the Church can learn from the world. The Vatican has taken the lead in learning from the world—modern communications, reaching out to the Society of Pius the X, building coalition with Anglicans, setting up a website and using modern means of communication to advance its ministry of evangelization. It is therefore appropriate to learn from modern forms of mergers, and training in cross cultural sensitivity and communication to enhance the work of evangelization and building one community from a diversity of cultures.

Borrowing a Leaf from a Mega Parish in Nigeria

St. Dominic parish in Lagos, Nigeria has about twenty thousand (20,000) parishioners. Many are not located within the geographic boundaries of the parish; they come from all over Lagos. The parish community is a mosaic of Nigeria's cultural and ethnic diversity. People from the East and West, middle belt, North and South come together and work together as a family; they have a common focus; they see themselves first and foremost as Catholics belonging to St. Dominic's parish. They take pride in belonging. Such a disposition pushes ethnic and linguistic differences into the background. Does this mean they have forgotten about or annulled their ethnic identities? Certainly not! Rather, they have brought their respective identities to fashion a much larger identity that is richer and more inclusive. The result is a vibrant faith community that continues to attract new members.

Catholic Christians need to learn how to work together; to see the Church family of God in the larger context; a context that transcends individual national and ethnic boundaries. This would be a true reading of the signs of the time in a world that is becoming more complex with among other things, increasing numbers of multi-racial individuals[21] and dual citizens which by themselves continue to challenge the traditional understanding of race and ethnicity; citizenship and nationality, and calls for redefining one's self in a given environment. Catholic Christians need to learn to read the signs of the time.

A Way Forward

African born Catholics retain a strong fidelity to the Church. They identify closely with the Church's teaching on marriage and family. Their rate of church attendance is much higher than that of American born Catholics. However, the participation of African born in parish life in the United States is generally limited to attendance at sacramental celebrations. Many are not incorporated as an integral part of the ecclesial community and thus few play a role within the Church; granted that they are limited as to the role they can play within the Church.

Given the American ethos of a self-made individual, the African born might be served better by applying President John Kennedy's famous inaugural statement which is restated and substituted here: "Ask not what the Church can do for you; rather ask what you can do for the Church" and of course with the understanding that there are limitations. There are instances where some African born have offered to be of service within the Church but were politely denied. There is a perception by some African born that the parish is self sufficient and therefore do not feel the need to support the church beyond the contributions to the Sunday collection. There is need to change this mentality and strive for self reliance. It seems that the onus of integration rests more on African born Catholics. They need to work harder at becoming an integral part of the Church so they can bring their gifts to enrich the Church Family of God in the United States.

Notes

1. The basic data is from 2010 US Census www.census.gov/2010census/data/
2. www.migrationpolicy.org/
3. The discrepancy is due to who gets included/excluded by the Census Bureau of which I shall explain shortly.
4. US Census 2010 www.census.gov/prod/2012pubs/acs-19. pdf Accessed March 20, 2013. See David Dixon (2006) *"Characteristics of the African Born in the United States,"* Migration Policy Institute;
5. Davidson (2006) op. cit.
6. US Census 2010; see: David Dixon (2006), The African born in the US, Migration Policy Institute (www.migrationinformation.org/usfocus/display.cfm?ID=366#13)

7. US Census 2010, See David Dixon (2006), The African born in the US, Migration Policy Institute
8. Gibson study of ethnic Groups in South Africa seems to suggest that this is not necessarily the case. See: James L. Gibson (2006) Do Strong Group Identities Fuel Intolerance? Evidence from South African Case; *Political Psychology* Vol. 27 No 5; 665–705
9. See Susan Fiske (2011) *Envy UP, Scorn Down: How Status Divides us,* New York, Russell Sage Foundation
10. The issue of identity is often misunderstood by those outside the "black" community and even by those within the "black" community. Negative media images of Africa on the one hand and hip-hop culture and the negative projection of images of African America youth, especially the projection of young women by rap music video generate mutual caution in regard to "belonging" within the community. See Fiske, op cit.
11. Jacob Olupona and Regina Geminacni ed. (2007), *African Immigrant Religions in America,* New York University Press
12. Michael W. Foley and Dean R. Hoge (2007) *Religion and the New Immigrants: How Faith Communities Form Our Newest Citizens,* New York, Oxford University Press
13. Olupona & Geminacni (2007), *African Immigrant Religions in America,* New York University Press
14. Olupona & Geminacni *op. cit.*
15. John Paul II (1994) *Ecclesia In Africa* Post-Synodal Apostolic Exhortation
16. *Ecclesia in Africa* §80
17. *Ecclesia in Africa* §63
18. *Lumen Gentium* Dogmatic Constitution On The Church, Promulgated By Paul VI on November 21, 1964 §1
19. Welcoming the Stranger Among Us: Unity In Diversity A Statement of the U.S. Catholic Bishops, Issued November 15, 2000 by the NCCB/USCC
20. See UN declaration of Human Rights www.un.org/en/documents/udhr/index.shtml#a2 Article 2: "Everyone is entitled to all the rights and freedoms set forth in this Declaration, without distinction of any kind, such as race, colour, sex, language, religion, political or other opinion, national or social origin, property, birth or other status. Furthermore, no distinction shall be made on the basis of the political, jurisdictional or international status of the country or territory to which a person belongs, whether it be independent, trust, non-self-governing or under any other limitation of sovereignty.
21. According to the 2010 Census, 1 in 12 marriages in United States are multi-cultural, accounting for 4.8 million interracial marriages. In 2010 15% of all new marriages were between persons of different race or ethnicity. Within the same period 9 million Americans or 3% of the US population identified themselves as multi-racial. For the US population under 18 years the percentage is 5.6. See: David Dixon (2006), *The African born in the US*, Migration Policy Institute; Wendy Wang (2012), "The Rise of Intermarriage Rates, Characteristics Vary by Race and Gender" From: www.pewsocialtrends.org/2012/02/16/the-rise-of-intermarriage/ Accessed March 20, 2013

Critical Thinking

1. What data sources were used in this article?
2. What challenges do immigrants from Africa face?

Create Central

www.mhhe.com/createcentral

Internet References

The International Center for Migration, Ethnicity, and Citizenship
www.newschool.edu/icmec

Library of Congress
www.loc.gov

National Catholic Bishops Conference
www.USCCB.org

Social Science Information Gateway
http://sosig.esrc.bris.ac.uk

Sociosite
www.sociosite.net

Article   Prepared by: John A. Kromkowski, *The Catholic University of America*

Police Stops in Ferguson: What Are the Numbers?

Walker Moskop

Learning Outcomes

After reading this article, you will be able to:

- Describe the documented policing patterns of Ferguson, Mo.

- Identify what determines police and community relations.

Ferguson police are much more likely to stop, search and arrest African-American drivers than white ones. Last year, blacks, who make up a little less than two-thirds of the driving-age population in the North County city, accounted for 86 percent of all stops. When stopped, they were almost twice as likely to be searched as whites and twice as likely to be arrested, though police were less likely to find contraband on them.

Pronounced as those statistics may seem, they don't necessarily make Ferguson an outlier.

The figures are provided by the state's attorney general's office, which collects the data from police agencies and creates a disparity index comparing the racial breakdown of drivers stopped to the racial breakdown of the driving age population in the police jurisdiction where they were stopped. An index of one means there is no disparity for a particular race. The index for blacks in Ferguson is 1.37.

Statewide, the disparity index for blacks—1.59—is higher than in Ferguson. The same is true for many other local police jurisdictions.

On the other hand, the disparity index for whites, at 0.38, is one of the lowest in the state. The statewide index is 0.96.

University of Missouri-St. Louis criminologist Rick Rosenfeld said the statistics for Ferguson don't stand out from many other St. Louis County municipalities.

"I don't think Ferguson would be at the top of many people's lists for racial tension between police and the community," he said.

Rosenfeld also noted that the attorney general's data has some limitations, specifically that it doesn't account for whether drivers live in the jurisdiction where they're stopped. This means that an index could be skewed in an area with interstate highways, busy roads or shopping centers. Additionally, an officer may not know the race of a driver when making the decision to stop someone.

Rosenfeld said the rate at which drivers are searched is a more useful metric. While the data doesn't prove the existence of racial profiling, the fact that Ferguson police were more likely to search a vehicle when the driver was black yet less likely to find contraband than when the driver was white could be more indicative of a problem, he said.

Breakdown of Driver Stops by Race in Ferguson

Local population %[*]: Whites: 34 percent; Blacks: 63 percent

Disparity Index[**]: Whites: 0.38; Blacks: 1.37

Search rate: Whites: 6.85 percent; Blacks: 12.13 percent

Contraband hit rate: Whites: 34.04 percent; Blacks: 21.71 percent

Arrest rate: Whites: 5.25 percent; Blacks: 10.43 percent

[*] Population figures are 2010 census estimates for persons 16 and older who designated a single race.

[**] The disparity index is the proportion of stops divided by the proportion of population for a given race.

Source: Missouri Attorney General's Office

Last year, Ferguson police searched 12.1 percent of black drivers they stopped, compared to 6.9 percent for whites. Contraband was found 22 percent of the time when the driver was black and 34 percent when the driver was white.

Rosenfeld said he was puzzled about why the stop rate for whites was so low in Ferguson. He said one possible factor is that the black population in the area, as a whole, is younger than the white population. Older people are less likely to be stopped, he said, and are less likely to be on the roads in general.

Critical Thinking

1. Are the policing practices documented in this case study widespread?

2. Does municipal fragmentation of metropolitan areas contribute to creating such practices?

3. What are the causes of racial segmentation and the racial gaps between the political/governmental leadership, the racial composition of the police department, and the residents of Ferguson?

Internet References

Community Oriented Policing Services (COPS) U.S. Department of Justice
   http://www.cops.usdoj.gov

Discover Policing Website
   www.discoverpolicing.org

LISC (Local Initiatives Support Corporation)
   www.lisc.org

NCJRS (National Criminal Justice Reference Service)
   www.ncjrs.gov

Urban Institute
   www.urban.org

Unit 2

UNIT

Prepared by: John A. Kromkowski, *The Catholic University of America*

Immigration: The Origin of Diversity, the Political Constructions of Disparities, and the Development of Pluralism

The political construction of disparities, immigration, and the formation of ethnic groups are the origins of ethnic and race relations. American diversity is embedded in the history and demography of America. In this unit, our attention shifts to the ongoing process of diversifying America as well as the key interventions of government that, at its outset, established and, more than a century later, disestablished the policy regime regarding race and ethnicity. Although ethnic variety was certainly a feature of colonial America, the U.S. Constitution is not focused on ethnic pluralism. The public sentiments of the founders suggested that the American idea was directed toward the creation of a new form of human order. They defined themselves not by "emigration from," but rather by "immigration to" America. Of course, aspirations and visions are more easily written than practiced. Reality and imagination clashed with the experiences of indigenous populations and the legalization of slavery. For these ethnicities and races, the American promise of dignity and freedom would be denied, deferred, and, at least legally, begun only centuries later.

The action of Congress, the Executive Branch, and the Supreme Court to redress the complex relationship between our constitutional system and the social and political facts of diversity has been an ongoing drama of governance of a pluralistic society geared toward equal justice under the law for all persons, in all states. Moreover, the history of American immigration legislation reveals a fundamental ambiguity as well as ambivalence toward the role of government and the best path toward equal justice for all. Diaspora, as a concept, provides a frame within which the clarification of the origins of diversity, disparities, and political development can be broached. The constitutional framework and the social and economic process, driven by a consumer market and the freedom it demands, have created an attractive ferment that is mirrored in the rise and fall of political forces that seek to influence the definition of citizenship and the constitutional and sociopolitical meanings of ethnicity and race.

This drama of definition finds contemporary Supreme Court challenges to voter rights and other aspects of civil rights consensus, which are embodied in the landmark actions of the Supreme Court. Concerns about immigration have turned to state legislatures, which may again turn to the Court for clarification about the significance of race and ethnic criteria in public affairs. Such expressions of popular ferment are played out in elections and referenda. The movement of public sentiment reflects the tension between the will of the people in particular states, the rule and supremacy of national law, equal protection, and due process. The mediation between laws and popular expression at the political nexus of state and federal legitimacy is a challenging and contentious aspect of race and ethnic relations.

The legal framework established by the original U.S. Constitution illustrates the way in which the American Founders handled ethnic pluralism. In most respects, they ignored the cultural and linguistic variety within and between the 13 original states, adopting, instead, a legal system that guaranteed religious exercise free from government interference, due process of law, and freedom of speech and the press. The founders, however, conspicuously compromised their claims of unalienable rights and democratic republicanism with regard to the constitutional status of Africans in bondage and indigenous Native Americans. Exclusionary practices continued even with constitutional amendments ending slavery established after the Civil War—thereby providing political inclusion of all persons—and the denial of representation in the House of Representatives to states who refused equal protection of the laws to all. Decisions by the U.S. Supreme Court helped to establish a legal system in which inequality and ethnic discrimination—both political and private—were legally permissible. The Supreme Court's attempt to redress patterns and practices of political leadership that has not persistently sought equal justice under the law for all persons, established a new politics that could mediate a relationship between our constitutional system and the diverse society it governs.

Moreover, the history of American immigration legislation, from the earlier Alien and Sedition Laws to the most recent statutes, reveals an ambiguous legacy. This legal framework continues to mirror the political forces that influence the definition of citizenship, ethnic identity, and ethnic groups in America. The legacies of African slavery, racial segregation, and ethnic discrimination established by the Constitution and by subsequent Court doctrines are traceable to U.S. Supreme Court opinions; congressional support for laws assures equal protection and the right to register and vote.

Two generations after the Civil Rights Era, our national public understanding of the thrust of that period can be obtained by reviewing the congressional deliberation in support of the Civil Rights Act and its goal of equal protection and equality before the law. Contemporary legal arguments, and the current judicial politics, pose a far more complex set of considerations. Careful analysis of our legal foundations and expectations for the next epoch of equality with the legal tradition will emerge from these reconsiderations and the new search for remedies. The implementation of desegregation, affirmative action, and voting rights have been challenged in judicial rulings, as well as in the decision to avoid court action that might compromise hard won gains for minority populations. The politics of affirmative action include advocates and opponents who have become more strident and exacerbated, competing for rewards and benefits. Thus, the claim to privilege and all that is implied in such has massively shifted public discourse and Even the most popular accounts of race in the American legal tradition have been changed and revalued in the crucible of persistent racism and ongoing political and media manipulation of racialist passion in the pursuit of remedies and privilege.

Over the last century, urbanization, metropolitanization, and central city isolation; the revival of immigration; and the expansion of the workforce, and the consumer market have, in a variety of ways, made three generations of Americans increasingly aware of the ways that group and personal identity are interwoven. These identities form complex networks of culture, economy, polity, and sociality. This perspective on American reality was fashioned from necessity and the moral imagination of the children and grandchildren of immigrants and others that constituted the demographic endowment of the United States. Their contribution was the articulation of the urban experience and its evocation of a new form of cultural pluralism—beyond the insularity, isolation, and dichotomous mentalities derived from the rural foundations of Anglo-Scot-Irish American culture. This Anglo-colonial cultural form, its language and practices of racial division, and ethnic group relations have been refashioned. However, the legacy of this dichotomous logic of social divisiveness has not entirely transformed. Xenophobia, racism, and color consciousness and their institutional legacies persist. Nonetheless, a re-interpretive project, in support of a more complex matrix of ethnicities, has emerged in research and in the practice of Americans. Moreover, the appreciation of various ethnic cultures and the legal defense of such claims to identity are constituting a new form of balanced citizenship and cultural democracy.

Article   Prepared by: John A. Kromkowski, *Catholic University of America*

Racial Restrictions in the Law of Citizenship

IAN F. HANEY LÓPEZ

Learning Outcomes

After reading this article, you will be able to:

- Explain the relations between the U.S. Congress, racial prejudice, and citizenship.

- Discuss the ways in which birthright, citizenship, and naturalization intersect with the development of race and gender in the development and change of the U.S. Constitution?

- Explain the ways that knowing the historical origin of government policy influences our understanding of current policy, debates, and directions?

The racial composition of the U.S. citizenry reflects in part the accident of world migration patterns. More than this, however, it reflects the conscious design of U.S. immigration and naturalization laws.

Federal law restricted immigration to this country on the basis of race for nearly one hundred years, roughly from the Chinese exclusion laws of the 1880s until the end of the national origin quotas in 1965.[1] The history of this discrimination can briefly be traced. Nativist sentiment against Irish and German Catholics on the East Coast and against Chinese and Mexicans on the West Coast, which had been doused by the Civil War, reignited during the economic slump of the 1870s. Though most of the nativist efforts failed to gain congressional sanction, Congress in 1882 passed the Chinese Exclusion Act, which suspended the immigration of Chinese laborers for ten years.[2] The Act was expanded to exclude all Chinese in 1884, and was eventually implemented indefinitely.[3] In 1917, Congress created "an Asiatic barred zone," excluding all persons from Asia.[4] During this same period, the Senate passed a bill to exclude "all members of the African or black race." This effort was defeated in the House only after intensive lobbying by the NAACP.[5] Efforts to exclude the supposedly racially undesirable southern and eastern Europeans were more successful. In 1921, Congress established a temporary quota system designed "to confine immigration as much as possible to western and northern European stock," making this bar permanent three years later in the National Origin Act of 1924.[6] With the onset of the Depression, attention shifted to Mexican immigrants. Although no law explicitly targeted this group, federal immigration officials began a series of round-ups and mass deportations of people of Mexican descent under the general rubric of a "repatriation campaign." Approximately 500,000 people were forcibly returned to Mexico during the Depression, more than half of them U.S. citizens.[7] This pattern was repeated in the 1950s, when Attorney General Herbert Brownell launched a program to expel Mexicans. This effort, dubbed "Operation Wetback," indiscriminately deported more than one million citizens and noncitizens in 1954 alone.[8]

Racial restrictions on immigration were not significantly dismantled until 1965, when Congress in a major overhaul of immigration law abolished both the national origin system and the Asiatic Barred Zone.[9] Even so, purposeful racial discrimination in immigration law by Congress remains constitutionally permissible, since the case that upheld the Chinese Exclusion Act to this day remains good law.[10] Moreover, arguably racial discrimination in immigration law continues. For example, Congress has enacted special provisions to encourage Irish immigration, while refusing to ameliorate the backlog of would-be immigrants from the Philippines, India, South Korea, China, and Hong Kong, backlogs created in part through a century of racial exclusion.[11] The history of racial discrimination in U.S. immigration law is a long and continuing one.

As discriminatory as the laws of immigration have been, the laws of citizenship betray an even more dismal record of racial exclusion. From this country's inception, the laws regulating who was or could become a citizen were tainted by racial prejudice. Birthright citizenship, the automatic acquisition of citizenship by virtue of birth, was tied to race until 1940. Naturalized citizenship, the acquisition of citizenship by any means other than through birth, was conditioned on race until 1952. Like immigration laws, the laws of birthright citizenship and naturalization shaped the racial character of the United States.

Birthright Citizenship

Most persons acquire citizenship by birth rather than through naturalization. During the 1990s, for example, naturalization will account for only 7.5 percent of the increase in the U.S. citizen population.[12] At the time of the prerequisite cases, the proportion of persons gaining citizenship through naturalization was probably somewhat higher, given the higher ratio of immigrants to total population, but still far smaller than the number of people gaining citizenship by birth. In order to situate the prerequisite laws, therefore, it is useful first to review the history of racial discrimination in the laws of birthright citizenship.

The U.S. Constitution as ratified did not define the citizenry, probably because it was assumed that the English common law rule of *jus soli* would continue.[13] Under *jus soli,* citizenship accrues to "all" born within a nation's jurisdiction. Despite the seeming breadth of this doctrine, the word "all" is qualified because for the first one hundred years and more of this country's history it did not fully encompass racial minorities. This is the import of the *Dred Scott* decision.[14] Scott, an enslaved man, sought to use the federal courts to sue for his freedom. However, access to the courts was predicated on citizenship. Dismissing his claim, the United States Supreme Court in the person of Chief Justice Roger Taney declared in 1857 that Scott and all other Blacks, free and enslaved, were not and could never be citizens because they were "a subordinate and inferior class of beings." The decision protected the slave-holding South and infuriated much of the North, further dividing a country already fractured around the issues of slavery and the power of the national government. *Dred Scott* was invalidated after the Civil War by the Civil Rights Act of 1866, which declared that "All persons born . . . in the United States and not subject to any foreign power, excluding Indians not taxed, are declared to be citizens of the United States."[15] *Jus soli* subsequently became part of the organic law of the land in the form of the Fourteenth Amendment: "All persons born or naturalized in the United States, and subject to the jurisdiction thereof, are citizens of the United States and of the state wherein they reside."[16]

Despite the broad language of the Fourteenth Amendment—though in keeping with the words of the 1866 act—some racial minorities remained outside the bounds of *jus soli* even after its constitutional enactment. In particular, questions persisted about the citizenship status of children born in the United States to noncitizen parents, and about the status of Native Americans. The Supreme Court did not decide the status of the former until 1898, when it ruled in *U.S. v. Wong Kim Ark* that native-born children of aliens, even those permanently barred by race from acquiring citizenship, were birthright citizens of the United States.[17] On the citizenship of the latter, the Supreme Court answered negatively in 1884, holding in *Elk v. Wilkins* that Native Americans owed allegiance to their tribe and so did not acquire citizenship upon birth.[18] Congress responded by granting Native Americans citizenship in piecemeal fashion, often tribe by tribe. Not until 1924 did Congress pass an act conferring citizenship on all Native Americans in the United States.[19] Even then, however, questions arose regarding the citizenship of those born in the United States after the effective date of the 1924 act. These questions were finally resolved, and *jus soli* fully applied, under the Nationality Act of 1940, which specifically bestowed citizenship on all those born in the United States

"to a member of an Indian, Eskimo, Aleutian, or other aboriginal tribe."[20] Thus, the basic law of citizenship, that a person born here is a citizen here, did not include all racial minorities until 1940.

Unfortunately, the impulse to restrict birthright citizenship by race is far from dead in this country. Apparently, California Governor Pete Wilson and many others seek a return to the times when citizenship depended on racial proxies such as immigrant status. Wilson has called for a federal constitutional amendment that would prevent the American-born children of undocumented persons from receiving birthright citizenship.[21] His call has not been ignored: thirteen members of Congress recently sponsored a constitutional amendment that would repeal the existing Citizenship Clause of the Fourteenth Amendment and replace it with a provision that "All persons born in the United States . . . of mothers who are citizens or legal residents of the United States . . . are citizens of the United States."[22] Apparently, such a change is supported by 49 percent of Americans.[23] In addition to explicitly discriminating against fathers by eliminating their right to confer citizenship through parentage, this proposal implicitly discriminates along racial lines. The effort to deny citizenship to children born here to undocumented immigrants seems to be motivated not by an abstract concern over the political status of the parents, but by racial animosity against Asians and Latinos, those commonly seen as comprising the vast bulk of undocumented migrants. Bill Ong Hing writes, "The discussion of who is and who is not American, who can and cannot become American, goes beyond the technicalities of citizenship and residency requirements; it strikes at the very heart of our nation's long and troubled legacy of race relations.[24] As this troubled legacy reveals, the triumph over racial discrimination in the laws of citizenship and alienage came slowly and only recently. In the campaign for the "control of our borders," we are once again debating the citizenship of the native-born and the merits of *Dred Scott.*[25]

Naturalization

Although the Constitution did not originally define the citizenry, it explicitly gave Congress the authority to establish the criteria for granting citizenship after birth. Article I grants Congress the power "To establish a uniform Rule of Naturalization."[26] From the start, Congress exercised this power in a manner that burdened naturalization laws with racial restrictions that tracked those in the law of birthright citizenship. In 1790, only a few months after ratification of the Constitution, Congress limited naturalization to "any alien, being a free white person who shall have resided within the limits and under the jurisdiction of the United States for a term of two years."[27] This clause mirrored not only the de facto laws of birthright citizenship, but also the racially restrictive naturalization laws of several states. At least three states had previously limited citizenship to "white persons": Virginia in 1779, South Carolina in 1784, and Georgia in 1785.[28] Though there would be many subsequent changes in the requirements for federal naturalization, racial identity endured as a bedrock requirement for the next

162 years. In every naturalization act from 1790 until 1952, Congress included the "white person" prerequisite.[29]

The history of racial prerequisites to naturalization can be divided into two periods of approximately eighty years each. The first period extended from 1790 to 1870, when only Whites were able to naturalize. In the wake of the Civil War, the "white person" restriction on naturalization came under serious attack as part of the effort to expunge *Dred Scott*. Some congressmen, Charles Sumner chief among them, argued that racial barriers to naturalization should be struck altogether. However, racial prejudice against Native Americans and Asians forestalled the complete elimination of the racial prerequisites. During congressional debates, one senator argued against conferring "the rank, privileges, and immunities of citizenship upon the cruel savages who destroyed [Minnesota's] peaceful settlements and massacred the people with circumstances of atrocity too horrible to relate."[30] Another senator wondered "whether this door [of citizenship] shall now be thrown open to the Asiatic population," warning that to do so would spell for the Pacific coast "an end to republican government there, because it is very well ascertained that those people have no appreciation of that form of government; it seems to be obnoxious to their very nature; they seem to be incapable either of understanding or carrying it out."[31] Sentiments such as these ensured that even after the Civil War, bars against Native American and Asian naturalization would continue.[32] Congress opted to maintain the "white person" prerequisite, but to extend the right to naturalize to "persons of African nativity, or African descent."[33] After 1870, Blacks as well as Whites could naturalize, but not others.

During the second period, from 1870 until the last of the prerequisite laws were abolished in 1952, the White-Black dichotomy in American race relations dominated naturalization law. During this period, Whites and Blacks were eligible for citizenship, but others, particularly those from Asia, were not. Indeed, increasing antipathy toward Asians on the West Coast resulted in an explicit disqualification of Chinese persons from naturalization in 1882.[34] The prohibition of Chinese naturalization, the only U.S. law ever to exclude by name a particular nationality from citizenship, was coupled with the ban on Chinese immigration discussed previously. The Supreme Court readily upheld the bar, writing that "Chinese persons not born in this country have never been recognized as citizens of the United States, nor authorized to become such under the naturalization laws."[35] While Blacks were permitted to naturalize beginning in 1870, the Chinese and most "other non-Whites" would have to wait until the 1940s for the right to naturalize.[36]

World War II forced a domestic reconsideration of the racism integral to U.S. naturalization law. In 1935, Hitler's Germany limited citizenship to members of the Aryan race, making Germany the only country other than the United States with a racial restriction on naturalization.[37] The fact of this bad company was not lost on those administering our naturalization laws. "When Earl G. Harrison in 1944 resigned as United States Commissioner of Immigration and Naturalization, he said that the only country in the world, outside the United States, that observes racial discrimination in matters relating to naturalization was Nazi Germany, 'and we all agree that this is not very desirable company.'"[38] Furthermore, the United States was open to charges of hypocrisy for banning from naturalization the nationals of many of its Asian allies. During the war, the United States seemed through some of its laws and social practices to embrace the same racism it was fighting. Both fronts of the war exposed profound inconsistencies between U.S. naturalization law and broader social ideals. These considerations, among others, led Congress to begin a process of piecemeal reform in the laws governing citizenship.

In 1940, Congress opened naturalization to "descendants of races indigenous to the Western Hemisphere."[39] Apparently, this "additional limitation was designed 'to more fully cement' the ties of Pan-Americanism" at a time of impending crisis.[40] In 1943, Congress replaced the prohibition on the naturalization of Chinese persons with a provision explicitly granting them this boon.[41] In 1946, it opened up naturalization to persons from the Philippines and India as well.[42] Thus, at the end of the war, our naturalization law looked like this:

The right to become a naturalized citizen under the provisions of this Act shall extend only to—

1. white persons, persons of African nativity or descent, and persons of races indigenous to the continents of North or South America or adjacent islands and Filipino persons or persons of Filipino descent;
2. persons who possess, either singly or in combination, a preponderance of blood of one or more of the classes specified in clause (1);
3. Chinese persons or persons of Chinese descent; and persons of races indigenous to India; and
4. persons who possess, either singly or in combination, a preponderance of blood of one or more of the classes specified in clause (3) or, either singly or in combination, as much as one-half blood of those classes and some additional blood of one of the classes specified in clause (1).[43]

This incremental retreat from a "Whites only" conception of citizenship made the arbitrariness of U.S. naturalization law increasingly obvious. For example, under the above statute, the right to acquire citizenship depended for some on blood-quantum distinctions based on descent from peoples indigenous to islands adjacent to the Americas. In 1952, Congress moved towards wholesale reform, overhauling the naturalization statute to read simply that "[t]he right of a person to become a naturalized citizen of the United States shall not be denied or abridged because of race or sex or because such person is married."[44] Thus, in 1952, racial bars on naturalization came to an official end.[45]

Notice the mention of gender in the statutory language ending racial restrictions in naturalization. The issue of women and citizenship can only be touched on here, but deserves significant study in its own right.[46] As the language of the 1952 Act implies, eligibility for naturalization once depended on a woman's marital status. Congress in 1855 declared that a foreign woman automatically acquired citizenship upon marriage to a U.S. citizen, or upon the naturalization of her alien husband.[47] This provision built upon the supposition that a woman's social and political status flowed from her husband. As an 1895 treatise on naturalization put it, "A woman partakes of her husband's nationality; her nationality is merged in that of her husband; her political status follows that of her husband."[48] A wife's acquisition of citizenship, however, remained subject to her individual qualification for naturalization—that is, on whether she was a "white person."[49] Thus, the Supreme Court held in 1868 that only "white women" could gain citizenship by marrying a citizen.[50] Racial restrictions further complicated matters for noncitizen women in that naturalization was denied to those married to a man racially ineligible for citizenship, irrespective of the woman's own qualifications, racial or otherwise.[51] The automatic naturalization of a woman upon her marriage to a citizen or upon the naturalization of her husband ended in 1922.[52]

The citizenship of American-born women was also affected by the interplay of gender and racial restrictions. Even though under English common law a woman's nationality was unaffected by marriage, many courts in this country stripped women who married noncitizens of their U.S. citizenship.[53] Congress recognized and mandated this practice in 1907, legislating that an American woman's marriage to an alien terminated her citizenship.[54] Under considerable pressure, Congress partially repealed this act in 1922.[55] However, the 1922 act continued to require the expatriation of any woman who married a foreigner racially barred from citizenship, flatly declaring that "any woman citizen who marries an alien ineligible to citizenship shall cease to be a citizen."[56] Until Congress repealed this provision in 1931,[57] marriage to a non-White alien by an American woman was akin to treason against this country: either of these acts justified the stripping of citizenship from someone American by birth. Indeed, a woman's marriage to a non-White foreigner was perhaps a worse crime, for while a traitor lost his citizenship only after trial, the woman lost hers automatically.[58] The laws governing the racial composition of this country's citizenry came inseverably bound up with and exacerbated by sexism. It is in this context of combined racial and gender prejudice that we should understand the absence of any women among the petitioners named in the prerequisite cases: it is not that women were unaffected by the racial bars, but that they were doubly bound by them, restricted both as individuals, and as less than individuals (that is, as wives).

Notes

1. U.S. COMMISSION ON CIVIL RIGHTS, THE TARNISHED GOLDEN DOOR: CIVIL RIGHTS ISSUES IN IMMIGRATION 1–12 (1990).

2. Chinese Exclusion Act, ch. 126, 22 Stat. 58 (1882). *See generally* Harold Hongju Koh, *Bitter Fruit of the Asian Immigration Cases,* 6 CONSTITUTION 69 (1994). For a sobering account of the many lynchings of Chinese in the western United States during this period, *see* John R. Wunder, *Anti-Chinese Violence in the American West, 1850–1910,* LAW FOR THE ELEPHANT, LAW FOR THE BEAVER: ESSAYS IN THE LEGAL HISTORY OF THE NORTH AMERICAN WEST 212 (John McLaren, Hamar Foster, and Chet Orloff eds., 1992). Charles McClain, Jr., discusses the historical origins of anti-Chinese prejudice and the legal responses undertaken by that community on the West Coast. Charles McClain, Jr., *The Chinese Struggle for Civil Rights in Nineteenth Century America: The First Phase, 1850–1870,* 72 CAL. L. REV. 529 (1984). For a discussion of contemporary racial violence against Asian Americans, *see* Note, *Racial Violence against Asian Americans,* 106 HARV. L. REV. 1926 (1993); Robert Chang, *Toward an Asian American Legal Scholarship: Critical Race Theory, Post-Structuralism, and Narrative Space,* 81 CAL. L. REV. 1241, 1251–58 (1993).

3. Act of July 9, 1884, ch. 220, 23 Stat. 115; Act of May 5, 1892, ch. 60, 27 Stat. 25; Act of April 29, 1902, ch. 641, 32 Stat. 176; Act of April 27, 1904, ch. 1630, 33 Stat. 428.

4. Act of Feb. 5, 1917, ch. 29, 39 Stat. 874.

5. U.S. COMMISSION ON CIVIL RIGHTS, *supra,* at 9.

6. *Id. See* Act of May 19, 1921, ch. 8, 42 Stat. 5; Act of May 26, 1924, ch. 190, 43 Stat. 153.

7. U.S. COMMISSION ON CIVIL RIGHTS, *supra,* at 10.

8. *Id.* at 11. *See generally* JUAN RAMON GARCIA, OPERATION WETBACK: THE MASS DEPORTATION OF MEXICAN UNDOCUMENTED WORKERS IN 1954 (1980).

9. Act of Oct. 2, 1965, 79 Stat. 911.

10. Chae Chan Ping v. United States, 130 U.S. 581 (1889). The Court reasoned in part that if "the government of the United States, through its legislative department, considers the presence of foreigners of a different race in this country, who will not assimilate with us, to be dangerous to its peace and security, their exclusion is not to be stayed." For a critique of this deplorable result, *see* Louis Henkin, *The Constitution and United States Sovereignty: A Century of Chinese Exclusion and Its Progeny,* 100 HARV. L. REV. 853 (1987).

11. For efforts to encourage Irish immigration, *see, e.g., Immigration Act of 1990, § 131, 104 Stat. 4978 (codified as amended at 8 U.S.C. § 1153 (c) [1994]).* Bill Ong Hing argues that Congress continues to discriminate against Asians. *"Through an examination of past exclusion laws, previous legislation, and the specific provisions of the Immigration Act of 1990, the conclusion can be drawn that Congress never intended to make up for nearly 80 years of Asian exclusion, and that a conscious hostility towards persons of Asian descent continues to pervade Congressional circles."* Bill Ong Hing, Asian Americans and Present U.S. Immigration Policies: A Legacy of Asian Exclusion, *ASIAN AMERICANS AND THE SUPREME COURT: A DOCUMENTARY HISTORY 1106, 1107 (Hyung-Chan Kim ed., 1992).*

12. Louis DeSipio and Harry Pachon, Making Americans: Administrative Discretion and Americanization, *12 CHICANO-LATINO L. REV. 52, 53 (1992).*

13. CHARLES GORDON AND STANLEY MAILMAN, IMMIGRATION LAW AND PROCEDURE § 92.03[1][b] (rev. ed. 1992).

14. Dred Scott v. Sandford, 60 U.S. (19 How.) 393 (1857). For an insightful discussion of the role of *Dred Scott* in the development of American citizenship, see JAMES KETTNER, *THE DEVELOPMENT OF AMERICAN CITIZENSHIP, 1608–1870, at 300–333 (1978); see also KENNETH L. KARST, BELONGING TO AMERICA: EQUAL CITIZENSHIP AND THE CONSTITUTION 43–61 (1989).*

15. Civil Rights Act of 1866, ch. 31, 14 Stat. 27.

16. U.S. Const. amend. XIV.

17. 169 U.S. 649 (1898).

18. 112 U.S. 94 (1884).

19. Act of June 2, 1924, ch. 233, 43 Stat. 253.

20. Nationality Act of 1940, § 201(b), 54 Stat. 1138. See generally *GORDON AND MAILMAN, supra, at § 92.03[3][e].*

21. Pete Wilson, Crack Down on Illegals, *USA TODAY, Aug. 20, 1993, at 12A.*

22. H. R. J. Res. 129, 103d Cong., 1st Sess. (1993). An earlier, scholarly call to revamp the Fourteenth Amendment can be found in PETER SCHUCK and ROGER SMITH, CITIZENSHIP WITHOUT CONSENT: ILLEGAL ALIENS IN THE AMERICAN POLITY (1985).

23. Koh, *supra, at 69–70.*

24. Bill Ong Hing, Beyond the Rhetoric of Assimilation and Cultural Pluralism: Addressing the Tension of Separatism and Conflict in an Immigration-Driven Multiracial Society, *81 CAL. L. REV. 863, 866 (1993).*

25. Gerald Neuman warns against amending the Citizenship Clause. Gerald Neuman, Back to *Dred Scott? 24 SAN DIEGO L. REV. 485, 500 (1987).* See also *Note,* The Birthright Citizenship Amendment: A Threat to Equality, *107 HARV. L. REV. 1026 (1994).*

26. U.S. Const. art. I, sec. 8, cl. 4.

27. Act of March 26, 1790, ch. 3, 1 Stat. 103.

28. KETTNER, *supra, at 215–16.*

29. One exception exists. In revisions undertaken in 1870, the "white person" limitation was omitted. However, this omission is regarded as accidental, and the prerequisite was reinserted in 1875 by "an act to correct errors and to supply omissions in the Revised Statutes of the United States." Act of Feb. 18, 1875, ch. 80, 18 Stat. 318. See *In re Ah Yup, 1 F.Cas. 223 (C.C.D.Cal. 1878) ("Upon revision of the statutes, the revisors, probably inadvertently, as Congress did not contemplate a change of the laws in force, omitted the words 'white persons.' ").*

30. Statement of Senator Hendricks, 59 CONG. GLOBE, 42nd Cong., 1st Sess. 2939 (1866). See also *John Guendelsberger,* Access to Citizenship for Children Born Within the State to Foreign Parents, *40 AM. J. COMP. L. 379, 407–9 (1992).*

31. Statement of Senator Cowan, 57 CONG. GLOBE, 42nd Cong., 1st Sess. 499 (1866). For a discussion of the role of anti-Asian prejudice in the laws governing naturalization, see generally *Elizabeth Hull,* Naturalization and Denaturalization, *ASIAN AMERICANS AND THE SUPREME COURT: A DOCUMENTARY HISTORY 403 (Hyung-Chan Kim ed., 1992).*

32. The Senate rejected an amendment that would have allowed Chinese persons to naturalize. The proposed amendment read: "That the naturalization laws are hereby extended to aliens of African nativity, and to persons of African descent, and to persons born in the Chinese empire." BILL ONG HING, MAKING AND REMAKING ASIAN AMERICA THROUGH IMMIGRATION POLICY, 1850–1990, at 239 n.34 (1993).

33. Act of July 14, 1870, ch. 255, § 7, 16 Stat. 254.

34. Chinese Exclusion Act, ch. 126, § 14, 22 Stat. 58 (1882).

35. Fong Yue Ting v. United States, 149 U.S. 698, 716 (1893).

36. Neil Gotanda contends that separate racial ideologies function with respect to "other non-Whites," meaning non-Black racial minorities such as Asians, Native Americans, and Latinos. Neil Gotanda, "Other Non-Whites" in American Legal History: A Review of *Justice at War, 85 COLUM. L. REV. 1186 (1985). Gotanda explicitly identifies the operation of this separate ideology in the Supreme Court's jurisprudence regarding Asians and citizenship. Neil Gotanda,* Asian American Rights and the "Miss Saigon Syndrome," *ASIAN AMERICANS AND THE SUPREME COURT: A DOCUMENTARY HISTORY 1087, 1096–97 (Hyung-Chan Kim ed., 1992).*

37. Charles Gordon, The Racial Barrier to American Citizenship, *93 U. PA. L. REV. 237, 252 (1945).*

38. MILTON KONVITZ, THE ALIEN AND THE ASIATIC IN AMERICAN LAW 80–81 (1946) (citation omitted).

39. Act of Oct. 14, 1940, ch. 876, § 303, 54 Stat. 1140.

40. Note, The Nationality Act of 1940, *54 HARV. L. REV. 860, 865 n.40 (1941).*

41. Act of Dec. 17, 1943, ch. 344, 3, 57 Stat. 600.

42. Act of July 2, 1946, ch. 534, 60 Stat. 416.

43. Id.

44. Immigration and Nationality Act of 1952, ch. 2, § 311, 66 Stat. 239 (codified as amended at 8 U.S.C. 1422 [1988]).

45. Arguably, the continued substantial exclusion of Asians from immigration not remedied until 1965, rendered their eligibility for naturalization relatively meaningless. "[T]he national quota system for admitting immigrants which was built into the 1952 Act gave the grant of eligibility a hollow ring." Chin Kim and Bok Lim Kim, Asian Immigrants in American Law: A Look at the Past and the Challenge Which Remains, *26 AM. U. L. REV. 373, 390 (1977).*

46. *See generally Ursula Vogel,* Is Citizenship Gender-Specific? *THE FRONTIERS OF CITIZENSHIP 58 (Ursula Vogel and Michael Moran eds., 1991).*

47. Act of Feb. 10, 1855, ch. 71, § 2, 10 Stat. 604. Because gender-based laws in the area of citizenship were motivated by the idea that a woman's citizenship should follow that of her husband, no naturalization law has explicitly targeted unmarried women. GORDON AND MAILMAN, *supra, at § 95.03[6] ("An unmarried woman has never been statutorily barred from naturalization.").*

48. PRENTISS WEBSTER, LAW OF NATURALIZATION IN THE UNITED STATES OF AMERICA AND OTHER COUNTRIES 80 (1895).

49. Act of Feb. 10, 1855, ch. 71, § 2, 10 Stat. 604.

50. Kelly v. Owen, 74 U.S. 496, 498 (1868).

51. GORDON AND MAILMAN, *supra at § 95.03[6].*

52. Act of Sept. 22, 1922, ch. 411, § 2, 42 Stat. 1021.

53. GORDON AND MAILMAN, *supra at § 100.03[4][m].*

54. Act of March 2, 1907, ch. 2534, § 3, 34 Stat. 1228. This act was upheld in MacKenzie v. Hare, 239 U.S. 299 (1915) (expatriating a U.S.-born woman upon her marriage to a British citizen).

55. Act of Sept. 22, 1922, ch. 411, § 3, 42 Stat. 1021.

56. *Id.* The Act also stated that "[n]o woman whose husband is not eligible to citizenship shall be naturalized during the continuance of the marriage."

57. Act of March 3, 1931, ch. 442, § 4(a), 46 Stat. 1511.

58. The loss of birthright citizenship was particularly harsh for those women whose race made them unable to regain citizenship through naturalization, especially after 1924, when the immigration laws of this country barred entry to any alien ineligible to citizenship. Immigration Act of 1924, ch. 190, § 13(c), 43 Stat. 162. *See, e.g.,* Ex parte (Ng) Fung Sing, 6 F.2d 670 (W. D. Wash. 1925). In that case, a U.S. birthright citizen

of Chinese descent was expatriated because of her marriage to a Chinese citizen, and was subsequently refused admittance to the United States as an alien ineligible to citizenship.

Critical Thinking

1. Explain the relationship between the U.S. Congress and racial prejudice and citizenship.
2. What does this article about American history have meaning for current events and contemporary society?
3. In what ways has birthright citizenship and naturalization intersected with race and gender in the development of the American Constitution?

Create Central

www.mhhe.com/createcentral

Internet References

Library of Congress
www.loc.gov
Social Science Information Gateway
http://sosig.esrc.bris.ac.uk
Sociosite
www.sociosite.net
Supreme Court/Legal Information Institute
http://supct.Iaw.cornell.edu/supct/index.html

Article   Prepared by: John A. Kromkowski, *Catholic University of America*

Dred Scott v. Sandford

December term 1856.

Learning Outcomes

After reading this article, you will be able to:

- Explain the strengths and weaknesses of the Congressional and Supreme Court in the process of governance.
- Explain the various roles and functions of the court in American political change.
- Discuss the current and past meaning of "the people of the United States."

Mr. Chief Justice Taney delivered the opinion of the court.

This case has been twice argued. After the argument at the last term, differences of opinion were found to exist among the members of the court; and as the questions in controversy are of the highest importance, and the court was at that time much pressed by the ordinary business of the term, it was deemed advisable to continue the case, and direct a reargument on some of the points, in order that we might have an opportunity of giving to the whole subject a more deliberate consideration. It has accordingly been again argued by counsel, and considered by the court; and I now proceed to deliver its opinion.

There are two leading questions presented by the record:

1. Had the Circuit Court of the United States jurisdiction to hear and determine the case between these parties? And
2. If it had jurisdiction, is the judgment it has given erroneous or not?

The plaintiff in error, who was also the plaintiff in the court below, was, with his wife and children, held as slaves by the defendant, in the State of Missouri; and he brought this action in the Circuit Court of the United States for that district, to assert the title of himself and his family to freedom.

The declaration is in the form usually adopted in that State to try questions of this description, and contains the averment necessary to give the court jurisdiction; that he and the defendant are citizens of different States; that is, that he is a citizen of Missouri, and the defendant a citizen of New York.

The defendant pleaded in abatement to the jurisdiction of the court, that the plaintiff was not a citizen of the State of Missouri, as alleged in his declaration, being a negro of African descent, whose ancestors were of pure African blood, and who were brought into this country and sold as slaves.

To this plea the plaintiff demurred, and the defendant joined in demurrer. The court overruled the plea, and gave judgment that the defendant should answer over. And he thereupon put in sundry pleas in bar, upon which issues were joined; and at the trial the verdict and judgment were in his favor. Whereupon the plaintiff brought this writ of error.

Before we speak of the pleas in bar, it will be proper to dispose of the questions which have arisen on the plea in abatement.

That plea denies the right of the plaintiff to sue in a court of the United States, for the reasons therein stated.

If the question raised by it is legally before us, and the court should be of opinion that the facts stated in it disqualify the plaintiff from becoming a citizen, in the sense in which that word is used in the Constitution of the United States, then the judgment of the Circuit Court is erroneous, and must be reversed.

It is suggested, however, that this plea is not before us; and that as the judgment in the court below on this plea was in favor of the plaintiff, he does not seek to reverse it, or bring it before the court for revision by his writ of error; and also that the defendant waived this defence by pleading over, and thereby admitted the jurisdiction of the court.

But, in making this objection, we think the peculiar and limited jurisdiction of courts of the United States has not been adverted to. This peculiar and limited jurisdiction has made it necessary, in these courts, to adopt different rules and principles of pleading, so far as jurisdiction is concerned, from those which regulate courts of common law in England, and in the different States of the Union which have adopted the common-law rules.

In these last-mentioned courts, where their character and rank are analogous to that of a Circuit Court of the United States; in other words, where they are what the law terms courts of general jurisdiction; they are presumed to have jurisdiction, unless the contrary appears. No averment in the pleadings of the plaintiff is necessary, in order to give jurisdiction. If the defendant objects to it, he must plead it specially, and unless the fact on which he relies is found to be true by a jury, or admitted to be true by the plaintiff, the jurisdiction cannot be disputed in an appellate court.

Now, it is not necessary to inquire whether in courts of that description a party who pleads over in bar, when a plea to the jurisdiction has been ruled against him, does or does not waive his plea; nor whether upon a judgment in his favor on the pleas in bar, and a writ of error brought by the plaintiff, the question upon the plea in abatement would be open for revision in the appellate court. Cases that may have been decided in such courts, or rules that may have been laid down by common-law pleaders, can have no influence in the decision in this court. Because, under the Constitution and laws of the United States, the rules which govern the pleadings in its courts, in questions of jurisdiction, stand on different principles and are regulated by different laws.

This difference arises, as we have said, from the peculiar character of the Government of the United States. For although it is sovereign and supreme in its appropriate sphere of action, yet it does not possess all the powers which usually belong to the sovereignty of a nation. Certain specified powers, enumerated in the Constitution, have been conferred upon it; and neither the legislative, executive, nor judicial departments of the Government can lawfully exercise any authority beyond the limits marked out by the Constitution. And in regulating the judicial department, the cases in which the courts of the United States shall have jurisdiction are particularly and specifically enumerated and defined; and they are not authorized to take cognizance of any case which does not come within the description therein specified. Hence, when a plaintiff sues in a court of the United States, it is necessary that he should show, in his pleading, that the suit he brings is within the jurisdiction of the court, and that he is entitled to sue there. And if he omits to do this, and should, by any oversight of the Circuit Court, obtain a judgment in his favor, the judgment would be reversed in the appellate court for want of jurisdiction in the court below. The jurisdiction would not be presumed, as in the case of a common-law English or State court, unless the contrary appeared. But the record, when it comes before the appellate court, must show, affirmatively, that the inferior court had authority under the Constitution, to hear and determine the case. And if the plaintiff claims a right to sue in a Circuit Court of the United States, under that provision of the Constitution which gives jurisdiction in controversies between citizens of different States, he must distinctly aver in his pleading that they are citizens of different States; and he cannot maintain his suit without showing that fact in the pleadings.

This point was decided in the case of *Bingham v. Cabot,* (in 3 Dall., 382,) and ever since adhered to by the court. And in *Jackson v. Ashton,* (8 Pet., 148,) it was held that the objection to which it was open could not be waived by the opposite party because consent of parties could not give jurisdiction.

It is needless to accumulate cases on this subject. Those already referred to, and the cases of *Capron v. Van Noorden,* (in 2 Cr., 126) and *Montalet v. Murray,* (4 Cr., 46,) are sufficient to show the rule of which we have spoken. The case of *Capron v. Van Noorden* strikingly illustrates the difference between a common-law court and a court of the United States.

If, however, the fact of citizenship is averred in the declaration, and the defendant does not deny it, and put it in issue by plea in abatement, he cannot offer evidence at the trial to disprove it, and consequently cannot avail himself of the objection in the appellate court, unless the defect should be apparent in some other part of the record. For if there is no plea in abatement, and the want of jurisdiction does not appear in any other part of the transcript brought up by the writ of error, the undisputed averment of citizenship in the declaration must be taken in this court to be true. In this case, the citizenship is averred, but it is denied by the defendant in the manner required by the rules of pleading, and the fact upon which the denial is based is admitted by the demurrer. And, if the plea and demurrer, and judgment of the court below upon it, are before us upon this record, the question to be decided is, whether the facts stated in the plea are sufficient to show that the plaintiff is not entitled to sue as a citizen in a court of the United States. . . .

We think they are before us. The plea in abatement and the judgment of the court upon it, are a part of the judicial proceedings in the Circuit Court, and are there recorded as such; and a writ of error always brings up to the superior court the whole record of the proceedings in the court below. And in the case of the *United States v. Smith,* (11 Wheat., 172) this court said, that the case being brought up by writ of error, the whole record was under the consideration of this court. And this being the case in the present instance, the plea in abatement is necessarily under consideration; and it becomes, therefore, our duty to decide whether the facts stated in the plea are or are not sufficient to show that the plaintiff is not entitled to sue as a citizen in a court of the United States.

This is certainly a very serious question, and one that now for the first time has been brought for decision before this court. But it is brought here by those who have a right to bring it, and it is our duty to meet it and decide it.

The question is simply this: Can a negro, whose ancestors were imported into this country, and sold as slaves, become a member of the political community formed and brought into existence by the Constitution of the United States, and as such become entitled to all the rights, and privileges, and immunities, guarantied by that instrument to the citizen? One of which rights is the privilege of suing in a court of the United States in the cases specified in the Constitution.

It will be observed, that the plea applies to that class of persons only whose ancestors were negroes of the African race, and imported into this country, and sold and held as slaves. The only matter in issue before the court, therefore, is, whether the descendants of such slaves, when they shall be emancipated, or who are born of parents who had become free before their birth, are citizens of a State, in the sense in which the word citizen is used in the Constitution of the United States. And this being the only matter in dispute on the pleadings, the court must be understood as speaking in this opinion of that class only, that is, of those persons who are the descendants of Africans who were imported into this country, and sold as slaves.

The situation of this population was altogether unlike that of the Indian race. The latter, it is true, formed no part of the colonial communities, and never amalgamated with them in social connections or in government. But although they were uncivilized, they were yet a free and independent people, associated together in nations or tribes, and governed by their own laws. Many of these political communities were situated in territories to which the white race claimed the ultimate right of dominion. But that claim was acknowledged to be subject to the right of the Indians to occupy it as long as they thought proper, and neither the English nor colonial Governments claimed or exercised any dominion over the tribe or nation by whom it was occupied, nor claimed the right to the possession of the territory, until the tribe or nation consented to cede it. These Indian Governments were regarded and treated as foreign Governments, as much so as if an ocean had separated the red man from the white; and their freedom has constantly been acknowledged, from the time of the first emigration to the English colonies to the present day, by the different Governments which succeeded each other. Treaties have been negotiated with them, and their alliance sought for in war; and the people who compose these Indian political communities have always been treated as foreigners not living under our Government. It is true that the course of events has brought the Indian tribes within the limits of the United States under subjection to the white race; and it has been found necessary, for their sake as well as our own, to regard them as in a state of pupilage, and to legislate to a certain extent over them and the territory they occupy. But they may, without doubt, like the subjects of any other foreign Government, be naturalized by the authority of Congress, and become citizens of a State, and of the United States; and if an individual should leave his nation or tribe, and take up his abode among the white population, he would be entitled to all the rights and privileges which would belong to an emigrant from any other foreign people.

We proceed to examine the case as presented by the pleadings.

The words "people of the United States" and "citizens" are synonymous terms, and mean the same thing. They both describe the political body who, according to our republican institutions, form the sovereignty and who hold the power and conduct the Government through their representatives. They are what we familiarly call the "sovereign people," and every citizen is one of this people, and a constituent member of this sovereignty. The question before us is, whether the class of persons described in the plea in abatement compose a portion of this people, and are constituent members of this sovereignty? We think they are not, and that they are not included, and were not intended to be included, under the word "citizens" in the Constitution, and can therefore claim none of the rights and privileges which that instrument provides for and secures to citizens of the United States. On the contrary, they were at that time considered as a subordinate and inferior class of beings, who had been subjugated by the dominant race, and, whether emancipated or not, yet remained subject to their authority, and had no rights or privileges but such as those who held the power and the Government might choose to grant them.

It is not the province of the court to decide upon the justice or injustice, the policy or impolicy, of these laws. The decision of that question belonged to the political or law-making power; to those who formed the sovereignty and framed the Constitution. The duty of the court is, to interpret the instrument they have framed, with the best lights we can obtain on the subject, and to administer it as we find it, according to its true intent and meaning when it was adopted.

In discussing this question, we must not confound the rights of citizenship which a State may confer within its own limits, and the rights of citizenship as a member of the Union. It does not by any means follow, because he has all the rights and privileges of a citizen of a State, that he must be a citizen of the United States. He may have all of the rights and privileges of the citizen of a State, and yet not be entitled to the rights and privileges of a citizen in any other State. For, previous to the adoption of the Constitution of the United States, every State had the undoubted right to confer on whomsoever it pleased the character of citizen, and to endow him with all its rights. But this character of course was confined to the boundaries of the State, and gave him no rights or privileges in other States beyond those secured to him by the laws of nations and the comity of States. Nor have the several States surrendered the power of conferring these rights and privileges by adopting the Constitution of the United States. Each State may still confer them upon an alien, or any one it thinks proper, or upon any class or description of persons; yet he would not be a citizen in the sense in which that word is used in the Constitution of the United States, nor entitled to sue as such in one of its courts, nor to the privileges and immunities of a citizen in the other States. The rights which he would acquire would be restricted to the State which gave them. The Constitution has conferred on Congress the right to establish a uniform rule of naturalization, and this right is evidently exclusive, and has always been held by this court to be so. Consequently, no State, since the adoption of the Constitution, can by naturalizing an alien invest him with the rights and privileges secured to a citizen of a State under the Federal Government, although, so far as the State alone was concerned, he would undoubtedly be entitled to the rights of a citizen, and clothed with all the rights and immunities which the Constitution and laws of the State attached to that character.

It is very clear, therefore, that no State can, by any act or law of its own, passed since the adoption of the Constitution, introduce a new member into the political community created by the Constitution of the United States. It cannot make him a member of this community by making him a member of its own. And for the same reason it cannot introduce any person, or description of persons, who were not intended to be embraced in this new political family which the Constitution brought into existence, but were intended to be excluded from it.

The question then arises, whether the provisions of the Constitution, in relation to the personal rights and privileges to which the citizen of a State should be entitled, embraced the negro African race, at that time in this country or who might afterwards be imported, who had then or should afterwards be made free in any State; and to put it in the power of a single State to make him a citizen of the United States, and endue him with the full rights of citizenship in every other State without their consent? Does the Constitution of the United States act upon him whenever he shall be made free under the laws of a State, and raised there to the rank of a citizen, and immediately clothe him with all the privileges of a citizen in every other State, and in its own courts?

The courts think the affirmative of these propositions cannot be maintained. And if it cannot, the plaintiff in error could not be a citizen of the State of Missouri, within the meaning of the Constitution of the United States, and, consequently, was not entitled to sue in its courts.

It is true, every person, and every class and description of persons, who were at the time of the adoption of the Constitution recognised as citizens in the several States, became also citizens of this new political body; but none other; it was formed by them, and for them and their posterity, but for no one else. And the personal rights and privileges guarantied to citizens of this new sovereignty were intended to embrace those only who were then members of the several State communities, or who should afterwards by birthright or otherwise become members, according to the provisions of the Constitution and the principles on which it was founded. It was the union of those who were at that time members of distinct and separate political communities into one political family, whose power, for certain specified purposes, was to extend over the whole territory of the United States. And it gave to each citizen rights and privileges outside of his State which he did not before possess, and placed him in every other State upon a perfect equality with its own citizens as to rights of person and rights of property; it made him a citizen of the United States.

It becomes necessary, therefore, to determine who were citizens of the several States when the Constitution was adopted. And in order to do this, we must recur to the Governments and institutions of the thirteen colonies, when they separated from Great Britain and formed new sovereignties, and took their places in the family of independent nations. We must inquire who, at that time, were recognised as the people or citizens of a State, whose rights and liberties had been outraged by the English Government; and who declared their independence, and assumed the powers of Government to defend their rights by force of arms.

In the opinion of the court, the legislation and histories of the times, and the language used in the Declaration of Independence, show, that neither the class of persons who had been imported as slaves, nor their descendants, whether they had become free or not, were then acknowledged as a part of the people, nor intended to be included in the general words used in that memorable instrument. . . .

Critical Thinking

1. What are the questions at issue in *Dred Scott v. Sandford?*
2. Explain in what ways does the Court view "the Indian race," "Negroes of African blood," and "people of the United States"?

Create Central

www.mhhe.com/createcentral

Internet References

Supreme Court/Legal Information Institute
   http://supct.Iaw.cornell.edu/supct/index.html

U.S. Census Bureau
   www.census.gov

U.S. Supreme Court Reports
   http://bulk.resource.orglcourts.gov/c/US

Supreme Court of the United States, 1856.

Article

Prepared by: John A. Kromkowski, *Catholic University of America*

Brown et al. v. Board of Education of Topeka et al.

347 U.S. 483 (1954).

Learning Outcomes

After reading this article, you will be able to:

- Explain the relationship between ending racial segregation in schools and housing policy.

- List the benefits associated with diversity.

- Explain the relationship of income, education and the cost of housing and the relevance of your findings for race and ethnic relations.

M
r. Chief Justice Warren delivered the opinion of the Court.

These cases come to us from the States of Kansas, South Carolina, Virginia, and Delaware. They are premised on different facts and different local conditions, but a common legal question justifies their consideration together in this consolidated opinion.[1]

In each of the cases, minors of the Negro race, through their legal representatives, seek the aid of the courts in obtaining admission to the public schools of their community on a nonsegregated basis. In each instance, they had been denied admission to schools attended by white children under laws requiring or permitting segregation according to race. This segregation was alleged to deprive the plaintiffs of the equal protection of the laws under the Fourteenth Amendment. In each of the cases other than the Delaware case, a three-judge federal district court denied relief to the plaintiffs on the so-called "separate but equal" doctrine announced by this Court in *Plessy v. Ferguson,* 163 U.S. 537. Under that doctrine, equality of treatment is accorded when the races are provided substantially equal facilities, even though these facilities be separate. In the Delaware case, the Supreme Court of Delaware adhered to that doctrine, but ordered that the plaintiffs be admitted to the white schools because of their superiority to the Negro schools.

The plaintiffs contend that segregated public schools are not "equal" and cannot be made "equal," and that hence they are deprived of the equal protection of the laws. Because of the obvious importance of the question presented, the Court took

jurisdiction.[2] Argument was heard in the 1952 Term, and reargument was heard this Term on certain questions propounded by the Court.[3]

Reargument was largely devoted to the circumstances surrounding the adoption of the Fourteenth Amendment in 1868. It covered exhaustively consideration of the Amendment in Congress, ratification by the states, then existing practices in racial segregation, and the views of proponents and opponents of the Amendment. This discussion and our own investigation convince us that, although these sources cast some light, it is not enough to resolve the problem with which we are faced. At best, they are inconclusive. The most avid proponents of the post–War Amendments undoubtedly intended them to remove all legal distinctions among "all persons born or naturalized in the United States." Their opponents, just as certainly, were antagonistic to both the letter and the spirit of the Amendments and wished them to have the most limited effect. What others in Congress and the state legislatures had in mind cannot be determined with any degree of certainty.

An additional reason for the inconclusive nature of the Amendment's history, with respect to segregated schools, is the status of public education at that time.[4] In the South, the movement toward free common schools, supported by general taxation, had not yet taken hold. Education of white children was largely in the hands of private groups. Education of Negroes was almost nonexistent, and practically all of the race were illiterate. In fact, any education of Negroes was forbidden by law in some states. Today, in contrast, many Negroes have achieved outstanding success in the arts and sciences as well as in the business and professional world. It is true that public school education at the time of the Amendment had advanced further in the North, but the effect of the Amendment on northern States was generally ignored in the congressional debates. Even in the North, the conditions of public education did not approximate those existing today. The curriculum was usually rudimentary; ungraded schools were common in rural areas; the school term was but three months a year in many states; and compulsory school attendance was virtually unknown. As a consequence, it is not surprising that there should be so little in the history of the Fourteenth Amendment relating to its intended effect on public education.

In the first cases in this Court construing the Fourteenth Amendment, decided shortly after its adoption, the Court interpreted it as proscribing all state-imposed discriminations against the Negro race.[5] The doctrine of "separate but equal" did not make its appearance in this Court until 1896 in the case of *Plessy v. Ferguson, supra,* involving not education but transportation.[6] American courts have since labored with the doctrine for over half a century. In this Court, there have been six cases involving the "separate but equal" doctrine in the field of public education.[7] In *Cumming v. County Board of Education,* 175 U.S. 528, and *Gong Lum v. Rice,* 275 U.S. 78, the validity of the doctrine itself was not challenged.[8] In more recent cases, all on the graduate school level, inequality was found in that specific benefits enjoyed by white students were denied to Negro students of the same educational qualifications. *Missouri ex rel. Gaines v. Canada,* 305 U.S. 337; *Sipuel v. Oklahoma,* 332 U.S. 631; *Sweatt v. Painter,* 339 U.S. 629; *McLaurin v. Oklahoma State Regents,* 339 U.S. 637. In none of these cases was it necessary to reexamine the doctrine to grant relief to the Negro plaintiff. And in *Sweatt v. Painter, supra,* the Court expressly reserved decision on the question whether *Plessy v. Ferguson* should be held inapplicable to public education.

In the instant cases, that question is directly presented. Here, unlike *Sweatt v. Painter,* there are findings below that the Negro and white schools involved have been equalized, or are being equalized, with respect to buildings, curricula, qualifications and salaries of teachers, and other "tangible" factors.[9] Our decision, therefore, cannot turn on merely a comparison of these tangible factors in the Negro and white schools involved in each of the cases. We must look instead to the effect of segregation itself on public education.

In approaching this problem, we cannot turn the clock back to 1868 when the Amendment was adopted, or even to 1896 when *Plessy v. Ferguson* was written. We must consider public education in the light of its full development and its present place in American life throughout the Nation. Only in this way can it be determined if segregation in public schools deprives these plaintiffs of the equal protection of the laws.

Today, education is perhaps the most important function of state and local governments. Compulsory school attendance laws and the great expenditures for education both demonstrate our recognition of the importance of education to our democratic society. It is required in the performance of our most basic public responsibilities, even service in the armed forces. It is the very foundation of good citizenship. Today it is a principal instrument in awakening the child to cultural values, in preparing him for later professional training, and in helping him to adjust normally to his environment. In these days, it is doubtful that any child may reasonably be expected to succeed in life if he is denied the opportunity of an education. Such an opportunity, where the state has undertaken to provide it, is a right which must be made available to all on equal terms.

We come then to the question presented: Does segregation of children in public schools solely on the basis of race, even though the physical facilities and other "tangible" factors may be equal, deprive the children of the minority group of equal educational opportunities? We believe that it does.

In *Sweatt v. Painter, supra,* in finding that a segregated law school for Negroes could not provide them equal educational opportunities, this Court relied in large part on "those qualities which are incapable of objective measurement but which make for greatness in a law school." In *McLaurin v. Oklahoma State Regents, supra,* the Court, in requiring that a Negro admitted to a white graduate school be treated like all other students, again resorted to intangible considerations: ". . . his ability to study, to engage in discussions and exchange views with other students, and, in general, to learn his profession." Such considerations apply with added force to children in grade and high schools. To separate them from others of similar age and qualifications solely because of their race generates a feeling of inferiority as to their status in the community that may affect their hearts and minds in a way unlikely ever to be undone. The effect of this separation on their educational opportunities was well stated by a finding in the Kansas case by a court which nevertheless felt compelled to rule against the Negro plaintiffs:

> "Segregation of white and colored children in public schools has a detrimental effect upon the colored children. The impact is greater when it has the sanction of the law; for the policy of separating the races is usually interpreted as denoting the inferiority of the negro group. A sense of inferiority affects the motivation of a child to learn. Segregation with the sanction of law, therefore, has a tendency to [retard] the educational and mental development of negro children and to deprive them of some of the benefits they would receive in a racial[ly] integrated school system."[10]

Whatever may have been the extent of psychological knowledge at the time of *Plessy v. Ferguson,* this finding is amply supported by modern authority.[11] Any language in *Plessy v. Ferguson* contrary to this finding is rejected.

We conclude that in the field of public education the doctrine of "separate but equal" has no place. Separate educational facilities are inherently unequal. Therefore, we hold that the plaintiffs and others similarly situated for whom the actions have been brought are, by reason of the segregation complained of, deprived of the equal protection of the laws guaranteed by the Fourteenth Amendment. This disposition makes unnecessary any discussion whether such segregation also violates the Due Process Clause of the Fourteenth Amendment.[12]

Because these are class actions, because of the wide applicability of this decision, and because of the great variety of local conditions, the formulation of decrees in these cases presents problems of considerable complexity. On reargument, the consideration of appropriate relief was necessarily subordinated to the primary question—the constitutionality of segregation in public education. We have now announced that such segregation is a denial of the equal protection of the laws. In order that we may have the full assistance of the parties in formulating decrees, the cases will be restored to the docket, and the parties are requested to present further argument on Questions 4 and 5 previously propounded by the Court for the reargument this Term.[13] The Attorney General of the United States is again invited to participate. The Attorneys General of the states requiring or permitting segregation in public education will also be permitted to appear as *amici curiae* upon request to do so by September 15, 1954, and submission of briefs by October 1, 1954.[14]

It is so ordered.

Notes

1. In the Kansas case, *Brown v. Board of Education,* the plaintiffs are Negro children of elementary school age residing in Topeka. They brought this action in the United States District Court for the District of Kansas to enjoin enforcement of a Kansas statute which permits, but does not require, cities of more than 15,000 population to maintain separate school facilities for Negro and white students. Kan. Gen. Stat. §72–1724 (1949). Pursuant to that authority, the Topeka Board of Education elected to establish segregated elementary schools. Other public schools in the community, however, are operated on a nonsegregated basis.

   In the South Carolina case, *Briggs v. Elliott,* the plaintiffs are Negro children of both elementary and high school age residing in Clarendon County. They brought this action in the United States District Court for the Eastern District of South Carolina to enjoin enforcement of provisions in the state constitution and statutory code which require the segregation of Negroes and whites in public schools. . . .

   In the Virginia case, *Davis v. County School Board,* the plaintiffs are Negro children of high school age residing in Prince Edward County. They brought this action in the United States District Court for the Eastern District of Virginia to enjoin enforcement of provisions in the state constitution and statutory code which require the segregation of Negroes and whites in public schools. . . .

   In the Delaware case, *Gebhart v. Belton,* the plaintiffs are Negro children of both elementary and high school age residing in New Castle county. They brought this action in the Delaware Court of Chancery to enjoin enforcement of provisions in the state constitution and statutory code which require the segregation of Negroes and whites in public schools. . . .

2. technical footnote deleted.
3. technical footnote deleted.
4. technical footnote deleted.
5. technical footnote deleted.
6. technical footnote deleted.
7. technical footnote deleted.
8. technical footnote deleted.
9. technical footnote deleted.
10. technical footnote deleted.
11. K. B. Clark, Effect of Prejudice and Discrimination on Personality Development (Midcentury White House Conference on Children and Youth, 1950); Witmer and Kotinsky, Personality in the Making (1952), c. VI; Deutscher and Chein, The Psychological Effects of Enforced Segregation: A Survey of Social Science Opinion, 26 *J. Psychol.* 259 (1948); Chein, What Are the Psychological Effects of Segregation Under Conditions of Equal Facilities?, 3 *Int. J. Opinion and Attitude Res.* 229 (1949); Brameld, Educational Costs, in Discrimination and National Welfare (MacIver, ed., 1949), 44–48; Frazier, The Negro in the United States (1949), 674–681. And see generally Myrdal, An American Dilemma (1944).
12. technical footnote deleted.
13. technical footnote deleted.
14. technical footnote deleted.

Critical Thinking

1. In retrospect, does ending racial segregation in schools without ending segregation in housing seem to be the fundamental constraint on the success desired and the type of fairness and equal protection sought by the Supreme Court in this case?

2. What are *de jure* and *de facto* forms or types of racial segregation?

Create Central

www.mhhe.com/createcentral

Internet References

Supreme Court/Legal Information Institute
http://supct.Iaw.cornell.edu/supct/index.html

U.S. Census Bureau
www.census.gov

U.S. Supreme Court Reports
http://bulk.resource.orglcourts.gov/c/US

Supreme Court of the United States, 1954.

Article   Prepared by: John A. Kromkowski, *Catholic University of America*

Historical Discrimination in the Immigration Laws

Learning Outcomes

After reading this article, you will be able to:

- Relate the history of immigration to the current debate on immigration reform.

- Discuss the implications, costs and benefits of unregulated immigration.

- Explain how people's attitudes about immigration differ in various parts of the country.

The Early Years

During the formative years of this country's growth, immigration was encouraged with little restraint. Any restrictions on immigration in the 1700s were the result of selection standards established by each colonial settlement. The only Federal regulation of immigration in this period lasted only 2 years and came from the Alien Act of 1798, which gave the President the authority to expel aliens who posed a threat to national security.[1]

Immigrants from northern and western Europe began to trickle into the country as a result of the faltering economic conditions within their own countries. In Germany, unfavorable economic prospects in industry and trade, combined with political unrest, drove many of its nationals to seek opportunities to ply their trades here.[2] In Ireland, the problems of the economy, compounded by several successive potato crop failures in the 1840s, sent thousands of Irish to seaports where ships bound for the United States were docked.[3] For other European nationals, the emigration from their native countries received impetus not only from adverse economic conditions at home but also from favorable stories of free land and good wages in America.[4]

The Nativist Movements

As a result of the large numbers of Catholics who emigrated from Europe, a nativist movement began in the 1830s.[5] It advocated immigration restriction to prevent further arrivals of Catholics into this country. Anti-Catholicism was a very popular theme, and many Catholics and Catholic institutions suffered violent attacks from nativist sympathizers. The movement, however, did not gain great political strength and its goal of curbing immigration did not materialize.

Immigrants in the mid-19th century did not come only from northern and western Europe. In China, political unrest and the decline in agricultural productivity spawned the immigration of Chinese to American shores.[6] The numbers of Chinese immigrants steadily increased after the so-called Opium War, due not only to the Chinese economy, but also to the widespread stories of available employment, good wages, and the discovery of gold at Sutter's Mill, which filtered in through arrivals from the Western nations.[7]

The nativist movement of the 1830s resurfaced in the late 1840s and developed into a political party, the Know-Nothing Party.[8] Its western adherents added an anti-Chinese theme to the eastern anti-Catholic sentiment.[9] But once again, the nativist movement, while acquiring local political strength, failed in its attempts to enact legislation curbing immigration. On the local level, however, the cry of "America for Americans" often led to discriminatory State statutes that penalized certain racially identifiable groups.[10] As an example, California adopted licensing statutes for foreign miners and fishermen, which were almost exclusively enforced against Chinese.[11]

In the mid-1850s, the Know-Nothing Party lost steam as a result of a division over the question of slavery, the most important issue of that time.[12] The nativist movement and antiforeign sentiment receded because of the slavery issue and the Civil War. It maintained this secondary role until the Panic of 1873 struck.

Chinese Exclusion

The depression economy of the 1870s was blamed on aliens who were accused of driving wages to a substandard level as well as taking away jobs that "belonged" to white Americans. While the economic charges were not totally without basis, reality shows that most aliens did not compete with white labor for "desirable" white jobs. Instead, aliens usually were relegated to the most menial employment.[13]

The primary target was the Chinese, whose high racial visibility, coupled with cultural dissimilarity and lack of political power, made them more than an adequate scapegoat for the economic problems of the 1870s.[14] Newspapers adopted the exhortations of labor leaders, blaming the Chinese for the economic plight of the working class. Workers released their frustrations and anger on the Chinese, particularly in the West.[15] Finally, politicians succumbed to the growing cry for exclusion of Chinese.

Congress responded by passing the Chinese Exclusion Act of 1882.[16] That act suspended immigration of Chinese laborers for 10 years, except for those who were in the country on November 17, 1880. Those who were not lawfully entitled to reside in the United States were subject to deportation. Chinese immigrants were also prohibited from obtaining United States citizenship after the effective date of the act.

The 1882 act was amended in 1884 to cover all subjects of China and Chinese who resided in any other foreign country.[17] Then in 1888, another act was enacted that extended the suspension of immigration for all Chinese except Chinese officials, merchants, students, teachers, and travelers for pleasure.[18] Supplemental legislation to that act also prohibited Chinese laborers from reentering the country, as provided for in the 1882 act, unless they reentered prior to the effective date of the legislation.[19]

Senator Matthew C. Butler of South Carolina summed up the congressional efforts to exclude Chinese by stating:

> [I]t seems to me that this whole Chinese business has been a matter of political advantage, and we have not been governed by that deliberation which it would seem to me the gravity of the question requires. In other words, there is a very important Presidential election pending. One House of Congress passes an act driving these poor devils into the Pacific Ocean, and the other House comes up and says, "Yes, we will drive them further into the Pacific Ocean, notwithstanding the treaties between the two governments."[20]

Nevertheless, the Chinese exclusion law was extended in 1892[21] and 1902,[22] and in 1904 it was extended indefinitely.[23]

Although challenged by American residents of Chinese ancestry, the provisions of these exclusion acts were usually upheld by judicial decisions. For example, the 1892 act[24] mandated that Chinese laborers obtain certificates of residency within 1 year after the passage of the act or face deportation. In order to obtain the certificate, the testimony of one credible white witness was required to establish that the Chinese laborer was an American resident prior to the passage of the act. That requirement was upheld by the United States Supreme Court in *Fong Yue Ting v. United States*.[25]

Literacy Tests and the Asiatic Barred Zone

The racial nature of immigration laws clearly manifested itself in further restrictions on prospective immigrants who were either from Asian countries or of Asian descent. In addition to extending the statutory life of the Chinese exclusion law, the 1902 act also applied that law to American territorial possessions, thereby prohibiting not only the immigration of noncitizen Chinese laborers from "such island territory to the mainland territory," but also "from one portion of the island territory of the United States to another portion of said island territory."[26] Soon after, Japanese were restricted from free immigration to the United States by the "Gentleman's Agreement" negotiated between the respective governments in 1907.[27] Additional evidence would be provided by the prohibition of immigration from countries in the Asia-Pacific Triangle as established by the Immigration Act of 1917.[28]

During this period, congressional attempts were also made to prevent blacks from immigrating to this country. In 1915 an amendment to exclude "all members of the African or black race" from admission to the United States was introduced in the Senate during its deliberations on a proposed immigration bill.[29] The Senate approved the amendment on a 29 to 25 vote,[30] but it was later defeated in the House by a 253 to 74 vote,[31] after intensive lobbying by the NAACP.[32]

In 1917 Congress codified existing immigration laws in the Immigration Act of that year.[33] That act retained all the prior grounds for inadmissibility and added illiterates to the list of those ineligible to immigrate, as a response to the influx of immigrants from southern and eastern Europe. Because of a fear that American standards would be lowered by these new immigrants who were believed to be racially "unassimilable" and illiterate, any alien who was over 16 and could not read was excluded. The other important feature of this statute was the creation of the Asia-Pacific Triangle, an Asiatic barred zone, designed to exclude Asians completely from immigration to the United States. The only exemptions from this zone were from an area that included Persia and parts of Afghanistan and Russia.

The 1917 immigration law reflected the movement of American immigration policy toward the curbing of free immigration. Free immigration, particularly from nations that were culturally dissimilar to the northern and western European background of most Americans, was popularly believed to be the root of both the economic problems and the social problems confronting this country.

The National Origins Quota System

Four years later, Congress created a temporary quota law that limited the number of aliens of any nationality who could immigrate to 3 percent of the United States residents of that nationality living in the country in 1910.[34] The total annual immigration allowable in any one year was set at 350,000. Western Hemisphere aliens were exempt from the quota if their country of origin was an independent nation and the alien had resided there at least 1 year.

The clear intent of the 1921 quota law was to confine immigration as much as possible to western and northern European stock. As the minority report noted:

> The obvious purpose of this discrimination is the adoption of an unfounded anthropological theory that the nations which are favored are the progeny of fictitious and hitherto unsuspected Nordic ancestors, while those discriminated against are not classified as belonging to that mythical ancestral stock. No scientific evidence worthy of consideration was introduced to substantiate this pseudoscientific proposition. It is pure fiction and the creation of a journalistic imagination....

The majority report insinuates that some of those who have come from foreign countries are non-assimilable or slow of assimilation. No facts are offered in support of such a statement. The preponderance of testimony adduced before the committee is to the contrary.[35]

Notwithstanding these objections, Congress made the temporary quota a permanent one with the enactment of the 1924 National Origins Act.[36] A ceiling of 150,000 immigrants per year was imposed. Quotas for each nationality group were 2 percent of the total members of that nationality residing in the United States according to the 1890 census.[37] Again, Western Hemisphere aliens were exempt from the quotas (thus, classified as "nonquota" immigrants). Any prospective immigrant was required to obtain a sponsor in this country and to obtain a visa from an American consulate office abroad. Entering the country without a visa and in violation of the law subjected the entrant to deportation without regard to the time of entry (no statute of limitation). Another provision, prohibiting the immigration of aliens ineligible for citizenship, completely closed the door on Japanese immigration, since the Supreme Court had ruled that Japanese were ineligible to become naturalized citizens.[38] Prior to the 1924 act, Japanese immigration had been subjected to "voluntary" restraint by the Gentleman's Agreement negotiated between the Japanese Government and President Theodore Roosevelt.

In addition to its expressed discriminatory provisions, the 1924 law was also criticized as discriminatory against blacks in general and against black West Indians in particular.[39]

The Mexican "Repatriation" Campaign

Although Mexican Americans have a long history of residence within present United States territory,[40] Mexican immigration to this country is of relatively recent vintage.[41] Mexican citizens began immigrating to this country in significant numbers after 1909 because of economic conditions as well as the violence and political upheaval of the Mexican Revolution.[42] These refugees were welcomed by Americans, for they helped to alleviate the labor shortage caused by the First World War.[43] The spirit of acceptance lasted only a short time, however.

Spurred by the economic distress of the Great Depression, Federal immigration officials expelled hundreds of thousands of persons of Mexican descent from this country through increased Border Patrol raids and other immigration law enforcement techniques.[44] To mollify public objection to the mass expulsions, this program was called the "repatriation" campaign. Approximately 500,000 persons were "repatriated" to Mexico, with more than half of them being United States citizens.[45]

Erosion of Certain Discriminatory Barriers

Prior to the next recodification of the immigration laws, there were several congressional enactments that cut away at the discriminatory barriers established by the national origins system.

In 1943 the Chinese Exclusion Act was repealed, allowing a quota of 105 Chinese to immigrate annually to this country and declaring Chinese eligible for naturalization.[46] The War Brides Act of 1945[47] permitted the immigration of 118,000 spouses and children of military servicemen. In 1946 Congress enacted legislation granting eligibility for naturalization to Pilipinos[48] and to races indigenous to India.[49] A Presidential proclamation in that same year increased the Pilipino quota from 50 to 100.[50] In 1948 the Displaced Persons Act provided for the entry of approximately 400,000 refugees from Germany, Italy, and Austria (an additional 214,000 refugees were later admitted to the United States).[51]

The McCarran-Walter Act of 1952

The McCarran-Walter Act of 1952,[52] the basic law in effect today, codified the immigration laws under a single statute. It established three principles for immigration policy:

1. the reunification of families,
2. the protection of the domestic labor force, and
3. the immigration of persons with needed skills.

However, it retained the concept of the national origins system, as well as unrestricted immigration from the Western Hemisphere. An important provision of the statute removed the bar to immigration and citizenship for races that had been denied those privileges prior to that time. Asian countries, nevertheless, were still discriminated against, for prospective immigrants whose ancestry was one-half of any Far Eastern race were chargeable to minimal quotas for that nation, regardless of the birthplace of the immigrant.

"Operation Wetback"

Soon after the repatriation campaigns of the 1930s, the United States entered the Second World War. Mobilization for the war effort produced a labor shortage that resulted in a shift in American attitudes toward immigration from Mexico. Once again Mexican nationals were welcomed with open arms. However, this "open arms" policy was just as short lived as before.

In the 1950s many Americans were alarmed by the number of immigrants from Mexico. As a result, then United States Attorney General Herbert Brownell, Jr., launched "Operation Wetback," to expel Mexicans from this country. Among those caught up in the expulsion campaign were American citizens of Mexican descent who were forced to leave the country of their birth. To ensure the effectiveness of the expulsion process, many of those apprehended were denied a hearing to assert their constitutional rights and to present evidence that would have prevented their deportation. More than 1 million persons of Mexican descent were expelled from this country in 1954 at the height of "Operation Wetback."[53]

The 1965 Amendments

The national origins immigration quota system generated opposition from the time of its inception, condemned for its attempts to maintain the existing racial composition of the United States. Finally, in 1965, amendments to the McCarran-Walter Act abolished the national origins system as well as the Asiatic barred zone.[54] Nevertheless, numerical restrictions were still imposed to limit annual immigration. The Eastern Hemisphere was subject to an overall limitation of 170,000 and a limit of 20,000 per country. Further, colonial territories were limited to 1 percent of the total available to the mother country (later raised to 3 percent or 600 immigrants in the 1976 amendments). The Western Hemisphere, for the first time, was subject to an overall limitation of 120,000 annually, although no individual per country limits were imposed. In place of the national origins system, Congress created a seven category preference system giving immigration priority to relatives of United States residents and immigrants with needed talents or skills.[55] The 20,000 limitation per country and the colonial limitations, as well as the preference for relatives of Americans preferred under the former selections process, have been referred to by critics as "the last vestiges of the national origins system" because they perpetuate the racial discrimination produced by the national origins system.

Restricting Mexican Immigration

After 1965 the economic conditions in the United States changed. With the economic crunch felt by many Americans, the cry for more restrictive immigration laws resurfaced. The difference from the 19th century situation is that the brunt of the attacks is now focused on Mexicans, not Chinese. High "guesstimates" of the number of undocumented Mexican aliens entering the United States, many of which originated from Immigration and Naturalization Service sources, have been the subject of press coverage.[56]

As a partial response to the demand for "stemming the tide" of Mexican immigration, Congress amended the Immigration and Nationality Act in 1976,[57] imposing the seven category preference system and the 20,000 numerical limitation per country on Western Hemisphere nations. Legal immigration from Mexico, which had been more than 40,000[58] people per year, with a waiting list 2 years long, was thus cut by over 50 percent.

Recent Revisions of the Immigrant Quota System

Although the annual per-country limitations have remained intact, Congress did amend the Immigration and Nationality Act in 1978 to eliminate the hemispheric quotas of 170,000 for Eastern Hemisphere countries and 120,000 for Western Hemisphere countries. Those hemispheric ceilings were replaced with an overall annual worldwide ceiling of 290,000.[59]

In 1980 the immigrant quota system was further revised by the enactment of the Refugee Act. In addition to broadening the definition of refugee, that statute eliminated the seventh preference visa category by establishing a separate worldwide ceiling for refugee admissions to this country. It also reduced the annual worldwide ceiling for the remaining six preference categories to 270,000 visas, and it increased the number of visas allocated to the second preference to 26 percent.[60]

Notes

1. Ch. 58, 1 Stat. 570 (1798).
2. Carl Wittke, *We Who Built America* (rev. 1964), p. 67.
3. Ibid., pp. 129–33.
4. Ibid., pp. 101–10.
5. Ibid., pp. 491–97.
6. Li Chien-nung, *The Political History of China, 1840–1928* (1956), pp. 48–49; Stanford Lyman, *Chinese Americans* (1974), pp. 4–5.
7. Mary Roberts Coolidge, *Chinese Immigration* (1909), pp. 16–17.
8. Wittke, *We Who Built America*, pp. 497–510.
9. Coolidge, *Chinese Immigration*, p. 58.
10. Ibid., pp. 69–82. Some municipalities also adopted ordinances that discriminated against Chinese. As an example, a San Francisco municipal ordinance, subsequently held unconstitutional in Yick Wo v. Hopkins, 118 U.S. 356 (1886), was enacted regulating the operation of public laundries but in practice was enforced almost exclusively against Chinese.
11. Ibid., pp. 33–38, 69–74.
12. Wittke, *We Who Built America*, pp. 509–10.
13. As one author noted, "[b]efore the late 1870s the Chinese engaged only in such work as white laborers refused to perform. Thus the Chinese not only were noninjurious competitors but in effect were benefactors to the white laborer." S.W. Kung, *Chinese in American Life: Some Aspects of Their History, Status, Problems, and Contributions* (1962), p. 68.
14. Carey McWilliams, *Brothers Under the Skin* (rev. 1951), pp. 101–03.
15. Coolidge, *Chinese Immigration*, p. 188.
16. Ch. 126, 22 Stat. 58 (1882).
17. Ch. 220, 23 Stat. 115 (1884).
18. Ch. 1015, 25 Stat. 476 (1888).
19. Ch. 1064, 25 Stat. 504 (1888).
20. 19 Cong. Rec. 8218 (1888).
21. Ch. 60, 27 Stat. 25 (1892).
22. Ch. 641, 32 Stat. 176 (1902).
23. Ch. 1630, 33 Stat. 428. (1904).
24. Ch. 60, 27 Stat. 25 (1892).
25. 149 U.S. 698 (1893).
26. Ch. 641, 32 Stat. 176 (1902).
27. The Gentleman's Agreement of 1907, U.S. Department of State, *Papers Relating to the Foreign Relations of the United States 1924* (1939), vol. 2, p. 339.
28. Ch. 29, 39 Stat. 874 (1917).
29. 52 Cong. Rec. 805 (1914).
30. *Id.* at 807.
31. *Id.* at 1138–39.
32. See *Crisis*, vol. 9 (February 1915), p. 190.
33. Ch. 29, 39 Stat. 874 (1917).
34. Ch. 8, 42 Stat. 5 (1921).
35. As reprinted in the legislative history of the INA [1952] U.S. Code Cong. and Ad. News 1653, 1668.
36. Ch. 190, 43 Stat. 153 (1924).

37. That act provided, however, that:

    The annual quota of any nationality for the fiscal year beginning July 1, 1927, and for each fiscal year thereafter, shall be a number which bears the same ratio to 150,000 as the number of inhabitants in continental United States in 1920 having that national origin (ascertained as hereinafter provided in this section) bears to the number of inhabitants in continental United States in 1920, but the minimum quota of any nationality shall be 100.

    Ch. 190, 43 Stat. 153, 159, § 11(b).

38. Early congressional enactments restricted eligibility for naturalization to free white persons (ch. 3, 1 Stat. 103 (1790)) and to persons of African nativity or descent (Rev. Stat. §2169 (1875)). But when Congress passed the Naturalization Act of June 29, 1906 (ch. 3592, 34 Stat. 596), persons of Japanese ancestry began submitting petitions to become naturalized citizens under the procedures established by that act. The Supreme Court, however, held that the 1906 act was limited by the prior congressional enactments and thus Japanese were ineligible for naturalization. Ozawa v. United States, 260 U.S. 178 (1922).

39. "West Indian Immigration and the American Negro," *Opportunity,* October 1924, pp. 298–99.

40. Under the Treaty of Guadalupe Hidalgo, many Mexican citizens became United States citizens after the annexation of territory by the United States following the Mexican War. Leo Grebler, Joan W. Moore, and Ralph C. Guzman, *The Mexican American People* (1970), pp. 40–41. The Treaty of Guadalupe Hidalgo is reprinted in Wayne Moquin, *A Documentary History of the Mexican Americans* (1971), p. 183.

41. Grebler, Moore, and Guzman, *The Mexican Americans People,* pp. 62–63.

42. Ibid.

43. Ibid., p. 64.

44. Ibid., pp. 523–26.

45. Moquin, *A Documentary History of the Mexican Americans,* p. 294.

46. Ch. 344, 57 Stat. 600 (1943).

47. Ch. 591, 59 Stat. 659 (1945).

48. 60 Stat. 1353.

49. Ch. 534, 60 Stat. 416 (1946).

50. Presidential Proclamation No. 2696, [1946] U.S. Code Cong. and Ad. News 1732.

51. Ch. 647, 62 Stat. 1009 (1948).

52. Ch. 477, 66 Stat. 163 (1952).

53. Grebler, Moore, and Guzman, *The Mexican American People,* pp. 521–22. Mark A. Chamberlin *et al.,* eds., "Our Badge of Infamy: A Petition to the United Nations on the Treatment of the Mexican Immigrant," in *The Mexican American and the Law* (1974 ed.), pp. 31–34.

54. Pub. L. No. 89–236, 79 Stat. 911 (1965).

55. The 1965 amendments to the Immigration and Nationality Act provided the following seven category preference system:

    First preference: unmarried sons and daughters of U.S. citizens. (20 percent)

    Second preference: spouses and unmarried sons and daughters of lawful resident aliens. (20 percent plus any visas not required for first preference)

    Third preference: members of the professions and scientists and artists of exceptional ability and their spouses and children. (10 percent)

    Fourth preference: married sons and daughters of U.S. citizens and their spouses and children. (10 percent plus any visas not required for first three preferences)

    Fifth preference: brothers and sisters of U.S. citizens and their spouses and children. (24 percent plus any visas not required for first four preferences)

    Sixth preference: skilled and unskilled workers in occupations for which labor is in short supply in this country, and their spouses and children. (10 percent)

    Seventh preference: refugees. (6 percent)

    Spouses and minor children of American citizens are exempt from the preference system.

56. "6–8 million," *New West Magazine,* May 23, 1977; "4–12 million," *Los Angeles Times,* Aug. 7, 1977.

57. Pub. L. No. 94–571, 90 Stat. 2703 (1976).

58. In 1976 there were 57,863 immigrants from Mexico; in 1975, 62,205. U.S., Immigration and Naturalization Service, *Annual Report 1976,* p. 89.

59. Pub. L. No. 95–412, 92 Stat. 907 (1978).

60. Refugee Act of 1980, Pub. L. No. 96–212 (to be codified in scattered sections of 8 U.S.C.). The Refugee Act also increased the allocation of refugee visas to 50,000 annually for the first three fiscal years under the statute and provided that the number of refugee admissions in the following years would be determined by the President after consultation with Congress.

Critical Thinking

1. From among the various historical actions taken to regulate immigration, select three that are particularly hard to understand?

2. What is "Operation Wetback?"

3. What is the National Origins Quota System?

Create Central

www.mhhe.com/createcentral

Internet References

Diversity.com
   www.diversity.com
Library of Congress
   www.loc.gov
Social Science Information Gateway
   http://sosig.esrc.bris.ac.uk
Sociosite
   www.sociosite.net
U.S. Census Bureau
   www.census.gov

Article   Prepared by: John A. Kromkowski, *The Catholic University of America*

Case Study: The American Immigrant Experiences

JOHN A. KROMKOWSKI, THADDEUS C. RADZILOWSKI, AND PAUL KOCHANOWSKI

Learning Outcomes

After reading this article, you will be able to:

- Describe the general features of large-scale immigration of Southern and Eastern Europeans into America.

- Describe the social contribution of neighborhoods to urban settlement.

- Describe the decline of urban ethnic neighborhoods in the 1960s and 1970s and the elements and process of neighborhood renewal.

Formative and guiding forces of experience teach profound lessons. What one learns and values at the first intersection of the personal in one's family and of the public in one's neighborhood shapes one's judgment and action in the urban arena of culture, government and economy that constitute the urbanized settlements in which larger and larger numbers of people live.

Periods of change often produce a conflict but more importantly they force us to define the commonweal we share. But groundless expectations for the future based in ideological images of the past eclipse honest-to-experience representations of reality, which ought to inform and guide us.

Thus the argument begins: If the neighborhood is the building block of a city and the neighborhood experiences are a value source of civility and important but currently neglected elements of models of economic and governmental development which drive mega-cities toward contemporary urban well-being, then, the gathering of human insight proposed in the guide to *The Communitas Process* should be assessed, tested, and its outcomes evaluated as a pathway toward a new flourishing

of Chinese culture and its new presence in the metropolitan age created by the economic and governmental action that has transformed not only China but countries throughout the world. The mega-cities of all countries are equally in need of recovering their cultures but also ought to be engaging in the plethora of cultural manifestation that the movement of populations brings into urban life. This work of re-engaging culture ought to be more systematically and artfully brought into the process of globalization, which has largely been economic and governmental and not attentive of the forms of sociality that are part of the human legacy of the world.

In the American experience, the small-scale settlement of urban areas—the neighborhood—not only mediated the passage of immigrants toward becoming American ethnics, citizens, producers and consumers, as importantly, it mediated the person from family into the public world of common culture, politics and economics. Through such interaction and relationship a society fashions bonds of association and exchange. The neighborhood is the initial locus of an interesting set of intersections, which may be fruitfully named the public, private and community sectors of the American reality. Thus the neighborhood is a social invention whose capacity for economic and cultural well-being appears to be pivotal for social formation, economic well-being and political development. Contemporary urban neighborhoods exist in uneasy tension with large-scale governmental, cultural and economic institutions. The agenda proposed for urban neighborhoods and the endorsement of social formation influenced by immigration and ethnicity does not invoke either of these sources as merely symbolic or as romantic political totems. The neighborhood agenda emerges from experiential analysis of the relation of immigration and ethnicity to the moral universe of exchange of goods and services. Such experiences informed by pragmatic common sense suggest the ground from which preference for the neighborhood can be determined without the sleight of hand employed by either romantic nostalgia or destructive progressivism

Feldstein and Costello, editors of *The Ordeal of Assimilation,* point to certain neglected aspects of social and economic practices of the early 20th century and argue against romantics who concentrate on the success stories and magnificent contributions made by the newcomers to American life. According to Feldstein and Costello, understanding the foreign-born's plight in America reveals ways in which these aliens have been affected by their new environment.

Immigration to America included experiences in 'uprooting' themselves from their native lands, making the arduous journey to America, trying to establish roots here, facing discrimination and privation, and attempting to adjust to a culture which was totally alien to the one they had left. They faced the threat and difficulty of detention or rejection at the port of debarkation, entrapment by unscrupulous shipping and boardinghouse agents, finding decent lodgings and employment and adjusting to a very unfamiliar life-style.[1]

During economic booms jobs in America were plentiful. Native-born Americans and immigrants from Northern and Western Europe were moving along the occupational scale and were no longer available to fill menial positions. Feldstein and Costello and others report that Eastern and Southern European newcomers generally lived in the worst urban tenements and were exposed to the ravages of periodic epidemics. Absentee slumlords and ruthless employers exploited them. The immigrant workingmen often toiled long hours and at very low wages, and many through no fault of their own, were the victims of serious industrial accidents.

Upon arrival in the United States, immigrants usually came under pressure to become "American," to conform to the actions, values and beliefs of the Anglo community. The pressure frequently caused the newcomers some uncertainty about the values and sense of community which they could develop in their new situation. Feldstein and Costello confirm the findings of many social historians:

> The aliens also were constantly under pressure to strip themselves of all aspects of their Old World backgrounds. Furthermore, the advocates of Americanization sought to divest them of their ethnic characteristics and have these new citizens of the republic adopt the customs and language of the predominant culture. While being discriminated against, the foreign-born found themselves in the paradoxical position of being forced to become part of the homogenized mass, which was victimizing them.[2]

While such influences were strong, closer-grain analysis of ethnicity and the American regime suggest an angle of vision which runs obliquely to, if not counter to, the lines of argument

of that focus upon the victimization of immigrants by the Anglo culture and the capitalist system. However, the success of immigrants in America cannot be denied. Closer attention to the diversity of culture and history that characterized Southern and Eastern European ethnic groups reflects their job experience after arrival in the United States. Some immigrants, such as the Armenians, were far more interested in entrepreneurial opportunities than others such as the Bulgarians who looked to employment in industry to make their living.[3] Certain groups such as the Greeks were attracted to service jobs, while others such the Poles were employed primarily in heavy industries as miners or steelmakers.[4] From 1890–1950 the occupational mobility rates of immigrants and their children also varied from group to group; for example, 43 percent of second generation Romanians moved into white-collar occupations, but only 16 percent of second generation Slovaks did the same.[5]

Almost all groups, however, shared certain aspects of the immigrant experience. All began at the bottom of American society; they endured difficult social and economic conditions, often for several generations; the rate of occupational mobility for most of them was low until relatively recently; and they were victims of social and economic discrimination at the hands of their fellow Americans.[6] The Kerner Commission Report summed up the experience of Southern and Eastern European immigrants in the course of its analysis of the problems of American cities in the 1960s. Eastern and Southern European ethnics, who came to America from rural backgrounds, as Negroes did, are only now, after three generations, in the final stages of escaping from poverty. Until the last 10 years or so, most of these were employed in blue-collar jobs, and only a small proportion of their children were able or willing to attend college. In other words, only the third and in many cases the fourth generation has been able to achieve the kind of middle-class income and status that allows it to send its children to college. Because of favorable economic and political conditions, these ethnic groups were able to escape from lower-class status to working class and lower middle-class status, but it has taken them three generations.[7]

Historical and local factors must be examined even more closely. The conditions under which the immigrants worked and lived remained difficult and marginal for the first two or three generations. The conditions in immigrant neighborhoods such as Manhattan's Mulberry Street or Chicago's Noble Street, rivaled in congestion and unhealthiness those of any urban slum in the world.[8] Chicago housing inspectors for 1900, 1910 and 1920 concluded that living conditions in the worse quarters of Calcutta or Tokyo were more favorable than in the Polish neighborhoods of the city.[9] As late as 1940, the infant mortality and tuberculosis death rates in Slavic and Italian immigrant districts were the highest or among the highest in the cities in which they lived.[10] In a city such as Detroit, the 1940 census showed that more than half the housing in immigrant areas was classified as substandard.[11] Working conditions were equally difficult and dangerous. The United States in the early part of the twentieth century had one of the worst industrial safety records among industrialized countries, and Eastern and Southern European immigrants who worked at the least desirable and most dangerous jobs suffered a disproportionate amount of the casualties.[12] For example, at the South Chicago mill of Illinois Steel for the five-year reporting period between 1906 and 1910 one out of every four immigrant workers was injured or killed each year. The victims numbered more than 3,000 men over the five-year period.[13]

The low occupational and social status of Southern and Eastern European immigrants was matched by equally low wages. For the years 1908 through 1910 the Commissioner General of Immigration reported that 58.2 percent of foreign-born Bulgarian, Greek, Croatian, Italian, Lithuanian, Macedonian, Magyar, Polish, Portuguese, Romanian, Russian, Ruthenian, Serbian, Slovak, Syrian or Turkish males earned on the average less than $400 per year, while only 15.2 percent of the foreign-born who were Dutch, English, Irish, Norwegian, Scotch, Swedish and Welsh earned less than $400 per year.[14]

Their low status is reflected in the fact that in many industries they earned less and held less skilled and prestigious jobs than the small number of obviously disadvantaged Black Americans in Northern cities with whom they worked.[15] Only during World War I did Eastern and Southern Europeans definitely begin to pass Black Americans in their occupational and economic status.[16] That advantage came just as large numbers of Blacks from the South began to migrate North to fill the growing demand for labor caused by the wartime suspension of immigration, and hence to replace gradually the Southern and Eastern Europeans at the bottom of the society. The presence of a new group may have served to push Americans of Southern and Eastern European ancestry a step or two up the ladder of occupational status as they themselves had boosted native white Americans and immigrants from Northwestern Europe a generation before.[17]

Thus, for several generations Eastern and Southern Europeans provided a major pool of cheap labor for the mines, mills and factories of America. As a result "many millions lived in abject poverty in the densely packed slums. They were also too often without the most simple comforts and conveniences which their own labor made possible for others. They struggled merely to maintain their families above the level of actual hunger and want."[18]

Social Mobility

The rate and patterns of occupational mobility for Southern and Eastern European ethnic groups varied considerably. Certain groups such as the Romanians showed a surprising mobility

and interest in education and a significant segment of second generation Romanians in the inter-war period moved into middle class occupations.[19] On the whole, however, the rate of mobility for most Americans of Southern and Eastern European ancestry was slow and gradual before the 1960s. It is interesting to note that in many cases second generation males of some of those groups showed a decline in status in relationship to the status achieved by their fathers.[20] This was especially true if the fathers had attained a precarious hold on a middle-class position. In his Cleveland study, Josef Barton notes, for example, that "Italian fathers who gained middle-class status . . . consistently failed to pass their status on to their children. As a result, the second generation started out the thirties with no better chances than those with which immigrants had begun."[21]

These conclusions are supported in general by Stephen Thernstrom's mobility study of the population of Boston, *The Other Bostonians.* Perhaps the most careful and extensive historical mobility study ever done, it covers the period between 1880 and 1970. Several of the findings are worth noting. First Thernstrom observes that the Great Depression had a particularly stunting effect on the occupational mobility of the cohort of men born during the first decade of the century who were beginning work at low-skilled occupations in the 1930s.[22] Northern cities in 1900 contained immigrant populations with high birth rates and a disproportionate concentration in the laboring classes.[23] It is clear that this disadvantage fell with heaviest consequences on many second generation Southern and Eastern European ethnics and retarded their upward mobility for life. Secondly, he concludes that there are sharp ethnic differences in economic opportunity. Immigrants consistently fared less well than natives in occupational competition, and the children of the immigrants were "distinctively less successful than men of old native stock."[24] He concludes that even though immigration restriction in the 1920s caused these differentials to blur, "half a century later they remain visible to some degree still."[25] Finally, Thernstrom found that there were variations in mobility rates between immigrants, second-generation men and Yankees. Certain groups such as English and the Jews "found their way into higher occupational strata with exceptional speed" while Catholic ethnic groups such as those from Southern and Eastern Europe "moved ahead economically only sluggishly and erratically."[26]

It appears that although by the middle of the twentieth century most Southern and Eastern European ethnic groups had established themselves solidly in the working class and had built stable and orderly communities, they had not yet moved in significant numbers into middle-class occupations.[27] Martin Mager's study of Detroit's elite graphically bears out that finding for one city. He concludes:

What is most striking is that by the mid-twentieth century Southern and Eastern Europeans still did not appear among the business, financial and industrial leadership of Detroit, in spite of the fact that two and in some cases three generations had passed.[28]

The explanations of the "slow and erratic" mobility of most Southern and Eastern European groups have revolved around a series of cultural factors. Observers have pointed to the obvious lack of skills useful in an industrial society, strong initial interest in returning to their European homes after a few years of work in America, poor educational preparation, inability to speak English and low social status as hindering the advancement of immigrants. These disadvantages carried over to their children.[29] In addition, particular features of their religious background and/or their rural or national cultures were often cited.[30] Some scholars using a Neo-Weberian analysis argued that Catholicism in general and the particular Catholic orientation and upbringing of the immigrants produced a worldview that placed less emphasis on worldly success and higher education than did Protestantism.[31] Others pointed to the relative importance of community rather than individualism, and of the accumulation of capital to purchase land and homes rather than to engage in entrepreneurial activity, as the product of value systems and mobility strategies characteristic of rural societies. These strategies were seen, at a number of points, as antagonistic to urban, secular or "modern" value systems.[32]

The value of these factors as sufficient and necessary explanations has been challenged. For example, Miriam Cohen has recently argued that the attitudes of Southern and Eastern European ethnic groups toward education was shaped not by deep-seated cultural factors, but by demographic and economic circumstances and the structural features of the job market.[33] She shows that when circumstances changed and the possibility of securing work and advancement as a result of education was perceived by Americans of Southern and Eastern European ancestry, they responded accordingly.[34] Cohen concludes that

> parental attitudes about education changed not because attitudes about females, males or children in general changed but because these parents had to adapt to changing social circumstances in an effort to do what they had always done—to prepare their children with the proper skills so that they would survive, even succeed as adults.[35]

The rather significant leap in income, education and middle class status in recent years for Americans of Southern and Eastern European ancestry—a phenomenon Andrew Greeley called "the Ethnic Miracle"[36]—also raises questions about the success of the cultural interpretation fully to explain their mobility patterns. Steven Steinberg's recent study, *The Ethnic Myth,* has argued that the establishment of strong ethnic communities and a stable working-class life pattern created the economic and cultural base from which third and fourth

generations could move up economically once they perceived that barriers to mobility such as discrimination had begun to fall.[37] Steinberg, in fact, points out that the cultural and economic base from which Eastern and Southern European ethnics have begun to move into professional occupations and academic life is much more narrow and precarious than that which afforded Jews the opportunity to make a similar move a generation before.[38] The children of Jewish immigrants from Eastern Europe who moved into academic life so successfully, came overwhelmingly out of the merchant and small shopkeeper class, not out of the Jewish working class. Catholic ethnics appear to be making their move primarily out of a working-class base.[39] These explanations of the "Ethnic Miracle" would strongly suggest that their mobility was not the result of rejection of the cultural background of the ethnic community and its values but rather of building upon them.

Conflict and Civility

During every major economic crisis since the 1880s, immigrants have become a target for complaints and frustrations. Such conflict, which even occurs between established ethnics and new immigrants of the same nationality, does more than reduce production and services: it destroys civic confidence and damages the moral universe of victims and victimizers. Group-based oppression and discrimination based on national origin in America have been ignored and neglected dimensions of our moral order. Economic, social and cultural conflicts that exist beneath the surface of passive civility explode during crises. Times of limited resources provoke competition for access to the sources of power that are presumed as remedies. Because explosions are rare in a society of abundance and well-orchestrated diversions, some recommend no moral therapy. Put simply: if it's not broke, don't fix it. This argument, however, discounts the importance of developing social consensus and dismisses approaches to cultural justice and the classical sense of civitas anchored in the experiences of lived cultural communities.

Sporadic reports of group violence and the demographics of immigration indicate that America is beginning a new round of population and cultural change. The number of Asian and South American immigrants has increased. The U.S. Census counted over 14 million foreign-born persons in 1980. In 1970 the Census revealed 9.6 million foreign-born persons. Yet Afro-Americans are isolated in urban areas and the expectation of an integrated society seems further off today than two decades ago. Such social indicators may induce fear and hatred. The challenge for leadership, however, is to channel the fresh and vital social energy of a new generation into attitudes, policies and programs, which reflect the convergent hopes for fairness, dignity and respect for all persons.

Before this society yields to internal disintegration, which may prompt extraordinary, and tyrannical corporate and governmental remedies, we need to address the task of enabling Americans to understand the non-governmental, "natural", "organic", neighborhood based, community character of civil society in America. What I propose is a new agenda and action thrust to understand, to protect and to encourage community-based institutions, which create a sense of human scale, cultural, grounding for personal efficacy and common citizenship. There is good historical-cultural evidence for the claim that community-based institutions have created wholesome and helpful bonds between persons as well as between people and large-scale governmental and corporate institutions.

Careful attention to what is left of the community-based reality in America may enable us to understand the forces leading to group conflicts and to seek new approaches to achieving liberty and justice. Without a new vision of civility, the rights of persons will become only forced behavior. Resources that can be bargained and accommodated can obviously be lost.

It is time to recall that civility and civil rights are not merely the products of inspired speech and law. They spring from the best and most generous impulses in human society and culture and are created by living in communities. It appears then that to establish justice means to awaken America to an understanding of its complexity, its pluralism and the importance of small-scale community-based institutions. That is the agenda for the renewal and recovery of solidarity in the pursuit of justice.

Neighborhoods Decline

In 1904 G.K. Chesterton published his first novel, *The Napoleon of Notting Hill*. It was a curious and prophetic book set in 1984 about a young leader of the Notting Hill neighborhood of London who leads his people in defense of the neighborhood against a proposed highway that would cut it apart. Chesterton had a great love for particular places and, though a man of universal vision, his essay proclaimed that, "Empires wax and wane and never provide the kind of local democratic loyalty that men need."

Chesterton loved those particular places. "There stood a row of shops. At one end was a public house . . . somewhere a church . . . there was a grocer's . . . a second hand bookstore . . . an old curiosity shop . . . shops supplying all the spiritual and bodily needs of men." By the turn of the century he came to understand that his "progressive" friends wanted to destroy the Notting Hill's of the world in the name of modernity and human advancement. At that point Chesterton discovered that he opposed these planners and idealists—as he said, "I drew my sword in defense of Notting Hill."

In the eighty years since Chesterton drew his rhetorical sword, the warning bells his art and insight sounded now resonate in the life and experience of neighborhood people. The neighborhood has not fared well in the United States. In fact, at the very time he was writing, the Progressive movement was readying its attack on ward government and neighborhood representation in city government in many American cities. As a result by 1920, in cities such as Detroit and Pittsburgh, the ward organization and the patronage system that supported it were replaced by city councils elected at large and by an extended civil service. The local political machine associated with bosses and immigrant and working-class politics disappeared in favor of a new, city-wide, middle-class machine based on educational qualifications, civic clubs, trade associations, men's groups associated with prestigious mainline Protestant churches and blue ribbon commissions. Even in cities that were not "reformed," the increasing centralization and professionalization of city administration and services diminished the role of local and ethnic institutions.

After the Second World War, the infusion into the cities of state and federal monies with their accompanying guidelines covering highway building, welfare and educational policy, industrial development and urban renewal destroyed local autonomy and initiative and completed the ruin of many neighborhoods. The growth of new suburban areas, fostered by some of the same politics, lured away many of the younger and more upwardly mobile of the neighborhood people. With the decline of the neighborhoods came the decline of the churches, schools, ethnic organizations, political clubs, shopping strips and entertainment centers that had tied them together and given them distinct identities. As a result, by the sixties many urban areas had been neglected, bulldozed, "redlined" and paved over into highways.

In addition to growing powerlessness and deterioration, neighborhoods faced demographic changes that altered their ethnic and racial composition, culture and social cohesion. This sometimes brought on and exacerbated conflict and competition for control of housing and local institutions. Moreover, racial and ethnic succession in urban neighborhoods was often poorly understood, misinterpreted and exaggerated by media and national leaders. Though neighborhood weakness still abounds, the struggle in defense of neighborhoods foreshadowed by Chesterton has begun and the defense of neighborhoods based on honest-to-experience analyses has yielded judgments and actions that are fueled by Chesterton's moral sensibility Yet, unlike his artful world of imagination, the praxis of contemporary defender of neighborhood is rewriting the agenda for urban life in the decades to come.

The neighborhood experiences of the 1970s indicate that there is a definable process of urban decay in American neighborhoods. And commercial disinvestment is a crucial component of this decay. The damage done to local, national and urban economies is severe. However, neighborhood revitalization, which began as an art, is now emerging as a science. Because commercial disinvestment is a key feature of decay, commercial revitalization is an indispensable part of the general revitalization. Neighborhood commercial revitalization can succeed under the right conditions and provided the appropriate development experiences are transferred to, and applied by, the private, public and community sectors of America.

The pattern of urban decline is well known and documented. Something like the following happens. When an older residential neighborhood begins to experience signs of distress, its commercial strip of retail and light manufacturing, although affected, still functions and provides jobs and services to the residents. However, a crucial stage is soon reached as the older population begins to die off or move out.

Signs of decay occur. The commercial strip, which is one—in some cases the only—source of capital accumulation for the neighborhood economy, begins to deteriorate as businesses begin to close or move out. Government sponsored urban renewal may occur, destroying residential and commercial buildings without replacing them. A local employer may move out due to the structural differences in taxes created by the federal system. Banks and insurance companies begin to reassess their risk in the area, perhaps denying insurance and access to capital at any price. The municipal government may begin to limit city services due to the decreased political clout of the area. The most affluent move out, commercial and residential closings accelerate, the area becomes less and less attractive and the speed of decay accelerates.

The cycle of decay does not usually limit its effect to the initial neighborhood. If left unchecked, the negative conditions begin to spill into adjoining neighborhoods; severe dislocations and distortions are introduced into the economy as jobs move out and workers follow. Many of the newly unemployed, especially those from lower income families, however, simply can't move in order to follow the jobs. Valuable existing facilities (commercial, industrial, and residential) are abandoned or underutilized, and replaced with costly new facilities in a more desirable location. The classic liberal response of government subsidies usually does little for the neighborhoods affected while further compounding inflation. As the government is forced into the political position of allocating a greater share of economic resources, the ability of the market to achieve efficiency and productivity is hampered.

The process can continue until the city and ultimately the nation find themselves in the now too frequent predicament of having unlivable neighborhoods with a large unemployed population. Without any agencies for internal capital formation, this population is dependent upon outside sources for permanent subsidies to maintain even subsistence levels. Usually the main government assistance comes in the form of costly ongoing subsidies such as welfare, food stamps, public health and temporary job programs.

To the extent that government tries to create permanent jobs, it has tended to concentrate on large-scale industrial projects through the Economic Development Administration or highly visible showcases in central business districts through HUD's Urban Development Action Grants. These have only marginal impact on the neighborhoods. It is well known that over 80% of net jobs created in this country in the last ten years came from the small business sector which is the keystone to neighborhood commerce. This fact suggests that neighborhood commercial revitalization is a prime development arena as well as a key to neighborhood salvage.

Neighborhood Revitalization

The success or failure of community and economic development activities throughout the cities and communities of the U.S. depends largely upon very localized characteristics, dynamics and developments. Federal agencies, state and local governments can provide various incentives and supportive programs, but they cannot supply directly the most critical need nor can they alone implement community and economic development ventures and processes. These public sector actors can, however, recognize needs and design programs, which eliminate bottlenecks and promote the development of those factors, which produce successful development.

The factors which ensure the steady increase in potential production and consumption, as well as participation and ownership in a given community, form a complex equation. Community and economic development depend on a host of interacting processes: entrepreneurial activity, the actual basis of all production, the availability of productive processes and resources, the accessible level of technique, social institutions and attitudes, capital, and sufficient population and level of consumption. The saliency of these various contextual factors shift from time to time, and their relationships to each other change. Some of the factors are of course external and beyond the influence of a community. But, experienced neighborhood analysts and proven practitioners of neighborhood revitalization have fashioned an understanding of this complex process. They can help discern what is meaningful, effective and needed to develop a community and to promote its full economic potential.

In addition to a correct analysis of economic and market factors, it is now more than obvious that the full use of community resources, in all their variety, is important to any particular local economic development endeavor. The non-participation of any sector, public, private or community, puts a venture at extreme risk. Citizen's groups, private businesses and other institutions can either oppose change and stifle development or be the primary impetus for development and improvement. Frequently, the difference between the adoption of one or another posture is determined by a group's self-interest and its understanding of its ability to share in the development.

It is clear then that the process by which a neighborhood economic development program is carried out requires this process of cooperative interaction. The public sector, primarily municipal government, must create the proper environment in order for business to operate effectively. The private sector, principally business people and financial institutions that indicate a desire to remain and invest in the neighborhood, must take a central position in the actual process of business development. Organized community groups must actively participate in the planning and implementation of the revitalization program, provide broad-based citizen support, relate the economic development program to the overall neighborhood revitalization process, and mediate between conflicting interests when and if the occasion arises. The three sectors should be jointly involved from the outset. The following narrative model includes a description of the public, the private and the community sectors each, and the role each must play in an effective economic revitalization program.

Public Sector

The primary responsibility of the public sector is the delivery of various types of services and actions, which are essential to a healthy community environment. In many cases, adequate delivery by the public sector can be a sufficient trigger for considerable private investment in the neighborhood. Provision of certain services and/or public actions by the municipality can spell the difference between the feasibility and non-feasibility of development projects. A partial listing of those necessary services and actions include:

- Police/security
- Parking
- Sanitation and neighborhood appearance
- Transportation facilities
- Code enforcement
- Other public actions—zoning, taxing, etc.

Adequate lines of communication should be established between public agencies and the private sector. Also because they are composed of, and represent, the interests of the residents of the area (who are the electorate), the community leadership must also play a vital role in this communication process.

Private Sector

In the context of the revitalization process, the private sector generally is made up of the local business and financial community. In any economic development program, this sector must carry the bulk of the development activity. The existence of a strong local merchants' association is often a precondition

for an effective program. The members of such associations should be expected to contribute to the support of their organizations by both financial involvement and the contribution of in-kind services.

Experience has shown that business development must involve all or most of the following aspects of the neighborhood economy. A neighborhood commercial revitalization program, as carried out by a local public/private partnership, must be able to deliver services in all the following areas.

Improving the Competitiveness of the Existing Merchants. Local merchants forced to compete with regional shopping centers, generally are unable to do so effectively. By forming and working through active merchants' associations patterned along the lines of those regional shopping centers, merchants can upgrade the physical appearance of their stores and the quality of merchandise, increase the scale of operations, promote the neighborhood as an interesting and convenient place to shop, institute building and equipment maintenance programs, and achieve cooperation in other programs of mutual benefit.

Providing Basic Commercial Services Lacking in the Neighborhood. Most old urban neighborhoods are under-serviced in terms of availability of basic goods and services. Treating the neighborhood essentially as a shopping center or district provides a way to analyze demand patterns, identify opportunities for new commercial activities, locate potential entrepreneurs, and assist in packaging and developing new business enterprises such as supermarkets, drug stores, junior department stores, hardware stores, etc.

Quality of Life Elements. A viable neighborhood economy should have interesting and entertaining commercial establishments such as restaurants, boutiques, and other shops, drawing heavily on the ethnic or cultural foundations in the neighborhood. These quality of life elements enhance life in the neighborhood and also attract customers from outside the neighborhood.

Involvement of Financial Institutions in the Local Economy. The local banks must play a central role in the revitalization process by providing loans to the merchants and property owners for rehabilitation and physical improvement. In most cases, banks are far more receptive to loan applications if they are properly packaged and part of a larger revitalization effort. For this reason, a local development organization should assist in individual business packaging and should help structure an overall development program. Its participation in establishing effective lines of communication between the financial institutions and the overall development effort can help assure an ongoing and mutually beneficial working relationship between the financial institutions and the local business community.

Upgrading the Employment Base in the Community. Except in very rare cases, the revitalization process will be severely limited if there is no expansion of the job base provided by the industrial sector. The city's overall economic development entity and community-based organizations should develop an active program to retain what industry is already in the neighborhood and to attract new industry by acquisition and relocation. In most cases, light assembly-type plants providing 50–70 jobs each are ideal for urban neighborhoods because they generally are nonpolluting and relatively labor intensive.

Community Sector

While the bulk of revitalization activity will come from the private sector, there are several aspects of the revitalization process in which community development organizations play a critical role. As part of their involvement in the planning process, community organizations must see that the economic revitalization program relates to, and supports, the overall neighborhood development program, especially as it pertains to land and physical development (e.g., housing) as well as to stability and neighborhood cohesion. Areas in which the community development organizations might be involved include the following.

Property maintenance. Just as maintenance of commercial property is critical to the success of a commercial revitalization program, overall neighborhood revitalization requires physical maintenance and improvement programs for residential property. By working with homeowners, the development organization can assist in arranging for property improvement loans through local banks and savings and loan associations. The confidence generated on the part of lending institutions toward the economic revitalization program should be transferable into other areas of a neighborhood revitalization program, including housing and home improvement programs. Certainly the lines of communication and working relationship established by the development organization between the financial institutions and the community should result in a closer partnership in these areas.

Development of Land and Physical Resources. Neighborhood revitalization cannot occur without reference to the land and physical resource needs of the area. These needs include living and working space (housing and building construction and rehabilitation), social services (e.g., medical and educational facilities), and recreational opportunities (places of entertainment, sport and relaxation). In each of these areas there are obvious opportunities, which a community development organization can help identify and package. Keep in mind

that local ownership or oversight of these resources is a primary goal and requirement for neighborhood stabilization.

Local Ownership of Commercial Real Estate. To allow for greater local participation in neighborhood land use, programs can be developed to increase the local ownership of commercial and industrial real estate. The development organization can assist in the development of investment syndicates, organize property management companies, and recommend methods for improving the attractiveness and marketability of the commercial locations. It is also felt that broad-based community ownership of commercial real estate could improve the quality of maintenance and reduce vandalism.

However, economic planners regularly neglect these strategies and techniques. Moreover, the impacts of investments, which improve the capacity of community-based economic development, are not factored into traditional approaches to unemployment, joblessness and poverty. New, yet tested, opportunity-creating approaches are needed to promote community development as an alternative to welfare dependency. Research and demonstration projects in neighborhoods, which are successfully revitalizing their commercial strips, suggest the validity of the following neighborhood economic revitalization (NER) approach. This approach replicates ordinary entrepreneurial processes, which take into account different variables in each neighborhood. It is structured around ordinary entrepreneurial processes so that performance can be measured by profit and loss and assessed by community satisfaction.

A Neighborhood Economic Revitalization Approach

There are four major steps in such an approach: 1) identification and capacity building; 2) development; 3) implementation; and 4) wrap-up. These steps parallel those a private developer/entrepreneur would take to revitalize a commercial strip.

1. Step one begins by focusing on a troubled but still robust neighborhood, which includes a neighborhood commercial area. The neighborhood residents and their institutions, along with local businesses, financial organizations and city officials are organized to shape their future through the initiatives of energized local leaders. Small seed grants and professional neighborhood organizers often assist local leaders. They begin a process of meeting local needs, addressing unfairness in public and private allocation of resources, and developing neighborhood confidence. At this point, a rudimentary plan of action is clear and a series of development sites and possibilities are proposed.

2. In step two, the development process, the leader's contract for a market analysis of the existing area, hire

an architect or engineer to review the physical plans and environment, expand the staff organization if necessary, and coordinate funding allocations and availability.

They also work with a planner, the city, businessmen and residents to draw up a plan for their area. Step three involves implementing the plan. The final step, wrap-up, includes grand opening ceremonies and management of the commercial operation.

The revitalization of an inner city commercial strip involves the same public and private sectors, which led to its decline in the first place. The major task is revitalizing the spirit of these forces to bring about a concerted, comprehensive program for the total rehabilitation of the social, economic and physical environment.

The selection criteria used in the identification process are comparable to the ordinary entrepreneur's identification of a suitable market place. The economic revitalization of a community depends on the existence of a host of preconditions, which ensure the profitable rebuilding. Profits must be measured not merely in cash flow balances of the merchants or cost benefits to city coffers, but also in the sense of place, dignity and freedom from fear of the inhabitants of the neighborhood. Initial and ongoing processes of community organizing and empowerment, leadership training and recruitment, as well as fashioning indigenous institutions to meet the challenges of rebuilding community cohesion, are needed to achieve optimum improvement.

Commercial revitalization will be most successful in an area where other programs for housing, crime control, jobs and health care exist. The ills of a ten to twenty year period of disinvestment cannot be cured piecemeal or quickly, even if all the people will it to happen. The pump can be primed with grant/subsidy dollars, but the successful operating cash flow mechanism for restoration of a neighborhood's lifeblood requires more dollars than it is politically possible to extract from the coffers of government. With an organized community, a series of coordinated programs and an active publicity campaign for communication between all sectors, the approach can operate successfully in the overall fabric for neighborhood economic revitalization.

The neighborhood economic revitalization approach will operate with few government controls or reviews, but it requires capital input at several points to ensure the successful capture of conventional funds. A careful balance, therefore, must be maintained between effective public control mechanisms and the allocation of limited public resources. It will take hard surveys and human energy for organizing groups into productive contributors in order to rebuild neighborhoods, cities and the nation; it is, therefore, important that local government be a sensitive, helping partner rather than a bureaucratic obstacle.

Although it requires only a small amount of seed funds to begin the process, an astute organizer is needed to entice the initial capital investment, which, in turn, is used to leverage other investments of capital. There are a number of sources of capital and matching capital funds, i.e. public and private sector funds, foundation funds, etc. An organization can afford to call in technical assistance to further its efforts at banding the neighborhood together, identifying revitalization processes and determining goals and objectives as some of these capital sources are identified and become available.

As a tool for the reversal of disinvestment in neighborhoods, the revitalization approach includes almost all applicable steps or activities necessary to affect reinvestment. It has taken at least ten to twelve years for neighborhood organizations in the inner city to coalesce, to identify themselves and their needs, and to learn the processes of reinvestment. This approach is an outgrowth of these decade-long efforts. Continued efforts of the sort and the consequent successful rebirth of inner cities for all peoples who live and work there can be accomplished during the next two decades.

Conventional approaches to development could be operational in inner city sites if redlining by bankers and insurance companies were not a counterproductive factor. The Home Mortgage Disclosure Act, the Community Reinvestment Act as well as some features of the tax code are rudimentary incentives for recapitalizing jobless and poor areas. The perceptions of large-scale financial institutions should be refocused so that dependency and decline may be abated. Building or restoring the participation of banks, insurance companies and other investing institutions as trusting partners is thus a key factor in this approach. The political machinery and bureaucratic process should also be refocused so that the faith of all the parties concerned and affected by the process of revitalization can be restored. Most successful efforts toward revitalization are achieved by joint efforts of community residents and merchants acting in concert with public agencies and public and private sources of investment capital.

An important difference between this and conventional approaches is the nature of the "entrepreneur." From one decisive, profit-motivated individual this approach goes to a tripartite group of various vested (and often conflicting) interests. Whereas the conventional entrepreneur works almost single-handedly and with single purpose of mind, in the neighborhood approach the entrepreneurial team must relate to a host of negative influences and obstructions. This challenges the simple-minded notion of the individualistic entrepreneurship, which neglects the effects of positive and negative external factors and fails to see that the neighborhood is a micro-market and economic multiplier. In point of fact the use of the neighborhood approach has begun the reexamination of conventional wisdom and market trends.

Reinvestment in urban neighborhoods by ordinary entrepreneurial interests will probably accelerate. However, this action for justice through development is not an automatic mechanism. It must be catalyzed and assisted by public, private and community resources. These must be targeted toward local projects that increase the flow of reinvestment and market activity in neighborhoods and encourage the development of viable establishments, which will increase the range and quality of goods and services available to the community.

Projects could accomplish such goals through various program components that:

- lend support to potential businesses that will employ neighborhood residents
- encourage an increase of local ownership and involvement in new businesses
- aid in making the commercial corridors more competitive with outside markets by supporting physical development programs that will improve the appearance of and help stabilize the district
- support the establishment of a strong and active business association to organize cooperative advertising and promotional events
- encourage the involvement of community residents supporting and developing the direction and programs of the project.

Thus the process and the project of neighborhood revitalization includes more than invocation of wholesome values and symbols. The celebrated recover of squandered practices is mostly imagery. In most respects neighborhood revitalization is a complex contemporary artifice—a contemporary social economic invention. The measures of success proposed in this agenda are articulated and exercised by the persons involved. That the large-scale mechanism of cultural, economic and social formation ought to be attentive to the presence of the social fabric that constitutes the lived experience of urban neighborhoods is as important today as it was in the early 20th century. The record of that era is as uneven as it is today. The ongoing work of social and economic justice is a task for each generation and each period of immigration. Honest-to-experience recollection of the immigrant experience, ethnic social mobility and neighborhood decline are the pathway to normative and practical prescription about multicultural social formation and neighborhood development.

Endnotes

1. Stanley Feldstein and Lawrence Costello, editors, *The Ordeal of Assimilation* (New York: Anchor & Doubleday, 1974), p. XIX.

2. Ibid., p. XX.

3. On the occupational and regional distribution of Southern and Eastern European immigrants prior to World War I see Caroline Golab, *Immigrant Destinations* (Philadelphia: Temple University Press, 1977), pp. 3–64.

4. Ibid.

5. Josef J. Barton, *Peasants and Strangers: Italians, Rumanians and Slovaks in an American City 1890–1950* (Cambridge, Mass.: Harvard University Press, 1974), pp. 137–141.

6. Philip Taylor, *The Distant Magnet: European Emigration to the U.S.A.* (New York: Harper & Row, Publishers, 1971), pp. 167–209.

7. "Comparing the Immigrant and Negro Experience," National Advisory Commission Report on Civil Disorders in the United States (Washington, D.C., 1968), p. 145.

8. J. Reis, *How the Other Half Lives* (New York, Sagamore Press, 1957).

9. The Chicago Homes Association reported an average of 339.8 tenants per acre and 2,716 families compressed into forty acres in which no building rose over four stories. The report concluded that the density of the "Polish Quarter was three times that of the most crowded portions of Tokyo, Calcutta and many other Asiatic cities." One block contained 1,349 children. Tenement Conditions in Chicago: Report by the Investigating Committee of the City Homes Association (1901) quoted in J. Parot, "Ethnic Census Black Metropolis" *Polish American Studies, XXIX* (no. 1–2, 1972), 7–12. The situation in the early 1920s had not changed dramatically with 50,000 people living per square mile in squalid, disease-ridden neighborhoods in which less than 10% owned their own homes. Edith Abbott, *The Tenements of Chicago 1908–1935* (Chicago: University of Chicago Press, 1936). Social workers and other observers often reported severe undernourishment and malnutrition in these areas well into the 1920's. For a report from Detroit, see City of Detroit, Annual Reports of the Departments of Public Welfare, 1922. On file, Benton Collection, Detroit Public Library. Helen Wendell, "Conditions in Hamtramck," *Pipps Weekly,* vol. 2 (Sept. 24, 1921).

10. For example, the infant mortality rates for Polish and other Eastern European neighborhoods in Detroit in 1940 ranged from 40 to 60 per 1,000 live births and the death rate from tuberculosis, a high of 70 per 100,000. City of Detroit, City Plan Commission, *Master Plan Reports: The People of Detroit* (Detroit, 1946), pp. 33–34.

11. U.S. Department of Commerce, Bureau of the Census, Housing Bulletin for Michigan Hamtramck Block Statistics (Washington, D.C.: U.S. Government Printing Office, 1942), pp. 5–8.

12. David Brody, *Steel Workers in America: The Non-Union Era* (New York: Harper Torchbooks, 1969), pp. 100–101.

13. Ibid.

14. Data summarized from a table abstracted from a report by the Commissioner General of Immigration in Peter Roberts, *The New Immigration: A Study of Industrial and Social Life of Southeastern Europeans in America* (New York: MacMillan, 1912), p. 366.

15. The Dillingham Commission on Immigration (1907–1911) reported that the average wages of Blacks in the industries surveyed were higher than immigrants in industries such as steel making or meatpacking. Blacks held higher positions and earned more money. For example in 1909 in the meat packing industry the average daily wage was $2.35 for native Whites, $2.05 for Blacks and $1.79 for Poles and Lithuanians. See David Brody, *The Butcher Workman* (Cambridge: Harvard University Press, 1957), p. 85. On the steel industry see John Bodnar, "The Impact of the 'new immigration' on the Black Worker," *Labor History,* vol. XVII, no. 2, (Spring, 1976), pp. 214–229. For a study that puts the overall wage for Southern and Eastern European Ethnics engaged in mining or manufacturing at the same level or a few cents a day higher than for Blacks, see Robert Higgs "Race, Skill and Earnings: American Immigrants in 1909" *The Journal of Economic History, XXXI* (1971), 424–426. The low status of Southern and Eastern European Ethnics is evidenced by that fact that Blacks, the most discriminated-against native American group, were not infrequently hired as armed guards to police Southern and Eastern European immigrants up to the end of World War I, often with resulting violence. For incidents that resulted in numbers dead and injured see T. Radzialowski, "Competition for Jobs and Racial Stereotypes: Poles and Blacks in Chicago" *Polish American Studies, XXXIII* (no. 2, 1976), pp. 5–18; and W. Tuttle, *Race Riot 1919* (New York: Athenaeum, 1974), p. 138.

16. Bodnar, "The Impact of the 'New Immigration' on the Black Worker" concludes that Southern and Eastern European Ethnic workers passed Blacks in their occupational status and wages by 1915. The increase in their numbers also displaced a significant number of Blacks working in this and a number of other industries. On this also see David Katzman, *Before the Ghetto: Black Detroit in the Nineteenth Century* (Urbana: University of Illinois Press, 1973), pp. 116, 120, and Gilbert Osofsky, *Harlem: The Making of a Ghetto* (New York: Harpers, 1971), pp. 196–198. Mobility rates for some Eastern and Southern European groups remained at the same level as that of Blacks even after World War I. A new study of Pittsburgh concludes "as late as 1920, half of the Russian Poles and nearly three quarters of the German Poles and Southern Blacks had failed to move from the bottom of the occupational classes . . . Northern born Blacks and Italians, conversely, moved out of the lower skilled levels with increasing frequency each decade." John Bodnar, Roger Simon and Michael Weber, *Lives of their Own: Blacks, Italians and Poles in Pittsburgh, 1900–1960* (Urbana, Ill.: University of Illinois Press, 1982).

17. On the "uplifting" effect of a new group of migrants on other workers see Theodore Hershberg, and others, "Occupation and Ethnicity in Five Nineteenth-Century Cities: A Collaborative Inquiry," *Historical Methods Newsletter, VII* (no. 3, 1974), 212–213. While the replacement of Southern and Eastern Europeans by Blacks at the bottom of the occupational scale may have had a significant impact on their mobility in some cities and some industries it is almost impossible to calculate and no detailed studies of this aspect of Black-Southern and Eastern European relations have been done. It is clear that such mobility would not have changed in any way the relative hierarchical ranking of any groups' occupational status. Bodnar, Simon and Weber, *Lives of their Own,* have recently called into question the thesis of the uplifting effect, p. 141.

18. Foster Rhea Dulles, *Labor in America: A History* (New York: Free Press of Glencoe, 1963), pp. 170–182.

19. Barton, *Peasants and Strangers,* pp. 172–173.

20. Stanley Lieberson, *Ethnic Patterns in American Cities* (New York: Free Press of Glencoe, 1963). pp. 170–182.

21. Barton, *Peasants and Strangers,* p. 172.

22. Stephen Thernstrom, *The Older Bostonians: Poverty and Progress in the American Metropolis 1880–1970* (Cambridge, Harvard University Press, 1973), p. 233.

23. U.S. Dept. of Commerce, Bureau of the Census, Sixteen Census of the Population, Special Reports, Differential Fertility 1940 and 1910 (Washington, D.C.: Govt. Printing Office, 1940). See tables 3 and 4 "Fertility for States and Large Cities."

24. Ibid., p. 250.

25. Ibid.

26. Ibid., pp. 250–251. Andrew Greeley argues that Thernstrom's findings on the Irish mobility rates may be true only for Boston and not for the Irish in the remainder of the country. A. Greeley, *The Irish Americans* (New York: Harper, 1981), p. 116.

27. Nathan Glazer and Daniel P. Moynihan, *Beyond the Melting Pot* (Cambridge, Mass.: MIT Press, 1964), pp. 181–207, 322. Herbert Gans, *Urban Villagers* (New York: The Free Press, 1962). Paul Wrobel, *Our Way* (Notre Dame, Ind., University of Notre Dame Press, 1979).

28. Martin Marger, "Ethnic Penetration of the Elite Structure of 1900–1950s" Diss. Michigan State University, 1973, p. 190. Two other studies of Detroit during the mid-1960s point to the still largely working class character of Southern and Eastern European groups twenty years ago. John Leggett, *Class, Race and Labor* (New York: Oxford, 1973) showed a Polish and Slavic sample that was more than 60% working class and with unemployment rates 40% higher than the white male population of Northwest European origin. Edward Laumann in his classic study *Bonds of Pluralism* (New York: John Wiley, 1973) studied the status and occupational distribution of major Southern and Eastern European groups in relation to the high prestige groups in the city. Using the Duncan index of socio-economic status he calculated the status of the fifteen major groups in Detroit. The highest three were Jews (63.4), Anglo-Presbyterians (59.2) and German Presbyterian (58.0). Slavic Catholics were ninth (46.5), Italian Catholics, tenth (44.1) and Polish Catholics, thirteenth (39.6). The occupational data from his sample showed in the 1960s in Detroit, Slavic Catholics with 60.5 percent in blue collar jobs, Italian Catholics with 56.4 percent and Polish Catholics with 67.3 percent in the same category. In the professions the representation of the three groups was 18.4 percent, 14.5 percent and 11.8 percent, respectively.

29. Taylor, *Distant Magnet,* pp. 167–209.

30. See, for example, the widely-quoted study by Gerhard Lenski, *The Religious Factor: A Sociologist's Inquiry* (Garden City, New York: Doubleday Anchor, 1963). See also Thomas O'Dea, *The American Catholic Dilemma* (New York: Sheed and Ward, 1959); H.C. Lehman and P.A. Witty "Scientific Eminence and Church Membership" *Scientific Monthly, XXXIII* (1933), 548–550 and Kenneth Hardy "Social Origins of American Scientists and Scholars" *Science,* 185 (1974) 497–506.

31. Lenski, *The Religious Factor.*

32. See, for example, U.S. Immigration Commission, *The Children of Immigrants in School,* vol. 4, Select Document 5074, 61st Congress, 2 cong. session, 1911; John Bodnar, "Immigration and Modernization: The Case of Slavic Peasants in Industrial America," *Journal of Social History, X* (1976), 44–71.

33. Miriam Cohen "Changing Education Strategies Among Immigrant Generations: New York Italians in Comparative Perspectives," *Journal of Social History, XV* (1981), 443–465.

34. Ibid.

35. Ibid., p. 464.

36. Andrew Greeley, "The Ethnic Miracle," *The Public Interest,* 45 (1976), 20–36.

37. Steven Steinberg, *The Ethnic Myth* (New York: Athenaeum, 1981), pp. 145–150.

38. Ibid., pp. 147–149.

39. Ibid. Steinberg's study calls into question the traditional argument that Jewish mobility was the product of a religious culture that stressed literacy and valued education. He argues that these factors should have worked regardless of class and occupation, if they were significant, but they did not according to his figures. The primary factors of Jewish mobility in his view were: greater skills than other Eastern and Southern

Europeans especially in those industries such as the garment industry, about to expand rapidly; greater familiarity with urban life; inclination toward entrepreneurial activity which created a shopkeeper class with the resources to educate children for the professions; and no interest in returning with their earnings to Europe.

Critical Thinking

1. Describe the central features of large-scale immigration and urbanization that created the context into which Eastern and Southern European peasants began to negotiate their cultural endowments within northern states and their industrial development strategies for transforming the social realities of America.

2. Describe and assess the concept "social construction of neighborhoods" and the claim that this notion of community fabric is a valued humanizing mode and locus for creating urban ethnicity.

3. Describe the decline of urban neighborhoods and the public policies that promoted the transformation of transportation and housing in America.

Internet References

Center for Migration Studies
www.Cmsny.org

First Suburbs Coalition
www.Marc.org/firstsuburbs

Immigration and Ethnic History Society
www.iehs.org

National Civic Review
www.ncl.org

Kromkowski, John A.; Radzilowski, Thaddeus C.; Kochanowski, Paul. "Case Study: The American Immigrant Experiences", *National Center for Urban Ethnic Affairs, Occasional Papers.* National Center for Urban Ethnic Affairs. Reprinted by permission.

Unit 3

UNIT

Prepared by: John A. Kromkowski, *The Catholic University of America*

American Demography: If You're Not Counted, You Don't Count: The U.S. Census, the Politics of Pluralism, and the Science of Social Indicators

This unit explores the demography of race and ethnic relations. The measuring of groups and socioeconomic aspects of race and ethnicity is quite different from the materials that reveal cultures, traditions, and legal constructions of groups. And yet, in one respect, it is the legal construction of the U.S. Census that provides some continuity to the influence of government on race and ethnic relations. The demography of race and ethnic relations would be impossible without the U.S. Census. Since its founding, the U.S. Census has been the premier standard source of American demography. With the addition in 2005 of the American Communities Survey, the decennial collection of information can be regularly and accurately updated for fact-based knowledge and evidence. This is required to make data-driven decisions in the economic marketplace, the realms of public policy making, and the evaluation of outcomes.

Unit 3 also addresses another aspect of race and ethnicity: the certification and validation of race and ethnicity in the United States by the U.S. Census. The historical documentation and account of the peculiarity of group designations and the creation and changing of methods and categories provides a retrospective glimpse and insight into the foundational ascriptions that are at the core of race and ethnicity in the public life of pluralistic countries. The elemental account of groups began

with the Constitutional origins of the Decennial Census. From the beginning of the Republic, the Census has provided a public record of various views of our demographic self as a country. From early Census makers and takers and their enumeration of the Census, to its current practice of self-identification, the Census has provided a mass of information. Ongoing rolling surveys, cross-tabs and geo-coding now provide an interactive data trove of geographic profiles spanning areas both small and large. Some significant profiles and cases are included in this unit. The importance of such data for marketing and electoral campaigning has institutionalized race and ethnicity in contemporary America. Now that race and ethnicity exist as "measured in population" it joins cultural tradition, identity, and legal construction as another way we speak about, analyze and understand race and ethnic relations.

American demography is a neglected dimension of race and ethnic relations. These aspects are broached in the articles selected for this unit. The following complex features of the American reality become more knowable because of attention to American demography:

- The variety and specificity of populations,

- The particular scale and region of demographic patterns of settlement, and

- The reinvestigation of historically embedded characteristics of dominant cultures and their interaction with minority groups.

The particular demography of a region clearly shapes its self-articulation, but demography alone cannot express the ongoing presence of the past and reveal its impact on current approaches to race relations. These aspects will be revisited in other units and will emerge from other forms of articulation, expression, and interpretation.

The U.S. Census reveals the ongoing process of peopling America and the remarkably "lumpy" distribution of geographic patterns in various states and regions. The persistence of ethnic identification and the arrival of new immigrants are measured in this data and can now be accessed and systematically analyzed. The specific dynamics of group isolation and integration point to the complexity generated by public policy, most importantly, the designations available for racial and ethnic identity, offered for the first time in the 2000 U.S. Census. The plentitude of resources and the social imagination of community leaders, as well as specific characteristics of race and ethnic populations—their size, scale, and scope—and the range of governmental policies, determine race and ethnic relations. As a guide for your own study, the U.S. Commission on Civil Rights has noted the following issues for both recent arrivals and Americans by birth:

- Employment: The areas of occupation selected by or imposed upon various ethnic populations trace ethnic group mobility strategies and ethnic succession in the workplace, especially in manufacturing, hospitals, restaurants, and maintenance and custodial positions. Some ethnic populations appear to have greater numbers of highly educated persons in professional or semiprofessional positions.
- Institutional and societal barriers: The job preferences and discrimination against the ethnic enclaves and persons install communities that are isolated from mainstream English-speaking society, suggesting the value of second-language competencies. Mutual accommodation is required to minimize the effect of inadequate language skills and training and difficulties in obtaining licenses, memberships, and certification.
- Exploitation of workers: The most common form is the payment of wages below minimum standards. Alien workers have been stereotyped as a drain on public services. Such scapegoating is insupportable.
- Taking jobs from Americans: Fact or fiction?: The stunning fact is that immigrants are a source of increased productivity and a significant, if not utterly necessary, addition to the workforce as well as to the consumer power that drives the American economy.

The U.S. Census in 1980 and 1990 began the systematic collection of ethnic data. Census data on ethnicity is derived from self-identification. This method captures the respondent's sense of personal and group identity. Prior to 1980 the paucity of quantified information on ethnic variety was a profound impediment to the analysis of the ethnic composition of America and to the electoral participation of ethnic voters and ethnic organizations. Appreciating the variety of ethnicities that constitute the American population begins with dispelling the conventional categories and counts. Personal reflections on the relevance of ethnicity to one's self-concept and the search for clearer expressions of group identity are included in this unit. Readers may be interested in exploring the concept of social distance and group affinity in relation to the information provided in these articles. This information can also serve as a tool for testing and discovering patterns of race and ethnic interest in various issues. In addition to those mentioned, recent concerns of ethnic groups include: language preservation, fair hearings for homeland interests, enclave neighborhoods, inclusion in ethnic studies, and their articulation of historical American expressions of fairness, justice, and equity, as well as the collection of accurate data from all ethnic groups in America. These values are thoroughly patterned into their worldview. These ethnic groups have appropriated the expansive promise of the American icon—the Statue of Liberty. The U.S. Census has unveiled complex features of American reality; and our grasp of demography has enabled us to distinguish the imaginative from the real and thus to know: the variety and specificity of populations, the scale and region of demographic patterns, and the historically embedded characteristics of dominant cultures and their interaction with minority groups.

The particular demography of a region clearly shapes regional cultures, but demography alone cannot express the ongoing presence of the past and reveal its impact on current approaches to race relations. In the 1990 Census, the South and West were the only regions of the United States that had measurable respondents that indicated "white" as an ancestry or ethnicity. The South had, by far, the largest percentage and absolute number of persons reporting "United States" as their ethnicity, race, or ancestry. Unlike other regions with large immigrant populations and descendants of the nineteenth-century immigrants, over 15 percent of the population of the South provided no answer to the ancestry question on the 1990 Census. The ongoing process of peopling America and the remarkably "lumpy" distribution of geographic patterns in various states and regions are important for race and ethnic relations. The persistence of ethnic identification and the arrival of new immigrants is measured in this data and can now be accessed and systematically analyzed. The specific dynamics of group isolation and integration point to the complexity generated by public policy and to differential outcomes among racial and ethnic groups, and thus our distance from liberty and justice for all.

Article   Prepared by: John A. Kromkowski, *Catholic University of America*

The American Community Survey: The New Dimensions of Race and Ethnicity in America

JOHN DAVID KROMKOWSKI

Learning Outcomes

After reading this article, you will be able to:

- Explain the various implications of data collection by the U.S. Census.

- List and discuss the benefits of easy access to information about the distribution and concentration of ethnic populations, as well as the various social and economic indicators.

Beginning in 1980, most ethnic and ancestry information was collected by the US Census Bureau from the 'Long Form' of the Decennial Enumeration of the Population of the The United States, when the "Ancestry Question" was added to the Census. The record of data collection regarding race, "ethnic," and color (bracketing the distinction between native or foreign-born) can be viewed in the US Census forms excerpts regarding classifications of race or color from 1790–2010. However, for the first time since 1940, the 2010 Census was short-form-only census. This is because the decennial long form has been replaced by the American Community Survey (ACS). The ACS is a nationwide, continuous survey designed to provide reliable and timely demographic, housing, social, and economic data every year.

Demographers and other data users have long viewed the collection interval of ten years between censuses as a severe constraint to understanding change in modern America. In 1995, the US Census Bureau began to address such limitations and to devise new approaches to generating national data that would more rapidly update information requirements of our contemporary society and economy and to measure the accelerating rates of social change and mobility. The mission, goal and objective was to institute a new data collection process for obtaining demographic, housing, social, and economic information previously obtained from the 'Long Form' of the Decennial Census. Congress authorized the American Community Survey

(ACS) and testing of the American Community Survey began in 1996. The ACS program began producing test data in 2000. In addition to the data base derived decennial censuses, the American Community Survey introduced an ongoing data collection process and the production of accurate and statistically sound surveys. The U.S. Census Bureau sends questionnaires to approximately 250,000 addresses monthly (or 3 million per year). The Bureau regularly gathers information previously contained only in the Long Form of the decennial census. This effort is the largest data collection project, except for the decennial census that the Census Bureau administers. The ACS will replace the long form in 2010 and thereafter by collecting long-form-type information throughout the decade rather than only once every 10 years.

Recently, the data produced by ACS has become available online via the Census Bureau web site. (See http://census.gov/acs/www/) The array of information available is stunning in its scope. A researcher can download data for over 7000 geographic units and over 175 ethnicities and develop cross-tabs and do statistical tests for a variety of general, social, economic and housing variables related to specific ethnicities. For any selected population group, data is available for hundreds of variables that are grouped under the following thirty-two major headings: total number of races reported, sex and age, relationship, households by type, marital status, school enrollment, educational attainment, fertility, responsibility for grandchildren under 18 years, veteran status, disability status, residence 1 year ago, place of birth, citizenship status and year of entry, world region of birth of foreign born, language spoken at home and ability to speak english, employment status, commuting to work, occupation, industry class of worker, income in the past 12 months, poverty rates for families and people for whom poverty status is determined, housing tenure, units in structure, year structure built, vehicles available, house heating fuel, selected housing characteristics, selected monthly owner costs as a percentage of household income in the past 12 months, owner characteristics, gross rent as a percentage of household income in the past 12 months, and gross rent. By 2002, the data collected by the sampling was encompassing enough to make national estimates. Because it includes the Ancestry Question, the Hispanic Origin Question as well as the "race" question, it is an increasingly important tool for a demographic understanding of race and ethnicity in America. The available data also provides sufficient information to obtain standard errors. As a result, doing statistical tests to determine significance is not difficult. The determination of statistical significance takes into account the difference between the two estimates as well as the standard errors of both estimates.

In broadest outline, what the data reveal is that America is diverse and that statistically meaningful distinctions continue to exist and to evolve in what can be characterized as remarkable "lumpy" society and a geographically clustering of ethnicities which can not be described by concepts such as integration and segregation. To understand population clustering of this sort and at this magnitude demands more detailed analysis of ethnic and race patterns along with other economic and social indicators. Why do differences remain and are they meaningful or merely statistical artifacts? Do we actually understand the analytical tools necessary for dealing with "big data"? See the American Factfinder website of the Census Bureau and tool to analyze data for example at http://www.nctr.usf.edu/abstracts/abs77802.htm.

Even the evolution of the kind of language we use reveals the cracks and faults with the concept of race. Two examples, may provide a starting point for discussion. In 2013, the U.S. Census Bureau announced that it was ending the use of "Negro" on its surveys and forms after more than 100 years of use. The government had considered ending usage of the word "Negro" for the 2010 Census but ultimately decided against it. The bureau reasoned that there was still a segment of the U.S. population that personally identified with the term. Most of them were older blacks living in the Southern states. But the description has come to be viewed as outdated and even offensive by many people in the black community, officials say, so the bureau will reduce the options to "black" or "African-American." The agency will include the new language next year in its annual American Community Survey. Also revealing, however, is the multitude of responses to the 2010 "race question" under "Some Other Race." Nearly 16 million Americans chose "some other race" alone and 21.7 million people chose it in combination with another response. These self reported responses include many of the ancestry groups identified in the Ancestry Question of the American Community Survey, for example - Polish, Italian, Irish, etc. Is it time to dump the race question and simply gather data through the ancestry question? If not, what are the reasons?

2010

→ NOTE: Please answer BOTH Question 5 about Hispanic origin and Question 6 about race. For this census, Hispanic origins are not races.

5. Is this person of Hispanic, Latino, or Spanish origin?
☐ No, not of Hispanic, Latino, or Spanish origin
☐ Yes, Mexican, Mexican Am., Chicano
☐ Yes, Puerto Rican
☐ Yes, Cuban
☐ Yes, another Hispanic, Latino, or Spanish origin — *Print origin, for example Argentinean, Colombian, Dominican, Nicaraguan, Salvadoran, Spaniard, and so on.*

6. What is this person's race? *Mark X one or more boxes.*
☐ White
☐ Black, African Am., or Negro
☐ American Indian or Alaska Native — *Print name of enrolled or Principal tribe.*

☐ Asian Indian ☐ Japanese ☐ Native Hawaiian
☐ Chinese ☐ Korean ☐ Guamanian or Chamorro
☐ Filipino ☐ Vietnamese ☐ Samoan
☐ Other Asian — *Print race, for example, Hmong, Laotian, Thai, Pakistani, Cambodian, and so on.* ☐ Other Pacific Islander — *Print race, for example, Fijan, Tongan, and so on.*

☐ Some other race — *Print race.*

2000

→ **NOTE: Please answer BOTH Questions 7 and 8.**

7. **Is person 1 Spanish/Hispanic/Latino?** *Mark ☒ the "No" box if **not** Spanish/Hispanic/Latino.*

☐ No, not Spanish/Hispanic/Latino   ☐ Yes, Puerto Rican
☐ Yes, Mexican, Mexican Am., Chicano ☐ Yes, Cuban
☐ Yes, other Spanish/Hispanic/Latino — *Print group.* ⟍

8. **What is Person 1's race?** *Mark ☒ one or more races to indicate what this person considers himself/herself to be.*

☐ White
☐ Black, African Am., or Negro
☐ American Indian or Alaska Native — *Print name of enrolled or principal tribe.* ⟍

☐ Asian Indian   ☐ Japanese   ☐ Native Hawaiian
☐ Chinese   ☐ Korean   ☐ Guamanian or Chamorro
☐ Filipino   ☐ Vietnamese ☐ Samoan
☐ Other Asian — *Print race.* ⟍   ☐ Other Pacific Islander — *Print race.* ⟍

☐ Some other race — *Print race.* ⟍

1990

4. Race

Fill ONE circle for the race that the person considers himself/herself to be.

If Indian (Amer.), print the name of the enrolled or principal tribe. ⟶

If Other Asian or Pacific Islander (API) print one group, for example: Hraong, Rjan, Laodan, Thai, Tongan, Paidsanl, Cambodan, and so on. ⟶

If Other race, print race. ⟶

○ White
○ Black or Negro
○ Indian (Amer.) (Print the name of the enrolled or principal tribe.) ⟍

○ Eskimo
○ Aleut

Asian or Pacific Islander (API)
○ Chinese   ○ Japanese
○ Filipino   ■   ○ Asian Indian
○ Hawaiian   ○ Samoan
○ Korean   ○ Guamanian
○ Vietnamese   ○ Other API ⟍

○ Other race (Print race) ⟍

7. Is this person of Spanish/Hispanic origin?

Fill ONE circle for each person.

If Yes, other Spanish/Hispanic, print one group, ⟶

○ No (not Spanish/Hispanic)
○ Yes, Mexican, Mexican-Am, Chicago
○ Yes, Pardo Rican ■
○ Yes, Cuban
○ Yes, other Spanish/Hispanic
(Print one group, for example: Argentinian, Colombian, Dominican, Nicaraguan, Salvadoran, Sparland and so on.) ⟍

1980

4. Is this person – *Fill one circle.*	O White O Black or Negro O Japanese O Chinese O Filipino O Korean O Vietnamese O Indian (Amer.) *Print tribe*	O Asian Indian O Hawaiian O Guamanian O Samoan O Eskimo O Aleut O Other – *Specify*
7. Is this person of Spanish/ Hispanic origin or descent? *Fill one circle.*	O No (not Spanish/Hispanic) O Yes, Mexican, Mexican-Amer., Chicano O Yes, Puerto Rican O Yes, Cuban O Yes, other Spanish/Hispanic	

1970

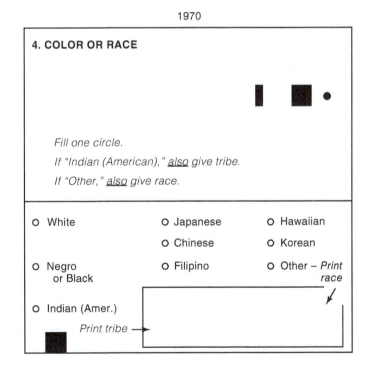

4. COLOR OR RACE

Fill one circle.
If "Indian (American)," <u>also</u> give tribe.
If "Other," <u>also</u> give race.

O White   O Japanese   O Hawaiian
           O Chinese   O Korean
O Negro   O Filipino   O Other – *Print race*
   or Black
O Indian (Amer.)
     Print tribe →

1960

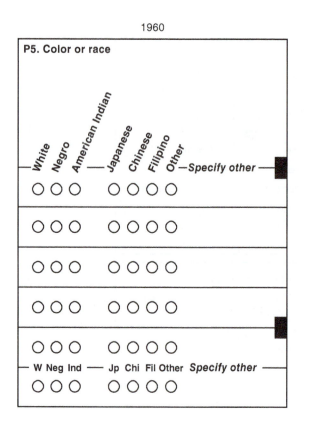

P5. Color or race

White Negro American Indian Japanese Chinese Filipino Other —Specify other —

○ ○ ○   ○ ○ ○ ○

○ ○ ○   ○ ○ ○ ○

○ ○ ○   ○ ○ ○ ○

○ ○ ○   ○ ○ ○ ○

○ ○ ○   ○ ○ ○ ○

— W Neg Ind — Jp Chi Fil Other *Specify other* —

○ ○ ○   ○ ○ ○ ○

1950

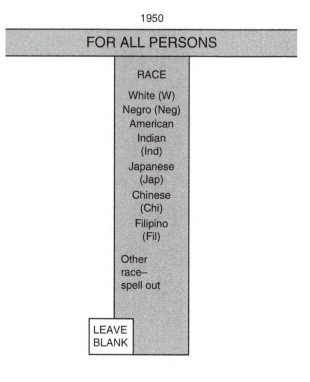

FOR ALL PERSONS

RACE

White (W)
Negro (Neg)
American
Indian
(Ind)
Japanese
(Jap)
Chinese
(Chi)
Filipino
(Fil)

Other
race—
spell out

LEAVE
BLANK

1940

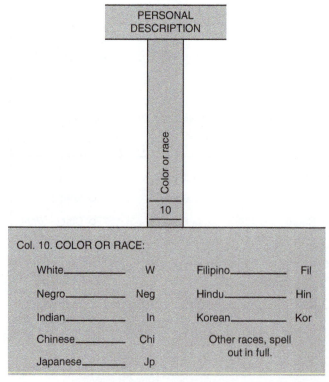

**PERSONAL
DESCRIPTION**

Color or race

10

Col. 10. COLOR OR RACE:

White_____	W	Filipino_____	Fil
Negro_____	Neg	Hindu_____	Hin
Indian_____	In	Korean_____	Kor
Chinese_____	Chi	Other races, spell	
Japanese_____	Jp	out in full.	

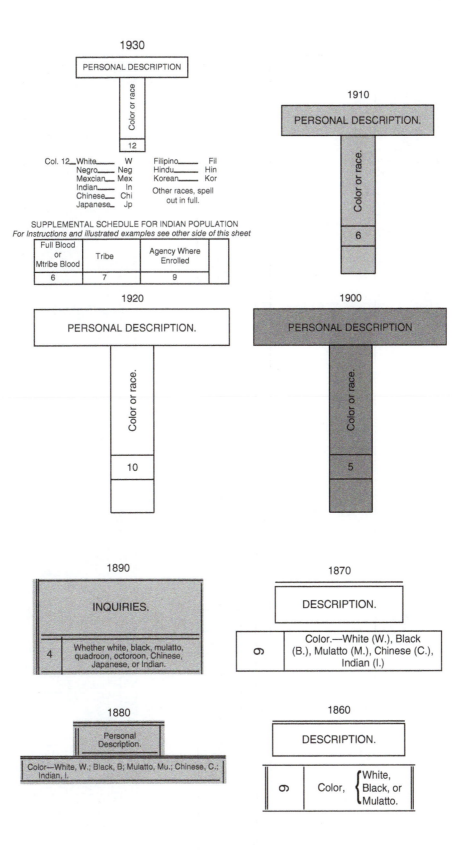

1850

NAMES OF SLAVE OWNERS.

Number of Slave.	DESCRIPTION.			Fugitives from the State.	Number manumitted.	Deaf & dumb, blind, insane, or idiotic.
	Age.	Sex.	Color.			

Color, { White, Black, or Mulatto.

1840

FREE WHITE PERSONS, INCLUDING HEADS OF FAMILIES.

MALES.

Under 5	5 & under 10	10 & under 15	15 & under 20	20 & under 30	30 & under 40	40 & under 50	50 & under 60	60 & under 70	70 & under 80	80 & under 90	90 & under 100	100 & upwards.

FEMALES.

Under 5	5 & under 10	10 & under 15	15 & under 20	20 & under 30	30 & under 40	40 & under 50	50 & under 60	60 & under 70	70 & under 80	80 & under 90	90 & under 100	100 & upwards.

FREE COLORED PERSONS.

MALES.

Under 10	10 & under 24	24 & under 36	36 & under 55	55 & under 100	100 & upwards.

FEMALES.

Under 10	10 & under 24	24 & under 36	36 & under 55	55 & under 100	100 & upwards.

1830

FREE COLORED PERSONS.

MALES

Under ten years of age.	Of ten and under twenty-four.	Of twenty-four and under thirty-six.	Of thirty-six and under fifty-five.	Of fifty-five and under one hundred.	Of one hundred and upwards.
under 10	10 to 24	24 to 36	35 to 55	55 to 100	100, inc

FEMALES

Under ten years of age.	Of ten and under twenty-four.	Of twenty-four and under thirty-six.	Of thirty-six and under fifty-five.	Of fifty-five and under one hundred.	Of one hundred and upwards.
under 10	10 to 24	24 to 35	35 to 55	55 to 100	100, inc

SLAVES.

MALES

Under ten years of age.	Of ten and under twenty-four.	Of twenty-four and under thirty-six.	Of thirty-six and under fifty-five.	Of fifty-five and under one hundred.	Of one hundred and upwards.
under 10	10 to 24	24 to 35	35 to 55	55 to 100	100, inc

FEMALES

Under ten years of age.	Of ten and under twenty-four.	Of twenty-four and under thirty-six.	Of thirty-six and under fifty-five.	Of fifty-five and under one hundred.	Of one hundred and upwards.
under 10	10 to 24	24 to 35	35 to 55	55 to 100	100, inc

TOTAL

Ms not clear

1820

Names of heads of families & Names of men of 21 years of age	Free White Males						Free White Females					Naturalised	Agricultural	Commercial	Manufactures	Free persons of soulder	Males of the age of 21 year & upwards	Remarks (33)
Delaware Co. Indiana. 1820.	under 10	Over 10 & under 16	Over 16 & under 18	Over 16 & under 26	Over 26 & under 44	Over 44 & upwards	Under 10	Over 10 & under 16	Over 16 & under 26	Over 26 & under 45	all over 45 years							
Benjamine-Cutbirth	2	—	—	3	—	/	—	2	/	—	/	—	4	—	—	—	2	

1810

FREE WHITE MALES.					FREE WHITE FEMALES.					All other free persons, except Indians, not taxed.	Slaves.
Under ten years of age	Of ten years, and under sixteen.	Of sixteen, and under twenty-six, including heads of families.	Of twenty-six, and under forty-five, including heads of families.	Of forty-five and upwards, including head of families.	Under ten years of age.	Of ten years, and under sixteen.	Of sixteen, and under twenty-six, including heads of families.	Of twenty-six, and under forty-five, including heads of families.	Of forty-five and upwards, including head of families.		
to 10.	to 16.	to 26.	to 45.	45 & c.	to 10.	to 16.	to 26.	to 45.	45 & c.		

1800

Free White Males					Free White Females					All other free persons except Indians not taxed	Slaves
to 10	10–16	16–26	26–45	45 &	to 10	10–16	16–26	26–45	45 &		
264	195	152	163	101	233	149	146	166	96	3	36

1790

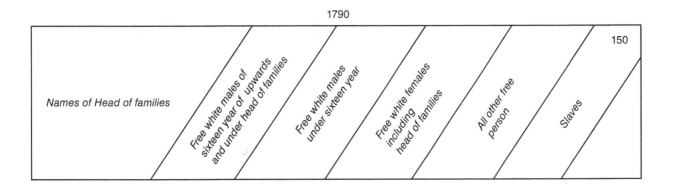

2010 American Community Survey 1-Year Estimates - Ancestry

Ancestry	Estimate	Margin of Error	Ancestry	Estimate	Margin of Error
Total:	309,349,689	*****	Latvian	84,664	+/−5,919
Afghan	79,775	+/−10,244	Lithuanian	660,071	+/−18,202
Albanian	193,813	+/−14,737	Luxemburger	40,975	+/−2,958
Alsatian	9,537	+/−1,490	Macedonian	61,287	+/−7,220
American	19,975,875	+/−105,096	Maltese	35,103	+/−4,237
Arab:	1,646,371	+/−36,587	New Zealander	19,961	+/−2,644
Egyptian	190,078	+/−14,249	Northern European	282,953	+/−13,422
Iraqi	105,981	+/−13,195	Norwegian	4,470,081	+/−44,484
Jordanian	61,664	+/−8,585	Pennsylvania German	332,341	+/−13,407
Lebanese	501,988	+/−14,992	Polish	9,569,207	+/−81,176
Moroccan	82,073	+/−8,848	Portuguese	1,405,909	+/−27,954
Palestinian	93,438	+/−11,185	Romanian	447,293	+/−14,196
Syrian	148,214	+/−10,956	Russian	2,971,599	+/−42,579
Arab	290,893	+/−18,004	Scandinavian	570,696	+/−15,941
Other Arab	223,020	+/−15,403	Scotch-Irish	3,257,161	+/−37,878
Armenian	474,559	+/−18,151	Scottish	5,460,679	+/−50,422
Assyrian/Chaldean/Syriac	106,298	+/−9,274	Serbian	187,739	+/−9,494
Australian	93,063	+/−6,325	Slavic	136,636	+/−6,696
Austrian	722,282	+/−16,851	Slovak	762,030	+/−17,141
Basque	53,052	+/−5,677	Slovene	171,923	+/−7,828
Belgian	360,912	+/−12,022	Soviet Union	1,749	+/−683
Brazilian	361,814	+/−16,826	Subsaharan African:	2,789,129	+/−44,560
British	1,181,340	+/−19,681	Cape Verdean	95,003	+/−8,865
Bulgarian	95,568	+/−8,384	Ethiopian	201,707	+/−15,456
Cajun	103,091	+/−6,726	Ghanaian	91,322	+/−8,350
Canadian	717,390	+/−17,498	Kenyan	51,749	+/−6,951
Carpatho Rusyn	8,934	+/−1,570	Liberian	51,296	+/−7,467
Celtic	50,919	+/−4,476	Nigerian	259,058	+/−17,258
Croatian	411,427	+/−13,210	Senegalese	11,369	+/−3,194
Cypriot	6,388	+/−1,597	Sierra Leonean	16,929	+/−4,726
Czech	1,525,187	+/−25,310	Somalian	120,102	+/−10,979
Czechoslovakian	304,020	+/−9,162	South African	57,327	+/−6,817
Danish	1,375,506	+/−24,059	Sudanese	42,147	+/−6,603
Dutch	4,645,131	+/−40,097	Ugandan	12,549	+/−3,711
Eastern European	489,534	+/−15,228	Zimbabwean	7,323	+/−2,525
English	25,926,451	+/−117,804	African	1,676,413	+/−35,051
Estonian	30,641	+/−4,238	Other Subsaharan African	143,867	+/−10,966
European	3,616,843	+/−44,797			
Finnish	647,697	+/−15,866	Swedish	4,088,555	+/−36,876
French (except Basque)	8,761,496	+/−55,528	Swiss	961,380	+/−20,027
French Canadian	2,042,808	+/−28,673	Turkish	195,283	+/−10,380
German	47,901,779	+/−110,936	Ukrainian	939,746	+/−23,848
German Russian	18,752	+/−2,946	Welsh	1,793,356	+/−25,237
Greek	1,315,775	+/−29,760	West Indian (Except Hispanic groups)	2,624,392	+/−41,889
Guyanese	214,315	+/−14,116			
Hungarian	1,501,736	+/−28,060	Bahamian	48,043	+/−6,299
Icelander	44,027	+/−3,947	Barbadian	58,215	+/−5,870
Iranian	463,552	+/−18,925	Belizean	54,925	+/−7,492
Irish	34,669,616	+/−132,430	Bermudan	4,730	+/−1,096
Israeli	129,359	+/−10,929	British West Indian	88,043	+/−7,258
Italian	17,235,941	+/−89,274	Dutch West Indian	54,260	+/−4,886

Ancestry	Estimate	Margin of Error
Haitian	881,488	+/−31,399
Jamaican	965,355	+/−27,254
Trinidadian & Tobagonian	197,520	+/−10,996
U.S. Virgin Islander	11,674	+/−2,496
West Indian	299,010	+/−15,401
Other West Indian	7,969	+/−1,884
Yugoslavian	326,576	+/−19,510
Other groups	120,017,996	+/−141,232
Unclassified or not reported	36,730,332	+/−134,914

Data are based on a sample and are subject to sampling variability. The degree of uncertainty for an estimate arising from sampling variability is represented through the use of a margin of error. The value shown here is the 90 percent margin of error. The margin of error can be interpreted roughly as providing a 90 percent probability that the interval defined by the estimate minus the margin of error and the estimate plus the margin of error (the lower and upper confidence bounds) contains the true value. In addition to sampling variability, the ACS estimates are subject to nonsampling error (for a discussion of nonsampling variability, see Accuracy of the Data). The effect of nonsampling error is not represented in these tables.

Starting in 2008, the Scotch-Irish category does not include Irish-Scotch. People who reported Irish-Scotch ancestry are classified under "Other groups," whereas in 2007 and earlier they were classified as Scotch-Irish.

The American Community Survey (ACS) implemented a variety of new race and ethnicity coding changes in 2010 to be consistent with the 2010 decennial census coding rules. Any changes in ancestry estimates for 2010 and beyond should be used with caution. For more information on these changes, please see "Coding Changes to the American Community Survey Between 2009 and 2010 and Their Potential Effect on the Estimates of Ancestry Groups" on the Ethnicity and Ancestry Branch website at http://www.census.gov/population/www/ancestry/.

S0201: Selected Population Profile in the United States of Groups with Over 1,000,000

2009–2011 American Community Survey 3-Year Estimates

Subject	White	Black or African American	Chinese	Filipino	Japanese	Korean	Vietnamese
TOTAL POPULATION	236,382,436	41,941,857	4,104,990	3,396,753	1,315,737	1,725,771	1,803,143
SEX AND AGE							
Median age (years)	39.2	30.9	35.0	33.7	37.5	33.1	34.3
HOUSEHOLDS BY TYPE							
Family households	66.0%	63.5%	70.1%	76.4%	60.0%	66.9%	80.3%
Married-couple family	51.6%	28.0%	57.1%	56.5%	46.8%	53.3%	60.6%
Female householder, no husband present, family	10.2%	29.4%	8.6%	14.8%	9.3%	9.8%	12.5%
Nonfamily households	34.0%	36.5%	29.9%	23.6%	40.0%	33.1%	19.7%
Average family size	3.11	3.42	3.39	3.76	3.09	3.22	3.91
SCHOOL ENROLLMENT							
Percent enrolled in college or graduate school	25.1%	21.4%	40.6%	29.4%	30.8%	39.6%	32.3%
Female 3 years and over enrolled in school	30,178,920	7,278,719	702,941	530,816	197,348	296,966	286,370
EDUCATIONAL ATTAINMENT							

(continued)

Subject	White	Black or African American	Chinese	Filipino	Japanese	Korean	Vietnamese
Less than high school diploma	12.3%	17.9%	17.9%	7.6%	5.0%	7.8%	30.0%
High school graduate (includes equivalency)	28.8%	31.2%	15.4%	16.1%	19.7%	18.6%	21.4%
Some college or associate's degree	29.4%	32.6%	15.7%	30.4%	28.9%	21.5%	22.9%
Bachelor's degree	18.6%	11.9%	25.4%	37.5%	30.8%	34.0%	18.7%
Graduate or professional degree	10.9%	6.4%	25.6%	8.4%	15.6%	18.0%	7.0%
RESPONSIBILITY FOR GRAND-CHILDREN UNDER 18 YEARS							
Living with grandchild(ren)	3.1%	6.1%	5.3%	7.1%	2.6%	2.9%	7.1%
RESIDENCE 1 YEAR AGO							
Same house	85.7%	80.5%	83.6%	84.3%	85.4%	80.2%	86.1%
PLACE OF BIRTH, CITIZENSHIP STATUS AND YEAR OF ENTRY							
Native	216,551,848	38,426,311	1,604,582	1,629,780	978,754	633,051	651,600
Foreign born	19,830,588	3,515,546	2,500,408	1,766,973	336,983	1,092,720	1,151,543
Foreign born; naturalized U.S. citizen	8,372,013	1,763,870	1,489,082	1,143,860	106,611	609,658	852,147
Foreign born; not a U.S. citizen	11,458,575	1,751,676	1,011,326	623,113	230,372	483,062	299,396
Population born outside the United States	19,830,588	3,515,546	2,500,408	1,766,973	336,983	1,092,720	1,151,543
LANGUAGE SPOKEN AT HOME AND ABILITY TO SPEAK ENGLISH							
English only	84.9%	91.4%	25.3%	44.3%	66.3%	29.6%	15.4%
Language other than English	15.1%	8.6%	74.7%	55.7%	33.7%	70.4%	84.6%
Speak English less than "very well"	6.1%	3.0%	41.1%	18.2%	15.7%	39.6%	51.0%
EMPLOYMENT STATUS							
Unemployed	5.8%	10.7%	5.0%	6.1%	4.2%	4.8%	6.4%
CLASS OF WORKER							
Self-employed workers in own not incorporated business	6.7%	3.6%	5.5%	3.2%	6.1%	10.3%	8.7%
INCOME							
Median household income (dollars)	54,387	34,826	67,118	77,147	67,620	52,674	54,525
Median income (dollars)	33,370	26,012	45,112	52,895	50,071	35,223	35,152
Per capita income (dollars)	29,408	17,688	30,217	26,219	32,322	26,115	20,996
POVERTY RATES							
All families	8.7%	23.0%	10.2%	5.4%	4.8%	11.8%	13.4%
Married-couple family	4.7%	8.0%	8.1%	2.7%	2.7%	8.9%	10.9%
Female householder, no husband present, family	26.4%	37.1%	21.6%	14.6%	15.3%	26.7%	25.6%

S0201: Selected Population Profile in the United States of Groups with Over 1,000,000

2009–2011 American Community Survey 3-Year Estimates

	Mexican	Puerto Rican	Cuban	Dominican	British	Czech	Danish
TOTAL POPULATION	32,869,887	4,749,070	1,829,495	1,485,465	1,181,125	1,543,514	1,394,031
SEX AND AGE							
Median age (years)	25.6	28.3	40.3	29.3	46.2	42.3	46.0
HOUSEHOLDS BY TYPE							
Family households	80.8%	70.0%	69.1%	79.1%	62.8%	62.9%	64.3%
Married-couple family	52.1%	36.5%	48.3%	34.8%	53.9%	52.1%	54.0%
Female householder, no husband present, family	19.2%	26.7%	14.9%	35.6%	6.4%	7.7%	7.6%
Nonfamily households	19.2%	30.0%	30.9%	20.9%	37.2%	37.1%	35.7%
Average family size	4.14	3.44	3.44	3.71	2.92	2.93	2.95
SCHOOL ENROLLMENT							
Percent enrolled in college or graduate school	14.4%	17.3%	27.4%	21.7%	38.9%	30.0%	30.0%
Female 3 years and over enrolled in school	5,514,839	801,842	226,358	244,553	130,089	194,893	165,135
EDUCATIONAL ATTAINMENT							
Less than high school diploma	43.4%	25.6%	23.5%	34.6%	3.1%	4.7%	3.8%
High school graduate (includes equivalency)	26.3%	29.6%	28.4%	25.8%	14.5%	24.6%	21.5%
Some college or associate's degree	20.9%	28.8%	24.1%	24.5%	27.9%	31.3%	34.5%
Bachelor's degree	6.8%	10.8%	15.0%	10.6%	30.0%	24.9%	25.1%
Graduate or professional degree	2.6%	5.3%	9.0%	4.5%	24.6%	14.5%	15.2%
RESPONSIBILITY FOR GRAND-CHILDREN UNDER 18 YEARS							
Living with grandchild(ren)	8.5%	5.9%	5.4%	8.5%	1.7%	1.6%	2.1%
RESIDENCE 1 YEAR AGO							
Same house	82.2%	80.3%	84.9%	83.1%	86.4%	87.2%	87.2%
PLACE OF BIRTH, CITIZENSHIP STATUS AND YEAR OF ENTRY							
Native	21,214,207	4,696,856	763,195	644,015	973,584	1,506,509	1,357,362
Foreign born	11,655,680	52,214	1,066,300	841,450	207,541	37,005	36,669
Foreign born; naturalized U.S. citizen	2,705,102	24,637	598,124	398,826	86,387	22,756	15,824
Foreign born; not a U.S. citizen	8,950,578	27,577	468,176	442,624	121,154	14,249	20,845
Population born outside the United States	11,655,680	52,214	1,066,300	841,450	207,541	37,005	36,669

(continued)

	Mexican	Puerto Rican	Cuban	Dominican	British	Czech	Danish
LANGUAGE SPOKEN AT HOME AND ABILITY TO SPEAK ENGLISH							
English only	24.7%	35.6%	18.2%	9.2%	95.9%	95.1%	95.6%
Language other than English	75.3%	64.4%	81.8%	90.8%	4.1%	4.9%	4.4%
Speak English less than "very well"	35.7%	18.4%	40.9%	45.2%	0.5%	0.9%	0.5%
EMPLOYMENT STATUS							
Unemployed	8.3%	9.6%	7.9%	9.6%	4.5%	4.9%	4.6%
CLASS OF WORKER							
Self-employed workers in own not incorporated business	6.1%	3.0%	6.9%	5.8%	7.6%	7.0%	8.3%
INCOME							
Median household income (dollars)	40,060	37,668	41,191	34,575	72,668	62,578	62,295
Median income (dollars)	24,209	22,572	30,524	23,130	48,357	42,024	45,043
Per capita income (dollars)	13,740	17,372	22,692	15,268	46,444	35,481	35,921
POVERTY RATES							
All families	24.0%	23.5%	13.9%	26.2%	3.7%	4.1%	4.4%
Married-couple family	17.6%	9.2%	9.8%	12.8%	2.1%	2.1%	2.5%
Female householder, no husband present, family	42.1%	43.1%	27.0%	40.9%	15.6%	17.0%	16.3%

S0201: Selected Population Profile in the United States of Groups with Over 1,000,000

2009–2011 American Community Survey 3-Year Estimates

	Greek	Hungarian	Irish	Italian	Norwegian	Polish	Portuguese
TOTAL POPULATION	1,311,844	1,484,821	35,186,074	17,488,984	4,491,712	9,660,864	1,420,978
SEX AND AGE							
Median age (years)	37.2	44.0	39.0	35.9	40.8	39.6	37.6
HOUSEHOLDS BY TYPE							
Family households	63.1%	62.2%	63.8%	64.3%	64.3%	63.4%	67.4%
Married-couple family	49.6%	50.8%	49.4%	50.2%	52.9%	51.2%	51.2%
Female householder, no husband present, family	9.3%	8.3%	10.6%	10.1%	8.1%	8.7%	11.9%
Nonfamily households	36.9%	37.8%	36.2%	35.7%	35.7%	36.6%	32.6%
Average family size	3.11	2.98	3.06	3.10	2.95	3.02	3.20
SCHOOL ENROLLMENT							
Percent enrolled in college or graduate school	29.7%	30.1%	26.2%	27.2%	27.3%	28.7%	25.1%

(continued)

	Greek	Hungarian	Irish	Italian	Norwegian	Polish	Portuguese
Female 3 years and over enrolled in school	190,604	180,496	4,773,621	2,589,185	580,916	1,291,236	194,149
EDUCATIONAL ATTAINMENT							
Less than high school diploma	9.7%	5.9%	7.5%	7.6%	4.4%	6.2%	17.1%
High school graduate (includes equivalency)	22.5%	25.7%	27.1%	27.9%	24.2%	27.2%	29.4%
Some college or associate's degree	27.7%	28.9%	32.7%	30.0%	34.6%	29.7%	30.0%
Bachelor's degree	24.1%	22.8%	20.7%	21.6%	24.1%	22.4%	15.6%
Graduate or professional degree	16.1%	16.6%	12.0%	12.9%	12.6%	14.6%	7.8%
RESPONSIBILITY FOR GRAND-CHILDREN UNDER 18 YEARS							
Living with grandchild(ren)	2.0%	1.8%	2.7%	2.1%	1.8%	1.9%	3.2%
RESIDENCE 1 YEAR AGO							
Same house	86.4%	87.7%	85.4%	86.3%	86.2%	87.8%	85.9%
PLACE OF BIRTH, CITIZENSHIP STATUS AND YEAR OF ENTRY							
Native	1,152,953	1,382,912	34,935,046	16,948,324	4,454,898	9,155,031	1,160,439
Foreign born	158,891	101,909	251,028	540,660	36,814	505,833	260,539
Foreign born; naturalized U.S. citizen	123,796	74,794	148,144	354,800	18,161	320,307	155,378
Foreign born; not a U.S. citizen	35,095	27,115	102,884	185,860	18,653	185,526	105,161
Population born outside the United States	158,891	101,909	251,028	540,660	36,814	505,833	260,539
LANGUAGE SPOKEN AT HOME AND ABILITY TO SPEAK ENGLISH							
English only	74.1%	89.5%	97.6%	93.0%	97.0%	91.6%	73.7%
Language other than English	25.9%	10.5%	2.4%	7.0%	3.0%	8.4%	26.3%
Speak English less than "very well"	6.3%	2.9%	0.3%	1.7%	0.4%	2.9%	9.7%
EMPLOYMENT STATUS							
Unemployed	6.1%	5.7%	6.2%	6.3%	5.1%	6.0%	7.1%
CLASS OF WORKER							
Self-employed workers in own not incorporated business	7.1%	6.7%	6.0%	5.9%	7.2%	5.8%	7.0%
INCOME							
Median household income (dollars)	63,099	61,458	58,311	63,934	61,310	63,016	59,587
Median income (dollars)	41,335	41,272	36,626	39,461	38,870	41,302	37,032
Per capita income (dollars)	34,207	37,211	31,411	32,637	33,300	34,465	29,137
POVERTY RATES							
All families	6.3%	5.6%	6.9%	6.3%	5.1%	5.0%	7.7%
Married-couple family	3.2%	3.4%	3.1%	2.8%	2.5%	2.5%	3.7%
Female householder, no husband present, family	21.3%	17.6%	22.5%	21.3%	19.4%	18.4%	22.9%

S0201: Selected Population Profile in the United States of Groups with Over 1,000,000

2009–2011 American Community Survey 3-Year Estimates

	Russian	Scotch-Irish	Scottish	Swedish	American
TOTAL POPULATION	3,027,065	3,308,414	5,562,022	4,128,135	20,875,080
SEX AND AGE					
Median age (years)	43.1	50.9	45.4	43.8	40.4
HOUSEHOLDS BY TYPE					
Family households	60.7%	61.1%	64.8%	63.6%	67.1%
Married-couple family	50.4%	50.0%	54.2%	52.4%	52.3%
Female householder, no husband present, family	7.4%	7.9%	7.1%	8.3%	10.8%
Nonfamily households	39.3%	38.9%	35.2%	36.4%	32.9%
Average family size	2.92	2.80	2.94	2.95	2.98
SCHOOL ENROLLMENT					
Percent enrolled in college or graduate school	30.1%	31.3%	33.2%	28.0%	19.8%
Female 3 years and over enrolled in school	384,415	325,628	602,549	516,287	2,672,602
EDUCATIONAL ATTAINMENT					
Less than high school diploma	3.7%	4.8%	4.2%	4.3%	14.4%
High school graduate (includes equivalency)	15.2%	21.5%	20.2%	22.8%	36.9%
Some college or associate's degree	23.8%	32.9%	32.9%	33.2%	28.2%
Bachelor's degree	29.0%	24.3%	26.0%	25.3%	13.6%
Graduate or professional degree	28.2%	16.5%	16.7%	14.4%	6.8%
RESPONSIBILITY FOR GRAND-CHILDREN UNDER 18 YEARS					
Living with grandchild(ren)	1.6%	2.3%	2.1%	2.1%	3.3%
RESIDENCE 1 YEAR AGO					
Same house	87.1%	88.2%	86.3%	86.8%	87.7%
PLACE OF BIRTH, CITIZENSHIP STATUS AND YEAR OF ENTRY					
Native	2,506,790	3,289,164	5,413,743	4,075,464	20,822,902
Foreign born	520,275	19,250	148,279	52,671	52,178
Foreign born; naturalized U.S. citizen	351,786	10,238	75,477	23,208	40,640
Foreign born; not a U.S. citizen	168,489	9,012	72,802	29,463	11,538
Population born outside the United States	520,275	19,250	148,279	52,671	52,178

(continued)

	Russian	Scotch-Irish	Scottish	Swedish	American
LANGUAGE SPOKEN AT HOME AND ABILITY TO SPEAK ENGLISH					
English only	79.7%	97.7%	97.3%	96.6%	96.9%
Language other than English	20.3%	2.3%	2.7%	3.4%	3.1%
Speak English less than "very well"	8.2%	0.3%	0.3%	0.4%	0.6%
EMPLOYMENT STATUS					
Unemployed	5.4%	4.9%	5.2%	5.0%	5.7%
CLASS OF WORKER					
Self-employed workers in own not incorporated business	9.6%	7.8%	7.5%	7.5%	6.5%
INCOME					
Median household income (dollars)	71,644	56,675	63,843	61,607	47,334
Median income (dollars)	45,995	42,643	42,187	41,936	30,073
Per capita income (dollars)	47,673	35,978	39,257	34,817	24,800
POVERTY RATES					
All families	5.2%	4.5%	4.6%	4.7%	9.7%
Married-couple family	3.1%	2.3%	2.6%	2.3%	5.2%
Female householder, no husband present, family	17.1%	15.9%	16.9%	18.2%	28.8%

Critical Thinking

1. Do you agree with the way data is collected by the U.S. Census?
2. In what ways is having all the ethnic data available in the U.S. Census helpful to seekers?

Create Central

www.mhhe.com/createcentral

Internet References

Library of Congress
www.loc.gov
Social Science Information Gateway
http://sosig.esrc.bris.ac.uk
Sociosite
www.sociosite.net
U. S. Bureau of Citizenship and Immigration Services
www.USCIS.gov/portaffsftefuscis

Article   Prepared by: John A. Kromkowski, *Catholic University of America*

Still Unmelted after All These Years

JOHN DAVID KROMKOWSKI

Learning Outcomes

After reading this article, you will be able to:

• Discuss the implication of population differences in the various regions of America.

• Explain the different purposes of State boundaries and regional clusters.

A re Polish Americans or Italian Americans or African Americans uniformly distributed through the United States? No; in fact, America is stunningly "unmelted." Just look. MAPS 1-4 Distribution by State of Polish, Italian, Irish, and "American."

A bowl of raw meat and uncooked potatoes, celery, carrots and onions is not per se appetizing. But even in a well simmered and tasty soup or stew, you can tell by looking that there are carrots, potatoes, celery, onions and meat. So let's not despair. Let's investigate.

The Ancestry Question on the US Census has produced a stunning array of information about how Americans self-describe themselves. The self-describing aspect of the US Census, especially The Ancestry Question is a highly important feature of data collection in a pluralistic democracy. Unlike the Race Question on the US Census which was constitutionally and historically imposed and rooted in pseudo-scientific and political assumptions of exclusion, the Ancestry Question emerged from a more current understanding[2] of ethnicity and its organic character and growth through the self-determined iterations rooted in the person, family, household and neighborhoods that constitute the American experience of immigration, urbanization and the attendant cultural pluralism of democratization and freedom fostered by a wide range of forces that accompanied American political development especially for the past seven decades. These social economic, political, and personal dynamics make the demography of ethnicity in America seem messy. Indeed, the ostensible messiness of immigration, the articulation of ancestry and identity rooted in ethnicity may well explain the slow evolutionary process and the significant impediments to collection of demographic information. Uniform data would be achieved by replacing the variety of Race and Ethnic Origin Questions associated with Hispanic, Asian, Indigenous

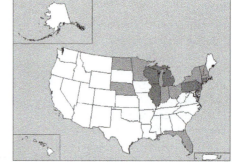

Legend

Data Classes
Percent
☐ 0.0–2.5
▨ 2.7–5.2
■ 6.7–9.3

TM-PCT037. Percent of Persons of Polish Ancestry: 2000.
Universe: Total population.
Data Set: Census 2000 Summary File 3 (SF 3)—Sample Data
United States by State.
Source: U.S. Census Bureau, Census 2000 Summary File 3, Matrices P1, and PCT18.

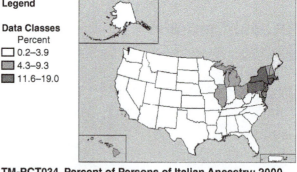

Legend

Data Classes
Percent
☐ 0.2–3.9
▨ 4.3–9.3
■ 11.6–19.0

TM-PCT034. Percent of Persons of Italian Ancestry: 2000.
Universe: Total population.
Data Set: Census 2000 Summary File 3 (SF 3)—Sample Data
United States by State.
Source: U.S. Census Bureau, Census 2000 Summary File 3, Matrices P1, and PCT18.

Peoples with a single Ancestry question and the tabulation of the multiple responses that are clearly evident in America. Nonetheless, now that Ancestry data has been collected for the last three Censuses and the computer driven computational revolution is firmly in place, demographic analysis can employ standard protocols and verifiable methods that enable

Legend

Data Classes
Percent
☐ 0.1–7.9
▨ 9.3–13.5
■ 14.8–22.5

TM-PCT033. Percent of Persons of Irish Ancestry: 2000.
Universe: Total population.
Data Set: Census 2000 Summary File 3(SF 3)—Sample Data
United States by State.

Source: U.S. Census Bureau, Census 2000 Summary File 3, Matrices P1, and
PCT18.

Legend

Data Classes
Percent
☐ 1.4–6.8
▨ 7.5–12.0
■ 13.5–20.9

TM-PCT047. Percent of Persons of United States or American Ancestry: 2000.
Universe: Total population.
Date Set: Census 2000 Summary File 3 (SF 3)—Sample Data
United States by State.

Source: U.S. Census Bureau, Census 2000 Summary File 3,
Matrices P1, and PCT18.

a fresh look at the data and thus establish connections, patterns and places and further discussion, interpretations and a scientific understanding of American pluralism.

This article investigates one such method: State Similarity Scores. A Similarity Score investigates the "distance" between States. Consider three cities: Baltimore, MD; Washington, DC and Chicago, IL. Baltimore is about a 40 mile drive from Washington. The driving distance between Washington and Chicago is roughly 710 miles. Chicago is 720 miles from Baltimore on the interstates. Knowing these distances, we can conceive of the triangle that these cities form and how they are geographically related.

In the two dimensional space of a map, a computer can now easily crunch out distances from a simple formula derived from Phythagoras.

$$\text{Distance}^2 = a^2 + b^2 \text{ or}$$
$$\text{Distance} = \sqrt{(a^2 + b^2)}$$

For example, using latitude and longitude to get the distance between Chicago and Baltimore, we find the difference between Chicago's latitude and Baltimore's latitude and the difference between Chicago's longitude and Baltimore's longitude.

$$a = \text{Lat}_{\text{Chicago}} - \text{Lat}_{\text{Baltimore}} \text{ and } b = \text{Long}_{\text{Chicago}} - \text{Long}_{\text{Baltimore}}$$

$$\text{So, Distance} = \sqrt{\begin{array}{l}\left(\text{Lat}_{\text{Chicago}} - \text{Lat}_{\text{Baltimore}}\right)^2 \\ + \left(\text{Long}_{\text{Chicago}} - \text{Long}_{\text{Baltimore}}\right)^2\end{array}}$$

In three dimensions, we'd add c^2, to handle perhaps altitude for Google Earth. The theorem isn't limited to our spatial definition of distance. It can apply to any orthogonal dimensions: space, time, movie tastes, colors, temperatures, and even ancestry responses. There is no limit to the number of variables. The focus, however, of this research is race, ethnicity and ancestry data from the US Census 2000. Appropriately, this type of investigation is also known as Nearest Neighbor Analysis. To find out how closely related any two states in terms of ethnicity, our equation would look like this:

$$\text{Distance} = \sqrt{\begin{array}{l}\left(\text{Ancestry1}_{\text{State 1}} - \text{Ancestry1}_{\text{State 2}}\right)^2 \\ + \left(\text{Ancestry2}_{\text{State 1}} - \text{Ancestry2}_{\text{State 2}}\right)^2 \\ + \cdots + \left(\text{Ancestry N}_{\text{State 1}} - \text{Ancestry N}_{\text{State 2}}\right)^2\end{array}}$$

For this paper I used 56 of the largest ethnicities[3] as orthogonal dimensions: Asian Indian, Asian Multiple Response, American Indian, "American", Arab, Austrian, Black or African American, Belgian, British, Canadian, Chinese, Cuban, Czech, Czechoslovakian, Danish, Dutch, English, Finnish, French excluding Basque, Filipino, French Canadian, German, Greek, Guamanian and/or Chamorrian, Jamaican, Japanese, Korean, Hawaiian, Hispanic or Latino Other, Hungarian, Irish, Lithuanian, Mexican, Native Not Specified, Norwegian, "Others", Other Asian, Other Pacific Islander, Puerto Rican, Polish, Portuguese, Russian, Samoan, Scandinavian, "Scotch Irish", Scottish, Slovak, Slovene, "Some Other Race", Sub Saharan African, Swedish, Ukrainian, Vietnamese, Welsh, and West Indian.[4]

For any two states, we can calculate a measure of similarity. A measure of 0, would mean that the two states are identical, i.e. they have exactly the same percentage of Polish American, Italian Americans, Irish Americans, African Americans, etc. The largest "distance" between two states was between DC and North Dakota at 91.429. The closest "distance" between two states was between Tennessee and Arkansas 3.720. Table 1 shows each state's "nearest cultural neighbors" and the "distance" metric.

If we look at only the closest connection for each of state, some distinct networks or groupings emerge. The largest of these clusters happens to correspond roughly to "The South."

Table 1 Nearest Neighbors along 56 dimensions of Ethnicity/Ancest

First Closest			Second Closest			Third Closest		
AL	SC	5.947	GA	7.213		NC	7.639	
AK	WA	12.354	OK	12.893		CO	15.157	
AZ	NV	9.405	TX	16.69		CO	17.233	
AR	TN	3.720	NC	7.809		VA	8.382	
CA	TX	10.344	AZ	19.1		NM	21.128	
CO	WA	9.759	OR	9.958		KS	12.213	
CT	MA	11.011	RI	14.181		NJ	14.499	
DC	MS	33.68	LA	37.691		GA	40.758	
DE	VA	10.625	MI	12.782		NJ	12.936	
FL	NY	10.115	VA	10.430		NJ	11.253	
GA	SC	4.179	AL	7.213		MS	9.648	
HI	CA	47.499	NM	49.38		TX	51.121	
ID	OR	7.619	WY	9.058		WA	10.961	
IL	NJ	13.474	MI	13.955		DE	14.214	
IN	MO	5.327	OH	6.3		KS	7.847	
IA	NE	8.916	MT	13.289		WI	13.514	
KS	IN	7.847	MO	8.337		OR	8.670	
KY	WV	6.661	TN	13.896		IN	14.001	
LA	MS	12.163	SC	13.077		GA	13.124	
ME	VT	4.781	NH	7.475		RI	19.544	
MD	VA	12.451	SC	12.606		GA	13.117	
MA	RI	7.942	CT	11.011		NH	16.286	
MI	OH	10.340	MO	10.977		PA	11.927	
MN	SD	11.895	WI	13.981		IA	15.716	
MS	GA	9.648	SC	9.947		LA	12.163	
MO	OH	4.801	IN	5.327		KS	8.337	
MT	WY	9.427	IA	13.289		OR	14.668	
NE	IA	8.916	WI	11.648		WY	15.914	
NV	AZ	9.405	CO	13.675		IL	14.786	
NH	VT	4.607	ME	7.475		MA	16.286	
NJ	NY	6.026	FL	11.253		DE	12.936	
NM	CA	21.128	TX	23.53		AZ	27.923	
NY	NJ	6.026	FL	10.115		DE	14.651	
NC	VA	5.9	AL	7.639		AR	7.809	
ND	SD	17.030	MN	17.407		WI	24.532	
OH	MO	4.801	IN	6.3		PA	6.692	
OK	AR	12.557	AK	12.893		FL	14.080	
OR	WA	4.784	ID	7.619		KS	8.670	
PA	OH	6.692	MO	10.27		IN	10.718	
RI	MA	7.942	CT	14.181		NH	16.638	
SC	GA	4.179	AL	5.947		NC	9.094	
SD	MN	11.895	WI	14.146		IA	14.527	
TN	AR	3.720	NC	9.043		VA	9.934	
TX	CA	10.344	AZ	16.69		NV	18.018	
UT	ID	14.655	OR	20.362		WA	21.495	
VT	NH	4.607	ME	4.781		MA	17.455	
VA	NC	5.9	AR	8.382		TN	9.934	
WA	OR	4.784	CO	9.759		KS	10.921	
WV	KY	6.661	IN	14.056		MO	17.644	
WI	NE	11.648	IA	13.514		MN	13.981	
WY	OR	8.960	ID	9.058		MT	9.427	

DC-MS-GA-SC-AL-NC-AR-TN
```
      |              |  |
      LA            VA  OK

           MD    DE
```

Other networks also emerged, when considering only the first closest connection:

Northeast Forest NH-VT-ME   Yellowstone MT-WY

Urban Northeast MA-RI-CT   Middle Prairie WI-IA-NE

Middle America KS-IN-MO   Upper Prairie MN-SD-ND
```
        |                    "Pacific Cal-Texico" TX-CA-NM
       MI-OH
        |                                    HI
        PA                   Coal Country KY-WV
```
Rocky Mountain Pacific   Southwest AZ-NV

UT-ID-OR-WA-AK   "Cosmopolitan Rural" IL-NJ-NY-FL
```
    |
    CO
```

We can also connect all of the States with the minimum possible distance among states, i.e a "minimum spanning tree," as follows:

"Ethnic Distance" to US

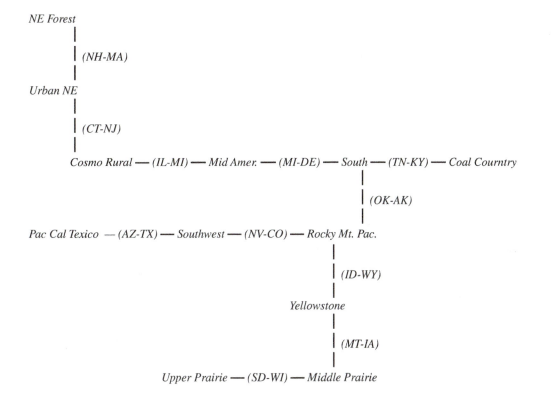

Figure 1   "Ethnic Distance" to US.

Finally, we can also measure the distance of each State to the United States as a whole. Illinois and Florida are very similar to the entire US, while North Dakota, DC and Hawaii are furthest in "distance" from the US in our 56 dimensional ethnic space. See Figure 1.

```
NE Forest
    |
    |  (NH-MA)
    |
Urban NE
    |
    |  (CT-NJ)
    |
Cosmo Rural —— (IL-MI) —— Mid Amer. —— (MI-DE) —— South —— (TN-KY) —— Coal Courntry
                                                     |
                                                     |  (OK-AK)
                                                     |
Pac Cal Texico — (AZ-TX) — Southwest — (NV-CO) — Rocky Mt. Pac.
                                                     |
                                                     |  (ID-WY)
                                                     |
                                                 Yellowstone
                                                     |
                                                     |  (MT-IA)
                                                     |
                            Upper Prairie —— (SD-WI) —— Middle Prairie
```

Notes

1. With acknowledgments to Michael Novak, The Rise of the Unmeltable Ethnics (1972) and Paul Simon's 1975 album and song.

2. Although, in some ways the Ancestry Question is arguably back to the future. See *Saint Francis College v. al-Khazraji*, 481 U.S. 604 (1987). A unanimous Court held that that persons of Arabian ancestry were protected from racial discrimination under Section 1981. The history of the definitions of "race," presented by the Court, is well worth reading because it shows how prior to the 20th century "race" and "ancestry" were synonymous concepts. After outlining the history and usage of the term "race," Justice White and the Court rejected the claim that "a distinctive physiognomy" is essential to qualify for 1981 protection and concluded: "We have little trouble in concluding that Congress intended to protect from discrimination identifiable classes of persons who are subjected to intentional discrimination solely because of their **ancestry or ethnic characteristics.**" William J. Brennan, Jr., in a separate concurrence, added that "Pernicious distinctions among individuals based solely on their **ancestry** are antithetical to the doctrine of equality upon which this nation is founded." (Emphasis supplied).

3. Some of these categories also come from the Race and Hispanic origin questions of the Census. Even though the Ancestry Question captures ethnic responses like Japanese, Korean, Cuban, Mexican and Black or African American, the Census Bureau sanitizes its Ancestry data, so that these responses are only readily available from the Race and Hispanic origin questions.

4. Older analysis of ethnic disimilarity differs from this method because it grouped ancestry responses into larger but far fewer categories such as "Old Stock," "Eastern and Southern European," "Asian," etc. Calculating similarity in 56 dimensional space was simply not possibly with hand calculations employed by previous researchers.

Critical Thinking

1. Were you surprised by the lack of uniform distribution of ethnic groups in America?

2. What is State Similarity Score?

3. Write a narrative that explains the "minimum spanning tree" or the other clustering of closest connections discerned from the Nearest Neighbor Analysis?

Create Central

www.mhhe.com/createcentral

Internet References

American Civil Liberties Union (ACLU)
www.aclu.org
Human Rights Web
www.hrweb.org
Sociosite
www.sociosite.net
U.S. Census Bureau
www.census.gov

The Size, Place of Birth, and Geographic Distribution of the Foreign-Born Population in the United States by Elizabeth M. Grieco et al.

79

Article

Prepared by: John A. Kromkowski, *The Catholic University of America*

The Size, Place of Birth, and Geographic Distribution of the Foreign-Born Population in the United States: 1960 to 2010

ELIZABETH M. GRIECO ET AL.

Learning Outcomes

After reading this article, you will be able to:

- Identify the most notable features found in this array of demographic data as well as the historical changes that are documented in this report.

- Point out the most striking geographic patterns in this report.

- Identify evidence for positive and negative interpretations of these data.

Introduction

During the last 50 years, the foreign-born population of the United States has undergone dramatic changes in size, origins, and geographic distribution.[1] Representing about 1 in 20 residents in 1960—mostly from countries in Europe who settled in the Northeast and Midwest—today's foreign-born population make up about 1 in 8 U.S. residents, composed mostly of immigrants from countries in Latin America and Asia who have settled in the West and South.[2] This transformation was triggered, at least in part, by U.S. immigration policy implemented after 1960.

New waves of immigrants began arriving in the United States following amendments to the Immigration Act in 1965 that abolished the national origins quota system, resulting in a shift away from traditional source countries to a greater diversity in the origins of the foreign born (CBO 2006; Vialet 1991). Unlike during the great migration of the late 1800s and early 1900s, when the majority of immigrants to the United States came from countries in Europe, most of the immigrants who arrived after 1970 were from countries in Latin America and Asia (Grieco 2009; Grieco and Trevelyan 2010; Walters and Cortes 2010). In addition to abolishing national quotas, the new law established a categorical preference system that prioritized admissions based on family relationships and needed skills and expanded the categories of family members who could enter without numerical limit (CBO 2006; Vialet 1991). The 1965 Act also restricted Eastern Hemisphere immigration to 170,000 and Western Hemisphere immigration to 150,000, but legislation enacted in 1978 combined the separate limits into a single annual worldwide ceiling of 290,000. In the 1980s and 1990s, growth in the foreign-born population was further augmented by the Immigration Reform and Control Act (IRCA) of 1986, which legalized approximately 2.7 million immigrants residing illegally in the United States, and the Immigration Act of 1990, which increased the worldwide immigration ceiling to a "flexible" cap of 675,000 per year (Rytina 2002; Vialet 1991).[3] Over the last four decades, the foreign-born population has continued to increase in size and as a percentage of the total U.S. population.

While not a direct result of immigration policy, the geographic distribution of the foreign-born population has also changed. In 1970, when the number of foreign born reached its lowest point in the 20th century, the majority of states had *less than* 5 percent foreign born in their total populations. Over two-thirds of the foreign-born population lived in the Northeast and Midwest regions.[4] As the nation's foreign-born population increased throughout the 1980s and 1990s, the greatest proportion resided in the "gateway" states of California, New York, Texas, and Florida, but there is evidence to suggest that by 2000 more had settled in nontraditional destinations, such as North Carolina, Georgia, and Nevada (Singer 2004). By 2010, most states had *at least* 5 percent foreign born in their total populations, and over two-thirds of the foreign born lived in the West and South.[5] As the foreign-born population increased and dispersed geographically, most of the United States—including places with little recent history of immigration—gained a greater immigrant presence.

The foreign-born population in the United States has undergone considerable transformation during the last 50 years. The purpose of this report is to describe in some detail changes in the size, origins, and geographic distribution that have occurred between 1960 and 2010. This paper begins by reviewing the historical growth of the foreign-born population, discussing the number of foreign born and the proportion of the total population they have represented through time. Next, broad shifts in the regions of origin will be reviewed, focusing on the simultaneous decline of the foreign born from Europe and increase from Latin America and Asia. Changes in the number of foreign born from specific source countries, such as Mexico, will also be discussed. The geographic distribution of the foreign-born population among the regions within the United States—Northeast, Midwest, South, and West—will then be reviewed, as will changes in the distribution among the states. The median age and age distribution of the foreign-born population will also be presented. This paper will conclude with a brief analysis of the role the growth in the foreign-born population has played in the increase in the total population of the United States over the last 50 years.

Historical Trends in the Size of the Foreign-Born Population

In 1960, there were 9.7 million foreign born in the United States, representing 5.4 percent of the total resident population. Between 1960 and 1970, the size of the foreign-born population declined to 9.6 million—or about 4.7 percent of the total population—and marked the end of a period of continuous decline that began in the 1930s. During the next four decades, the foreign-born population increased in size and as a percent of the total population: from 14.1 million (or 6.2 percent) in 1980 to 40.0 million (or 12.9 percent) in 2010. While the number of foreign born in 2010 represented a historical high,

the proportion of the total population was lower than during the great migration wave of the later 1800s to early 1900s, when it fluctuated between 13 and 15 percent. Between 1910 and 1930, the foreign-born population ranged from 13.5 to 14.2 million, then experienced continual decline until 1970, when it reached its lowest number in the 20th century. By comparison, between 1970 and 2010, the foreign-born population experienced continual growth, increasing to its current historical high.[6]

Changes in the Origins of the Foreign-Born Population

Perhaps more notable than the growth in the foreign-born population is the change in distribution of origin countries over time. During the 1960 to 2010 period, the number of foreign born from Latin America and Asia grew rapidly, while the number from Europe first declined then remained relatively stable. In 1960, there were fewer than 1 million foreign born from Latin America, but by 2010, there were 21.2 million. For the foreign born from Asia, there were fewer than one-half million in 1960, but by 2010 there were 11.3 million. By comparison, the foreign-born population from Europe declined from 7.3 million in 1960 to 5.1 million in 1980, then ranged between 4 and 5 million from 1990 to 2010.

When compared with the change in the number of foreign born from Europe. Latin America, and Asia, change in the proportional distribution among the regions of origin is more dramatic. In 1960, 75 percent of the foreign-born population was born in Europe. In 1980, 39 percent were born in Europe, while over half (52 percent) were born in Latin America or Asia. By 2010, more than 80 percent of the foreign-born population were born in either Latin America or Asia, with over half (53 percent) from Latin America alone.

Another significant trend in the shift in origins since 1960 has been the increase in the foreign born from Central America.[7] In 1960, the foreign born from Central America represented 6 percent of the total foreign-born population. By 2010, they represented 37 percent of the total foreign born. The growth was fueled primarily by immigration from a single source country: Mexico. While the decline in the size of the foreign-born population from Europe after 1960 was notable, the growth in the foreign-born population from Mexico during this 50-year period was equally remarkable. In 1960, there were about 576,000 foreign born from Mexico residing in the United States; by 1980, there were 2.2 million; and by 2010, there were 11.7 million. The greatest change occurred between 1970 and 2000, when the number of foreign born from Mexico increased rapidly, nearly tripling in size between 1970 and 1980, nearly doubling in size between 1980 and 1990, and more than doubling again between 1990 and 2000.

Perhaps more important than the increase in the number of foreign born from Mexico, however, is the increased proportion this population represents of the total foreign born. In 1960, the foreign born from Mexico represented just under 6 percent of the total foreign-born population; by 1980, about 16 percent; and by 2010, 29 percent. Not since the late 1800s and early 1900s has any one country-of-origin group represented such a high proportion of the total foreign-born population: for example, between 1870 and 1900, the foreign born from Germany represented between 26 percent and 30 percent of the total foreign-born population, while the foreign born from Ireland represented between 16 percent and 33 percent.[8] However, for a single place-of-birth group, the number of foreign born from Mexico in 2010 does represent a historical high.

Unlike immigration from Latin America, movement from Asia to the United States has not been dominated by a single sub-region or country of birth but has been more evenly distributed among several groups. Since 1960, the foreign-born populations from China (including Hong Kong and Taiwan), India, the Philippines, Vietnam, and Korea have increased steadily, each reaching 1.0 million or more by 2010. Combined, these five country-of-birth groups represented 71 percent of the Asian foreign born and about 20 percent of the total foreign born. At 2.2 million, the foreign born from China was the largest of these groups, comprising about 19 percent of the foreign born from Asia and 5 percent of the total foreign-born.

Although the foreign-born population from countries in Africa remained relatively small, it has continued to increase, from about 35,000 in 1960 to about 1.6 million in 2010. As a percentage of the total foreign-born population, the foreign born from Africa represented less than one percent in 1960, 1.5 percent in 1980, and 4.0 percent in 2010. African countries in 2010 with foreign-born populations in the United States estimated to be more than 100,000 included Nigeria, Ethiopia, Egypt, and Ghana. However, as a percentage of the total population, the foreign born from Africa represented less than 1 percent in 2010.

The foreign born from Mexico has remained the largest country-of-birth group over the last 30 years. By comparison, in 1960 and 1970, the foreign born from Italy, Germany, and Canada represented the three largest groups. After 1970, however, the size of some of the European country-of-birth groups began to decline. For example, 1.3 million foreign born from Italy in 1960 declined to 832,000 by 1980 and 365,000 by 2010; 990,000 foreign born from Germany in 1960 declined to 849,000 by 1980 and 605,000 by 2010. Other European countries, such as Ireland, Austria, and Hungary, exhibited a similar pattern of decline, while the United Kingdom and Poland declined early in the period then remained at about the same size. For example, the size of the foreign-born population from the United Kingdom declined from 833,000 in 1960 to 669,000 in 1980 then ranged from about 640,000 to about 678,000. The size of the foreign born from Canada demonstrated a similar pattern of decline then stabilization.

When these changes in origin country distribution since 1960 are viewed as a whole, another trend emerges: as the number of foreign born increased through time, fewer and fewer countries of birth represented more than 5 percent of the total foreign-born population. In 1960, there were seven countries representing 5 percent or more, including Italy, Germany, Canada, the United Kingdom, Poland, the Soviet Union, and Mexico. By 1980, there were four: Mexico, Germany, Canada, and Italy. Paradoxically, as the number of foreign born continued to increase after 1980 and the regions of origins shifted to include more countries in Latin America and Asia, the foreign born became proportionally concentrated into fewer country-of-birth groups. In 1990 and 2000, only Mexico represented at least 5 percent of the foreign born. By 2010, there were two countries: Mexico and China. Over 1 in 3 foreign born came from either Mexico or China in 2010, while over 1 in 4 came from Mexico alone.

The Geographic Distribution of the Foreign-Born Population

Between 1960 and 1970, the size of the foreign-born population residing in the United States declined, from 9.7 million to 9.6 million. Of the four regions of the country—Northeast, Midwest, West and South—only the Northeast and Midwest experienced declines in their foreign-born populations during this decade, driving the national trend, while the West and South grew. Despite the decline experienced over the decade, by 1970, the Northeast remained the region with the largest number of foreign born; however, the West had surpassed the Midwest as the region with the second largest foreign-born population.

Between 1970 and 2010, the foreign-born populations of all regions increased.[9] By 1980, the West had surpassed the Northeast as the region with the greatest number of foreign born, and the South exceeded the Midwest as the region with the third largest foreign-born population. By 2000, the number of foreign born in the West was greater than both the Northeast and Midwest *combined*, while the South had a larger foreign-born population than the Northeast. As of 2010, there were 14.1 million foreign born in the West, 12.7 million in the South, 8.6 million in the Northeast, and 4.5 million in the Midwest. Since 1990, the South has experienced the greatest numeric growth in its total foreign-born population, growing by at least 4 million between 1990 and 2000 and again between 2000 and 2010.

Over the last 50 years, the distribution of the foreign-born population has shifted from the Northeast and Midwest regions of the country to the West and South. In 1960, over two-thirds of the foreign-born population lived in either the Northeast (47 percent) or the Midwest (23 percent). Throughout this period, the proportion of foreign born residing in these two regions continued to decline, dropping by more than one half. By 2010, about 33 percent of the foreign-born population lived in the Northeast (22 percent) and Midwest (11 percent). By comparison, the proportion residing in the West and South regions more than doubled, from 30 percent in 1960 to 67 percent in 2010. The proportion of the foreign-born population residing in the West increased from about 20 percent in 1960 to 40 percent in 1990, declining to 35 percent by 2010. The South was the only region that exhibited a continuous increase in its proportion of foreign born, tripling from about 10 percent in 1960 to 32 percent in 2010.[10]

Distribution of the Foreign-Born Population by Geographic Region and Country of Birth

The size, origins, and geographic distribution of the foreign-born population have changed considerably since 1960. As the number of foreign born increased, especially after 1970, the geographic distribution of the foreign born moved from the Northeast and Midwest to the West and South. At the same time, the leading immigrant source countries shifted from Europe to Latin America and Asia. In general, this pattern of change in the distribution of source countries can be seen within each geographic region of the United States, although the timing and the particular countries of birth represented does vary.

Between 1960 and 1990, Italy was the largest foreign-born group in the Northeast, followed by other countries from Europe—such as Poland, Germany, and the United Kingdom—and Canada. Starting in 1990, the foreign born from countries in the Caribbean and Asia—including the Dominican Republic, China, India, and Jamaica—were among the largest groups. Unlike all other geographic regions in the United States, the Northeast is notable for its diversity of foreign born: no single country-of-birth group has represented more than 10 percent of the foreign-born population since 1980.

In the Midwest, the foreign-born from Europe—including Germany, Poland, Italy, and the United Kingdom—and Canada were among the largest foreign-born groups between 1960 and 2000. During this period, Germany represented the largest single country-of-birth group in 1960 (13 percent) and 1970 (12 percent). However, by 1980, the foreign born from Mexico was the largest group, with 10 percent of the foreign-born population. This proportion increased over the next 30 years, reaching 30 percent in 2010. Since 1980, no other country-of-birth

group besides Mexico has represented more than 10 percent of the foreign-born population in the Midwest.

There was little change in the distribution of the foreign-born population in the South between 1960 and 1990. Mexico, Cuba, Germany, the United Kingdom, and Canada remained among the largest groups throughout this 30-year period. Since 2000, about one-third of the foreign born in the South has been from Mexico, with all other countries representing less than 10 percent each, including Cuba, India, El Salvador, and Vietnam.

In the West, the foreign born from Mexico has remained the dominant group over the last 50 years, increasing from 16 percent in 1960 to 42 percent by 2010. The foreign born from Canada and the United Kingdom were also among the largest groups in 1960, 1970, and 1980. Since 1970, only Mexico has exceeded 10 percent of the regional total. Other large groups in the West since 1990 include the Philippines, China, Vietnam, and El Salvador.

Distribution and Growth of the Foreign-Born Population by State

Since 1960, two states—California and New York—have had the largest foreign-born populations among all other states and represented the largest share of the total foreign born.[11] New York had the largest number of foreign born until 1970 but by 1980 was surpassed by California, which has remained the state with the largest foreign-born population through 2010. Today, over one-fourth of the total foreign-born population lives in the state of California alone.

During the decades between 1960 and 1990, the foreign-born populations of seven states, including Michigan, Montana, North Dakota, Ohio, Pennsylvania, South Dakota, and Wisconsin, continuously declined in size. By comparison, 20 states experienced continuous increases in their foreign-born population during these three decades, and 19 were located in either the South or West.[12] Over the next two decades—1990 through 2010—the number of foreign born in *every* state and the District of Columbia increased. The six states that experienced the greatest growth in number of foreign born between 2000 and 2010 included California, Texas, Florida, New York, New Jersey, and Georgia.

The Foreign Born as a Percent of State Population

As the foreign-born population increased in size and dispersed geographically, most states—including those with little recent immigrant history—experienced a greater immigrant presence.

In 1960, the populations of two-thirds of all states included less than 5 percent foreign born. Six states (New York, Massachusetts, Connecticut, New Jersey, Rhode Island, and

Hawaii) had 10 percent or more foreign born in their total populations, but no state in 1960 had 15 percent or more foreign born. In 1970, when the number of foreign born reached its lowest point in the 20th century, 80 percent of all states had less than 5 percent foreign born. New York, with 12 percent, was the state with the highest percent foreign born in its total population.

By 1980, most states still had relatively small foreign-born populations, but the proportion of foreign born in several states in the West and South increased to above 5 percent. California replaced New York as the state with the highest percent foreign born. By 1990, 22 percent of California's population and 16 percent of New York's population was foreign born. However, less than two-thirds of all states, especially those in the Midwest and South, remained at less than 5 percent foreign born in their total populations.

Between 1990 and 2000, the foreign-born population of the United States grew by 11.3 million persons, representing the largest numeric increase of any decade in U.S. history. By 2000, over half of all states included 5 percent or more foreign born in their total populations, with six states including 15 percent or more. Between 2000 and 2010, the foreign-born population increased by an additional 8.8 million persons. By 2010, the foreign-born population represented more than 5 percent in about two-thirds of all states. There were eight states with 15 percent or more foreign born in their total populations, including California, New York, New Jersey, Florida, Nevada, Hawaii, Texas, and Massachusetts.

The Foreign-Born as a Percent of the County Population: 2010

In 2010, the foreign-born population represented 12.9 percent of the national population. There were 13 states where the foreign-born population represented a greater share of the state population than the national average, including California (27 percent), New York (22 percent), New Jersey (21 percent), Florida (19 percent), Nevada (19 percent), Hawaii (18 percent), and Texas (16 percent).[13] These were also the states where, in general, counties with the highest proportion foreign born were concentrated.

There were 3,143 counties in the United States in 2010, including 2,425 with a population of 10,000 or more. Of these 2,425 counties, there were 146 where the foreign-born population represented more than 12.9 percent of the county population, including 30 where the foreign born comprised more than one-fourth and 9 where the foreign born comprised more than one-third of the population. Most of these counties were in the states of California (33 counties), Texas (23 counties), Florida (13 counties), New Jersey (10 counties), New York (9 counties), and Virginia (8 counties). There was only one county—Miami-Dade County, Florida—where the

foreign born comprised more than half (52 percent) of the total population. Additional counties with a population of at least 10,000 and a percent foreign born greater than one-third included: Queens County, New York; Hudson County, New Jersey; Kings County (Brooklyn), New York; Santa Clara County, California; San Francisco County, California; Los Angeles County, California; San Mateo County, California; and Bronx County, New York.

The Foreign-Born Population by Age

Over the past 50 years, the foreign-born population has become, in general, a younger population. This was especially true between 1960 and 1990, when the median age of the foreign-born population declined from 57 years in 1960 to 37 years in 1990. This decline in median age reflects the shift over time to a greater proportion of foreign born in the younger age groups. In 1960, over half (55 percent) of all foreign born were aged 55 and over, but by 2000, 20 percent were in this age category. In addition, the proportion of foreign born between the ages of 18 and 54 continuously increased from 39 percent in 1960 to 70 percent in 2000. Also notable during this period was the change in the proportion of foreign born under 18, which nearly doubled from 6.4 percent in 1960 to 12.2 percent in 1980, declining to and remaining at about 10 percent through 2000. In contrast to this 40 year trend, the foreign-born population actually aged between 2000 and 2010, as demonstrated by the increase in the median age to 41.4 years and the increase in the proportion aged 55 and over to 25 percent.

When the age distribution of the foreign born from Europe is compared with that of the foreign born from Latin America and Asia, there are considerable differences. For the last 50 years, while the foreign born from Europe has become increasingly juvenescent, it has remained a population older than either the foreign born from Latin America or Asia, with a higher median age and greater proportion in the older ages. The average difference between the median age of the foreign born from Latin America and the foreign born from Europe for the entire period was about 20 years, ranging from about 13 years to about 26 years. By comparison, the difference in the median age between the foreign born from Latin America and the foreign born from Asia ranged from about the same to about 5 years younger. Also throughout the period, the proportion of the foreign-born population from Latin America and Asia who were under age 55 was considerably higher than the proportion of the foreign-born population from Europe. By 2010, 81 percent of the foreign born from Latin America and 73 percent of the foreign born from Asia were under age 55 compared with 55 percent of the foreign born from Europe.

In general, between 1960 and 2010, the foreign born as a whole became a younger population. While the median age did increase after 2000, reaching 41 years in 2010, it has yet to return to the levels seen in 1960 and 1970, when more than half of all foreign born were older than 50 years of age. The juvenescence after 1960 was due, in part, to the death of older foreign born, especially those from Europe, who had immigrated to the United States in the decades before 1950.[14] Even as the proportion of younger European immigrants grew through time, the foreign born from Europe remained an older population, especially relative to the foreign born from Latin America and Asia, and represented an increasingly diminishing share of the total foreign born. By comparison, the foreign born from Latin America became a younger population, with higher proportions in the younger age groups, and grew to represent over half of all foreign born. Although the pattern of aging was different for the foreign-born population from Asia, it remained younger than the foreign born from Europe and, like Latin America, represented an increasing share of the total foreign born through time. Thus, the increasing juvenescence of the foreign-born population, especially after 1970, is attributable in large part to the shift over time to a greater proportion of younger immigrants from Latin America and Asia.

Conclusion: The Foreign Born and the Growth of the U.S. Population

During the last 50 years, the foreign-born population of the United States has undergone dramatic changes, shifting from an older, predominantly European population settled in the Northeast and Midwest to a younger, predominantly Latin American and Asian population settled in the West and South. These qualitative changes occurred simultaneously with a quantitative growth in the total number of foreign born. In 1960, there were 9.7 million foreign born in the United States, representing 5 percent of the total population. By 2010, the population had grown to 40 million, representing about 13 percent of the total population.

As the foreign-born population increased, the native-born population grew as well, from 169.6 million in 1960 to 269.4 million in 2010. One important difference between the patterns of growth in the two populations is the rate of change throughout the period, which was higher for the foreign-born population. Between 1960 and 2010, the foreign-born population increased by 310 percent, or by about an average of 34 percent per decade, while the native-born population increased by 59 percent, or on average about 10 percent per decade. Recall that the number of foreign born in the United States actually

declined between 1960 and 1970, so the percent change was higher for the 40-year period between 1970 and 2010: 315 percent, or by an average of about 43 percent per decade. By comparison, the native-born population increased by 39 percent between 1970 and 2010, or by about 9 percent per decade.[15]

Although the foreign-born population demonstrated a greater percent increase than the native population over the last 40 years, as a *proportion* of the total growth, the foreign born accounted for less than one-third of the change. The total population—including both native and foreign born—increased from 203.2 million in 1970 to 309.3 million in 2010, or by about 106.1 million.

The native population represented 71 percent of that growth, with 29 percent accounted for by the increase in the number of foreign born. The foreign-born from Latin America and Asia comprised 98 percent of the growth in the total foreign-born population during this period. Mexico alone accounted for 36 percent of the growth in the foreign-born population and 10 percent of the growth in the total population after 1970.

While the increase in the number of foreign born has contributed to the growth of the total population since 1970, its impact is mitigated by the fact that children of immigrants born in the United States are, by definition, native. An alternative way to assess the absolute impact of immigration on total growth is to consider the proportion of increase represented by *both* the foreign born and their children. According to the results of the 1970 census, the "first generation" (i.e., the foreign born) and "second generation" (i.e., the native born with at least one foreign-born parent) summed to 32.4 million, representing 16 percent of the population. By 2010, according to the Current Population Survey (CPS), there were 71.7 million persons in the first and second generations, comprising 24 percent of the population.[16] The difference between the 1970 Census and 2010 CPS suggests the size of the combined first and second generations increased by approximately 39.3 million persons over this 40-year period. While the proportion of total growth represented by the increase in the number of foreign born was 29 percent, when combined with the second generation, the proportion increases to about 37 percent. In other words, over one-third of the growth in the total population of the United States between 1970 and 2010 was due to the increase in the foreign-born population and their native-born children.

Source of the Data and Accuracy of the Estimates

Many of the findings presented in this report were based on the American Community Survey (ACS) data collected in 2010. The ACS is a nationwide survey designed to provide communities with reliable and timely demographic, social, economic, and housing data for the nation, states, congressional districts, counties, places, and other localities every year. It has an annual sample size of about 3 million addresses across the United States and Puerto Rico and includes both housing units and group quarters (e.g., nursing facilities and prisons). The ACS is conducted in every county throughout the nation, and every municipio in Puerto Rico, where it is called the Puerto Rico Community Survey. For information on the ACS sample design and other topics, visit <www.census.gov/acs/www>. For information on sampling and estimation methods, confidentiality protection, and sampling and nonsampling errors, see the "2010 ACS Accuracy of the Data" document located at <http://www.census.gov/acs/www/Downloads/data_documentation/Accuracy/ACS_Accuracy_of_Data_2010.pdf>. For additional information about the design and methodology of the ACS, see U.S. Census Bureau (2009).

Other findings presented in this report that were not derived from the 2010 ACS were collected from previously published findings based on data from each decennial census conducted by the Census Bureau since 1850. Because the structure of the decennial census has changed over time, some of the data were based on complete censuses (100 percent of the population, from 1850 to 1930) and some were based on sample populations of various sizes (ranging from 5 percent to 20 percent from 1940 to 2000). In general, the decennial censuses collected data from the population living in households as well as those living in group quarters. For more information about the source and accuracy details of the decennial censuses, see Gibson and Jung (2006) and U.S. Census Bureau (2002a, 2002b).

For additional information about the design and methodology of the Current Population Survey, see U.S. Census Bureau (2006). Additional information about the Annual Social and Economic (ASEC) supplement is available at <http://www.census.gov/cps/methodology/techdocs.html>. All comparisons presented in this report have taken sampling error into account and are significant at the 90 percent confidence interval unless otherwise noted. Due to rounding, some details may not sum to totals.

References

Congressional Budget Office. 2006. *Immigration Policy in the United States.* Washington, D.C.: Congressional Budget Office <http://www.cbo.gov/ftpdocs/70xx/doc7051/02-28-Immigration.pdf>

Gibson, Campbell and Kay Jung. 2006. "Historical Census Statistics on the Foreign-Born Population in the United States: 1850 to 2000." Population Division Working Paper Number 81. Washington, D.C.: U.S. Census Bureau. <http://www.census.gov/population/www/techpap.html>.

Grieco, Elizabeth M. 2009. *Race and Hispanic Origin of the Foreign-Born Population in the United States: 2007.* American Community Survey Reports, ACS-11. Washington, D.C.: U.S. Census Bureau. <http://www.census.gov/prod/2010pubs/acs-11.pdf>

Grieco, Elizabeth M. and Edward N. Trevelyan. 2010. *Place of Birth of the Foreign-Born Population: 2009.* American Community Survey Briefs, ACSBR/09-15. Washington, D.C.: U.S. Census Bureau. <http://www.census.gov/prod/2010pubs/acsbr09-15.pdf>

Rytina, Nancy. 2002. "IRCA Legalization Effects: Lawful Permanent Residence and Naturalization through 2001." Paper presented at *The Effects of Immigrant Legalization Programs on the United States: Scientific Evidence on Immigrant Adaptation and Impact on the U.S. Economy and Society,* The Cloister, Mary Woodward Lasker Center, National Institutes of Health Main Campus, October 25, 2002.

Singer, Audrey. 2004. *The Rise of New Immigrant Gateways.* Washington, D.C.: Brookings Institution. <http://www.brookings.edu/urban/pubs/20040301_gateways.pdf>

U.S. Census Bureau, American Community Survey. 2010. Information about the American Community Survey is available on the U.S. Census Bureau's Web site at: <http://www.census.gov/acs/www>

U.S. Census Bureau. 2002a. *Measuring America: The Decennial Censuses from 1790 to 2000.* Washington, D.C.: U.S. Census Bureau. <http://www.census.gov/prod/www/abs/ma.html>

U.S. Census Bureau. 2002b. *2000 Census of Population and Housing, Summary File 3: Technical Documentation.* Washington, D.C.: U.S. Census Bureau. <http://www.census.gov/prod/cen2000/doc/sf3.pdf>

U.S. Census Bureau. 2006. *Design and Methodology: Current Population Survey.* Technical Paper 66. Washington, D.C.: U.S. Census Bureau. <http://www.census.gov/prod/2006pubs/tp-66.pdf>

U.S. Census Bureau. 2009. *Design and Methodology: American Community Survey.* Washington, D.C.: U.S. Census Bureau. <http://www.census.gov/acs/www/Downloads/survey_methodology/acs_design_methodology.pdf>.

Vialet, Joyce C. 1991. "A Brief History of U.S. Immigration Policy." *Congressional Research Service Report for Congress,* number 91–141 EPW. Washington, D.C.: Library of Congress.

Walters, Nathan P. and Rachel T. Cortes. 2010. *Year of Entry of the Foreign-Born Population: 2009.* American Community Survey Briefs, ACSBR/09-17. Washington, D.C.: U.S. Census Bureau. <http://www.census.gov/prod/2010pubs/acsbr09-17.pdf>

Notes

1. The foreign-born population includes anyone who was not a U.S. citizen at birth, including those who have become U.S. citizens through naturalization. Conversely, the native-born population includes anyone who is a U.S. citizen at birth. Respondents who were born in the United States, Puerto Rico, a U.S. Island Area (U.S. Virgin Islands, Guam, American

Samoa, or the Commonwealth of the Northern Mariana Islands), or abroad of a U.S. citizen parent or parents, are defined as native. In this paper, the terms "native" and "native born" are used interchangeably.

2. Unless otherwise noted, the data presented in this, report were derived from the 1960 through 2000 decennial censuses, as presented by Gibson and Jung (2006), and the 2010 American Community Survey 1-year estimates.

3. The cap is "flexible" because it can exceed 675,000 in any year when unused visas from the family-sponsored and employment-based categories are available from the previous year. If only 625,000 people were admitted during the year, for example, the cap would be raised to 725,000 the following year.

4. The Northeast region includes the states of Connecticut, Maine, Massachusetts, New Hampshire, New Jersey, New York, Pennsylvania, Rhode Island, and Vermont. The Midwest region includes the states of Illinois, Indiana, Iowa, Kansas, Michigan, Minnesota, Missouri, Nebraska, North Dakota, Ohio, South Dakota, and Wisconsin.

5. The West region includes the states of Alaska, Arizona, California, Colorado, Hawaii, Idaho, Montana, Nevada, New Mexico, Oregon, Utah, Washington, and Wyoming. The South region includes the states of Alabama, Arkansas, Delaware, Florida, Georgia, Kentucky, Louisiana, Maryland, Mississippi, North Carolina, Oklahoma, South Carolina, Tennessee, Texas, Virginia, West Virginia and the District of Columbia.

6. According to Gibson and Jung (2006), the data on the total foreign-born population of the United States are generally comparable from 1850 to 2000. Since 1890, however, individuals who were born in a foreign country but had a least one parent who was an American citizen have been defined as native rather than foreign born. For additional information, see U.S. Census Bureau (2002a).

7. Central America includes the countries of Belize, Costa Rica, El Salvador, Guatemala, Honduras, Mexico, Nicaragua, and Panama.

8. See Gibson and Jung (2006), table 4.

9. For the Midwest, the size of the foreign-born population for 1980 and 1990 are not statistically different.

10. From 1960 to 2010, the foreign-born population of the five boroughs of New York City (Bronx, Brooklyn, Manhattan, Queens, and Staten Island) consistently represented over two-thirds of the foreign-born population of the state of New York (ranging between 68 percent and 74 percent) and over one-third of the foreign-born population in the Northeast (ranging between 34 percent and 40 percent). However, while the number of foreign born in New York City doubled in size during this period, increasing from 1.5 million in 1960 to 3 million in 2010, it represented an increasingly smaller share

of the total foreign-born population, declining from 16 percent in 1960 to about 8 percent in 2010.

11. In this paper, the term *states* refers to the 50 states plus the District of Columbia.

12. The states where the foreign-born populations continually increased in size between 1960 to 1970, 1970 to 1980, and 1980 to 1990 included: Alabama, Arizona, Arkansas, California, Colorado, Delaware, Florida, Georgia, Hawaii, Louisiana, Maryland, Nevada, New Jersey, New Mexico, North Carolina, Oklahoma, South Carolina, Tennessee, Texas, and Virginia.

13. The estimates for Nevada and Hawaii are not statistically different.

14. The decline in the number of foreign born from Europe was also due, in part, to emigration. Unfortunately, the U.S Census Bureau does not collect data on the number of people, either native or foreign born, who emigrate from the United States, or enumerate Americans living overseas.

15. For each decade, of course, the native-born population exhibited a greater numeric increase than the foreign born: between 1970 and 2010, the native population grew by an average of 18.9 million per decade, while the foreign born grew by an average of 7.6 million. However, as a change in the percent of the base population at the beginning of each decade after 1970, the foreign-born population grew at a faster rate.

16. Note that both the 1970 Census and 2010 Current Population Survey estimates of the population by generation groups refer to the civilian noninstitutionalized population.

Critical Thinking

1. What do demographic indicators reveal about an ethnic group?

2. Examine the origin and sources of misinformation about Asian Americans.

3. Does public attention to the activities of Asian Americans associated with Islamic countries seem to be increasing?

Internet References

Immigration and Ethnic History Society
www.iehs.org

Immigration Policy Center
www.immigrationpolicy.org

The International Center for Migration, Ethnicity, and Citizenship
www.newschool.edu/icmec/?v=

U. S. Bureau of Citizenship and Immigration Services
www.uscis.gov

U.S. Census Bureau
www.census.gov

Grieco, Elizabeth M., et al. "The Size, Place of Birth and Geographic Distribution of the Foreign-Born Population in the United States: 1960–2010", *U.S. Census Bureau*, October 2012.

Article   Prepared by: John A. Kromkowski, *The Catholic University of America*

The Foreign-Born Population from Africa: 2008–2012

CHRISTINE P. GAMBINO, EDWARD N. TREVELYAN, AND JOHN THOMAS FITZWATER

Learning Outcomes

After reading this article, you will be able to:

- Identify from which African counties the largest numbers of immigrants are coming to America.

- Understand in what respect these immigrants are different from American-born African Americans.

Introduction

According to the 2008–2012 American Community Survey (ACS), 39.8 million foreign-born people resided in the United States, including 1.6 million from Africa, or about 4 percent of the total foreign-born population. In 1970, there were about 80,000 African foreign born, representing less than 1 percent of the total foreign-born population (Figure 1). During the following four decades, the number of foreign born from Africa grew rapidly, roughly doubling each decade.

About three-fourths of the foreign-born population from Africa came to live in the United States after 1990.[1] The timing of this movement was driven in part by historical changes. Outmigration from Africa increased rapidly after World War II, as migrants responded to the pull of educational opportunities and jobs abroad.[2] While the first waves of postwar migrants went to other African countries and former colonial powers of Europe, migration to the United States increased in the 1970s as economies faltered and new restrictions were placed upon immigration in Western Europe.[3] More immigrants from Africa were admitted to the United States after the U.S. Immigration Act of 1965, which replaced the national origin quota system favoring immigration from Europe with a new law prioritizing skilled labor, family unification, and humanitarianism.[4]

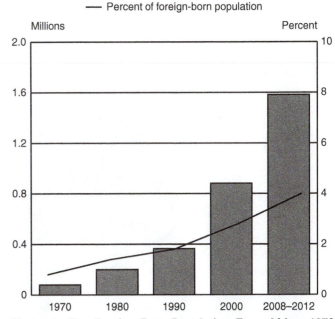

Figure 1. **The Foreign-Born Population From Africa: 1970 to 2008–2012** (Data based on sample. For information on confidentiality protection, sampling error, nonsampling error, and definitions, see www.census.gov/acs/www)

Source: U. S. Census Bureau, Decennial Censuses, 1970 to 2000 and 2008–2012 American Community Survey, 5-year estimates.

In addition, nearly a quarter of all immigrants from Africa to the United States in 2010 entered as refugees or received asylum as a result of ethnic conflict or civil war, particularly in countries such as Somalia, Liberia, and Sudan.[5] The rate of African-born immigrants arriving and staying in the

United States accelerated further as immigrant networks grew and pathways were established.[6]

This brief discusses the size, place of birth, geographical distribution, and educational attainment of the foreign born from Africa. Data are presented at the national, state, and metropolitan levels based on the 2008–2012 ACS 5-year file.

African Regions and Countries of Birth

Of the 1.6 million foreign born from Africa in the United States, 36 percent were from Western Africa, 29 percent were from Eastern Africa, and 17 percent were from Northern Africa, followed by Southern Africa (5 percent), Middle Africa (5 percent), and other Africa (7 percent) (Figure 2).[7] Since 2000, the foreign born from Africa increased by over 700,000 persons, up from a total of 881,300. Over 490,000, or about 70 percent of that growth, has been from countries in Western and Eastern Africa.

The largest African-born populations were from Nigeria and Ghana in Western Africa; Ethiopia, Kenya, and Somalia in Eastern Africa; Egypt in Northern Africa; and South Africa in Southern Africa. Of these seven, the four largest were

Nigeria (221,000 or 14 percent of the African-born population), Ethiopia (164,000 or 10 percent), Egypt (143,000 or 9 percent), and Ghana (121,000 or 8 percent), together constituting 41 percent of the African-born total.

Geographic Distribution of the Foreign-Born Population from Africa

Four states had more than 100,000 foreign born from Africa: New York (164,000), California (155,000), Texas (134,000), and Maryland (120,000). When combined, these four states represented over one-third (36 percent) of the foreign born from Africa.

Among states with at least 2,500 foreign born from Africa, Rhode Island had the highest percentage of the African born from Western Africa (82 percent), while over half of the African born in Massachusetts and New York (each 52 percent) were from this region. Over half of the foreign born from Africa in three states—Minnesota, Nevada, and Washington—were from Eastern Africa. Minnesota's Eastern African born represented 61 percent of its African-born population, over

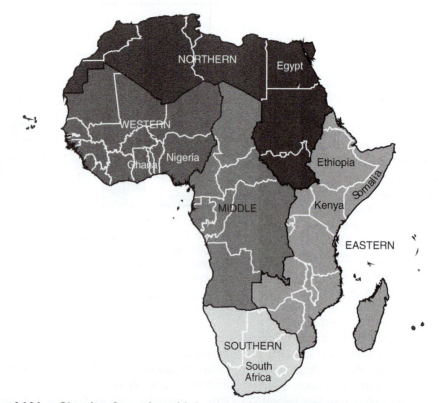

Figure 2.   Regions of Africa, Showing Countries with Largest African-Born Populations in the United States: 2008–2012
Source: U.S. Census Bureau, 2008–2012 American Community Survey, 5-year estimates.

double the national percentage and included a Somali-born population of 21,000. Florida and New Jersey (each 33 percent) and Iowa (30 percent) were among the states with the highest percentage of their African-born populations from Northern Africa. California's large Egyptian-born population (31,000) contributed to its Northern African representation (29 percent), notably higher than the national percentage (17 percent).[8]

The states with the highest percentage foreign born from Africa in their foreign-born populations included North Dakota and Minnesota (both 19 percent), South Dakota (17 percent), Maryland and the District of Columbia (both 15 percent).[9] Arkansas, California, Florida, Hawaii, and New Mexico each had less than 2 percent foreign born from Africa in their foreign-born populations.

Of the ten states with the largest African-born populations, five had percentages of African born in their foreign-born populations that were at least twice the national percentage: Minnesota (19 percent), Maryland (15 percent), Virginia (9 percent), and Georgia and Massachusetts (both 8 percent).

Distribution by Metropolitan Statistical Area

Metropolitan areas with the largest African-born population included New York, NY (212,000); Washington, DC (161,000); Atlanta, GA (68,000); Los Angeles, CA (68,000); and Minneapolis-St. Paul, MN (64,000). In addition to having a high number of African born, the percentage of the foreign-born population from Africa in the Washington, DC, metro area (13 percent) was more than three times the national percentage (4 percent), and Minneapolis-St. Paul, MN (20 percent), was five times the national percentage.

In several metropolitan areas with relatively small African-born populations, the African born nevertheless represented a high proportion of the total foreign born. These included Columbus, OH (23 percent); Baltimore, MD (13 percent); and Providence, RI (11 percent), with between 20,000 and 35,000 African foreign born.[10] Most metropolitan areas with a high percentage of African born in their foreign-born populations were in the Midwest and Northeast regions in states such as Minnesota, Ohio, and Maine. It is notable that in many metropolitan areas in the western half of the country, the concentrations of African born were well below the national average. These included Los Angeles (1.5 percent), San Francisco (1.8 percent), and San Diego (2.2 percent).

With the exception of Nigeria, there was considerable variation in the top countries of birth in metropolitan areas with the largest African-born populations. For example, both Dallas-Ft. Worth and Houston showed large numbers of Nigerians and Ethiopians. Chicago, Columbus, and New York had significant

Ghanaian populations, while foreign born from Cabo Verde figured prominently in Boston and Providence (half of the African born in Providence). The largest African-origin countries for Washington, DC, were Ethiopia and Nigeria. The largest African-born populations in Minneapolis-St. Paul were from Somalia and Ethiopia. In Los Angeles and San Francisco, leading African countries of birth included Egypt, Nigeria, and Ethiopia. The largest African-origin countries in the New York metropolitan area were Egypt and Ghana, each composing just under 20 percent of the total African born.[11]

Educational Attainment

Compared with the overall foreign-born population, the foreign born from Africa had higher levels of educational attainment (Figure 6). High levels of educational attainment among the African born are in part due to the large number of educated Africans who have chosen to emigrate and to many who come to the United States to pursue academic studies.[12,13] Forty-one percent of the African-born population had a bachelor's degree or higher in 2008–2012, compared with 28 percent of the overall foreign born. Egypt (64 percent) and Nigeria (61 percent) were among the African countries of birth with the highest proportion of bachelor's and higher degrees.

Nearly one-third of the overall foreign-born population (32 percent) had less than a high school education. This contrasts with only 12 percent for the African-born population, as represented by such countries as South Africa (3 percent), Nigeria (4 percent), and Egypt and Kenya (each 5 percent).[14]

The difference in educational attainment among the populations from different African countries in part reflects how they immigrated to the United States. A relatively high proportion of immigrants from Africa entered the United States on diversity visas (24 percent as compared with 5 percent of the overall foreign born), which require a high school diploma or equivalent work experience.[15] The foreign born from Somalia, who mostly entered the United States as refugees or asylees (82 percent in 2010), not as diversity migrants (1 percent in 2010), were an exception to this overall pattern.[16] Forty percent of the Somali born had less than a high school education.

Summary

The foreign-born population from Africa is small relative to other foreign-born groups, but has experienced rapid growth in the last 40 years. Among the African-born population, the majority were born in Western Africa (36 percent), Eastern Africa (29 percent), or Northern Africa (17 percent). While traditional immigrant destinations such as New York and California have attracted the largest number of African

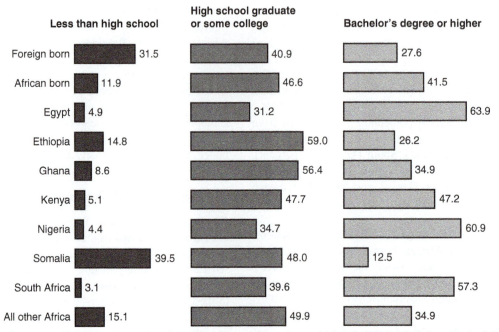

	Less than high school	High school graduate or some college	Bachelor's degree or higher
Foreign born	31.5	40.9	27.6
African born	11.9	46.6	41.5
Egypt	4.9	31.2	63.9
Ethiopia	14.8	59.0	26.2
Ghana	8.6	56.4	34.9
Kenya	5.1	47.7	47.2
Nigeria	4.4	34.7	60.9
Somalia	39.5	48.0	12.5
South Africa	3.1	39.6	57.3
All other Africa	15.1	49.9	34.9

Figure 3. Educational Attainment of the Foreign-Born Population from Africa by Selected Country of Birth: 2008–2012 (Percentage distribution of the population 25 and older. Percents may not add to 100 due to rounding. Data based on sample. For information on confidentiality protection, sampling error, nonsampling error, and definitions, see www.census.gov/acs/www)

Source: U.S. Census Bureau, 2008–2012 American Community Survey, 5-year estimates.

immigrants, they account for a relatively small percentage of the total foreign born in those states. Higher concentrations of the African born in a state's total foreign-born population are instead found in North Dakota, Minnesota, South Dakota, Maryland, and the District of Columbia. Compared with the overall foreign-born population, a higher proportion of African born have completed a bachelor's degree or higher level of education.

What is the American Community Survey?

The American Community Survey (ACS) is a nationwide survey designed to provide communities with reliable and timely demographic, social, economic, and housing data for the nation, states, congressional districts, counties, places, and other localities every year. It has an annual sample size of about 3.5 million addresses across the United States and Puerto Rico and includes both housing units and group quarters (e.g., nursing facilities and prisons). The 5-year file of the ACS is designed to provide reliable statistics for small populations and small geographical areas of the United States. For information on the ACS sample design and other topics, visit <www.census.gov/acs/www/>.

Source and Accuracy

The data presented in this report are based on the ACS sample interviewed from January 2008 through December 2012. The estimates based on this sample describe the average values of person, household, and housing unit characteristics over this period of collection. Sampling error is the uncertainty between an estimate based on a sample and the corresponding value that would be obtained if the estimate were based on the entire population (as from a census). Measures of sampling error are provided in the form of margins of error for key estimates included in this report. All comparative statements in this report have undergone statistical testing, and comparisons are significant at the 90 percent level unless otherwise noted. In addition to sampling error, nonsampling error may be introduced during any of the operations used to collect and process survey data such as editing, reviewing, or keying data from questionnaires. For more information on sampling and estimation methods, confidentiality protection, and sampling and nonsampling errors, please see the ACS Multiyear Accuracy of the Data document located at <www.census.gov/acs/www/Downloads/data_documentation/Accuracy/MultiyearACSAccuracyofData2012.pdf>.

Notes

1. Elizabeth M. Grieco, et al., *The Foreign-Born Population in the United States: 2010,* American Community Survey Reports, U.S. Census Bureau, May 2012, page 10, <www.census.gov/prod/2012pubs/acs-19.pdf>, accessed on August 15, 2014.

2. John A. Arthur, *Invisible Sojourners: African Immigrant Diaspora in the United States,* Praeger Publishers, 2000, pp. 20–26.

3. April Gordon, "The New Diaspora: African Immigration to the United States," *Journal of Third World Studies,* 1998, 15(1): 81–87, <www.inmotionaame.org/texts/viewer .cfm?id=13_011T&page=79>, accessed on August 15, 2014.

4. Congressional Budget Office, *Immigration Policy in the United States,* Washington, DC, 2006, <www.cbo.gov/ftpdocs/70xx/doc7051/02-28-Immigration.pdf>, accessed on August 15, 2014.

5. Randy Capps, Kristen McCabe, and Michael Fix, *Diverse Streams: African Migration to the United States,* Migration Policy Institute, 2012, pp. 8–9, <www.migrationpolicy.org/sites/default/files/publications/CBI-AfricanMigration.pdf>, accessed on August 15, 2014.

6. John A. Arthur, "Transnational African Immigrant Lives and Identities," *African Diaspora Identities,* Lexington Books, 2010, pp. 79–87.

7. African subregional geographic divisions are the same as defined by the United Nations prior to the independence of South Sudan in 2011. Western Africa includes Benin, Burkina Faso, Cabo Verde, Cote d'Ivoire, The Gambia, Ghana, Guinea, Guinea-Bissau, Liberia, Mali, Mauritania, Niger, Nigeria, St. Helena, Senegal, Sierra Leone, and Togo. Eastern Africa includes the British Indian Ocean Territory, Burundi, Comoros, Djibouti, Eritrea, Ethiopia, Kenya, Madagascar, Malawi, Mauritius, Mayotte, Mozambique, Reunion, Rwanda, Seychelles, Somalia, Tanzania, Uganda, Zambia, and Zimbabwe. Northern Africa includes Algeria, Egypt, Libya, Morocco, Sudan (includes South Sudan), Tunisia, and Western Sahara. Southern Africa includes Botswana, Lesotho, Namibia, South Africa, and Swaziland. Middle Africa includes Angola, Cameroon, Central African Republic, Chad, Republic of the Congo (Congo-Brazzaville), Democratic Republic of the Congo (Congo-Kinshasa), Equatorial Guinea, Gabon, and Sao Tome and Principe.

8. The Northern African percentage of California's African-born population (29 percent) was not statistically different from the Northern African percentage of Iowa's African-born population (30 percent).

9. The African-born percentage of South Dakota's foreign-born population (17 percent) was not statistically different from the African-born percentages of North Dakota's and Minnesota's foreign-born populations (both 19 percent).

10. The African-born percentage of the Baltimore, MD, metropolitan statistical area's foreign-born population (13 percent) was not statistically different from the African-born percentage of the Providence, RI, metropolitan statistical area's foreign-born population (11 percent).

11. In the New York metropolitan statistical area, the percentage of the African-born population born in Ghana (17.0) was not statistically different from the percentage of the African-born population born in Nigeria (16.4).

12. Amandu Jacky Kaba, "Africa's Migration Brain Drain: Factors Contributing to the Mass Emigration of Africa's Elite to the West," in Isidore Okpewho and Nzegwu Nkiru, Eds., *The New African Diaspora,* Indiana University Press, 2009, pp. 109–118.

13. John A. Arthur, "Transnational African Immigrant Lives and Identities," *African Diaspora Identities,* Lexington Books, 2010, pp. 81–82.

14. The percentage of the Nigerian born with less than a high school education (4 percent) was not statistically different from the percentage of the Egyptian born and Kenyan born with less than a high school education (each 5 percent).

15. Capps, op. cit., pp. 8–12.

16. Capps, op. cit., p. 12.

Critical Thinking

1. Do changes in transportation and ease of maintaining communication with countries of origin suggest that the acculturation of immigrants in the 21st century will be substantively different from early eras of large-scale migration?

2. Does the discussion of citizenship by birth pose political challenges?

3. Explore age cohorts and country of origin patterns for clues about the future.

Internet References

Diversity.com
www.diversity.com

U.S. Census Bureau
www.census.gov

Gambino, Christine P.; Trevelyan, Edward N.; Fitzwater, John Thomas. "The Foreign-Born Population From Africa: 2008–2012", *U.S. Census Bureau,* October 2014.

Article   Prepared by: John A. Kromkowski, *The Catholic University of America*

Irish-American Heritage Month (March) and St. Patrick's Day (March 17): 2015

Learning Outcomes

After reading this article, you will be able to:

- Identify the historical changes documented in this report.
- Understand the most notable findings of this report.

Congress proclaimed March as Irish-American Heritage Month in 1991, and the President issues a proclamation commemorating the occasion each year.

Originally, a religious holiday to honor St. Patrick, who introduced Christianity to Ireland in the fifth century, St. Patrick's Day has evolved into a celebration for all things Irish. The world's first St. Patrick's Day parade occurred on March 17, 1762, in New York City, featuring Irish soldiers serving in the English military. This parade became an annual event, with President Truman attending in 1948.

Population Distribution

33.3 million

Number of U.S. residents who claimed Irish ancestry in 2013. This number was more than seven times the population of Ireland itself (4.6 million). Irish was the nation's second-most frequently reported European ancestry, trailing German.

Sources: 2013 American Community Survey
http://factfinder2.census.gov/bkmk/table/1.0/en/ACS/13_1YR/S0201/0100000US/popgroup~541
http://factfinder.census.gov/bkmk/table/1.0/en/ACS/13_1YR/B04003/0100000US
Ireland Central Statistics Office
http://www.cso.ie/en/releasesandpublications/er/pme/populationandmigrationestimatesapril2014/#.VInESmNsgtM

21.2%

Percentage of the population in Massachusetts that claimed Irish ancestry, which is among the highest in the nation. California has 2.5 million people claiming Irish ancestry, which is the highest of any state.

Source: 2013 American Community Survey
http://factfinder2.census.gov/bkmk/table/1.0/en/ACS/13_1YR/DP02/0100000US.04000

251,033

Number of foreign-born U.S. residents with Irish ancestry in 2013. Of these, 150,256 had become naturalized citizens.

Source: 2013 American Community Survey
http://factfinder2.census.gov/bkmk/table/1.0/en/ACS/13_1YR/S0201/0100000US/popgroup~541

39.7 years old

Median age of those who claimed Irish ancestry, which is higher than U.S. residents as a whole at 37.5 years.

Source: 2013 American Community Survey
http://factfinder2.census.gov/bkmk/table/1.0/en/ACS/13_1YR/S0201/0100000US/popgroup~541
http://factfinder2.census.gov/bkmk/table/1.0/en/ACS/13_1YR/S0201/0100000US/

Irish-Americans Today

35.1%

Percentage of people of Irish ancestry, 25 or older, who had a bachelor's degree or higher. In addition, 93.6 percent of Irish-Americans in this age group had at least a high school diploma. For the nation as a whole, the corresponding rates were 29.6 percent and 86.6 percent, respectively.

Source: 2013 American Community Survey

http://factfinder2.census.gov/bkmk/table/1.0/en/ACS/13_1YR/S0201/0100000US/popgroup~001|541

$60,967

Median income for households headed by an Irish-American, higher than the median household income of $52,250 for all households. In addition, 7.3 percent of family households of Irish ancestry were in poverty, lower than the rate of 11.6 percent for all Americans.

Source: 2013 American Community Survey

http://factfinder2.census.gov/bkmk/table/1.0/en/ACS/13_1YR/S0201/0100000US/popgroup~001|541

41.9%

Percentage of employed civilian Irish-Americans 16 or older who worked in management, business, science and arts occupations. Additionally, 25.5 percent worked in sales and office occupations; 15.6 percent in service occupations; 9.4 percent in production, transportation and material moving occupations; and 7.6 percent in natural resources, construction and maintenance occupations.

Source: 2013 American Community Survey

http://factfinder2.census.gov/bkmk/table/1.0/en/ACS/13_1YR/S0201/0100000US/popgroup~001|541

68.6%

Percentage of householders of Irish ancestry who owned the home in which they live, with the remainder renting. For the nation as a whole, the homeownership rate was 63.5 percent.

Source: 2013 American Community Survey

http://factfinder2.census.gov/bkmk/table/1.0/en/ACS/13_1YR/S0201/0100000US/popgroup~001|541

Sports Celebration of Irish Heritage
101,975

Population of South Bend, Ind., home to the Fighting Irish of the University of Notre Dame. About 11.0 percent of South Bend's population claims Irish ancestry.

Source: 2013 American Community Survey

http://factfinder2.census.gov/bkmk/table/1.0/en/ACS/13_1YR/DP02/1600000US1871000

22.1%

Percentage of the Boston metropolitan area population that claims Irish ancestry, one of the highest percentages for the top 50 metro areas by population. Boston is home to the Celtics of the National Basketball Association.

Source: 2013 American Community Survey

http://factfinder.census.gov/bkmk/table/1.0/en/ACS/13_1YR/DP02/0100000US.31000.005

79,446 and 16,771

Population of New Rochelle, N.Y., and Moraga, Calif., home to the Gaels of Iona University and St. Mary's College of California, respectively. About 9.5 percent of the New Rochelle population and 13.3 percent of the Moraga population claim Irish ancestry.

Sources: 2013 Population Estimates and 2013 American Community Survey

http://www.census.gov/popest/data/cities/totals/2013/SUB-EST2013.html

http://factfinder.census.gov/bkmk/table/1.0/en/ACS/13_5YR/DP02/1600000US0649187|1600000US3650617

Places to Spend the Day
16

Number of places (incorporated places and census designated places) or county subdivisions in the United States that share the name of Ireland's capital, Dublin. The most populous of the places named Dublin in 2013 was Dublin, Calif., at 52,105.

Source: 2013 Population Estimates

http://factfinder2.census.gov/bkmk/table/1.0/en/PEP/2013/PEPANNRES/0400000US06.16200

If you're still not into the spirit of St. Paddy's Day, then you might consider paying a visit to Emerald Isle, N.C., with 3,714 residents.

Source: 2013 Population Estimates

http://factfinder2.census.gov/bkmk/table/1.0/en/PEP/2013/PEPANNRES/0400000US37.16200

Other appropriate places in which to spend the day: the township of Irishtown, Ill., several places or county subdivisions named Clover (in South Carolina, Illinois, Minnesota, Pennsylvania, Virginia, West Virginia, and Wisconsin) or one of the six places that are named Shamrock (in Oklahoma, Texas (2), Minnesota, Missouri and Nebraska).

Source: http://www.census.gov/geo/maps-data/data/gazetteer.html

Following is a list of observances typically covered by the Census Bureau's *Facts for Features* series:

African-American History Month (February)
Super Bowl
Valentine's Day (Feb. 14)
Women's History Month (March)
Irish-American Heritage Month (March)/
  St. Patrick's Day (March 17)
Earth Day (April 22)
Asian/Pacific American Heritage Month (May)
Older Americans Month (May)
Cinco de Mayo (May 5)
Mother's Day
Hurricane Season Begins (June 1)
Father's Day
The Fourth of July (July 4)
Anniversary of Americans with Disabilities Act (July 26)
Back to School (August)
Labor Day
Grandparents Day
Hispanic Heritage Month (Sept. 15–Oct. 15)
Unmarried and Single Americans Week
Halloween (Oct. 31)
American Indian/Alaska Native Heritage Month
  (November)
Veterans Day (Nov. 11)

Thanksgiving Day
The Holiday Season (December)

Critical Thinking

1. Do large and apparently mainstream ethnic populations understand group relations in fundamentally different ways than minority groups?
2. Is it true that everyone is Irish on Saint Patrick's Day, March 17?

Editor's note—The preceding data were collected from a variety of sources and may be subject to sampling variability and other sources of error. Facts for Features are customarily released about two months before an observance in order to accommodate magazine production timelines. Questions or comments should be directed to the Census Bureau's Public Information Office: telephone: 301-763-3030; or e-mail: <pio@census.gov>.

Internet References

The American Irish Historical Society
  www.aihs.org
The Ancient Order of Hibernians
  www.aoh.org
National Catholic Bishops Conference
  www.USCCB.org

U.S. Department of Commerce, Economics and Statistics Administration. "Irish American Heritage Month (March) and St. Patrick Day (March 17) 2015", *U.S. Census Bureau*, January 2015.

Unit 4

UNIT

Prepared by: John A. Kromkowski, *The Catholic University of America*

Indigenous Ethnic Groups: The Native Americans

The contemporary issues of Native Americans are clearly a particular case of race and ethnic relations in America. Unlike other ethnic groups in the United States, relations between the United States and Native Americans are regulated by treaties, laws, and specific relations between various states. The Native American reality can be viewed in comparative perspective to descendants of all conquered indigenous peoples. Similarly, they add their weight to the claims for cultural justice, equal protection, and due process throughout the record of human conflict in race and ethnic relations. The history of indigenous peoples in the American hemisphere as well as other colonized areas throughout the world included various contested issues and conquests. The consequences of these conflicts were the extension of power over populations that became marginalized and isolated within larger scale regimes. New worlds of meaning eventually emerged from the conquests of small scale communities, but the expectation of revival and renewal of meaning from earlier periods and more compact forms of social cohesion continued. The reclaiming of the history of pre- and post-conquest indigenous cultures is a contemporary effort. In part, this is informed by the search for meaning and justice rooted in the deepest stirring of human consciousness, and its access to symbolization embedded in traditions. Such traditions have been articulated in folkloric fashion and have been challenged by acculturation, assimilation, mobility, and new patterns of interaction with other ethnic groups and with mainstream America. Identity politics in 1978 prompted Congress to venture into family law. Congress outlawed the practice of removing Native American children through adoption by non-native-Americans by privileging placement of children within their tribes. In 2013, the Supreme Court decided to hear *Adoptive Couple v. Baby Girl* and ruled on the constitutionality of protection for an unwed father to claim a child adopted outside the tribe.

Ethnicity is built upon the truth and strength of a tradition. A sense of family and community, and an unwillingness to give up, have led to standoffs with many forces within America. From this perspective, this unit details ways in which an ethnic group maintains its rights and heritage to preserve an ancient culture from amnesia and extinction. Indigenous ethnic communities have encountered a complex array of historical, social, cultural, and economic forces. As a result, in the late twentieth century, the traditions of indigenous ethnic groups have been renegotiated by yet another generation. Some find interaction easy, but others avoid striking a balance between traditional values and new demands. Native Americans have increasingly interfaced with the American legal system at the state level on issues of land use and gaming, which represent part of this current redefinition. Finally, however, they are challenging themselves to be themselves; examples of indigenous self-help reveal insights into how personal leadership and service to the community weave the social fabric of civil society.

With new cultural confidence and economic capacity, most notably in the gaming industry, the descendants of native peoples entered a new epoch, as did the entire country. Native Americans are part of the social texture of American pluralism. Some may argue that the reclamation and revival of tradition and power are unique social and political events. However, a wider view suggests that native populations are but another manifestation of ethnicity and ethnic groups articulating their agenda within the contexts of the American legal and economic order. Popular consciousness of indigenous peoples was heightened by the development of a National Museum on the Mall in Washington, DC. The expansion and profitability of Native American gambling casinos, their attendant impact on state and local economies, and the tax exemptions enjoyed by these ventures, appear to be headed toward contentions that may spill over into new issues of public order.

Questions of race and ethnic relations extend to claims regarding the rights of sovereign nations and the interests of the U.S. government and its citizens, which also include various Native Americans. These discussions are no longer at the margin of public affairs. The selections in this unit include demographics, self-help, philanthropy, governance, and identity. On one level, the descendants of indigenous peoples are a wide variety of peoples living in various states. On another level, these nations and tribes have been grouped into one category and have organized as an interest group that engages in the policy arenas of state and the national government.

Does this complex of particulars and definitions, including group-specific protections beyond individual rights and tradition, transform this instance of ethnicity into an issue of foreign and not domestic policy? Should the claims of ethnic groups in defense of culture, territory, and unique institutions be honored and protected by law and public policy? Why or why not? Is sovereignty real without the power to utilize authoritative force? In fact, this is a worldwide phenomenon that can be viewed as part of a wider continuum—one that that includes those populations comprised of thousands of ethnic groups on all continents and islands that have been conquered by the development of the modern state and the creation of large countries and, in some situations, empires. The process of extending the reach of a regime, which on one level may be described as a political military phenomena, is certainly not restricted to modern times. In fact, such conquests in the ancient world bear comparison. Most interestingly, in the ancient world, the intersections of ethnic groups with overwhelming powers reverberated in the moral, religious, and intellectual imagination in ways that continue into our time, and have shaped the search for meaning and justice in history and human affairs. The claims that power determines righteousness, and that power and ethno-religious superiority are woven into the engines of history and its progress, frame many conversations about human affairs that move beyond the horizon of the instruments of successful and efficacious outcomes of various forms of contention.

Article   Prepared by: John A. Kromkowski, *The Catholic University of America*

American Indian and Alaska Native Heritage Month: November 2014

U.S. CENSUS BUREAU

Learning Outcomes

After reading this article, you will be able to:

- Identify the central findings of this report.

- Identify the primary legislative recommendations of this report.

- Understand in what respects this report changed or confirmed general notions and assessments of the conditions that shape the opportunities of Native American children.

T he first American Indian Day was celebrated in May 1916 in New York. Red Fox James, a Blackfeet Indian, rode horseback from state to state, getting endorsements from 24 state governments, to have a day to honor American Indians. In 1990, President George H.W. Bush signed a joint congressional resolution designating November 1990 as "National American Indian Heritage Month." Similar proclamations have been issued every year since 1994. This Facts for Features presents statistics for American Indians and Alaska Natives, as this is one of the six major Office of Management and Budget race categories.

Note: Unless otherwise specified, the statistics in the "Population" section refer to the population who reported a race alone or in combination with one or more other races.

Population
5.2 million

The nation's population of American Indians and Alaska Natives, including those of more than one race. They made up about 2 percent of the total population in 2013. Of this total, about 49 percent were American Indian and Alaska Native only, and about 51 percent were American Indian and Alaska Native in combination with one or more other races.

Source: 2011–2013 American Community Survey

<http://factfinder2.census.gov/faces/tableservices/jsf/pages/productview.xhtml?pid=ACS_13_3YR_S0201&prodType=table>

11.2 million

The projected population of American Indians and Alaska Natives, alone or in combination, on July 1, 2060. They would comprise 2.7 percent of the total population.

Source: Population projections

<http://www.census.gov/population/projections/files/summary/NP2012-T4.xls>

432,343

The American Indian and Alaska Native population, alone or in combination, 65 and over.

Source: 2013 American Community Survey

<http://factfinder2.census.gov/faces/tableservices/jsf/pages/productview.xhtml?pid=ACS_13_3YR_S0201&prodType=table>

14

Number of states with more than 100,000 American Indian and Alaska Native residents, alone or in combination, in 2013. These states were California, Oklahoma, Arizona, Texas, New Mexico, Washington, New York, North Carolina, Florida, Alaska, Michigan, Oregon, Colorado and Minnesota.

Source: 2013 American Community Survey

<http://factfinder2.census.gov/bkmk/table/1.0/en/ACS/12_1YR/S0201/0100000US.04000/popgroup~009>

14.3%

The proportion of Alaska's population identified as American Indian and Alaska Native, alone or in combination, in 2013, the highest share for this race group of any state. Alaska was followed by Oklahoma (7.5 percent), New Mexico (9.1), South Dakota (8.5 percent) and Montana (6.8 percent).

Source: 2013 American Community Survey

<http://factfinder2.census.gov/faces/tableservices/jsf/pages/productview.xhtml?pid=ACS_13_1YR_DP05&prodType=table>

30.8

Median age for those who were American Indian and Alaska Native, alone or in combination, in 2013. This compares with a median age of 37.5 for the U.S. population as a whole.

Source: 2011–2013 American Community Survey

<http://factfinder2.census.gov/faces/tableservices/jsf/pages/productview.xhtml?pid=ACS_13_3YR_S0201&prodType=table>

Reservations
325

Number of federally recognized American Indian reservations in 2012. All in all, excluding Hawaiian Home Lands, there are 630 American Indian and Alaska Native legal and statistical areas for which the Census Bureau provides statistics.

Source: Census Bureau Geography Division

<https://www.census.gov/geo/reference/gtc/gtc_aiannha.html>

Tribes
566

Number of federally recognized Indian tribes.

Data courtesy of the Bureau of Indian Affairs, 2013

<http://www.bia.gov/cs/groups/public/documents/text/idc015898.pdf>

Families
1,698,815

The number of American Indian and Alaska Native family households in 2013 (households with a householder who was American Indian and Alaska Native alone or in combination with another race). Of these, 38.5 percent were married-couple families, including those with children.

Source: 2011–2013 American Community Survey

<http://factfinder2.census.gov/faces/tableservices/jsf/pages/productview.xhtml?pid=ACS_13_3YR_S0201&prodType=table>

6.1%

The percentage of American Indian and Alaska Natives, alone or in combination with other races, who were grandparents living with at least one of their grandchildren in 2013.

Source: 2011–2013 American Community Survey

<http://factfinder2.census.gov/faces/tableservices/jsf/pages/productview.xhtml?pid=ACS_13_3YR_S0201&prodType=table>

Housing
53.9%

The percentage of single-race American Indian and Alaska Native householders who owned their own home in 2013. This is compared with 64.0 percent of the overall population.

Source: 2011–2013 American Community Survey

<http://factfinder2.census.gov/faces/tableservices/jsf/pages/productview.xhtml?pid=ACS_13_3YR_S0201&prodType=table>

Languages
20.0%

Percentage of American Indians and Alaska Natives, alone or in combination, age 5 and older who spoke a language other than English at home in 2011–2013, compared with 21 percent for the nation as a whole.

Source: 2011–2013 American Community Survey

<http://factfinder2.census.gov/faces/tableservices/jsf/pages/productview.xhtml?pid=ACS_13_3YR_S0201&prodType=table>

Education
82.2%

The percentage of American Indians and Alaska Natives 25 and older who had at least a high school diploma, GED certificate or alternative credential. In addition, 17.6 percent obtained a bachelor's degree or higher. In comparison, 86.3 percent of the overall population had a high school diploma or higher and 29.1 percent had a bachelor's degree or higher.

Source: 2011–2013, American Community Survey
<http://factfinder2.census.gov/faces/tableservices/jsf/pages/productview.xhtml?pid=ACS_13_3YR_S0201&prodType=table>

39.8%

Single-race American Indians and Alaska Natives 25 and older whose bachelor's degree or higher was in science and engineering, or science and engineering-related fields in 2013. This compares with 43.7 percent for all people 25 and older with a bachelor's degree or higher.

Source: 2013 American Community Survey
<http://factfinder2.census.gov/bkmk/table/1.0/en/ACS/12_1YR/C15010C>

Source: 2001–2013 American Community Survey
<http://factfinder2.census.gov/faces/tableservices/jsf/pages/productview.xhtml?pid=ACS_13_3YR_C15010&prodType=table>

13.5%

Percentage of single-race American Indians and Alaska Natives 25 and older who had a bachelor's degree, graduate or professional degree in 2013.

Source: 2013 American Community Survey
<http://factfinder2.census.gov/faces/tableservices/jsf/pages/productview.xhtml?pid=ACS_13_3YR_S0201&prodType=table>

Jobs
25.9%

The percentage of civilian-employed single-race American Indian and Alaska Native people 16 and older who worked in management, business, science and arts occupations in 2013. In addition, 25.2 percent worked in service occupations and 22.7 percent in sales and office occupations.

Source: 2011–2013 American Community Survey
<http://factfinder2.census.gov/faces/tableservices/jsf/pages/productview.xhtml?pid=ACS_13_3YR_S0201&prodType=table>

Veterans
152,897

The number of single-race American Indian and Alaska Native veterans of the U.S. armed forces in 2011–2013.

Source: 2011–2013 American Community Survey
<http://factfinder2.census.gov/faces/tableservices/jsf/pages/productview.xhtml?pid=ACS_13_3YR_B21001C&prodType=table>

Income and Poverty
$36,252

The median household income of single-race American Indian and Alaska Native households in 2013. This compares with $52,176 for the nation as a whole.

Source: 2013 American Community Survey
<http://factfinder2.census.gov/faces/tableservices/jsf/pages/productview.xhtml?pid=ACS_13_3YR_S0201&prodType=table>

29.2%

The percent of single-race American Indians and Alaska Natives that were in poverty in 2013, the highest rate of any race group. For the nation as a whole, the poverty rate was 15.9 percent.

Source: 2011–2013 American Community Survey
<http://factfinder2.census.gov/bkmk/table/1.0/en/ACS/12_1YR/S0201//popgroup~002|004|006|009|012>

<http://factfinder2.census.gov/faces/tableservices/jsf/pages/productview.xhtml?pid=ACS_13_3YR_S0201&prodType=table>

Health Insurance
26.9%

The percentage of single-race American Indians and Alaska Natives who lacked health insurance coverage in 2013. For the nation as a whole, the corresponding percentage was 14.5 percent.

Source: 2013 Current Population Survey
<http://www.census.gov/hhes/www/cpstables/032014/health/People%20Without%20Health%20Insurance%20Coverage%20by%20Race%20and%20Hispanic%20Origin.xls>

Following is a list of observances typically covered by the Census Bureau's *Facts for Features* series:

African-American History Month (February)
Super Bowl
Valentine's Day (Feb. 14)
Women's History Month (March)
Irish-American Heritage Month (March)/ St. Patrick's Day (March 17)
Earth Day (April 22)
Asian/Pacific American Heritage Month (May)
Older Americans Month (May)
Mother's Day
Hurricane Season Begins (June 1)
Father's Day
The Fourth of July (July 4)
Anniversary of Americans with Disabilities Act (July 26)
Back to School (August)
Labor Day

Grandparents Day
Hispanic Heritage Month (Sept. 15–Oct. 15)
Unmarried and Single Americans Week
Halloween (Oct. 31)
American Indian/Alaska Native Heritage Month
   (November)
Veterans Day (Nov. 11)
Thanksgiving Day
The Holiday Season (December)

Critical Thinking

1. What are the causes of population distribution among the various Native Americans and the States?

2. Discuss the various profiles of Native Americans that emerge from the various categories and indicators collected by the Census.

Internet References

Library of Congress
   www.loc.gov
Social Science Information Gateway
   http://sosig.esrc.bris.ac.uk
Sociosite
   www.sociosite.net

U.S. Census Bureau, November 2014.

Article   Prepared by: John A. Kromkowski, *The Catholic University of America*

Ending Violence So Children Can Thrive

BYRON L. DORGAN ET AL.

Learning Outcomes

After reading this article, you will be able to:

- Identify the central findings of this report.

- Identify its primary legislative and administrative recommendations.

- Understand in what respects this report changed or confirmed general notions and assessments of the conditions that shape the opportunities of Native American children.

D ay in and day out, despite the tremendous efforts of tribal[1] governments and community members, many of them hindered by insufficient funding, American Indian and Alaska Native (AI/AN) children suffer exposure to violence at rates higher than any other race in the United States. The immediate and long term effects of this exposure to violence includes increased rates of altered neurological development, poor physical and mental health, poor school performance, substance abuse, and overrepresentation in the juvenile justice system. This chronic exposure to violence often leads to toxic stress reactions and severe trauma; which is compounded by historical trauma. Sadly, AI/AN children experience posttraumatic stress disorder at the same rate as veterans returning from Iraq and Afghanistan and triple the rate of the general population.[2] With the convergence of exceptionally high crime rates, jurisdictional limitations, vastly under-resourced programs, and poverty, service providers and policy makers should assume that *all* AI/AN children have been exposed to violence.

Through hearings and Listening Sessions over the course of 2013–14, the Attorney General's Advisory Committee on American Indian and Alaska Native Children Exposed to Violence[3] examined the current epidemic of violence and evaluated suggestions for preventing violence and alleviating its impact on AI/AN children. This report presents the Advisory Committee's policy recommendations that are intended to serve as a blueprint for preventing AI/AN children's exposure to violence and for mitigating the negative effects experienced by AI/AN children exposed to violence across the United States and throughout Indian country. The primary focus of the report is the thirty-one wide-ranging findings and recommendations that emerged from hearings and Listening Sessions. The Advisory Committee also examines the reports of the Attorney General's National Task Force on Children Exposed to Violence in 2012[4] and the Indian Law and Order Commission (ILOC) in 2013,[5] and incorporates some of the recommendations from these important reports that most strongly impact AI/AN children exposed to violence.

This report contains five chapters: (1) "Building a Strong Foundation"; (2) "Promoting Well-Being for American Indian and Alaska Native Children in the Home"; (3) "Promoting Well-Being for American Indian and Alaska Native Children in the Community"; (4) "Creating a Juvenile Justice System that Focuses on Prevention, Treatment, and Healing"; and (5) "Empowering Alaska Tribes,[6] Removing Barriers, and Providing Resources." Each chapter contains a discussion of the topics, providing background information, data, examples of problems as well as promising practices, and the Advisory Committee's recommendations.

This Advisory Committee was charged with making recommendations to the Attorney General of the United States. Many of the recommendations in this report are addressed to Congress and executive branch agencies outside the Department of Justice because solutions to the dire situation faced by AI/AN children must be comprehensive and will require efforts beyond the Department of Justice. Therefore, the Committee recommends that the Attorney General work with the legislative and executive branches of government to implement the recommendations. A summary of each chapter is presented below.

Building a Strong Foundation

We must transform the broken systems that re-traumatize children into systems where American Indian and Alaska Native (AI/AN) tribes are empowered with authority and resources to prevent exposure to violence and to respond to and promote healing of their children who have been exposed. Current barriers that prevent tribes from leading in protecting and healing their children must be eliminated before real change can begin.

Leaders at the highest levels of the executive and legislative branches of the federal government should coordinate and implement the recommendations in this report consistent with three core principles—Empowering Tribes, Removing Barriers, and Providing Resources—identified by the Advisory Committee.

There is a vital connection between tribal sovereignty and protecting AI/AN children. The Advisory Committee is convinced that state and federal governments must recognize and respect the primacy of tribal governments in responding to AI/AN children. Jurisdictional restrictions on tribes must be eliminated to allow tribes to exercise their inherent sovereign authority to prevent AI/AN children's exposure to violence. Resource limitations must be adequately addressed. The barriers that currently limit tribes' response to exposure to violence must be removed. Tribes should be supported in this effort with the assistance, collaboration, and resources needed to build their capacity to fully implement and sustain tribal-controlled, trauma-informed prevention and treatment models and systems. These barriers must be removed in order to empower individual tribal communities to prevent their children from being exposed to violence along with sufficient tools to respond and promote healing in their children who have been exposed.

The White House should establish—no later than May 2015—a permanent fully-staffed Native American Affairs Office within the White House Domestic Policy Council. This new Native American Affairs Office should include a senior position specializing in AI/AN children exposed to violence. This office should be responsible for coordination across the executive branch of all services provided for the benefit and protection of AI/AN children and the office lead should report directly to the Director of the Domestic Policy Council as a Special Assistant to the President. The Native American Affairs Office should have overall executive branch responsibility for coordinating and implementing the recommendations in this report including conducting annual tribal consultations.

The Advisory Committee believes that a permanent fully-staffed Native American Affairs Office, including a senior position specializing in AI/AN children exposed to violence, is required in order to comply with the federal government's trust responsibility and to effectively address the current inability of the federal government to serve the needs of AI/AN children exposed to violence. The new White House Native American Affairs Office should provide the essential executive branch coordination and collaboration required to effectively implement the recommendations in this report. The current "stovepipe organizational structure" of the executive branch restricts the flow of information and cross-organizational communication, making essential collaboration extremely difficult.

The White House Native American Affairs Office should conduct annual consultations with tribal governments, including discussion of:

1. Administering tribal funds and programs;
2. Enhancing the safety of AI/AN children exposed to violence in the home and in the community;
3. Enhancing child protection services through traumainformed practice;
4. Enhancing research and evaluation to address behavioral health needs and explore tribal cultural interventions and best practices;
5. Enhancing substance abuse services for caregivers and youth that addresses exposure to violence; and
6. Evaluating the implementation status of the recommendations in this report.

Congress should restore the inherent authority of American Indian and Alaska Native (AI/AN) tribes to assert full criminal jurisdiction over all persons who commit crimes against AI/AN children in Indian country.

In May 2013, Congress passed the Violence against Women Reauthorization Act (VAWA).[7] Among its provisions, Congress amended the Indian Civil Rights Act (ICRA) to authorize "special domestic violence criminal jurisdiction" to tribal courts over non- Indian offenders who (1) commit domestic violence, (2) commit dating violence, or (3) violate a protection order. It is troubling that tribes have no criminal jurisdiction over non-Indians who commit heinous crimes of sexual and physical abuse of AI/AN children in Indian country. Congress has restored criminal jurisdiction over non-Indians who commit domestic violence, commit dating violence, and violate protection orders. Congress should now similarly restore the inherent authority of AI/AN tribes to assert full criminal jurisdiction over all persons who commit crimes against AI/AN children in Indian country including both child sexual abuse and child physical abuse.

Congress and the executive branch shall direct sufficient funds to AI/AN tribes to bring funding for tribal criminal and civil justice systems and tribal child protection systems into parity with the rest of the United States and shall

remove the barriers that currently impede the ability of AI/AN Nations to effectively address violence in their communities. *The Advisory Committee believes that treaties, existing law and trust responsibilities are not discretionary and demand this action.*

The Advisory Committee believes that this investment is necessary to create an environment in which AI/AN children, today and for generations to come, may thrive. This investment is not only the right thing to do, but is part of the legal obligations of this nation to those communities. In order to more effectively address the needs of AI/AN children exposed to violence, substantial changes must be made in the methods by which AI/AN tribes are able to access federal funding. Substantially increased levels of federal funding will be required.

Funding for child maltreatment prevention and child protection efforts is especially limited in Indian country. Meanwhile, states receive proportionately more funding for prevention and child protection while tribes receive little to no federal support for these activities. Tribes are not even eligible for the two major programs that fund these state programs—Title XX of the Social Services Block Grant and the Child Abuse Prevention and Treatment Act.

The U.S. Department of the Interior (DOI) through the Bureau of Indian Affairs (BIA) provides limited funding for tribal court systems but the funding level is far too low. The BIA has historically denied any tribal law enforcement and tribal court funding to tribes in jurisdictions—such as Public Law 280 (PL-280) jurisdictions[8]— where congressionally authorized concurrent state jurisdiction has been established. Furthermore, efforts to fund tribal justice systems such as the Indian Tribal Justice Act of 1993 (which authorized an additional $50 million per year in tribal court base funding) have repeatedly *authorized* increased tribal court funding, but the long-promised funding has never materialized in the form of actual *appropriations*.

Since the late 1990s, the U.S. Department of Justice (DOJ) has also become a significant federal source of tribal justice funding. Tribes have utilized DOJ grant funding to enhance various and diverse aspects of their tribal justice systems, from tribal codes to Juvenile Healing to Wellness Courts (tribal drug courts) to unique tribal youth programs. While these grants have offered immense support, they are far from the consistent, tribally driven approach that is needed in Indian country. The Advisory Committee heard repeated frustration from hearing witnesses concerning the competitive funding approach that DOJ utilizes.

It is important to note that DOJ funding for tribal justice systems has been consistently decreasing in recent years. It is particularly troubling that the Consolidated Tribal Assistance Solicitation (CTAS) grant program with the closest direct connection to AI/AN children exposed to violence—the Office of Juvenile Justice and Delinquency Prevention (OJJDP) Tribal Youth Program (TYP)—has suffered the greatest decrease in funding levels. In a four-year period, OJJDP TYP funding has plummeted from $25 million in FY 2010 down to only $5 million in FY 2014. Tribes, like their state and local counterparts, deserve the benefit of reliability in their quest to build robust tribal justice systems that can adequately serve their youth. Base funding from resources pooled across various federal agencies would offer tribes the reliability and flexibility that is needed.

AI/AN children are generally served best when tribes have the opportunity to take ownership of the programs and resources that they provide. PL-93-638 contracts, self-governance compacts, and PL-102-477 funding agreements, are examples of successful federal programs that afford tribes the option to take over the management of federal funds for an array of programs. However, currently none of these programs applies to the DOJ.

Congress and the executive branch shall provide recurring mandatory, not discretionary, base funding for all tribal programs that impact AI/AN children exposed to violence, including tribal criminal and civil justice systems and tribal child protection systems, and make it available on equal terms to all federally recognized tribes, whether their lands are under federal jurisdiction or congressionally authorized state jurisdiction.

The United States' trust responsibility to AI/AN tribes requires the provision of basic governmental services in Indian country. Funding to fulfill this obligation, however, is currently provided in the *discretionary* portion of the federal budget despite the fact that the treaties that made promises to Indian tribes did not promise "*discretionary*" support and the trust responsibility is not *discretionary*. Because the spending is discretionary and not mandatory as it should be, public policies like sequestration reduce or eliminate programs that clearly should not be cut.

Congress shall appropriate, not simply authorize, sufficient substantially increased funding to provide reliable tribal base funding for all tribal programs that impact AI/AN children exposed to violence. This includes tribal criminal and civil justice systems and tribal child protection systems. At a minimum, and as a helpful starting point, Congress shall enact the relevant funding level requests in the National Congress of American Indians (NCAI) Indian Country Budget Request for FY 2015.

Substantially increased levels of federal funding will be required to more effectively address the needs of AI/AN children exposed to violence. For the past ten years, NCAI has published an annual Indian Country Budget Request Report that reflects collaboration with tribal leaders, Native organizations, and tribal budget consultation bodies. That budget request should serve as a helpful starting point for the initial minimum levels of increased funding that will be needed. The annual NCAI budget reports also provide further insightful detail concerning a wide range of federal programs that will be required to implement these recommendations.

Congress shall authorize all federal agencies, beginning with the Department of Justice (DOJ), to enter into 638 self-determination and self-governance compacts with tribes to ensure that all tribal system funding, including both justice and child welfare, is subject to tribal management. Further, the Department of Health and Human Services (HHS) should fully utilize its current 638 self-determination and self-governance authority to the greatest extent feasible for flexible funding programs in the Department of Health and Human Services (HHS) beyond the Indian Health Service (IHS) and seek additional legislative authority where needed.

Expanding the option for self-governance would translate to greater flexibility for tribes to provide critical social services within agencies such as the Administration on Aging, Administration on Children and Families, Substance Abuse and Mental Health Services Administration, and the Health Resources and Services Administration. HHS must work closely with tribes to strengthen current self-governance programs and advance initiatives that will streamline and improve HHS program delivery in Indian country.

Congress shall end all grant-based and competitive Indian country criminal justice funding in the Department of Justice (DOJ) and instead establish a permanent, recurring base funding system for tribal law enforcement and justice services.

As soon as possible, Congress should end all grant-based and competitive Indian country criminal justice funding in the DOJ and instead pool these monies to establish a permanent, recurring base funding system for tribal law enforcement and justice services. Federal base funding for tribal justice systems should be made available on equal terms to all federally recognized tribes, whether their lands are under federal jurisdiction or congressionally authorized state jurisdiction.

Congress shall establish a much larger commitment than currently exists to fund tribal programs through the Department of Justice's Office of Justice Programs (OJP) and the Victims of Crime Act (VOCA) funding. As an initial step towards the much larger commitment needed, Congress shall establish a minimum 10 percent tribal set-aside, as per the Violence Against Women Act (VAWA) tribal set-aside, from funding for all discretionary Office of Justice Programs (OJP) and Victims of Crime Act (VOCA) funding

making clear that the tribal set-aside is the minimum tribal funding and not in any way a cap on tribal funding. President Obama's annual budget request to Congress has included a 7 percent tribal set-aside for the last few years. This is a very positive step and Congress should authorize this request immediately. However, the tribal set-aside should be increased to 10 percent in subsequent appropriations bills. Until Congress acts, the Department of Justice shall establish this minimum 10 percent tribal setaside administratively.

After determining that AI/AN women face the highest level of violence in the nation—along with the highest rate of unmet needs—Congress set aside a percentage of VAWA funding for tribal governments. Since the 2005 VAWA Reauthorization, the tribal set-aside has been 10 percent. The Advisory Committee finds that the 10 percent VAWA tribal set-aside is a highly relevant precedent that should be applied to all discretionary OJP programs that impact AI/AN children exposed to violence. The same rationale applies to the VOCA funding, which has served as a major funding source for states to provide services to victims of crime since its establishment in 1984. However, it should be noted that this is a minimum initial amount with the expectation that substantially increased levels of funding will be forthcoming.

The Department of Justice (DOJ) and Department of Interior (DOI) should, within one year, conduct tribal consultations to determine the feasibility of implementing Indian Law and Order Commission (ILOC) Recommendation 3.8 to consolidate all DOI tribal criminal justice programs and all DOJ Indian country programs and services into a single "Indian country component" in the DOJ and report back to the President and AI/AN Nations on how tribes want to move forward on it.

While the Advisory Committee is in general agreement with the ILOC's Recommendation 3.8 to consolidate all DOI tribal criminal justice programs and all DOJ Indian country programs and services into a single DOJ "Indian country component," the Advisory Committee recommends that tribal consultation be conducted prior to making such a significant and far-reaching move.

The legislative branch of the federal government along with the executive branch, under the direction and oversight of the White House Native American Affairs Office, should provide adequate funding for and assistance with Indian country research and data collection.

Research and data collection is a critical component of developing effective responses to AI/AN children exposed to violence. Tribal governments, like every government, need the ability to track and access data involving their citizens across service areas and to accept the responsibility of gathering data. Tribal governments currently do not have adequate access to accurate, comprehensive data regarding key areas affecting AI/AN children exposed to violence. Even when data is gathered, it is often not shared with tribes. In order to remedy this situation, federal leadership is required and data should be co-owned with tribes.

Tribal Nations also need access to research initiatives that will help create and develop effective prevention and intervention strategies for children exposed to violence. Currently, many tribal communities are developing and implementing culturally based prevention and intervention programs. However, most do not have the resources necessary to evaluate the effectiveness of these programs.

The legislative and executive branches of the federal government should encourage tribal-state collaborations to meet the needs of AI/AN children exposed to violence.

The criminal justice, juvenile justice, and child welfare systems are too often ineffective because tribes and states do not always act collaboratively. The federal government should use its power and funds to encourage tribal-state collaborations.

The federal government should provide training for AI/AN Nations and for the federal agencies serving AI/AN communities on the needs of AI/AN children exposed to violence. Federal employees assigned to work on issues pertaining to AI/AN communities should be required to obtain training on tribal sovereignty, working with tribal governments, and the impact of historical trauma and colonization on tribal Nations within the first sixty days of their job assignment.

The federal trust responsibility should include ensuring that all service providers attending to the needs of AI/AN children receive appropriate training and technical assistance. Properly credentialed professionals who lack the cultural knowledge to identify and understand tribal familial needs face challenges in providing effective services. Further, AI/AN communities struggle to ensure access to a qualified AI/AN workforce in the trauma treatment area.

Promoting Well-Being for American Indian and Alaska Native Children in the Home

Every single day, a majority of American Indian and Alaska Native (AI/AN) children are exposed to violence within the walls of their own homes. This exposure not only contradicts traditional understandings that children are to be protected and viewed as sacred, but it leaves hundreds of children traumatized and struggling to cope over the course of their lifetime. Despite leadership from tribal governments, parents and families,

domestic violence in the homes of AI/AN children and physical abuse, sexual abuse, and neglect of children is more common than in the general population. Unfortunately, the response of child-serving systems often re-traumatizes the child.

The legislative and executive branches of the federal government should ensure Indian Child Welfare Act (ICWA) compliance and encourage tribal-state ICWA collaborations.

> **Within two years of the publication of this report, the Administration for Children and Families (ACF) in the Department of Health and Human Services (HHS), the Bureau of Indian Affairs (BIA) in the Department of the Interior (DOI), and tribes should develop a modernized unified data-collection system designed to collect Adoption and Foster Care Analysis and Reporting System (AFCARS) (ICWA and tribal dependency) data on all AI/AN children who are placed into foster care by their agency and share that data quarterly with tribes to allow tribes and the BIA to make informed decisions regarding AI/AN children.**
>
> **The Secretaries of the Department of Interior (DOI) and Health and Human Services (HHS) should compel BIA and ACF to work together collaboratively to collect data regarding compliance with ICWA in state court systems. The ACF and BIA should work collaboratively to ensure state court compliance with ICWA.**
>
> **The BIA should issue regulations (not simply update guidelines) and create an oversight board to review ICWA implementation and designate consequences of noncompliance and/or incentives for compliance with ICWA to ensure the effective implementation of ICWA.**
>
> **The Department of Justice (DOJ) should create a position of Indian Child Welfare Specialist to provide advice to the Attorney General and DOJ staff on matters relative to AI/AN child welfare cases, to provide case support in cases before federal, tribal, and state courts, and to coordinate ICWA training for federal, tribal, and state judges; prosecutors; and other court personnel.**

If AI/AN children today are to be provided with a reliable safety net, the letter and the spirit of ICWA must be enforced. ICWA provides critical legal protections for AI/AN children when intervention and treatment is deemed necessary by state child protection agencies. The most significant provisions seek to keep AI/AN children safely in their homes and provide AI/AN children with certain civil protections as members of their respective tribes.

The lack of accurate, relevant data on tribal children and families often results in AI/AN children being left out of discussions about policy development, resource allocation, and decision making at the federal level. Or, because of the lack of such data regarding AI/AN children, policy makers delay or decline to make decisions and resource allocations because they cannot "justify" the services. By increasing tribal capacity (through tribal child protection agencies in BIA and IHS) in the area of data collection, tribal engagement and federal responsiveness to AI/AN children's needs can be increased.

ICWA noncompliance is at least in part a result of minimal oversight of ICWA implementation and no enforcement mechanism. ICWA was enacted without providing sanctions for noncompliance, incentives for effective compliance, a data-collection requirement, and a mandate for an oversight committee or authority to monitor compliance. ICWA is the only federal child welfare law that does not include legislatively mandated oversight or periodic review.[9] These deficits in ICWA should be corrected.

The DOJ existing structure does not include a position that allows for investigation and research on Indian child welfare cases. The current environment is litigious and recent Indian child welfare cases have risen to the state and federal Supreme Courts. In addition to monitoring state compliance with ICWA included in other recommendations in this chapter, a position within the DOJ dedicated to supporting challenges to ICWA will improve child welfare outcomes and play a direct role in reducing trauma and violence experienced by AI/AN children in the child welfare system. Requirements for the position should include ICWA and family law experience. The position should be filled immediately.

The Bureau of Indian Affairs (BIA) in the Department of the Interior (DOI), the Administration for Children and Families (ACF) in the Department of Health and Human Services (HHS), and tribes, within one year of the publication of this report, should develop and submit a written plan to the White House Domestic Policy Council, to work collaboratively and efficiently to provide trauma-informed, culturally appropriate tribal child welfare services in Indian country.

When federal agencies fail to work together with tribes to confront problems in Indian country, the result is ineffective and inefficient systems. Child welfare services in Indian country are a good example of this inefficiency. Cooperation and collaboration among agencies that focus on tribal families and children must be thoughtfully planned and consistently delivered.

The Administration for Children and Families (ACF) in the Department of Health and Human Services (HHS), Bureau

of Indian Affairs (BIA) in the Department of the Interior (DOI), and tribes should collectively identify child welfare best practices and produce an annual report on child welfare best practices in AI/AN communities that is easily accessible to tribal communities.

Tribal child protection and prevention teams need AI/AN-specific research about the intersection of domestic violence, trauma exposure, and child maltreatment in order to create and promote effective prevention strategies, interventions, treatment, and policy change. Tribal communities have traditional methods of practice-based evidence to deal with trauma and healing. These practices have been used for centuries, but are not acknowledged as "evidence-based" treatments. Although promising practices exist throughout tribal communities, we do not have enough information about the effectiveness of such programs and methods of implementation, which makes success hard to replicate.

The Indian Health Service (IHS) in the Department of Health and Human Services (HHS), state public health services, and other state and federal agencies that provide pre- or postnatal services should provide culturally appropriate education and skills training for parents, foster parents, and caregivers of AI/ AN children. Agencies should work with tribes to culturally adapt proven therapeutic models for their unique tribal communities (e.g., adaptation of home visitation service to include local cultural beliefs and values).

Due to the prevalence of violence in AI/AN homes and communities and the influence of historical trauma, many AI/AN parents, foster parents, and prospective parents may need help developing traditional parenting skills. Caregivers may have experienced trauma as children or may continue to be victims of violence in their homes. Assistance for families experiencing violence or at risk for violence is most accessible when it is brought directly into the home.

The Bureau of Indian Affairs (BIA) in the Department of the Interior (DOI), tribal social service agencies, and state social service agencies should have policies that permit removal of children from victims of domestic violence for "failure to protect" only as a last resort as long as the child is safe.

Children are often removed from both parents when domestic violence occurs, even when one parent was also a victim of violence. Children who witness domestic violence have a greater need for stability and security; however when the child is removed from the nonoffending parent, it can produce the opposite effect.. To ensure stability and permanency for children in a home with domestic violence, children should remain with the non-offending parent (caregiver) whenever possible, as long as the child is safe.

The Secretary of Health and Human Services (HHS) should increase and support access to culturally appropriate behavioral health and substance abuse prevention and treatment services in all AI/AN communities, especially the use of traditional healers and helpers identified by tribal communities.

Substance abuse related to child abuse and neglect is more likely to be reported for AI/AN families. Treatment programs that work with AI/AN populations should incorporate AI/AN tribal customs and spiritual ceremonies, be trauma-informed, and be holistic. AI/ AN people in recovery may have experienced multiple traumas in their lifetimes, suffer from historical and intergenerational trauma, and abuse alcohol and drugs as a way of coping with those traumas. Without treatment to heal from the underlying traumas, alcohol and drug abuse treatment may be ineffective.

Promoting Well-Being for American Indian and Alaska Native Children in the Community

Violence in American Indian and Alaska Native (AI/AN) communities occurs at very high rates compared with non-AI/AN communities—higher for AI/AN people than for all other races. AI/AN children are exposed to many types of communitybased violence, including simple assaults, violent threats, sexual assault, and homicide. Additionally, suicide, gang violence, sex and drug trafficking, and bullying are especially problematic for AI/AN youth. Coupling that rate of exposure with the high rate of homelessness makes AI/AN youth especially vulnerable to community violence. The recommendations in this chapter speak to increasing capacity and infrastructure in AI/AN communities to allow those communities to confront the impact of current and past violence and to prevent future violence.

The White House Native American Affairs Office (see Recommendation 1.2) and executive branch agencies that are responsible for addressing the needs of AI/AN children, in consultation with tribes, should develop a strategy to braid (integrate) flexible funding to allow tribes to create comprehensive violence prevention, intervention, and treatment programs to serve the distinct needs of AI/AN children and families.

The White House Native American Affairs Office, the U.S. Attorney General, the Secretaries of the Department of Interior (DOI) and Health and Human Services (HHS), and the heads of other agencies that provide funds that serve AI/AN children should annually consult with tribal governments to solicit recommendations on the mechanisms that would provide flexible funds for the assessment of local needs, and for the development and adaptation of promising practices that allow for the integration of the unique cultures and healing traditions of the local tribal community.

The White House Native American Affairs Office and the U.S. Attorney General should work with the organizations that specialize in treatment and services for traumatized children, for example, National Child Traumatic Stress Network, to ensure that services for AI/AN children exposed to violence are trauma-informed.

The White House Native American Affairs Office should coordinate the development and implementation of federal policy that mandates exposure to violence trauma screening and suicide screening be a part of services offered to AI/AN children during medical, juvenile justice, and/or social service intakes.

Although children exposed to violence in AI/AN communities are similar to all children exposed to violence, solutions to the exposure to traumatic events may vary greatly among the 566 distinct federally recognized tribes across the United States. Federal, tribal, and state agencies and organizations must collaborate to ensure that tribal communities are allowed the flexibility to implement solutions that work and are culturally and locally relevant to meet the challenges, the circumstances, and the unique characteristics of their children and communities.

Policies must be developed and implemented to ensure that screening for exposure to violence takes place in numerous settings and issues of confidentiality are resolved. Confidentiality issues will arise as children are screened by various child-serving organizations in the communities that serve them. The need for confidentiality must be balanced with the need for service providers to have information that will permit them to more effectively serve the child. The Advisory Committee urges federal, tribal, and state programs that collect these data to seek creative ways to monitor and use information for the benefit of the child rather than use confidentiality as an excuse to inappropriately refuse to share information.

The Department of Justice's National Institute of Justice (NIJ) and other Justice Department agencies with statutory research funding should set aside 10 percent of their annual research budgets for partnerships between tribes and research entities to develop, adapt, and validate trauma screens for use among AI/AN children and youth living in rural, tribal, and urban communities. Trauma screens should be tested and validated for use in schools, juvenile justice (law enforcement and courts), mental health, primary care, Defending Childhood Tribal Grantee programs, and social service agencies and should include measures of trauma history, trauma symptoms, recognizing trauma triggers, recognizing trauma reactions, and developing positive coping skills for both the child and the caregivers.

Early identification of exposure to violence, timely intervention and treatment, and especially prevention can protect a child from being trapped in a cycle of repeated exposure to violence.[10] Identification of children who have been traumatized by exposure to violence is the first step toward healing and recovery. Children must be screened in schools, clinics, social service agencies, juvenile justice facilities, wherever children are found. An AI/AN child's response to a trauma may be intensified because of the legacy of historical trauma. Tribal communities need assistance from research partnerships to develop, validate, and use instruments to screen for trauma symptoms and design an effective path forward for children.

The White House Native American Affairs Office and responsible federal agencies should provide AI/AN youth-serving organizations such as schools, Head Starts, daycares, foster care programs, and so forth with the resources needed to create and sustain safe places where AI/AN children exposed to violence can obtain services. Every youth-serving organization in tribal and urban Native communities should receive mandated trauma-informed training and have trauma-informed staff and consultants providing school-based trauma-informed treatment in bullying, suicide, and gang prevention/intervention.

Tribal child-serving systems and school staff are often unaware of the impact trauma has on the psychological and emotional health of their students. Schools that are trauma-informed can establish safe and nurturing environments where children can learn.

The Secretary of Housing and Urban Development (HUD) should designate and prioritize Native American Housing Assistance and Self-Determination Act (NAHSDA) funding for construction of facilities to serve AI/AN children exposed to violence and structures for positive youth activities. This will help tribal communities create positive environments such as shelters, housing, cultural facilities, recreational facilities, sport centers, and theaters through the Indian Community Development Block Grant Program and the Housing Assistance Programs.

The Advisory Committee repeatedly heard testimony about the need for safe houses for youth in tribal communities—safe settings for youth escaping violence and places where a youth's basic needs for safety, nutrition, mental health treatment, and

education can be assessed and met. Safe houses may provide for their cultural and spiritual needs as well. Providing a safe place where violenceexposed youth can focus on healing is the first step toward helping a young person recover from trauma.

The White House Native American Affairs Office should work with the Congress and executive branch agencies in consultation with tribes to develop, promote, and fund youth-based afterschool programs for AI/AN youth. The programs must be culturally based and trauma-informed, must partner with parents/ caregivers, and, when necessary, provide referrals to traumainformed behavioral health providers. Where appropriate, local capacity should also be expanded through partnerships with America's volunteer organizations, for example, AmeriCorps.

Community-based and afterschool programs for youth that teach culture, prevention, and life skills will help AI/AN youth develop healthy lifestyles and values and strengthen their resiliency.

The White House Native American Affairs Office and the Secretary of Health and Human Services (HHS) should develop and implement a plan to expand access to Indian Health Service (IHS), tribal, and urban Indian centers to provide behavioral health services to AI/AN children in schools. This should include the deployment of behavioral health services providers to serve students in the school setting.

Federal, tribal, state, and for-profit agencies that provide behavioral health services must cooperate to develop and deliver school-based services for AI/AN students. Federal agencies should work with public schools and Bureau of Indian Education (BIE)–funded schools to ensure that services are offered, preferably in the schools, to students attending BIE-funded schools. School-based services increase the availability and utilization of services and will increase safety in schools.

Creating a Juvenile Justice System that Focuses on Prevention, Treatment, and Healing

Children entering the juvenile justice system are exposed to violence at staggeringly high rates. Many American Indian and Alaska Native (AI/AN) people believe that the Western criminal/ juvenile justice system is inappropriate for children, particularly AI/AN children, as it is contrary to AI/AN values in raising children.

The Advisory Committee concludes that the standard way juvenile justice has been administered by state jurisdictions is a failure and it re-traumatizes AI/AN children. The Advisory Committee supports substantial reform of the juvenile justice systems impacting AI/AN youth. A reformed juvenile justice system should be tribally operated or strongly influenced by tribes within the local region.

Congress should authorize additional and adequate funding for tribal juvenile justice programs, a grossly underfunded area, in the form of block grants and self-governance compacts that would support the restructuring and maintenance of tribal juvenile justice systems.

> **Congress should create an adequate tribal set-aside that allows access to all expanded federal funding that supports juvenile justice at an amount equal to the need in tribal communities. As an initial step towards the much larger commitment needed, Congress should establish a minimum 10 percent tribal set-aside, as per the Violence Against Women Act (VAWA) tribal set aside, from funding for all Office of Juvenile Justice and Delinquency Prevention (OJJDP) funding making clear that the tribal set-aside is the minimum tribal funding and not in any way a cap on tribal funding. President Obama's annual budget request to Congress has included a 7 percent tribal set aside for the last few years. This is a very positive step and Congress should authorize this request immediately. However, the tribal set-aside should be increased to 10 percent in subsequent appropriations bills. Until Congress acts, the Department of Justice should establish this minimum 10 percent tribal set-aside administratively.**
>
> **Federal funding for state juvenile justice programs should require that states engage in and support meaningful and consensual consultation with tribes on the design, content, and operation of juvenile justice programs to ensure that programming is imbued with cultural integrity to meet the needs of tribal youth.**
>
> **Congress should direct the Department of Justice (DOJ) and the Department of Interior (DOI) to determine which agency should provide funding for both the construction and operation of jails and juvenile detention facilities in AI/AN communities, require consultation with tribes concerning selection process, ensure the trust responsibilities for these facilities and services are assured, and appropriate the necessary funds.**

The funding tribes receive for juvenile justice programming must be adequate and stable. Currently, tribes need to rely on inadequate base funding from the BIA, thus forcing them to compete for grant funds to support the most basic components of a juvenile justice system. It is unacceptable for federal agencies to provide grant funding for a tribal program and limit the funding to three years, requiring tribes to re-compete or lose funding at the end of the grant period. Flexibility and stability in funding is important to allow local communities to utilize the funding in creative, impactful ways.

Programming offered in state juvenile justice systems is not meeting the needs of AI/AN youth and in some cases is harming these youth. Even those states with significant AI/AN populations fail to meaningfully consult with tribes about their juvenile justice systems to ensure that their programming is thoughtful and culturally based. One way to ensure that states with significant AI/AN populations involve the tribes in important decisions regarding AI/AN children is to tie federal funding to meaningful consultation with tribes.

Currently the DOJ and DOI have divided responsibilities to construct, operate, staff, and maintain jails and juvenile detention centers. This has resulted in dozens of facilities being constructed that are vacant or seriously underutilized because operating funds have not been provided. The split responsibility that exists now is not workable.

Federal, state, and private funding and technical assistance should be provided to tribes to develop or revise traumainformed, culturally specific tribal codes to improve tribal juvenile justice systems.

Developing a tribal juvenile justice system requires developing tribal codes that fit the culture and community. Technical assistance should be provided to develop culturally appropriate, trauma-informed juvenile justice codes and systems.

Federal, tribal, and state justice systems should provide publicly funded legal representation to AI/AN children in the juvenile justice systems to protect their rights and minimize the harm that the juvenile justice system may cause them. The use of technology such as videoconferencing could make such representation available even in remote areas.

AI/AN youth need to be provided with counsel due to the impact of immaturity, the effects of exposure to violence and trauma, and caregivers who are no more likely to understand the system, rights, and process than the youth. Given the overrepresentation of AI/AN youth in state and federal justice systems and in secure confinement, it is critical that culturally competent, well-trained defense counsel be afforded to the youth at public expense in all federal, tribal, and state juvenile proceedings.

Federal, tribal, and state justice systems should only use detention of AI/AN youth when the youth is a danger to themselves or the community. It should be close to the child's community and provide trauma-informed, culturally appropriate, and individually tailored services, including reentry services. Alternatives to detention such as "safe houses" should be significantly developed in AI/AN urban and rural communities.

The use of juvenile detention is not effective as a deterrent to delinquent behavior, risky behavior, or truancy and should only be used when there is clear evidence that the youth is a danger to themselves or the community.

Federal, tribal, and state justice systems and service providers should make culturally appropriate trauma-informed screening, assessment, and care the standard in juvenile justice systems. The Indian Health Service (IHS) in the Department of Health and Human Services (HHS) and tribal and urban Indian behavioral health service providers must receive periodic training in culturally adapted trauma-informed interventions and cultural competency to provide appropriate services to AI/AN children and their families.

Behavioral health services for AI/AN youth may be handled by different agencies with different priorities. Youth in the juvenile justice system are typically not a priority to those community-based agencies. Culturally appropriate, trauma-informed screening and care must become the standard in all juvenile justice systems that impact AI/AN youth if the system is to treat children as sacred and promote wellness and resilience.

Congress should amend the Indian Child Welfare Act (ICWA) to provide that when a state court initiates any delinquency proceeding involving an Indian child for acts that took place on the reservation, all of the notice, intervention, and transfer provisions of ICWA will apply. For all other Indian children involved in state delinquency proceedings, ICWA should be amended to require notice to the tribe and a right to intervene. As a first step, the Department of Justice (DOJ) should establish a demonstration pilot project that would provide funding for three states to provide ICWA-type notification to tribes within their state whenever the state court initiates a delinquency proceeding against a child from that tribe which includes a plan to evaluate the results with an eye toward scaling it up for all AI/AN communities.

States have jurisdiction over AI/AN children when a violation occurs outside of Indian country, or within Indian country in PL-280 states or states that have a settlement act or other similar federal legislation. An overarching concern voiced at hearings conducted by the Advisory Committee was that states are not required to notify the tribe or involve the tribe in a juvenile delinquency proceeding. That concern is exacerbated because states generally do not provide the cultural support necessary for Native youth's rehabilitation and reentry into the tribal community.

Congress should amend the Federal Education Rights and Privacy Act (FERPA) to allow tribes to access their members' school attendance, performance, and disciplinary records.

FERPA[11] generally allows federal, state, and local education agencies the ability to access student records and other personally identifiable information kept by state public schools without the advance consent of the parents; it does not afford the same access to tribes. Tribes need this access in order to be informed enough to intervene early and respond to the red flags raised by truancy and disciplinary problems in schools as it pertains to AI/AN children exposed to violence.

Empowering Alaska Tribes, Removing Barriers, and Providing Resources

Problems with children exposed to violence in American Indian and Alaska Native (AI/AN) communities are severe across the United States—but they are systemically worse in Alaska. Issues related to Alaska Native children exposed to violence are different for a variety of reasons including regional vastness and geographical isolation, extreme weather, exorbitant transportation costs, lack of economic opportunity and access to resources, a lack of respect for Alaska tribal sovereignty, and a lack of understanding and respect for Alaska Native history and culture, all of which have contributed to high levels of recurring violence. Alaska Tribes are best positioned to effectively address these problems so long as the current barriers are removed and Alaska Tribes are empowered to protect Alaska Native children.

The federal government should promptly implement all five recommendations in Chapter 2 (Reforming Justice for Alaska Natives: The Time Is Now) of the Indian Law and Order Commission's 2013 Final Report, A Roadmap for Making Native America Safer, and assess the cost of implementation. This will remove the barriers that currently inhibit the ability of Alaska Native Tribes to exercise criminal jurisdiction and utilize criminal remedies when confronting the highest rates of violent crime in the country.

(Indian Law and Order Commission Recommendation 2.1): Congress should overturn the U.S. Supreme Court's decision in *Alaska v. Native Village of Venetie Tribal Government,* by amending the Alaska Native

Claims Settlement Act (ANCSA) to provide that former reservation lands acquired in fee by Alaska Native villages and other lands transferred in fee to Native villages pursuant to ANCSA are Indian country.

(Indian Law and Order Commission Recommendation 2.2): Congress and the President should amend the definitions of Indian country to clarify (or affirm) that Native allotments and Native-owned town sites in Alaska are Indian country.

(Indian Law and Order Commission Recommendation 2.3): Congress should amend the Alaska Native Claims Settlement Act to allow a transfer of lands from Regional Corporations to Tribal governments; to allow transferred lands to be put into trust and included within the definition of Indian country in the Federal criminal code; to allow Alaska Native Tribes to put tribally owned fee simple land similarly into trust; and to channel more resources directly to Alaska Native Tribal governments for the provision of governmental services in those communities.

(Indian Law and Order Commission Recommendation 2.4): Congress should repeal Section 910 of Title IX of the Violence Against Women Reauthorization Act of 2013 (VAWA Amendments), and thereby permit Alaska Native communities and their courts to address domestic violence and sexual assault committed by Tribal members and non-Natives, just as in the lower 48.

(Indian Law and Order Commission Recommendation 2.5): Congress should affirm the inherent criminal jurisdiction of Alaska Native Tribal governments over their members within the external boundaries of their villages.

The Advisory Committee agrees with each of the five Alaskaspecific Indian Law and Order Commission (ILOC) recommendations and the Commission's rationale for each recommendation. Until and unless these barriers are removed, the state of Alaska will continue to assert that Alaska Tribes do not have any criminal jurisdiction and thereby continue to contend that Alaska Tribes are only empowered to utilize civil courts and civil remedies when confronting the highest rates of violent crime in the country. The Advisory Committee recommends that these five ILOC recommendations be enacted as soon as possible in order to ensure that Alaska Tribes are also empowered to exercise criminal jurisdiction and criminal remedies when confronting such incredibly high rates of violent crime.

The Department of Justice (DOJ) and the Department of Interior (DOI) should provide recurring base funding for Alaska Tribes to develop and sustain both civil and criminal tribal court systems, assist in the provision of law enforcement and related services, and assist with intergovernmental agreements.

As a first step, the DOJ and the DOI should—within one year—conduct a current inventory and a needs/cost assessment of law enforcement, court, and related services for every Alaska Tribe.

The DOJ and the DOI should provide the funding necessary to address the unmet need identified, and ensure that each Alaska Tribe has the annual base funding level necessary to provide and sustain an adequate level of law enforcement, tribal court, and related funding and services.

Congress should enact legislation along the lines of the current bipartisan bill sponsored by both Alaska senators (S. 1474 to be titled Alaska Safe Families and Villages Act of 2014) that supports the development, enhancement, and sustainability of Alaska tribal courts including full faith and credit for Alaska tribal court acts and decrees and the establishment of specific Alaska tribal court base funding streams and grants to Alaska Native Tribes carrying out intergovernmental agreements with the state of Alaska.

The federal government should work together with Alaska Tribes and the state of Alaska to improve coordination and collaboration on a broad range of public safety measures that cause Alaska Native children to be exposed to high rates of violence.

The development, enhancement, and sustainment of Alaska tribal courts, and truly cooperative relationships between the state of Alaska and Alaska Tribes, are required to reduce violent crime and protect Alaska Native children from exposure to violence. Villagebased tribal courts are the culturally appropriate provider. Alaska tribal courts must be developed, enhanced, and sustained in order to effectively address issues concerning Alaska Native children exposed to violence.

The state of Alaska should prioritize law enforcement responses and related resources for Alaska Tribes, and recognize and collaborate with Alaska tribal courts.

The state of Alaska should prioritize the state law enforcement response and resources for Alaska Tribes. At a minimum, there must be at least one law enforcement official onsite in each village.

The state of Alaska should prioritize the provision of needed village-based services including village-based women's shelters (which allow children to stay with their mothers), child advocacy centers, and alcohol and drug treatment services.

> The state of Alaska should recognize and collaborate with Alaska tribal courts including following existing federal laws designed to protect Alaska Native children and families such as VAWA protection order authority, which requires states to recognize and enforce tribal protection orders that have been issued by tribal courts—including Alaska Native tribal courts—without first requiring a state court certification of the tribal protection order.
>
> The state of Alaska should enter into self-governance intergovernmental agreements with Alaska Tribes in order to provide more local tools and options to combat village public safety issues and address issues concerning Alaska Native children exposed to violence.

The state of Alaska must increase the level of protection in Alaska Tribes. Village-based services are needed in law enforcement and victim protection. Approximately 370 State Troopers have primary responsibility for law enforcement in rural Alaska, but have a full-time presence in less than half of the remote Alaska Tribes. Seventy-five villages lack any law enforcement at all.[12]

The Administration for Child and Families (ACF) in the Department of Health and Human Services (HHS) and the State of Alaska Office of Children's Services (OCS) should jointly respond to the extreme disproportionality of Alaska Native children in foster care by establishing a time-limited, outcome-focused task force to develop real-time, Native inclusive strategies to reduce disproportionality.

Issues of foster care disproportionality are huge problems for many tribes. Inadequate numbers of Native foster families to assure compliance with ICWA impacts most state child welfare agencies as well. But this problem takes on added dimensions and particular significance in Alaska—not only due to the high level of removals of Alaska Native children and the fact that it has been increasing at an alarming rate—but also due to many other factors including the remoteness of Alaska Tribes, Alaska's vast size, the exorbitant cost of transportation, the financial limitations of subsistence economy, the lack of village-based foster care options, the lack of village-based services and resources, the lack of tribal courts, and the historic refusal of the state of Alaska to collaborate with Alaska Tribes and, until recently to recognize that Alaska Tribes even exist.

The Department of Interior (DOI) and the State of Alaska should empower Alaska Tribes to manage their own subsistence hunting and fishing rights, remove the current barriers, and provide Alaska Tribes with the resources needed to effectively manage their own subsistence hunting and fishing.

Regulations that limit the ability of Alaska Natives to conduct traditional subsistence hunting and fishing are directly connected to violence in Alaska Tribes and the exposure of Alaska Native children to that violence. Violence is essentially nonexistent during the times in which the communities are engaging in traditional subsistence hunting and fishing activities, and violence spikes during times when Alaska Natives are unable to provide for their families. Beyond providing basic food, subsistence fishing and hunting has been essential to Alaska Native families' way of life for generations. Like language and cultural traditions, it has been passed down from one generation to the next and is an important means of reinforcing tribal values and traditions and binding families together in common spirit and activity. Interfering with these traditions erodes culture, family, a sense of purpose and ability to provide for one's own, and a sense of pride.

Notes

1. For purposes of this report, we use the term "tribe" to refer to federally recognized tribes from the Secretary of Interior's list. 79 Fed. Reg. 4,748 (Jan. 29, 2014), *available at* http://www. gpo.gov/ fdsys/pkg/FR-2014-01-29/pdf/2014-01683.pdf.

2. Indian Law and Order Commission, *A Roadmap for Making Native America Safer: Report to the President and Congress of the United States* (November 2013): 154, available at: http://www.aisc.ucla. edu/iloc/report/index.html.

3. The Advisory Committee is the anchor of the AI/AN Task Force established in 2013 by the Attorney General. The Advisory Committee consists of nonfederal experts in the area of AI/AN children exposed to violence.

4. Listenbee, Robert L., Jr., et al., *Report of the Attorney General's National Task Force on Children Exposed to Violence*, Washington, D.C.: U.S. Department of Justice, Office of Juvenile Justice and Delinquency Prevention, December 2012.

5. Indian Law and Order Commission, *A Roadmap for Making Native America Safer: Report to the President and Congress of the United States* (November 2013), available at: http://www. aisc.ucla.edu/ iloc/report/index.html.

6. The Native peoples of Alaska are commonly referred to as "Alaska Natives," and "Alaska Native Villages." For the purposes of this report, we will use the term "Alaska Tribe" to refer to federally recognized tribes in the State of Alaska. 79 Fed. Reg. 4,748 (Jan. 29, 2014), *available at* http://www. gpo. gov/fdsys/pkg/FR-2014-01-29/pdf/2014-01683.pdf.

7. The Violence Against Women Reauthorization Act of 2013, PL-113-4, 127 Stat. 54 (March 7, 2013).

8. See Chapter 11 (Funding) of Final Report—Law Enforcement and Criminal Justice under Public Law 280 available at: http:// www.tribal-institute.org/download/pl280_study.pdf.

9. Written Testimony of Sarah Hicks Kastelic (Alutiiq), Hearing of the Task Force on American Indian/Alaska Native Children Exposed to Violence, Anchorage, AK, June 11, 2014 at 23, available at: http://www.justice.gov/defendingchildhood/4th-hearing/hearing4-briefing-binder.pdf.

10. Listenbee, Robert L., Jr., et al., *Report of the Attorney General's National Task Force on Children Exposed to Violence,* Washington, D.C.: U.S. Department of Justice, Office of Juvenile Justice and Delinquency Prevention (December 2012): 66.

11. 20 U.S.C. 1232(g).

12. S. Rep. No. 113-260, at 2 (2014), *to accompany* S. 1474, 113th Cong. 2d Sess. (2014).

Critical Thinking

1. Who is primarily responsible for the safety and well-being of children?
2. Discuss the various causes of this troubling situation that prompted this report.
3. What are the cultural and economic roots of social problems and the rural isolation?

Internet References

Native American Heritage Association
www.naha-inc.org
Native American Home Pages
www.nativeculturelinks.com/nations.html

Dorgan, Byron L. et al. "Ending Violence so Children Can Thrive", *United States Department of Justice,* November 2014.

Article   Prepared by: John A. Kromkowski, *The Catholic University of America*

Does the Fate of the Navajo Nation Depend on Its Language?

Elaine Teng

Learning Outcomes

After reading this article, you will be able to:

- Understand in what respects this case study changed or confirmed your understanding of self-governance among Native Americans.

- Identify what notions about traditional societies and the importance of language this article addresses.

On Thursday, a Navajo court in Window Rock, Arizona removed tribal presidential candidate Chris Deschene from the ballot for refusing to prove his fluency in the Navajo language, as is required by Navajo law. The decision highlights a growing dispute over the future of the country's largest Native American community, the role of language in establishing its identity, and what it means to be Navajo in modern society. According to the 2010 census-http://www.census.gov/prod/2011pubs/acsbr10-10.pdf-, around 169,000 people say they speak Navajo; yet fewer and fewer of those under 50, like 43-year-old Deschene, are fluent, stoking fears that the language—and the Navajo identity—could die out. In an interview with *The New Republic*, Dr. Evangeline Parsons-Yazzie, a 61-year-old Navajo professor emeritus of Navajo (the language) at Northern Arizona University, discusses the generational divide, how to define fluency, and the future of the Navajo Nation.

Elaine Teng: Can you explain to our readers what's at stake in this dispute over Chris Deschene's eligibility for the presidency?

Evangeline Parsons-Yazzie: I can see both sides of the argument. On one hand, the Navajo language has been declared an endangered language, which means that the children are

no longer speaking the language. I think Chris Deschene represents many of those young people who speak very little but understand quite a bit, not that he necessarily is one of them. The people who brought this dispute against him have shut out all other young Navajos who would have liked to have him represent their people. [These young people] are very good orators in English and would have represented their people very, very well on a state, national, and international level. At this point, that's what's needed.

On the other hand, I can understand why the people who created the dispute are saying what they are, because our language does represent sovereignty. Sovereignty is something we inherited and we're supposed to maintain. It's a gift to us, and that's how the elders who are fluent speakers see it. Therefore, they want their youth to be able to come back before them and speak in their language. It's the elders who make up the voting public, and they feel that the president of the Navajo Nation should be able to explain to them in Navajo the issues that are facing them.

ET: So this seems to be a generational question. If young people feel shut out from the process, do you think this will create change?

EPY: I think the people who brought about this dispute are not considering their own children and grandchildren. If this becomes part of the Navajo code, which is the set of laws that govern the Navajo people and is part of our sovereignty, then they're doing a disservice to their children.

Maybe this will challenge the young voters to vote for Chris Deschene as a write-in option. I just hope the young people do challenge this and try to voice their wishes, too, and say, "Hey, we want to be represented too. We don't speak the language."

There are different degrees of fluency. The language tests that are provided across the reservation vary[1]; some include religious and philosophical aspects, which are very, very difficult and at a high level of speech. Whereas what a candidate needs is conversational Navajo. If they move around in political circles, they can acquire that language.

The Navajo people are not allowing for that acquisition to take place, or to trust that acquisition will take place, and therefore they're distrusting the younger generation as well.

ET: Chris Deschene has conversational fluency then, but not an in-depth political vocabulary?

EPY: I haven't heard him speak. I met him once, but because there were non-Navajos in the room, he spoke in English. He greeted me in Navajo, and his greeting was nice. I didn't detect any sign of an accent. A lot of people, when they're just beginning to pick up the language, they have an accent in their Navajo. I didn't detect that at all. Had I known he was going to be challenged in this way, I would have chatted with him. He's a very respectful young man. He has a really wonderful command of the English language, which is what we also need. We need new ideas, new blood coming into the Navajo Nation.

ET: He seems very qualified, having been in the Marines and the Arizona State House of Representatives. Other than the language requirement, he seems like a very good candidate.

EPY: I believe he is, and I hope that the Navajo youth and the non-fluent Navajos challenge this and say that we want him as a write-in candidate, and show the people: We want to be represented, too. We're Navajos as well.

I think a lot of young people who are willing to take a political stance for their people are really confused right now because we didn't count on two very important issues.[2] They [the Navajo Nation Council] didn't listen to our wishes, and now they're pushing us out even more, so our voices don't mean anything. We need somebody who can interface at the state and national level, and you don't need Navajo fluency for that. These people who created the dispute are not looking down the road. They're looking right before their noses, and that's it. And it's just so, so sad.

ET: How is the language taught today? Is it taught in schools or mostly at home?

EPY: It's still being spoken at home quite a bit. If you travel across the reservation, you can hear parents speaking to their children, elders speaking to children, and you hear children speaking past as well. It's taught in the schools quite extensively across the reservation.

The youth themselves are creating a new dialect, which is pleasing. A dying language is one that stays completely the same. A language that is still alive is constantly changing, so that's encouraging.

ET: How many Navajo people live on or off the reservation?

EPY: More people are moving off the reservation for economic reasons. They've applied for jobs and they've been told, "Sorry, you don't speak Navajo. You're highly qualified, but we're going to hire this less qualified person [because they speak Navajo], so sorry." I've taught twenty-four years. The youth want to come back, but they go back to the university to work on a master's degree because they were not wanted on their own reservation because they couldn't speak. We're really doing a disservice to ourselves, to our wholeness as a people, and to our own economic system. We chase the youth away just for the sake of understanding. I feel for Mr. Deschene, but on the other hand I feel for the elders who have that expectation that he needs to communicate with us. Because they are the majority of the voters.

The median age was 21 in the 2000 Census, I believe.[3] We are an extremely young nation. The people who brought about this dispute are discriminating against the majority of the population, and that's scary. The language needs to be protected, but it shouldn't be used to discriminate against people.

This interview has been edited and condensed.

Notes

1. Dr. Parsons-Yazzie helped design one of the language tests used on the reservation.
2. The two issues were changing the nation's name-http://articles.latimes.com/1993-12-16/news/mn-2405_1_navajo-nation from Navajo to *Dine,* and bringing casinos to the reservation.
3. In fact, in the 2010 Census, the median age was 28.

Critical Thinking

1. Discuss the meaning of stereotypes?
2. Can stereotypes be negative and positive? Who decides?
3. Can ethnic humor be defamatory? What does irony do to our interpretations of ethnicity?

Internet References

AAIA Association on American Indian Affairs
www.indian-affairs.org
NCAI National Tribal Organizations
www.ncai.org

Native American Rights Fund
www.Narf.org

Unit 5

UNIT

Prepared by: John A. Kromkowski, *The Catholic University of America*

African Americans

An article by Lerone Bennett, published in *Ebony* more than a decade before the election of president Barack Obama, expressed the thrust of an argument that has defined the discussion within Negro, black, and African American communities. Bennett's argument is that historical moments define a people's identity. A series of pivotal dramatic events inform the identity of African Americans; and because of the centrality of this group, these moments have shaped the character of group relations as a whole. The key moments include the following epoch-defining experiences of race and ethnicity: the arrival, the founding of communities and settlements, Nat Turner's War, the multiple moments and venues of emancipation, the Booker T. Washington and W.E.B. Dubois strategic crossroads, migrations, *Brown vs. Board of Education*, the events in Montgomery, Little Rock, and that day in Memphis when time and everything else stopped. Of course, The March on Washington and *Brown vs. Topeka* are central to the Civil Rights Era. And the memory and national holiday devoted to Martin Luther King Jr. are ongoing public memorials. A few moments of legal history are explored in this unit to illustrate the role of government in race and ethnic relations.

Ethnic group discrimination and prejudice, rooted in the brutal and inhumane conquest and slavery that brought Africans to America, are a profound and searing legacy. Eighteenth- and nineteenth-century laws and practices of defining race-shaped legal doctrine regarding citizenship and the mentalities of color consciousness, prejudice, and racism in America. Today, differentiation by race and ethnicity are aspects of understanding intergroup and intragroup relations, dynamics, and definitions. In this respect, the process of definition has come a long way since the 1988 *New York Times* editorial that provided the following account of a group that traces its American ancestry to initial participation as three-fifths of a person status in the U.S. Constitution to its later exclusion from the freedoms of this polity altogether by the U.S. Supreme Court's *Dred Scott* decision. The editors of the *Times* wrote (December 22, 1988): "The archaeology is dramatically plain to older adults who in one lifetime, have already heard preferred usage shift from colored to Negro to black. The four lingual layers provided an abbreviated history of naming race and ethnicity in this century." And this process continues. Early in 2013, the U.S. Census acknowledged that their polling indicated that the classification "Negro" was offensive and announced that the U.S. Census would no longer use

this term in its data collection. Thus, another layer of the language of group identity has emerged from popular practice into public policy.

But language and reality intersect to reveal other types of measurable differentiations: income, education, location, occupation, profession, wealth, recent immigration from the Caribbean or an African country, mother tongue, languages, dialects, and inter-ethnic marriage. The final item is a topic that is rarely broached in mainstream media. Ethnic media address audiences that are radically different populations interested in other ethnic-specific topics: skin tone, color, hue, and hair texture and musical and cultural aesthetics. Thus, the African American community or communities and the various gatekeepers, framers of issues, fashioners of the language of blackness/post-blackness/Afro-centric/cultural–religious markers are essentially more complex and complicated. Discrimination and consciousness of the African American ethnicity and accounts of African American traditions are, like all American ethnicities, works in progress. This intellectual and cultural ferment suggests that a model of exploration is most appropriate for understanding personal and group identity and the various invocations of tradition and current concerns related to race and ethnic relations. Ethnic groups share different perspectives and experiences about the functions of faith and community-based initiatives and solidarity, the extended family, the efficacy of government as guarantor of civil liberties and civil rights, and the political role of the religious ministry. Such dimensions are woven into mentalities and behavior that constitute an ethnic endowment of depth and meaning that is permanent and in flux. These languages of race and ethnic relations are articulated by elected leaders as race-shaped well as the self-anointed and self-appointed who influence the direction of social change and ongoing reconfiguring of race and ethnic relations in America.

The preceding glimpses into the context and content of the African American reality, its struggles, its tradition and community, its achievements, and its perceptions of strains and stresses reveal a dense set of dimensions and concerns. These pieces of an authentic identity, rather than stereotype, have replaced earlier dichotomies: "slave/free, black/white, poor/rich," but vestiges are still evident. A variety of group relations based on historic and regional, as well as institutional, agendas to preserve cultural and racial consciousness have complicated the simple hope for liberty and justice that is shared by many Americans. Many African Americans still face challenges in housing, employment, mobility, and education. Growing gaps in education, financial status and class, crime, and death rates of young black men paint daunting pictures of past policies and the future.

Discrimination and prejudice based on skin color are issues rarely broached in mainstream media. Evidence of inter-racial marriage and the influence of skin hue within the African American community raise attendant issues of discrimination and consciousness of color. This concern is reflected in eighteenth- and nineteenth-century laws and practices of defining race that shaped the mentalities of color consciousness, prejudice, and racism in America. Other dimensions of the African American experience have been explored, such as fragmentation based on immigration, economic and professional mobility, the tenuous hold that the middle class has experienced due to wage stag-nation, and finally the persistent isolation of very low income households and collapse of educational support. These factors suggest that convergence among these segments of the African American population is subject to the overall clustering of the American population into cohorts measured by level of educa-tion, income, and value of housing, as well as macro-region of the country. New perspectives on the post–Civil Rights Era can be gained from reflective accounts of the leaders who influ-enced the direction of social change that reconfigured race and ethnic relations in America. As this debate continues, patterns of change within African American populations compel discussion of the black middle class, the purpose and influence of the his-torically black universities, and the reopening of the discussion of slavery and reparations for the measurable lack of participa-tion in esteem, rewards, and benefits. The changing structure of the African American family has stubbornly eluded researchers and parents who confront the realities of pride and prejudice. What are the implications of the continual discovery of prejudice and discrimination in universities, corporations, political atti-tudes, and especially relations of young men to law enforcement and other parts of the criminal justice system?

Article   Prepared by: John A. Kromkowski, *The Catholic University of America*

Rachel Dolezal Case Exposes Fault Lines over Racial Identity

Eric Gorski

Learning Outcomes

After reading this article, you will be able to:

- Describe the circumstance of Rachel Dolezal's emergence as a focal point or explaining racial identity and the limits of self-invention as well as the social political consequences of contesting identity.

- Explain and assess practical implications of self-identification and the ascription of race and ethnicity by others as personal and social phenomena.

Every day, Alisha Kwon Hammett is reminded of her otherness. A black woman on light rail wonders aloud where she's from. The ladies at the Korean market ask, "What kind of Asian are you?" Hammett—part Korean, part black and adopted as a child by white parents—knows curiosity is human nature.

But imagine, she said, the constant feeling of strangers trying to squeeze you into a nice little box. That otherness could be internalized as marginalization, she said.

"I don't get to choose who I am when someone sees me," said Hammett, 31, of Denver, an instructor in the University of Colorado's ethnic living and learning community leadership studies program.

For several days running, an embattled Spokane, Wash., civil rights leader's choice to pass herself off as black has provided grist for social media and cable TV while setting off a complex national conversation about racial identity, privilege and the appropriation of blackness.

The bizarre story of former NAACP branch leader Rachel Dolezal has baffled, angered and intrigued—sometimes all at once—and raised questions about how racial identity is forged in an increasingly multicultural society haunted by racism past and present.

"I was just really disappointed that someone who could be a powerful white ally chose deception," Hammett said. "I think when you see that, it's a critique of everything. As a community of color, are we open to white allies? Are those tools there to walk in solidarity with each other? Or is it so difficult for white people to be in solidarity with people of color that they have gone to the extent that they are in blackface?"

In an interview Tuesday with NBC's Today show, Dolezal said she has identified as black since she was 5—when she used brown instead of peach crayons in self-portraits—and is not trying to deceive.

Doris Walker, communications director for the Denver branch of the NAACP, which from its inception has been an interracial organization, said that is not how racial identity works.

Walker, 33, grew up the daughter of civil rights attorneys. She said she has been molded by experiences both beautiful and painful.

Marching in Martin Luther King Jr. Day parades. Watching a cross burn in her father's front yard while living in Oklahoma.

"My belief as far as being black is it's not a choice—it's an experience," said Walker, 33. "If you are black by selection, if you are black by scenario, I don't feel that is appropriate."

At first, Walker thought Dolezal was doing little harm. She viewed it as just another embrace of black culture—nothing new. But as more details have emerged, her view of Dolezal has turned more critical.

"It's a huge deal to stand in front of hundreds of thousands of people to represent an organization that specifically focuses on fairness, and to take that opportunity away from someone who is actually black and lived the black experience their entire lives," she said.

A Discourse

Shifting views about race coupled with the very American idea of self-invention are helping shape discourse over the Dolezal story, said Claire Garcia, director of the race, ethnicity and migration studies program at Colorado College.

No longer is the notion of race viewed as something that resides in blood or genes as some biological or physiological fact, Garcia said. There is recognition that race is a construct, a discourse, she said.

"It is kind of hard to wrap our heads around the fact that race is fiction, that it is nothing, that it is not a thing—but it is everything in our society," said Garcia, who is black. "We have seen recently it can have life-and-death consequences."

At the same time, no one has complete control over their racial identities, she said—it's a give-and-take, a combination of being perceived as well as reacting to how people perceive you.

"Obviously, race is more than skin pigmentation," said Miguel De La Torre, a professor of social ethics and Latino/a studies at Iliff School of Theology in Denver. "It is also the social struggles, what you deal with as a small child trying to figure it out. It's more than a claim."

Still others point out that Dolezal, "passing" as black, enjoyed a privilege not extended to members of minority groups.

"If the going gets tough, you can be like, 'Wait, I was just playing—I am white,' " said Ronda Belen, a Denver community activist.

Belen and others note that black people throughout history have passed for white when they could, with far different stakes.

"It was a matter of survival. It wasn't a matter of convenience," she said. "When black people 'passed,' they lost culture, they lost familial connections. You could be outed at any moment and lose your life."

Community Acceptance

Daryl Joji Maeda, chair of CU Boulder's Department of Ethnic Studies, said there is no one arbiter of racial identity, particularly among African-Americans.

That differs from the system that governs the Native American community, with tribes setting protocols for who qualifies for membership in a legal sense, he said.

"In Rachel Dolezal's case, the question would be, 'Does her community accept her as African-American?'" he said. "Knowing the full story, does her community accept her as a member of the community? That is not something you or I should pass judgment on."

Critical Thinking

1. Discuss the social "scientistic" concept and claim that reality is socially constructed.
2. What are the implications of color consciousness on self-identity and the historical fact that various types of "whiteness" have been socially and politically used to differentiate populations?

Internet References

Act for Youth
   www.actforyouth.net
Identity issues
   www.goodtherapy.org
National Association for the Advancement of Colored People (NAACP)
   www.naacp.org
National Center for Biotechnology
   www.ncbi.nlm.nih.gov

Article Prepared by: John A. Kromkowski, *The Catholic University of America*

Black (African-American) History Month: February 2015

To commemorate and celebrate the contributions to our nation made by people of African descent, American historian Carter G. Woodson established Black History Week. The first celebration occurred on Feb. 12, 1926. For many years, the second week of February was set aside for this celebration to coincide with the birthdays of abolitionist/editor Frederick Douglass and Abraham Lincoln. In 1976, as part of the nation's bicentennial, the week was expanded into Black History Month. Each year, U.S. presidents proclaim February as National African-American History Month.

Note: The reference to the black population in this publication is to single-race blacks ("black alone") except in the first section on "Population." In that section the reference is to black alone or in combination with other races; a reference to respondents who said they were one race (black) or more than one race (black plus other races).

Learning Outcomes

After reading this article, you will be able to:

- Identify from which African countries the largest numbers of immigrants are coming to America.

- Discuss in what respect these immigrants are different from American-born African Americans.

Population
45.0 million
The number of blacks, either alone or in combination with one or more other races, on July 1, 2013, up 1.0 percent from July 1, 2012.

Source: Population Estimates

<http://factfinder2.census.gov/bkmk/table/1.0/en/PEP/2013/PEPSR5H?slice=Year~est72013>

74.5 million
The projected black, either alone or in combination, population of the United States (including those of more than one race) for July 1, 2060. On that date, according to the projection, blacks would constitute 17.9 percent of the nation's total population.

Source: Population Projections Table 10

<http://www.census.gov/population/projections/data/national/2014/summarytables.html>

3.7 million
The black population in New York, which led all states as of July 1, 2013. Texas had the largest numeric increase since 2012 (78,000). The District of Columbia had the highest percentage of blacks (51.0 percent), followed by Mississippi (38.1 percent).

Source: Population Estimates

<http://www.census.gov/newsroom/press-releases/2014/cb14-118.html>

1.3 million
Cook County, Ill. (Chicago) had the largest black population of any county in 2013 (1.3 million), and Harris, Texas (Houston) had the largest numeric increase since 2012 (18,000). Holmes, Miss., was the county with the highest percentage of blacks in the nation (83.2 percent).

Source: Population Estimates

<http://www.census.gov/newsroom/press-releases/2014/cb14-118.html>

Serving Our Nation
2.2 million
Number of black military veterans in the United States in 2013.
    Source: 2013 American Community Survey
    <http://factfinder.census.gov/bkmk/table/1.0/en/ACS/13_1YR/C21001B>

Education
83.7%
The percentage of blacks 25 and over with a high school diploma or higher in 2013.
    Source: 2013 American Community Survey
    <http://factfinder.census.gov/bkmk/table/1.0/en/ACS/13_1YR/S0201//popgroup~004>

19.3%
The percentage of blacks 25 and over who had a bachelor's degree or higher in 2013.
    Source: 2013 American Community Survey
    <http://factfinder.census.gov/bkmk/table/1.0/en/ACS/13_1YR/S0201//popgroup~004>

1.7 million
Among blacks 25 and over, the number who had an advanced degree in 2013.
    Source: 2013 American Community Survey
    <http://factfinder2.census.gov/bkmk/table/1.0/en/ACS/13_1YR/B15002B>

3.0 million
Number of blacks enrolled in undergraduate college in 2013 compared with 2.6 million in 2008, a 17.5 percent increase.
    Source: 2013 American Community Survey
    <http://factfinder2.census.gov/bkmk/table/1.0/en/ACS/13_1YR/B14007B>
    <http://factfinder2.census.gov/bkmk/table/1.0/en/ACS/08_1YR/B14007B>

Voting
17.8 million
The number of blacks who voted in the 2012 presidential election. In comparison to the 2008 election, about 1.7 million additional black voters reported going to the polls in 2012.
    Source: The Diversifying Electorate—Voting Rates by Race and Hispanic Origin 2012
    <http://www.census.gov/prod/2013pubs/p20-568.pdf>

66.2%
The percentage of blacks who voted in the 2012 presidential election, higher than the 64.1 percent of non-Hispanic whites who did so. This marks the first time that blacks have voted at a higher rate than whites since the Census Bureau started publishing statistics on voting by the eligible citizen population in 1996.
    Source: The Diversifying Electorate—Voting Rates by Race and Hispanic Origin 2012
    <http://www.census.gov/prod/2013pubs/p20-568.pdf>

Income, Poverty and Health Insurance
$34,598
The annual median income of black households in 2013, compared with the nation at $51,939.
    Source: U.S. Census Bureau, Income, Poverty and Health Insurance Coverage in the United States: 2013
    <http://www.census.gov/content/dam/Census/library/publications/2014/demo/p60-249.pdf>

27.2%
Poverty rate in 2013 for blacks, while nationally it was 14.5 percent.
    Source: U.S. Census Bureau, Income, Poverty and Health Insurance Coverage in the United States: 2013
    <http://www.census.gov/content/dam/Census/library/publications/2014/demo/p60-249.pdf>

84.1%
Percentage of blacks that were covered by health insurance during all or part of 2013. Nationally, 86.6 percent of all races were covered by health insurance.
    Source: U.S. Census Bureau, Health Insurance Coverage in the United States: 2013
    <http://www.census.gov/content/dam/Census/library/publications/2014/demo/p60-250.pdf>

Families and Children
61.8%
Among households with a black householder, the percentage that contained a family in 2013. There were 9.8 million black family households.
    Source: 2013 Current Population Survey, Families and Living Arrangements, Table HH-1 and F1
    <http://www.census.gov/hhes/families/data/cps2013H.html>

45.7%

Among families with black householders, the percentage that were married couples in 2013.

Source: 2013 Current Population Survey, Families and Living Arrangements, Table F1

<http://www.census.gov/hhes/families/data/cps2013F.html>

1.3 million

Number of black grandparents who lived with their own grandchildren younger than 18 in 2013. Of this number, 45.2 percent were also responsible for their care.

Source: 2013 American Community Survey

<http://factfinder2.census.gov/bkmk/table/1.0/en/ACS/13_1YR/B10051B>

Jobs

28.1%

The percentage of civilian employed blacks 16 and over who worked in management, business, science and arts occupations, while 36.3 percent of the total civilian employed population worked in these occupations.

Source: 2013 American Community Survey

<http://factfinder2.census.gov/bkmk/table/1.0/en/ACS/13_1YR/S0201//popgroup~004>

<http://factfinder2.census.gov/bkmk/table/1.0/en/ACS/13_1YR/S0201>

Following is a list of observances typically covered by the Census Bureau's *Facts for Features* series:

African-American History Month (February)
Super Bowl
Valentine's Day (Feb. 14)
Women's History Month (March)
Irish-American Heritage Month (March)/St. Patrick's Day (March 17)

Earth Day (April 22)
Asian/Pacific American Heritage Month (May)
Older Americans Month (May)
Mother's Day
Hurricane Season Begins (June 1)
Father's Day
The Fourth of July (July 4)
Anniversary of Americans with Disabilities Act (July 26)
Back to School (August)
Labor Day
Grandparents Day
Hispanic Heritage Month (Sept. 15–Oct. 15)
Unmarried and Single Americans Week
Halloween (Oct. 31)
American Indian/Alaska Native Heritage Month (November)
Veterans Day (Nov. 11)
Thanksgiving Day
The Holiday Season (December)

Critical Thinking

1. How is Black History month celebrated in your area?
2. Which of the various demographic indicators are most important?

Internet References

National Association for the Advancement of Colored People (NAACP)
   www.naacp.org
National Urban League
   www.nul.org
Sociosite
   www.sociosite.net

U.S Census Bureau. February 2013.

African-Born Population in U.S. Roughly Doubled Every Decade Since 1970, Census Bureau Reports by United States Census Bureau

127

Article   Prepared by: John A. Kromkowski, *The Catholic University of America*

African-Born Population in U.S. Roughly Doubled Every Decade Since 1970, Census Bureau Reports

U.S. DEPARTMENT OF COMMERCE, ECONOMICS, AND STATISTICS ADMINISTRATION

Learning Outcomes

After reading this article, you will be able to:

- Identify from which African countries the largest numbers of immigrants are coming to America.

- Identify in what respect these immigrants differ from American-born African Americans.

The foreign-born population from Africa has grown rapidly in the United States during the last 40 years, increasing from about 80,000 in 1970 to about 1.6 million in the period from 2008 to 2012, according to a U.S. Census Bureau brief released today. The population has roughly doubled each decade since 1970, with the largest increase happening from 2000 to 2008–2012.

The Foreign-born Population from Africa: 2008–2012, a brief based on American Community Survey statistics, shows that the African foreign-born population accounts for 4 percent of the total U.S. foreign-born population. No African country makes up the majority of these immigrants, but four countries—Nigeria, Ethiopia, Egypt and Ghana—make up 41 percent of the African-born total.

"The brief—the Census Bureau's first focusing on the African foreign-born population—highlights the size, growth, geographic distribution and educational attainment of this group," said Christine Gambino of the Census Bureau's Foreign-born Population Branch, who is one of the brief's authors. "We have found that the African-born population tends to be more educated and accounts for a relatively large proportion of the foreign-born population in some nontraditional immigrant gateway states such as Minnesota and the Dakotas."

The foreign-born population from Africa had a higher level of educational attainment than the overall foreign-born population: 41 percent of African-born had a bachelor's degree or higher compared with 28 percent overall. Within the foreign-born population from Africa, educational attainment varied by place of birth. For example, 40 percent of the Somali-born population had less than a high school education, while 64 percent of Egyptian-born individuals had a bachelor's degree or higher.

This brief is one of several focusing on the foreign-born population from world regions of birth. Previous reports include *"The Foreign Born from Asia: 2011"* and *"The Foreign Born from Latin America and the Caribbean: 2010."* In addition, supplemental tables are now available for the African-born population by metropolitan statistical area. Below are highlights of the geographic distribution of the African-born population from the brief:

Geographic Distribution

- The four states with African-born populations over 100,000 were New York (164,000), California (155,000), Texas (134,000) and Maryland (120,000).
- Of the 10 states with the largest African-born populations, Minnesota (19 percent), Maryland (15 percent), Virginia (9 percent), Georgia (8 percent) and Massachusetts (8 percent) had percentages of

African-born in their foreign-born populations that were at least twice the national percentage of 4 percent.
- Metropolitan areas with the largest African-born populations were New York (212,000), Washington (161,000), Atlanta (68,000), Los Angeles (68,000), Minneapolis-St. Paul (64,000), Dallas-Fort Worth (61,000) and Boston (60,000).
- Among the 10 metro areas with the largest African-born populations, Nigerians were the most populous group and constituted a high proportion (20 percent or more) of the African-born in the Atlanta, Chicago, Dallas-Fort Worth and Houston metros. Similarly, Ethiopians were a high proportion and the largest group in the Washington D.C. metro, Cabo Verdeans in Boston, Somalis in Minneapolis-St. Paul, Egyptians in Los Angeles and Liberians in Philadelphia.

About the American Community Survey

The information in this release comes from data collected from the American Community Survey from 2008 to 2012. The questions asked include:

- Where was this person born?
- Is this person a citizen of the United States?
- When did this person come to live in the United States?

Organizations use this information to develop programs for refugees, immigrants and other foreign-born individuals.

Federal and state agencies require these statistics to support enforcement of nondiscrimination policies and to allocate funds for school districts based on limited English proficiency, immigrant, low income and minority student populations.

Ever since Thomas Jefferson directed the first census in 1790, the census has collected detailed characteristics about our nation's people. Questions about jobs and the economy were added 20 years later under James Madison, who said such information would allow Congress to "adapt the public measures to the particular circumstances of the community," and over the decades allow America "an opportunity of marking the progress of the society."

Critical Thinking

1. Do changes in transportation and ease of maintaining communication with countries of origin suggest that the acculturation of immigrants in the 21st century will be substantively different from early eras of large-scale migration?
2. Does the discussion of citizenship by birth pose political challenges?
3. What does the expansion of dual citizenship meaning for political participation?

Internet References

Immigration and Ethnic History Society
www.iehs.org

U.S. Census Bureau
www.census.gov

Article   Prepared by: John A. Kromkowski, *The Catholic University of America*

The Case for Reparations

Two hundred fifty years of slavery. Ninety years of Jim Crow. Sixty years of separate but equal. Thirty-five years of racist housing policy. Until we reckon with our compounding moral debts, America will never be whole.

TA-NEHISI COATES

Learning Outcomes

After reading this article, you will be able to:

- Explain the central core arguments for reparations.
- Discuss the legal and moral claims and imperatives of the case.

And if thy brother, a Hebrew man, or a Hebrew woman, be sold unto thee, and serve thee six years; then in the seventh year thou shalt let him go free from thee. And when thou sendest him out free from thee, thou shalt not let him go away empty: thou shalt furnish him liberally out of thy flock, and out of thy floor, and out of thy winepress: of that wherewith the LORD thy God hath blessed thee thou shalt give unto him. And thou shalt remember that thou wast a bondman in the land of Egypt, and the LORD thy God redeemed thee: therefore I command thee this thing today.

— Deuteronomy 15: 12–15

Besides the crime which consists in violating the law, and varying from the right rule of reason, whereby a man so far becomes degenerate, and declares himself
to quit the principles of human nature, and to be a noxious creature, there is commonly injury done to some person or other, and some other man receives damage by his transgression: in which case he who hath received any damage, has, besides the right of punishment common to him with other men, a particular right to seek reparation.

— John Locke, "Second Treatise"

By our unpaid labor and suffering, we have earned the right to the soil, many times over and over, and now we are determined to have it.

— Anonymous, 1861

"So That's Just One of My Losses"

Clyde Ross was born in 1923, the seventh of 13 children, near Clarksdale, Mississippi, the home of the blues. Ross's parents owned and farmed a 40-acre tract of land, flush with cows, hogs, and mules. Ross's mother would drive to Clarksdale to do her shopping in a horse and buggy, in which she invested all the pride one might place in a Cadillac. The family owned another horse, with a red coat, which they gave to Clyde. The Ross family wanted for little, save that which all black families in the Deep South then desperately desired—the protection of the law.

In the 1920s, Jim Crow Mississippi was, in all facets of society, a kleptocracy. The majority of the people in the state were perpetually robbed of the vote—a hijacking engineered through the trickery of the poll tax and the muscle of the lynch mob. Between 1882 and 1968, more black people were lynched in Mississippi than in any other state. "You and I know what's the best way to keep the nigger from voting," blustered Theodore Bilbo, a Mississippi senator and a proud Klansman. "You do it the night before the election."

The state's regime partnered robbery of the franchise with robbery of the purse. Many of Mississippi's black farmers lived in debt peonage, under the sway of cotton kings who were at once their landlords, their employers, and their primary merchants. Tools and necessities were advanced against the return on the crop, which was determined by the employer. When farmers were deemed to be in debt—and they often were—the negative balance was then carried over to the next season. A man or woman who protested this arrangement did so at the risk of grave injury or death. Refusing to work meant arrest under vagrancy laws and forced labor under the state's penal system.

Well into the 20th century, black people spoke of their flight from Mississippi in much the same manner as their runagate ancestors had. In her 2010 book, *The Warmth of Other Suns*, Isabel Wilkerson tells the story of Eddie Earvin, a spinach picker who fled Mississippi in 1963, after being made to work at gunpoint. "You didn't talk about it or tell nobody," Earvin said. "You had to sneak away."

When Clyde Ross was still a child, Mississippi authorities claimed his father owed $3,000 in back taxes. The elder Ross could not read. He did not have a lawyer. He did not know anyone at the local courthouse. He could not expect the police to be impartial. Effectively, the Ross family had no way to contest the claim and no protection under the law. The authorities seized the land. They seized the buggy. They took the cows, hogs, and mules. And so for the upkeep of separate but equal, the entire Ross family was reduced to sharecropping.

This was hardly unusual. In 2001, the Associated Press published a three-part investigation into the theft of black-owned land stretching back to the antebellum period. The series documented some 406 victims and 24,000 acres of land valued at tens of millions of dollars. The land was taken through means ranging from legal chicanery to terrorism. "Some of the land taken from black families has become a country club in Virginia," the AP reported, as well as "oil fields in Mississippi" and "a baseball spring training facility in Florida."

Clyde Ross was a smart child. His teacher thought he should attend a more challenging school. There was very little support

for educating black people in Mississippi. But Julius Rosenwald, a part owner of Sears, Roebuck, had begun an ambitious effort to build schools for black children throughout the South. Ross's teacher believed he should attend the local Rosenwald school. It was too far for Ross to walk and get back in time to work in the fields. Local white children had a school bus. Clyde Ross did not, and thus lost the chance to better his education.

Then, when Ross was 10 years old, a group of white men demanded his only childhood possession—the horse with the red coat. "You can't have this horse. We want it," one of the white men said. They gave Ross's father $17.

"I did everything for that horse," Ross told me. "Everything. And they took him. Put him on the racetrack. I never did know what happened to him after that, but I know they didn't bring him back. So that's just one of my losses."

The losses mounted. As sharecroppers, the Ross family saw their wages treated as the landlord's slush fund. Landowners were supposed to split the profits from the cotton fields with sharecroppers. But bales would often disappear during the count, or the split might be altered on a whim. If cotton was selling for 50 cents a pound, the Ross family might get 15 cents, or only five. One year Ross's mother promised to buy him a $7 suit for a summer program at their church. She ordered the suit by mail. But that year Ross's family was paid only five cents a pound for cotton. The mailman arrived with the suit. The Rosses could not pay. The suit was sent back. Clyde Ross did not go to the church program.

It was in these early years that Ross began to understand himself as an American—he did not live under the blind decree of justice, but under the heel of a regime that elevated armed robbery to a governing principle. He thought about fighting. "Just be quiet," his father told him. "Because they'll come and kill us all."

Clyde Ross grew. He was drafted into the Army. The draft officials offered him an exemption if he stayed home and worked. He preferred to take his chances with war. He was stationed in California. He found that he could go into stores without being bothered. He could walk the streets without being harassed. He could go into a restaurant and receive service.

Ross was shipped off to Guam. He fought in World War II to save the world from tyranny. But when he returned to Clarksdale, he found that tyranny had followed him home. This was 1947, eight years before Mississippi lynched Emmett Till and tossed his broken body into the Tallahatchie River. The Great Migration, a mass exodus of 6 million African Americans that spanned most of the 20th century, was now in its second wave. The black pilgrims did not journey north simply seeking better wages and work, or bright lights and big adventures. They were fleeing the acquisitive warlords of the South. They were seeking the protection of the law.

Clyde Ross was among them. He came to Chicago in 1947 and took a job as a taster at Campbell's Soup. He made a stable wage. He married. He had children. His paycheck was his own. No Klansmen stripped him of the vote. When he walked down the street, he did not have to move because a white man was walking past. He did not have to take off his hat or avert his gaze. His journey from peonage to full citizenship seemed near-complete. Only one item was missing—a home, that final badge of entry into the sacred order of the American middle class of the Eisenhower years.

In 1961, Ross and his wife bought a house in North Lawndale, a bustling community on Chicago's West Side. North Lawndale had long been a predominantly Jewish neighborhood, but a handful of middle-class African Americans had lived there starting in the '40s. The community was anchored by the sprawling Sears, Roebuck headquarters. North Lawndale's Jewish People's Institute actively encouraged blacks to move into the neighborhood, seeking to make it a "pilot community for interracial living." In the battle for integration then being fought around the country, North Lawndale seemed to offer promising terrain. But out in the tall grass, highwaymen, nefarious as any Clarksdale kleptocrat, were lying in wait.

Three months after Clyde Ross moved into his house, the boiler blew out. This would normally be a homeowner's responsibility, but in fact, Ross was not really a homeowner. His payments were made to the seller, not the bank. And Ross had not signed a normal mortgage. He'd bought "on contract": a predatory agreement that combined all the responsibilities of homeownership with all the disadvantages of renting—while offering the benefits of neither. Ross had bought his house for $27,500. The seller, not the previous homeowner but a new kind of middleman, had bought it for only $12,000 six months before selling it to Ross. In a contract sale, the seller kept the deed until the contract was paid in full—and, unlike with a normal mortgage, Ross would acquire no equity in the meantime. If he missed a single payment, he would immediately forfeit his $1,000 down payment, all his monthly payments, and the property itself.

The men who peddled contracts in North Lawndale would sell homes at inflated prices and then evict families who could not pay—taking their down payment and their monthly installments as profit. Then they'd bring in another black family, rinse, and repeat. "He loads them up with payments they can't meet," an office secretary told *The Chicago Daily News* of her boss, the speculator Lou Fushanis, in 1963. "Then he takes the property away from them. He's sold some of the buildings three or four times."

Ross had tried to get a legitimate mortgage in another neighborhood, but was told by a loan officer that there was no financing available. The truth was that there was no financing for people like Clyde Ross. From the 1930s through the 1960s, black people across the country were largely cut out of the legitimate home-mortgage market through means both legal and extralegal. Chicago whites employed every measure, from "restrictive covenants" to bombings, to keep their neighborhoods segregated.

Their efforts were buttressed by the federal government. In 1934, Congress created the Federal Housing Administration. The FHA insured private mortgages, causing a drop in interest rates and a decline in the size of the down payment required to buy a house. But an insured mortgage was not a possibility for Clyde Ross. The FHA had adopted a system of maps that rated neighborhoods according to their perceived stability. On the maps, green areas, rated "A," indicated "in demand" neighborhoods that, as one appraiser put it, lacked "a single foreigner or Negro." These neighborhoods were considered excellent prospects for insurance. Neighborhoods where black people lived were rated "D" and were usually considered ineligible for FHA backing. They were colored in red. Neither the percentage of black people living there nor their social class mattered. Black people were viewed as a contagion. Redlining went beyond FHA-backed loans and spread to the entire mortgage industry, which was already rife with racism, excluding black people from most legitimate means of obtaining a mortgage.

"A government offering such bounty to builders and lenders could have required compliance with a nondiscrimination policy," Charles Abrams, the urban-studies expert who helped create the New York City Housing Authority, wrote in 1955. "Instead, the FHA adopted a racial policy that could well have been culled from the Nuremberg laws."

The devastating effects are cogently outlined by Melvin L. Oliver and Thomas M. Shapiro in their 1995 book, *Black Wealth/White Wealth*:

> Locked out of the greatest mass-based opportunity for wealth accumulation in American history, African Americans who desired and were able to afford home ownership found themselves consigned to central-city communities where their investments were affected by the "self-fulfilling prophecies" of the FHA appraisers: cut off from sources of new investment[,] their homes and communities deteriorated and lost value in comparison to those homes and communities that FHA appraisers deemed desirable.

In Chicago and across the country, whites looking to achieve the American dream could rely on a legitimate credit system backed by the government. Blacks were herded into the sights of unscrupulous lenders who took them for money and for sport. "It was like people who like to go out and shoot lions in Africa. It was the same thrill," a housing attorney told the historian Beryl Satter in her 2009 book, *Family Properties*. "The thrill of the chase and the kill."

The kill was profitable. At the time of his death, Lou Fushanis owned more than 600 properties, many of them in North Lawndale, and his estate was estimated to be worth $3 million. He'd made much of this money by exploiting the frustrated hopes of black migrants like Clyde Ross. During this period, according to one estimate, 85 percent of all black home buyers who bought in Chicago bought on contract. "If anybody who is well established in this business in Chicago doesn't earn $100,000 a year," a contract seller told *The Saturday Evening Post* in 1962, "he is loafing."

Contract sellers became rich. North Lawndale became a ghetto.

Clyde Ross still lives there. He still owns his home. He is 91, and the emblems of survival are all around him—awards for service in his community, pictures of his children in cap and gown. But when I asked him about his home in North Lawndale, I heard only anarchy.

"We were ashamed. We did not want anyone to know that we were that ignorant," Ross told me. He was sitting at his dining-room table. His glasses were as thick as his Clarksdale drawl. "I'd come out of Mississippi where there was one mess, and come up here and got in another mess. So how dumb am I? I didn't want anyone to know how dumb I was.

"When I found myself caught up in it, I said, 'How? I just left this mess. I just left no laws. And no regard. And then I come here and get cheated wide open.' I would probably want to do some harm to some people, you know, if I had been violent like some of us. I thought, 'Man, I got caught up in this stuff. I can't even take care of my kids.' I didn't have enough for my kids. You could fall through the cracks easy fighting these white people. And no law."

But fight Clyde Ross did. In 1968 he joined the newly formed Contract Buyers League—a collection of black homeowners on Chicago's South and West Sides, all of whom had been locked into the same system of predation. There was Howell Collins, whose contract called for him to pay $25,500 for a house that a speculator had bought for $14,500. There was Ruth Wells, who'd managed to pay out half her contract, expecting a mortgage, only to suddenly see an insurance bill materialize out of thin air—a requirement the seller had added without Wells's knowledge. Contract sellers used every tool at their disposal to pilfer from their clients. They scared white residents into selling low. They lied about properties' compliance with building codes, then left the buyer responsible when city inspectors arrived. They presented themselves as real-estate brokers, when in fact they were the owners. They guided their clients to lawyers who were in on the scheme.

The Contract Buyers League fought back. Members—who would eventually number more than 500—went out to the posh suburbs where the speculators lived and embarrassed them by knocking on their neighbors' doors and informing them of the details of the contract-lending trade. They refused to pay their installments, instead holding monthly payments in an escrow account. Then they brought a suit against the contract sellers, accusing them of buying properties and reselling in such a manner "to reap from members of the Negro race large and unjust profits."

In return for the "deprivations of their rights and privileges under the Thirteenth and Fourteenth Amendments," the league demanded "prayers for relief"—payback of all moneys paid on contracts and all moneys paid for structural improvement of properties, at 6 percent interest minus a "fair, nondiscriminatory" rental price for time of occupation. Moreover, the league asked the court to adjudge that the defendants had "acted willfully and maliciously and that malice is the gist of this action."

Ross and the Contract Buyers League were no longer appealing to the government simply for equality. They were no longer fleeing in hopes of a better deal elsewhere. They were charging society with a crime against their community. They wanted the crime publicly ruled as such. They wanted the crime's executors declared to be offensive to society. And they wanted restitution for the great injury brought upon them by said offenders. In 1968, Clyde Ross and the Contract Buyers League were no longer simply seeking the protection of the law. They were seeking reparations.

"A Difference of Kind, Not Degree"

According to the most-recent statistics, North Lawndale is now on the wrong end of virtually every socioeconomic indicator. In 1930 its population was 112,000. Today it is 36,000. The halcyon talk of "interracial living" is dead. The neighborhood is 92 percent black. Its homicide rate is 45 per 100,000—triple the rate of the city as a whole. The infant-mortality rate is 14 per 1,000—more than twice the national average. Forty-three percent of the people in North Lawndale live below the poverty line—double Chicago's overall rate. Forty-five percent of all households are on food stamps—nearly three times the rate of the city at large. Sears, Roebuck left the neighborhood in 1987, taking 1,800 jobs with it. Kids in North Lawndale need not be confused about their prospects: Cook County's Juvenile Temporary Detention Center sits directly adjacent to the neighborhood.

North Lawndale is an extreme portrait of the trends that ail black Chicago. Such is the magnitude of these ailments that it can be said that blacks and whites do not inhabit the same city. The average per capita income of Chicago's white neighborhoods is almost three times that of its black neighborhoods. When the Harvard sociologist Robert J. Sampson examined incarceration rates in Chicago in his 2012 book, *Great*

American City, he found that a black neighborhood with one of the highest incarceration rates (West Garfield Park) had a rate more than 40 times as high as the white neighborhood with the highest rate (Clearing). "This is a staggering differential, even for community-level comparisons," Sampson writes. "A difference of kind, not degree."

In other words, Chicago's impoverished black neighborhoods—characterized by high unemployment and households headed by single parents—are not simply poor; they are "ecologically distinct." This "is not simply the same thing as low economic status," writes Sampson. "In this pattern Chicago is not alone."

The lives of black Americans are better than they were half a century ago. The humiliation of WHITES ONLY signs are gone. Rates of black poverty have decreased. Black teen-pregnancy rates are at record lows—and the gap between black and white teen-pregnancy rates has shrunk significantly. But such progress rests on a shaky foundation, and fault lines are everywhere. The income gap between black and white households is roughly the same today as it was in 1970. Patrick Sharkey, a sociologist at New York University, studied children born from 1955 through 1970 and found that 4 percent of whites and 62 percent of blacks across America had been raised in poor neighborhoods. A generation later, the same study showed, virtually nothing had changed. And whereas whites born into affluent neighborhoods tended to remain in affluent neighborhoods, blacks tended to fall out of them.

This is not surprising. Black families, regardless of income, are significantly less wealthy than white families. The Pew Research Center estimates that white households are worth roughly 20 times as much as black households, and that whereas only 15 percent of whites have zero or negative wealth, more than a third of blacks do. Effectively, the black family in America is working without a safety net. When financial calamity strikes—a medical emergency, divorce, job loss—the fall is precipitous.

And just as black families of all incomes remain handicapped by a lack of wealth, so too do they remain handicapped by their restricted choice of neighborhood. Black people with upper-middle-class incomes do not generally live in upper-middle-class neighborhoods. Sharkey's research shows that black families making $100,000 typically live in the kinds of neighborhoods inhabited by white families making $30,000. "Blacks and whites inhabit such different neighborhoods," Sharkey writes, "that it is not possible to compare the economic outcomes of black and white children."

The implications are chilling. As a rule, poor black people do not work their way out of the ghetto—and those who do often face the horror of watching their children and grandchildren tumble back.

Even seeming evidence of progress withers under harsh light. In 2012, the Manhattan Institute cheerily noted that segregation had declined since the 1960s. And yet African Americans still remained—by far—the most segregated ethnic group in the country.

With segregation, with the isolation of the injured and the robbed, comes the concentration of disadvantage. An unsegregated America might see poverty, and all its effects, spread across the country with no particular bias toward skin color. Instead, the concentration of poverty has been paired with a concentration of melanin. The resulting conflagration has been devastating.

One thread of thinking in the African American community holds that these depressing numbers partially stem from cultural pathologies that can be altered through individual grit and exceptionally good behavior. (In 2011, Philadelphia Mayor Michael Nutter, responding to violence among young black males, put the blame on the family: "Too many men making too many babies they don't want to take care of, and then we end up dealing with your children." Nutter turned to those presumably fatherless babies: "Pull your pants up and buy a belt, because no one wants to see your underwear or the crack of your butt.") The thread is as old as black politics itself. It is also wrong. The kind of trenchant racism to which black people have persistently been subjected can never be defeated by making its victims more respectable. The essence of American racism is disrespect. And in the wake of the grim numbers, we see the grim inheritance.

The Contract Buyers League's suit brought by Clyde Ross and his allies took direct aim at this inheritance. The suit was rooted in Chicago's long history of segregation, which had created two housing markets—one legitimate and backed by the government, the other lawless and patrolled by predators. The suit dragged on until 1976, when the league lost a jury trial. Securing the equal protection of the law proved hard; securing reparations proved impossible. If there were any doubts about the mood of the jury, the foreman removed them by saying, when asked about the verdict, that he hoped it would help end "the mess Earl Warren made with *Brown v. Board of Education* and all that nonsense."

The Supreme Court seems to share that sentiment. The past two decades have witnessed a rollback of the progressive legislation of the 1960s. Liberals have found themselves on the defensive. In 2008, when Barack Obama was a candidate for president, he was asked whether his daughters—Malia and Sasha—should benefit from affirmative action. He answered in the negative.

The exchange rested upon an erroneous comparison of the average American white family and the exceptional first family. In the contest of upward mobility, Barack and Michelle Obama have won. But they've won by being twice as good—and enduring twice as much. Malia and Sasha Obama enjoy privileges beyond the average white child's dreams. But that comparison is incomplete. The more telling question is how they compare with Jenna and Barbara Bush—the products of many generations of privilege, not just one. Whatever the Obama children achieve, it will be evidence of their family's singular perseverance, not of broad equality.

"We Inherit Our Ample Patrimony"

In 1783, the freedwoman Belinda Royall petitioned the commonwealth of Massachusetts for reparations. Belinda had been born in modern-day Ghana. She was kidnapped as a child and sold into slavery. She endured the Middle Passage and 50 years of enslavement at the hands of Isaac Royall and his son. But the junior Royall, a British loyalist, fled the country during the Revolution. Belinda, now free after half a century of labor, beseeched the nascent Massachusetts legislature:

> The face of your Petitioner, is now marked with the furrows of time, and her frame bending under the oppression of years, while she, by the Laws of the Land, is denied the employment of one morsel of that immense wealth, apart whereof hath been accumulated by her own industry, and the whole augmented by her servitude.

> WHEREFORE, casting herself at your feet if your honours, as to a body of men, formed for the extirpation of vassalage, for the reward of Virtue, and the just return of honest industry—she prays, that such allowance may be made her out of the Estate of Colonel Royall, as will prevent her, and her more infirm daughter, from misery in the greatest extreme, and scatter comfort over the short and downward path of their lives.

Belinda Royall was granted a pension of 15 pounds and 12 shillings, to be paid out of the estate of Isaac Royall—one of the earliest successful attempts to petition for reparations. At the time, black people in America had endured more than 150 years of enslavement, and the idea that they might be owed something in return was, if not the national consensus, at least not outrageous.

"A heavy account lies against us as a civil society for oppressions committed against people who did not injure us," wrote the Quaker John Woolman in 1769, "and that if the particular case of many individuals were fairly stated, it would appear that there was considerable due to them."

As the historian Roy E. Finkenbine has documented, at the dawn of this country, black reparations were actively considered and often effected. Quakers in New York, New England, and Baltimore went so far as to make "membership contingent upon compensating one's former slaves." In 1782, the Quaker Robert Pleasants emancipated his 78 slaves, granted

them 350 acres, and later built a school on their property and provided for their education. "The doing of this justice to the injured Africans," wrote Pleasants, "would be an acceptable offering to him who 'Rules in the kingdom of men.'"

Edward Coles, a protégé of Thomas Jefferson who became a slaveholder through inheritance, took many of his slaves north and granted them a plot of land in Illinois. John Randolph, a cousin of Jefferson's, willed that all his slaves be emancipated upon his death, and that all those older than 40 be given 10 acres of land. "I give and bequeath to all my slaves their freedom," Randolph wrote, "heartily regretting that I have been the owner of one."

In his book *Forever Free,* Eric Foner recounts the story of a disgruntled planter reprimanding a freedman loafing on the job:

Planter: "You lazy nigger, I am losing a whole day's labor by you."

Freedman: "Massa, how many days' labor have I lost by you?"

In the 20th century, the cause of reparations was taken up by a diverse cast that included the Confederate veteran Walter R. Vaughan, who believed that reparations would be a stimulus for the South; the black activist Callie House; black-nationalist leaders like "Queen Mother" Audley Moore; and the civil-rights activist James Forman. The movement coalesced in 1987 under an umbrella organization called the National Coalition of Blacks for Reparations in America (N'COBRA). The NAACP endorsed reparations in 1993. Charles J. Ogletree Jr., a professor at Harvard Law School, has pursued reparations claims in court.

But while the people advocating reparations have changed over time, the response from the country has remained virtually the same. "They have been taught to labor," the *Chicago Tribune* editorialized in 1891. "They have been taught Christian civilization, and to speak the noble English language instead of some African gibberish. The account is square with the ex slaves."

Not exactly. Having been enslaved for 250 years, black people were not left to their own devices. They were terrorized. In the Deep South, a second slavery ruled. In the North, legislatures, mayors, civic associations, banks, and citizens all colluded to pin black people into ghettos, where they were overcrowded, overcharged, and undereducated. Businesses discriminated against them, awarding them the worst jobs and the worst wages. Police brutalized them in the streets. And the notion that black lives, black bodies, and black wealth were rightful targets remained deeply rooted in the broader society. Now we have half-stepped away from our long centuries of despoilment, promising, "Never again." But still we are haunted. It is as though we have run up a credit-card bill and, having pledged to charge no more, remain befuddled that the balance does not disappear. The effects of that balance, interest accruing daily, are all around us.

Broach the topic of reparations today and a barrage of questions inevitably follows: Who will be paid? How much will they be paid? Who will pay? But if the practicalities, not the justice, of reparations are the true sticking point, there has for some time been the beginnings of a solution. For the past 25 years, Congressman John Conyers Jr., who represents the Detroit area, has marked every session of Congress by introducing a bill calling for a congressional study of slavery and its lingering effects as well as recommendations for "appropriate remedies."

A country curious about how reparations might actually work has an easy solution in Conyers's bill, now called HR 40, the Commission to Study Reparation Proposals for African Americans Act. We would support this bill, submit the question to study, and then assess the possible solutions. But we are not interested.

"It's because it's black folks making the claim," Nkechi Taifa, who helped found N'COBRA, says. "People who talk about reparations are considered left lunatics. But all we are talking about is studying [reparations]. As John Conyers has said, we study everything. We study the water, the air. We can't even study the issue? This bill does not authorize one red cent to anyone."

That HR 40 has never—under either Democrats or Republicans—made it to the House floor suggests our concerns are rooted not in the impracticality of reparations but in something more existential. If we conclude that the conditions in North Lawndale and black America are not inexplicable but are instead precisely what you'd expect of a community that for centuries has lived in America's crosshairs, then what are we to make of the world's oldest democracy?

One cannot escape the question by hand-waving at the past, disavowing the acts of one's ancestors, nor by citing a recent date of ancestral immigration. The last slaveholder has been dead for a very long time. The last soldier to endure Valley Forge has been dead much longer. To proudly claim the veteran and disown the slaveholder is patriotism à la carte. A nation outlives its generations. We were not there when Washington crossed the Delaware, but Emanuel Gottlieb Leutze's rendering has meaning to us. We were not there when Woodrow Wilson took us into World War I, but we are still paying out the pensions. If Thomas Jefferson's genius matters, then so does his taking of Sally Hemings's body. If George Washington crossing the Delaware matters, so must his ruthless pursuit of the runagate Oney Judge.

In 1909, President William Howard Taft told the country that "intelligent" white southerners were ready to see blacks as "useful members of the community." A week later Joseph Gordon, a black man, was lynched outside Greenwood, Mississippi. The high point of the lynching era has passed.

But the memories of those robbed of their lives still live on in the lingering effects. Indeed, in America there is a strange and powerful belief that if you stab a black person 10 times, the bleeding stops and the healing begins the moment the assailant drops the knife. We believe white dominance to be a fact of the inert past, a delinquent debt that can be made to disappear if only we don't look.

There has always been another way. "It is in vain to alledge, that *our ancestors* brought them hither, and not we," Yale President Timothy Dwight said in 1810.

> We inherit our ample patrimony with all its incumbrances; and are bound to pay the debts of our ancestors. *This* debt, particularly, we are bound to discharge: and, when the righteous Judge of the Universe comes to reckon with his servants, he will rigidly exact the payment at our hands. To give them liberty, and stop here, is to entail upon them a curse.

"The Ills That Slavery Frees Us From"

America begins in black plunder and white democracy, two features that are not contradictory but complementary. "The men who came together to found the independent United States, dedicated to freedom and equality, either held slaves or were willing to join hands with those who did," the historian Edmund S. Morgan wrote. "None of them felt entirely comfortable about the fact, but neither did they feel responsible for it. Most of them had inherited both their slaves and their attachment to freedom from an earlier generation, and they knew the two were not unconnected."

When enslaved Africans, plundered of their bodies, plundered of their families, and plundered of their labor, were brought to the colony of Virginia in 1619, they did not initially endure the naked racism that would engulf their progeny. Some of them were freed. Some of them intermarried. Still others escaped with the white indentured servants who had suffered as they had. Some even rebelled together, allying under Nathaniel Bacon to torch Jamestown in 1676.

One hundred years later, the idea of slaves and poor whites joining forces would shock the senses, but in the early days of the English colonies, the two groups had much in common. English visitors to Virginia found that its masters "abuse their servantes with intollerable oppression and hard usage." White servants were flogged, tricked into serving beyond their contracts, and traded in much the same manner as slaves.

This "hard usage" originated in a simple fact of the New World—land was boundless but cheap labor was limited. As life spans increased in the colony, the Virginia planters found in the enslaved Africans an even more efficient source of cheap labor. Whereas indentured servants were still legal subjects of the English crown and thus entitled to certain protections, African slaves entered the colonies as aliens. Exempted from the protections of the crown, they became early America's indispensable working class—fit for maximum exploitation, capable of only minimal resistance.

For the next 250 years, American law worked to reduce black people to a class of untouchables and raise all white men to the level of citizens. In 1650, Virginia mandated that "all persons except Negroes" were to carry arms. In 1664, Maryland mandated that any Englishwoman who married a slave must live as a slave of her husband's master. In 1705, the Virginia assembly passed a law allowing for the dismemberment of unruly slaves—but forbidding masters from whipping "a Christian white servant naked, without an order from a justice of the peace." In that same law, the colony mandated that "all horses, cattle, and hogs, now belonging, or that hereafter shall belong to any slave" be seized and sold off by the local church, the profits used to support "the poor of the said parish." At that time, there would have still been people alive who could remember blacks and whites joining to burn down Jamestown only 29 years before. But at the beginning of the 18th century, two primary classes were enshrined in America.

"The two great divisions of society are not the rich and poor, but white and black," John C. Calhoun, South Carolina's senior senator, declared on the Senate floor in 1848. "And all the former, the poor as well as the rich, belong to the upper class, and are respected and treated as equals."

In 1860, the majority of people living in South Carolina and Mississippi, almost half of those living in Georgia, and about one-third of all Southerners were on the wrong side of Calhoun's line. The state with the largest number of enslaved Americans was Virginia, where in certain counties some 70 percent of all people labored in chains. Nearly one-fourth of all white Southerners owned slaves, and upon their backs the economic basis of America—and much of the Atlantic world—was erected. In the seven cotton states, one-third of all white income was derived from slavery. By 1840, cotton produced by slave labor constituted 59 percent of the country's exports. The web of this slave society extended north to the looms of New England, and across the Atlantic to Great Britain, where it powered a great economic transformation and altered the trajectory of world history. "Whoever says Industrial Revolution," wrote the historian Eric J. Hobsbawm, "says cotton."

The wealth accorded America by slavery was not just in what the slaves pulled from the land but in the slaves themselves. "In 1860, slaves as an asset were worth more than all of America's manufacturing, all of the railroads, all of the productive capacity of the United States put together," the Yale historian David W. Blight has noted. "Slaves were the single largest, by far,

financial asset of property in the entire American economy." The sale of these slaves—"in whose bodies that money congealed," writes Walter Johnson, a Harvard historian—generated even more ancillary wealth. Loans were taken out for purchase, to be repaid with interest. Insurance policies were drafted against the untimely death of a slave and the loss of potential profits. Slave sales were taxed and notarized. The vending of the black body and the sundering of the black family became an economy unto themselves, estimated to have brought in tens of millions of dollars to antebellum America. In 1860 there were more millionaires per capita in the Mississippi Valley than anywhere else in the country.

Beneath the cold numbers lay lives divided. "I had a constant dread that Mrs. Moore, her mistress, would be in want of money and sell my dear wife," a freedman wrote, reflecting on his time in slavery. "We constantly dreaded a final separation. Our affection for each was very strong, and this made us always apprehensive of a cruel parting."

Forced partings were common in the antebellum South. A slave in some parts of the region stood a 30 percent chance of being sold in his or her lifetime. Twenty-five percent of interstate trades destroyed a first marriage and half of them destroyed a nuclear family.

When the wife and children of Henry Brown, a slave in Richmond, Virginia, were to be sold away, Brown searched for a white master who might buy his wife and children to keep the family together. He failed:

> The next day, I stationed myself by the side of the road, along which the slaves, amounting to three hundred and fifty, were to pass. The purchaser of my wife was a Methodist minister, who was about starting for North Carolina. Pretty soon five waggon-loads of little children passed, and looking at the foremost one, what should I see but a little child, pointing its tiny hand towards me, exclaiming, "There's my father; I knew he would come and bid me good-bye." It was my eldest child! Soon the gang approached in which my wife was chained. I looked, and beheld her familiar face; but O, reader, that glance of agony! may God spare me ever again enduring the excruciating horror of that moment! She passed, and came near to where I stood. I seized hold of her hand, intending to bid her farewell; but words failed me; the gift of utterance had fled, and I remained speechless. I followed her for some distance, with her hand grasped in mine, as if to save her from her fate, but I could not speak, and I was obliged to turn away in silence.

In a time when telecommunications were primitive and blacks lacked freedom of movement, the parting of black families was a kind of murder. Here we find the roots of American wealth and democracy—in the for-profit destruction of the most important asset available to any people, the family. The destruction was not incidental to America's rise; it facilitated that rise. By erecting a slave society, America created the economic foundation for its great experiment in democracy. The labor strife that seeded Bacon's rebellion was suppressed. America's indispensable working class existed as property beyond the realm of politics, leaving white Americans free to trumpet their love of freedom and democratic values. Assessing antebellum democracy in Virginia, a visitor from England observed that the state's natives "can profess an unbounded love of liberty and of democracy in consequence of the mass of the people, who in other countries might become mobs, being there nearly altogether composed of their own Negro slaves."

The Quiet Plunder

The consequences of 250 years of enslavement, of war upon black families and black people, were profound. Like home-ownership today, slave ownership was aspirational, attracting not just those who owned slaves but those who wished to. Much as homeowners today might discuss the addition of a patio or the painting of a living room, slaveholders traded tips on the best methods for breeding workers, exacting labor, and doling out punishment. Just as a homeowner today might subscribe to a magazine like *This Old House,* slaveholders had journals such as *De Bow's Review,* which recommended the best practices for wringing profits from slaves. By the dawn of the Civil War, the enslavement of black America was thought to be so foundational to the country that those who sought to end it were branded heretics worthy of death. Imagine what would happen if a president today came out in favor of taking all American homes from their owners: the reaction might well be violent.

"This country was formed for the *white,* not for the black man," John Wilkes Booth wrote, before killing Abraham Lincoln. "And looking upon *African slavery* from the same standpoint held by those noble framers of our Constitution, I for one have ever considered *it* one of the greatest blessings (both for themselves and us) that God ever bestowed upon a favored nation."

In the aftermath of the Civil War, Radical Republicans attempted to reconstruct the country upon something resembling universal equality—but they were beaten back by a campaign of "Redemption," led by White Liners, Red Shirts, and Klansmen bent on upholding a society "formed for the *white,* not for the black man." A wave of terrorism roiled the South. In his massive history *Reconstruction,* Eric Foner recounts incidents of black people being attacked for not removing their hats; for refusing to hand over a whiskey flask; for disobeying church procedures; for "using insolent language"; for disputing labor contracts; for refusing to be "tied like a slave." Sometimes the attacks were intended simply to "thin out the niggers a little."

Terrorism carried the day. Federal troops withdrew from the South in 1877. The dream of Reconstruction died. For the next century, political violence was visited upon blacks wantonly, with special treatment meted out toward black people of ambition. Black schools and churches were burned to the ground. Black voters and the political candidates who attempted to rally them were intimidated, and some were murdered. At the end of World War I, black veterans returning to their homes were assaulted for daring to wear the American uniform. The demobilization of soldiers after the war, which put white and black veterans into competition for scarce jobs, produced the Red Summer of 1919: a succession of racist pogroms against dozens of cities ranging from Longview, Texas, to Chicago to Washington, D.C. Organized white violence against blacks continued into the 1920s—in 1921 a white mob leveled Tulsa's "Black Wall Street," and in 1923 another one razed the black town of Rosewood, Florida—and virtually no one was punished.

The work of mobs was a rabid and violent rendition of prejudices that extended even into the upper reaches of American government. The New Deal is today remembered as a model for what progressive government should do—cast a broad social safety net that protects the poor and the afflicted while building the middle class. When progressives wish to express their disappointment with Barack Obama, they point to the accomplishments of Franklin Roosevelt. But these progressives rarely note that Roosevelt's New Deal, much like the democracy that produced it, rested on the foundation of Jim Crow.

"The Jim Crow South," writes Ira Katznelson, a history and political-science professor at Columbia, "was the one collaborator America's democracy could not do without." The marks of that collaboration are all over the New Deal. The omnibus programs passed under the Social Security Act in 1935 were crafted in such a way as to protect the southern way of life. Old-age insurance (Social Security proper) and unemployment insurance excluded farmworkers and domestics—jobs heavily occupied by blacks. When President Roosevelt signed Social Security into law in 1935, 65 percent of African Americans nationally and between 70 and 80 percent in the South were ineligible. The NAACP protested, calling the new American safety net "a sieve with holes just big enough for the majority of Negroes to fall through."

The oft-celebrated G.I. Bill similarly failed black Americans, by mirroring the broader country's insistence on a racist housing policy. Though ostensibly color-blind, Title III of the bill, which aimed to give veterans access to low-interest home loans, left black veterans to tangle with white officials at their local Veterans Administration as well as with the same banks that had, for years, refused to grant mortgages to blacks. The historian Kathleen J. Frydl observes in her 2009 book, *The GI Bill,* that so many blacks were disqualified from receiving Title III benefits "that it is more accurate simply to say that blacks could not use this particular title."

In Cold War America, homeownership was seen as a means of instilling patriotism, and as a civilizing and anti-radical force. "No man who owns his own house and lot can be a Communist," claimed William Levitt, who pioneered the modern suburb with the development of the various Levittowns, his famous planned communities. "He has too much to do."

But the Levittowns were, with Levitt's willing acquiescence, segregated throughout their early years. Daisy and Bill Myers, the first black family to move into Levittown, Pennsylvania, were greeted with protests and a burning cross. A neighbor who opposed the family said that Bill Myers was "probably a nice guy, but every time I look at him I see $2,000 drop off the value of my house."

The neighbor had good reason to be afraid. Bill and Daisy Myers were from the other side of John C. Calhoun's dual society. If they moved next door, housing policy almost guaranteed that their neighbors' property values would decline.

Whereas shortly before the New Deal, a typical mortgage required a large down payment and full repayment within about 10 years, the creation of the Home Owners' Loan Corporation in 1933 and then the Federal Housing Administration the following year allowed banks to offer loans requiring no more than 10 percent down, amortized over 20 to 30 years. "Without federal intervention in the housing market, massive suburbanization would have been impossible," writes Thomas J. Sugrue, a historian at the University of Pennsylvania. "In 1930, only 30 percent of Americans owned their own homes; by 1960, more than 60 percent were home owners. Home ownership became an emblem of American citizenship."

That emblem was not to be awarded to blacks. The American real-estate industry believed segregation to be a moral principle. As late as 1950, the National Association of Real Estate Boards' code of ethics warned that "a Realtor should never be instrumental in introducing into a neighborhood . . . any race or nationality, or any individuals whose presence will clearly be detrimental to property values." A 1943 brochure specified that such potential undesirables might include madams, bootleggers, gangsters—and "a colored man of means who was giving his children a college education and thought they were entitled to live among whites."

The federal government concurred. It was the Home Owners' Loan Corporation, not a private trade association, that pioneered the practice of redlining, selectively granting loans and insisting that any property it insured be covered by a restrictive covenant—a clause in the deed forbidding the sale

of the property to anyone other than whites. Millions of dollars flowed from tax coffers into segregated white neighborhoods.

"For perhaps the first time, the federal government embraced the discriminatory attitudes of the marketplace," the historian Kenneth T. Jackson wrote in his 1985 book, *Crabgrass Frontier,* a history of suburbanization. "Previously, prejudices were personalized and individualized; FHA exhorted segregation and enshrined it as public policy. Whole areas of cities were declared ineligible for loan guarantees." Redlining was not officially outlawed until 1968, by the Fair Housing Act. By then the damage was done—and reports of redlining by banks have continued.

The federal government is premised on equal fealty from all its citizens, who in return are to receive equal treatment. But as late as the mid-20th century, this bargain was not granted to black people, who repeatedly paid a higher price for citizenship and received less in return. Plunder had been the essential feature of slavery, of the society described by Calhoun. But practically a full century after the end of the Civil War and the abolition of slavery, the plunder—quiet, systemic, submerged—continued even amidst the aims and achievements of New Deal liberals.

Making the Second Ghetto

Today Chicago is one of the most segregated cities in the country, a fact that reflects assiduous planning. In the effort to uphold white supremacy at every level down to the neighborhood, Chicago—a city founded by the black fur trader Jean Baptiste Point du Sable—has long been a pioneer. The efforts began in earnest in 1917, when the Chicago Real Estate Board, horrified by the influx of southern blacks, lobbied to zone the entire city by race. But after the Supreme Court ruled against explicit racial zoning that year, the city was forced to pursue its agenda by more discreet means.

Like the Home Owners' Loan Corporation, the Federal Housing Administration initially insisted on restrictive covenants, which helped bar blacks and other ethnic undesirables from receiving federally backed home loans. By the 1940s, Chicago led the nation in the use of these restrictive covenants, and about half of all residential neighborhoods in the city were effectively off-limits to blacks.

It is common today to become misty-eyed about the old black ghetto, where doctors and lawyers lived next door to meatpackers and steelworkers, who themselves lived next door to prostitutes and the unemployed. This segregationist nostalgia ignores the actual conditions endured by the people living there—vermin and arson, for instance—and ignores the fact that the old ghetto was premised on denying black people privileges enjoyed by white Americans.

In 1948, when the Supreme Court ruled that restrictive covenants, while permissible, were not enforceable by judicial action, Chicago had other weapons at the ready. The Illinois state legislature had already given Chicago's city council the right to approve—and thus to veto—any public housing in the city's wards. This came in handy in 1949, when a new federal housing act sent millions of tax dollars into Chicago and other cities around the country. Beginning in 1950, site selection for public housing proceeded entirely on the grounds of segregation. By the 1960s, the city had created with its vast housing projects what the historian Arnold R. Hirsch calls a "second ghetto," one larger than the old Black Belt but just as impermeable. More than 98 percent of all the family public-housing units built in Chicago between 1950 and the mid 1960s were built in all-black neighborhoods.

Governmental embrace of segregation was driven by the virulent racism of Chicago's white citizens. White neighborhoods vulnerable to black encroachment formed block associations for the sole purpose of enforcing segregation. They lobbied fellow whites not to sell. They lobbied those blacks who did manage to buy to sell back. In 1949, a group of Englewood Catholics formed block associations intended to "keep up the neighborhood." Translation: keep black people out. And when civic engagement was not enough, when government failed, when private banks could no longer hold the line, Chicago turned to an old tool in the American repertoire—racial violence. "The pattern of terrorism is easily discernible," concluded a Chicago civic group in the 1940s. "It is at the seams of the black ghetto in all directions." On July 1 and 2 of 1946, a mob of thousands assembled in Chicago's Park Manor neighborhood, hoping to eject a black doctor who'd recently moved in. The mob pelted the house with rocks and set the garage on fire. The doctor moved away.

In 1947, after a few black veterans moved into the Fernwood section of Chicago, three nights of rioting broke out; gangs of whites yanked blacks off streetcars and beat them. Two years later, when a union meeting attended by blacks in Englewood triggered rumors that a home was being "sold to niggers," blacks (and whites thought to be sympathetic to them) were beaten in the streets. In 1951, thousands of whites in Cicero, 20 minutes or so west of downtown Chicago, attacked an apartment building that housed a single black family, throwing bricks and firebombs through the windows and setting the apartment on fire. A Cook County grand jury declined to charge the rioters—and instead indicted the family's NAACP attorney, the apartment's white owner, and the owner's attorney and rental agent, charging them with conspiring to lower property values. Two years after that, whites picketed and planted explosives in South Deering, about 30 minutes from downtown Chicago, to force blacks out.

When terrorism ultimately failed, white homeowners simply fled the neighborhood. The traditional terminology, *white flight,* implies a kind of natural expression of preference. In fact, white flight was a triumph of social engineering, orchestrated by the shared racist presumptions of America's public and private sectors. For should any nonracist white families decide that integration might not be so bad as a matter of principle or practicality, they still had to contend with the hard facts of American housing policy: When the mid-20th-century white homeowner claimed that the presence of a Bill and Daisy Myers decreased his property value, he was not merely engaging in racist dogma—he was accurately observing the impact of federal policy on market prices. Redlining destroyed the possibility of investment wherever black people lived.

"A Lot of People Fell by the Way"

Speculators in North Lawndale, and at the edge of the black ghettos, knew there was money to be made off white panic. They resorted to "block-busting"—spooking whites into selling cheap before the neighborhood became black. They would hire a black woman to walk up and down the street with a stroller. Or they'd hire someone to call a number in the neighborhood looking for "Johnny Mae." Then they'd cajole whites into selling at low prices, informing them that the more blacks who moved in, the more the value of their homes would decline, so better to sell now. With these white-fled homes in hand, speculators then turned to the masses of black people who had streamed northward as part of the Great Migration, or who were desperate to escape the ghettos: the speculators would take the houses they'd just bought cheap through block-busting and sell them to blacks on contract.

To keep up with his payments and keep his heat on, Clyde Ross took a second job at the post office and then a third job delivering pizza. His wife took a job working at Marshall Field. He had to take some of his children out of private school. He was not able to be at home to supervise his children or help them with their homework. Money and time that Ross wanted to give his children went instead to enrich white speculators.

"The problem was the money," Ross told me. "Without the money, you can't move. You can't educate your kids. You can't give them the right kind of food. Can't make the house look good. They think this neighborhood is where they supposed to be. It changes their outlook. My kids were going to the best schools in this neighborhood, and I couldn't keep them in there."

Mattie Lewis came to Chicago from her native Alabama in the mid-'40s, when she was 21, persuaded by a friend who told her she could get a job as a hairdresser. Instead she was hired by Western Electric, where she worked for 41 years. I met Lewis in the home of her neighbor Ethel Weatherspoon. Both had owned homes in North Lawndale for more than 50 years. Both had bought their houses on contract. Both had been active with Clyde Ross in the Contract Buyers League's effort to garner restitution from contract sellers who'd operated in North Lawndale, banks who'd backed the scheme, and even the Federal Housing Administration. We were joined by Jack Macnamara, who'd been an organizing force in the Contract Buyers League when it was founded, in 1968. Our gathering had the feel of a reunion, because the writer James Alan McPherson had profiled the Contract Buyers League for *The Atlantic* back in 1972.

Weatherspoon bought her home in 1957. "Most of the whites started moving out," she told me. "'The blacks are coming. The blacks are coming.' They actually said that. They had signs up: DON'T SELL TO BLACKS."

Before moving to North Lawndale, Lewis and her husband tried moving to Cicero after seeing a house advertised for sale there. "Sorry, I just sold it today," the Realtor told Lewis's husband. "I told him, 'You know they don't want you in Cicero,'" Lewis recalls. "'They ain't going to let nobody black in Cicero.'"

In 1958, the couple bought a home in North Lawndale on contract. They were not blind to the unfairness. But Lewis, born in the teeth of Jim Crow, considered American piracy—black people keep on making it, white people keep on taking it—a fact of nature. "All I wanted was a house. And that was the only way I could get it. They weren't giving black people loans at that time," she said. "We thought, 'This is the way it is. We going to do it till we die, and they ain't never going to accept us. That's just the way it is.'

"The only way you were going to buy a home was to do it the way they wanted," she continued. "And I was determined to get me a house. If everybody else can have one, I want one too. I had worked for white people in the South. And I saw how these white people were living in the North and I thought, 'One day I'm going to live just like them.' I wanted cabinets and all these things these other people have."

Whenever she visited white co-workers at their homes, she saw the difference. "I could see we were just getting ripped off," she said. "I would see things and I would say, 'I'd like to do this at my house.' And they would say, 'Do it,' but I would think, 'I can't, because it costs us so much more.'"

I asked Lewis and Weatherspoon how they kept up on payments.

"You paid it and kept working," Lewis said of the contract. "When that payment came up, you knew you had to pay it."

"You cut down on the light bill. Cut down on your food bill," Weatherspoon interjected.

"You cut down on things for your child, that was the main thing," said Lewis. "My oldest wanted to be an artist and my other wanted to be a dancer and my other wanted to take music."

Lewis and Weatherspoon, like Ross, were able to keep their homes. The suit did not win them any remuneration. But it forced contract sellers to the table, where they allowed some members of the Contract Buyers League to move into regular

mortgages or simply take over their houses outright. By then they'd been bilked for thousands. In talking with Lewis and Weatherspoon, I was seeing only part of the picture—the tiny minority who'd managed to hold on to their homes. But for all our exceptional ones, for every Barack and Michelle Obama, for every Ethel Weatherspoon or Clyde Ross, for every black survivor, there are so many thousands gone.

"A lot of people fell by the way," Lewis told me. "One woman asked me if I would keep all her china. She said, 'They ain't going to set you out.'"

"Negro Poverty Is Not White Poverty"

On a recent spring afternoon in North Lawndale, I visited Billy Lamar Brooks Sr. Brooks has been an activist since his youth in the Black Panther Party, when he aided the Contract Buyers League. I met him in his office at the Better Boys Foundation, a staple of North Lawndale whose mission is to direct local kids off the streets and into jobs and college. Brooks's work is personal. On June 14, 1991, his 19-year-old son, Billy Jr., was shot and killed. "These guys tried to stick him up," Brooks told me. "I suspect he could have been involved in some things . . . He's always on my mind. Every day."

Brooks was not raised in the streets, though in such a neighborhood it is impossible to avoid the influence. "I was in church three or four times a week. That's where the girls were," he said, laughing. "The stark reality is still there. There's no shield from life. You got to go to school. I lived here. I went to Marshall High School. Over here were the Egyptian Cobras. Over there were the Vice Lords."

Brooks has since moved away from Chicago's West Side. But he is still working in North Lawndale. If "you got a nice house, you live in a nice neighborhood, then you are less prone to violence, because your space is not deprived," Brooks said. "You got a security point. You don't need no protection." But if "you grow up in a place like this, housing sucks. When they tore down the projects here, they left the high-rises and came to the neighborhood with that gang mentality. You don't have nothing, so you going to take something, even if it's not real. You don't have no street, but in your mind it's yours."

We walked over to a window behind his desk. A group of young black men were hanging out in front of a giant mural memorializing two black men: IN LOVIN MEMORY QUENTIN AKA "Q," JULY 18, 1974 MARCH 2, 2012. The name and face of the other man had been spray-painted over by a rival group. The men drank beer. Occasionally a car would cruise past, slow to a crawl, then stop. One of the men would approach the car and make an exchange, then the car would drive off. Brooks had known all of these young men as boys.

"That's their corner," he said.

We watched another car roll through, pause briefly, then drive off. "No respect, no shame," Brooks said. "That's what they do. From that alley to that corner. They don't go no farther than that. See the big brother there? He almost died a couple of years ago. The one drinking the beer back there . . . I know all of them. And the reason they feel safe here is cause of this building, and because they too chickenshit to go anywhere. But that's their mentality. That's their block."

Brooks showed me a picture of a Little League team he had coached. He went down the row of kids, pointing out which ones were in jail, which ones were dead, and which ones were doing all right. And then he pointed out his son—"That's my boy, Billy," Brooks said. Then he wondered aloud if keeping his son with him while working in North Lawndale had hastened his death. "It's a definite connection, because he was part of what I did here. And I think maybe I shouldn't have exposed him. But then, I had to," he said, "because I wanted him with me."

From the White House on down, the myth holds that fatherhood is the great antidote to all that ails black people. But Billy Brooks Jr. had a father. Trayvon Martin had a father. Jordan Davis had a father. Adhering to middle-class norms has never shielded black people from plunder. Adhering to middle-class norms is what made Ethel Weatherspoon a lucrative target for rapacious speculators. Contract sellers did not target the very poor. They targeted black people who had worked hard enough to save a down payment and dreamed of the emblem of American citizenship—homeownership. It was not a tangle of pathology that put a target on Clyde Ross's back. It was not a culture of poverty that singled out Mattie Lewis for "the thrill of the chase and the kill." Some black people always will be twice as good. But they generally find white predation to be thrice as fast.

Liberals today mostly view racism not as an active, distinct evil but as a relative of white poverty and inequality. They ignore the long tradition of this country actively punishing black success—and the elevation of that punishment, in the mid-20th century, to federal policy. President Lyndon Johnson may have noted in his historic civil-rights speech at Howard University in 1965 that "Negro poverty is not white poverty." But his advisers and their successors were, and still are, loath to craft any policy that recognizes the difference.

After his speech, Johnson convened a group of civil-rights leaders, including the esteemed A. Philip Randolph and Bayard Rustin, to address the "ancient brutality." In a strategy paper, they agreed with the president that "Negro poverty is a special, and particularly destructive, form of American poverty." But when it came to specifically addressing the "particularly destructive," Rustin's group demurred, preferring to advance programs that addressed "all the poor, black and white."

The urge to use the moral force of the black struggle to address broader inequalities originates in both compassion and pragmatism. But it makes for ambiguous policy. Affirmative action's precise aims, for instance, have always proved elusive. Is it meant to make amends for the crimes heaped upon black people? Not according to the Supreme Court. In its 1978 ruling in *Regents of the University of California v. Bakke*, the Court rejected "societal discrimination" as "an amorphous concept of injury that may be ageless in its reach into the past." Is affirmative action meant to increase "diversity"? If so, it only tangentially relates to the specific problems of black people—the problem of what America has taken from them over several centuries.

This confusion about affirmative action's aims, along with our inability to face up to the particular history of white-imposed black disadvantage, dates back to the policy's origins. "There is no fixed and firm definition of affirmative action," an appointee in Johnson's Department of Labor declared. "Affirmative action is anything that you have to do to get results. But this does not necessarily include preferential treatment."

Yet America was built on the preferential treatment of white people—395 years of it. Vaguely endorsing a cuddly, feel-good diversity does very little to redress this.

Today, progressives are loath to invoke white supremacy as an explanation for anything. On a practical level, the hesitation comes from the dim view the Supreme Court has taken of the reforms of the 1960s. The Voting Rights Act has been gutted. The Fair Housing Act might well be next. Affirmative action is on its last legs. In substituting a broad class struggle for an anti-racist struggle, progressives hope to assemble a coalition by changing the subject.

The politics of racial evasion are seductive. But the record is mixed. Aid to Families With Dependent Children was originally written largely to exclude blacks—yet by the 1990s it was perceived as a giveaway to blacks. The Affordable Care Act makes no mention of race, but this did not keep Rush Limbaugh from denouncing it as reparations. Moreover, the act's expansion of Medicaid was effectively made optional, meaning that many poor blacks in the former Confederate states do not benefit from it. The Affordable Care Act, like Social Security, will eventually expand its reach to those left out; in the meantime, black people will be injured.

"All that it would take to sink a new WPA program would be some skillfully packaged footage of black men leaning on shovels smoking cigarettes," the sociologist Douglas S. Massey writes. "Papering over the issue of race makes for bad social theory, bad research, and bad public policy." To ignore the fact that one of the oldest republics in the world was erected on a foundation of white supremacy, to pretend that the problems of a dual society are the same as the problems of unregulated capitalism, is to cover the sin of national plunder with the sin of national lying. The lie ignores the fact that reducing American poverty and ending white supremacy are not the same. The lie ignores the fact that closing the "achievement gap" will do nothing to close the "injury gap," in which black college graduates still suffer higher unemployment rates than white college graduates, and black job applicants without criminal records enjoy roughly the same chance of getting hired as white applicants *with* criminal records.

Chicago, like the country at large, embraced policies that placed black America's most energetic, ambitious, and thrifty countrymen beyond the pale of society and marked them as rightful targets for legal theft. The effects reverberate beyond the families who were robbed to the community that beholds the spectacle. Don't just picture Clyde Ross working three jobs so he could hold on to his home. Think of his North Lawndale neighbors—their children, their nephews and nieces—and consider how watching this affects them. Imagine yourself as a young black child watching your elders play by all the rules only to have their possessions tossed out in the street and to have their most sacred possession—their home—taken from them.

The message the young black boy receives from his country, Billy Brooks says, is " 'You ain't shit. You not no good. The only thing you are worth is working for us. You will never own anything. You not going to get an education. We are sending your ass to the penitentiary.' They're telling you no matter how hard you struggle, no matter what you put down, you ain't shit. 'We're going to take what you got. You will never own anything, nigger.' "

Toward a New Country

When Clyde Ross was a child, his older brother Winter had a seizure. He was picked up by the authorities and delivered to Parchman Farm, a 20,000-acre state prison in the Mississippi Delta region.

"He was a gentle person," Clyde Ross says of his brother. "You know, he was good to everybody. And he started having spells, and he couldn't control himself. And they had him picked up, because they thought he was dangerous."

Built at the turn of the century, Parchman was supposed to be a progressive and reformist response to the problem of "Negro crime." In fact it was the gulag of Mississippi, an object of terror to African Americans in the Delta. In the early years of the 20th century, Mississippi Governor James K. Vardaman used to amuse himself by releasing black convicts into the surrounding wilderness and hunting them down with bloodhounds. "Throughout the American South," writes David M. Oshinsky in his book *Worse Than Slavery*, "Parchman Farm is synonymous with punishment and brutality, as well it should

be . . . Parchman is the quintessential penal farm, the closest thing to slavery that survived the Civil War."

When the Ross family went to retrieve Winter, the authorities told them that Winter had died. When the Ross family asked for his body, the authorities at Parchman said they had buried him. The family never saw Winter's body.

And this was just one of their losses.

Scholars have long discussed methods by which America might make reparations to those on whose labor and exclusion the country was built. In the 1970s, the Yale Law professor Boris Bittker argued in *The Case for Black Reparations* that a rough price tag for reparations could be determined by multiplying the number of African Americans in the population by the difference in white and black per capita income. That number—$34 billion in 1973, when Bittker wrote his book—could be added to a reparations program each year for a decade or two. Today Charles Ogletree, the Harvard Law School professor, argues for something broader: a program of job training and public works that takes racial justice as its mission but includes the poor of all races.

To celebrate freedom and democracy while forgetting America's origins in a slavery economy is patriotism à la carte.

Perhaps no statistic better illustrates the enduring legacy of our country's shameful history of treating black people as sub-citizens, sub-Americans, and sub-humans than the wealth gap. Reparations would seek to close this chasm. But as surely as the creation of the wealth gap required the cooperation of every aspect of the society, bridging it will require the same.

Perhaps after a serious discussion and debate—the kind that HR 40 proposes—we may find that the country can never fully repay African Americans. But we stand to discover much about ourselves in such a discussion—and that is perhaps what scares us. The idea of reparations is frightening not simply because we might lack the ability to pay. The idea of reparations threatens something much deeper—America's heritage, history, and standing in the world.

The early American economy was built on slave labor. The Capitol and the White House were built by slaves. President James K. Polk traded slaves from the Oval Office. The laments about "black pathology," the criticism of black family structures by pundits and intellectuals, ring hollow in a country whose existence was predicated on the torture of black fathers, on the rape of black mothers, on the sale of black children. An honest assessment of America's relationship to the black family reveals the country to be not its nurturer but its destroyer.

And this destruction did not end with slavery. Discriminatory laws joined the equal burden of citizenship to unequal distribution of its bounty. These laws reached their apex in the mid-20th century, when the federal government—through housing policies—engineered the wealth gap, which remains with us to this day. When we think of white supremacy, we picture Colored Only signs, but we should picture pirate flags.

On some level, we have always grasped this.

"Negro poverty is not white poverty," President Johnson said in his historic civil-rights speech.

> Many of its causes and many of its cures are the same. But there are differences—deep, corrosive, obstinate differences—radiating painful roots into the community and into the family, and the nature of the individual. These differences are not racial differences. They are solely and simply the consequence of ancient brutality, past injustice, and present prejudice.

We invoke the words of Jefferson and Lincoln because they say something about our legacy and our traditions. We do this because we recognize our links to the past—at least when they flatter us. But black history does not flatter American democracy; it chastens it. The popular mocking of reparations as a harebrained scheme authored by wild-eyed lefties and intellectually unserious black nationalists is fear masquerading as laughter. Black nationalists have always perceived something unmentionable about America that integrationists dare not acknowledge—that white supremacy is not merely the work of hotheaded demagogues, or a matter of false consciousness, but a force so fundamental to America that it is difficult to imagine the country without it.

And so we must imagine a new country. Reparations—by which I mean the full acceptance of our collective biography and its consequences—is the price we must pay to see ourselves squarely. The recovering alcoholic may well have to live with his illness for the rest of his life. But at least he is not living a drunken lie. Reparations beckons us to reject the intoxication of hubris and see America as it is—the work of fallible humans.

Won't reparations divide us? Not any more than we are already divided. The wealth gap merely puts a number on something we feel but cannot say—that American prosperity was ill-gotten and selective in its distribution. What is needed is an airing of family secrets, a settling with old ghosts. What is needed is a healing of the American psyche and the banishment of white guilt.

What I'm talking about is more than recompense for past injustices—more than a handout, a payoff, hush money, or a reluctant bribe. What I'm talking about is a national reckoning that would lead to spiritual renewal. Reparations would mean the end of scarfing hot dogs on the Fourth of July while denying the facts of our heritage. Reparations would mean the end of yelling "patriotism" while waving a Confederate flag. Reparations would mean a revolution of the American consciousness, a reconciling of our self-image as the great democratizer with the facts of our history.

"There Will Be No 'Reparations' from Germany"

We are not the first to be summoned to such a challenge.

In 1952, when West Germany began the process of making amends for the Holocaust, it did so under conditions that should be instructive to us. Resistance was violent. Very few Germans believed that Jews were entitled to anything. Only 5 percent of West Germans surveyed reported feeling guilty about the Holocaust, and only 29 percent believed that Jews were owed restitution from the German people.

"The rest," the historian Tony Judt wrote in his 2005 book, *Postwar,* "were divided between those (some two-fifths of respondents) who thought that only people 'who really committed something' were responsible and should pay, and those (21 percent) who thought 'that the Jews themselves were partly responsible for what happened to them during the Third Reich.'"

Germany's unwillingness to squarely face its history went beyond polls. Movies that suggested a societal responsibility for the Holocaust beyond Hitler were banned. "The German soldier fought bravely and honorably for his homeland," claimed President Eisenhower, endorsing the Teutonic national myth. Judt wrote, "Throughout the fifties West German officialdom encouraged a comfortable view of the German past in which the Wehrmacht was heroic, while Nazis were in a minority and properly punished."

Konrad Adenauer, the postwar German chancellor, was in favor of reparations, but his own party was divided, and he was able to get an agreement passed only with the votes of the Social Democratic opposition.

Among the Jews of Israel, reparations provoked violent and venomous reactions ranging from denunciation to assassination plots. On January 7, 1952, as the Knesset—the Israeli parliament—convened to discuss the prospect of a reparations agreement with West Germany, Menachem Begin, the future prime minister of Israel, stood in front of a large crowd, inveighing against the country that had plundered the lives, labor, and property of his people. Begin claimed that all Germans were Nazis and guilty of murder. His condemnations then spread to his own young state. He urged the crowd to stop paying taxes and claimed that the nascent Israeli nation characterized the fight over whether or not to accept reparations as a "war to the death." When alerted that the police watching the gathering were carrying tear gas, allegedly of German manufacture, Begin yelled, "The same gases that asphyxiated our parents!"

Begin then led the crowd in an oath to never forget the victims of the Shoah, lest "my right hand lose its cunning" and "my tongue cleave to the roof of my mouth." He took the crowd through the streets toward the Knesset. From the rooftops, police repelled the crowd with tear gas and smoke bombs. But the wind shifted, and the gas blew back toward the Knesset, billowing through windows shattered by rocks. In the chaos, Begin and Prime Minister David Ben-Gurion exchanged insults. Two hundred civilians and 140 police officers were wounded. Nearly 400 people were arrested. Knesset business was halted.

Begin then addressed the chamber with a fiery speech condemning the actions the legislature was about to take. "Today you arrested hundreds," he said. "Tomorrow you may arrest thousands. No matter, they will go, they will sit in prison. We will sit there with them. If necessary, we will be killed with them. But there will be no 'reparations' from Germany."

Survivors of the Holocaust feared laundering the reputation of Germany with money, and mortgaging the memory of their dead. Beyond that, there was a taste for revenge. "My soul would be at rest if I knew there would be 6 million German dead to match the 6 million Jews," said Meir Dworzecki, who'd survived the concentration camps of Estonia.

Ben-Gurion countered this sentiment, not by repudiating vengeance but with cold calculation: "If I could take German property without sitting down with them for even a minute but go in with jeeps and machine guns to the warehouses and take it, I would do that—if, for instance, we had the ability to send a hundred divisions and tell them, 'Take it.' But we can't do that."

The reparations conversation set off a wave of bomb attempts by Israeli militants. One was aimed at the foreign ministry in Tel Aviv. Another was aimed at Chancellor Adenauer himself. And one was aimed at the port of Haifa, where the goods bought with reparations money were arriving. West Germany ultimately agreed to pay Israel 3.45 billion deutsche marks, or more than $7 billion in today's dollars. Individual reparations claims followed—for psychological trauma, for offense to Jewish honor, for halting law careers, for life insurance, for time spent in concentration camps. Seventeen percent of funds went toward purchasing ships. "By the end of 1961, these reparations vessels constituted two-thirds of the Israeli merchant fleet," writes the Israeli historian Tom Segev in his book *The Seventh Million*. "From 1953 to 1963, the reparations money funded about a third of the total investment in Israel's electrical system, which tripled its capacity, and nearly half the total investment in the railways."

Israel's GNP tripled during the 12 years of the agreement. The Bank of Israel attributed 15 percent of this growth, along with 45,000 jobs, to investments made with reparations money. But Segev argues that the impact went far beyond that. Reparations "had indisputable psychological and political importance," he writes.

Reparations could not make up for the murder perpetrated by the Nazis. But they did launch Germany's reckoning with itself, and perhaps provided a road map for how a great civilization might make itself worthy of the name.

Assessing the reparations agreement, David Ben-Gurion said:

> For the first time in the history of relations between people, a precedent has been created by which a great State, as a result of moral pressure alone, takes it upon itself to pay compensation to the victims of the government that preceded it. For the first time in the history of a people that has been persecuted, oppressed, plundered and despoiled for hundreds of years in the countries of Europe, a persecutor and despoiler has been obliged to return part of his spoils and has even undertaken to make collective reparation as partial compensation for material losses.

Something more than moral pressure calls America to reparations. We cannot escape our history. All of our solutions to the great problems of health care, education, housing, and economic inequality are troubled by what must go unspoken. "The reason black people are so far behind now is not because of now," Clyde Ross told me. "It's because of then." In the early 2000s, Charles Ogletree went to Tulsa, Oklahoma, to meet with the survivors of the 1921 race riot that had devastated "Black Wall Street." The past was not the past to them. "It was amazing seeing these black women and men who were crippled, blind, in wheelchairs," Ogletree told me. "I had no idea who they were and why they wanted to see me. They said, 'We want you to represent us in this lawsuit.'"

A commission authorized by the Oklahoma legislature produced a report affirming that the riot, the knowledge of which had been suppressed for years, had happened. But the lawsuit ultimately failed, in 2004. Similar suits pushed against corporations such as Aetna (which insured slaves) and Lehman Brothers (whose co-founding partner owned them) also have thus far failed. These results are dispiriting, but the crime with which reparations activists charge the country implicates more than just a few towns or corporations. The crime indicts the American people themselves, at every level, and in nearly every configuration. A crime that implicates the entire American people deserves its hearing in the legislative body that represents them.

John Conyers's HR 40 is the vehicle for that hearing. No one can know what would come out of such a debate. Perhaps no number can fully capture the multi-century plunder of black people in America. Perhaps the number is so large that it can't be imagined, let alone calculated and dispensed. But I believe that wrestling publicly with these questions matters as much as—if not more than—the specific answers that might be produced. An America that asks what it owes its most vulnerable citizens is improved and humane. An America that looks away is ignoring not just the sins of the past but the sins of the present and the certain sins of the future. More important than any single check cut to any African American, the payment of reparations would represent America's maturation out of the childhood myth of its innocence into a wisdom worthy of its founders.

In 2010, Jacob S. Rugh, then a doctoral candidate at Princeton, and the sociologist Douglas S. Massey published a study of the recent foreclosure crisis. Among its drivers, they found an old foe: segregation. Black home buyers—even after controlling for factors like creditworthiness—were still more likely than white home buyers to be steered toward subprime loans. Decades of racist housing policies by the American government, along with decades of racist housing practices by American businesses, had conspired to concentrate African Americans in the same neighborhoods. As in North Lawndale half a century earlier, these neighborhoods were filled with people who had been cut off from mainstream financial institutions. When subprime lenders went looking for prey, they found black people waiting like ducks in a pen.

"High levels of segregation create a natural market for subprime lending," Rugh and Massey write, "and cause riskier mortgages, and thus foreclosures, to accumulate disproportionately in racially segregated cities' minority neighborhoods."

Plunder in the past made plunder in the present efficient. The banks of America understood this. In 2005, Wells Fargo promoted a series of Wealth Building Strategies seminars. Dubbing itself "the nation's leading originator of home loans to ethnic minority customers," the bank enrolled black public figures in an ostensible effort to educate blacks on building "generational wealth." But the "wealth building" seminars were a front for wealth theft. In 2010, the Justice Department filed a discrimination suit against Wells Fargo alleging that the bank had shunted blacks into predatory loans regardless of their creditworthiness. This was not magic or coincidence or misfortune. It was racism reifying itself. According to *The New York Times,* affidavits found loan officers referring to their black customers as "mud people" and to their subprime products as "ghetto loans."

"We just went right after them," Beth Jacobson, a former Wells Fargo loan officer, told *The Times.* "Wells Fargo mortgage had an emerging-markets unit that specifically targeted black churches because it figured church leaders had a lot of influence and could convince congregants to take out subprime loans."

In 2011, Bank of America agreed to pay $355 million to settle charges of discrimination against its Countrywide unit. The following year, Wells Fargo settled its discrimination suit for more than $175 million. But the damage had been done. In 2009, half the properties in Baltimore whose owners had been granted loans by Wells Fargo between 2005 and 2008 were vacant; 71 percent of these properties were in predominantly black neighborhoods.

Critical Thinking

1. What is genocide?
2. Discuss the parallels that are made to reparations payments to Japanese Americans.
3. Have reparations for broken treaties and misallocated or unpaid mineral royalties claims to Native American nations been settled?

Internet References

National Association for the Advancement of Colored People (NAACP)
  www.naacp.org
National Urban League
  www.nul.org

Article   Prepared by: John A. Kromkowski, *Catholic University of America*

Poverty Rates for Selected Detailed Race and Hispanic Groups by State and Place: 2007–2011

Suzanne Macartney, Alemayehu Bishaw, and Kayla Fontenot

Learning Outcomes

After reading this article, you will be able to:

- Identify the five concentrations of poverty.

- Determine whether the measurement of poverty reveals race and ethnic or place-specific causes and/or correlations.

Introduction

Poverty rates are important indicators of community well-being and are used by government agencies and organizations to allocate need-based resources. The American Community Survey (ACS) 5-year data allow for the analysis of poverty rates by race arid Hispanic origin for many levels of geography.

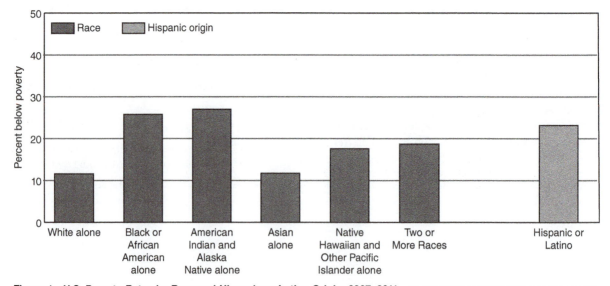

Figure 1   U.S. Poverty Rates by Race and Hispanic or Latino Origin: 2007–2011   (For information on confidentiality protection, sampling error, nonsampling error, and definitions, see *www.census.gov/acs/www/*)

Note: Persons who report only one race among the six defined categories are referred to as the race-alone population, while persons who report more than one race category are referred to as the Two or More Races population. This figure shows data using the race-alone approach. Use of the single-race population does not imply that it is the preferred method of presenting or analyzing data. The Census Bureau uses a variety of approaches. Because Hispanics may be of any race, data in this figure for Hispanics overlap with data for race groups.

Source: U.S. Census Bureau, 2007–2011 American Community Survey.

In this report, poverty rates are summarized by race and Hispanic origin for the United States, each state, and the District of Columbia.

Poverty rates are also presented for selected retailed race and origin groups in the cities and towns with the largest populations of these groups. For the nation and selected places, poverty rates are summarized for detailed Asian groups with populations of 750,000 or more, detailed Native Hawaiian and Other Pacific Islander groups with populations of 25,000 or more, and detailed Hispanic groups with populations of 1 million or more.

Highlights

- According to the 2007–2011 ACS, 42.7 million people or 14.3 percent of the U.S. population had income below the poverty level.
- By race, the highest national poverty rates were for American Indians and Alaska Natives (27.0 percent) and Blacks or African Americans (25.8 percent).
- Native Hawaiians and Other Pacific Islanders had a national poverty rate of 17.6 percent.
- For the Asian population, poverty rates were higher for Vietnamese (14.7 percent) and Koreans (15.0 percent), and lower for Filipinos (5.8 percent).[1]
- Among Hispanics, national poverty rates ranged from a low of 16.2 percent for Cubans to a high of 26.3 percent for Dominicans.
- Nine states had poverty rates of about 30 percent or more for American Indians and Alaska Natives (Arizona, Maine, Minnesota, Montana, Nebraska, New Mexico, North Dakota, South Dakota, and Utah).
- For Asians, nine states had poverty rates of about 10 percent or less (Connecticut, Delaware, Hawaii, Maryland, Nevada, New Hampshire, New Jersey, Virginia, and South Carolina).
- The 2007–2011 national poverty rate for Whites was 11.6 percent, and most states (43) as well as the District of Columbia had poverty rates lower than 14.0 percent for this group.

Understanding Race and Hispanic Origin Concepts

Individuals who responded to the question on race by indicating only one race are referred to as the race-alone population or the group who reported only one race category. The text and figures of this report show estimates for the race-alone population. Six categories make up this population: White alone, Black or African American alone, American Indian and Alaska Native alone, Asian alone, Native Hawaiian and Other Pacific Islander alone, and Some Other Race alone. Individuals who chose more than one of the six race categories are referred to as the Two or More Races population. All respondents who indicated more than one race can be collapsed into the Two or More Races category which, combined with the six race-alone categories, yields seven mutually exclusive and exhaustive categories. Thus, the six race-alone categories and the Two or More Races category sum to the total population.

Hispanics may be of any race. For each race group, data in this report include people who reported they were of Hispanic origin and people who reported they were not Hispanic. Because Hispanics may be of any race, data in this report for Hispanics overlap with data for race groups. For more information on the concepts of race and Hispanic origin, see Humes, K., N. Jones, and R. Ramirez, "Overview of Race and Hispanic Origin: 2010," U.S. Census Bureau, 2010 Census Briefs, 2011, available at www.census.gov/prod/cen2010/briefs/c2010br-02.pdf.

See Census Briefs and Reports, 2010 Census, at www.census.gov/2010census/ discussed in this for more information on the race and origin groups report.

The estimates contained in this report are based on the 2007-2011 ACS. The ACS is conducted every month with income data collected for the 12 months preceding the interview. The 5-year estimates are period estimates. They represent the characteristics of the population and housing over the specific data collection period.

National

During the 2007 to 2011 period, 42.7 million people or 14.3 percent of the U.S. population had income below the poverty level (Table 1). National poverty rates differed widely across race groups and by Hispanic or Latino origin.[2]

Two groups had poverty rates more than 10 percentage points higher than the U.S. rate for the total population: American Indian and Alaska Native (27.0 percent) and Black or African American (25.8 percent). Rates were above the overall national average for Native Hawaiians and Other Pacific Islanders (17.6 percent) while poverty rates for Whites (11.6 percent) and Asians (11.7 percent) were lower than the overall rate (14.3 percent).[3] The Hispanic population had a poverty rate of 23.2 percent, about 9 percentage points higher than the overall U.S. rate (Figure 1).

For a particular race group, poverty rates may differ by detailed race or origin. Some detailed race or origin groups are listed on the ACS questionnaire such as Filipino, Native Hawaiian, or Puerto Rican.

Categories not listed may be handwritten and the responses tabulated within major race groups. Poverty differed across detailed Asian groups. Poverty rates also differed by detailed Native Hawaiian and Other Pacific Islander groups.

An estimated 17.6 percent of the Native Hawaiian and Other Pacific Islander population had income below the poverty level over the 2007 to 2011 period (Figure 2). Within this group, poverty rates ranged from a low of 6.4 percent for Fijians to a high of about 18.0 percent for Samoans and Tongans.[4] The largest detailed group, Native Hawaiian, had a poverty rate of 14.4 percent, a rate not statistically different from the U.S. average for the total population. For Guamanians or Chamorros, poverty was estimated at 11.6 percent, a rate lower than the U.S. average for the total population.

Figure 3 shows that for the Asian population, poverty was estimated at 8.2 percent for both Asian Indians and Japanese. Higher rates were found for Vietnamese (14.7 percent) and Koreans (15.0 percent),[5] and lower rates were found for Filipinos (5.8 percent).

Many Hispanic groups had poverty rates higher than the overall U.S. rate for the 2007 to 2011 period (Figure 4). Salvadorans and Cubans had poverty rates of 18.9 percent and 16.2 percent, respectively. For Mexicans and Guatemalans, the rates were about 25.0 percent. Similar rates were found for Puerto Ricans (25.6 percent) and Dominicans (26.3 percent).

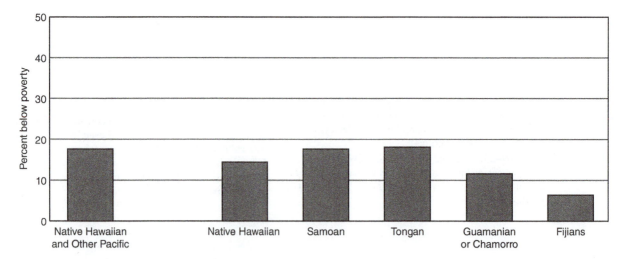

Figure 2.   U.S. Poverty Rates for the Native Hawaiian and Other Pacific Islander Alone Population and Selected Detailed Groups: 2007–2011 (For information on confidentiality protection, sampling error, nonsampling error, and definitions, see www.census.gov/acs/www/)

Note: Persons who report only one race among the six defined categories are referred to as the race-alone population, while persons who report more than one race category are referred to as the Two or More Races population. This figure shows data using the race-alone approach. Use of the single-race population does not imply that it is the preferred method of presenting or analyzing data. The Census Bureau uses a variety of approaches.

Source: U.S. Census Bureau, 2007–2011 American Community Survey.

Poverty Rates for Selected Detailed Race and Hispanic Groups by State and Place: 2007-2011 by S. Macartney, A. Bishaw, and K. Fontenot

149

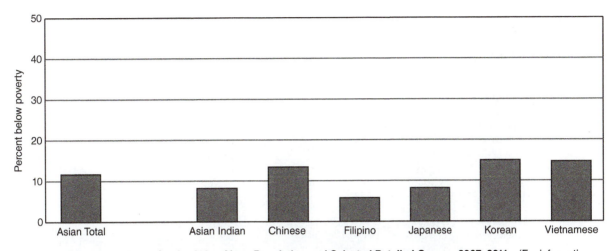

Figure 3.   U.S. Poverty Rates for the Asian Alone Population and Selected Detailed Groups: 2007–2011   (For information on confidentiality protection, sampling error, nonsampling error, and definitions, see www.census.gov/acs/www/)

Note: Persons who report only one race among the six defined categories are referred to as the race-alone population, while persons who report more than one race category are referred to as the Two or More Races population. This figure shows data using the race-alone approach. Use of the single-race population does not imply that it is the preferred method of presenting or analyzing data. The Census Bureau uses a variety of approaches.

Source: U.S. Census Bureau, 2007–2011 American Community Survey.

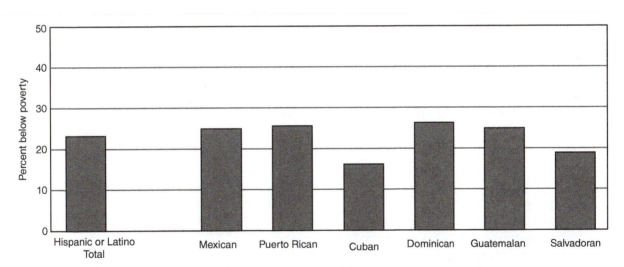

Figure 4.   U.S. Poverty Rates for the Hispanic Population and Selected Detailed Groups: 2007–2011   (For information on confidentiality protection, sampling error, nonsampling error, and definitions, see www.census.gov/acs/www/)

Note: Hispanics may be of any race. For more information, see Ennis, S., M. Rios-Vargas, and N. Albert, "The Hispanic Population: 2010," U.S. Census Bureau, *2010 Census Briefs,* C2010BR-04, 2011, available at www.census.gov/prod/cen2010/briefs/c2010br-04.pdf.

Source: U.S. Census Bureau, 2007–2011 American Community Survey.

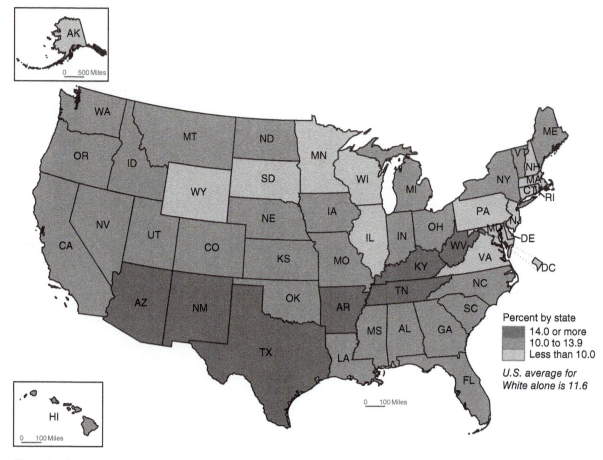

Figure 5.   Percentage of the White Alone Population in Poverty for the United States: 2007–2011

Source: U.S. Census Bureau, 2007–2011 American Community Survey.

States

State-level poverty rates also differed widely across race and Hispanic groups for the 2007 to 2011 period. Tables 2 through 8 show poverty rates by race and Hispanic origin for the 50 states and the District of Columbia. Figures 5 through 9 show the variation in poverty levels across the United States for selected race and Hispanic groups.

White

Figure 5 shows the distribution of poverty for the White population. Forty-three states and the District of Columbia had poverty rates for the White population lower than 14.0 percent for

2007 to 2011. Seven states had poverty rates of 14.0 percent or more (Arizona, Arkansas, Kentucky, New Mexico, Tennessee, Texas, and West Virginia).[6]

Black

Figure 6 shows that during the 2007 to 2011 period for the Black population, 43 states and the District of Columbia had poverty rates of 20.0 percent or higher. Iowa, Maine, Mississippi, and Wisconsin had rates above 35.0 percent. Six states had poverty rates for Blacks that were about 20.0 percent or less (Alaska, Delaware, Hawaii, Maryland, New Jersey, and Virginia).

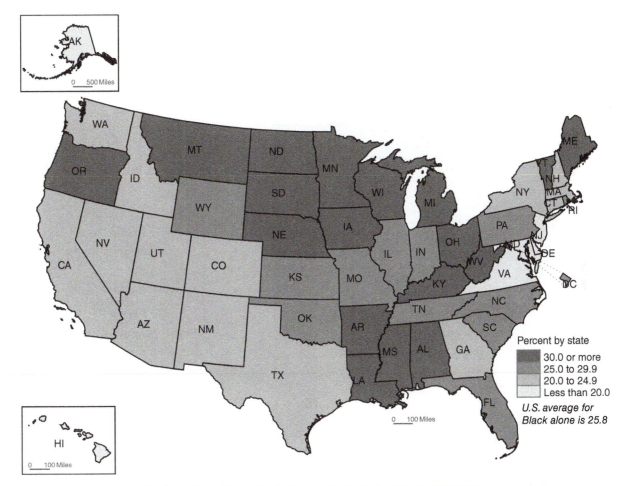

Figure 6. Percentage of the Black Alone Population in Poverty for the United States: 2007–2011

Source: U.S. Census Bureau, 2007–2011 American Community Survey.

American Indian and Alaska Native

Table 2 shows poverty rates for the American Indian and Alaska Native alone population. For American Indians and Alaska Natives, the poverty rates in Maryland (13.9 percent), New Hampshire (15.8 percent), and Virginia (13.8 percent) were among the lowest of any states.[7] By comparison, South Dakota (48.3 percent) had the highest poverty rate for this group. North Dakota was next at 41.6 percent.[8] Seven other states had poverty rates of about 30.0 percent or more (Arizona, Maine, Minnesota, Montana, Nebraska, New Mexico, and Utah) (Figure 7). Table 3 shows poverty rates for persons identified as American Indian and Alaska Native alone or in combination with one or more other races.[9]

Native Hawaiian and Other Pacific Islander

The 2007-20 ACS poverty rates for the Native Hawaiian and Other Pacific Islander alone population are shown in Table 4. Connecticut (7.0 percent), Illinois (8.6 percent), and New Hampshire (6.6 percent) were among the states with the lowest poverty rates for this group.[10] Poverty rates for Arkansas (41.8 percent), Nebraska (50.8 percent), and Oklahoma (37.0 percent) were among the highest rates.[11] Table 5 shows poverty rates for persons identified as Native Hawaiian and Other Pacific Islander alone or in combination with one or more other races.

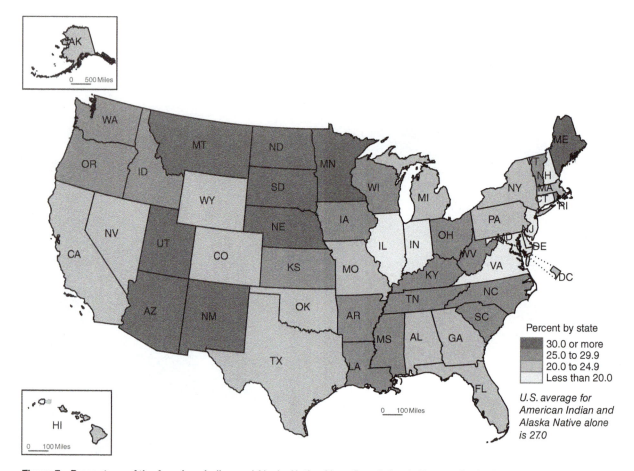

Figure 7   Percentage of the American Indian and Alaska Native Alone Population in Poverty for the United States: 2007–2011

Source: U.S. Census Bureau, 2007–2011 American Community Survey.

Asian

Table 6 shows that for the Asian alone population, Delaware (7.9 percent), Hawaii (6.4 percent), and New Jersey (6.8 percent) had some of the lowest state poverty rates for the 2007 to 2011 periodY Figure 8 shows six other states with poverty rates of about 10.0 percent or less for Asians (Connecticut, Maryland, New Hampshire, Nevada, South Carolina, and Virginia). By comparison, Idaho (19.7 percent), Indiana (19.2 percent), and North Dakota (22.3 percent) had some of the highest poverty rates.[13] Table 7 shows poverty rates for persons identified as Asian alone or in combination with one or more other races.

Hispanic or Latino

For the Hispanic or Latino population, Alaska (10.3 percent) had the lowest level of poverty during the 2007 to 2011 period while Kentucky (31.5 percent), Pennsylvania (31.6 percent), and

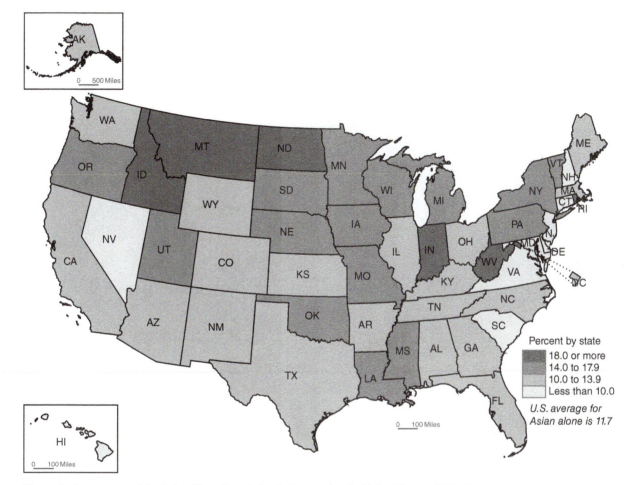

Figure 8   Percentage of the Asian Alone Population in Poverty for the United States: 2007–2011

Source: U.S. Census Bureau, 2007–2011 American Community Survey.

Tennessee (32.2 percent) were among the states with the highest levels (Table 8).[14] Figure 9 shows the other states with poverty rates at 30.0 percent or higher for the Hispanic population (Alabama, Arkansas, Georgia, North Carolina, and Rhode Island).

Cities

Poverty rates for selected detailed race and Hispanic groups by city or place are shown in Figures 10, 11, and 12.

Figure 10 shows that the poverty rate was about 30.0 percent or greater for the American Indian and Alaska Native population in 6 of the 20 places most populated by this group (Gallup, New Mexico; Minneapolis, Minnesota; Rapid City, South Dakota; Shiprock, New Mexico; Tucson, Arizona; and Zuni Pueblo, New Mexico). The poverty rate in Rapid City, South Dakota (50.9 percent) for American Indians and Alaska Natives was around three times the rate in Anchorage, Alaska (16.6 percent).

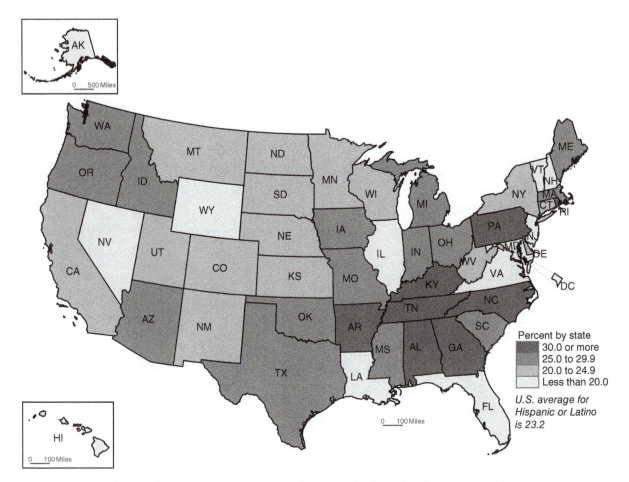

Figure 9   Percentage of the Hispanic or Latino Population in Poverty for the United States: 2007–2011

Source: U.S. Census Bureau, 2007–2011 American Community Survey.

Poverty rates for the Vietnamese population are shown in Figure 11. Fountain Valley, California (8.2 percent); Oklahoma City, Oklahoma (7.7 percent); and San Francisco, California (11.9 percent), had poverty rates lower than the group's national rate (14.7 percent). By comparison, the poverty rate for Vietnamese in Boston, Massachusetts (35.8 percent), was around three times the U.S. rate for this group.

In cities or places with large populations of Dominicans, poverty rates for this group ranged from 43.2 percent to 10.0 percent (Figure 12). Poverty was around 30.0 percent or greater in 8 of the 20 places most populated by Dominicans (Boston, Massachusetts; Lawrence, Massachusetts; Lynn, Massachusetts; New York, New York; Passaic, New Jersey; Philadelphia, Pennsylvania; Providence, Rhode Island; and Reading, Pennsylvania).

(For additional poverty rates by city or place for selected detailed race and Hispanic groups, please see the appendix tables.)

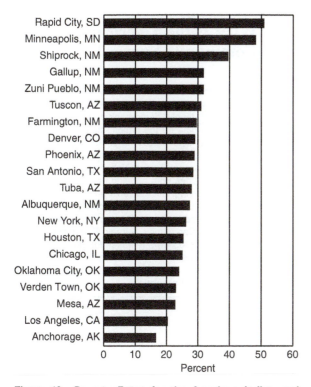

Figure 10. Poverty Rates for the American Indian and Alaska Native (AIAN) Alone Population in 20 U.S. Cities Most Populated by AIAN Alone: 2007–2011 (For information on confidentiality protection, sampling error, nonsampling error, and definitions, see www.census.gov/acs/www/)

Source: U.S. Census Bureau, 2007–2011 American Community Survey.

How Poverty Is Measured

Poverty status is determined by comparing annual income to a set of dollar values called poverty thresholds that vary by family size, number of children, and the age of the householder. If a family's before-tax money income is less than the dollar value of their threshold, then that family and every individual in it are considered to be in poverty. For people not living in families, poverty status is determined by comparing the individual's income to his or her poverty threshold.

The poverty thresholds are updated annually to allow for changes in the cost of living using the Consumer Price Index (CPI-U). They do not vary geographically.

The ACS is a continuous survey and people respond throughout the year. Since income is reported for the previous 12 months, the appropriate poverty threshold for each family is determined by multiplying the base-year poverty threshold (1982) by the average of monthly CPI-U values for the 12 months preceding the survey month.

For more information see "ACS Poverty Definition" and "How Poverty is Calculated in the ACS" at www/census.gov/hhes/www/poverty/methods/definitions.html.

Figure 11. Poverty Rates for the Vietnamese Alone Population in the 20 U.S. Cities Most Populated by Vietnamese Alone: 2007–2011 (For information on confidentiality protection, sampling error, nonsampling error, and definitions, see www.census.gov/acs/www/)

Note: To illustrate the data available in the appendix tables of this report, selected groups with comparatively higher rates of poverty and geographic dispersion are highlighted in these figures.

Persons who report only one race among the six defined categories are referred to as the race-alone population, while persons who report more than one race category are referred to as the Two or More Races population. This figure shows data using the race-alone approach. Use of the single-race population does not imply that it is the preferred method of presenting or analyzing data. The Census Bureau uses a variety of approaches.

Source: U.S. Census Bureau, 2007–2011 American Community Survey.

What Is the American Community Survey?

The American Community Survey (ACS) is a nationwide survey designed to provide communities with reliable and timely demographic, social, economic, and housing data for the nation, states, congressional districts, counties, places, and other localities every year. It has an annual sample size of about 3.3 million addresses across the United States and Puerto Rico and includes both housing units and group quarters (e.g., nursing facilities and prisons). The ACS is conducted in every county throughout the nation, and every municipio in Puerto Rico, where it is called the Puerto Rico Community Survey. Beginning in 2006, ACS data for 2005 were released for geographic areas with populations of 65,000 and greater. For information on the ACS sample design and other topics, visit www.census.gov/acs/www.

Figure 12. Poverty Rates for the Dominican Population in the 20 U.S. Cities Most Populated by Dominicans: 2007–2011 (For information on confidentiality protection, sampling error, nonsampling error, and definitions, see www.census.gov/acs/www/)

Note: To illustrate the data available in the appendix tables of this report, selected groups with comparatively higher rates of poverty and geographic dispersion are highlighted in these figures.

Source: U.S. Census Bureau, 2007–2011 American Community Survey.

Source and Accuracy

The data presented in this report are based on the ACS sample interviewed between 2007 and 2011. The estimates based on this sample approximate the actual values and represent the entire household and group quarters population. Sampling error is the difference between an estimate based on a sample and the corresponding value that would be obtained if the estimate were based on the entire population (as from a census). Measures of the sampling errors are provided in the form of margins of error for all estimates included in this report. All comparative statements in this report have undergone statistical testing, and comparisons are significant at the 90 percent level unless otherwise noted. In addition to sampling error, nonsampling error may be introduced during any of the operations used to collect and process survey data such as editing, reviewing, or keying data from questionnaires. For more information on sampling and estimation methods, confidentiality protection, and sampling and nonsampling errors, please see the 2011 ACS Accuracy of the Data document located at www.census.gov/acs/www/Downloads/data_documentation/Accuracy/ACS_Accuracy_of_Data_2011.pdf.

Table 1
U.S. Poverty Rates by Race, Selected Detailed Race, and Hispanic Origin Groups: 2007–2011[1,2]

(For information on confidentiality protection, sampling error, nonsampling error, and definitions, see www.census.gov/acs/www/)

Race and Hispanic or Latino origin	Population	Number below poverty	Margin of error (±)[3]	Percent below poverty	Margin of error (±)[3]
Total	298,787,989	42,739,924	277,336	14.3	0.1
White alone	222,007,105	25,659,922	193,148	11.6	0.1
White alone, non-Hispanic	192,160,374	18,959,814	152,602	9.9	0.1
Black or African American alone	36,699,584	9,472,583	50,241	25.8	0.1
American Indian and Alaska Native alone or in combination	4,738,750	1,130,661	12,413	23.9	0.3
American Indian and Alaska Native alone	2,414,908	651,226	9,734	27.0	0.4
Asian alone or in combination	16,389,524	1,899,448	19,805	11.6	0.1
Asian alone	14,223,507	1,663,303	19,470	11.7	0.1
Asian Indian	2,743,999	224,343	7,718	8.2	0.3
Chinese	3,162,573	424,322	7,305	13.4	0.2
Filipino	2,517,885	146,113	4,685	5.8	0.2
Japanese	782,469	64,553	2,727	8.2	0.3
Korean	1,378,830	206,241	5,340	15.0	0.3
Vietnamese	1,554,143	228,381	6,674	14.7	0.4
Native Hawaiian and Other Pacific Islander alone or in combination	992,614	156,717	5,039	15.8	0.5
Native Hawaiian and Other Pacific Islander alone	485,892	85,346	3,634	17.6	0.7
Native Hawaiian	151,905	21,937	1,485	14.4	1.0
Samoan	99,860	17,606	1,616	17.6	1.6
Tongan	39,893	7,221	1,421	18.1	3.0
Guamanian or Chamorro	70,669	8,197	1,007	11.6	1.4
Fijians	27,158	1,738	488	6.4	1.8
Other Pacific Islander[4]	96,407	28,647	2,643	29.7	2.3
Some Other Race alone	15,393,344	3,792,156	47,496	24.6	0.2
Two or More Races	7,563,658	1,415,388	13,717	18.7	0.2
Hispanic origin	48,190,992	11,197,648	77,014	23.2	0.2
Mexican	31,157,323	7,744,050	65,971	24.9	0.2
Guatemalan	1,054,350	262,575	7,506	24.9	0.6
Salvadoran	1,708,491	323,317	8,870	18.9	0.5
Cuban	1,727,550	279,011	5,969	16.2	0.4
Dominican	1,387,724	364,523	6,591	26.3	0.5
Puerto Rican	4,466,054	1,142,216	13,907	25.6	0.3

[1]Poverty status is determined for individuals in housing units and noninstitutional group quarters. The poverty universe excludes children under age 15 who are not related to the householder, people living in institutional group quarters, and people living in college dormitories or military barracks.

[2]The Census Bureau does not advocate the use of the alone population over the alone-or-in-combination population or vice versa. The use of the alone population in sections of this brief does not imply that it is the preferred method of presenting or analyzing data. Data on race from the American Community Survey can be presented and discussed in a variety of ways. Hispanics and Latinos may be of any race. For more information see the 2010 Census Brief, Overview of Race and Hispanic Origin, at www.census.gov/prod/cen2010/briefs/c2010br-02.pdf.

[3]Data are based on a sample and are subject to sampling variability. A margin of error is a measure of an estimate's variability. The larger the margin of error in relation to the size of the estimate, the less reliable the estimate. This number when added to or subtracted from the estimate forms the 90 percent confidence interval.

[4]Includes Other Micronesian (25,000), Other Pacific Islander not specified (17,000), Marshallese (17,000), Other Native Hawaiian (8,000), Other Pacific Islander (7,000), Palauan (6,000), Other Polynesian (5,000), Chuukese (2,000), Pohnpeian (1,000), Tahitian (1,000), and other detailed groups.

Source: U.S. Census Bureau, 2007–2011 American Community Survey.

Table 2
Poverty Rates for the American Indian and Alaska Native Alone Population by State: 2007–2011[1]

(For information on confidentiality protection, sampling error, nonsampling error, and definitions, see www.census.gov/acs/www/)

State	Population	American Indian and Alaska Native alone[2]			
		Number below poverty	Margin of error (±)[3]	Percent below poverty	Margin of error (±)[3]
United States.................................	2,414,908	651,226	9,734	27.0	0.4
Alabama	25,905	5,746	1,049	22.2	3.4
Alaska..	94,670	19,896	918	21.0	0.9
Arizona	272,710	95,654	3,469	35.1	1.3
Arkansas	16,962	4,242	551	25.0	2.7
California	277,564	60,743	3,014	21.9	1.0
Colorado	45,497	10,775	1,219	23.7	2.4
Connecticut..................................	7,578	1,504	386	19.8	4.3
Delaware......................................	3,076	588	260	19.1	7.6
District of Columbia	1,711	370	155	21.6	8.8
Florida	56,251	13,118	1,264	23.3	2.0
Georgia	23,011	5,410	823	23.5	3.3
Hawaii	2,807	585	210	20.8	7.0
Idaho...	18,627	4,947	681	26.6	3.1
Illinois...	24,269	4,448	495	18.3	2.1
Indiana..	14,173	2,519	349	17.8	2.2
Iowa..	9,122	2,351	357	25.8	3.1
Kansas..	22,097	5,606	728	25.4	2.8
Kentucky......................................	8,489	2,147	418	25.3	4.3
Louisiana	27,618	7,263	1,013	26.3	3.2
Maine..	6,814	2,257	294	33.1	4.1
Maryland......................................	15,985	2,222	475	13.9	2.5
Massachusetts..............................	11,665	2,789	560	23.9	3.9
Michigan......................................	52,770	13,128	1,017	24.9	1.8
Minnesota....................................	54,191	20,795	1,174	38.4	1.9
Mississippi	13,488	3,437	750	25.5	5.5
Missouri.......................................	21,535	4,804	580	22.3	2.4
Montana.......................................	59,102	21,469	1,497	36.3	2.4
Nebraska	15,074	5,738	665	38.1	3.9
Nevada	28,633	5,883	657	20.5	2.0
New Hampshire	2,530	399	154	15.8	5.7
New Jersey...................................	19,998	3,365	742	16.8	3.1
New Mexico	183,672	57,585	2,904	31.4	1.5
New York......................................	65,396	15,955	1,531	24.4	2.1
North Carolina	106,000	29,526	2,031	27.9	1.8
North Dakota	34,151	14,195	896	41.6	2.5
Ohio..	20,331	5,679	605	27.9	2.7
Oklahoma	251,022	55,559	2,064	22.1	0.8
Oregon...	55,341	15,874	1,664	28.7	2.5
Pennsylvania................................	17,196	3,996	489	23.2	2.7
Rhode Island	4,396	1,307	482	29.7	9.2
South Carolina..............................	14,394	3,737	571	26.0	3.5
South Dakota................................	65,779	31,792	1,563	48.3	2.3
Tennessee	14,836	4,264	814	28.7	4.4
Texas..	120,664	24,476	1,678	20.3	1.2
Utah..	29,570	9,366	995	31.7	3.0
Vermont	1,722	435	153	25.3	8.0
Virginia..	24,342	3,370	608	13.8	2.0
Washington...................................	90,775	23,342	1,654	25.7	1.6
West Virginia	2,749	756	214	27.5	6.7
Wisconsin	46,330	13,071	956	28.2	1.9
Wyoming......................................	12,320	2,743	595	22.3	4.6

[1]Poverty status is determined for individuals in housing units and noninstitutional group quarters. The poverty universe excludes children under age 15 who are not related to the householder, people living in institutional group quarters, and people living in college dormitories or military barracks.

[2]Persons who report only one race among the six defined categories are referred to as the race-alone population, while persons who report more than one race category are referred to as the Two or More Races population. This table shows data using the race-alone approach. Use of the single-race population does not imply that it is the preferred method of presenting or analyzing data. The Census Bureau uses a variety of approaches.

[3]Data are based on a sample and are subject to sampling variability. A margin of error is a measure of an estimate's variability. The larger the margin of error in relation to the size of the estimate, the less reliable the estimate. This number when added to or subtracted from the estimate forms the 90 percent confidence interval.

Source: U.S. Census Bureau, 2007–2011 American Community Survey.

Table 3
Poverty Rates for the American Indian and Alaska Native Alone or in Combination Population by State: 2007–2011[1]

(For information on confidentiality protection, sampling error, nonsampling error, and definitions, see www.census.gov/acs/www/)

State	American Indian and Alaska Native alone or in combination[2]				
	Population	Number below poverty	Margin of error (±)[3]	Percent below poverty	Margin of error (±)[3]
United States.....................	**4,738,750**	**1,130,661**	**12,413**	**23.9**	**0.3**
Alabama	56,295	12,919	1,310	22.9	2.2
Alaska.................................	131,007	24,959	1,090	19.1	0.8
Arizona	323,816	107,026	3,906	33.1	1.1
Arkansas............................	45,783	11,447	903	25.0	1.9
California	630,094	122,663	4,458	19.5	0.6
Colorado	98,741	21,175	1,479	21.4	1.4
Connecticut........................	27,868	3,989	691	14.3	2.4
Delaware	8,276	1,366	414	16.5	4.7
District of Columbia	4,587	977	248	21.3	5.2
Florida	142,232	29,727	2,017	20.9	1.3
Georgia	65,927	12,979	1,457	19.7	2.0
Hawaii	31,673	5,987	1,051	18.9	2.9
Idaho	34,867	9,136	838	26.2	2.3
Illinois	74,187	13,959	1,072	18.8	1.4
Indiana	52,897	10,526	742	19.9	1.3
Iowa	26,040	8,022	806	30.8	2.5
Kansas	58,099	13,650	988	23.5	1.5
Kentucky	29,163	8,488	951	29.1	2.7
Louisiana	52,740	13,021	1,345	24.7	2.3
Maine	18,940	5,659	467	29.9	2.4
Maryland	51,675	7,503	1,334	14.5	2.4
Massachusetts	40,200	8,413	873	20.9	2.0
Michigan	133,069	32,588	1,739	24.5	1.1
Minnesota	93,419	30,553	1,423	32.7	1.5
Mississippi	26,625	6,233	968	23.4	3.3
Missouri	76,974	17,971	1,499	23.3	1.6
Montana	73,585	25,096	1,512	34.1	2.0
Nebraska	30,471	10,528	1,105	34.6	3.0
Nevada	49,984	9,812	902	19.6	1.6
New Hampshire	9,565	1,270	270	13.3	2.7
New Jersey	57,876	8,615	1,235	14.9	1.9
New Mexico	208,247	63,107	3,157	30.3	1.4
New York	154,839	34,498	2,040	22.3	1.1
North Carolina	169,155	45,587	2,210	26.9	1.2
North Dakota	39,848	15,384	876	38.6	2.2
Ohio	87,119	24,136	1,604	27.7	1.6
Oklahoma	466,618	101,415	3,284	21.7	0.7
Oregon	111,593	29,403	1,966	26.3	1.4
Pennsylvania	67,249	15,209	1,183	22.6	1.7
Rhode Island	11,718	2,985	602	25.5	5.0
South Carolina	36,831	8,586	807	23.3	1.9
South Dakota	76,671	34,623	1,498	45.2	2.0
Tennessee	54,978	13,496	1,226	24.5	2.0
Texas	272,544	49,386	2,358	18.1	0.8
Utah	44,921	12,106	1,169	26.9	2.4
Vermont	7,029	1,301	212	18.5	3.0
Virginia	69,782	9,834	1,017	14.1	1.3
Washington	184,571	42,025	1,882	22.8	1.0
West Virginia	18,379	5,390	619	29.3	2.8
Wisconsin	79,938	21,746	1,129	27.2	1.3
Wyoming	20,045	4,187	695	20.9	3.5

[1]Poverty status is determined for individuals in housing units and noninstitutional group quarters. The poverty universe excludes children under age 15 who are not related to the householder, people living in institutional group quarters, and people living in college dormitories or military barracks.

[2]Persons who report only one race among the six defined categories are referred to as the race-alone population, while persons who report more than one race category are referred to as the Two or More Races population. This table shows data using the race-alone-or-in-combination approach. The race alone-or-in-combination population is the total number of people who reported a particular race, whether or not they reported any other races. Use of this approach does not imply that it is the preferred method of presenting or analyzing data. The Census Bureau uses a variety of approaches.

[3]Data are based on a sample and are subject to sampling variability. A margin of error is a measure of an estimate's variability. The larger the margin of error in relation to the size of the estimate, the less reliable the estimate. This number when added to or subtracted from the estimate forms the 90 percent confidence interval.

Source: U.S. Census Bureau, 2007–2011 American Community Survey.

Table 4
Poverty Rates for the Native Hawaiian and Other Pacific Islander Alone Population by State: 2007–2011[1]

(For information on confidentiality protection, sampling error, nonsampling error, and definitions, see www.census.gov/acs/www/)

| State | Population | Native Hawaiian and Other Pacific Islander alone[2] | | | |
		Number below poverty	Margin of error (±)[3]	Percent below poverty	Margin of error (±)[3]
United States......................	485,892	85,346	3,634	17.6	0.7
Alabama	1,210	230	116	19.0	8.2
Alaska.................................	6,677	1,183	490	17.7	7.4
Arizona	10,827	2,041	625	18.9	5.6
Arkansas	4,960	2,071	539	41.8	10.8
California	138,273	18,221	1,831	13.2	1.3
Colorado	5,492	893	444	16.3	8.0
Connecticut.........................	1,268	89	105	7.0	7.8
Delaware.............................	(NA)	(NA)	(NA)	(NA)	(NA)
District of Columbia	(NA)	(NA)	(NA)	(NA)	(NA)
Florida	10,619	1,604	457	15.1	4.1
Georgia...............................	4,294	1,120	334	26.1	7.6
Hawaii.................................	126,799	24,213	1,993	19.1	1.5
Idaho..................................	2,413	352	181	14.6	7.5
Illinois.................................	3,090	265	138	8.6	4.4
Indiana................................	1,197	299	169	25.0	11.9
Iowa	986	357	196	36.2	14.1
Kansas................................	1,550	190	101	12.3	5.7
Kentucky	2,274	490	319	21.5	11.9
Louisiana	1,644	421	324	25.6	16.0
Maine.................................	296	81	66	27.4	18.0
Maryland.............................	2,417	265	143	11.0	5.1
Massachusetts.....................	1,471	305	189	20.7	12.0
Michigan	2,461	586	270	23.8	9.1
Minnesota...........................	2,088	379	154	18.2	7.3
Mississippi..........................	557	90	67	16.2	14.2
Missouri..............................	5,491	941	395	17.1	7.0
Montana..............................	571	119	92	20.8	11.8
Nebraska	1,121	569	195	50.8	14.5
Nevada	16,112	2,924	819	18.1	4.9
New Hampshire	288	19	16	6.6	7.5
New Jersey	1,959	261	168	13.3	8.3
New Mexico	1,105	247	153	22.4	12.5
New York.............................	6,347	1,160	390	18.3	6.6
North Carolina	4,429	445	211	10.0	4.5
North Dakota	340	59	50	17.4	14.0
Ohio...................................	2,035	303	148	14.9	6.9
Oklahoma	4,151	1,536	472	37.0	10.1
Oregon................................	13,111	4,119	767	31.4	5.0
Pennsylvania........................	2,513	609	214	24.2	6.8
Rhode Island	436	163	117	37.4	27.0
South Carolina.....................	1,802	332	226	18.4	11.4
South Dakota.......................	(NA)	(NA)	(NA)	(NA)	(NA)
Tennessee	3,054	395	246	12.9	7.8
Texas	19,121	3,195	677	16.7	3.4
Utah...................................	24,705	4,767	1,061	19.3	4.3
Vermont	(NA)	(NA)	(NA)	(NA)	(NA)
Virginia	4,981	619	229	12.4	4.1
Washington..........................	36,379	6,568	1,050	18.1	2.8
West Virginia	(NA)	(NA)	(NA)	(NA)	(NA)
Wisconsin	1,435	216	97	15.1	6.7
Wyoming..............................	158	26	30	16.5	17.3

(NA) Not available. Data cannot be displayed because the number of sample cases is too small.

[1]Poverty status is determined for individuals in housing units and noninstitutional group quarters. The poverty universe excludes children under age 15 who are not related to the householder, people living in institutional group quarters, and people living in college dormitories or military barracks.

[2]Persons who report only one race among the six defined categories are referred to as the race-alone population, while persons who report more than one race category are referred to as the Two or More Races population. This table shows data using the race-alone approach. Use of the single-race population does not imply that it is the preferred method of presenting or analyzing data. The Census Bureau uses a variety of approaches.

[3]Data are based on a sample and are subject to sampling variability. A margin of error is a measure of an estimate's variability. The larger the margin of error in relation to the size of the estimate, the less reliable the estimate. This number when added to or subtracted from the estimate forms the 90 percent confidence interval.

Source: U.S. Census Bureau, 2007–2011 American Community Survey.

Table 5
Poverty Rates for the Native Hawaiian and Other Pacific Islander Alone or in Combination Population by State: 2007–2011[1]

(For information on confidentiality protection, sampling error, nonsampling error, and definitions, see www.census.gov/acs/www/)

State	Native Hawaiian and Other Pacific Islander alone or in combination[2]				
	Population	Number below poverty	Margin of error (±)[3]	Percent below poverty	Margin of error (±)[3]
United States............................	992,614	156,717	5,039	15.8	0.5
Alabama	2,746	538	184	19.6	5.6
Alaska....................................	9,797	1,793	581	18.3	5.5
Arizona..................................	20,234	3,107	675	15.4	3.2
Arkansas................................	6,041	2,312	551	38.3	9.2
California	240,453	29,709	2,156	12.4	0.9
Colorado	12,003	1,670	496	13.9	3.9
Connecticut............................	2,767	279	185	10.1	6.1
Delaware................................	1,005	53	55	5.3	5.4
District of Columbia	(NA)	(NA)	(NA)	(NA)	(NA)
Florida	23,077	3,419	733	14.8	3.1
Georgia..................................	8,508	2,038	509	24.0	5.6
Hawaii....................................	331,970	52,044	2,977	15.7	0.9
Idaho.....................................	4,845	966	357	19.9	6.9
Illinois...................................	8,523	782	306	9.2	3.5
Indiana..................................	3,368	668	270	19.8	7.2
Iowa......................................	2,525	623	254	24.7	9.1
Kansas..................................	3,102	435	182	14.0	5.8
Kentucky	3,536	865	312	24.5	7.5
Louisiana...............................	2,994	806	367	26.9	9.8
Maine....................................	786	119	91	15.1	10.2
Maryland................................	5,738	737	286	12.8	4.1
Massachusetts........................	4,491	828	266	18.4	5.8
Michigan	6,657	1,379	361	20.7	4.7
Minnesota..............................	5,342	931	275	17.4	5.0
Mississippi	1,110	217	128	19.5	9.6
Missouri	8,800	1,357	447	15.4	5.0
Montana................................	1,602	373	186	23.3	10.0
Nebraska...............................	1,874	713	216	38.0	10.7
Nevada..................................	30,228	4,700	952	15.5	3.3
New Hampshire	939	78	73	8.3	8.3
New Jersey	6,531	1,151	416	17.6	5.8
New Mexico	2,508	472	223	18.8	8.3
New York................................	13,842	2,307	546	16.7	4.0
North Carolina	10,071	1,951	514	19.4	4.1
North Dakota	826	112	78	13.6	8.6
Ohio......................................	6,551	1,185	355	18.1	5.0
Oklahoma	7,793	2,402	583	30.8	7.3
Oregon..................................	23,492	6,227	967	26.5	3.8
Pennsylvania..........................	6,713	1,357	365	20.2	4.9
Rhode Island	1,116	339	176	30.4	16.4
South Carolina	3,764	860	534	22.8	11.3
South Dakota	(NA)	(NA)	(NA)	(NA)	(NA)
Tennessee	5,538	800	307	14.4	5.6
Texas....................................	33,684	5,665	755	16.8	2.2
Utah......................................	33,825	6,390	1,197	18.9	3.5
Vermont.................................	(NA)	(NA)	(NA)	(NA)	(NA)
Virginia..................................	12,080	1,412	405	11.7	3.0
Washington.............................	62,461	9,642	1,193	15.4	1.9
West Virginia..........................	936	183	122	19.6	12.1
Wisconsin	3,730	558	181	15.0	4.6
Wyoming................................	539	66	67	12.2	12.0

(NA) Not available. Data cannot be displayed because the number of sample cases is too small.

[1] Poverty status is determined for individuals in housing units and noninstitutional group quarters. The poverty universe excludes children under age 15 who are not related to the householder, people living in institutional group quarters, and people living in college dormitories or military barracks.

[2] Persons who report only one race among the six defined categories are referred to as the race-alone population, while persons who report more than one race category are referred to as the Two or More Races population. This table shows data using the race-alone-or-in-combination approach. The race alone-or-in-combination population is the total number of people who reported a particular race, whether or not they reported any other races. Use of this approach does not imply that it is the preferred method of presenting or analyzing data. The Census Bureau uses a variety of approaches.

[3] Data are based on a sample and are subject to sampling variability. A margin of error is a measure of an estimate's variability. The larger the margin of error in relation to the size of the estimate, the less reliable the estimate. This number when added to or subtracted from the estimate forms the 90 percent confidence interval.

Source: U.S. Census Bureau, 2007–2011 American Community Survey.

Poverty Rates for Selected Detailed Race and Hispanic Groups by State and Place: 2007-2011 by S. Macartney, A. Bishaw, and K. Fontenot

163

Table 6
Poverty Rates for the Asian Alone Population by State: 2007–2011[1]

(For information on confidentiality protection, sampling error, nonsampling error, and definitions, see www.census.gov/acs/www/)

State	Population	Asian alone[2]			
		Number below poverty	Margin of error (±)[3]	Percent below poverty	Margin of error (±)[3]
United States	14,223,507	1,663,303	19,470	11.7	0.1
Alabama	51,579	6,752	913	13.1	1.8
Alaska	35,533	3,606	820	10.1	2.3
Arizona	169,293	21,147	1,895	12.5	1.1
Arkansas	34,273	4,316	715	12.6	2.0
California	4,758,104	521,442	9,163	11.0	0.2
Colorado	131,648	13,680	1,268	10.4	0.9
Connecticut	128,737	10,020	1,245	7.8	0.9
Delaware	28,433	2,238	536	7.9	1.9
District of Columbia	19,143	2,671	436	14.0	2.2
Florida	449,557	53,911	3,097	12.0	0.7
Georgia	301,347	34,804	2,569	11.5	0.8
Hawaii	515,593	33,153	1,727	6.4	0.3
Idaho	18,300	3,607	742	19.7	3.9
Illinois	571,519	60,800	3,011	10.6	0.5
Indiana	94,842	18,172	1,374	19.2	1.4
Iowa	50,461	7,126	778	14.1	1.5
Kansas	65,265	9,076	1,154	13.9	1.7
Kentucky	46,559	6,087	879	13.1	1.8
Louisiana	68,009	10,949	1,077	16.1	1.6
Maine	13,154	1,621	404	12.3	3.1
Maryland	307,872	22,761	1,774	7.4	0.6
Massachusetts	330,917	45,624	2,456	13.8	0.7
Michigan	237,499	33,233	2,052	14.0	0.8
Minnesota	203,691	34,965	2,229	17.2	1.1
Mississippi	24,891	4,379	847	17.6	3.3
Missouri	89,889	13,455	1,123	15.0	1.2
Montana	5,731	1,085	294	18.9	4.9
Nebraska	29,669	4,222	676	14.2	2.2
Nevada	189,126	15,835	1,612	8.4	0.8
New Hampshire	26,703	2,514	567	9.4	2.1
New Jersey	705,933	48,140	2,948	6.8	0.4
New Mexico	26,739	3,391	670	12.7	2.5
New York	1,383,969	229,552	5,208	16.6	0.4
North Carolina	197,435	25,447	1,870	12.9	0.9
North Dakota	6,247	1,394	246	22.3	3.9
Ohio	185,506	22,400	1,552	12.1	0.8
Oklahoma	61,837	8,972	897	14.5	1.4
Oregon	136,765	20,259	1,473	14.8	1.1
Pennsylvania	329,095	48,723	2,410	14.8	0.7
Rhode Island	29,347	5,563	1,010	19.0	3.4
South Carolina	54,679	4,798	660	8.8	1.2
South Dakota	7,307	1,048	369	14.3	5.0
Tennessee	88,464	10,202	1,072	11.5	1.2
Texas	928,236	109,895	3,840	11.8	0.4
Utah	53,973	9,508	1,181	17.6	2.1
Vermont	6,989	1,267	358	18.1	4.9
Virginia	422,299	34,165	2,354	8.1	0.5
Washington	463,863	51,854	2,641	11.2	0.6
West Virginia	11,159	1,932	369	17.3	3.3
Wisconsin	122,474	21,082	1,549	17.2	1.3
Wyoming	3,854	460	158	11.9	4.0

[1]Poverty status is determined for individuals in housing units and noninstitutional group quarters. The poverty universe excludes children under age 15 who are not related to the householder, people living in institutional group quarters, and people living in college dormitories or military barracks.

[2]Persons who report only one race among the six defined categories are referred to as the race-alone population, while persons who report more than one race category are referred to as the Two or More Races population. This table shows data using the race-alone approach. Use of the single-race population does not imply that it is the preferred method of presenting or analyzing data. The Census Bureau uses a variety of approaches.

[3]Data are based on a sample and are subject to sampling variability. A margin of error is a measure of an estimate's variability. The larger the margin of error in relation to the size of the estimate, the less reliable the estimate. This number when added to or subtracted from the estimate forms the 90 percent confidence interval.

Source: U.S. Census Bureau, 2007–2011 American Community Survey.

Table 7
overty Rates for the Asian Alone or in Combination Population by State: 2007–2011[1]

(For information on confidentiality protection, sampling error, nonsampling error, and definitions, see www.census.gov/acs/www/)

| State | Population | Asian alone or in combination[2] | | | |
		Number below poverty	Margin of error (±)[3]	Percent below poverty	Margin of error (±)[3]
United States	16,389,524	1,899,448	19,805	11.6	0.1
Alabama	62,319	8,281	964	13.3	1.5
Alaska	46,317	4,663	949	10.1	2.0
Arizona	214,481	26,481	2,100	12.3	1.0
Arkansas	40,761	5,567	920	13.7	2.1
California	5,321,945	575,061	9,712	10.8	0.2
Colorado	174,187	18,548	1,612	10.6	0.9
Connecticut	144,994	11,309	1,297	7.8	0.9
Delaware	32,567	2,564	559	7.9	1.7
District of Columbia	23,182	3,107	447	13.4	1.8
Florida	544,305	63,704	3,332	11.7	0.6
Georgia	339,803	39,355	2,744	11.6	0.8
Hawaii	757,432	59,509	2,805	7.9	0.4
Idaho	27,498	5,515	810	20.1	2.8
Illinois	635,049	67,473	3,267	10.6	0.5
Indiana	114,356	21,148	1,526	18.5	1.3
Iowa	59,364	8,684	840	14.6	1.4
Kansas	77,992	10,823	1,211	13.9	1.5
Kentucky	56,810	7,822	1,036	13.8	1.8
Louisiana	78,678	12,539	1,184	15.9	1.5
Maine	16,947	2,107	456	12.4	2.7
Maryland	351,143	25,454	1,920	7.2	0.5
Massachusetts	365,383	49,109	2,572	13.4	0.7
Michigan	276,666	39,319	2,199	14.2	0.8
Minnesota	232,548	37,814	2,284	16.3	1.0
Mississippi	28,942	5,089	842	17.6	2.9
Missouri	113,583	17,500	1,286	15.4	1.1
Montana	10,019	1,815	360	18.1	3.3
Nebraska	37,761	5,547	749	14.7	2.0
Nevada	229,015	19,955	1,699	8.7	0.7
New Hampshire	32,248	3,064	616	9.5	1.9
New Jersey	759,407	52,013	3,067	6.8	0.4
New Mexico	35,700	4,492	772	12.6	2.1
New York	1,495,346	243,108	5,515	16.3	0.4
North Carolina	232,911	29,980	1,943	12.9	0.8
North Dakota	8,273	1,866	351	22.6	4.1
Ohio	222,707	27,624	1,601	12.4	0.7
Oklahoma	78,957	11,955	1,052	15.1	1.3
Oregon	176,765	24,985	1,677	14.1	0.9
Pennsylvania	370,657	53,682	2,479	14.5	0.7
Rhode Island	33,252	6,029	1,031	18.1	3.1
South Carolina	68,383	6,754	949	9.9	1.4
South Dakota	9,091	1,454	425	16.0	4.6
Tennessee	105,470	12,677	1,101	12.0	1.1
Texas	1,041,268	121,643	4,084	11.7	0.4
Utah	73,059	12,162	1,118	16.6	1.5
Vermont	9,189	1,635	400	17.8	4.2
Virginia	489,098	38,829	2,541	7.9	0.5
Washington	571,426	62,376	2,970	10.9	0.5
West Virginia	14,376	2,686	421	18.7	2.8
Wisconsin	142,298	23,876	1,673	16.8	1.2
Wyoming	5,596	696	220	12.4	3.9

[1]Poverty status is determined for individuals in housing units and noninstitutional group quarters. The poverty universe excludes children under age 15 who are not related to the householder, people living in institutional group quarters, and people living in college dormitories or military barracks.

[2]Persons who report only one race among the six defined categories are referred to as the race-alone population, while persons who report more than one race category are referred to as the Two or More Races population. This table shows data using the race-alone-or-in-combination approach. The race alone-or-in-combination population is the total number of people who reported a particular race, whether or not they reported any other races. Use of this approach does not imply that it is the preferred method of presenting or analyzing data. The Census Bureau uses a variety of approaches.

[3]Data are based on a sample and are subject to sampling variability. A margin of error is a measure of an estimate's variability. The larger the margin of error in relation to the size of the estimate, the less reliable the estimate. This number when added to or subtracted from the estimate forms the 90 percent confidence interval.

Source: U.S. Census Bureau, 2007–2011 American Community Survey.

Table 8
Poverty Rates for the Hispanic or Latino Population by State: 2007–2011[1]

(For information on confidentiality protection, sampling error, nonsampling error, and definitions, see www.census.gov/acs/www/)

State	Population	Hispanic or Latino[2]			
		Number below poverty	Margin of error (±)[3]	Percent below poverty	Margin of error (±)[3]
United States	48,190,992	11,197,648	77,014	23.2	0.2
Alabama	170,351	53,203	3,032	31.2	1.8
Alaska	37,976	3,925	614	10.3	1.6
Arizona	1,817,790	469,009	10,185	25.8	0.6
Arkansas	174,123	53,978	2,833	31.0	1.6
California	13,503,094	2,803,788	25,767	20.8	0.2
Colorado	985,873	240,274	6,643	24.4	0.7
Connecticut	449,691	110,895	3,844	24.7	0.9
Delaware	68,418	15,645	1,859	22.9	2.7
District of Columbia	51,852	7,268	958	14.0	1.9
Florida	4,057,788	790,397	13,282	19.5	0.3
Georgia	804,180	240,966	7,118	30.0	0.9
Hawaii	114,599	17,869	1,541	15.6	1.3
Idaho	164,689	45,994	2,208	27.9	1.3
Illinois	1,959,070	376,023	8,442	19.2	0.4
Indiana	367,774	100,729	3,823	27.4	1.0
Iowa	139,236	35,990	1,962	25.8	1.4
Kansas	280,455	68,985	3,426	24.6	1.2
Kentucky	119,640	37,685	2,232	31.5	1.9
Louisiana	177,171	35,182	2,196	19.9	1.2
Maine	16,612	4,774	560	28.7	3.4
Maryland	442,416	56,112	3,267	12.7	0.7
Massachusetts	587,872	175,533	5,106	29.9	0.9
Michigan	420,184	117,043	3,324	27.9	0.8
Minnesota	237,023	58,356	2,601	24.6	1.1
Mississippi	70,914	19,714	1,615	27.8	2.2
Missouri	199,949	50,199	2,563	25.1	1.3
Montana	26,996	6,708	750	24.8	2.7
Nebraska	154,497	37,563	2,104	24.3	1.4
Nevada	689,331	136,444	4,921	19.8	0.7
New Hampshire	34,822	6,051	868	17.4	2.5
New Jersey	1,487,862	268,776	6,940	18.1	0.5
New Mexico	915,122	220,754	5,430	24.1	0.6
New York	3,282,749	818,211	10,517	24.9	0.3
North Carolina	747,738	235,175	6,769	31.5	0.9
North Dakota	12,443	2,703	392	21.7	3.1
Ohio	333,626	95,465	3,969	28.6	1.2
Oklahoma	308,731	87,596	3,285	28.4	1.1
Oregon	427,756	113,281	4,504	26.5	1.1
Pennsylvania	662,044	209,169	5,812	31.6	0.9
Rhode Island	123,727	37,085	2,020	30.0	1.6
South Carolina	214,207	63,858	3,236	29.8	1.5
South Dakota	20,286	4,632	653	22.8	3.2
Tennessee	270,686	87,068	3,610	32.2	1.3
Texas	9,035,286	2,340,708	23,191	25.9	0.3
Utah	336,479	75,690	3,562	22.5	1.1
Vermont	8,886	1,618	269	18.2	3.0
Virginia	588,949	87,109	3,904	14.8	0.7
Washington	710,202	185,613	5,723	26.1	0.8
West Virginia	19,725	4,399	633	22.3	3.2
Wisconsin	314,991	75,040	3,197	23.8	1.0
Wyoming	45,111	7,396	901	16.4	2.0

[1] Poverty status is determined for individuals in housing units and noninstitutional group quarters. The poverty universe excludes children under age 15 who are not related to the householder, people living in institutional group quarters, and people living in college dormitories or military barracks.

[2] Because Hispanics may be any race, data in this report for Hispanics overlap with data for race groups. Data users should exercise caution when interpreting aggregate results for race groups or for the Hispanic population because these populations consist of many distinct groups that differ in socioeconomic characteristics, culture, and recency of immigration. For more information see the 2010 Census Brief, Overview of Race and Hispanic Origin, at www.census.gov/prod/cen2010/briefs/c2010br-02.pdf.

[3] Data are based on a sample and are subject to sampling variability. A margin of error is a measure of an estimate's variability. The larger the margin of error in relation to the size of the estimate, the less reliable the estimate. This number when added to or subtracted from the estimate forms the 90 percent confidence interval.

Source: U.S. Census Bureau, 2007-2011 American Community Survey.

Notes

1. Poverty rates for Vietnamese and Koreans were not statistically different from one another.

2. Definitions of the race and Hispanic-origin groups used in this brief are available in the 2010 ACS Subject Definitions Guide available at www.census.gov/acs/www/data_documentation/documentation_main/.

   Individuals who responded to the question on race by indicating only one race are referred to as the race-alone population (e.g., "White alone," "Black alone," etc.). As a matter of policy, the U.S. Census Bureau does not advocate the use of the alone population over the alone-or-in-combination population or vice versa. The text and figures of this report focus on the race-alone population. This approach does not imply that it is a preferred method of presenting or analyzing data. The tables in this report show data using both approaches.

   Because Hispanics may be of any race, data for Hispanics overlap with data for race groups. Therefore, data users should exercise caution when comparing aggregate results for race population groups and the Hispanic population.

3. Poverty rates for Whites and Asians were not statistically different from one another.

4. Poverty rates for Samoans (17.6 percent) and Tongans (18.1 percent) were not statistically different from one another.

5. Poverty rates for Vietnamese and Koreans were not statistically different from one another.

6. Poverty rates for the White population in Arizona and Tennessee were not statistically different from one another. The poverty rate for the White population in Idaho was not statistically different from Tennessee.

7. Poverty rates for American Indian and Alaska Native (AlAN) in Maryland, New Hampshire, and Virginia were not statistically different from one another.

8. The poverty rate for AlAN in North Dakota was not statistically different from the rate for AlAN in Nebraska.

9. The maximum number of people who reported a particular race is reflected in the race alone-or-in-combination population. The race alone-or-in-combination population is the total number of people who reported a particular race, whether or not they reported any other races.

10. Poverty rates for the White population in Arizona and Tennessee were not statistically different from one another. The poverty rate for the White population in Idaho was not statistically different from Tennessee.

11. Poverty rates for Asians in Idaho, Indiana, and North Dakota were not statistically different from one another.

12. Poverty rates for Hispanics in Kentucky, Pennsylvania, and Tennessee were not statistically different from one another.

13. Poverty rates for Native Hawaiian and Other Pacific Islander (NHPI) in Connecticut, Illinois, and New Hampshire were not statisti- cally different from one another.

14. Poverty rates for NHPI in Arkansas, Nebraska, and Oklahoma were not statistically different from one another.

Critical Thinking

1. Evaluate the causes and remedies for poverty.
2. Discuss the opportunities and obstacles of entering the workforce.

Create Central

www.mhhe.com/createcentral

Internet References

National Association for the Advancement of Colored People (NAACP)
   www.naacp.org
Sociosite
   www.sociosite.net
The National Urban League
   www.nul.org

U.S Census Bureau, 2013.

Unit 6

UNIT

Prepared by: John A. Kromkowski, *The Catholic University of America*

Hispanic/Latino Americans

Hispanic/Latino Americans are a composite of ethnicities. "The clustering of these ethnicities and nationalities are based upon their mutually shared relationship with the Spanish Language as well as their similar experiences as either recent immigrants, refugees, or populations coercively incorporated into the United States. This seems to be sufficient evidence of the commonalities that constitute the shared expression of this complex of memory and contemporary politics." Yet the terms "Hispanic" and "Latino", used to differentiate them from Anglo-American foundations, are but the surface of the process of inter-group dynamics in the United States. The social expressions of these groups, as they search for cultural and political terrain, are certainly not monolithic. A wider horizon into which this topic can be placed can be gained by recalling that the term "Hispanic" emerged from an act of political will and cultural entrepreneurship. This substantive and consequential emergence of community leadership and coalition building during the urban ferment of the 1960s is most relevant to understanding race and ethnic relations.

The overall and interrelated character and mobility of ethnic groups and the particularity of locations are both relevant for the serious consideration of the Hispanic/Latino presence in the United States. The following examples frame the importance of a place-specific approach to understanding ethnicity in general and, in this case, variations found in the Hispanic presence.

- The Hispanic presence in New York, Connecticut, and Cleveland could focus on Puerto Ricans.
- The Hispanic presence in New York could focus on relations among newer Hispanics, such as Mexicans and Dominicans, and long-time residents of New York, the Puerto Ricans.
- The Hispanic presence in Miami could not ignore Cubans.
- The Hispanic presence in Texas, Arizona, California, and New Mexico could focus on border cities.
- The Hispanic presence in New Mexico and Arizona could address the differences in state political cultures that seem to drive fundamentally different approaches to governance and ethnic relations.
- The Hispanic presence in Hazelton, Pennsylvania and Arizona and Alabama could address other very recent uses of city ordinances and state laws that terrorized and removed populations.
- The Hispanic presence in the executive suites of major corporations could be assessed as measures of economic mobility from the margin to the mainstream.
- The Hispanic presence in prisons and gangs and criminal action could be assessed.
- The Hispanic presence in arts, music, film, and literature could be tracked and translations of classics of various ethnic/national traditions, as well as new literature from the experiences of immigrant and ethnic communities, could be reviewed.
- The Hispanic presence in the restaurant industry could be compared to the Italian American presence.
- The Hispanic presence in professional baseball could be assessed as a mobility strategy.
- The Hispanic presence in the faculties of higher education and in other professions and various private sector segments of the economy can be measured, and indices of dissimilarity can be tabulated.
- The Hispanic presence can be used to assess levels of social distance by context, across groups, and by location.
- The Hispanic presence of immigrants from Caribbean and Central American countries could be contrasted with immigrants from Mexico and South American countries.
- The social and economic mobility of Hispanic immigrants from Caribbean and Central American countries can be measured against immigrants from Caribbean countries that were part of French, Dutch, and British empires.
- The Hispanic presence and the immigration experiences could be compared to immigrant experiences of recent African American immigrants whose experiences and traditional memories do not include the trauma and struggle to overcome slavery, peonage, *de jure* segregation, large scale incarceration, and generations of encounters with economic and governmental sectors of America.
- The Hispanic presence of immigrants from Caribbean, Central American, and South American countries and Mexico could be compared to the grandchildren of immigrants from these and other countries.
- The Hispanic presence in Congress and the President's cabinet; their role as ambassadors; their involvement in policy development, as well as leadership positions in Congressional staffs, federal agencies, national advocacy, and research organizations; and their involvement with major public affair journals, media, and communication organizations could be analyzed.

- The Hispanic presence in military services could be compared to the African American and Polish American presence in the armed forces. This could be compared without attention to race and ethnicity, but to economic class and age cohorts.
- The Hispanic presence that emerges from content analysis of local radio, television, and advertising and its impact on self-image, identity, and community building could be analyzed. In addition, an inventory of ownership and origins of positive and negative programming could be analyzed.
- The Hispanic presence in a directory of institutions, organizations, and associations, including religious congregations and religiously affiliated institutions and their funding and fields of action, range of capacities, and measures of adequacy, importance, and short falls could be considered.
- The Hispanic presence as measured by a full social, economic, and housing demography and comparative indicia for each ethnic group and each location could be analyzed.

- The Hispanic presence located in Virginia, Maryland, and the Federal District, as well as disaggregation by counties, cities, towns, and neighborhoods could be considered.

What does Hispanic/Latino really mean? Am I Hispanic because I am a fluent Spanish speaking person and an immigrant from Romania and Brazil? If not, then what does Hispanic/Latino really mean? What purposes do such meanings and questions of meaning, belonging, or participating in a Hispanic aspect serve? Posing such questions, and other less cosmic and exotic inquiries about various dimensions of ethnic identity and ethnic issues, provocatively shifts perspectives toward the fact of immigration and group participation of immigrants, their children, and grandchildren in the United States. American mentalities vary from region to region. What may be clear in many Eastern and Midwestern states are contentious concerns in many Western and southwestern states, as well as sources of confusion, bafflement, and anger in some Southern states.

Article   Prepared by: John A. Kromkowski, *The Catholic University of America*

Facts for Features: Hispanic Heritage Month 2014: Sept. 15–Oct. 15

U.S. Census Bureau

Learning Outcomes

After reading this article, you will be able to:

- Identify the most troubling demographic indicators and the most celebrated aspects of Hispanic Heritage.

- Name what ethnic groups comprise and in what ways these ethnicities constitute Hispanic Heritage.

- Explain the role of language in the development of a culture and heritage.

In September 1968, Congress authorized President Lyndon B. Johnson to proclaim National Hispanic Heritage Week, observed during the week that included Sept. 15 and Sept. 16. Congress expanded the observance in 1989 to a monthlong celebration (Sept. 15–Oct. 15) of the culture and traditions of those who trace their roots to Spain, Mexico and the Spanish-speaking nations of Central America, South America and the Caribbean.

Sept. 15 is the starting point for the celebration because it is the anniversary of independence of five Latin American countries: Costa Rica, El Salvador, Guatemala, Honduras and Nicaragua. In addition, Mexico and Chile celebrate their independence days on Sept. 16 and Sept. 18, respectively.

Population

54 million

The Hispanic population of the United States as of July 1, 2013, making people of Hispanic origin the nation's largest ethnic or racial minority. Hispanics constituted 17 percent of the nation's total population.

Source: 2013 Population Estimates

<http://factfinder2.census.gov/faces/tableservices/jsf/pages/productview.xhtml?pid=PEP_2013_PEPASR6H&prodType=table>

1.1 million

Number of Hispanics added to the nation's population between July 1, 2012, and July 1, 2013. This number is close to half of the approximately 2.3 million people added to the nation's population during this period.

Source: 2013 Population Estimates

National Characteristics: Population by Sex, Race, and Hispanic origin

<http://www.census.gov/popest/data/national/asrh/2013/index.html>, See first bullet under "Sex, Race, and Hispanic Origin"

2.0%

Percentage increase in the Hispanic population between 2012 and 2013.

Source: 2013 Population Estimates

National Characteristics: Population by Sex, Race, and Hispanic origin

<http://www.census.gov/popest/data/national/asrh/2013/index.html>, See first bullet under "Sex, Race, and Hispanic Origin"

128.8 million

The projected Hispanic population of the United States in 2060. According to this projection, the Hispanic population will constitute 31 percent of the nation's population by that date.

Source: Population Projections

<http://www.census.gov/newsroom/releases/archives/population/cb12-243.html>

2nd
Ranking of the size of the U.S. Hispanic population worldwide, as of 2010. Only Mexico (120 million) had a larger Hispanic population than the United States (54 million).

Source: International Data Base
<http://www.census.gov/population/international/data/idb/informationGateway.php>

64%
The percentage of those of Hispanic origin in the United States who were of Mexican background in 2012. Another 9.4 percent were of Puerto Rican background, 3.8 percent Salvadoran, 3.7 percent Cuban, 3.1 percent Dominican and 2.3 percent Guatemalan. The remainder was of some other Central American, South American or other Hispanic/Latino origin.

Source: U.S. Census Bureau, 2012 American Community Survey: Table B03001
<http://factfinder2.census.gov/faces/tableservices/jsf/pages/productview.xhtml?pid=ACS_12_1YR_B03001&prodType=table>

States and Counties
34.4 years
Median age of Hispanics in Florida, the highest of any state in the country.

Source: 2013 Population Estimates
State Characteristics: Median Age by Race and Hispanic Origin
<http://factfinder2.census.gov/faces/tableservices/jsf/pages/productview.xhtml?pid=PEP_2013_PEPASR6H&prodType=table>

10 million
The estimated population for those of Hispanic origin in Texas as of July 1, 2013.

Source: 2013 Population Estimates
State Characteristics: Population by Sex, Race, and Hispanic Origin
<http://www.census.gov/popest/data/national/asrh/2013/index.html>

8
The number of states with a population of 1 million or more Hispanic residents in 2013—Arizona, California, Colorado, Florida, Illinois, New Jersey, New York and Texas.

Source: 2013 Population Estimates
State Characteristics: Population by Race and Hispanic Origin

<http://www.census.gov/popest/data/national/asrh/2013/index.html>

55%
The percentage of all the Hispanic population that lived in California, Florida and Texas as of July 1, 2013.

Source: 2013 Population Estimates
State Characteristics: Population by Race and Hispanic Origin
<http://www.census.gov/popest/data/national/asrh/2013/index.html>

47.3%
The percentage of New Mexico's population that was Hispanic as of July 1, 2013, the highest of any state.

Source: 2013 Population Estimates
State Characteristics: Population by Race and Hispanic Origin
<http://www.census.gov/popest/data/national/asrh/2013/index.html>

14.7 million
The Hispanic population of California. This is the largest Hispanic population of any state.

Source: 2013 Population Estimates
<http://www.census.gov/newsroom/press-releases/2013/cb13-112.html>

4.8 million
Los Angeles County had the largest Hispanic population of any county in 2013.

Source: 2013 Population Estimates
<http://www.census.gov/newsroom/press-releases/2014/cb14-118.html>

50,000
Miami-Dade County in Florida had the largest numeric increase of Hispanics from 2012 to 2013.

Source: 2013 Population Estimates
<http://www.census.gov/newsroom/press-releases/2014/cb14-118.html>

22
Number of states in which Hispanics were the largest minority group. These states were Arizona, California, Colorado, Connecticut, Florida, Idaho, Illinois, Iowa, Kansas, Massachusetts, Nebraska, Nevada, New Hampshire, New Jersey, New Mexico, New York, Oregon, Rhode Island, Texas, Utah, Washington and Wyoming.

Source: 2013 Population Estimates, PEPSR6H and PEPSR5H
<http://factfinder2.census.gov/faces/tableservices/
jsf/pages/productview.xhtml?pid=PEP_2013_PEPSR5H&
prodType=table> and
<http://factfinder2.census.gov/faces/tableservices/
jsf/pages/productview.xhtml?pid=PEP_2013_PEPSR6H&
prodType=table>

Families and Children
11.9 million
The number of Hispanic family households in the United States
in 2013.

Source: Families and Living Arrangements: Table F1
<http://www.census.gov/hhes/families/files/cps2013/tabF1-
hisp.xls>

62.4%
The percentage of Hispanic family households that were
married-couple households in 2013. For the total population in
the U.S., it was 73.2 percent.

Source: Families and Living Arrangements: Table F1
<http://www.census.gov/hhes/families/files/cps2013/tabF1-
hisp.xls>
<http://www.census.gov/hhes/families/data/cps2013F.html>

58.5%
The percentage of Hispanic married-couple households that
had children younger than 18 present in 2013, whereas for the
nation it was 40.3 percent.

Source: Families and Living Arrangements: Table F1
<http://www.census.gov/hhes/families/files/cps2013/tabF1-
hisp.xls>
<http://www.census.gov/hhes/families/data/cps2013F.html>

65.1%
Percentage of Hispanic children living with two parents in
2013, whereas nationwide it was 68.5 percent.

Source: Families and Living Arrangements: Table C9
<http://www.census.gov/hhes/families/files/cps2013/tabC9-
hispanic.xls>
<http://www.census.gov/hhes/families/data/cps2013C.html>

43.1%
Percentage of Hispanic married couples with children under 18
where both spouses were employed in 2013, whereas nationwide it was 58.0 percent.

Source: Families and Living Arrangements: Table FG-1
<http://www.census.gov/hhes/families/data/cps2013FG
.html>

Spanish Language
38.3 million
The number of U.S. residents 5 and older who spoke Spanish
at home in 2012. This is a 121 percent increase since 1990
when it was 17.3 million. Those who *hablan español en casa*
constituted 13.0 percent of U.S. residents 5 and older. More
than half (58 percent) of these Spanish speakers spoke English
"very well."

Source: U.S. Census Bureau, 2012 American Community
Survey: Table B16001 and Table DP02
<http://factfinder2.census.gov/faces/tableservices/jsf/pages/
productview.xhtml?pid=ACS_12_1YR_DP02&prodType=
table> and Language Use in the United States: 2012
<http://www.census.gov/prod/2013pubs/acs-22.pdf>

73.9%
Percentage of Hispanics 5 and older who spoke Spanish at
home in 2012.

Source: U.S. Census Bureau, 2012 American Community
Survey: Table B16006
<http://factfinder2.census.gov/faces/tableservices/jsf/
pages/productview.xhtml?pid=ACS_12_1YR_B16006&
prodType=table>

Income, Poverty and Health Insurance
$39,005
The median income of Hispanic households in 2012.

Source: Income, Poverty, and Health Insurance Coverage in
the United States: 2012, Table A
<http://www.census.gov/newsroom/press-releases/2013/
cb13-165.html>

25.6%
The poverty rate among Hispanics in 2012 was 25.6 percent.

Source: Income, Poverty, and Health Insurance Coverage in
the United States: 2012, Table B
<http://www.census.gov/newsroom/press-releases/2013/
cb13-165.html>

29.1%
The percentage of Hispanics who lacked health insurance in
2012, down from 30.1 percent in 2011

Source: Income, Poverty, and Health Insurance Coverage
in the United States: 2012, Table C <http://www.census.gov/
newsroom/press-releases/2013/cb13-165.html>

Education
64.0%
The percentage of Hispanics 25 and older that had at least a high school education in 2012.

Source: American Community Survey: 2012 Table S0201 (Hispanic Origin)

<http://factfinder2.census.gov/faces/tableservices/jsf/pages/productview.xhtml?pid=ACS_12_1YR_S0201&prodType=table>

13.8%
The percentage of the Hispanic population 25 and older with a bachelor's degree or higher in 2012. American Community Survey: 2012 Table S0201 (Hispanic Origin)

<http://factfinder2.census.gov/faces/tableservices/jsf/pages/productview.xhtml?pid=ACS_12_1YR_S0201&prodType=table>

4 million
The number of Hispanics 25 and older who had at least a bachelor's degree in 2012.

Source: American Community Survey: 2012 Table C1502I

<http://factfinder2.census.gov/faces/tableservices/jsf/pages/productview.xhtml?pid=ACS_12_1YR_C15002I&prodType=table>

1.3 million
Number of Hispanics 25 and older with advanced degrees in 2012 (e.g., master's, professional, doctorate).

Source: American Community Survey: 2012 Table B150021 (Hispanic origin)

<http://factfinder2.census.gov/faces/tableservices/jsf/pages/productview.xhtml?pid=ACS_12_1YR_B15002I&prodType=table>

6.8%
Percentage of students (both undergraduate and graduate) enrolled in college in 2012 who were Hispanic.

Source: School Enrollment Data Current Population Survey: October 2012, Table1

<http://www.census.gov/hhes/school/data/cps/2012/tables.html>

23.3%
Percentage of elementary and high school students that were Hispanic in 2012.

Source: School Enrollment Data Current Population Survey: October 2012, Table 1

<http://www.census.gov/hhes/school/data/cps/2012/tables.html>

Foreign-Born
35.6%
Percentage of the Hispanic population that was foreign-born in 2012.

Source: U.S. Census Bureau, 2012 American Community Survey, Table: S0201

<http://factfinder2.census.gov/bkmk/table/1.0/en/ACS/12_1YR/S0201//popgroup~400>

64.3%
Percentage of the 10.3 million noncitizens under the age of 35 who were born in Latin America and the Caribbean and are living in the United States in 2010–2012.

<http://www.census.gov/prod/2014pubs/acsbr12-06.pdf>

Jobs
67.1%
Percentage of Hispanics or Latinos 16 and older who were in the civilian labor force in 2012.

Source: U.S. Census Bureau, 2012 American Community Survey, Table: S0201 (Hispanic) and B23002i

<http://factfinder2.census.gov/faces/tableservices/jsf/pages/productview.xhtml?pid=ACS_12_1YR_S0201&prodType=table>

<http://factfinder2.census.gov/faces/tableservices/jsf/pages/productview.xhtml?pid=ACS_12_1YR_B23002I&prodType=table>

19.5%
The percentage of civilian employed Hispanics or Latinos 16 and older who worked in management, business, science and arts occupations in 2012.

Source: U.S. Census Bureau, 2012 American Community Survey, Table C24010I

<http://factfinder2.census.gov/bkmk/table/1.0/en/ACS/12_1YR/C24010I?>

Voting
8.4%
The percentage of voters in the 2012 presidential election who were Hispanic. Hispanics comprised 7 percent of voters in 2010.

Source: News Release: Census Bureau Reports Hispanic Voter Turnout Reaches Record High for Congressional Election

<http://www.census.gov/newsroom/releases/archives/voting/cb11-164.html> and Voting and Registration in the Election of November 2012: Table 2

<http://www.census.gov/hhes/www/socdemo/voting/publications/p20/2012/tables.html>

Serving Our Country

1.2 million

The number of Hispanics or Latinos 18 and older who are veterans of the U.S. armed forces.

Source: U.S. Census Bureau, 2012 American Community Survey: Table B21001I

<http://factfinder2.census.gov/faces/tableservices/jsf/pages/productview.xhtml?pid=ACS_12_1YR_B21001I&prodType=table>

Businesses

Source for statements in this section: Statistics for All U.S. Firms by Industry, Gender, Ethnicity, and Race for the United States, States, Metro Areas, Counties, and Places: 2007, Table SB0700CSA01

<http://factfinder2.census.gov/faces/tableservices/jsf/pages/productview.xhtml?pid=SBO_2007_00CSA01&prodType=table> Data for 2012 are being collected.

2.3 million

The number of Hispanic-owned businesses in 2007, up 43.6 percent from 2002.

$350.7 billion

Receipts generated by Hispanic-owned businesses in 2007, up 58.0 percent from 2002.

23.7%

The percentage of businesses in New Mexico in 2007 that were Hispanic-owned, which led all states. Florida (22.4 percent) and Texas (20.7 percent) were runners-up.

The following is a list of observances typically covered by the Census Bureau's *Facts for Features* series:

African-American History Month (February)
Super Bowl
Valentine's Day (Feb. 14)
Women's History Month (March)

Irish-American Heritage Month (March)/St. Patrick's Day (March 17)
Earth Day (April 22)
Asian/Pacific American Heritage Month (May)
Older Americans Month (May)
Mother's Day
Hurricane Season Begins (June 1)
Father's Day
The Fourth of July (July 4)
Anniversary of Americans with Disabilities Act (July 26)
Back to School (August)
Labor Day
Grandparents Day
Hispanic Heritage Month (Sept. 15–Oct. 15)
Unmarried and Single Americans Week
Halloween (Oct. 31)
American Indian/Alaska Native Heritage Month (November)
Veterans Day (Nov. 11)
Thanksgiving Day
The Holiday Season (December)

Critical Thinking

1. What do demographic indicators reveal about an ethnic group?
2. Is there evidence for improving outcomes?
3. How important is the official recognition and acknowledgment of an ethnic group?

Internet References

Hispanic Access Foundation
www.haf.org
Latino American Network Information Center (LANIC)
http://lanic.utexas.edu
League of United Latino Citizens
www.lulac.org
National Association of Latin American Elected Officials
www.naleo.org
National Council of La Raza (NCLR)
www.nclr.org

Profile America Facts. "Facts for Features: Hispanic Heritage Month 2014: Sept 15–Oct 15", *U.S. Department of Commerce, Economics, and Statistics Administration,* September 2014.

Article   Prepared by: John A. Kromkowski, *Catholic University of America*

The Foreign Born from Latin America and the Caribbean: 2010

Learning Outcomes

After reading this article, you will be able to:

- Identify the most troubling demographic indicators about the foreign-born population from Central America.

- Explain whether this report is hopeful or pessimistic about the future for Hispanic/Latino/a Americans?

- List the countries from which Hispanic/Latino/a immigrants are coming to the United States.

Introduction

During the last 50 years, the number of foreign born from Latin America and the Caribbean has increased rapidly, from less than 1 million in 1960 to 21.2 million in 2010.[1] Currently, the foreign born from Latin America represent over half of the total foreign-born population. This brief will discuss the size, place of birth, citizenship status, and geographic distribution of the foreign born from Latin America in the United States. It presents data on the foreign born from Latin America at the national and state levels based on the 2010 American Community Survey (ACS).

Defining Nativity Status: Who Is Foreign Born?

Nativity status refers to whether a person is native or foreign born. The native-born population includes anyone who was a U.S. citizen at birth. Respondents who were born in the United States, Puerto Rico, a U.S. Island Area (U.S. Virgin Islands, Guam, American Samoa, or the Commonwealth of the Northern Mariana Islands), or abroad of a U.S. citizen parent or parents, are defined as native born. The foreign-born population includes anyone who was not a U.S. citizen at birth, including those who have become U.S. citizens through naturalization.

In 2010, 309.3 million people lived in the United States, including 40.0 million foreign born (13 percent of the total population). In 2000, 31.1 million of the 281.4 million U.S. residents were foreign—born—11 percent of the total population.[2] Over the decade, the foreign-born population increased by 8.8 million.

Over half (53 percent) of all foreign-born U.S. residents in 2010 were from Latin America (Table 1). Another 28 percent were from Asia. The next largest world region-of-birth group, the foreign born from Europe, represented 12 percent of all foreign born—less than half the size of the foreign born from Asia. About 4 percent of the foreign born were born in Africa and 3 percent were from other regions, including Oceania and Northern America. The single largest country-of-birth group was from Mexico (29 percent of all foreign born).

Findings

In 2000, 16.1 million foreign born from Latin America lived in the United States. Over the last 10 years, the foreign-born population from Latin America increased by 5.1 million, reaching 21.2 million in 2010.

The majority of the foreign born from Latin America were from Central America (70 percent), followed by the Caribbean (18 percent), and South America (13 percent) (Table 2). Mexico accounted for more than half (55 percent) of the foreign born from Latin America. El Salvador and Cuba each represented more than 5 percent. Among the foreign born from the Caribbean, those born in Cuba (30 percent) and the Dominican Republic (24 percent) represented the largest proportion of all foreign born. Over three-fourths of all foreign born from Central America were born in Mexico (79 percent). Colombia represented the largest share of the foreign born from South America (23 percent).

Although the foreign born from Latin America were found across the country, most were concentrated in only a few states. In 2010, 26 percent (or 5.5 million) of the foreign born from Latin America lived in California, 14 percent (or 3.0 million) in Texas, 13 percent (or 2.8 million) in Florida, and 10 percent (or 2.2 million) in New York (Figure 1). When combined, these four states accounted for 63 percent (or 13.4 million) of the total Latin American foreign born.

Table 1 Foreign-Born Population by Region of Birth: 2010

Region of birth	Number		Percent	
	Estimate	Margin of error (±)[1]	Estimate	Margin of error (±)[1]
Total	39,956	115	100.0	(X)
Africa	1,607	33	4.0	0.1
Asia..	11,284	47	28.2	0.1
Europe...	4,817	44	12.1	0.1
Latin America and the Caribbean	21,224	90	53.1	0.1
Caribbean	3,731	42	9.3	0.1
Central America	14,764	90	36.9	0.2
Mexico	11,711	83	29.3	0.2
Other Central America[2]	3,053	46	7.6	0.1
South America	2,730	42	6.8	0.1
Other regions[3].....................................	1,024	19	2.6	—

(Numbers in thousands. Data based on sample. For information on confidentiality protection, sampling error, nonsampling error, and definitions, see *www.census.gov/acs/www*)

— Represents or rounds to zero.

(X) Not applicable.

[1]Data are based on a sample and are subject to sampling variability. A margin of error is a measure of an estimate's variability. The larger the margin of error is in relation to the size of the estimate, the less reliable the estimate. This number when added to and subtracted from the estimate forms the 90 percent confidence interval.

[2]Other Central America includes Belize, Costa Rica, El Salvador, Guatemala, Honduras, Nicaragua, and Panama.

[3]Other regions includes Oceania and Northern America.

Source: U.S. Census Bureau, 2010 American Community Survey.

In 19 states, the foreign-born population from Latin America composed over half of the state's foreign-born population (Figure 2). In the South and West, the foreign-born population from Latin America represented 65 percent or more of the total foreign-born population in Arizona, Arkansas, Florida, New Mexico, and Texas. In Florida and New Mexico, approximately 75 percent of the foreign-born population were born in Latin America. In just nine states, the foreign-born population from Latin America represented less than 25 percent of the foreign-born population. In Maine and North Dakota, they were approximately 10 percent. In Hawaii, they were less than 10 percent.

In over three-fourths of all states and the District of Columbia, the foreign-born populations from Central America represented more than half of the Latin American foreign born (Table 3). The foreign born from Mexico represented about 9 out of 10 foreign born from Latin America in New Mexico, Arizona, and Idaho. The foreign born from the Caribbean represented about one-third of the Latin American foreign born in seven states. Two of these states—Florida (55 percent) and New York (49 percent)—each have Latin American foreign-born populations of 2 million or more.

In 2010, 32 percent of the foreign-born population from Latin America were naturalized citizens (Table 4). The foreign-born population from Central America had the lowest percent

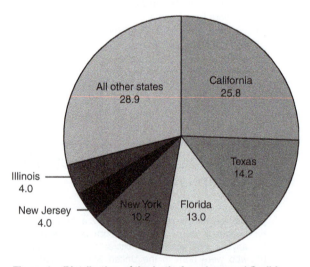

Figure 1. Distribution of the Latin American and Caribbean Foreign Born by State: 2010 (Percent distribution. Data based on sample. For information on confidentiality protection, sampling error, nonsampling error, and definitions, see *www. census.gov/acs/www*)

Source: U.S. Census Bureau, 2010 American Community Survey.

Table 2 Foreign-Born Population From Latin America and the Caribbean by Country of Birth: 2010

Region and country of birth	Number		Percent of total		Percent of region	
	Estimate	Margin of error (±)[1]	Estimate	Margin of error (±)[1]	Estimate	Margin of error (±)[1]
Total	21,224	90	100.0	(X)	(X)	(X)
Caribbean...................................	3,731	42	17.6	0.2	100.0	(X)
Cuba	1,105	27	5.2	0.1	29.6	0.6
Dominican Republic	879	24	4.1	0.1	23.6	0.6
Haiti	587	21	2.8	0.1	15.7	0.6
Jamaica.......................................	660	20	3.1	0.1	17.7	0.5
Other Caribbean[2]	500	17	2.4	0.1	13.4	0.4
Central America...........................	14,764	90	69.6	0.2	100.0	(X)
Mexico	11,711	83	55.2	0.3	79.3	0.3
El Salvador.................................	1,214	34	5.7	0.2	8.2	0.2
Guatemala	831	29	3.9	0.1	5.6	0.2
Honduras	523	24	2.5	0.1	3.5	0.2
Other Central America[3]	485	17	2.3	0.1	3.3	0.1
South America	2,730	42	12.9	0.2	100.0	(X)
Brazil..	340	15	1.6	0.1	12.4	0.5
Colombia.....................................	637	19	3.0	0.1	23.3	0.6
Ecuador......................................	443	20	2.1	0.1	16.2	0.6
Peru	429	18	2.0	0.1	15.7	0.6
Other South America[4]	882	23	4.2	0.1	32.3	0.7

(Numbers in thousands. Data based on sample. For information on confidentiality protection, sampling error, nonsampling error, and definitions, see *www.census.gov/acs/www*)

(X) Not applicable.

[1]Data are based on a sample and are subject to sampling variability. A margin of error is a measure of an estimate's variability. The larger the margin of error is in relation to the size of the estimate, the less reliable the estimate. This number when added to and subtracted from the estimate forms the 90 percent confidence interval.

[2]Other Caribbean includes Anguilla, Antigua and Barbuda, Aruba, Bahamas, Barbados, British Virgin Islands, Cayman Islands, Dominica, Grenada, the former country of Guadeloupe (including St. Barthélemy and Saint-Martin), Martinique, Montserrat, the former country of the Netherlands Antilles (including Bonaire, Curaçao, Saba, Sint Eustatius, and Sint Maarten), St. Kitts and Nevis, St. Lucia, St. Vincent and the Grenadines, Trinidad and Tobago, and Turks and Caicos Islands.

[3]Other Central America includes Belize, Costa Rica, Nicaragua, and Panama.

[4]Other South America includes Argentina, Bolivia, Chile, Falkland Islands, French Guiana, Guyana, Paraguay, Suriname, Uruguay, and Venezuela.

Source: U.S. Census Bureau, 2010 American Community Survey.

naturalized of all regions of birth (24 percent). Of those born in the Caribbean, 54 percent were naturalized citizens. About 44 percent of the foreign born from South America were naturalized citizens. Among the country-of-birth groups shown, Jamaica (61 percent) and Cuba (56 percent) had the highest percent naturalized. By comparison, Mexico (23 percent) and Honduras (21 percent) were among the countries with the lowest percent naturalized.

Source and Accuracy

Data presented in this report are based on people and households that responded to the ACS in 2010. The resulting estimates are representative of the entire population. All comparisons presented in this report have taken sampling error into account and are significant at the 90 percent confidence level unless

otherwise noted. Due to rounding, some details may not sum to totals. For information on sampling and estimation methods, confidentiality protection, and sampling and nonsampling errors, please see the "2010 ACS Accuracy of the Data" document located at www.census.gov/acs/www/Downloads/data_documentation/Accuracy/ACS_Accuracy_of_Data_2010.pdf.

What is the American Community Survey?

The American Community Survey (ACS) is a nationwide survey designed to provide communities with reliable and timely demographic, social, economic, and housing data for the nation, states, congressional districts, counties, places, and other localities every year. It has an annual sample size of about 3 million addresses across the United States and Puerto

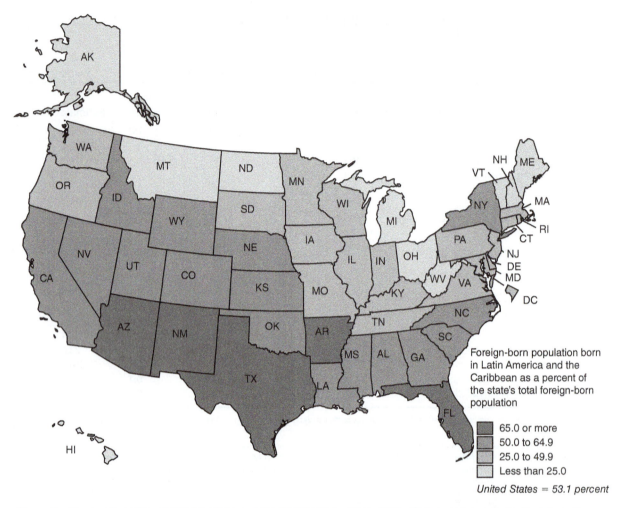

Figure 2. Foreign Born From Latin American and the Caribbean by State: 2010 (Data based on sample. For information on confidentiality protection, sampling error, nonsampling error, and definitions, see *www.census.gov/acs/www*)
Source: U.S. Census Bureau, 2010 American Community Survey.

Rico and includes both housing units and group quarters (e.g., nursing facilities and prisons). The ACS is conducted in every county throughout the nation, and every municipio in Puerto Rico, where it is called the Puerto Rico Community Survey. Beginning in 2006, ACS data for 2005 were released for geographic areas with populations 65,000 and greater. For information on the ACS sample design and other topics, visit www.census.gov/acs/www.

Table 3 Percent Distribution of the Foreign Born From Latin America and the Caribbean by Region of Birth and State: 2010

Area	Latin America		Caribbean		Central America						South America	
					Total		Mexico		Other Central America[1]			
	Number	Margin of error (±)²	Percent of total	Margin of error (±)²	Percent of total	Margin of error (±)²	Percent of total	Margin of error (±)²	Percent of total	Margin of error (±)²	Percent of total	Margin of error (±)²
United States	21,224	90	17.6	0.2	69.6	0.2	55.2	0.3	14.4	0.2	12.9	0.2
Alabama	98	5	5.4	1.6	86.8	2.6	70.0	3.8	16.7	3.5	7.8	2.1
Alaska	9	2	16.4	9.3	68.0	9.0	56.2	11.5	11.8	8.2	15.6	6.2
Arizona	572	13	2.2	0.5	94.9	0.7	90.4	1.0	4.5	0.9	2.9	0.5
Arkansas	88	5	1.7	0.9	94.4	1.6	73.4	3.6	21.0	3.6	3.9	1.5
California	5,477	43	1.3	0.1	94.4	0.2	78.8	0.5	15.6	0.4	4.4	0.2
Colorado	275	11	2.4	0.6	93.1	1.0	84.5	1.7	8.6	1.4	4.5	0.9
Connecticut	205	11	36.3	2.6	26.2	3.0	10.2	1.9	16.0	2.7	37.5	3.2
Delaware	34	3	16.5	4.1	65.9	6.3	49.7	7.9	16.2	5.6	17.6	5.4
District of Columbia	36	3	20.8	4.8	59.8	6.7	10.8	5.1	49.0	7.5	19.4	5.1
Florida	2,752	30	55.1	0.9	21.5	0.8	9.6	0.5	11.9	0.6	23.4	0.7
Georgia	515	12	16.4	1.3	72.5	1.5	56.3	2.0	16.2	1.6	11.1	1.0
Hawaii	13	3	14.7	7.9	55.6	9.0	41.0	9.1	14.6	5.8	29.7	7.9
Idaho	54	4	1.2	0.9	93.4	2.0	88.2	3.1	5.2	3.1	5.4	1.8
Illinois	842	16	3.0	0.4	90.2	0.9	84.1	1.1	6.1	0.8	6.8	0.8
Indiana	143	6	4.9	1.1	89.2	1.8	76.9	2.6	12.3	2.1	5.9	1.4
Iowa	60	4	2.1	1.2	91.0	2.6	75.0	4.4	16.0	3.8	6.9	2.5
Kansas	106	6	1.0	0.5	94.0	1.5	83.8	2.5	10.2	2.5	5.0	1.4
Kentucky	60	4	16.3	3.3	76.0	3.9	60.7	4.8	15.3	3.7	7.8	2.1
Louisiana	93	5	11.3	2.4	79.2	2.8	32.6	3.5	46.6	3.6	9.5	2.4
Maine	4	1	34.5	12.6	25.2	14.0	11.8	10.9	13.4	8.8	40.4	14.2
Maryland	312	9	16.9	1.6	63.0	1.9	11.3	1.5	51.7	2.5	20.1	1.7
Massachusetts	356	13	42.6	2.1	24.0	1.9	4.4	0.9	19.6	1.9	33.4	2.1
Michigan	118	7	11.9	2.2	78.3	2.9	67.7	3.5	10.6	2.1	9.8	1.7
Minnesota	104	5	4.7	1.4	77.5	3.1	63.4	3.7	14.1	2.7	17.8	2.8
Mississippi	32	3	8.9	4.4	78.5	5.5	64.3	6.5	14.3	5.1	12.5	4.9
Missouri	72	6	11.9	3.0	77.2	3.6	62.5	4.2	14.7	3.2	10.9	2.5
Montana	2	1	6.7	6.7	45.0	16.2	41.5	17.3	3.6	4.5	48.3	16.1
Nebraska	61	4	1.9	1.1	94.2	1.8	75.0	4.8	19.3	4.7	3.9	1.6
Nevada	291	8	6.7	1.0	88.4	1.4	75.1	1.8	13.3	1.7	5.0	0.9

(continued)

| | Latin America | | Caribbean | | Central America | | | | | | South America | |
Area	Number	Margin of error (±)²	Percent of total	Margin of error (±)²	Total Percent of total	Margin of error (±)²	Mexico Percent of total	Margin of error (±)²	Other Central America¹ Percent of total	Margin of error (±)²	Percent of total	Margin of error (±)²
New Hampshire	14	3	31.4	9.9	35.2	11.0	20.8	11.0	14.4	6.0	33.5	10.8
New Jersey	852	15	32.4	1.5	30.9	1.3	15.2	1.1	15.6	1.1	36.8	1.5
New Mexico	163	9	2.2	0.7	95.1	1.4	91.4	1.6	3.7	1.3	2.7	1.0
New York	2,155	28	49.3	0.9	23.9	0.9	11.7	0.8	12.1	0.7	26.8	0.8
North Carolina	414	11	7.1	1.2	83.2	1.5	63.5	2.3	19.7	1.8	9.7	1.1
North Dakota	1	1	25.4	17.6	63.7	18.4	50.7	18.5	13.0	13.9	10.9	8.9
Ohio	101	6	13.7	3.6	70.3	4.3	53.8	4.8	16.5	3.0	16.0	3.1
Oklahoma	121	6	1.6	0.9	93.4	1.7	83.3	2.8	10.1	2.4	5.0	1.5
Oregon	175	8	2.2	0.8	94.0	1.1	86.2	2.0	7.9	2.0	3.7	0.8
Pennsylvania	221	11	39.6	2.8	38.2	2.7	26.7	2.3	11.5	1.7	22.2	2.3
Rhode Island	60	4	45.4	5.3	36.1	4.9	6.9	2.5	29.2	4.8	18.5	4.7
South Carolina	120	6	7.6	1.8	81.6	2.8	57.8	4.0	23.8	3.8	10.7	2.1
South Dakota	6	1	1.5	1.9	87.0	6.2	64.1	15.4	22.9	14.8	11.5	6.0
Tennessee	143	7	5.3	1.4	87.4	2.4	63.3	4.7	24.1	3.8	7.3	1.7
Texas	3,013	35	2.0	0.2	94.0	0.3	82.5	0.5	11.5	0.5	4.0	0.3
Utah	139	6	1.6	0.9	82.5	2.4	73.8	2.7	8.8	1.7	15.9	2.3
Vermont	3	1	18.0	11.9	40.1	20.5	33.7	22.0	6.5	5.7	41.9	15.7
Virginia	338	9	8.5	1.1	63.7	2.1	19.1	2.3	44.6	2.6	27.8	2.1
Washington	277	8	2.0	0.5	91.5	1.1	84.2	1.6	7.4	1.1	6.4	1.0
West Virginia	5	1	21.5	9.7	57.7	11.7	22.9	8.9	34.8	13.0	20.8	10.0
Wisconsin	110	6	3.7	1.0	88.1	2.3	80.3	2.5	7.7	1.8	8.2	2.0
Wyoming	9	2	—	—	84.4	9.5	75.1	10.3	9.3	6.7	15.6	9.5

(Numbers in thousands. Data based on sample. For information on confidentiality protection, sampling error, nonsampling error, and definitions, see www.census.gov/acs/www)

— Represents or rounds to zero.

¹Other Central America includes Belize, Costa Rica, El Salvador, Guatemala, Honduras, Nicaragua, and Panama.

²Data are based on a sample and are subject to sampling variability. A margin of error is a measure of an estimate's variability. The larger the margin of error is in relation to the size of the estimate, the less reliable the estimate. This number when added to and subtracted from the estimate forms the 90 percent confidence interval.

Source: U.S. Census Bureau, 2010 American Community Survey.

Table 4 Percent of the Foreign Born From Latin America and the Caribbean Who Are Naturalized U.S. Citizens by Place of Birth: 2010

	Percent	
Region and country of birth	**Estimate**	**Margin of error (±)[1]**
Total	32.1	0.3
Caribbean	54.1	0.6
Cuba.	55.7	1.2
Dominican Republic	47.7	1.4
Haiti	50.0	1.6
Jamaica	61.2	1.5
Other Caribbean[2]	57.7	1.6
Central America	24.3	0.3
Mexico	22.9	0.3
El Salvador.	27.9	1.0
Guatemala.	24.1	1.3
Honduras	21.1	1.4
Other Central America[3]	52.1	1.5
South America	44.4	0.6
Brazil.	28.2	1.7
Colombia.	48.2	1.3
Ecuador	40.7	1.8
Peru	43.2	1.7
Other South America[4]	50.3	1.1

(Data based on sample. For information on confidentiality protection, sampling error, nonsampling error, and definitions, see *www.census.gov/acs/www*)

[1]Data are based on a sample and are subject to sampling variability. A margin of error is a measure of an estimate's variability. The larger the margin of error is in relation to the size of the estimate, the less reliable the estimate. This number when added to and subtracted from the estimate forms the 90 percent confidence interval.

[2]Other Caribbean includes Anguilla, Antigua and Barbuda, Aruba, Bahamas, Barbados, British Virgin Islands, Cayman Islands, Dominica, Grenada, the former country of Guadeloupe (including St. Barthélemy and Saint-Martin), Martinique, Montserrat, the former country of the Netherlands Antilles (including Bonaire, Curaçao, Saba, Sint Eustatius, and Sint Maarten), St. Kitts and Nevis, St. Lucia, St. Vincent and the Grenadines, Trinidad and Tobago, and Turks and Caicos Islands.

[3]Other Central America includes Belize, Costa Rica, Nicaragua, and Panama.

[4]Other South America includes Argentina, Bolivia, Chile, Falkland Islands, French Guiana, Guyana, Paraguay, Suriname, Uruguay, and Venezuela.

Source: U.S. Census Bureau, 2010 American Community Survey.

Notes

1. The term *Latin America and the Caribbean* includes countries in Central and South America and the Caribbean. *Central America* includes Belize, Costa Rica, El Salvador, Guatemala, Honduras, Mexico, Nicaragua, and Panama. *South America* includes Argentina, Bolivia, Brazil, Chile, Colombia, Ecuador, Falkland Islands, French Guiana, Guyana, Paraguay, Peru, Suriname, Uruguay, and Venezuela. *Caribbean* includes Anguilla, Antigua and Barbuda, Aruba, Bahamas, Barbados, British Virgin Islands, Cayman Islands, Cuba, Dominica, Dominican Republic, Grenada, the former country of Guadeloupe (including St. Barthélemy and Saint-Martin), Haiti, Jamaica, Martinique, Montserrat, the former country of the Netherlands Antilles (including Bonaire, Curaçao, Saba, Sint Eustatius, and-Sint Maarten), St. Kitts and Nevis, St. Lucia, St. Vincent and the Grenadines, Trinidad and Tobago, and Turks and Caicos Islands. Note that people born in Puerto Rico and the U.S. Virgin Islands are native born to the United States and are not included in the list of countries in the Caribbean. Throughout the remainder of this report, the term *Latin America* refers to all of these areas.

2. Gibson, Campbell and Kay Jung, 2006. "Historical Census Statistics on the Foreign-Born Population in the United States: 1850 to 2000." U.S. Census Bureau: Population Division Working Paper, Number 81 available on the Census Bureau's Web site at www.census.gov/population/www/techpap.html.

Critical Thinking

1. Explain troubling and hopeful evidence in this report.

2. Do the concentrations of populations from countries of origin have positive and negative consequences?

Create Central

www.mhhe.com/createcentral

Internet References

Hispanic Access Foundation
www.haf.org

Latino American Network Information Center (LANIC)
http:Illanic.utexas.edu

League of United Latino Citizens
www.lulac.org

National Association of Latin American Elected Officials
www.naleo.org

National Catholic Bishops Conference
www.USCCB.org

National Council of La Raza (NCLR)
www.nclrorg

Social Science Information Gateway
http://sosig.esrc.bris.ac.uk

Sociosite
www.sociosite.net

The International Center for Migration, Ethnicity, and Citizenship
www.newschool.edu/icmec

U.S Census Bureau, 2010.

Article   Prepared by: John A. Kromkowski, *Catholic University of America*

A Promised Land, A Devil's Highway: The Crossroads of the Undocumented Immigrant

DANIEL G. GROODY

Learning Outcomes

After reading this article, you will be able to:

- Describe the condition of immigrants at the border.

- Explain the motivation and values of religious organizations who work with immigrants in need.

The great legacy of Archbishop Oscar Romero's life was his identification with the crucified Christ. While his witness to the God of life reached its ultimate expression during his last liturgy, the sacrifice of his own life on the altar of God was the culmination of his solidarity with those who suffer on the altar of the world. Among the many poor people for whom he laid down his life are those who eventually emigrated from his country in search of more dignified lives. As we reflect on the contribution of Oscar Romero's life, I would like to do so in light of what Ignacio Ellacuría calls "the people crucified in history." In particular, I would like to look at the physical, spiritual, and theological terrain of the undocumented immigrant coming across the Mexican-American border today.

The context of Romero's death leaves much room for reflection, but in the very least, it prompts us to consider the integral relationship that his faith expressed at liturgy and that his commitment to the poor expressed in the struggle for justice. As a starting point, I would like to look at the relationship between the Eucharist and immigration. While, on the surface, there does not appear to be an obvious connection between what happens at Mass and what happens on the border, the correlation became clearer the first time I attended a Eucharistic celebration in El Paso, Texas, where Mexico meets the United States. We celebrated Mass outside on November 1, in the open air, in the dry, rugged, and sun-scorched terrain where the two countries meet. In this liturgy, we remembered all the saints and the souls who had gone before us. We also remembered the thousands of Mexican immigrants who died at the crossroads of the border in recent years. Like other liturgies, a large crowd gathered to pray and worship. Unlike at other liturgies, however, a sixteen foot iron fence divided this coummunity in half, with one side in Mexico and the other side in the United States.

To give expression to our common solidarity as a people of God beyond our political constructions, we joined altars on both sides of the wall. Even while border patrol agents and helicopters surrounded us and kept a strict vigilance—lest any Mexicans cross over—we sang, we worshiped, and we prayed. We prayed for our governments. We prayed for those who died. And we prayed to understand better our interconnectedness to each other. I remember in particular the sign of peace, when one normally shakes a hand or shares a hug with one's neighbor. Unable to touch my Mexican neighbor except through some small holes in the fence, I became acutely aware of the unity that we celebrated but also the divisions that we experience. Even while this Eucharist testified to our unity in Christ, the wall between us revealed the dividedness of our current reality, for no other reason than that we were born on different sides of the fence.

A Faith Perspective on a Complex Reality

For the last few decades, I have been talking to immigrants, border patrol agents, *coyote smugglers* (those who transport people across), ranchers, vigilante groups, educators, congresspersons, medical personnel, social workers, human rights advocates, and others involved in this immigration drama. Ranchers have seen their property trashed by immigrants who parade through their land and leave behind water jugs, litter, and discarded clothing. Educators and hospital administrators have felt increasing financial pressure from the influx of newly arrived immigrants. Border patrol agents have told stories of being pinned down by gunfire from drug smugglers of cocaine and marijuana. Congressional leaders have felt pressure, especially since September 11, to establish policies that aim at safeguarding a stable economy and protecting the common good. Coyote smugglers have talked about guiding people across the treacherous terrain along the border and gaining a profit while doing so. But most of all, migrants have shared what it is like to break from home, cross the border, and enter the United States as undocumented immigrants. In the process, they have revealed not only much about the physical terrain of the immigrant journey but also the spiritual terrain of their faith lives.

In speaking with these different groups along the border, I have learned that each constituency believes that it has certain rights. Each group has a point to make, a truth to defend. These include the rights to private property, jobs, national security, civil law and order, and other such rights. The legitimacy of each claim makes it clear that immigration is a complex reality and that it is not easy to untangle a web of competing interests. Yet, it is here that theology can offer some important reflection about what it means to be human before God and what it means to live together in society.

From a theological perspective, while every truth claim merits consideration, not every claim has equal authority. Christian theology asserts that as a starting point, those who suffer the most deserve the greatest hearing (Matthew 25:31–46), even though, ironically, the voice of the "least" is often the last one to be heard, if it is heard at all. Oscar Romero learned throughout his life that the poor themselves not only deserve to be heard but are key to gaining an accurate grasp of reality, without which wise choices cannot be made. In the context of immigration, this is where the stories of the immigrants themselves are particularly important. As some of the most vulnerable members of society, immigrants clarify that whatever "rights" are at stake in this debate, one of the most neglected is the right to a more dignified life. These rights become clearer when one listens to the stories as they emerge from various crisis points along the border, including detention centers, hospitals, shelters, train stations, deserts, mountains, and along rivers and highways and other areas. Their stories have made me look at the immigration issue differently. They have helped me see that the journey of an undocumented immigrant is not a camping trip through a scenic part of the American Southwest but a descent into the vast expanses of hell; their journey toward a promised land" takes place on what Luis Alberto Urrea calls "a devil's highway."

The Evolution of the Mexican-American Border

The pathways of this highway have been carved out slowly over time. The Mexican-American border has undergone a complex evolution, especially over the last century. Up until the end of the Mexican-American War in 1848, when Mexico ceded what is now much of the Southwestern United States, people moved freely and cyclically throughout the current border states and Mexico. The border area remained relatively porous, and enforcement was relatively light through most of the nineteenth and twentieth centuries, except for a vigilante organization in 1880 that tried to keep the Chinese out. In 1924, the U.S. Border Patrol began tightening the border through more systematic

enforcement efforts. In time, stricter border policies emerged, especially in the 1980s when President Reagan declared a "war on drugs." This "war" made the border an increasingly militarized zone as American drug enforcement entities battled against wealthy, organized drug cartels for superiority in firepower and surveillance.

An important development for the border was the devaluation of the Mexican peso in 1983, which triggered an explosion of foreign-owned factories along the Mexican side of the border. U.S. companies took advantage of the exchange rate by moving their assembly plants from the states to Mexico in pursuit of cheap labor. Hundreds of thousands of Mexican citizens, many of whom had lost their land because of Mexican agricultural policies, came north to work in *maquiladoras*. In the last few years, however, more than a quarter of these plants have closed down as companies have discovered even cheaper labor in Asia. Consequently, hundreds of thousands of jobs along the border have disappeared, digging the Mexican economy into a deeper hole and making unemployment and underemployment more the norm than the exception.

In the 1990s, the Clinton administration, fueled by much anti-immigrant sentiment that was brewing in California such as that reflected in proposition 187, further intensified border control with policies such as Operation Hold the Line, in El Paso, and Operation Gatekeeper, in San Diego, and later, other similar initiatives. By erecting walls and fences, by stationing border patrol agents every quarter mile along the border in the major urban areas, and by the increased use of military technology, including drone planes, infrared technology, motion sensors, and other such instruments, crossing outside of normal ports of entry became much more difficult, which, by design, has significantly raised the stakes of migrating illegally. To avoid detection, immigrants are pushed to the most remote areas of the border where surveillance is thin.

While policies such as Operation Gatekeeper in 1994 and similar initiatives along the border were meant to deter immigrants from crossing illegally, they have not changed the flows at all but merely redirected migrants into more life-threatening territory, such as waterless deserts and mountains. With temperatures exceeding 120 degrees in the shade, many have to walk fifty miles or longer in treacherous conditions. In such surroundings, one's body cooks like an egg, which causes heat stroke, brain damage, and even death. Because it is physically impossible to carry the food and water necessary for this type of trek, many do not make it. I realized how extreme this journey was when one day, a coyote offered me a "ride-along scholarship" so that I could see what the journey was like. Instead of paying the going rate of $1,800 to take me across the border, he said he was going to "teach" me what it was like, for free. His words were as follows:

> *We'll walk for three or four days, and all you will have with you are a few tortillas, some sardines, and water. The food is so bad you won't want to eat, and you will get so tired you won't think you are going to make it. If you push on, you can do it, but if you fall behind, we will leave you behind. And*

you should wear high heel, leather boots, because
we come across rattlesnakes in the desert at night,
but if you have the right boots on, the snake's teeth
won't penetrate your skin and you'll be okay.

Because of such dangers, every day, immigrants dehydrate in deserts, drown in canals, freeze in mountains, and suffocate in tractor trailers. As a result, the death toll has increased 1,000 percent in some places. When asked what he thought about the dangers, an immigrant named Mario said,

Sure, I think about the dangers. I think about them
all the time. But I have no choice if I am going to
move forward with my life. The fact is, amidst the
poverty in Mexico, I am already dead. Crossing the
desert gives me the hope of living, even if I die.

If they make it across the border, most immigrants will work at low-paying jobs that no one else wants except the most desperate. They will debone chickens in poultry plants, pick crops in fields, and build houses in construction. As one person noted, "it looks like entering the U.S. through the desert as undocumented immigrants do is some kind of employment screening test administered by the U.S. government for the hospitality, construction, and recreation industries." Willing to work at the most dangerous jobs, an immigrant a day will die in the workplace, even while for others, the workplace has become safer over the last decade. Immigrants die cutting North Carolina tobacco and Nebraska beef, chopping down trees in Colorado, welding a balcony in Florida, trimming grass at a Las Vegas golf course, and falling from scaffolding in Georgia.

With an economic gun at their backs, they leave their homes because hunger and poverty push them to cross the border. Mario told me in an immigration detention center,

Sometimes my kids come to me and say, "Daddy,
I'm hungry." And I don't have enough money to buy
them food. And I can't tell them I don't have any
money, but I don't. I can barely put beans, pota-
toes, and tortillas on the table with what I make.
But I feel so bad that I sometimes will go into a
store, even if it is two or three blocks away, or even
three or four kilometers away, or even another
country in order to get food for my family. I feel
awful, but nothing is worse than seeing your hun-
gry child look you in the eyes, knowing you don't
have enough food to give them.

Immigrants are pushed by economic poverty, pulled by the hope of a better life in the United States, and blocked by an iron wall at the border. At this border, where the ideals of freedom in America are safeguarded, many immigrants clash with a form of slavery embedded in the contemporary American imagination.

Crossing the Borders of our Own Mind

While many Americans hailed the crumbling of the Berlin Wall in 1989 and mourned the death of sixty-eight people who died trying to cross it over a period of twenty-eight years, many of us have stood idle as we have constructed a new wall between Mexico and the United States. Since 1994, more than 4,000 undocumented immigrants have died trying to find their way into America. The tragic loss of life along the Mexican-American border is a challenge to the national consciences of Mexico, the United States, and, indeed, the global community. While it raises serious questions about structural injustice, it challenges all of us to reflect on how we regard those labeled as "different" by mainstream society.

Despite the obstacles that immigrants face in crossing the border, perhaps the more difficult borders to cross today are the borders of our own minds, especially, those that guard our deep-seated biases and prejudices and those we put up when we encounter someone who we consider to be totally "other" than we are. Mexican immigrants bear some of the worst stereotypes in today's society and are some of the first to be typecast in a negative light. Not infrequently in mainstream media, they are typecast as illegal, nontaxpaying "leaches" who suck dry the funds of local communities while selling drugs, committing crimes, and taking jobs away from Americans. Some even lump immigrants into the same category as terrorists, as an unwelcome threat, without ever realizing that the terrorists of September 11 came into the country with legal visas. Nonetheless, in the popular mind, immigrants are perceived as a menace to the common good and the preservation of U.S. culture. Absurdly, some—apparently unaware of the last battle against indigenous Americans at Wounded Knee—argue that immigrants are taking away "Native American" culture.

Whatever one's perceptions about these popular impressions, sadly, many of the immigrants themselves begin to believe the stereotypes spread about them. Often looked at as uneducated, lazy, and inferior, they begin to internalize many of these labels. Such stereotypes have their origin from the time of the Spanish conquest in the early sixteenth century. Unfortunately, many immigrants come to believe some of the ways that contemporary society typecasts them. Perhaps, one of the more challenging roads to conversion for them is not only believing in God but believing in themselves. Lydia comments,

We are constantly reminded that we are less than
everybody else, that we are poor, that we don't
have an education, that we don't speak right, that
we are lesser human beings in one way or another.
Sometimes, we even begin to wonder whether God
thinks that way about us too.

The more challenging road to conversion for many Americans often means unlearning the negative stereotypes and seeing more clearly the inner worth, dignity, and respective contributions that immigrants bring to this country.

A Day without a Mexican

Despite the tide of anti-immigrant sentiment, the economic undercurrent is such that immigrants are an essential and vital part of our current economic reality. We have effectively walled off the truth about the role that immigrants play in sustaining the infrastructure of America. As Pastor Robin Hoover of

Humane Borders says, "our nation virtually posts two signs on its southern border: 'Help Wanted: Inquire Within' and 'Do Not Trespass.'" Without the help of immigrant labor, the U.S. economy would virtually collapse. We want and need cheap immigrant labor, but we do not want the immigrants.

A few years ago an interesting documentary came out called *A Day without a Mexican*. It attempted to show what the American economy would look like if there were no Mexicans working here anymore. There would be no maids in hotels. No people to wash dishes in restaurants. No landscapers to mow grass. No cheap hands to do construction. No people to pick vegetables in the fields. As a result, lettuce would cost more than eight dollars a head; industries would shut down; various sectors of the economy would be paralyzed. Even though the U.S. economy needs these immigrants and even though multinational corporations profit from their labor, immigrants today are not afforded the same opportunities or open doors that immigrants experienced in previous generations. In fact, the opposite is true. Instead of receiving hospitality and openness, many immigrants find scapegoating and rejections, hostility and fear.

Today, some immigrants are greeted by vigilante groups and civilian border patrols who hunt them down, treat them like animals, and even threaten to kill them. In parts of the Southwest, racist violence runs deep in groups such as the Civil Homeland Defense, Ranch Rescue, and American Border Patrol (not to be confused with the U.S. Border Patrol). "If I had my way," one rancher reportedly bellowed at a meeting with U.S. Border Patrol officials, "I'd shoot every single one of 'em." The fact is that most immigrants are not stealing jobs from Americans; they are doing work that most Americans do not want to do. Moreover, not only are immigrants not a drain on the U.S. economy, but they also contribute with direct and indirect taxes. Even though immigrants collectively pay more than $90 billion in taxes, many are afraid to use social services for fear that it will expose their undocumented status.

Nonetheless, like previous immigrants from Ireland, Italy, Germany, Eastern Europe, China, and Japan, these Mexican immigrants, as Jorge Bustamante notes, are often valued for their cheap labor but are not afforded the human rights due to them as contributing members of society. They become a "disposable commodity" when they are no longer useful. It is here in particular that the Scriptures and Catholic social teaching have something important to say.

The Relationship of Immigration to Revelation

According to the Judeo-Christian Scriptures, immigration is not simply a sociological fact but also a theological event. In the process of immigrating, God revealed his covenant to his people. This covenant was a gift and a responsibility; it reflected God's goodness to them, but it also called them to respond to newcomers in the same way that Yahweh responded to them when they were in slavery: "So you too must befriend the alien, for you were once aliens yourselves in the land of Egypt" (Deuteronomy 10:19).

Building on this same foundation, Catholic social teaching has reiterated that the true moral worth of any society is how it treats its most vulnerable members. John Paul II consistently underscored the moral responsibility of richer nations to help poor nations, particularly with regard to more open immigration policies. While some in America claim that these undocumented immigrants have no right to be here, the church believes that a person's true homeland is that which provides the person with bread.

When Moisés reached Tijuana, he said that the reason why he wanted to come to the United States was that he could barely put food on the table with what he earned. He said that his ambition was simply to provide "bread" for his family. On this same day, a few miles away on the other side of the border near a very popular resort hotel on Coronado Island, a woman said that she had come to the area because she was looking for a "specialty bread," a delicacy that she could not find anywhere else. The contradictions of the moment were striking: two people can live in the same geographical place but live in two totally different worlds. These two lives are microcosms of a larger contrast between Mexico and the United States, between the First World and the Third World.

While the church recognizes the right of a nation to control its borders, it does not see this right as an absolute right, nor does it see sovereign rights as having priority over basic human rights. It acknowledges that the ideal is that people find work in their home countries; however, it also teaches that if their countries of birth do not afford the conditions necessary to lead a fully human life, then those persons have a right to emigrate. While border reform does not mean naively opening our borders to everyone, as if there were no need to take into account other political and socioeconomic factors, the church makes every effort to put human life at the forefront of the discussion. It critically asks why barriers have been steadily lowered when it comes to commerce but have steadily risen when it comes to labor. If Oscar Romero were alive today, he would likely challenge those unjust social structures that benefit the elite at the expense of the poor or that calculate financial costs but ignore the human costs of economic systems and political policies. He would indict a society that values goods and money more than it does human beings and human rights, which directly contradicts the biblical narrative. While some Americans and some Christians may see our privileged life in the United States as a divine right, a scriptural reading of reality offers an entirely different perspective.

The gospel vision challenges the prevailing consumerist mentality of American culture, which seeks meaning through a seemingly endless accumulation of goods, even while the rest of the world suffers for want of basic needs. Jesus, in his life and ministry, went beyond borders of all sorts, including those defined by the authorities of his own day, such as clean/unclean, saintly/sinful, and rich/poor. In doing so, he called into being a community of magnanimity and generosity that would reflect God's unlimited love for all people (Acts 2). He called people "blest," not when they have received the most, but when they have shared the most and needed the least. Christians, as such, distinguish themselves not by the quantity of their possessions but the quality of their heart, which expresses itself in service. Above all, this quality of the heart is measured by the extent to which one loves the least significant among us.

In many respects, immigrants sit at America's door like Lazarus sat at the gate of the rich man (Luke 16:19–31), hoping for scraps to fall from the American table of prosperity. While there are many texts through which to analyze today's reality along the border, the Judgment of the Nations (Matthew 25:31–46) is a particularly challenging text through which to read the issue of immigration. In this passage, Jesus says, "I was hungry and you gave me food, I was thirsty and you gave me drink, a stranger and you welcomed me, naked and you clothed me, ill and you cared for me, in prison and you visited me." The corollaries to the immigrant experience are striking. Hungry in their homelands, thirsty in the treacherous deserts in which they cross, naked after being robbed at gunpoint by *bandito* gangs, sick in the hospitals from heat-related illnesses, imprisoned in immigration detention centers, and, finally, if they make it across, estranged in a new land, they bear many of the marks of the crucified Christ in our world today.

Migrants undergo a way of the cross every day. They experience an economic crucifixion when they realize that they can no longer subsist in their homeland. They experience a social crucifixion when they have to leave their families and friends behind. They undergo a cultural crucifixion when they leave behind the familiar and come into a new and strange land. They experience a legal crucifixion when they cross the border and become "illegal aliens." For those who die in the deserts and mountains, they experience an actual crucifixion, dying some of the most horrible deaths imaginable. And they even experience a religious crucifixion of sorts when they experience themselves as strangers, outsiders, and even threats to church communities, if they are welcomed there. As an archbishop, Romero was one that welcomed the excluded and put them at the center of his pastoral attention and ministry. His own spirituality and identification with the crucified Christ compelled him to go the poor as his response of love to the God of love.

Spirituality and theology are built into the struggles of immigration, particularly, migrants, even if the situation does not look that way on the surface. John Paul II notes,

> The immediate reasons for the complex reality of human migration differ widely; its ultimate source, however, is the longing for a transcendent horizon of justice, freedom and peace. In short, it testifies to an anxiety which, however indirectly, refers to God, in whom alone humans can find the full satisfaction of all his expectations ("Message for World Migration Day," no. 1).

What appears to be simply a sociological, political, and economic phenomenon has a deep theological current under the surface. Theology, above all, engages the hopes and struggles of the human heart, and from there, it seeks to find God's revelation in the midst of everyday life, even and especially in those "godless" areas where God seems disturbingly absent. Theology takes flesh in the ordinariness of life, and because it is rooted in everyday life, it is also rooted in the everyday sufferings of people.

Theology, as it is disclosed in history, has always evolved in this way. While Christians today regard the cross as the one symbol that summarizes God's redemptive love for the world, at the time of Jesus, it held no initial theological significance. In biblical times, the cross was a form of capital punishment, which, in the Old Testament, reflected more of God's curse than his blessing (Deuteronomy 21:23). However, upon deeper reflection, a theological truth emerged about the cross, symbolizing God's self-giving love to God's people. In a similar way, migration, like the cross, has deep theological dimensions. Immigrants hold much potential to be bearers of new life. In response to the challenge of immigration, the U.S. bishops, as expressed in their pastoral letter *Strangers No Longer: Together on the Journey of Hope,* have sought "to awaken our peoples to the mysterious presence of the crucified and risen Lord in the person of the migrant and to renew in them the values of the Kingdom of God that he proclaimed" (Catholic Bishops of Mexico and the United States, no. 3). Building on this similar spirit, Romero not only reached out to those on the edge of society but realized that the church is born on the margins, where those who are crucified live and suffer today.

Amid such difficult conditions, many immigrants offer a surprising but compelling witness of faith. When María came north from Guatemala, she wanted to work in the United States for only two years, then return home to her family. I met her on the Mexican side of the border, just before her third attempt to cross. In the previous ten days, she had tried twice to cross the border through a remote route in southern Arizona. On her first attempt, she was mugged at the border by a *bandito* gang. Though bruised and beaten, she continued her journey through the desert and ran out of food. Just before she reached the road, she was apprehended by the border patrol and put into an immigration detention center. A few days later, she tried again. This time, her coyote smuggler tried to rape her, but she managed to free herself and push her way through the desert once again. After four days of walking, she ran out of food, water, and even strength. After almost dying in the desert, the border patrol found her, helped her, and then sent her back to Mexico.

After chronicling her story to me for a long time and after telling me about her suffering in detail, I was curious about how she dealt with these trials before God, so I asked her, "If you had fifteen minutes to speak to God, what would you say to Him?" Thinking that she would have given Him a long litany of complaints, María surprised me when she said,

> First of all, I do not have fifteen minutes to speak to God. I am always conversing with Him, and I feel His presence with me always. Yet, if I saw God face to face, the first thing I would do is thank Him, because He has been so good to me and has blest me so abundantly.

It is extraordinary to ponder that thousands of years ago, Israel's strongest affirmations about God's faithfulness often came in the midst of its own exile in Babylon, not in the midst of prosperity. Given that many immigrants live as exiles in the United States, it is striking to witness such faith amid such adversity and to see such revelation in unsuspected places.

Migration as a Journey of Hope

Archbishop Romero understood that salvation was intimately intertwined with a commitment to the crucified peoples of today. He testified to the mercy of God in a merciless world. "In my life," he said, "I have only been a poem of the love of God, and I have become in Him what He has wanted me to be." Standing in solidarity with Christ on the altar and through Christ as crucified with the poor, Romero came to be known as an *entregado*, one who not only gives one's life for his people but also reveals through faithful witness the life of the Savior, known in Spanish as *El Salvador*. He also understood that following this Savior led him to a migration of hope, even and especially when his labors for justice took place amid a seemingly hopeless situation.

As immigrants such as those from Mexico and other parts of Latin America fight for more dignified lives, it is helpful to remember that the term *immigrant* is built into the church's very self-definition. It sees itself as comprising a "pilgrim people" moving from sin to grace, from cross to resurrection, and from this world to the next. In the Eucharist, the church protests against the walls and barriers that we set up between ourselves, and it affirms again and again that we are one body in Christ. It realizes that, this side of heaven, we all live in the same country; we all live on the same side of the fence. To the church, death is the ultimate border; the journey of faith is the ultimate migration; and God is the ultimate promised land. Christ teaches that we will be able to cross over this final border to the extent that we have been able to cross over the smaller borders in this life and see our interconnectedness to each other (Luke 16:19–31). In the very least, we need a new imagination to bring about a new immigration policy.

Life itself, if we live it well, is a process of endless migration. Movement toward the promised land inevitably calls us to cross borders of every sort, and it makes us vulnerable in the process. As undocumented immigrants remind us, this journey is not a road for the fainthearted. Each day, God calls us out of our comfort zones as we move from the known to the unknown, from the secure to the insecure, from the land of our physical birth to the land of our spiritual birth. It is only when we choose not to migrate, when we stagnate, when we seek to save our lives rather than lose them in God, that we spiritually die. If "migration" is worked into the self-definition of all peoples, then we might find those who come to us as immigrants less threatening than we often do. And we might see not only a reflection of ourselves but that of God, who, even when we were lost, did not abandon us to die. Rather, in love, God "migrated" to us in the Incarnation so that, through Him, we might migrate with Him across all borders into the fullness of God's loving embrace and find our true homeland in God's Kingdom.

Discussion Questions

1. Given the complexity of the immigration question, why do you think that the church has taken the stance of defending the immigrant—even the undocumented immigrant? Since most Americans are the offspring of immigrants, why do you think the anti-immigration sentiment is so strong?
2. Discuss: Have you had personal or business dealings with undocumented immigrants? Do they work hard? If legislation were passed that prohibited helping undocumented immigrants, would you be willing to break the law and still help them? Why? Why not?
3. How is the Eucharist a sign that breaks down walls and barriers? Discuss Father Groody's point that the term *immigrant* is "built into the church's very self-definition."

Resources and Further Study

Catholic Bishops of Mexico and the United States. *Strangers No Longer: Together on the Journey of Hope.* Washington D.C.: United States Conference of Catholic Bishops, 2003. www.usccb.org/mrs/stranger.shtml (accessed May 2, 2007).

Elizondo, Virgil. *Galilean Journey.* Maryknoll, N.Y.: Orbis Books, 1983.

Groody, Daniel G. *Border of Death, Valley of Life: An Immigrant Journey of Heart and Spirit.* Lanham, Md.: Rowman & Littlefield, 2002.

———, prod. *Dying to Live: A Migrant's Journey.* Video/DVD. Notre Dame, Ind.: University of Notre Dame, 2005.

———. *Globalization, Spirituality, and Justice: Navigating the Path to Peace.* Maryknoll, N.Y.: Orbis Books, 2007.

———, ed. *The Option for the Poor in Christian Theology.* Notre Dame, Ind.: University of Notre Dame Press, 2007.

Groody, Daniel G., and Gioacchino Campese, eds. *A Promised Land, a Perilous Journey: Theological Perspectives on Migration.* Notre Dame, Ind.: University of Notre Dame Press, 2007.

John Paul II. "Message for World Migration Day." United States Conference of Catholic Bishops, November 21, 1999. www.usccb.org/pope/wmde.htm (accessed May 2, 2007).

Skylstad, William. "Comprehensive Immigration Reform." United States Conference of Catholic Bishops, January 15, 2006. www.usccb.org/bishops/immigrationreform.shtml (accessed May 2, 2007).

Critical Thinking

1. Describe conditions of migrants near the border?
2. Why are religious organizations engaged in this situation?

Create Central

www.mhhe.com/createcentral

Internet References

The Council for Research in Values and Philosophy
www.crvp.org

Diversity.com
www.diversity.com

The International Center for Migration, Ethnicity, and Citizenship
www.newschool.edu/icmec

Article Prepared by: John A. Kromkowski, *The Catholic University of America*

Cuban-Americans: Politics, Culture and Shifting Demographics

Kristiana Mastropasqua

Learning Outcomes

After reading this article, you will be able to:

- Explain in what respects Cuban Americans are different from other Hispanic/Latino ethnic groups.

- Identify the central aspects of US-Cuba relations.

The announcement that the United States and Cuba would resume relations has brought renewed focus to the complex and politically fraught history of the two countries. Cuban-Americans have long held intense feelings about their ancestral country, and deep issues of identity will continue to evolve as the political situation shifts.

One recent incident, perhaps, crystallizes the complications of identity. In May 2013, former New Mexico governor Bill Richardson, who is of Mexican descent, stated that Texas senator Ted Cruz, of Cuban origin, should not "be defined as Hispanic." The discussion centered on Cruz's anti-immigration Position and Richardson later clarified his remark, saying he meant that Cruz shouldn't be defined as "just a Hispanic." Still, the dispute was a reflection of the deep cultural and political divide between the two communities, a split highlighted earlier at the 2012 national conventions: To give its keynote address, the Democratic National Committee chose San Antonio mayor Julian Castro, who is Mexican-American. The Republican National Committee chose Cuban-American senator Marco Rubio of Florida to introduce candidate Mitt Romney.

The history of Cuban migration to the U.S. is dramatically different than that of other immigrant groups. In 1910, the number of Cubans living in the U.S. was estimated at a little more than 15,000. When Fidel Castro took power in 1959, the Cuban-American population in the United States exploded: 215,000 arrived in the years immediately following the revolution. A 2013 article in *Daedalus* by Marta Tienda and Susana M. Sanchez, "Latin American Immigration to the United States," gives a history of Cuban immigration to the United States.

In 1966 the U.S. government passed the Cuban Adjustment Act, which codified a fast-track path to permanent residency for Cuban exiles, essentially providing immediate naturalization regardless of quotas and visa procedures. After the fall of the Soviet Union, Cuban migration to the U.S. accelerated: In 1994 alone, 33,000 Cubans were intercepted by the U.S. Coast Guard. In response, U.S. and Cuban governments worked to establish a solution that would prevent Cubans from risking their lives at sea.

The result, in 1995, came to be known as the "wet foot, dry foot" policy: Any Cuban who successfully arrives on U.S. soil is accepted; those stopped at sea are repatriated. The policy remains in effect today. A 2011 article in *Connecticut Public Interest Law Journal* explores the preferential immigration treatment provided to Cuban migrants. A report by the Congressional Research Service, "Cuban Migration to the United States: Policy and Trends," looks at past policies and potential future directions.

Latinos of Cuban origin are highly politically active—they've created one of the nation's strongest ethnic lobbies, the Cuban American National Foundation—and they have a higher average income than any other Latino group. These two characteristics have been attributed in part to the consequences of the Cuban revolution for the island's elites. According to pollster Fernand R. Amandi, the "first waves of Cuban immigrants fleeing the Castro revolution came from the top echelons of society: the successful, the highly educated and the politically active." According to the Pew Hispanic Center, while 48% of all eligible Hispanics voted in the 2012 election, the rate was approximately 67% for Latinos of Cuban descent.

Cuban-Americans are not only more politically active than other Hispanics, they're also more conservative: A 2012 report by the Pew Hispanic Center found that more than 70% of Latino voters supported Barack Obama, but Florida's Cuban-American voters split, with 49% supporting Obama and 47% in favor of Mitt Romney. But attitudes are changing: Second- and third-generation Cuban-Americans feel more connected to their adopted country, and the newest arrivals come for economic opportunity rather than political asylum. There continues to be a growing debate about American foreign policy toward Cuba within the Cuban American community, with some groups actively speaking out against prevailing policies. A 2009 study by Benajamin G. Bishin, "Miami Dade's Cuban American Voters in the 2008 election," explores at length the changing nature of the Cuban electorate.

In 2012, the Pew Hispanic Center produced a detailed statistical profile of Hispanics of Cuban origin. Approximately 1.9 million live in the United States, accounting for 3.7% of the overall Latino population. Of all the Latino groups, Cubans are the most regionally concentrated, with nearly 70% of the population in Florida. While 37% of U.S. Latinos are foreign born, nearly 60% of Cubans were born outside of the United States. More than half of Cuban immigrants arrived later than 1990, and more than half are U.S. citizens. The median age for Cubans in the United States is 40, compared to the overall U.S. median age of 37 and the Hispanic median age of 27. Cubans in the U.S. are more proficient in English: 58% speak the language proficiently, compared to 35% of the overall Hispanic population. They're also more educated: 24% of Cubans ages 25 and older have obtained at least a bachelor's degree compared to 13% of the total Hispanic population. The average annual income for Cubans is $25,000, higher than the median earnings for the overall Latino population, which is $20,000.

Below is a selection of recent studies that explore the history, political convictions and culture of persons of Cuban origin in the United States.

"Exile Politics and Republican Party Affiliation: The Case of Cuban Americans in Miami"
Girard, Chris; Grenier, Guillermo J.; Gladwin, Hugh. *Social Science Quarterly,* March 2012, Vol. 93, Issue 1, 42–57. doi: 10.1111/j.1540-6237.2011.00835.x.

Abstract: "Objectives: We test the hypothesis that exile politics—measured by support for anti-Castro policies—contribute to the overwhelming preference for the Republican Party among South Florida's Cuban Americans. Results: Among Cuban Americans in Miami-Dade County, measures of exile politics account for a recent downward shift in Republican registration, as well as for much of the variation in Republican registration by race and age. Also, measures of exile politics

partly explain differences between Cubans and non-Cubans with regard to partisan preference."

"The Political Incorporation of Cuban Americans: Why Won't Little Havana Turn Blue?"
Bishin, Benjamin G.; Klofstad, Casey A. *Political Research Quarterly,* September 2012, vol. 65, No. 3, 586–599. doi: 10.1177/1065912911414589.

Abstract: "This article examines the political implications of the changing demographics of the Cuban American community. Over the past decade, pundits have predicted a massive shift in Cuban American voting behavior owing to demographic changes in the community. The authors find evidence that the attitudes of Cuban Americans have undergone significant changes, driven largely by the increased number of post-Mariel (1980) immigrants. The authors also find, however, that these dramatic changes have not yet been reflected at the ballot box, nor are they likely to be soon, owing to the slow process of immigrant political incorporation."

"Miami Dade's Cuban American Voters in the 2008 Election"
Bishin, Benjamin; Cherif, Feryal M.; Gomez, Andy S.; Lofstad, Casey. Working paper, Social Science Research Network, March 4, 2009.

Abstract: "In this paper we describe the behavior and attitudes of Cuban American voters in the 2008 election by presenting data from the 2008 Miami-Dade County Exit Poll (Bishin and Klofstad 2008). Our findings suggest that while the seismic shift in the political preferences of the Cuban American community predicted by the national news media was not realized, modest changes in vote preferences and more dramatic changes in attitudes toward U.S. Cuba foreign policy did occur. In general, these results are consistent with our expectations articulated in previous research, in which we held that large scale changes in Cuban American's voting preferences were unlikely to occur since they seem most likely to be driven by replacement of older Cuban American voters by younger, more recent immigrants and their relatives. . . ."

"Cuba: U.S. Policy and Issues for the 113th Congress"
Sullivan, Mark P. *Congressional Research Service,* June 2013.

Abstract: "Cuba remains a one-party communist state with a poor record on human rights. The country's political succession in 2006 from the long-ruling Fidel Castro to his brother Raúl was characterized by a remarkable degree of stability. In February 2013, Castro was reappointed to a second five-year term as president (until 2018, when he would be 86 years old), and selected a 52-year old former Education Minister Miguel Díaz-Canel as his First Vice President, making him the official successor in the event that Castro cannot serve out his term. Raúl Castro has implemented a number of gradual economic policy changes over the past several years, including an expansion of self-employment. A party congress held in April 2011 laid out numerous economic goals that, if implemented, could significantly alter Cuba's state-dominated economic model. Few observers, however, expect the government to ease its tight control over the political system. While the government reduced the number of political prisoners in 2010–2011, the number increased in 2012; moreover, short-term detentions and harassment have increased significantly."

"President or Dictator? A Comparison of Cuban-American Media Coverage of Cuban News"

Peterson, Geoffrey; Lopez Ortega, Etzel; Rojas, Giney; Callahan, Kara. American Political Science Association, 2012.

Abstract: "This paper examines the content of the Spanish-language press in two cities and compares how various newspapers portray various elements of Cuban political culture. Our findings indicate there are significant differences in the tenor of the coverage between the English and Spanish news outlets. We also find significant differences between the two Spanish-language news outlets, with the Miami-based newspaper being significantly more negative in their portrayal of Fidel Castro and the Cuban political system compared to the coverage targeting the Cuban-American population in New York City. Overall, we find significant evidence to show that the coverage of Cuban politics varies dramatically across sources."

"The Personal Is Political: The Cuban Ethnic Electoral Policy Cycle"

Eckstein, Susan, *Latin American Politics and Society,* spring 2009, Vol. 51, Issue 1, 119–148 doi: 10.1111/j.1548-2456.2009.00042.x.

Abstract: "This article documents a U.S. Cuban foreign policy cycle that operated in tandem with the presidential electoral cycle between 1992 and 2004. During these post–Cold War years, when Cuba posed no threat to U.S. national security, influential, well-organized Cuban Americans leveraged political contributions and votes to tighten the embargo on travel and trade, especially at the personal level. U.S. presidential candidates, most notably incumbent presidents seeking reelection, responded to their demands with discretionary powers of office. When presidential candidates supported policies that made good electoral sense but conflicted with concerns of state, they subsequently reversed or left unimplemented Cuba initiatives. After describing the logic behind an ethnic electoral policy cycle and U.S. personal embargo policy between 1992 and 2004, this article examines Cuban American voter participation, political and policy preferences, lobbying, political contributions, and the relationship between the ethnic policy and presidential election cycles."

"Paradise Lost: Older Cuban American Exiles' Ambiguous Loss of Leaving the Homeland"

Perez, Rose M., *Journal of Gerontological Social Work,* 2013. doi: 10.1080/01634372.2013.817496.

Summary: "To explore the experience of leaving Cuba, two Cuban American émigrés interviewed 20 Cuban exiles aged 65 or older, who left Cuba between 1959 and 1971. The interviews were conducted in New York and New Jersey using a phenomenological approach (Moutsakas, 1994). Themes included feeling betrayed by the Revolution, the inevitability of leaving, the expectation of a temporary refuge, and longing [for], and idealizing the past. The psychological presence that participants expressed, along with an endless sense of loss, resonates with ambiguous loss theory (Boss, 2006)—themes that have yet to be explored in the literature and that have research and practice implications."

"The Cuban Experience in Public Health: Does Political Will Have a Role?"

Pagliccia, Nino; Alvarez Perez, Adolfo. *International Journal of Health Services,* Nov. 2012, Vol. 42, No. 1, 77–94. doi: 10.2190/HS.42.1.h.

Abstract: "The role of political will in public health has been largely ignored. In Cuba, however, for the past 50 years, political will has been the ultimate, encompassing intersectoral action in public health. The excellent achievements in population health in Cuba during these 50 years have been widely recognized. Researchers have sought to explain this "Cuban paradox" by focusing on a large array of public health factors, including health promotion, primary care activities, and intersectoral action on health determinants. These factors constitute necessary but not sufficient conditions to achieve good health outcomes. This article defines political will and uses the experience of Cuba to illustrate the potential role of political will in public health."

"The Politics of Perception: An Investigation of the Presence and Sources of Perceptions of Internal Discrimination Among Latinos"

Monforti, Jessica Lavariega; Sanchez, Gabriel R. *Scoial Science Quarterly,* March 2010, Vol. 91, Issue 1, 245–265. doi: 10.1111/j.1540-6237.2010.00691.x.

Abstract: "Utilizing data from the 2002 Kaiser/Pew Latino National Survey of Latinos, we explore the presence and motivating factors of perceptions of internal discrimination within the Latino population in the United States through descriptive statistics and multivariate regression analysis. We find that

84% of Latinos in the survey sample believe that Latino internal discrimination is problematic, and also find support for our theories that perceptions of internal discrimination are greater for those who are less integrated into U.S. society, as well as for Latinos who self-identify as black."

Critical Thinking

1. What are the particular circumstances of Cuban Americans?
2. Do all ethnic groups share affinities to countries of origin?

3. Differentiate what it means to be an immigrant, a refugee, in exile, a tourist, and a short-term or seasonal worker in a country other than your own.

Internet References

Cuban American National Foundation
www.canf.org
Cuba Study Group
www. cubastudygroup.org
Havana Cuba Business Travel Culture and Politics
www.havanajournal.com

Mastropasqua,Kristiana. "Cuban-American: Politics, culture and shifting demographics", *Journalist's Resource*. December 18, 2014 Creative Common Attribution 3.0 license. http://journalistsresource.org/studies/government/immigration/cuban-americans-politics-culture-demographics.

Unit 7

UNIT

Prepared by: John A. Kromkowski, *The Catholic University of America*

Asian Americans

The Asian American ethnic groups provide unique and varied perspectives on the adjustment of immigrants and their reception in various regimes and cultures. Asian Americans are engaged in the ongoing issue of cultural formation, the recovery of tradition, and the incorporation of new ethnicities from Asian into mainstream cultural entertainment. The political and economic forces that frame relationships at the personal and cultural levels pose dilemmas and attendant choices that define current situations and the artifices used to heighten or diminish Asian ethnicities in America. The variety of religious traditions that Asian immigrants bring to America adds another dimension of cultural and moral importance. In what respect are non-Judeo-Christian/Islamic faith traditions issues of consequence? The aftermath of conflict and resulting analysis have riveted attention on the ethnic factor. The details of familial and cultural development within these Asian American communities compose worlds of meaning that are rich sources of material from which both insights and troubling questions of personal and group identity emerge. Pivotal periods of conflict in the drama of the American experience provide an occasion for learning as much about us as about one of the newest clusters of ethnicities—the Asian Americans.

The intrinsic complexity of immigration as a social issue is one reason for the lack of comprehensive and long-range planning evidenced by U.S. immigration laws. The extreme diversity in our immigration sources clearly adds to the complexity of this issue. Throughout this nation's history, immigration has been both praised and reviled. Immigrant success stories are mingled with fear that the foreigner will take jobs and that our infrastructure will be strained.

The late 1800s was a turning point in U.S. immigration history, not only because it signalled the beginning of direct federal controls, but also because it reflected new immigrant sources whose ability to assimilate would be questioned. The first general immigration law was enacted in 1882. Generally, it established a 50-cent head tax per immigrant and gave the treasury secretary jurisdiction over immigration matters. The 1882 act also excluded convicts, paupers, and mentally defective aliens. Earlier that year, Congress had passed the Chinese Exclusion Act, which based ineligibility for admission to the United States on national origin. The act also prohibited foreign-born Chinese from becoming citizens and placed a 10-year ban on the admission of Chinese workers. In 1890 there were 107,488 Chinese

aliens on the American mainland; because of the Exclusion Act, that number had dwindled to 61,639 by 1920. Thousands of Chinese aliens had come to the West Coast as contract laborers to build the railroads in the mid-1850s. By 1880, there were 189,000 Chinese in the United States. Their sheer numbers, coupled with the fact that most were unskilled and worked for low wages, generated hostility and adverse public opinion. Calls for restrictive measures grew until Congress responded with the 1882 act. However, the issue did not disappear after the act's passage.

In the next several decades, Congress would take further restrictive measures against the Chinese. In 1884, in fact, Congress amended the Chinese Exclusion Act. The section dealing with Chinese workers was extended to cover all Chinese, regardless of whether they were Chinese subjects. The immigrant head tax increased to $1.00 in 1884. Thousands of Japanese immigrants arrived in the late 1800s. Initially, Hawaiian sugar plantations were their destination, where they worked as contract laborers. Congress amended the 1882 Chinese Exclusion Act again in 1892, as it was about to expire. The 1892 act extended the exclusion provisions for an additional 10 years and required all Chinese workers to obtain a residence certificate within one year.

In 1893, Congress passed an act that reinforced prior immigration laws. It also required ship owners to collect information about incoming aliens to help identify those who were excludable. Boards of inquiry were established in 1893 to deal with immigration problems, including deportation.

Calls for more regulation and restriction of immigrants continued through the turn of the century. Various members of Congress proposed a literacy test again and again as an immigration control to exclude aliens who were unable to read in any language. Legislation to accomplish this was vetoed by presidents Cleveland, Taft, and Wilson. In 1917, a literacy test for incoming aliens was enacted over President Wilson's veto.

Between 1901 and 1920, 14,531,197 immigrants entered the United States. In 1901, an immigrant anarchist assassinated President McKinley. Theodore Roosevelt, who succeeded McKinley, told Congress that U.S. policy should be to systematically exclude and deport anarchists. Two years later, Congress responded by adding anarchists to the growing list of excludable aliens; this was the first federal law making political ideas and beliefs grounds for deportation. The 1903 immigration act also barred epileptics, insane persons, and professional beggars from entry. In addition, it raised the head tax to $2.00 and re-codified the contract labor law. Congress passed a subsequent statute in 1907, which raised the head tax to $4.00 and earmarked these revenues for use in defraying the costs of enforcing U.S. immigration laws. The 1907 act also created a commission to study immigration, which came to be known as the Dillingham Commission after the senator who chaired it.

The commission submitted a 42-volume report in 1911. It concluded that the immigrants who started coming to the United States in the late 1800s adversely affected the American labor movement. The growth of the Asian American population since the immigration reform of 1965, the emergence of China as an international financial power, and the image of Asian American intellectual and financial success have heightened interest in this cluster of ethnic groups.

Article   Prepared by: John A. Kromkowski, *Catholic University of America*

Profile America: Facts for Features, Asian/Pacific American Heritage Month: May 2013

In 1978, a joint congressional resolution established Asian/Pacific American Heritage Week. The first 10 days of May were chosen to coincide with two important milestones in Asian/Pacific American history: the arrival in the United States of the first Japanese immigrants (May 7, 1843) and contributions of Chinese workers to the building of the transcontinental railroad, completed May 10, 1869. In 1992, Congress expanded the observance to a monthlong celebration. Per a 1997 Office of Management and Budget directive, the Asian or Pacific Islander racial category was separated into two categories: one being Asian and the other Native Hawaiian and Other Pacific Islander. Thus, this Facts for Features contains a section for each.

Learning Outcomes

After reading this article, you will be able to:

- Know when Congress established Asian/Pacific American Heritage Week.

- Identify the most troubling demographic indicators about Asian/Pacific Americans.

Asians

18.2 million

The estimated number of U.S. residents in 2011 who were Asian, either alone or in combination with one or more additional races.

Source: 2011 Population Estimates Table 3 www.census .gov/popest/data/index.html. For additional information, see www.census.gov/popest/data/national/asrh/2011/index.html.

5.8 million

The Asian alone or in combination population in California in 2011. The state had the largest Asian population, followed by New York (1.7 million). The Asian alone-or-in-combination population represented 57 percent of the total population in Hawaii.

Source: 2011 Population Estimates Table 5 www.census .gov/popest/data/index.html. For additional information, see www.census.gov/popest/data/state/asrh/2011/index.html.

46%

Percentage growth of the Asian alone or in combination population between the 2000 and 2010 censuses, which was more than any other major race group.

Source: U.S. Census Bureau, 2010 Census Redistricting Data (Public Law 94–171) Summary File, Custom Table 3, www .census.gov/2010census/news/xls/cbllcn123_us_2010redistr. xls. For additional details, see Hoeffel, E., S. Rastogi, M. Kim, and H. Shahid. 2011. *The Asian Population: 2010*, U.S. Census Bureau, 2010 Census Briefs, C2010BR-11, available at www .census.gov/prod/cen2010/briefs/c2010br-ll.pdf.

4 million

Number of Asians of Chinese, except Taiwanese, descent in the U.S. in 2011. The Chinese (except Taiwanese) population was the largest Asian group, followed by Filipinos (3.4 million), Asian Indians (3.2 million), Vietnamese (1.9 million), Koreans (1.7 million) and Japanese (1.3 million). These estimates represent the number of people who reported a specific detailed Asian group alone, as well as people who reported that detailed Asian group in combination with one or more other detailed Asian groups or another race(s).

Source: U.S. Census Bureau, 2011 American Community Survey, Table B02018
http://factfinder2.census.gov/bkmk/table/1.0/en/ACS/ 11_1YR/B02018

Income, Poverty and Health Insurance

$67,885

Median household income for the Asian alone population in 2011.

Source: U.S. Census Bureau, 2011 American Community Survey, Table S0201, http://factfinder2.census.gov/bkmk/table/ 1.0/en/ACS/11_1YR/S020l//popgroup~031 Median household income differed greatly by Asian group. For Asian Indians, for example, the median income in 2011 was $92,418; for Bangladeshi, it was $45,185. (These figures represent the Asian alone population.)

Source: U.S. Census Bureau, 2011 American Community Survey, Table S0201,
http://factfinder2.census.gov/bkmk/table/1.0/en/ACS/ 11_1YR/S0201//popgroup~013 and
http://factfinder2.census.gov/bkmk/table/1.0/en/ACS/ 11_1YR/S0201//popgroup~014

12.8%

The poverty rate for the Asian alone population in 2011.

Source: U.S. Census Bureau, 2011 American Community Survey, Table S1701
http://factfinder2.census.gov/faces/tableservices/jsf/pages/productview.xhtml?pid=ACS_11_1YR_S1701

15.4

Percentage of single-race Asians without health insurance coverage in 2011.

Source: U.S. Census Bureau, 2011 American Community Survey, Table S0201
http://factfinder2.census.gov/bkmk/table/1.0/en/ACS/11_1YR/ S0201/popgroup~012

Education
50%

The percentage of the Asian alone population 25 and older who had a bachelor's degree or higher level of education. This compared with 28.5 percent for all Americans 25 and older.

Source: U.S. Census Bureau, 2011 American Community Survey, Table S0201,
http://factfinder2.census.gov/bkmk/table/1.0/en/ACS/ 11_1YR/S0201//popgroup~012 and
http://factfinder2.census.gov/bkmk/table/1.0/en/ACS/ 11_1YR/S0201

85.1%

The percentage of the Asian alone population 25 and older who had at least a high school diploma. This is not statistically different from the percentage for the total population or the percentage of Native Hawaiian or Other Pacific Islander alone, 86 and 85 percent, respectively.

Source: U.S. Census Bureau, 2011 American Community Survey, Table S0201,
http://factfinder2.census.gov/bkmk/table/1.0/en/ACS/ 11_1YR/S0201

20.7%

The percentage of the Asian alone population 25 and older who had a graduate (e.g., master's) or professional degree. This compared with 10.6 percent for all Americans 25 and older.

Source: U.S. Census Bureau, 2011 American Community Survey, Table S0201,

http://factfinder2.census.gov/bkmk/table/1.0/en/ACS/ 11_1YR/S0201 and
http://factfinder2.census.gov/bkmk/table/1.0/en/ACS/ 11_1YR/S020l//popgroup~031

Voting
589,000

The additional number of the Asian alone population who voted in the 2008 presidential election than in the 2004 election. All in all, 48 percent of Asians turned out to vote in 2008—up 4 percentage points from 2004. A total of 3.4 million Asians voted.

Source: U.S. Census Bureau, Voting and Registration in the Election of November 2008,
www.census.gov/newsroom/releases/archives/voting/cb09-110.html

Businesses

Source for the statements referenced in this section, unless otherwise indicated: U.S. Census Bureau, 2007 Survey of Business Owners via American FactFinder,

http://factfinder2.census.gov/bkmk/table/1.0/en/ SBO/2007/00CSA01/0100000US/naics~00

1.5 million

Number of businesses owned by Asians in 2007, an increase of 40.4 percent from 2002.

$506.0 billion

Total receipts of businesses owned by Asians in 2007, up 54.9 percent from 2002.

44.7%

Percentage of Asian-owned businesses that operated in repair and maintenance, personal and laundry services; professional, scientific and technical services; and retail trade in 2007.

47.2%

Percentage of businesses in Hawaii owned by people of Asian descent. It was 14.9 percent in California and 10.1 percent in New York.

508,969

California had the most Asian-owned firms at 508,969 (32.8 percent of all such firms), followed by New York with 196,825 (12.7 percent) and Texas with 114,297 (7.4 percent).

Serving Our Nation
264,695

The number of the Asian alone population military veterans in 2011. About one in three veterans was 65 and older.

Source: U.S. Census Bureau, 2011 American Community Survey, Table B21001D, http://factfinder2.census.gov/bkmk/ table/1.0/en/ACS/11_1YR/B21001D

Jobs

48.5%

The proportion of civilian employed single-race Asians 16 and older who worked in management, business, science and arts occupations, such as financial managers, engineers, teachers and registered nurses in 2011. Additionally, 17.4 percent worked in service occupations, 21.1 percent in sales and office occupations, 9.6 percent in production, transportation and material moving occupations and 3.3 percent in natural resources, construction and maintenance occupations.

Source: U.S. Census Bureau, 2011 American Community Survey, Table S0201,
http://factfinder2.census.gov/bkmk/table/1.0/en/ACS/11_1YR/S0201//popgroup~012

Internet Use

80%

Percentage of Asians in 2009 living in a household with Internet use—the highest rate among race and ethnic groups.

Source: U.S. Census Bureau, Reported Internet Usage for Households, by selected Householder Characteristics; Current Population Survey: 2009
www.census.gov/population/www/socdemo/computer/2009.html

Age Distribution

33.5

Median age of the Asian alone or in combination population in 2011. The corresponding figure was 37.3 years for the population as a whole.

Source: U.S. Census Bureau, 2011 American Community Survey, Tables S0201,
http://factfinder2.census.gov/bkmk/table/1.0/en/ACS/11_1YR/S0201//popgroup~031 and
http://factfinder2.census.gov/bkmk/table/1.0/en/ACS/11_1YR/S0201

25.6%

Percent of the Asian alone or in combination population that was under age 18 in 2011, while 9.0 percent was 65 or older.

Source: U.S. Census Bureau, 2011 American Community Survey, Table S0201
http://factfinder2.census.gov/bkmk/table/1.0/en/ACS/11_1YR/S0201//popgroup~031

Native Hawaiians and Other Pacific Islanders

1.4 million

The estimated number of U.S. residents in 2011 who were Native Hawaiian or Other Pacific Islander, either alone or in combination with one or more additional races.

Source: 2011 Population Estimates Table 3
www.census.gov/popest/data/index.html. For additional information, see
www.census.gov/popest/data/national/asrh/2011/index.html.

359,000

Hawaii had the largest population of Native Hawaiians and Other Pacific Islanders among the alone or in combination population with 359,000, followed by California (329,000) in 2011. Hawaii had the largest proportion of Native Hawaiians and Other Pacific Islanders (26 percent).

Source: 2011 Population Estimates Table 4
www.census.gov/popest/data/index.html. For additional information, see
www.census.gov/popest/data/state/asrh/2011/index.html.

40%

Percentage growth of the Native Hawaiian and Other Pacific Islander alone or in combination population between the 2000 and 2010 censuses.

Source: U.S. Census Bureau, 2010 Census Redistricting Data (Public Law 94–171) Summary File, Custom Table 3, www.census.gov/2010census/news/xls/cb11cn123_us_2010redistr.xls. For additional details, see Hixson, L., B. Hepler, and M. Kim. 2011. *The Native Hawaiian and Other Pacific Islander Population: 2010,* U.S. Census Bureau, 2010 Census Briefs, C2010BR-12, available at
www.census.gov/prod/cen2010/briefs/c2010br-12.pdf.

518,000

Number of Native Hawaiians in the U.S. in 2011. The Native Hawaiian population was the largest detailed Native Hawaiian and Other Pacific Islanders (NHPI) group, followed by Samoan (174,000) and Guamanian or Chamorro (108,000). These estimates represent the number of people who reported a specific detailed NHPI group alone, as well as people who reported that detailed NHPI group in combination with one or more other detailed NHPI groups or another race(s).

Source: U.S. Census. Bureau, 2011 American Community Survey, Table B02019
http://factfinder2.census.gov/bkmk/table/1.0/en/ACS/11_1YR/B02019

Income, Poverty and Health Insurance

$49,378

The median income of households headed by the Native Hawaiians and Other Pacific Islanders alone in 2011.

Source: U.S. Census Bureau, 2011 American Community Survey, Table S0201

http://factfinder2.census.gov/bkmk/table/1.0/en/ACS/
11_1YR/S0201//popgroup~050

21.5%

The poverty rate in 2011 Native Hawaiians and Other Pacific Islanders alone population.

Source: U.S. Census Bureau, 2011 American Community Survey, Table S0201,
http://factfinder2.census.gov/bkmk/table/1.0/en/ACS/
11_1YR/S0201//popgroup~050

18.5%

The percentage without health insurance in 2011 for single-race Native Hawaiians and Other Pacific Islanders.

Source: U.S. Census Bureau, 2011 American Community Survey, Table S0201,
http://factfinder2.census.gov/bkmk/table/1.0/en/ACS/
11_1YR/S0201//popgroup~050

Education
14.5%

The percentage of the Native Hawaiians and Other Pacific Islanders alone 25 and older who had a bachelor's degree or higher in 2011. This compared with 28.5 percent for the total population.

Source: U.S. Census Bureau, 2011 American Community Survey, Tables S020I
http://factfinder2.census.gov/bkmk/table/1.0/en/ACS/
11_1YR/S0201//popgroup~050 and
http://factfinder2.census.gov/bkmk/table/1.0/en/ACS/
11_1YR/S0201

85.1%

The percentage of the Native Hawaiians and Other Pacific Islanders alone 25 and older who had at least a high school diploma in 2011. This compared with 85.9 percent of the total population.

Source: U.S. Census Bureau, 2011 American Community Survey Tables S0201
http://factfinder2.census.gov/bkmk/table/1.0/en/ACS/
11_1YR/S020l//popgroup~050 and
http://factfinder2.census.gov/bkmk/table/1.0/en/ACS/
11_1YR/S0201

4.3%

The percentage of the Native Hawaiians and Other Pacific Islanders alone 25 and older who had obtained a graduate or professional degree in 2011. This compared with 10.6 percent for the total population this age.

Source: U.S. Census Bureau, 2011 American Community Survey, Tables S0201
http://factfinder2.census.gov/bkmk/table/1.0/en/ACS/
11_1YR/S0201//popgroup~050 and

http://factfinder2.census.gov/bkmk/table/1.0/en/ACS/
11_1YR/S0201

Businesses

Source for the statements referenced in this section, unless otherwise indicated: U.S. Census Bureau, 2007 Survey of Business Owners via American FactFinder
http://factfinder2.census.gov/bkmk/table/1.0/en/SBO/
2007/00CSA01/0100000US/naics~00

37,687

The number of Native Hawaiian and Other Pacific Islander-owned businesses in 2007, up 30.2 percent from 2002.

$6.3 billion

Total receipts of these businesses in 2007, up 47.7 percent from 2002.

44.5%

The percent of all Native Hawaiian and Other Pacific Islander-owned business revenue that construction and retail trade accounted for in 2007.

9.5%

The percent of businesses in Hawaii owned by Native Hawaiian and Other Pacific Islanders in 2007, highest among all states.

Serving Our Nation
27,469

The number of the Native Hawaiian and Other Pacific Islander alone military veterans. About one in five veterans was 65 years and older.

Source: U.S. Census Bureau, 2011 American Community Survey, B21001E,
http://factfinder2.census.gov/bkmk/table/1.0/en/ACS/
10_1YR/B21001E

Jobs
24%

The proportion of civilian employed the Native Hawaiians and Other Pacific Islanders alone 16 and older who worked in management, business, science and arts occupations, such as financial managers, engineers, teachers and registered nurses in 2011. The percents for management, business, science and arts occupations, sales and office occupations and service occupations are not statistically different from one another. Additionally, 25.7 percent worked in service occupations, while 26.6 percent worked in sales and office occupations, 15.2 percent in production, transportation and material moving occupations and 8.6 percent in natural resources, construction and maintenance occupation.

Source: U.S. Census Bureau, 2011 American Community Survey, Table S0201,

http://factfinder2.census.gov/bkmk/table/1.0/en/ACS/
11_1YR/S0201//popgroup~050

Age Distribution

27.1

The median age of the Native Hawaiian and Other Pacific
Islander population alone or in combination in 2011. The
median age was 37.3 for the population as a whole.

Source: U.S. Census Bureau, 2011 American Community
Survey,
http://factfinder2.census.gov/bkmk/table/1.0/en/ACS/
11_1YR/S0201//popgroup~060 and
http://factfinder2.census.gov/bkmk/table/1.0/en/ACS/
11_1YR/S0201

33.5%

Percentage of the Native Hawaiian and Other Pacific Islander
alone or in combination population that was under age 18 in
2011, while 5.5 percent was 65 or older.

Source: U.S. Census Bureau, 2011 American Community Survey, Table S0201,
http://factfinder2.census.gov/bkmk/table/1.0/en/ACS/
11_1YR/S0201//popgroup~060

Following is a list of observances typically covered by the
Census Bureau's *Facts for Features* series:

- Black History Month (February)
- Super Bowl
- Valentine's Day (Feb. 14)
- Women's History Month (March)
- Irish-American Heritage Month (March)/
- St. Patrick's Day (March 17)
- Asian/Pacific American Heritage Month (May)
- Older Americans Month (May)
- Cinco de Mayo (May 5)
- Mother's Day
- Hurricane Season Begins (June 1)
- Father's Day
- The Fourth of July (July 4)
- Anniversary of Americans with Disabilities Act
  (July 26)

- Back to School (August)
- Labor Day
- Grandparents Day
- Hispanic Heritage Month (Sept. 15–Oct. 15)
- Halloween (Oct. 31)
- American Indian/Alaska Native Heritage Month
  (November)
- Veterans Day (Nov. 11)
- Thanksgiving Day
- The Holiday Season (December)

Critical Thinking

1. Are Asian immigrants acculturating and assimilating or are
   these concepts irrelevant in a globalized world?
2. Discuss the positive and troubling consequences related to
   highly skilled immigrants.

Create Central

www.mhhe.com/createcentral

Internet References

Asian American for Equality
   www.aafe.org

Asian American Studies Center
   www.aasc.ucla.eduldefault.asp

Asian-Nation
   www.asian-nation.orglindex_shtml

Social Science Information Gateway
   http://sosig.esrc.bris.ac.uk

Sociosite
   www.sociosite.net

Editor's note—As a matter of policy, the Census Bureau does not
advocate the use of the *alone* population over the *alone-or-in-
combination* population or vice versa. The use of the *alone* population
in sections of this report does not imply that it is a preferred method
of presenting or analyzing data. The same is true for sections of this
report that focus on the *alone-or-in-combination* population. Data on
race can be presented and discussed in a variety of ways.

The preceding data were collected from a variety of sources and may
be subject to sampling variability and other sources of error.

U.S Census Bureau, 2013.

Article   Prepared by: John A. Kromkowski, *The Catholic University of America*

With No Trademark, Sriracha Name Is Showing Up Everywhere

DAVID PIERSON

Learning Outcomes

After reading this article, you will be able to:

- Understand the origins of "sriracha."

- Discuss the legal aspects of this case study.

Wander down almost any supermarket aisle and it's easy to spot one of the food industry's hottest fads. Sriracha, the fiery red Asian chili sauce, has catapulted from a cult hit to flavor du jour, infusing burgers, potato chips, candy, vodka and even lip balm.

That would seem like a boon for the man who made the sauce a household name. Except for one glaring omission.

David Tran, a Vietnamese refugee who built the pepper empire from nothing, never trademarked the term, opening the door for others to develop their own sauce or seasoning and call it Sriracha.

That's given some of the biggest names in the food business such as Heinz, Frito-Lay, Subway and Jack in the Box license to bank off the popularity of a condiment once named *Bon Appétit* magazine's ingredient of the year.

Restaurant chains and candy and snack makers aren't buying truckloads of Tran's green-capped condiment emblazoned with the rooster logo. Nor are they paying Tran a dime in royalties to use the word "Sriracha" (pronounced "see-RAH-cha").

"In my mind, it's a major misstep," said Steve Stallman, president of Stallman Marketing, a food business consultancy. "Getting a trademark is a fundamental thing."

Tran, who now operates his family-owned company Huy Fong Foods out of a 650,000-squarefoot facility in Irwindale,

doesn't see his failure to secure a trademark as a missed opportunity. He says it's free advertising for a company that's never had a marketing budget. It's unclear whether he's losing out: Sales of the original Sriracha have grown from $60 million to $80 million in the last two years alone.

"Everyone wants to jump in now," said Tran, 70. "We have lawyers come and say 'I can represent you and sue' and I say 'No. Let them do it.'"

Tran is so proud of the condiment's popularity that he maintains a daily ritual of searching the Internet for the latest Sriracha spinoff.

He believes all the exposure will lead more consumers to taste the original spicy, sweet concoction—which was inspired by flavors from across Southeast Asia and named after a coastal city in Thailand. Tran also said he was discouraged to seek a trademark because it would have been difficult getting one named after a real-life location.

That hasn't stopped competitors from scratching their heads.

Tony Simmons, chief executive of the McIlhenny Co., makers of Tabasco, said Tran's Sriracha sauce was the "gold standard" for Sriracha-style sauces, which has largely come to mean any dressing that packs a piquant punch of chili paste, vinegar, garlic and sugar.

Simmons was reassured by his lawyers that Tabasco would have no problem releasing a similar sauce using the name Sriracha.

"We spend enormous time protecting the word 'Tabasco' so that we don't have exactly this problem," Simmons said. "Why Mr. Tran did not do that, I don't know."

There are now a slew of sauces on the market labeled Sriracha, including variations by Frank's Red Hot, Kikkoman and Lee Kum Kee.

The category has helped ignite U.S. hot sauce sales, which have jumped from $229 million in 2000 to $608 million last year, according to Euromonitor.

"What we're seeing among consumers is demand, not just for heat, but more complex, regional flavors," said Beth Bloom, a food and drink analyst for Mintel. "With Sriracha, Huy Fong introduced a new style and a whole new category of hot sauce."

Although Taco Bell and Pizza Hut are some of the latest national brands to experiment with their own Sriracha seasoning in tacos, nachos and pizza sauce, it's Tabasco's that has Tran admittedly sweating.

"My 'rooster killer' jumped into the market," said Tran, borrowing a description he saw on a food blog. "They're a big company. They have a lot of money and a lot of advertising."

Simmons isn't counting on toppling Sriracha any time soon.

"Mr. Tran got an awful big head start," he said.

After a limited release, Tabasco will distribute its Sriracha sauce nationwide sometime in the first quarter of this year, Simmons said.

It may be too late for Tran to successfully argue that the trademark belongs to him.

Two dozen applications to use the word have been filed with the United States Patent and Trademark Office. None has been granted for Sriracha alone. The word is now too generic, the agency determined.

"The ship has probably sailed on this, which is unfortunate because they've clearly added something to American cuisine that wasn't there before," said Kelly P. McCarthy, a partner and expert on brand protection and trademark issues at the law firm Sideman & Bancroft.

She said it's not uncommon for popular products to lose their trademarks because they've become "genericized," such as Otis Elevator Co.'s use of "escalator" and Bayer AG's loss of "aspirin."

Tran's attorney isn't so sure the same applies to Sriracha.

Rod Berman, who was primarily retained 10 years ago to tackle counterfeiters, thinks many consumers still associate Sriracha with Huy Fong. He cited the mountain of publicity, films and growing sales as evidence.

"My instinct is to want to go after the people that used the Sriracha name," said Berman, an intellectual property lawyer who has represented the Los Angeles Lakers, Pom Wonderful and Nordstrom.

But that's not realistic, he says, especially for a medium-size company like Huy Fong.

"Large companies, the Mattels and Disneys of the world, try to protect everything and have the budget for that," Berman

said. "With smaller enterprises like Huy Fong, you have to pick and choose."

That's why Tran has gone after knockoffs of Huy Fong's Sriracha from China. Unlike the name, Tran trademarked his rooster logo and distinctive bottle.

At the same time, Tran has signed licensing agreements with a handful of specialty producers such as Rogue, which brews a Sriracha hot stout beer packaged in a red bottle and green cap to look like Huy Fong's signature sauce, and Pop Gourmet, which makes a Sriracha popcorn and will soon release a Sriracha seasoning spice.

Even with these partnerships, Tran doesn't charge any royalty fees. All he asks is that they use his sauce and stay true to its flavor.

"I wanted to bring people the real stuff," said David Israel, chief executive of Pop Gourmet in Kent, Wash.

The Sriracha popcorn is the company's No. 1 seller, and Israel has high hopes for the new seasoning, which took nine months to develop.

For the Rogue stout, Sriracha is added during the fermentation process. The beer quickly sold out.

"We could have gone and just used Huy Fong's sauce, but we also wanted to use their name" and logo, said Brett Joyce, president of the Newport, Ore., company.

Randy Clemens, author of "The Sriracha Cookbook" and "The Veggie-Lover's Sriracha Cookbook," said the licensed products preserve Huy Fong's flavor, unlike the mass-market efforts.

"A little kick, but to put Sriracha in the title is a little disingenuous," Clemens said. "What makes the original so great is that it's bold and kicks you in the face."

Tran agreed his imitators fall short in flavor and spice, but like the trademark, he isn't losing any sleep over it.

"David is fine with that since in some indirect way, we will still reap the benefit of the word 'Sriracha' being used," said Donna Lam, Tran's longtime deputy. "We seem to be the best-known Sriracha out there, and everyone seems to use our brand as the gold standard. If anything, we are proud we started the Sriracha craze."

Critical Thinking

1. What is a patent? What is a trademark?
2. What do you make of narratives of ethnic entrepreneurs and how such tales have become a robust dimension of popular journalism?
3. Discuss negative and positive stereotypes from this case.

Internet References

12 Weird Facts You Didn't Know About Sriracha
www.thrillist.com

AWIB Asian & Asian American Organizations
www.awib.org/index.cfm?fuseaction=page.viewpage&pageid=816

American-Thai Foundation
www.americanthaifoundation.org

Sriracha: A documentary
http://srirachamovie.com

The Sriracha Cookbook
http://thesrirachacookbook.com

Article   Prepared by: John A. Kromkowski, *The Catholic University of America*

Finally a Movie That Captures What It's Like to Be Asian American

ELAINE TENG

Learning Outcomes

After reading this article, you will be able to:

- Discuss this movie and its impact.
- Discuss the meaning of representation in art, especially film, that this account proposes.

O ver the last few decades, American television and film have opened up, so much so that my colleague Esther Breger recently argued that TV is more diverse than it's ever been. But the one group that's still notably absent is Asian Americans. The Asian-American family hasn't been the subject of a sitcom since Margaret Cho's "All-American Girl" was canceled after disastrous reviews 20 years ago.

Critics are now looking ahead to ABC's family sitcom "Fresh Off the Boat," debuting this spring. Based on celebrity chef Eddie Huang's memoirs, the show should go a long [way] toward representing the 18 million Asian Americans who are virtually invisible in mainstream media. But it remains to be seen if the show can be as groundbreaking as many hope; it's already received criticism for its title (which most would recognize as an offensive term for Asian immigrants).

The struggle for Asian-American representation on network television, though, doesn't mean it's impossible to effectively capture the immigrant experience. Though set across the pond, British indie film, *Lilting,* which premiered this fall, covers the immigrant reality in a way that should both resonate with Asian Americans and pull back the curtain for white audiences.

While other minority groups also suffer from stereotyping and underrepresentation on TV, blacks and Latinos appear more frequently, at least in recent seasons (see shows like "Jane the Virgin," "Orange is the New Black," "Blackish").

"All-American Girl" remains to date the only attempt to depict Asian-American family life on TV, and it failed spectacularly. It was canceled after one season, and almost the entire cast had been fired by the time the finale aired. The show's producers actually asked star Margaret Cho to act "more Asian"—and brought in an Asian expert to coach her.

If represented at all, Asian American characters find their identity either fetishized or ignored completely. There is no middle ground. Shows like "Selfie" or "The Mindy Project" are essentially race blind; the characters just happen to be Asian Americans who live and interact in very white worlds. But, as E. Alex Jung recently put it in the *LA Review of Books,* the problem with these shows is: "Taking the 'Asian' out of Asian American doesn't make its characters more American, but less so."

Then there's the opposite approach, where shows exoticize race or simply use racism as a substitute for humor. CBS's "2 Broke Girls" is particularly guilty of this with its racist depiction of a Korean-American character. "Every time Han gets to say something on '2 Broke Girls,' the undercurrent is that it's funny because it's broken English," wrote Tim Goodman at *The Hollywood Reporter.*

Movies are typically even worse than TV—Asian Americans basically don't appear. Movies with Asian protagonists are invariably period dramas about a China or a Japan totally removed from the real, present-day experience. If Asians only existed according to Hollywood, they would all be warriors who can fly through trees.

Lilting, however, manages to be a movie about the modern immigrant experience, about how first- and second-generation Asian immigrants encounter life in the West. This, in fact, represents the majority of Asian Americans, who are overwhelmingly first- and second-generation immigrants; the two groups make up 91 percent of the Asian-American population—with the exception of the Japanese, who largely emigrated earlier.

The film is the debut full-length feature from writer-director Hong Khaou, whose Cambodian-Chinese family left Asia for the U.K. when he was a boy (and who I interviewed). The movie follows Richard (Ben Whishaw), a young British man, and Junn (Cheng Pei-Pei), an older Chinese immigrant, as they mourn and clash over the death of Kai, Richard's partner and Junn's son. To complicate matters, Junn and Richard do not speak the same language, and the movie floats elegantly between Chinese and English, with a scattering of subtitles, as the two rely on an amiable translator to communicate.

The film presents identity as we actually experience it, as something we carry with us every moment that informs our thoughts and our reactions. But at the same time, being Asian is one factor of many that make up a full person. Junn, who struggles to adapt to English society and rejects Richard's attempts to help her overcome her grief, is an extremely complex woman whose hostility and sorrow are informed by her immigrant background, but not defined by it. She's an immigrant, but also a bereaved mother, a widow, and a woman, one whose obstinacy and fiery personality have nothing to do with her racial identity.

Still, the movie doesn't shy away from depicting Asian culture in a realistic way, and, to go one step further, shows how it subtly affects each character in the movie. Like many second-generation immigrants, Kai speaks Chinese with a slight English accent, and his mother lovingly corrects his pronunciation from time to time. Richard, who was exposed to East Asian culture through Kai, cooks bacon with chopsticks and says it's the only real way to do so. (Funnily enough, I have friends who learned the same trick from me.) These brief moments capture the funny little ways culture spreads and evolves, familiar to so many immigrants who have seen their traditions and values blend and change with those of their adopted country.

The very fact that the director chose to film *Lilting* in both Chinese and English shows the importance he places in capturing the authentic immigrant experience. He could easily have decided to have Junn speak English, or to rely only on subtitles to relay her thoughts, which would have undoubtedly been easier to write than the complicated translation scenes.

But instead, by placing the act of translation at the heart of the movie, Khaou makes his audience experience everyday communication the way most immigrant families do. Like many Asian Americans, I speak to my parents in a mixture of English and Chinese, and grew up filling out forms and translating things like DMV documents and rental agreements. For us, translation is just a part of life, as our parents rely on us to communicate with their new world, and in turn, impart our heritage to us through their native tongue.

Lilting shows people as they really are, whose identities inform who they are but are ever shifting and evolving. Unlike most of its peers, the movie understands that racial identity is not all or nothing. These characters, like real people, are complex and changing, and they can belong to a group—be it Asian, black, white, Hispanic, gay, straight, etc.—but also be more than that.

When movies and television acknowledge and bring that to life, they will not only have diversified their audience, but they will impact the way we look at each other in the world. No group is a stereotype, and it's time our media reflected that.

Critical Thinking

1. Are Asian immigrants acculturating and assimilating or are these concepts irrelevant in a globalized world?

2. Discuss the positive and troubling consequences related to high-skilled immigrants.

Internet References

Asian Americans for Equality
www.aafe.org

Asian American Studies Center
www.aasc.ucla.edu

Asian-Nation
http://www.asian-nation.org

ELAINE TENG is the managing editor of *The New Republic*.

Unit 8

UNIT

Prepared by: John A. Kromkowski, *The Catholic University of America*

Euro/Mediterranean Ethnic Americans

The American experience from 1870 to 1924 addressed the influence of these groups and in so doing shifted the American consciousness of itself. Even 100 years later, America's public mind continues to identify and divide its history as an immigrant-receiving country into two periods: The Old Immigration, meaning Northern Europeans, and the New Immigration, meaning Others—the Mediterranean and Eastern Europeans, as well as Asian and Hispanic populations. One marker of this division can be found in the 1910 report of the Dillingham Commission. This congressional and presidential blue ribbon panel warned America that the Eastern European and Mediterranean character was less capable of Americanization than the Nordics and Teutonics who had populated America earlier.

Due to the considerable fluidity of immigrant experiences, as well as the complex processes of cultural identity and political use of cultural symbols, such as race and ethnicity, the search for more analytical rigor in this field is far from complete. One guide to discernible and measurable features of ethnic phenomena and characteristics that are attributes of ethnicity was developed in a fine collection of materials on this topic, *The Harvard Encyclopedia of American Ethnic Groups*. It lists the following markers of ethnic groups: common geographic origin; migratory status; language/dialect; religious faith(s); ties that transcend kinship, neighborhood, and community boundaries; shared traditions, values, and symbols; literature; folklore; music; food preferences; settlement and employment patterns; special interests in regard to politics in the homeland and in the United States; institutions that specifically serve and maintain the group; an internal sense of distinctiveness; and an external perception of distinctiveness. With the addition of a demographic database developed by the U.S. Census, a much more rigorous set of analytics can be applied to anthropological and humanistic approaches to ethnic groups.

Moynihan and Glazer, in *Beyond the Melting Pot* (1964), the report of the Kerner Commission, and findings of the National Center for Urban Ethnic Affairs, confirmed that ethnicity was a salient factor. The descendants of Mediterranean and Eastern European immigrants, even into the fourth generation, were just barely moving toward the middle class. They were absent in the professions and rarely admitted into prestigious universities or colleges. More specifically, Italian and Polish people, like blacks and Hispanics/Latinos, were found to be excluded from the executive suites and boardrooms of America's largest corporations, publicly regulated utilities, and philanthropies.

Ethnicity is often associated with immigrants and with importation of culture, language, stories, and foods from foreign shores. Appalachian, Western, and other regional ethnicities are evidence of multigenerational ethnic cultural developments within the American reality. The persistent, ongoing process of cultural formation and personal identity are expressed locally in unique and intriguing folkways, dialects, languages, myths, festivals, food displays, and other enduring monuments and visible signs of the past and of the public dimension of cultural consciousness that constitutes ethnicity. After all, it was this American promise that resonated in their hearts and minds in 1965 when a coalition of Mediterranean and Eastern European Americans in the national government supported the 1965 Voting Rights Act that ensured fair elections for the disenfranchised in the South. This legislative coalition was accomplished through deliberative democracy. In the same year as immigration reform, America instituted fundamental change that significantly altered the terms of race and ethnic relations. The massive migration of people during the past decades, which has included significantly large Mediterranean and Eastern European populations, has reengaged the issue of immigration in American politics. The ethnic factor now reaches nearly all Americans. Should ethnic populations be denied their distinctiveness through absorption into the mass of modernity, or can their distinctiveness accompany them into mainstream modern America?

To address this question is to step into the search for a normative base for resolving dilemmas and contentions among groups. Significant clarification can be gained by defining ethnicity. What constitutes ethnic identity? Are ancestry and place of origin important? Are contextual factors, such as other populations, ethnicities, and economic, educational, cultural, and social dynamics, as well as traditions, determinative? Are the influences of such factors on ethnic groups and the manifestations of their presence in a metropolitan region firmly congealed?

Certain lines of clarification to these introductory issues were drafted for a project sponsored by the National Center for Urban Ethnic Affairs focused on the Detroit metropolitan region. The regional chair of this project, Thaddeus Radzilowski, President of the Piast Institute, proposed the following deep description of the experience of American ethnicity:

> Ethnicity is one of the deepest and most enduring of human identities because it is based on language, religion, culture, family, common history and local community. It can have political salience and as such can play both negative and positive roles. However, political or public salience is not necessary for its survival. It can be the basis of community formation and a generous pluralism on the one hand, or divisiveness and prejudice on the other.
>
> Ethnicity in America is a creative adaptation to life in the New World by immigrants, both free and coerced. It was an attempt by newcomers to make themselves "at home" in a new place, often under difficult and challenging conditions. Out of the process came cultures that were born out of preservation, adaptation, direct borrowing, and invention, often reinforced by prejudice and interest. Successful ethnicities have kept the ability to change themselves to meet new conditions, as well as to modify the dominant society in which they are embedded and to affect other ethnic cultures with whom they coexist.
>
> Ethnic adaptation to preserve core values and to mobilize group members in times of difficulty has happened with remarkable speed given the usually more leisurely pace of historical change. To be able to anticipate and use ethnicity in ways beneficial to the evolution of our society requires a clear understanding of recent history and current prospects if it is to succeed. At this point, it is not utopian to suggest the possibility of the repolarization of ethnicity and its return as a vehicle to talk about civic values, community, and multiculturalism. This discourse will require rethinking of multiculturalism at the same time. The postulation of the incomprehensibility and irreconcilability of cultures to each other is useless for any civic dialogue. Multiculturalism in its soft form is, at this time, too superficial and vapid to carry any meaningful concepts of community development. Neither has a language or a story fashioned a political dialogue, any more than race, embedded in institutions in which people can act in the civic arena.

Article   Prepared by: John A. Kromkowski, *Catholic University of America*

Comparison on Ethnic Pride: Irish Catholic, Eastern European, Arab, Hispanic, Italian, Chinese, and other Mixed Ethnicities: The Zogby Center Polls 2000–2004

Learning Outcomes

After reading this article, you will be able to:

- Determine whether measures of public opinion are good indicators of values and behaviors. Under what conditions and about what sorts of issues?

- Discuss those findings that you found surprising and explain why you were surprised.

We compared the polling results on ethnic pride across seven ethnic groups within the populace of the United States: Arab, Hispanic, Italian, Chinese, Irish Catholic, Eastern European Catholic and Catholic with mixed ethnic background. Certain categories excluded one or more of these groups.

A. Ethnic Pride

Americans maintain a tremendous sense of recognition with regards to their ethnic origins and make-up. When we asked individuals in four of our seven groups to assess "How strong are your emotional ties to your family's country of origin?" over 70% of those polled said they maintained at least somewhat

Table 1   Emotional Ties to Country of Origin

	Arab	Hispanic	Italian	Chinese
Very strong	39.7	36.8	34.3	40.1
Somewhat Strong	38.7	33.5	41.4	41.8
Not strong	21.5	29.1	23.8	18.1

strong emotional ties. And while Chinese Americans appear to have the greatest connection with their country of origin at 40.1% (followed shortly thereafter by Arabs, Hispanics and lastly Italians), more than a third of each group claimed to have very strong emotional ties.

As was reported in Zogby's 2000 Culture Poll entitled *What Ethnic Americans Really Think,* most Americans would appear to be very proud of their ethnic heritage, a fact that would seem to corroborate the strong emotional ties that many Ethnic Americans maintain with their country of origin. When asked, "On a scale of 1 to 5, with 1 being not at all and 5 being extremely, how proud are you of your ethnic heritage?" Between 70% and 90% of each one of our target

Table 2   Ethnic Pride

	Irish Catholic	Eastern European	Mixed	Arab	Hispanic	Italian	Chinese
Proud	81.6	80.7	70.4	85.5	90.0	90.7	85.2
Average pride	12.8	12.3	17.9	10.1	8.2	6.6	10.3
Not proud	5.2	6.6	10.9	3.8	1.4	2.4	3.0

groups expressed some degree of pride (4 or 5 on the scale) with regards to their ethnicity. Inversely, less than 11% of each respective group said they are not at all proud of their ethnic composition. Italian and Hispanic Americans are most likely to say that they are very proud of their origins at 90.7% and 90.0% respectively, while Catholics with mixed ethnic background are least likely to do so (70.4%).

When asked, "How important is your ethnic heritage in defining you as a person?" a majority of those polled responded that their ethnicity did in fact contribute in at least some way to their persona. This was especially true of Arab, Hispanic and Chinese-Americans, of whom over 50% went so far as to say that their ethnic heritage was very important in defining them as a person. Catholics with mixed ethnic background would seem to place the least amount of importance on ethnicity, with 40.5% claiming that their ethnic heritage is not at all important in defining them as a person. A large chunk of Eastern European Catholics (35.0%) and Irish Catholics (32.4%) also see their ethnic heritage as irrelevant to their self-definition.

B. Discrimination

While the majority of our respective target groups expressed a similar sense of recognition and pride regarding their ethnic heritage, responses were somewhat more polarizing as they pertained to discrimination. In response to the question "Have you personally experienced discrimination in the past because of your ethnicity/ancestral heritage?" an overwhelming majority of Irish Catholics, Eastern European Catholics, Catholics with mixed origins and Italian-Americans (88.6%, 91.6%, 90.8% and 79.1% respectively) said that they had never been victimized on account of their ethnic background. On the contrary, nearly half of those Hispanic and Chinese-American individuals polled (48.9% and 49.0%) respectively) claim to have been discriminated against.

When asked "How worried are you about the long-term effects of discrimination?" our results mirrored those of the previous question regarding the subject. As might be expected, for example, Hispanic and Chinese-Americans appear to be the most concerned by discrimination in the long-term, with 56.9% of the former and 46.3% of the latter at least somewhat worried. Italian-Americans are markedly less concerned, demonstrated by the fact that over 80% of those polled expressed no concern about the long-term effects of discrimination.

Arab-Americans would seem to be the most concerned about the contentious issue of discrimination, with an astonishing 25% very worried about the long-term effects of discriminatory behavior. This reality is perhaps less surprising in view of the

Table 3 Importance of Ethnic Heritage in Self-Definition

	Irish Catholic	Eastern European	Mixed	Arab	Hispanic	Italian	Chinese
Very important	24.5	25.0	20.1	55.6	55.6	48.1	54.0
Somewhat important	43.1	39.7	38.7	29.9	30.6	37.4	31.7
Not important	32.4	35.0	40.5	14.0	13.5	14.0	13.6

Table 4 Discrimination

	Irish Catholic	Eastern European	Mixed	Hispanic	Italian	Chinese
Yes	11.2	8.2	9.2	48.9	20.2	49.0
No	88.6	91.6	90.8	50.8	79.1	49.7

Table 5 Discrimination: Long-Term Effects

	Arab	Hispanic	Italian	Chinese
Very worried	25.0	15.4	3.8	5.4
Somewhat worried	34.6	41.5	14.3	40.9
Not worried	38.8	42.3	81.4	53.5

political and social climate in the post-911 era. A significant majority of Arab Americans (60%) consider the events since September 11 to have negatively affected the public display of their heritage.

C. Taking a Closer Look at Ethnic Pride

1. Compared by Age

All of the groups we studied registered strong emotional ties to their land of heritage, regardless of the age of the respondent.

In general the strength of those ties decreased with age, with individuals aged 18 to 29 claiming to have the strongest emotional ties and those aged 65 and above having the weakest. The exception to the rule was the Chinese American population, where 18 to 29 year-olds actually recorded the weakest emotional ties (73.8%) and 50 to 64 year-olds the strongest (88.5%). Amongst Italian Americans 50 to 64 year-olds registered the weakest emotional ties (70.55%), although 18 to 29 year-olds maintained the strongest ties (83.0%).

Table 6   Emotional Ties

	Arab	Hispanic	Italian	Chinese
18–29	89.0	91.0	83.0	73.8
30–49	80.2	88.1	77.2	83.6
50–64	77.9	84.2	70.5	88.5
65+	70.6	81.0	75.1	79.6

Among Arab, Hispanic and Chinese Americans, younger generations appear to have the most pride in their ethnic heritage. For the three Catholic groups, the trend is reversed. It is those over 65 years old who seem to exhibit the most ethnic pride. The age gap is most remarkable in the case of Catholics with mixed background. Only 52.7% of its 18 to 29 year-olds claim to be proud of their ethnic heritage compared to 81.9% of those over 65 years old. For Italian Americans, the percentage of those proud of their ethnic heritage does not vary much across the age categories, although the older generations do seem to show slightly more pride than the younger ones.

For Arab, Hispanic and Chinese Americans, the relative importance of ethnic heritage decreases with age, with few exceptions. This is not the case with regards to the other four groups. In fact, quite to the contrary, those aged 65 and above were most concerned by the importance of their ethnic heritage among Eastern European Catholics, Catholics with mixed background and Italian Americans. For Irish Catholics, the age difference is not obvious among those over 30, although there is a significant dip for those aged 18 to 29.

2. Compared by Political Party Affiliation

There does not appear to be any generality to assess the relationship between political party affiliation and the emotional ties held to one's land of heritage. Amongst Hispanic and Italian Americans registered Democrats had the strongest emotional ties, while Republicans and/or independents had the strongest

Table 7   Pride in Ethnic Heritage

	Irish Catholic	Eastern European	Mixed	Arab	Hispanic	Italian	Chinese
18–29	72.0	61.7	52.7	94.0	91.6	90.0	90.2
30–49	83.8	83.1	65.5	84.2	91.1	87.7	83.7
50–64	77.0	77.4	74.5	81.5	90.8	93.0	83.0
65+	87.2	89.6	81.9	87.6	83.4	93.6	77.8

Table 8   Importance of Ethnic Heritage

	Irish Catholic	Eastern European	Mixed	Arab	Hispanic	Italian	Chinese
18–29	52	51.9	61.8	94.0	91.6	90.0	90.2
30–49	69.8	66.0	57.8	84.2	91.1	87.7	83.7
50–64	67.1	61.9	53.8	81.5	90.8	93.0	83.0
65+	69.4	73.4	66.9	87.6	83.4	93.6	77.8

ties in the Arab and Chinese American communities. Emotional ties do not, however, vary extraordinarily with party affiliation, as evidenced by the fact that over 70% of all respondents supposedly maintain strong ties to their land of heritage.

Generally, registered democrats exhibit the greatest pride in their ethnic heritage within the groups that we examined. There are a few exceptions. First, among Arab Americans, a greater percentage of republicans and independents claim to be proud

Table 9   Emotional Ties

	Arab	Hispanic	Italian	Chinese
Democrat	73.3	88.9	80.1	78.4
Republican	75.5	82.1	72.9	80.0
Independent	84.3	83.3	72.9	81.3

Table 10 Pride in Ethnic Heritage

	Irish Catholic	Eastern European	Mixed	Arab	Hispanic	Italian	Chinese
Democrat	83.3	81.2	71.6	82.5	90.6	92.2	90.3
Republican	84.4	83.2	69.5	87.0	87.0	91.8	81.3
Independent	75.4	76.7	69.9	86.7	90.8	86.7	82.4

of their ethnic heritage. Then for Irish and Eastern European Catholics, it is also the republicans that lead. Democrats are slightly behind while independents are left at the bottom.

Different from the case with ethnic pride, democrats seem to lead in almost all groups in their emphasis on the importance of ethnic heritage. The only exception was Chinese Americans, where democrats lagged almost ten percent behind independent voters. Between the groups of democrats, Arab, Hispanic and Italian Americans were most likely to claim that their ethnic heritage was very important to them. The groups that are least likely to see the importance of ethnic heritage are independent Catholics with eastern European or mixed ethnic background (56.4% and 53.8% respectively).

Table 12 Emotional Ties

	Arab	Hispanic	Italian	Chinese
Male	72.9	69.7	72.4	82.3
Female	83.9	70.9	78.7	81.5

proud of their ethnic background. On the contrary, Chinese American men are slightly more proud of their heritage than their female counterparts (87.7% and 82.9% respectively).

Among 5 of the 7 groups, female respondents are more likely to view their ethnic heritage as important or somewhat

Table 11 Importance of Ethnic Heritage

	Irish Catholic	Eastern European	Mixed	Arab	Hispanic	Italian	Chinese
Democrat	71.1	70.0	64.3	87.8	88.9	86.8	83.7
Republican	69.1	65.4	57.1	81.8	82.1	86.2	81.3
Independent	60.7	56.4	53.8	84.8	83.3	82.4	93.1

3. Compared by Gender

With the exception of Chinese Americans, women appear to maintain stronger emotional ties with their country of origin than do men. With that said, the difference between the emphasis that men and women place on their emotional ties is negligible. Only Arab Americans exhibited any significant gap between male and female respondents, with 11.0% more females claiming to have strong emotional ties to their land of origin than men (83.9% and 72.9%) respectively).

Women appear slightly more likely to exhibit a tremendous sense of pride in their ethnic heritage than men do. Indeed, amongst all Catholic groups, Arab, Hispanic and Italian Americans, a greater percentage of females claimed that they are very

important in defining themselves. The gender gap varies between 6% and 8.4%. One exception is the Catholics with mixed background where males lead females by 7.1%. There is little gender difference among eastern European Catholics. For both genders, the Catholic groups lag far behind the other four ethnic groups in their perceived importance of ethnic heritage.

4. Compared by Income

Income does not have a consistent impact upon the respondents' emotional ties to their country of origin. The Italians exhibit the least variation across the income groups. The group difference is less than 4.6%. Those with an annual income less than $50,000 exhibit the strongest emotional attachment. Within

Table 13 Pride in Ethnic Heritage

	Irish Catholic	Eastern European	Mixed	Arab	Hispanic	Italian	Chinese
Male	79.5	78.9	66.6	83.6	87.7	89.1	87.7
Female	83.6	82.4	73.9	87.4	91.8	92.1	82.9

Table 14 Importance of Ethnic Heritage

	Irish Catholic	Eastern European	Mixed	Arab	Hispanic	Italian	Chinese
Male	63.2	65.1	62.5	81.7	82.2	82.4	82.0
Female	71.0	64.4	55.4	89.3	89.6	88.4	89.5

the other three ethnic populations, the difference in emotional ties varies greatly across the income groups. For the *Hispanics,* those who earn less than $35,000 a year profess stronger attachment to their country of origin while those who have an annual income over $75,000 allege the least affection. Among the *Chinese Americans,* however, it is the lowest income group that claims weakest emotional ties to their motherland. As to the Arabs, those making between $50,000 and $75,000 a year are most estranged from their country of origin.

Table 15 Emotional Ties

	Arab	Hispanic	Italian	Chinese
>$35K	78.1	76.8	78.3	76.1
$35–50K	82.2	69.4	78.3	87.3
$50–75K	72.9	68.0	74.7	84.5
$75K+	78.7	62.7	73.7	87.3

The income group that shows the least pride in ethnic heritage are the Catholics with mixed background who earn more than $75,000 a year. Only 63.2% of this group claim to be proud of their ethnic heritage. On the other hand, those with an income of less than $35,000 see the highest percentage of respondents within this group taking pride in their ethnic background. Similarly, among eastern Europeans, those that exhibit the most pride in their ethnic heritage are also from the lowest income group. Irish Catholics, however, see a different pattern

here. Almost all its income groups exhibit immense pride in their ethnic heritage except those making less than $35,000 per year. Those from the lowest income category lag behind other groups by more than 10% in terms of their ethnic pride.

Among the Arab Americans, the group that lags behind are those making between $50,000 and $75,000, which is consistent with our previous findings on emotional ties—this group also happens to be the one that exhibits the weakest emotional ties to their country of origin.

The same cannot be said for Hispanic Americans and Chinese Americans though. Among the Hispanic group, those with an annual income less than $35,000 exhibit the least pride in ethnic heritage while those making more than $75,000 per year show almost equally strong pride as the other two groups. However, as we show earlier, the same lowest-income group has the strongest emotional ties to their country of origin while the highest-income group has the weakest. It shows that emotional ties to the country of origin and pride in ethnic heritage do not always go hand in hand. Similarly, those Chinese Americans with an annual income under $35,000 show the least emotional attachment to China yet the most pride in ethnic heritage. On the whole, we do not see great variation across income groups among the Chinese Americans on their pride in ethnic heritage.

Among Italian Americans, income does not seem to have a strong impact upon their pride in ethnic heritage. All groups exhibit immense pride although the income group making between $50,000 and $75,000 per year falls slightly behind. The same group shows relatively weaker ties to their country of origin in our previous findings.

Table 16 Pride in Ethnic Heritage

	Irish Catholic	Eastern European	Mixed	Arab	Hispanic	Italian	Chinese
<$35K	69.1	86.5	79.3	78.1	86.3	93.1	86.9
$35–50K	83.8	74	78.8	82.2	91.7	91.6	86.1
$50–75K	86.6	75.7	66.0	72.9	92.5	89.2	83.2
$75K+	82.7	78.5	63.2	78.7	90.2	92.1	85.0

Income does not have a uniform impact upon the importance respondents attach to their ethnic heritage. Catholic groups, in general, attach much less importance to their ethnic heritage compared to other ethnic groups. Among the Catholics, the two groups that attach most importance to their ethnic heritage are those with Eastern European or mixed background and an annual income under $35,000 (74.9% and 71.4% respectively).

Also for the Catholics with mixed background, one's income level and the importance of ethnic heritage are negatively correlated. In other words, the higher one's income is, the less likely it is for one to consider their ethnicity important in defining themselves. For Irish Catholics, the importance of their ethnic heritage does not vary much across income groups. The only exception is the group who make between $35,000 and $50,000 per year. This group tends to rate the importance of their ethnic heritage particularly low compared to others. Only 58.3% of this group believe that ethnic heritage plays an important role in their self-definition. As to east European Catholics, those with an income between $35,000 and $50,000 are least likely to acknowledge the importance of ethnic heritage.

For all income groups of Hispanic Americans, ethnic heritage plays an important role in their self-definition. The group that attaches the greatest importance to their ethnicity are those with an income between $35,000 and $50,000. Like their Hispanic counterparts, all groups of Italian Americans consider their ethnicity an important part of their self-definition. The group that lags behind slightly are those making between $50,000 and $75,000 a year—82.4% of them declare that ethnic heritage is important or somewhat important in defining themselves.

Among the Chinese Americans, those least likely to acknowledge the importance of ethnic heritage earn between $50,000 and $75,000. Only 76.4% of them claim that ethnic heritage is important for their self-definition. On the other hand, the group most likely to see the importance of their ethnic heritage are those with an income between $35,000 and $50,000.

emotional ties to China, compared to 80.9% of those who are not unionized.

The difference in ethnic pride between union members and nonunion members varies across the groups. For 4 of the 6 groups, the trend seems to be that the unionized respondents are more likely to be proud of their ethnic heritage than their non-unionized counterparts. Big gaps are found among Italian

Tabe 18 Emotional Ties

	Hispanic	Italian	Chinese
Yes	70.0	77.4	86.4
No/NS	70.5	75.0	80.9

Americans and Catholics with mixed background. Among the former, 90.2% of their union members claim to be proud of their ethnicity compared to only 78.5% of their non-unionized counterparts who say so. For the latter, the percentages are 77.0% for union members as against 68.7% for non-union members. There is little difference between unionized eastern

Table 17 Importance of Ethnic Heritage

	Irish Catholic	Eastern European	Mixed	Arab	Hispanic	Italian	Chinese
<$35K	68.1	74.9	71.4	78.2	86.8	87.9	83.3
$35–50K	58.3	52.6	65.2	83.3	90.5	89.2	90.3
$50–75K	66.4	56.9	60.4	84.7	85.4	82.4	76.4
$75K+	65.2	64.9	50.9	92.5	82.4	86.8	87.6

Table 19 Pride in Ethnic Heritage

	Irish Catholic	Eastern European	Mixed	Hispanic	Italian	Chinese
Yes	80.0	80.2	77.0	91.7	90.2	88.9
No/NS	82.1	82.1	80.9	68.7	89.2	84.2

5. Compared by Union Membership

Union membership does not seem to have an impact on Hispanic Americans' emotional affinity to their country of origin. For both union members and non-union members, about 70% of the respondents acknowledge strong or somewhat strong emotional ties.

Union membership has a minor effect upon Italian American's emotional ties. Those who are union members are slightly more likely to declare their emotional attachment, but the difference of merely 2.4% between the union members and the non-union member is almost negligible.

The gap between unionized Chinese Americans and their non-unionized counterparts is more pronounced. 86.4% of the unionized Chinese Americans claim strong or somewhat strong

European Catholics and their non-unionized counterparts. For Irish Catholics, non-union members are slightly more likely to show pride in their ethnic heritage.

For almost all ethnic groups, union members are somewhat more likely to acknowledge the importance of ethnic heritage in self-definition than non-union members. The difference varies from 1.0% to 15.5%. The greatest difference is found among Catholics with mixed ethnic background.

The only exception are the Hispanic Americans, among whom the non-union members are slightly more likely to declare the importance of their ethnic heritage than union members are.

Generally, within each ethnic group, union members are more likely to declare strong emotional ties to their country of

Table 20 Importance of Ethnic Heritage

	Irish Catholic	Eastern European	Mixed	Hispanic	Italian	Chinese
Yes	68.3	67.4	71.2	84.8	88.8	90.9
No/NS	67.3	63.9	55.7	86.7	84.1	84.6

origin; they are more likely to be proud of their ethnic heritage; they are more inclined to consider ethnic heritage important in their self-defmition.

6. Compared by Relationship Status

Relationship status seems to affect the ethnic groups' emotional ties differently. Among the Hispanics, those who are single, divorced, widowed or separated (D/S/W) are more likely to claim strong emotional ties to their country of origin. The Chinese Americans are just the opposite. Those who are married see the highest percentage of respondents with strong emotional ties.

86.1% of Chinese Americans in matrimony acknowledge their emotional attachment to China compared to 74.5% among the single and 74.6% among the D/W/S. We see a more homogeneous picture among the Italians with the singles slightly ahead of the other groups by 2 to 6 percent.

Among the Catholics and Chinese Americans, those who are on D/W/S status are most likely to take pride in their ethnic

heritage. For the Hispanics, the group that shows least pride in their ethnic heritage are those who are single. The Italian Americans who are married are most likely to be proud of their ethnic heritage, followed closely by those who are on D/W/S status. The percentages are 91.8% and 90.4% respectively. Out of all the groups, those least likely to be proud of their ethnic heritage are Catholics with mixed ethnic background who are married or single.

Taken as a whole, Catholics do not see their ethnic heritage as important as Hispanic Americans, Italian Americans or Chinese Americans do. The group that deviates most are the single Irish Catholics. Less than half of this group believe that their ethnic heritage is important in defining themselves. Other groups that are unlikely to acknowledge the importance of their ethnic heritage are single/married Catholics with mixed ethnic background as well as single eastern European Catholics. The group with the highest percentage of respondents acknowledging the importance of their ethnicity are single Hispanic Americans. More than 90% of them consider their ethnicity an important part of their self-definition. Italian Americans do not see much of a variation across the groups. Whatever their relationship status is, Italian Americans tend to see their ethnic heritage an important part of their self-definition. Almost the same can be said about Chinese Americans with an exception of those who are on D/W/S status. 73.2% of Chinese Americans who are divorced, widowed or separated consider their ethnicity important, which is more than 10% lower than those who are married or single.

Table 21 Emotional Ties

	Hispanic	Italian	Chinese
Married	67.2	74.2	86.1
Single	78.3	80.2	74.5
D/W/S	74.2	75.4	74.6

Table 22 Pride in Ethnic Heritage

	Irish Catholic	Eastern European	Mixed	Hispanic	Italian	Chinese
Married	82.1	78.5	68.1	90.3	91.8	84.2
Single	76.5	86.6	68.6	80.0	86.5	85.9
D/W/S	86.3	90.7	81.4	88.5	90.4	88.8

Table23 Importance of Ethnic Heritage

	Irish Catholic	Eastern European	Mixed	Hispanic	Italian	Chinese
Married	71.6	64.7	57.2	85.3	85.7	86.7
Single	49.6	60.0	58.0	90.3	83.9	85.4
D/W/S	70.2	74.0	67.6	84.9	85.1	73.2

Critical Thinking

1. Are measures of public opinion good indicators of values and behaviors? Under what conditions and about what sorts of issues?
2. Discuss those findings that you found surprising. Why were you surprised?

Create Central

www.mhhe.com/createcentral

Internet References

The Ancient Order of Hibernians
www.aoh.org
The Anti Defamation League
www.ADC.org
The Chicago Jewish News Online
www.chicagojewishnews.org
www.polamcon.org

The International Center for Migration, Ethnicity, and Citizenship
www.newschool.edu/icmec
The Jewish American Committee
www.ajc.org
The Jewish American Congress
www.Ajcongress.org
League of United Latino Citizens
www.lulac.org
National Association of Arab Americans
www.naaa.org
www.aai.org
The National Italian American Foundation
www.niaf.org
National Urban League
www.nul.org
Order Sons of Italy in America
www.osia.org
Polish American Journal
www.polamioumal.com

Article   Prepared by: John A. Kromkowski, *The Catholic University of America*

American Attitudes toward Arabs and Muslims

Learning Outcomes

After reading this article, you will be able to:

• Based on the findings of this study, fashion a profile of American attitudes about Arabs and Muslims.

• Identify what a review of press accounts on Arabs and Muslims tells us about images of both groups.

Since we first began our polling on American attitudes toward Arabs and Muslims in 2010, there has been continued erosion in the favorable ratings given to both communities, posing a threat to the rights of Arab Americans and American Muslims. Favorable attitudes have continued to decline—from 43% in 2010 to 32% in 2014 for Arabs; and from 35% in 2010 to 27% in 2014 for Muslims.

A direct consequence of this disturbing trend is that a significant number of Americans (42%) support the use of profiling by law enforcement against Arab Americans and American Muslims and a growing percentage of Americans say that they lack confidence in the ability of individuals from either community to perform their duties as Americans should they be appointed to an important government position. 36% of respondents felt that Arab Americans would be influenced by their ethnicity and 42% of respondents felt that American Muslims would be influenced by their religion.

While the persistence of negative Arab and Muslim stereotypes is a factor in shaping attitudes toward both groups, our polling establishes that lack of direct exposure to Arab Americans and American Muslims also plays a role in shaping attitudes. What we find is that Americans who say they know either Arabs or Muslims have significantly higher favorable attitudes toward

both (33% higher in both cases) and also have greater confidence in their ability to serve in important government positions. This is especially true among younger and non-white Americans, greater percentages of whom indicate knowing Arabs and Muslims and having more favorable attitudes toward both communities.

Another of the poll's findings establishes that a majority of Americans say that they feel they do not know enough about Arab history and people (57%) or about Islam and Muslims (52%). Evidence of this comes through clearly in other poll responses where respondents wrongly conflate the two communities—with significant numbers assuming that most Arab Americans are Muslim (in reality, less than a third are) or that most American Muslims are Arab (less than one-quarter are).

The way forward is clear. Education about and greater exposure to Arab Americans and American Muslims are the keys both to greater understanding of these growing communities of American citizens and to insuring that their rights are secured.

Methodology

Zogby Analytics conducted an online survey of 1110 likely voters in the United States between June 27, 2014 and June 29, 2014. Based on a confidence interval of 95%, the margin of error for 1110 is +/−3.0 percentage points.

I. Attitudes toward Arabs and Muslims

Please tell me your opinion on each of the following—is it very favorable, somewhat favorable, somewhat unfavorable, very unfavorable, or are you not familiar enough to make a judgment?

Religion/Group		Total	Dem	Rep	Independent	18–29	65+	White	Non-White
Roman Catholics	Favorable	58	55	67	53	54	73	62	49
	Unfavorable	21	20	21	21	24	16	21	21
Presbyterians	Favorable	60	55	69	55	52	79	64	48
	Unfavorable	14	14	13	14	15	9	13	15
Born Again Christians	Favorable	57	50	72	51	62	58	57	58
	Unfavorable	23	26	17	26	17	30	25	18
Jews	Favorable	66	64	75	62	63	84	71	56
	Unfavorable	12	10	13	14	16	5	11	17
Arabs	Favorable	**32**	38	28	27	**42**	32	30	**38**
	Unfavorable	**39**	30	**54**	34	38	**50**	**40**	27
Hindus	Favorable	44	47	45	41	50	52	45	44
	Unfavorable	23	18	35	17	16	23	24	20
Chinese	Favorable	47	50	56	43	52	49	45	53
	Unfavorable	25	19	36	21	15	35	29	15
Buddhists	Favorable	51	55	47	49	55	57	52	48
	Unfavorable	19	14	30	13	20	19	19	19
Muslims	Favorable	**27**	35	21	22	**38**	23	25	32
	Unfavorable	**45**	33	**63**	39	25	**58**	**50**	33

Religion/Group		2010	2012	2014
Arabs	Favorable	43	41	32
	Unfavorable	41	39	39
Muslims	Favorable	35	40	27
	Unfavorable	55	41	45

1. Arabs and Muslims have the lowest favorable/highest unfavorable ratings among the groups covered.
2. Note that one in four Americans were either unfamiliar with or not sure of their attitudes toward these two communities.
3. There is a deep partisan divide on unfavorable attitudes towards Arabs and Muslims. While Democrats give Arabs a net 38%/30% favorable rating and Muslims a net 35%/33% rating, Republicans give Arabs a net 28%/54% unfavorable rating and Muslims a 21%/63% unfavorable rating.
4. The partisan divide masks a generational and racial divide. Younger Americans (18–29) view Arabs and Muslims more favorably than older Americans (65+). Favorable attitudes toward Arabs and Muslims are significantly higher among African Americans, Hispanics, and Asian Americans.

II. Do You Know Arabs or Muslims?

Do you personally know anyone who is Arab or Muslim?

Response	Total	Dem	Rep	Ind	18–29	65+	White	Non-White
Yes, I know*	**47**	49	46	45	**53**	44	43	59
No, I don't know	41	39	43	40	34	46	45	28

*Includes those who know either an Arab or a Muslim, and those who know both.

Attitudes toward Arabs and Muslims by those who know and those who do not know anyone who is Arab or Muslim.

Religion/Group		Yes, I Know	No, I don't know
Arabs	Favorable	42	23
	Unfavorable	39	44
Muslims	Favorable	36	19
	Unfavorable	45	49

1. More respondents know an Arab or Muslim than don't know an Arab or Muslim.

2. Young people are more likely to know an Arab or Muslim than older Americans.
3. Those who do not know an Arab or Muslim are more likely to view the groups unfavorably, in both instances, favorable attitudes nearly double.

III. Arab Americans and American Muslims Working in the Government

If an Arab American were to attain an important position of influence in the government, would you feel confident that person would be able to do the job, or would you feel that any ethnic loyalty would influence their decision-making?

Arab American	Total	Dem	Rep	Ind	18–29	65+	White	Non-White
Confident they could do the job	36	48	25	33	44	34	35	40
Their ethnicity would influence their decision-making	36	24	50	36	30	41	58	32

If an American Muslim were to attain an important position of influence in the government, would you feel confident that person would be able to do the job, or would you feel that their religion would influence their decision-making?

American Muslim	Total	Dem	Rep	Ind	18–29	65+	White	Non-White
Confident they could do the job	34	45	23	31	53	27	31	42
Their religion would influence their decision-making	42	29	57	42	23	53	45	32

Group	Response	2010	2014
Arab Americans	Confident they could do the job.	42	36
	Their ethnicity would influence their decision-making.	32	36
American Muslims	Confident they could do the job.	38	34
	Their religion would influence their decision-making.	38	42

Confidence in Arab Americans and American Muslims by those who know and those who do not know anyone who is Arab or Muslim.

Group	Response	Yes, I know	No, I don't know
Arab American	Confident they could do the job	46	30
	Their ethnicity would influence their decision-making	37	37
American Muslim	Confident they could do the job	43	29
	Their religion would influence their decision-making	43	46

1. Respondents, as a whole, are divided as to whether Arab Americans and American Muslims, if appointed to a government post, could do the job without their ethnicity or religion influencing their work. Again, there is a deep partisan divide on this question.

2. Democrats and Republicans are deeply divided. Their assessments of an Arab American's or an American Muslim's ability to do the job are mirror images of each other. In both cases, Republicans fear that the ethnicity and religion of members of these communities would influence their work.

3. There is a significant generational divide between younger and older generations.

4. Overall, White Americans felt that ethnicity or religion would influence decision-making, whereas Non-White Americans were confident that Arab Americans and American Muslims could do the job.

5. Those who do not know an Arab or Muslim are less confident that the two groups could perform the job without their religion or ethnicity influencing their decision-making.

IV. Knowledge of Arabs and Muslims

Do you know enough about Arab countries and Arab people or do you feel you need to know more?

Response	Total	Dem	Rep	Ind	18–29	65+	White	Non-White
Know enough	31	29	36	30	30	27	31	33
Need to know more	57	59	54	57	55	64	59	50

Do you know enough about Islam and Muslims or do you feel you need to know more?

Response	Total	Dem	Rep	Ind	18–29	65+	White	Non-White
Know enough	36	29	48	34	25	41	39	29
Need to know more	52	59	43	52	59	50	52	52

1. Every category said they need to know more about Arabs, and every category (except Republicans) said they need to know more about Muslims. Today's numbers are nearly identical to numbers from four years ago.

2. When comparing, older Americans feel they need to know more about Arabs, but younger Americans feel they need to know more about Muslims.

3. Compared with other groups, more Republicans felt they already knew enough about Muslims than those who felt the need to know more.

Critical Thinking

1. Are measures of public opinion good indicators of values and behaviors? Under what conditions and about what sorts of issues?

2. Discuss those findings that you found surprising. Why were you surprised?

Internet References

Arab American Institute
www.aaiusa.org

National Association of Arab Americans
www.nnaac.org

Article

Prepared by: John A. Kromkowski, *The Catholic University of America*

Italian American Stereotypes in U.S. Advertising

The Order Sons of Italy in America

Learning Outcomes

After reading this article, you will be able to:

- Identify the central concerns of Italian American leaders regarding public images.

- Discuss approaches and remedies to negative stereotypical portrayal.

Background

- A recent Zogby poll of American teenagers 13 to 18 years old revealed that 78% associate Italian Americans with either criminal activities or blue-collar work.

- An earlier poll by the Princeton-based Response Analysis Corporation revealed that 74% of adult Americans believe most Italian Americans have some connection to organized crime.

The Problem

Advertising campaigns that feature Italian Americans use stereotypes that present an unbalanced portrayal of people of Italian heritage.

- The men are uneducated, dishonest and/or violent.

- The women are elderly, overweight housewives and grandmothers wearing black dresses, housecoats or aprons.

- Thanks to the popularity of "The Sopranos" and entertainment like it, most advertising that uses Italian Americans portrays them as gangsters.

- Even Mafia-themed advertising that may not include specific references to Italian Americans are perceived by the general public to be about Italian Americans.

The Facts

- The U.S. Department of Justice estimates that less than .0025 percent of the **26 million Americans of Italian descent** are involved in organized crime.

- The U.S. Census Bureau reports that two-thirds of the Italian Americans in the work force are in white-collar jobs as executives, physicians, teachers, attorneys, administrators, etc.

- Italian Americans are the nation's fifth largest ethnic group, according to the Year 2000 Census.

The following is a random sampling of commercials and print ads featuring Italian American characters, or Mafia-related themes, that were seen nationally between 1999 and 2003.

- **LYCOS INTERNET SEARCH ENGINE TV COMMERCIAL**
  As a mandolin plays Italian music in the background, an older man carries furniture up the steps of a brownstone apartment while his dark-haired daughter and grandchild look on. He tells his daughter that the furniture "fell off a truck."

  In the next scene, more furniture is being moved in, but the daughter holds up a bill of sale so that FBI agents in a parked car nearby can see that she bought it on the Internet, using Lycos.

- **RAGU RICH & MEATY MEAT SAUCE PRINT AD**
  Graphic shows three butchers with olive complexions scowling into the camera. Behind them hang sausages and

a salami. "We asked these butchers what they thought of our new meat sauce," the ad reads. "They beat us up."

- **UNCLE BEN'S PASTA BOWL PRINT AD**
  "If you eat an Uncle Ben's pasta bowl," the ad reads, "don't be surprised ifa youa starta talking likea this afterwards."

- **BUDWEISER BEER TV COMMERCIAL**
  Several swarthy men in an Italian restaurant ask each other "Howya doin'?" and "Didcha take care a dat ting?"

- **OPTIMUM ONLINE COMMERCIAL**
  An African American woman is having her refrigerator repaired by a dark, hairy, white man named "Joe." The woman asks how much the job will cost. "Two hundred dollars," he replies. When she checks on Optimum Online, she learns it only costs $25.

- **THE INTERNATIONAL DAIRY FOOD TV COMMERCIAL**
  "Vinny" and a friend try to break the bones of a man who owes them money, but since the intended victim drinks milk, they can't hurt him.

- **THE INTERNATIONAL DAIRY FOOD TV COMMERCIAL**
  Four dark, heavy, hairy young men wearing gold chains menace a group of senior citizen men in a diner. The elderly men route the bullies because milk makes them strong.

- **STACKER 2 DIET PILLS TV COMMERCIAL**
  As an Italian melody plays, a man enters a store with two bodyguards and a buxom blonde. Peppering his speech with "*capisci*," he strong-arms another customer and the store clerk.

- **RAGU PASTA SAUCE TV COMMERCIAL**
  Several elderly, overweight Italian American women in housedresses are so delighted with Ragu's meat sauce that they turn somersaults and play leapfrog in a meadow. The camera zooms in on the generous proportions of one woman's rear quarters and the bloomers of another.

- **BUITONI PASTA TV COMMERCIAL**
  A very old, very wrinkled woman, dressed in black, drags her overweight adult son by the ear through the streets to a supermarket where she berates him in English and Italian for selling the secret family pasta recipe to Buitoni.

- **RUBBERMAID TV COMMERCIAL**
  Five older women dressed in black with their hair in buns dance a Tarantella because the new Rubbermaid containers do not stain when they put tomato sauce in them.

- **TODAY'S MAN TV COMMERCIAL**
  An Italian woman goes through her husband's closet, yelling at him about the state of his wardrobe. The husband, who is

supposed to be Michael Corleone of "The Godfather," stares coldly at her as she rants.

- **AT&T BROADBAND TV COMMERCIAL**
  A teacher warns a student that he will fail her class because his assignment is late. Two characters from "The Sopranos" appear and threaten the teacher if the student doesn't receive an "A."

- **BLISTEX TV COMMERCIAL**
  A swarthy man in a black suit asks another man if he took care of "that thing." The lackey pulls out a tube of lip balm, but his boss tells him only Blistex supplies the protection he needs. "Believe me, I know about protection," he says.

- **EVEREADY BATTERY TV COMMERCIAL**
  A photographer's camera battery dies during the birthday party of a mobster's child. The photographer is stuffed into a tuba.

- **GODFATHER'S PIZZA PRINT AD**
  Ad presents a man dressed in a pinstripe suit, black shirt, white tie and a fedora. Ad reads: "Stay home with da family" in large letters and features a coupon for a pizza dubbed "the Mob Pleaser."

- **INFOSEEK TV COMMERCIAL**
  To promote Infoseek's Internet services, commercial presents a mini-drama in which mobsters accuse a man of being part of the CIA.

- **JERRY'S SUBS & PIZZA RADIO COMMERCIAL**
  An actor impersonating Tony Soprano threatens a Jerry Subs storeowner who is competing with a pizzeria owned by the gangster's friend. After tasting Jerry's pizza, the gangster offers to take the owner for a ride on his boat.

- **NETFLIX.COM TV COMMERCIAL**
  Mobsters conspire to discuss what to do with a dead body. The commercial is promoting DVD rentals.

- **ROUND-UP HERBICIDE TV COMMERCIAL**
  Voice-over announces that the product will "kill off the Weed Family." The Weed mobsters, speaking with exaggerated New York accents, air their fears of being killed.

- **SHOPPERS DRUG MART TV COMMERCIAL**
  A man refuses to shake hands with a sick Mafia "Godfather."

- **SUPERIOR QUICK DRY CEMENT TV COMMERCIAL**
  "Jack gets a permanent vacation" during a boat ride with mobsters who use the cement product to "bury" Jack at sea.

- **TCI/AT&T TV COMMERCIAL**
  To promote its digital cable service, advertiser presents a Mafia boss questioning a "not so Wiseguy."

- **VANILLA COKE TV COMMERCIAL**
  Actor Chazz Palminteri, reprising his role as mob boss Sonny in "A Bronx Tale," threatens a nosy young man, who has peeked behind a fence. The gangster rewards the young man's curiosity, however, with a can of the new Vanilla Coke.

- **VERMONT TEDDY BEAR PRINT AD**
  For Valentine's Day, the company offers a "Gangster of Love" bear, wearing spats, a fedora and carrying a violin case. Ad reads: "Be a goodfella. Send her this bear and she'll be singing like a soprano."

- **VITAMIN SHOPPE TV COMMERCIAL**
  As gangsters "sell" products, a voice over warns, "Make sure you know who you're dealing with online."

- **WRIGLEY'S ECLIPSE TV COMMERCIAL**
  Men burst into an Italian restaurant, shouting, "Die, bad breath!"

APPENDIX I: *Ragu response to a consumer complaining about the Ragu commercial featuring elderly Italian American women turning somersaults.*

——Original Message——
From:xxxx
Sent: Tuesday, June 10, 2003 4:35 AM
To: ddesanctis@osia.org
Subject: Response from Ragu

I have attached the response that I rec'd back from Ragu, for your review and perusal, after I e-mailed them my thoughts and comments on their commercials. It seems to be a general form letter.

Dear Ms. xxx:

Thank you for taking the time to contact us about our Ragú Rich & Meaty advertising. As one of the country's largest advertisers, we take seriously our responsibility to meet our consumer's needs while maintaining the highest standards in our business practices. Let us provide you with some background on our Rich & Meaty products and advertising.

Ragú cooks one-half pound of meat and combines it with the perfect amount of Italian seasonings for a taste that is reminiscent of the homemade meat sauce our grandmothers used to make.

At www.ragu.com you can see how the Ragú brand uses the fictional character "Mama", an Italian-American grandmother, as a trusted symbol of high-quality and great taste. The Rich & Meaty experience is meant to take us back to the days when grandmothers spent hours in the kitchen preparing their special meat sauce. Because Rich & Meaty does the work for you and it is such a great-tasting, high-quality product, we feel that even "Mama" would approve.

The Ragú Rich & Meaty ad was designed to appeal to a diverse group of consumers, and underwent rigorous testing to evaluate consumer reaction. This ad was previewed among a wide range of consumers from different parts of the country, including Italian-Americans.

The commercial was intended to portray a humorous celebration of how the quality of Rich & Meaty has freed the grandmothers from their kitchens, and reflect the Ragú Rich & Meaty brand image of a high-quality, great-tasting meat sauce. In fact, we have received many calls and e-mails complimenting the ad for its entertaining, comical depiction of women being liberated from the drudgery of cooking pasta sauce. When it comes to brand communications, we work hard to match our message with the right medium, using extensive insights from our consumers, but recognize that not everyone will be satisfied with the outcome.

We highly value your feedback as a part of the market research we conduct routinely about consumers' attitudes and preferences. You can be assured that your comments are appreciated and will be shared with appropriate staff.

Regards,
Your friends at Ragu

APPENDIX II: *Matthew Kauffman, who writes a business column for the* **Hartford Courant,** *criticizes the advertising world's stereotyping of Italian Americans in this column, which ran in the* **Hartford Courant** *on May 28, 2003.*

RUB OUT THOSE ADS THAT SPOOF THE MOB
Matthew Kauffman—May 28, 2003

There's a new TV ad for Prestone that features a timid man innocently washing his car until he is confronted by two imposing Italian Mafiosi in dark suits.

In Gag No. 1, one of the mobsters clicks open a briefcase—and here we're supposed to fear that the timid man is about to be shot to death in his driveway. But, big relief, the briefcase merely holds some Prestone tire cleaner.

In Gag No. 2, a dog briefly considers urinating on the timid man's wheels, but turns tail and runs when the hit men reach menacingly into their suit jackets.

"Smart dog," one mobster says.

"Lucky dog," the other replies.

Ah, the Italian mobster motif. How original.

Madison Avenue tolerates a dwindling number of stereotypes. Gays are still fair game. Blondes rarely stand a chance. And then there are Italians, and the seemingly irresistible desire to paint them as silk-suit-wearing, pinky-ring-waving, New Joisey-talking galoots with a penchant for violence.

"It's horrible," says Roy L. De Barbieri, a lawyer in New Haven and the Connecticut area coordinator for the National Italian American Foundation. "In 2003, it's absolutely incredible that people have such low ideas about an ethnic group."

But those ideas are rampant in the ad world. Coca-Cola introduced Vanilla Coke with a creepy ad campaign in which a mobster snatches curious people off the street—and then rewards them for their curiosity with a bottle of pop. It's irrelevant to the brand, but how 'bout that Italian accent!

A few years back, a Diet Dr Pepper spot featured wiseguys in a game show parody called "Crime Family Feud." "Name a popular family activity," the host intones. And the No. 1 answer? "Racketeering."

The examples run on and on. Eclipse gum used hit men and the tagline "Die, bad breath. Die." Red Lobster ordered up a spot with mobsters titled "Breakin' Legs." A national driving school ran with a gag about a hooked-up instructor asking his young charge for help with a body in the trunk.

And AT&T ran a spot featuring an actor from "The Sopranos" who threatens a high school teacher on behalf of a kid who failed to turn in a science project.

That last one was an especially sore point with some Italian Americans, who blame "The Sopranos" for the latest run of mobbed-up commercials. Although most critics and viewers adore the HBO series, a number of Italian American groups just despise it.

In Chicago, a group even filed a novel lawsuit seeking a declaration that the show violates the state constitution's "Individual Dignity Clause," which condemns the portrayal of particular groups as criminals.

The suit went nowhere. But it was always a symbolic act, more likely to generate publicity than a favorable ruling. Still, it's a message worth hearing: that cheap shots in entertainment and advertising are just that—cheap.

This is not a plea for runaway political correctness and the blandness it engenders. More than a decade ago, *Adweek* magazine lamented that creativity in advertising was being jeopardized by a paralyzing fear of hurting somebody's feelings. Honda, the magazine noted, was trying to keep humans out of its ads altogether rather than risk offending some group.

That's silly. But the fact that it may be difficult to navigate the sensitivities of consumers doesn't mean advertisers shouldn't try.

Setting the bar can, indeed, be tough. De Barbieri hates the Alka-Seltzer ad in which a television pitchman keeps flubbing his line, "Mama Mia! That's a spicy meatball!" (The ad's a classic, but it didn't run long, pulled off the air after Italian Americans complained.) He's horrified by another ad featuring "ill-kempt and fat" Italian women doing cartwheels over Ragu's spaghetti sauce. And don't get him started on the accents in the Olive Garden restaurant ads.

Me, I'm not especially bothered by those. All three certainly supersize the clichés, but, to me, there's nothing particularly mean-spirited or demeaning about, say, the stereotype of Italian grandmothers as whizzes in the kitchen.

But wrestling over the propriety of those iffy portrayals is a far cry from routinely endorsing the image of Italian Americans as violent gangsters.

"Could you imagine anyone opening a 'Black Sambo's Chicken Shack?'" De Barbieri asks. "You couldn't get away with that for one day. But everyone thinks it's OK to use Italian American negative stereotypes."

Society is astonishingly adept at doling out offensive stereotypes: the lazy Mexican, the cheap Jew, the drunk Irishman, the dangerous African American. They are broad-brush depictions that make decent people shudder. And you're not likely to find them in mainstream ads.

So what is it that makes the stereotype of the violent Italian so embraceable?

Note to marketers: Next time you're tempted to reach for the well worn image of the Italian mobster, think about the message you're sending to customers. Think about the reception that ad may get from Italian American consumers.

And then fuhgeddaboutit.

Copyright 2003, Hartford Courant

Source

This survey of recent advertising campaigns using Italian American characters was prepared by the Order Sons of Italy in America (OSIA), the largest and longest established national organization in the United States for people of Italian descent.

We are grateful for assistance from OSIA's Commission for Social Justice, UNICO National, the Italian American One Voice Coalition and Italian American Pride.

Critical Thinking

1. Are measures of public opinion good indicators of values and behaviors? Under what conditions and about what sorts of issues?
2. Discuss those findings that you found surprising. Why were you surprised?

Internet References

The National Italian American Foundation
www.niaf.org

Order Sons of Italy in America
www.osia.org

Article   Prepared by: John A. Kromkowski, *The Catholic University of America*

Made In Hollywood: Italian Stereotypes in the Movies

Rosanne De Luca Braun

Learning Outcomes

After reading this article, you will be able to:

- Identify the contributions Italian Americans made to the development of American movies.

- Identify what typecasting is, and what popular images of Italian Americans were created by movies.

*B*ehind the camera, the early Italian immigrants helped launch Hollywood's film industry while on-screen they were typecast in roles still recognizable today.

Among the Italians who immigrated to America 100 years ago were men and women whose talents were useful to the brand-new American movie business. Their training in stonecutting and sculpture, church decoration and garment-making made them natural resources as costume designers, set decorators, painters, masons, and the all-purpose artisans desperately needed on the movie set.

Their long history with spectacle and festivals made them comfortable with filmmaking's monumental tasks while their natural inventiveness and mechanical aptitude were essential to an industry creating itself at breakneck speed.

Italian Americans like director Fred Niblo, cinematographer Tony Gaudio and writer/director Frank Capra rose to the top even before talking pictures were invented. But on-screen, Italian Americans fared very differently. Why?

Foreign Invaders

While Italian Americans behind the scenes were largely unknown to early moviegoers, onscreen Italian characters were highly visible and evoked the American audience's complicated feelings about the foreigners "invading" their shores.

Between 1870 and 1920, the United States absorbed nearly 18 million immigrants—by 1930, more than five million were Italian—80 percent of whom settled in New York City, home of the first American filmmakers and audiences.

To the established American population, descended from earlier British, Scandinavian and German immigrants, these foreigners were a new breed who looked, dressed, spoke and prayed differently. In fact, because of Italians' olive skin, the Americans thought they were racially different, too—somewhere "in-between" black and white—and attributed to them different emotional traits and sexual behavior.

The Italians themselves did not help. Unlike the immigrant Jews, southern Italians had little experience assimilating into a foreign culture and lived tightly inside their own communities. The Americans thus marked them as a stubbornly separate group, probably dangerous and destined to remain outside mainstream society forever.

Sensationalized newspaper reports of urban crimes and brutalities fanned this flame, and history bears witness to a cruel pattern of anti-Italian discrimination. Between 1890 and 1915, for example, at least 47 Italians were lynched in the South.

Italian Typecasting

But the Italians also fascinated Americans, who considered them as passionate, sensual, violent, exotic and deeply familial—characteristics that differed markedly from their own Protestant mores. Repelled and yet attracted, they wanted to see this world in action, from a close but safe vantage point. Enter the movies.

When movies with Italian American characters began appearing early in the 20th century, they were written, cast and directed by the first New York-based movie makers: white, Anglo-Saxon Protestants who shared their audience's fears and biases. Set in New York, the films tended to be about love and betrayal, sex outside marriage, sacrifice for the family and impulsive behavior that sometimes stepped outside the law.

Although the Italian American gangster didn't fully surface until talking pictures, a few early films had Mafia themes: *The Black Hand* in 1906, *The Italian Blood* in 1911, *The Last of the Mafia* in 1915. Most movies featuring Italians, however, were operatic melodramas of love and revenge set on the Lower East Side such as *The Italian* of 1915 (originally titled *The Dago*) or *Sin* (1915) with Theda Bara. Sometimes parts of the stories took place in Italy, featuring seductive but evil Italian noblemen.

With few exceptions, Italian and Italian American characters were portrayed by Anglo American actors, who used exaggerated gestures, seemed to speak at the top of their lungs and behaved melodramatically, throwing themselves on their loved ones' graves in anguish. By the 1920s more than 50 American films presented Italian characters from this Anglo Protestant perspective. Work for Italian actors was limited to small, cartoonish parts—organ grinders and barbers, and even these parts often went to actors of other ethnicities.

Valentino's Role

It was no accident that Rudolph Valentino's popularity coincided with the beginning of the Roaring Twenties, when American society in general and women in particular were struggling to break free of hundred-year-old sexual, gender and racial taboos.

America needed a groundbreaker and the movies produced him. Darkly handsome, muscular yet lithe and graceful, Valentino's on-screen persona represented long-forbidden eroticism to American women, and on his slender shoulders his fans hung the mantles of passionate lover, sex icon and exotic liberator of sexual mores.

Ironically, his real life bore no resemblance to his screen persona: biographers have since speculated that Valentino was probably impotent, his professional and personal life managed by a succession of powerful wives.

Nevertheless, the stir Valentino created helped Americans redefine the boundaries of acceptable romantic behavior; his ambiguous sexuality (men were certain he was homosexual) and foreignness enabled movie audiences to explore their own repressed emotions at a safe distance.

But his unprecedented popularity set in motion a film icon— the Latin lover—that has lived on in characters as diverse as those played by Dean Martin, Armand Assante and John Travolta. By the late 1920s, then, even though newly-minted laws restricting immigration were reducing Americans' anxiety over a foreign invasion, the Italian "types" were already established on American movie screens: urban brute, Latin lover, sensual earth mother, musical clown, gluttonous outsider.

Sad Consequences

When talking pictures arrived in the early 1930s, these stereotypes became fixed and live on today, more than 70 years later, as the gangster and the boxer, the buffoon and the sex goddess. The early Italian immigrants who sat in the darkened movie theaters looked at themselves through their new countrymen's eyes and were humiliated. They taught their children to reject their own backgrounds and "become an American!"

These two parallel histories—the invisibility of the Italian American filmmakers who help create American film art and commerce, and the visibility of rigid Italian American on-screen stereotypes—continue to this day.

According to the Italic Studies Institute, of the more than 1,000 Hollywood films featuring Italian or Italian American characters made between 1928 and 2000, nearly three-quarters portray them as gangsters, boors, buffoons, bigots or bimbos.

These characters are instantly recognizable to both American and international movie audiences, the same audiences that don't know the names Vincente Minnelli, Henry Mancini, Santo Loquasto or Richard La Gravenese—and or those of the legions of Italian American film artists who create the American movie experiences we all share.

One story has been told all too often, the other not at all. It's a story whose time has come.

Critical Thinking

1. Discuss the meaning of stereotype.
2. Can stereotypes be negative and positive? Who decides?
3. Can ethnic humor be defamatory? What does irony do to our interpretations of ethnicity?

Internet References

Order Sons of Italy in America
www.osia.org

The National Italian American Foundation
www.niaf.org

Article   Prepared by: John A. Kromkowski, *The Catholic University of America*

Polonia: Today's Profile Tomorrow's Promise

DOMINIK STECULA AND THADDEUS C. RADZILOWSKI

Learning Outcomes

After reading this article, you will be able to:

- Identify the constraints researchers encounter in the study of small yet differentiated ethnic groups.

- Identify the range of indicators used to construct a comprehensive profile of Polonia.

- Identify the core values of Polish Americans.

Introduction and Methodology

According to the United States Census Bureau, there are approximately 10,000,000 people who self-identify as being Polish by ancestry. This is a significant group of people who are willing to publicly acknowledge being Polish American. It numbers about 3% of the population of the country. Unfortunately, as important as that figure is, it cannot tell us about the intensity of that identification, or how it plays out in the daily lives of those who say they are Polish Americans, as that community is rather diverse. For example, about 5% of Polish Americans are foreign born and about half of those are US citizens. The dynamics of the community are therefore complicated.

There are no significant population studies or surveys that provide information of any kind on the attitudes and opinions of Polish Americans. Most of the surveys we have are of those ethnic groups or conglomerations of ethnic groups such as "Hispanics" who are covered as "protected classes" under US Civil Rights laws and regulations. The surveys done by the National Opinion Research Center (NORC) of the University of Chicago, which did sample ancestry groups, had ceased to do so by the 1980s. By the end of the 20th century, the national

election exit polls also dropped questions about ancestry. Although the US Census continues to ask about ancestry, the question which was only added to the National Census in 1980, albeit on the so-called "long form" (a one out of six sample) was moved to the rolling three-year American Community Survey (ACS) in 2004. The ACS is based on a 1 out of 19 sample. While the ACS does provide useful information on Poles and other "ancestry" groups (largely people belonging to European and Middle Eastern groups who fall under the default racial category of "White") it is not as extensive as that available on "Racial" or "Ethnic" groups (there is only one ethnic group—"Hispanic"—known to the US Census).

We thus have limited ways of getting information about the Polish Americans in the United States. No national polling company uses ancestry as a survey variable. The exit polling in national elections dropped the ancestry category by 2000 and the NORC the major research center which used ancestry in its national surveys no longer does so. At this point, an attempt to design and implement a statistically valid survey of the national Polish American communities is beyond our resources. We have chosen, therefore, to survey those Polish Americans who have a strong commitment to a Polish identity in the US, who can be mobilized to support Polish American and Polish causes and who are interested in and keep abreast of issues that concern Polonia as well as Poland. The respondents to our two major national surveys are people who are the leaders and activists at the grassroots level. We feel that this is this group upon whom the present and future of Polonia depends. To reach this group we relied on what is called "snowballing sampling." Those who participated were reached through press releases and other communications of the Piast Institute, information from other Polish institutions, and via media, forums and list serves, and personal contacts with colleagues. It is not an ideal methodology but the results of our 2010 and 2013 surveys and an earlier 2009 more limited survey (900 respondents) we did in conjunction with a study of the 2008 election have shown in a number of significant areas a remarkable consistency of responses that we feel we can speak with some surety about Polish Americans and their opinions. By no means, however, is such methodological approach unusual. As a matter of fact, a growing number of works in the academic fields of political science, sociology and other social sciences. The rise of the convenience sampling is an understandable extension of the prominence of the Internet, and it allows researchers to closely examine populations that were previously diffcult to reach. The limitation of this approach is a serious one, however, as the statistical leverage that is present in analysis on random samples is not available with this approach. In other words, one cannot use this data to run explanatory models, as the underlying assumption of that methodology is rooted in the randomness of the sample. Most of the analysis, therefore, has to be limited to basic descriptive statistics and any generalizations should be taken with a grain of salt.

The underlying theoretical assumption of the study, as well as the other work done by the Piast Institute, is that Polish America—Polonia—is a modern American ethnic group with strong and abiding Polish roots and a long and distinctive American experience. It was founded in the US almost 160 years ago and it has continued to evolve in response to new immigrants and challenges from Europe as well as to an ever-changing American environment which Polonia in itself has played a significant role in shaping. It also has its own internal dynamics. Polonia was and continues to be a new creation.

Demographics

The online survey was answered by 1344 people who self-identify as Polish American. These people came from 47 different states, which is comparable to our previous surveys. However, just as was the case with the previous study, the bulk of the respondents came from a handful of states. 60% of all respondents came from the top five states (which are, in order, Michigan, Illinois, New York, Virginia and New Jersey). 77% of all respondents came from the top ten states, which are, in addition to the previously mentioned states: California, Pennsylvania, Maryland, Connecticut and Ohio. None of these should be surprising, as the census data indicates that these are the states with the largest Polish American populations.

In terms of variations, this year's survey yielded a much more substantial response from California and Connecticut—both major Polonia centers—than did the 2010 survey.

The survey indicates that most Polish Americans live in urban and suburban areas, with only 20% of the respondents indicating living in small towns or rural areas.

The breakdown of all respondents indicates that 54% are women and 46% are men. 57% of respondents are married. The majority of respondents were born in the United States (70%), but a substantial 26% were born in Poland. The rest indicated another country as their place of birth. The overwhelming majority are US citizens (95%). Most respondents have also lived in the United States their whole lives (69%) and only 2% have been in the US for less than 10 years.

It is worth noting that in the previous survey 35% of the respondents were born in Poland or another foreign country. This year's survey thus shows a greater participation of American-born respondents.

The age distribution of the respondents is skewed towards older people, with the youngest respondents being 18 (by survey definition, as it was open to voting age adults) and the oldest being 88. Mean age is 50.4 years while median age is 53.5. This indicates that older members of the community remain active in Polonia and are technologically savvy. However, still over 15% of respondents were below 30 years old. A plurality of respondents are between the ages of 50 and 64 and over 21% are 65 or older.

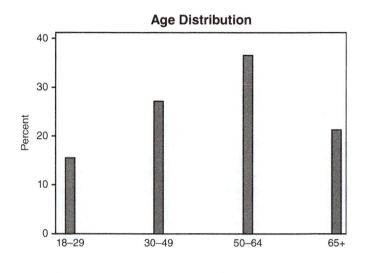

The income distribution indicates that the majority of Polonia seems to be well within the confines of the middle class, although that is obviously a somewhat ambiguous category. 8% of the respondents report incomes of $200,000 dollars or more per year, while close to 10% refused to answer the question.

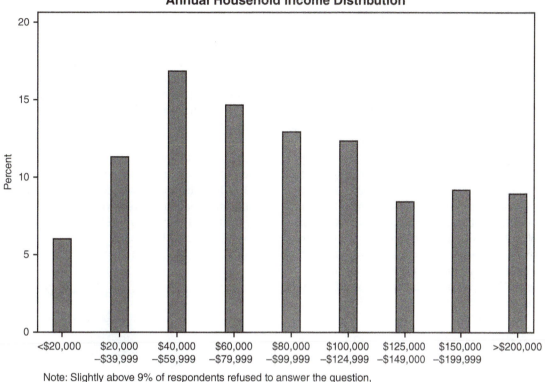

Annual Household Income Distribution

Note: Slightly above 9% of respondents refused to answer the question, their responses were coded as missing and excluded from this analysis

Religious Affliation

In terms of religious affliation, the majority of Polish Americans indicated Roman Catholic faith (71%). Close to 15% of respondents indicated affliation with a different Christian religion, such as Polish National Catholic Church, Protestant Church, etc. Less than 1% are Jewish but close to 14% indicate no religious preference. That number is slightly higher than the previous survey and indicates that this group of people is a considerable group within Polonia.

Politics, Participation and Ideology

Ideologically, a plurality of Polonia is conservative (38.5%), although compared to the last study, this group shrank from 44%. 37% of Polonia is liberal while about a fourth indicates being in the political center. On the extreme ends of the political spectrum, almost 6% of respondents indicate being very conservative, while a comparable 7% indicate being very liberal.

In terms of party affliation, a plurality of respondents indicates affliation with the Democratic Party (36%, which is almost identical to the last survey's result). Almost 36% of the respondents, however, indicate that they are independent.

23% of Polish Americans indicate affliation with the Republican Party (which is slightly less than the last study indicated) and almost 6% indicate other party affliation.

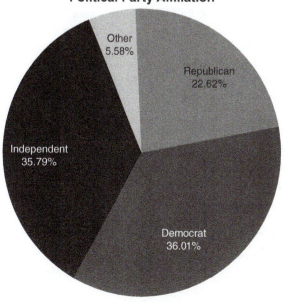

Political Party Affiliation

Other 5.58%
Republican 22.62%
Independent 35.79%
Democrat 36.01%

Examination of the vote choice in the last election reveals that 92.5% of Polish Americans are registered voters. Political science literature is usually reluctant about self-reported turnout numbers, as people tend to report voting even though they have not actually voted. As a result, that number is probably inflated, although we don't know by how much. Among self-reported registered voters, 5% did not vote in the last election. The majority of those who took part in the election voted for President Barack Obama, 40% preferred Mitt Romney and 6.7% voted for third party candidates. Compared to the national election results, Polish Americans preferred Obama slightly more than voters nationally (53.1% compared to 51.1%), Romney significantly less than voters nationally (40% compared to 47.2%) and third party candidates significantly more than the national electorate (6.7% compared to 1.7%). A much higher preference for third party candidates by Polish American voters than the electorate at large has been a characteristic for more than a third of a century as recorded by surveys and exit polls, exemplified by an astounding 13% vote of the Polish American community for John Anderson in 1980.

Vote choice in 2012	No.	%
Didn't Vote	63	5.1
B. Obama	627	50.4
M. Romney	473	38.1
3rd Party Candidate	80	6.4
Total	1243	100

Respondents were also asked specifically: "Regardless of which candidate you voted for or preferred in this past election, which presidential candidate do you believe was better suited to deal with Polish-American issues?" Results indicate that people were not thrilled with either of the major party candidates and 21% indicated that other (unspecified) candidates were better suited to deal with Polish-American issues. Despite his attempts to reach Polonia, Mitt Romney's efforts to cater to the community appear to have fallen flat.

Better suited for Polish American Issues	No.	%
B. Obama	577	42.9
M. Romney	486	36.2
Other Candidate	281	20.9
Total	1344	100

The survey also asked about other political participation of Polish Americans. The results indicate that Poles are not very involved in the political process. Majority (68%) did not participate in the political process in any way outside of voting. 21% participated by donating money to a political party, candidate or a PAC. 7% both donated and volunteered, while 3% only volunteered for a campaign.

This year's survey also introduced questions about Polish politics in addition to the battery of questions about American politics. Initial analysis reveals that over 10% of the respondents voted in Polish elections in the last decade. When asked about specific party affliation with a Polish political party, a substantial majority of respondents (72%) revealed a lack of interest in Polish politics and hence no party affliation. Once the people who lack enough interest to develop a partisan affliation are removed from the analysis, 38% identify with Platforma Obywatelska (PO) and 32% with Prawo i Sprawiedliwość (PiS).

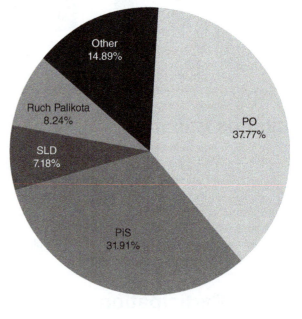

Polish Political Party Affiliation

The high percentage of respondents indicating a lack of interest in Polish politics is consistent across questions. When asked directly about interest in politics, on a 1 to 10 scale, with 1 being least interested while 10 being most interested, most people indicated great interest in American politics but very few seem interested in Polish politics. The direct comparison of the distribution of both variables are almost mirror opposites of each other, as the graph below indicates.

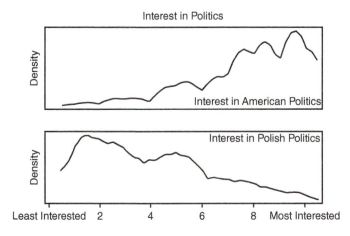

Interest in Politics

Issues

There were a variety of specific issue questions that were asked on the survey which are not analyzed here. However, the respondents were also asked to examine a list of important issues and rank them in order of importance to them personally.

Issue	% Indicating it as MOST important	% Indicating it as LEAST important
Balancing the federal budget	43	3
Gun ownership reforms	24	12
Climate change	12	31
Visa waiver for Poland	8	29
Unemployment/Jobs	6	18
Immigration reform	8	7

The analysis indicates that respondents are primarily concerned with major issues facing the United States. When given a choice between these issues and including Poland in the visa waiver, only 8% ranked it as their priority issue. 29% listed the issue as their least important personal issue. Only climate change was deemed less important with 31% of respondents indicating this specific issue as their least important problem.

When examining issues in the context of the Poland-US relations specifically, the visa waiver for Poland is clearly the most important issue, although surprisingly only a plurality

of the respondents pointed to this issue (and not an expected majority).

MIP in Poland - US Relations	No.	%
The Visa Waiver for Polish citizens	469	34.9
The so-called Missile shield placement in Poland	139	10.3
Military and Intelligence Cooperation	161	12
Economic cooperation	380	28.3
Cultural and educational exchanges	163	12.1
Other	32	2.4
Total	*1344*	*100*

Polish American Experience

A majority of respondents identify as Polish Americans or Americans of Polish descent. 14% say they are Polish and about 10% identify only as American.

Slightly above 44% of respondents reveal no membership in any Polish American organization. Social and cultural organizations are most popular, with 31% indicating membership in an organization of this type. Least popular are sports organizations, with only 3% of respondents indicating membership. Only 6% of respondents indicate membership in a political Polonia organization.

The 2013 results show a considerable variation from the Piast 2010 in which only 24% of respondents said they belonged to no Polish American organization. In that same survey 39% indicated they belonged to a social or cultural organization as opposed to the 2013 results which showed only 31% identifying as members of such groups. On the other hand, more than twice as many respondents said they held membership in a Polish American political organization in 2013 as in 2010.

Somewhat surprisingly, a majority of the respondents get their news from Internet sources. This trend is consistent with general American population patterns, but the fact that it was revealed in an Internet based survey casts doubt on its generalizability. Nevertheless, it is worth noting that the number of people who said their main news source was the Internet was almost 20 points higher in 2013 than in 2010. The age distribution of the sample indicates that the respondents are not mainly young people accustomed to the Internet, but also elderly foreign born people, who did not grow up with the Internet. Furthermore, a question about social media usage also supports the thesis that Polish Americans are generally technologically savvy, with 78% of respondents indicating social media usage.

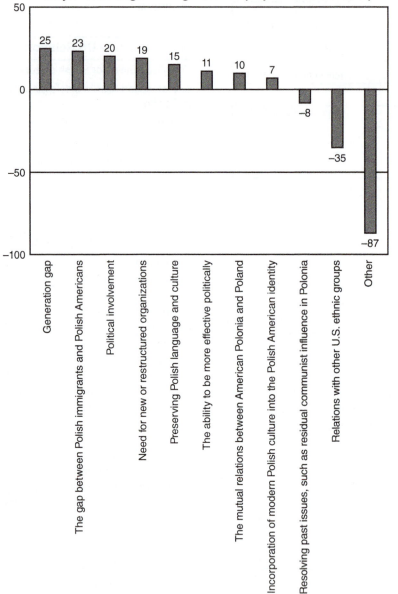

Major Challenge Facing Polonia (Top 3 - Bottom 3; %)

While a direct comparison with the results of the 2010 survey on this question with the current survey is not possible because of a different methodology and a slight change in the challenges presented, it can be said that, in general, the results are relatively the same in terms of ranking. The one notable variation is the significantly higher ranking given to the issue of "Closing the Generation Gap" in 2013 as opposed to the 2010 survey.

Core Polish American Values	% indicating a given value as one of their five choices
Honor	46
Importance of family	82
Social justice	22
Sense of community	43
High value of status recognition inside of the community	9
Catholic faith	57
Uniqueness of Polish culture and historical experience	65
Commitment to freedom	50
Tenacity	29
Ethnic pride	53
Other	3

The same top 5 core values surfaced in 2013 as in 2010. The only variation is that "The importance of the Polish historical experience" and "The Catholic faith" exchanged places on the 2013 survey. The latter formerly number 2 in the ranks slipped to number 3 while the former moved up one ranking to number 2. The importance of family remained solidly the number 1 core value in both surveys.

The following is a new question which did not appear in 2010. We asked the respondents to identify the events or people in the "Polish American Experience" that were most salient for them as Polish Americans. The respondents preferred general aspects of their history and self-image such as work ethic, community building, heritage preservation and success in America over more specific historical accomplishments which seemed to have faded somewhat from the collective memory. The responses also recorded the continuing importance of Pulaski and Kosciuszko to Polish American identity.

Key aspects, people or events that shape the Polish American Experience (choice of 5)	% indicating a given aspect as one of their five choices
Making the immigration journey to America.	46
Building of over 1,000 Polish churches and 800 parochial schools.	36
Creating communities which shaped the culture of American neighborhoods.	54
Being a major force in establishing the largest CIO Labor Unions.	16
Serving in America's Wars, in particular the highest service per capita in World War II.	46
The high educational and professional attainments of 3rd and 4th generations Polish Americans.	54
Polonia's role in the Resurrection of Poland in 1918 and the support of Polish aspirations for freedom and independence during the cold war.	36
Preservation of Polish heritage and culture in U.S. for over 150 years.	64
Role in building the American industrial system.	21
The Polish work ethic.	63
Polish commitment to home ownership.	16
Thaddeus Kosciuszko & Casmir Pulaski and their contr. to US Independence.	47
Thousand-year history of Poland and its identity with the Catholic Church over the centuries.	36
The 400 year Polish—Lithuanian Union and Commonwealth with its traditions of rights, local assemblies and national parliament (Sejm), elective kingship and religious toleration.	15
The unusual religious and ethnic diversity of the peoples of Commonwealth that came together to create the Modern Polish Nation.	22
May 3, 1791 Constitution—The second in the World after the U.S. Constitution and the first in Europe.	39
The long Defense of Europe from invasion from the East culminating in Sobieski's Victory at Vienna over the Turks in 1683.	19
The Polish struggle for independence during the Partitions. (Insurrections of 1830, 1846, 1848, 1863).	25
The Role of Poles in fighting for freedom in other lands ("For your freedom and ours").	29

Key aspects, people or events that shape the Polish American Experience (choice of 5) (Continued)	% indicating a given aspect as one of their five choices
Polish Independence in 1918 and the Second Republic.	12
The Warsaw Uprising 1944 and underground struggle against Nazism.	47
Poland's role in World War II (Monte Cassino, Poles in RAF, battle of Falaise Gap, etc.)	39
Poland's struggle against Communism.	51
The Solidarity Movement	49
John Paul II.	48
Modern Post Communist Poland.	15
Polish Culture, Art and Literature.	44

This question asked the respondents to identify those events or persons in Polish history which have the most meaning for them or with which they strongly identify. This is a new question that did not appear in 2010. The ones that resonated most strongly, not surprisingly, were those of most recent memory and which placed Poland on the world stage. The one exception was the general identification with Polish Culture. Clearly many Polish Americans, whatever the extent of their knowledge of Polish Culture and/or it contributions to World Culture, feel it is something to be proud of and to identify with.

Conclusion

The full results of the 2013 survey with a more extensive analysis of the data will be published later on in 2014 in a book form. This paper represents a preliminary reconnaissance of the data, drawing comparisons with the previous surveys conducted by the Piast Institute, and highlighting some of the newer questions asked. Overall, it aims to paint a picture of modern Polonia that is impossible to assess with the Census data. The bigger questions, such as whether there is such a thing as one Polonia, although pressing, is beyond the scope of this preliminary paper. These bigger questions will be given their due diligence in the upcoming book.

Critical Thinking

1. Does the designation of core values of an ethnic group by meaningful events and dominant experiences provide a solid foundation for credible measures of its orientations? Can you propose other methods?

2. Does the percentage of an ethnic group's population that is foreign born suggest a meaningful difference that should be accounted for in comparative studies of ethnic values?

3. In what respect does the collection of group values and common disposition to a set of memories contribute to the economic and social indicators and general demographics of ethnic populations?

Internet References

Polish American Congress
www.pac1944.org
Polish American Journal
www.polamjournal.com

DOMINIK STECUTA is a doctoral student in the Department of Political Science at The University of British Columbia in Vancouver, Canada and a Director of Research and Data Analysis at the Piast Institute in Hamtramck, Michigan. Dominik's research interests are comparative politics and political behavior, with an emphasis on public opinion formation, political psychology and political communications. Prior to his doctoral studies, Dominik attended McGill University in Montreal where he obtained a Master's Degree in comparative politics.

DR. THADDEUS RADZILOWSKI is the President and co-founder of the Piast Institute, An Institute for Polish and Polish American Affairs. He is President Emeritus of Saint Mary's College in Orchard Lake, Michigan. Radzilowski is a historian who holds a PhD in History from the University of Michigan. During his career he has taught at Madonna University, Heidelberg College and Southwest Minnesota State University in Minnesota. At Southwest Minnesota State he served as Chair of the Department of History, Director of the Regional History Center, Director of Rural Studies and Associate Vice President for Academic Affairs.

Unit 9

UNIT

Prepared by: John A. Kromkowski, *The Catholic University of America*

Contemporary Dilemmas and Contentions: The Search for Convergent Issues and Common Values

In a very provocative book by Michael Novak, *The Rise of the Unmeltable Ethnics*, written at the very beginning of the 1970s, the following observation is made: *"The eyes of others, Hegel noted, are mirrors in which we learn our own identity. The first eyes into which the immigrants from Southern and Eastern Europe looked were Nordic eyes, the eyes of 'old Americans' or 'nativists'. . . . two forms of prejudice stamped the immigrants. Both had a peculiar "northern" quality: one was racial and the other "progressive." According to one view, it was his race and religion that made the Southern European inferior. According to the other, it was his social and political backwardness."*

Though acknowledgment of ethnicity and cultural pluralism emerged as an intellectual and cultural force in the mid 1960s, its origins were formed even before the period of massive Mediterranean and Eastern European immigration to America. As the articles in this unit illustrate, ethnic experiences may be less foreign and alien than most imagine them to be. The American South has experienced considerably less immigration and undergone less urbanization than the North. Its persistent small towns, its ethos of agriculture, its rurality, its isolation and independence from currents of Northern intellectual and literary expression rooted in other traditions have differentiated its culture and arts and architecture, its folkways and learning. The South, unlike New England and many of the Northern industrial states, has deeper ambiguities about the uprooting force of bourgeois and market-driven universalism. The absence of large-scale immigration and urbanization has limited its historical experience with diversity and pluralism.

Southern regional culture is not homogeneous. However, it does have embedded in it a particularity that is well worth exploring in more detail. Its impact on ethnic and racial group formation and interaction in the context of the Southern experience, and the process of separation and integration is uniquely its own. The contextual character of group relations is well established in the social sciences as a powerful explanatory variable. In fact, ethnicity as a local identity may be utterly and entirely contextual. The ongoing emergence of Southern cultural and social histories produced by Lewis P. Simpson and Joel Williamson and the location and the ongoing impact of the social imagination of Southern narrative and poetic voices and traditions in the works of William Faulkner, Toni Morrison, Sarah Orne Jewett, Alice Walker, Flannery O'Connor, Maya Angelou, Robert Penn Warren, John Crowe Ransom, and Cleanth Brooks fashion a profound interpretative ground upon which a fuller understanding of this regional clustering of group relations rests. Today, another layer of self-articulation and new voices engaging old themes and practices related to slavery and colors have entered public life. Change and ethnicity are not contradictory, for each generation creates anew its ethnicity, which, alongside other affinities, affiliations, and loyalties constitutes the fabric of civil society.

Perhaps the most obvious characterization of these ancestry-conscious persons and groups is their oscillation between self-celebration of achievements and anguished concern about their marginality. Their uncertain relationships with their ancestral homelands and their long-standing love affair with America and its promise of liberty and justice for all is inspired by their inheritance of this legacy from energetic, risk-taking, forebears who left Europe. They left small southern towns and enclave/ghetto neighborhoods in search of the American promise of liberty and justice—to own land and houses in a better economy, a freer polity, and a less status-bound culture.

The impetus of new waves of immigration, the influence of globalization, divisiveness, the practices of "winner take all" competition in the market and for political power, public ferment, tension, and violence must be considered. In addition, the decline of community spiritedness among neighbors and the broken bonds of trust between first line law enforcement and the collapsing, dominated, and marginalized residential and commercial areas they patrol all intersect with some level of race and ethnic passion. This passion can be purposefully or inadvertently triggered.

Ethnicity in America for immigrants and ethnics became a complex of identifications and loyalties that included sentimental attachment to home village, region, or nation; a certain religious affiliation; and the notion of being part of a distinct religious culture. But immigrant and ethnic attitudes in America included loyalty to America and an identification with a particular city, district, or neighborhood in which a particular group settled. This represented membership in the local ethnic community and its institutional expressions. Ethnicity offers a sense of belonging to a certain class or distinct occupation. Thus, ethnicity was essentially a local identity. The relative saliency of its components and each of these elements of ethnic and religious identity changed under the impact of events and with the passing generations.

Article   Prepared by: John A. Kromkowski, *The Catholic University of America*

The Ugly Truth about Hate Crimes—in 5 Charts and Maps

CHRISTOPHER INGRAHAM

Learning Outcomes

After reading this article, you will be able to:

- Compose a profile of hate crime in America.
- Identify the sources of hate crimes.

N ine black church congregants were killed by a white shooter last night in Charleston, S.C., a shocking event that local police are characterizing as a hate crime. Below are several pieces of critical context on hate crimes and hate groups from the Southern Poverty Law Center, the FBI and other sources. While the number of active hate groups in the United States has fallen in recent years, the hate crime rate remains steady and blacks remain the racial group most likely to experience racially motivated violence.

1. Among racial groups, blacks experience the most hate crime.

FBI hate crime data how that more than 50 out of every 1 million black citizens was the victim of a racially motivated hate crime in 2012, the highest among any racial group.

But this is almost certainly an undercount. The FBI is reliant on state and local law enforcement agencies to categorize and report hate crimes correctly. Some agencies do a much better job of this than others, and there is general agreement that the FBI numbers are significantly lower than they should be.

Blacks experience the most hate crime.
Number of hate crime victims per 1 million members of each group, 2012

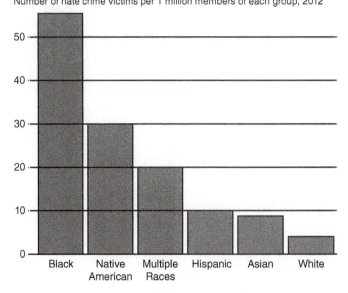

Source: FBI, U.S Census. Gallup. UCLA School of Law

2. Hate crime rates have remained stable over the past decade.

Hate crime rates hold steady
Total number of hate crimes reported per year

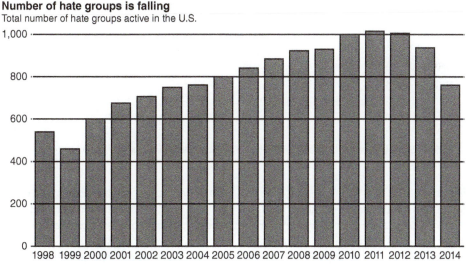

Source: Bureau of Justice Statistics

The Bureau of Justice Statistics provides the most comprehensive overall count of hate crime incidents. Its data, drawn from interviews with victims, shows the number of hate crimes has remained fairly constant over the past 10 years, hovering between 200,000 and 300,000 annually.

3. The number of active hate groups has fallen in recent years.

According to the Southern Poverty Law Center, the number of active hate groups, which it defines as groups having "beliefs or practices that attack or malign an entire class of people, typically for their immutable characteristics," more than doubled from 457 in 1999 to 1018 in 2011.

Since then, the number of active groups has declined to 784. The SPLC attributes this to various causes—including an improving economy and recent law enforcement crackdowns, as well as widespread internecine squabbling and splintering within the groups themselves.

Number of hate groups is falling
Total number of hate groups active in the U.S.

Source: Southern Poverty Law Center

4. Hate groups are most concentrated in the Deep South, Northern Plains.

Hate groups aren't distributed evenly by geography. Controlling for the population in each state, hate groups are concentrated most in the Deep South and in the Montana/Idaho region.

Vermont and New Hampshire also stand out on this map. Partially, this is a function of low population—Vermont has fewer than 700,000 residents, which combined with its four active hate groups gives it a high per-capita value. But this may not just be an artifact of low population. Researchers at Humboldt State University recently mapped geocoded tweets containing hate speech, and their map does appear to show a high incidence of hate-tweets originating in Vermont.

Number of active hate groups per 1 million residents

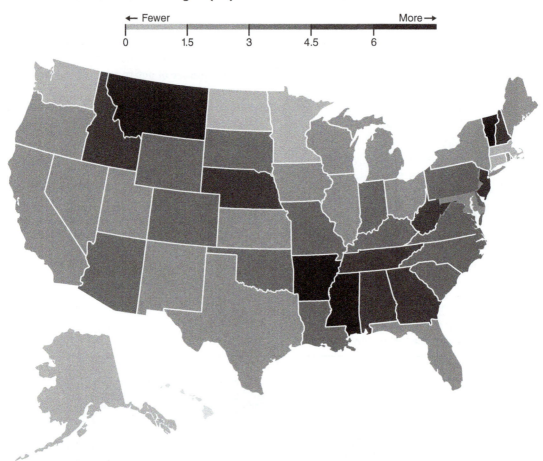

← Fewer   More →

0   1.5   3   4.5   6

Source: Southern Poverty Law Center, U.S Census, GRAPHIC: The Washington Post, Published April 14, 2014.

5. Hardship breeds hatred.

Researchers have tried to suss out the causes of hate crime over the years. A 2002 review of hate crime literature by Princeton economist Alan Krueger looked at the economic determinants of hate crime—whether these crimes rose and fell in response to economic conditions such as the poverty rate and unemployment. Krueger concludes that "rather than economic conditions, the hate crimes literature points to a breakdown in law enforcement and official sanctioning and encouragement of civil disobedience as significant causes of the occurrence of hate crimes."

Not so fast, say economists Matt Ryan and Peter Leeson. In 2010 they examined the links between hate groups and hate crime in the United States. Perhaps surprisingly, they find no relationship between the number of hate groups in a state

and the number of hate crimes that occur within that state in a given year. Instead, the primary determinants seem to be economic. "Our results suggest that unemployment and, to a lesser extent, poverty, are strongly associated with more hate crime, particularly crimes that are sexually, racially and religiously motivated," they conclude.

The most recent SPLC data on hate groups also seems to show a relationship between active hate groups and economic conditions in a state. The chart below plots number of active KKK chapters against the percentage of state residents living in poverty, and shows a positive relationship between the two. This fits with an analysis Richard Florida did a few years back in the *Atlantic* magazine, where he found that the prevalence of hate groups corresponds with various political and economic factors.

Poverty and hate

Poverty rate vs. number of active Ku Klux Klan chapters, by state.

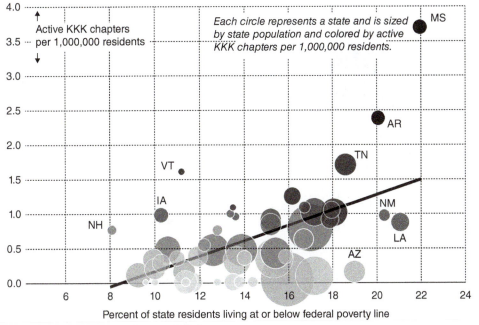

Source: Southern Poverty Law Center and US Census

Critical Thinking

1. Clarify the moral and legal roles of intentionality in violence against another person.
2. What can be done to heal hatred?

Internet References

American Civil Liberties Union (ACLU)
www.aclu.org

The Leadership Conference
www.civilrights.org

Not in Our Town
www.niot.org

Southern Poverty Law Center
www.splcenter.org

U.S. Department of Justice Civil Rights Division
www.justice.gov

Article   Prepared by: John A. Kromkowski, *Catholic University of America*

Judge Upholds Most of Arizona Law Banning Ethnic Studies

LINDSEY COLLOM

Learning Outcomes

After reading this article, you will be able to:

- Identify the reasons for legal control of school curriculum in Arizona.

- Describe the concern of those that support ethnic studies in school.

State officials have won a significant legal battle in a long-running saga over a controversial Tucson schools ethnic-studies program, with a federal judge ruling that a law designed to ban it is constitutional.

Authorities instrumental in the law's passage said Monday that they feel vindicated in their efforts to ban what they deemed to be racially divisive courses in public schools.

Arizona Attorney General Tom Horne, who helped craft the law and personally argued the case in Tucson, called the decision "a victory for ensuring that public education is not held captive to radical, political elements and that students treat each other as individuals—not on the basis of the race they were born into."

The challenge to the new state law was initially launched in 2010 by teachers of the Tucson Unified School District's Mexican-American studies program, which offered a slate of history, government and literature classes at four high schools. They had claimed the law infringed the constitutional rights of Hispanic teachers and students to free speech and equal protection.

The program was discontinued by the Tucson Unified School District's governing board in January 2012 after an administrative law judge determined that the program presented material in a "biased, political and emotionally charged manner."

Proponents of the curriculum said the classes connected students—including those with Native American, Mexican-American, Asian-American and African-American heritages—to their cultural past and their roles in American history. District data showed that students who took the courses performed better on standardized tests.

A former student of the program intervened to carry the case on the teachers' behalf when they were dismissed as plaintiffs.

Judge A. Wallace Tashima. in a ruling released Friday, said objections to the law did not "meet the high threshold to establish a constitutional violation."

But Tashima said a subsection that prohibits courses designed for a particular ethnic group is "unconstitutionally vague" and could have a chilling effect on "legitimate and objective ethnic studies courses." The judge declined to issue a permanent injunction on that portion of the law and said the court has jurisdiction on any future proceedings, if warranted.

The state law, which took effect in January 2011, prohibits Arizona school districts and charter schools from offering classes that promote overthrowing the U.S. government, promote resentment for a certain race or class of people, are geared for students of a particular ethnic background, or advocate ethnic solidarity instead of recognizing students as individuals.

TUSD was not a party to the case, but spokeswoman Cara Rene said Monday that the ruling allows the district to move forward with curriculum requirements of a recently finalized desegregation plan. The plan was the outgrowth of a 40-year-old case in which several families had accused the district of discrimination.

Critical Thinking

1. Why is banning ethnic studies an important issue in Arizona?
2. Is learning an ethnic tradition achieved in school or in an ethnic family and community?

Create Central

www.mhhe.com/createcentral

Internet References

American Indian Ritual Object Repatriation Foundation
   www.repatriationfoundation.on.org

Center for Research in Ethnic Relations
www.warwickac.ukllaclsoc/CRER_RC

Diversity.com
www.diversity.com

Social Science Information Gateway
http://sosig.esrc.bris.ac.uk

Sociosite
www.sociosite.net

Yale University Guide to American Ethnic Studies
www.library.yale.edulrsc/ethniclintemet html

Article

Prepared by: John A. Kromkowski, *The Catholic University of America*

Hard Truths: Law Enforcement and Race

REMARKS AS DELIVERED BY JAMES B. COMEY, DIRECTOR, FEDERAL BUREAU OF INVESTIGATION, GEORGETOWN UNIVERSITY, WASHINGTON, D.C., FEBRUARY 12, 2015

Learning Outcomes

After reading this article, you will be able to:

- Understand how Father Patrick Francis Healy, a Jesuit priest and former president of Georgetown University, is related to the topic of this speech.

- Identify what current issues in law enforcement are addressed by James B. Comey, Director of the Federal Bureau of Investigation.

T hank you, President DeGioia. And good morning, ladies and gentlemen. Thank you for inviting me to Georgetown University. I am honored to be here. I wanted to meet with you today, as President DeGioia said, to share my thoughts on the relationship between law enforcement and the diverse communities we serve and protect. Like a lot of things in life, that relationship is complicated. Relationships often are.

Beautiful Healy Hall—part of, and all around where we sit now—was named after this great university's 29th President, Patrick Francis Healy. Healy was born into slavery, in Georgia, in 1834. His father was an Irish immigrant plantation owner and his mother, a slave. Under the laws of that time, Healy and his siblings were considered to be slaves. Healy is believed to be the first African-American to earn a PhD, the first to enter the Jesuit order, and the first to be president of Georgetown University or any predominantly white university.

Given Georgetown's remarkable history, and that of President Healy, this struck me as an appropriate place to talk about the difficult relationship between law enforcement and the communities we are sworn to serve and protect.

With the death of Michael Brown in Ferguson, the death of Eric Garner in Staten Island, the ongoing protests throughout the country, and the assassinations of NYPD Officers Wenjian Liu and Rafael Ramos, we are at a crossroads. As a society, we can choose to live our everyday lives, raising our families and going to work, hoping that someone, somewhere, will do something to ease the tension—to smooth over the conflict. We can roll up our car windows, turn up the radio and drive around these problems, or we can choose to have an open and honest discussion about what our relationship is today—what it should be, what it could be, and what it needs to be—if we took more time to better understand one another.

Current Issues Facing Law Enforcement

Unfortunately, in places like Ferguson and New York City, and in some communities across this nation, there is a disconnect between police agencies and many citizens—predominantly in communities of color.

Serious debates are taking place about how law enforcement personnel relate to the communities they serve, about the appropriate use of force, and about real and perceived biases, both within and outside of law enforcement. These are important debates. Every American should feel free to express an informed opinion—to protest peacefully, to convey frustration and even anger in a constructive way. That's what makes our democracy great. Those conversations—as bumpy and uncomfortable as they can be—help us understand different perspectives, and better serve our communities. Of course, these are only conversations in the true sense of that word if we are willing not only to talk, but to listen, too.

I worry that this incredibly important and incredibly difficult conversation about race and policing has become focused entirely on the nature and character of law enforcement officers, when it should also be about something much harder to discuss. Debating the nature of policing is very important, but I worry that it has become an excuse, at times, to avoid doing something harder.

The Hard Truths

Let me start by sharing some of my own hard truths:

First, all of us in law enforcement must be honest enough to acknowledge that much of our history is not pretty. At many points in American history, law enforcement enforced the status quo, a status quo that was often brutally unfair to disfavored groups. It was unfair to the Healy siblings and to countless others like them. It was unfair to too many people.

I am descended from Irish immigrants. A century ago, the Irish knew well how American society—and law enforcement—viewed them: as drunks, ruffians, and criminals. Law enforcement's biased view of the Irish lives on in the nickname we still use for the vehicles we use to transport groups of prisoners. It is, after all, the "paddy wagon."

The Irish had tough times, but little compares to the experience on our soil of black Americans. That experience should be part of every American's consciousness, and law enforcement's role in that experience—including in recent times—must be remembered. It is our cultural inheritance.

There is a reason that I require all new agents and analysts to study the FBI's interaction with Dr. Martin Luther King, Jr., and to visit his memorial in Washington as part of their training. And there is a reason I keep on my desk a copy of Attorney General Robert Kennedy's approval of J. Edgar Hoover's request to wiretap Dr. King. It is a single page. The entire application is five sentences long, it is without fact or substance, and is predicated on the naked assertion that there is "communist influence in the racial situation." The reason I do those things is to ensure that we remember our mistakes and that we learn from them.

One reason we cannot forget our law enforcement legacy is that the people we serve and protect cannot forget it, either. So we must talk about our history. It is a hard truth that lives on.

A second hard truth: Much research points to the widespread existence of unconscious bias. Many people in our white-majority culture have unconscious racial biases and react differently to a white face than a black face. In fact, we all, white and black, carry various biases around with us. I am reminded of the song from the Broadway hit, Avenue Q: "Everyone's a Little Bit Racist." Part of it goes like this:

Look around and you will find
No one's really color blind.
Maybe it's a fact

We all should face
Everyone makes judgments
Based on race.

You should be grateful I did not try to sing that.

But if we can't help our latent biases, we can help our behavior in response to those instinctive reactions, which is why we work to design systems and processes that overcome that very human part of us all. Although the research may be unsettling, it is what we do next that matters most.

But racial bias isn't epidemic in law enforcement any more than it is epidemic in academia or the arts. In fact, I believe law enforcement overwhelmingly attracts people who want to do good for a living—people who risk their lives because they want to help other people. They don't sign up to be cops in New York or Chicago or L.A. to help white people or black people or Hispanic people or Asian people. They sign up because they want to help all people. And they do some of the hardest, most dangerous policing to protect people of color.

But that leads me to my third hard truth: something happens to people in law enforcement. Many of us develop different flavors of cynicism that we work hard to resist because they can be lazy mental shortcuts. For example, criminal suspects routinely lie about their guilt, and nearly everybody we charge is guilty. That makes it easy for some folks in law enforcement to assume that everybody is lying and that no suspect, regardless of their race, could be innocent. Easy, but wrong.

Likewise, police officers on patrol in our nation's cities often work in environments where a hugely disproportionate percentage of street crime is committed by young men of color. Something happens to people of good will working in that environment. After years of police work, officers often can't help but be influenced by the cynicism they feel.

A mental shortcut becomes almost irresistible and maybe even rational by some lights. The two young black men on one side of the street look like so many others the officer has locked up. Two white men on the other side of the street—even in the same clothes—do not. The officer does not make the same association about the two white guys, whether that officer is white or black. And that drives different behavior. The officer turns toward one side of the street and not the other. We need to come to grips with the fact that this behavior complicates the relationship between police and the communities they serve.

So why has that officer—like his colleagues—locked up so many young men of color? Why does he have that life-shaping experience? Is it because he is a racist? Why are so many black men in jail? Is it because cops, prosecutors, judges, and juries are racist? Because they are turning a blind eye to white robbers and drug dealers?

The answer is a fourth hard truth: I don't think so. If it were so, that would be easier to address. We would just need to change the way we hire, train, and measure law enforcement and that would substantially fix it. We would then go get those white criminals we have been ignoring. But the truth is significantly harder than that.

The truth is that what really needs fixing is something only a few, like President Obama, are willing to speak about, perhaps because it is so daunting a task. Through the "My Brother's Keeper" initiative, the President is addressing the disproportionate challenges faced by young men of color. For instance, data shows that the percentage of young men not working or not enrolled in school is nearly twice as high for blacks as it is for whites. This initiative, and others like it, is about doing the hard work to grow drug-resistant and violence-resistant kids, especially in communities of color, so they never become part of that officer's life experience.

So many young men of color become part of that officer's life experience because so many minority families and communities are struggling, so many boys and young men grow up in environments lacking role models, adequate education, and decent employment—they lack all sorts of opportunities that most of us take for granted. A tragedy of American life—one that most citizens are able to drive around because it doesn't touch them—is that young people in "those neighborhoods" too often inherit a legacy of crime and prison. And with that inheritance, they become part of a police officer's life, and shape the way that officer—whether white or black—sees the world. Changing that legacy is a challenge so enormous and so complicated that it is, unfortunately, easier to talk only about the cops. And that's not fair.

Let me be transparent about my affection for cops. When you dial 911, whether you are white or black, the cops come, and they come quickly, and they come quickly whether they are white or black. That's what cops do, in addition to all of the other hard and difficult and dangerous and frightening things that they do. They respond to homes in the middle of the night where a drunken father, wielding a gun, is threatening his wife and children. They pound up the back stairs of an apartment building, not knowing whether the guys behind the door they are about to enter are armed, or high, or both.

I come from a law enforcement family. My grandfather, William J. Comey, was a police officer. Pop Comey is one of my heroes. I have a picture of him on my wall in my office at the FBI, reminding me of the legacy I've inherited and that I must honor.

He was the child of immigrants. When he was in the sixth grade, his father was killed in an industrial accident in New York. Because he was the oldest, he had to drop out of school so that he could go to work to support his mom and younger siblings. He could never afford to return to school, but when

he was old enough, he joined the Yonkers, New York, Police Department.

Over the next 40 years, he rose to lead that department. Pop was the tall, strong, silent type, quiet and dignified, and passionate about the rule of law. Back during Prohibition, he heard that bootleggers were running beer through fire hoses between Yonkers and the Bronx.

Now, Pop enjoyed a good beer every now and again, but he ordered his men to cut those hoses with fire axes. Pop had to have a protective detail, because certain people were angry and shocked that someone in law enforcement would do that. But that's what we want as citizens—that's what we expect. And so I keep that picture of Pop on my office wall to remind me of his integrity, and his pride in the integrity of his work.

Law enforcement ranks are filled with people like my grandfather. But, to be clear, although I am from a law enforcement family, and have spent much of my career in law enforcement, I'm not looking to let law enforcement off the hook. Those of us in law enforcement must redouble our efforts to resist bias and prejudice. We must better understand the people we serve and protect—by trying to know, deep in our gut, what it feels like to be a law-abiding young black man walking on the street and encountering law enforcement. We must understand how that young man may see us. We must resist the lazy shortcuts of cynicism and approach him with respect and decency.

We must work—in the words of New York City Police Commissioner Bill Bratton—to really see each other. Perhaps the reason we struggle as a nation is because we've come to see only what we represent, at face value, instead of who we are. We simply must see the people we serve.

But the "seeing" needs to flow in both directions. Citizens also need to really see the men and women of law enforcement. They need to see what police see through the windshields of their squad cars, or as they walk down the street. They need to see the risks and dangers law enforcement officers encounter on a typical late-night shift. They need to understand the difficult and frightening work they do to keep us safe. They need to give them the space and respect to do their work, well and properly.

If they take the time to do that, what they will see are officers who are human, who are overwhelmingly doing the right thing for the right reasons, and who are too often operating in communities—and facing challenges—most of us choose to drive around.

One of the hardest things I do as FBI Director is call the chiefs and sheriffs in departments around the nation when officers have been killed in the line of duty. I call to express my sorrow and offer the FBI's help. Officers like Wenjian Liu and Rafael Ramos, two of NYPD's finest who were gunned down by a madman who thought his ambush would avenge the deaths of Michael Brown and Eric Garner. I make far too many calls. And, there are far too many names of fallen officers on the National Law Enforcement Officers Memorial and far too many names etched there each year.

Officers Liu and Ramos swore the same oath all in law enforcement do, and they answered the call to serve the people, all people. Like all good police officers, they moved toward danger, without regard for the politics or passions or race of those who needed their help—knowing the risks inherent in their work. They were minority police officers, killed while standing watch in a minority neighborhood—Bedford-Stuyvesant—one they and their fellow officers had rescued from the grip of violent crime.

Twenty years ago, Bed-Stuy was shorthand for a kind of chaos and disorder in which good people had no freedom to walk, shop, play, or just sit on the front steps and talk. It was too dangerous. But today, no more, thanks to the work of those who chose lives of service and danger to help others.

But despite this selfless service—of these two officers and countless others like them across the country—in some American communities, people view the police not as allies, but as antagonists, and think of them not with respect or gratitude, but with suspicion and distrust.

We simply must find ways to see each other more clearly. And part of that has to involve collecting and sharing better information about encounters between police and citizens, especially violent encounters.

Not long after riots broke out in Ferguson late last summer, I asked my staff to tell me how many people shot by police were African-American in this country. I wanted to see trends. I wanted to see information. They couldn't give it to me, and it wasn't their fault. Demographic data regarding officer-involved shootings is not consistently reported to us through our Uniform Crime Reporting Program. Because reporting is voluntary, our data is incomplete and therefore, in the aggregate, unreliable.

I recently listened to a thoughtful big city police chief express his frustration with that lack of reliable data. He said he didn't know whether the Ferguson police shot one person a week, one a year, or one a century, and that in the absence of good data, "all we get are ideological thunderbolts, when what we need are ideological agnostics who use information to try to solve problems." He's right.

The first step to understanding what is really going on in our communities and in our country is to gather more and better data related to those we arrest, those we confront for breaking the law and jeopardizing public safety, and those who confront us. "Data" seems a dry and boring word but, without it, we cannot understand our world and make it better.

How can we address concerns about "use of force," how can we address concerns about officer-involved shootings if we do not have a reliable grasp on the demographics and circumstances of those incidents? We simply must improve the way we collect and analyze data to see the true nature of what's happening in all of our communities.

The FBI tracks and publishes the number of "justifiable homicides" reported by police departments. But, again, reporting by police departments is voluntary and not all departments participate. That means we cannot fully track the number of incidents in which force is used by police, or against police, including non-fatal encounters, which are not reported at all.

Without complete and accurate data, we are left with "ideological thunderbolts." And that helps spark unrest and distrust and does not help us get better. Because we must get better, I intend for the FBI to be a leader in urging departments around this country to give us the facts we need for an informed discussion, the facts all of us need, to help us make sound policy and sound decisions with that information.

***

America isn't easy. America takes work. Today, February 12, is Abraham Lincoln's birthday. He spoke at Gettysburg about a "new birth of freedom" because we spent the first four score and seven years of our history with fellow Americans held as slaves—President Healy, his siblings, and his mother among them. We have spent the 150 years since Lincoln spoke making great progress, but along the way treating a whole lot of people of color poorly. And law enforcement was often part of that poor treatment. That's our inheritance as law enforcement and it is not all in the distant past.

We must account for that inheritance. And we—especially those of us who enjoy the privilege that comes with being the majority—must confront the biases that are inescapable parts of the human condition. We must speak the truth about our shortcomings as law enforcement, and fight to be better. But as a country, we must also speak the truth to ourselves. Law enforcement is not the root cause of problems in our hardest hit neighborhoods. Police officers—people of enormous courage and integrity, in the main—are in those neighborhoods, risking their lives, to protect folks from offenders who are the product of problems that will not be solved by body cameras.

We simply must speak to each other honestly about all these hard truths.

In the words of Dr. King, "We must learn to live together as brothers or we will all perish together as fools."

We all have work to do—hard work, challenging work—and it will take time. We all need to talk and we all need to listen, not just about easy things, but about hard things, too. Relationships are hard. Relationships require work. So let's begin that work. It is time to start seeing one another for who and what we really are. Peace, security, and understanding are worth the effort. Thank you for listening to me today.

Critical Thinking

1. What can the FBI do to improve policy at the local and state level?
2. Docs municipal fragmentation of metropolitan areas contribute to creating such practices?
3. What are the causes of racial segmentation and the racial gaps between the political/governmental leadership, the racial composition of the police department and the residents of Ferguson?

Internet References

Bureau of Justice Statistics (BJS)
www.bjs.gov

Discover Policing
http://discoverpolicing.org

The Role of Traditional Policing in Community
www.cops.usdoj.gov

Comey, James B. "Hard Truths: Law Enforcement and Race", February 2015, Federal Bureau of Investigation.

Article   Prepared by: John A. Kromkowski, *The Catholic University of America*

Investigation of the Ferguson Police Department

United States Department of Justice Civil Rights Division

Learning Outcomes

After reading this article, you will be able to:

- Describe the policing practices of the Ferguson, MO police department presented in the report.

- Identify what recommendations and remedies are proposed.

Report Summary

The Civil Rights Division of the United States Department of Justice opened its investigation of the Ferguson Police Department ("FPD") on September 4, 2014. This investigation was initiated under the pattern-or-practice provision of the Violent Crime Control and Law Enforcement Act of 1994, 42 U.S.C. § 14141, the Omnibus Crime Control and Safe Streets Act of 1968, 42 U.S.C. § 3789d ("Safe Streets Act"), and Title VI of the Civil Rights Act of 1964, 42 U.S.C. § 2000d ("Title VI"). This investigation has revealed a pattern or practice of unlawful conduct within the Ferguson Police Department that violates the First, Fourth, and Fourteenth Amendments to the United States Constitution, and federal statutory law.

Over the course of the investigation, we interviewed City officials, including City Manager John Shaw, Mayor James Knowles, Chief of Police Thomas Jackson, Municipal Judge Ronald Brockmeyer, the Municipal Court Clerk, Ferguson's Finance Director, half of FPD's sworn officers, and others. We spent, collectively, approximately 100 person-days onsite in Ferguson. We participated in ride-alongs with on-duty officers, reviewed over 35,000 pages of police records as well as thousands of emails and other electronic materials provided by the police department. Enlisting the assistance of statistical experts, we analyzed FPD's data on stops, searches, citations,

and arrests, as well as data collected by the municipal court. We observed four separate sessions of Ferguson Municipal Court, interviewing dozens of people charged with local offenses, and we reviewed third-party studies regarding municipal court practices in Ferguson and St. Louis County more broadly. As in all of our investigations, we sought to engage the local community, conducting hundreds of in-person and telephone interviews of individuals who reside in Ferguson or who have had interactions with the police department. We contacted ten neighborhood associations and met with each group that responded to us, as well as several other community groups and advocacy organizations. Throughout the investigation, we relied on two police chiefs who accompanied us to Ferguson and who themselves interviewed City and police officials, spoke with community members, and reviewed FPD policies and incident reports.

We thank the City officials and the rank-and-file officers who have cooperated with this investigation and provided us with insights into the operation of the police department, including the municipal court. Notwithstanding our findings about Ferguson's approach to law enforcement and the policing culture it creates, we found many Ferguson police officers and other City employees to be dedicated public servants striving each day to perform their duties lawfully and with respect for all members of the Ferguson community. The importance of their often-selfless work cannot be overstated.

We are also grateful to the many members of the Ferguson community who have met with us to share their experiences. It became clear during our many conversations with Ferguson residents from throughout the City that many residents, black and white, genuinely embrace Ferguson's diversity and want to reemerge from the events of recent months a truly inclusive, united community. This Report is intended to strengthen those efforts by recognizing the harms caused by Ferguson's law enforcement practices so that those harms can be better understood and overcome.

Ferguson's law enforcement practices are shaped by the City's focus on revenue rather than by public safety needs. This emphasis on revenue has compromised the institutional character of Ferguson's police department, contributing to a pattern of unconstitutional policing, and has also shaped its municipal court, leading to procedures that raise due process concerns and inflict unnecessary harm on members of the Ferguson community. Further, Ferguson's police and municipal court practices both reflect and exacerbate existing racial bias, including racial stereotypes. Ferguson's own data establish clear racial disparities that adversely impact African Americans. The evidence shows that discriminatory intent is part of the reason for these disparities. Over time, Ferguson's police and municipal court practices have sown deep mistrust between parts of the community and the police department, undermining law enforcement legitimacy among African Americans in particular.

Focus on Generating Revenue

The City budgets for sizeable increases in municipal fines and fees each year, exhorts police and court staff to deliver those revenue increases, and closely monitors whether those increases are achieved. City officials routinely urge Chief Jackson to generate more revenue through enforcement. In March 2010, for instance, the City Finance Director wrote to Chief Jackson that "unless ticket writing ramps up significantly before the end of the year, it will be hard to significantly raise collections next year. . . . Given that we are looking at a substantial sales tax shortfall, it's not an insignificant issue." Similarly, in March 2013, the Finance Director wrote to the City Manager: "Court fees are anticipated to rise about 7.5%. I did ask the Chief if he thought the PD could deliver 10% increase. He indicated they could try." The importance of focusing on revenue generation is communicated to FPD officers. Ferguson police officers from all ranks told us that revenue generation is stressed heavily within the police department, and that the message comes from City leadership. The evidence we reviewed supports this perception.

Police Practices

The City's emphasis on revenue generation has a profound effect on FPD's approach to law enforcement. Patrol assignments and schedules are geared toward aggressive enforcement of Ferguson's municipal code, with insufficient thought given to whether enforcement strategies promote public safety or unnecessarily undermine community trust and cooperation. Officer evaluations and promotions depend to an inordinate degree on "productivity," meaning the number of citations issued. Partly as a consequence of City and FPD priorities, many officers appear to see some residents, especially those who live in Ferguson's predominantly African-American neighborhoods, less as constituents to be protected than as potential offenders and sources of revenue.

This culture within FPD influences officer activities in all areas of policing, beyond just ticketing. Officers expect and demand compliance even when they lack legal authority. They are inclined to interpret the exercise of free-speech rights as unlawful disobedience, innocent movements as physical threats, indications of mental or physical illness as belligerence. Police supervisors and leadership do too little to ensure that officers act in accordance with law and policy, and rarely respond meaningfully to civilian complaints of officer misconduct. The result is a pattern of stops without reasonable suspicion and arrests without probable cause in violation of the Fourth Amendment; infringement on free expression, as well as retaliation for protected expression, in violation of the First Amendment; and excessive force in violation of the Fourth Amendment.

Even relatively routine misconduct by Ferguson police officers can have significant consequences for the people whose rights are violated. For example, in the summer of 2012, a 32-year-old African-American man sat in his car cooling off after playing basketball in a Ferguson public park. An officer pulled up behind the man's car, blocking him in, and demanded the man's Social Security number and identification. Without any cause, the officer accused the man of being a pedophile, referring to the presence of children in the park, and ordered the man out of his car for a pat-down, although the officer had no reason to believe the man was armed. The officer also asked to search the man's car. The man objected, citing his constitutional rights. In response, the officer arrested the man, reportedly at gunpoint, charging him with eight violations of Ferguson's municipal code. One charge, Making a False Declaration, was for initially providing the short form of his first name (e.g., "Mike" instead of "Michael"), and an address which, although legitimate, was different from the one on his driver's license. Another charge was for not wearing a seat belt, even though he was seated in a parked car. The officer also charged the man both with having an expired operator's license, and with having no operator's license in his possession. The man told us that, because of these charges, he lost his job as a contractor with the federal government that he had held for years.

Municipal Court Practices

Ferguson has allowed its focus on revenue generation to fundamentally compromise the role of Ferguson's municipal court. The municipal court does not act as a neutral arbiter of the law or a check on unlawful police conduct. Instead, the court primarily uses its judicial authority as the means to compel the payment of fines and fees that advance the City's financial interests. This has led to court practices that violate the Fourteenth Amendment's due process and equal protection requirements. The court's practices also impose unnecessary harm, overwhelmingly on African-American individuals, and run counter to public safety.

Most strikingly, the court issues municipal arrest warrants not on the basis of public safety needs, but rather as a routine response to missed court appearances and required fine payments. In 2013 alone, the court issued over 9,000 warrants on cases stemming in large part from minor violations such as parking infractions, traffic tickets, or housing code violations. Jail time would be considered far too harsh a penalty for the great majority of these code violations, yet Ferguson's municipal court routinely issues warrants for people to be arrested and incarcerated for failing to timely pay related fines and fees. Under state law, a failure to appear in municipal court on a traffic charge involving a moving violation also results in a license suspension. Ferguson has made this penalty even more onerous by only allowing the suspension to be lifted after payment of an owed fine is made in full. Further, until recently, Ferguson also added charges, fines, and fees for each missed appearance and payment. Many pending cases still include such charges that were imposed before the court recently eliminated them, making it as difficult as before for people to resolve these cases.

The court imposes these severe penalties for missed appearances and payments even as several of the court's practices create unnecessary barriers to resolving a municipal violation. The court often fails to provide clear and accurate information regarding a person's charges or court obligations. And the court's fine assessment procedures do not adequately provide for a defendant to seek a fine reduction on account of financial incapacity or to seek alternatives to payment such as community service. City and court officials have adhered to these court practices despite acknowledging their needlessly harmful consequences. In August 2013, for example, one City Councilmember wrote to the City Manager, the Mayor, and other City officials lamenting the lack of a community service option and noted the benefits of such a program, including that it would "keep those people that simply don't have the money to pay their fines from constantly being arrested and going to jail, only to be released and do it all over again."

Together, these court practices exacerbate the harm of Ferguson's unconstitutional police practices. They impose a particular hardship upon Ferguson's most vulnerable residents, especially upon those living in or near poverty. Minor offenses can generate crippling debts, result in jail time because of an inability to pay, and result in the loss of a driver's license, employment, or housing.

We spoke, for example, with an African-American woman who has a still-pending case stemming from 2007, when, on a single occasion, she parked her car illegally. She received two citations and a $151 fine, plus fees. The woman, who experienced financial difficulties and periods of homelessness over several years, was charged with seven Failure to Appear offenses for missing court dates or fine payments on her parking tickets between 2007 and 2010. For each Failure to Appear, the court issued an arrest warrant and imposed new fines and fees. From 2007 to 2014, the woman was arrested twice, spent six days in jail, and paid $550 to the court for the events stemming from this single instance of illegal parking. Court records show that she twice attempted to make partial payments of $25 and $50, but the court returned those payments, refusing to accept anything less than payment in full. One of those payments was later accepted, but only after the court's letter rejecting payment by money order was returned as undeliverable. This woman is now making regular payments on the fine. As of December 2014, over seven years later, despite initially owing a $151 fine and having already paid $550, she still owed $541.

Racial Bias

Ferguson's approach to law enforcement both reflects and reinforces racial bias, including stereotyping. The harms of Ferguson's police and court practices are borne disproportionately by African Americans, and there is evidence that this is due in part to intentional discrimination on the basis of race.

Ferguson's law enforcement practices overwhelmingly impact African Americans. Data collected by the Ferguson Police Department from 2012 to 2014 shows that African Americans account for 85% of vehicle stops, 90% of citations, and 93% of arrests made by FPD officers, despite comprising only 67% of Ferguson's population. African Americans are more than twice as likely as white drivers to be searched during vehicle stops even after controlling for non-race based variables such as the reason the vehicle stop was initiated, but are found in possession of contraband 26% less often than white drivers, suggesting officers are impermissibly considering race as a factor when determining whether to search. African Americans are more likely to be cited and arrested following a stop regardless of why the stop was initiated and are more likely to receive multiple citations during a single incident. From 2012 to 2014, FPD issued four or more citations to African Americans on 73 occasions, but issued four or more citations to non-African Americans only twice. FPD appears to bring certain offenses almost exclusively against African Americans. For example, from 2011 to 2013, African Americans accounted for 95% of

Manner of Walking in Roadway charges, and 94% of all Failure to Comply charges. Notably, with respect to speeding charges brought by FPD, the evidence shows not only that African Americans are represented at disproportionately high rates overall, but also that the disparate impact of FPD's enforcement practices on African Americans is 48% larger when citations are issued not on the basis of radar or laser, but by some other method, such as the officer's own visual assessment.

These disparities are also present in FPD's use of force. Nearly 90% of documented force used by FPD officers was used against African Americans. In every canine bite incident for which racial information is available, the person bitten was African American.

Municipal court practices likewise cause disproportionate harm to African Americans. African Americans are 68% less likely than others to have their cases dismissed by the court, and are more likely to have their cases last longer and result in more required court encounters. African Americans are at least 50% more likely to have their cases lead to an arrest warrant, and accounted for 92% of cases in which an arrest warrant was issued by the Ferguson Municipal Court in 2013. Available data show that, of those actually arrested by FPD only because of an outstanding municipal warrant, 96% are African American.

Our investigation indicates that this disproportionate burden on African Americans cannot be explained by any difference in the rate at which people of different races violate the law. Rather, our investigation has revealed that these disparities occur, at least in part, because of unlawful bias against and stereotypes about African Americans. We have found substantial evidence of racial bias among police and court staff in Ferguson. For example, we discovered emails circulated by police supervisors and court staff that stereotype racial minorities as criminals, including one email that joked about an abortion by an African-American woman being a means of crime control.

City officials have frequently asserted that the harsh and disparate results of Ferguson's law enforcement system do not indicate problems with police or court practices, but instead reflect a pervasive lack of "personal responsibility" among "certain segments" of the community. Our investigation has found that the practices about which area residents have complained are in fact unconstitutional and unduly harsh. But the City's personal-responsibility refrain is telling: it reflects many of the same racial stereotypes found in the emails between police and court supervisors. This evidence of bias and stereotyping, together with evidence that Ferguson has long recognized but failed to correct the consistent racial disparities caused by its police and court practices, demonstrates that the discriminatory effects of Ferguson's conduct are driven at least in part by discriminatory intent in violation of the Fourteenth Amendment.

Community Distrust

Since the August 2014 shooting death of Michael Brown, the lack of trust between the Ferguson Police Department and a significant portion of Ferguson's residents, especially African Americans, has become undeniable. The causes of this distrust and division, however, have been the subject of debate. Police and other City officials, as well as some Ferguson residents, have insisted to us that the public outcry is attributable to "outside agitators" who do not reflect the opinions of "real Ferguson residents." That view is at odds with the facts we have gathered during our investigation. Our investigation has shown that distrust of the Ferguson Police Department is long-standing and largely attributable to Ferguson's approach to law enforcement. This approach results in patterns of unnecessarily aggressive and at times unlawful policing; reinforces the harm of discriminatory stereotypes; discourages a culture of accountability; and neglects community engagement. In recent years, FPD has moved away from the modest community policing efforts it previously had implemented, reducing opportunities for positive police-community interactions, and losing the little familiarity it had with some African-American neighborhoods. The confluence of policing to raise revenue and racial bias thus has resulted in practices that not only violate the Constitution and cause direct harm to the individuals whose rights are violated, but also undermine community trust, especially among many African Americans. As a consequence of these practices, law enforcement is seen as illegitimate, and the partnerships necessary for public safety are, in some areas, entirely absent.

Restoring trust in law enforcement will require recognition of the harms caused by Ferguson's law enforcement practices, and diligent, committed collaboration with the entire Ferguson community. At the conclusion of this report, we have broadly identified the changes that are necessary for meaningful and sustainable reform. These measures build upon a number of other recommended changes we communicated verbally to the Mayor, Police Chief, and City Manager in September so that Ferguson could begin immediately to address problems as we identified them. As a result of those recommendations, the City and police department have already begun to make some changes to municipal court and police practices. We commend City officials for beginning to take steps to address some of the concerns we have already raised. Nonetheless, these changes are only a small part of the reform necessary. Addressing the deeply embedded constitutional deficiencies we found demands an entire reorientation of law enforcement in Ferguson. The City must replace revenue-driven policing with a system grounded in the principles of community policing and police legitimacy, in which people are equally protected and treated with compassion, regardless of race.

Background

The City of Ferguson is one of 89 municipalities in St. Louis County, Missouri.[1] According to United States Census Data from 2010, Ferguson is home to roughly 21,000 residents.[2] While Ferguson's total population has stayed relatively constant in recent decades, Ferguson's racial demographics have changed dramatically during that time. In 1990, 74% of Ferguson's population was white, while 25% was black.[3] By 2000, African Americans became the new majority, making up 52% of the City's population.[4] According to the 2010 Census, the black population in Ferguson has grown to 67%, whereas the white population has decreased to 29%.[5] According to the 2009–2013 American Community Survey, 25% of the City's population lives below the federal poverty level.[6]

Residents of Ferguson elect a Mayor and six individuals to serve on a City Council. The City Council appoints a City Manager to an indefinite term, subject to removal by a Council vote. *See* Ferguson City Charter § 4.1. The City Manager serves as chief executive and administrative officer of the City of Ferguson, and is responsible for all affairs of the City. The City Manager directs and supervises all City departments, including the Ferguson Police Department.

The current Chief of Police, Thomas Jackson, has commanded the police department since he was appointed by the City Manager in 2010. The department has a total of 54 sworn officers divided among several divisions. The patrol division is the largest division; 28 patrol officers are supervised by four sergeants, two lieutenants, and a captain. Each of the four patrol squads has a canine officer. While all patrol officers engage in traffic enforcement, FPD also has a dedicated traffic officer responsible for collecting traffic stop data required by the state of Missouri. FPD has two School Resource Officers ("SROs"), one who is assigned to the McCluer South-Berkeley High School and one who is assigned to the Ferguson Middle School. FPD has a single officer assigned to be the "Community Resource Officer," who attends community meetings, serves as FPD's public relations liaison, and is charged with collecting crime data. FPD operates its own jail, which has ten individual cells and a large holding cell. The jail is staffed by three non-sworn correctional officers. Of the 54 sworn officers currently serving in FPD, four are African American.

FPD officers are authorized to initiate charges—by issuing citations or summonses, or by making arrests—under both the municipal code and state law. Ferguson's municipal code addresses nearly every aspect of civic life for those who live in Ferguson, and regulates the conduct of all who work [in], travel through, or otherwise visit the City. In addition to mirroring some non-felony state law violations, such as assault, stealing, and traffic violations, the code establishes housing violations, such as High Grass and Weeds; requirements for permits to rent an apartment or use the City's trash service; animal control

ordinances, such as Barking Dog and Dog Running at Large; and a number of other violations, such as Manner of Walking in Roadway. *See, e.g.,* Ferguson Mun. Code §§ 29-16 et seq.; 37-1 et seq.; 46-27; 6-5, 6-11; 44-344.

FPD files most charges as municipal offenses, not state violations, even when an analogous state offense exists. Between July 1, 2010, and June 30, 2014, the City of Ferguson issued approximately 90,000 citations and summonses for municipal violations. Notably, the City issued nearly 50% more citations in the last year of that time period than it did in the first. This increase in enforcement has not been driven by a rise in serious crime. While the ticketing rate has increased dramatically, the number of charges for many of the most serious offenses covered by the municipal code—e.g., Assault, Driving While Intoxicated, and Stealing—has remained relatively constant.[7]

Because the overwhelming majority of FPD's enforcement actions are brought under the municipal code, most charges are processed and resolved by the Ferguson Municipal Court, which has primary jurisdiction over all code violations. Ferguson Mun. Code § 13-2. Ferguson's municipal court operates as part of the police department. The court is supervised by the Ferguson Chief of Police, is considered part of the police department for City organizational purposes, and is physically located within the police station. Court staff report directly to the Chief of Police. Thus, if the City Manager or other City officials issue a court-related directive, it is typically sent to the Police Chief's attention. In recent weeks, City officials informed us that they are considering plans to bring the court under the supervision of the City Finance Director.

A Municipal Judge presides over court sessions. The Municipal Judge is not hired or supervised by the Chief of Police, but is instead nominated by the City Manager and elected by the City Council. The Judge serves a two-year term, subject to reappointment. The current Municipal Judge, Ronald Brockmeyer, has presided in Ferguson for approximately ten years. The City's Prosecuting Attorney and her assistants officially prosecute all actions before the court, although in practice most cases are resolved without trial or a prosecutor's involvement. The current Prosecuting Attorney was appointed in April 2011. At the time of her appointment, the Prosecuting Attorney was already serving as City Attorney, and she continues to serve in that separate capacity, which entails providing general counsel and representation to the City. The Municipal Judge, Court Clerk, Prosecuting Attorney, and all assistant court clerks are white.

While the Municipal Judge presides over court sessions, the Court Clerk, who is employed under the Police Chief's supervision, plays the most significant role in managing the court and exercises broad discretion in conducting the court's daily operations. Ferguson's municipal code confers broad authority on the Court Clerk, including the authority to collect all fines and fees, accept guilty pleas, sign and issue subpoenas, and approve bond determinations. Ferguson Mun. Code § 13-7. Indeed, the Court Clerk and assistant clerks routinely perform duties that are, for all practical purposes, judicial. For example, documents indicate that court clerks have disposed of charges without the Municipal Judge's involvement.

The court officially operates subject to the oversight of the presiding judge of the St. Louis County Circuit Court (21st Judicial Circuit) under the rules promulgated by that Circuit Court and the Missouri Supreme Court. Notwithstanding these rules, the City of Ferguson and the court itself retain considerable power to establish and amend court practices and procedures. The Ferguson municipal code sets forth a limited number of protocols that the court must follow, but the code leaves most aspects of court operations to the discretion of the court itself. *See* Ferguson Mun. Code Ch. 13, Art. III. The code also explicitly authorizes the Municipal Judge to "make and adopt such rules of practice and procedure as are necessary to hear and decide matters pending before the municipal court." Ferguson Mun. Code § 13-29.

The Ferguson Municipal Court has the authority to issue and enforce judgments, issue warrants for search and arrest, hold parties in contempt, and order imprisonment as a penalty for contempt. The court may conduct trials, although it does so rarely, and most charges are resolved without one. Upon resolution of a charge, the court has the authority to impose fines, fees, and imprisonment when violations are found. Specifically, the court can impose imprisonment in the Ferguson City Jail for up to three months, a fine of up to $1,000, or a combination thereof. It is rare for the court to sentence anyone to jail as a *penalty* for a violation of the municipal code; indeed, the Municipal Judge reports that he has done so only once. Rather, the court almost always imposes a monetary penalty payable to the City of Ferguson, plus court fees. Nonetheless, as discussed in detail below, the court issues arrest warrants when a person misses a court appearance or fails to timely pay a fine. As a result, violations that would normally not result in a penalty of imprisonment can, and frequently do, lead to municipal warrants, arrests, and jail time.

As the number of charges initiated by FPD has increased in recent years, the size of the court's docket has also increased. According to data the City reported to the Missouri State Courts Administrator, at the end of fiscal year 2009, the municipal court had roughly 24,000 traffic cases and 28,000 non-traffic cases pending. As of October 31, 2014, both of those figures had roughly doubled to 53,000 and 50,000 cases, respectively. In fiscal year 2009, 16,178 new cases were filed, and 8,727 were resolved. In 2014, by contrast, 24,256 new offenses were filed, and 10,975 offenses were resolved.

The court holds three or four sessions per month, and each session lasts no more than three hours. It is not uncommon for as many as 500 people to appear before the court in a single session, exceeding the court's physical capacity and leading individuals to line up outside of court waiting to be heard. Many people have multiple offenses pending; accordingly, the court typically considers 1,200–1,500 offenses in a single session, and has in the past considered over 2,000 offenses during one sitting. Previously there was a cap on the number of offenses that could be assigned to a particular docket date. Given that cap, and the significant increase in municipal citations in recent years, a problem developed in December 2011 in which more citations were issued than court sessions could timely accommodate. At one point court dates were initially scheduled as far as six months after the date of the citation. To address this problem, court staff first raised the cap to allow 1,000 offenses to be assigned to a single court date and later eliminated the cap altogether. To handle the increasing caseload, the City Manager also requested and secured City Council approval to fund additional court positions, noting in January 2013 that "each month we are setting new all-time records in fines and forfeitures," that this was overburdening court staff, and that the funding for the additional positions "will be more than covered by the increase in revenues."

Ferguson Law Enforcement Efforts are Focused on Generating Revenue

City officials have consistently set maximizing revenue as the priority for Ferguson's law enforcement activity. Ferguson generates a significant and increasing amount of revenue from the enforcement of code provisions. The City has budgeted for, and achieved, significant increases in revenue from municipal code enforcement over the last several years, and these increases are projected to continue. Of the $11.07 million in general fund revenue the City collected in fiscal year 2010, $1.38 million came from fines and fees collected by the court; similarly, in fiscal year 2011, the City's general fund revenue of $11.44 million included $1.41 million from fines and fees. In its budget for fiscal year 2012, however, the City predicted that revenue from municipal fines and fees would increase over 30% from the previous year's amount to $1.92 million; the court exceeded that target, collecting $2.11 million. In its budget for fiscal year 2013, the City budgeted for fines and fees to yield $2.11 million; the court exceeded that target as well, collecting $2.46 million. For 2014, the City budgeted for the municipal court to generate $2.63 million in revenue. The City has not yet made public the actual revenue collected that year, although budget documents forecasted lower revenue than was budgeted. Nonetheless, for fiscal year 2015, the City's budget anticipates fine and fee revenues to account for

$3.09 million of a projected $13.26 million in general fund revenues.[8]

City, police, and court officials for years have worked in concert to maximize revenue at every stage of the enforcement process, beginning with how fines and fine enforcement processes are established. In a February 2011 report requested by the City Council at a Financial Planning Session and drafted by Ferguson's Finance Director with contributions from Chief Jackson, the Finance Director reported on "efforts to increase efficiencies and maximize collection" by the municipal court. The report included an extensive comparison of Ferguson's fines to those of surrounding municipalities and noted with approval that Ferguson's fines are "at or near the top of the list." The chart noted, for example, that while other municipalities' parking fines generally range from $5 to $100, Ferguson's is $102. The chart noted also that the charge for "Weeds/Tall Grass" was as little as $5 in one city but, in Ferguson, it ranged from $77 to $102. The report stated that the acting prosecutor had reviewed the City's "high volume offenses" and "started recommending higher fines on these cases, and recommending probation only infrequently." While the report stated that this recommendation was because of a "large volume of non-compliance," the recommendation was in fact emphasized as one of several ways that the code enforcement system had been honed to produce more revenue.

In combination with a high fine schedule, the City directs FPD to aggressively enforce the municipal code. City and police leadership pressure officers to write citations, independent of any public safety need, and rely on citation productivity to fund the City budget. In an email from March 2010, the Finance Director wrote to Chief Jackson that "unless ticket writing ramps up significantly before the end of the year, it will be hard to significantly raise collections next year. What are your thoughts? Given that we are looking at a substantial sales tax shortfall, it's not an insignificant issue." Chief Jackson responded that the City would see an increase in fines once more officers were hired and that he could target the $1.5 million forecast. Significantly, Chief Jackson stated that he was also "looking at different shift schedules which will place more officers on the street, which in turn will increase traffic enforcement per shift." Shortly thereafter, FPD switched to the 12-hour shift schedule for its patrol officers, which FPD continues to use. Law enforcement experience has shown that this schedule makes community policing more difficult— a concern that we have also heard directly from FPD officers. Nonetheless, while FPD heavily considered the revenue implications of the 12-hour shift and certain other factors such as its impact on overtime and sick time usage, we have found no evidence that FPD considered the consequences for positive community engagement. The City's 2014 budget itself stated

that since December 2010, "the percent of [FPD] resources allocated to traffic enforcement has increased," and "[a]s a result, traffic enforcement related collections increased" in the following two years. The 2015 budget added that even after those initial increases, in fiscal year 2012–2013, FPD was once again "successful in increasing their proportion of resources dedicated to traffic enforcement" and increasing collections.

As directed, FPD supervisors and line officers have undertaken the aggressive code enforcement required to meet the City's revenue generation expectations. FPD officers routinely conduct stops that have little relation to public safety and a questionable basis in law. FPD officers routinely issue multiple citations during a single stop, often for the same violation. Issuing three or four charges in one stop is not uncommon in Ferguson. Officers sometimes write six, eight, or, in at least one instance, fourteen citations for a single encounter. Indeed, officers told us that some compete to see who can issue the largest number of citations during a single stop.

The February 2011 report to the City Council notes that the acting prosecutor—with the apparent approval of the Police Chief—"talked with police officers about ensuring all necessary summonses are written for each incident, i.e. when DWI charges are issued, are the correct companion charges being issued, such as speeding, failure to maintain a single lane, no insurance, and no seat belt, etc." The prosecutor noted that "[t]his is done to ensure that a proper resolution to all cases is being achieved and that the court is maintaining the correct volume for offenses occurring within the city." Notably, the "correct volume" of law enforcement is uniformly presented in City documents as related to revenue generation, rather than in terms of what is necessary to promote public safety.[9] Each month, the municipal court provides FPD supervisors with a list of the number of tickets issued by each officer and each squad. Supervisors have posted the list inside the police station, a tactic officers say is meant to push them to write more citations.

The Captain of FPD's Patrol Division regularly communicates with his Division commanders regarding the need to increase traffic "productivity," and productivity is a common topic at squad meetings. Patrol Division supervisors monitor productivity through monthly "self-initiated activity reports" and instruct officers to increase production when those reports show they have not issued enough citations. In April 2010, for example, a patrol supervisor criticized a sergeant for his squad only issuing 25 tickets in a month, including one officer who issued "a grand total" of 11 tickets to six people on three days "devoted to traffic stops." In November 2011, the same patrol supervisor wrote to his patrol lieutenants and sergeants that "[t]he monthly self-initiated activity totals just came out," and they "may want to advise [their] officers who may be interested in the open detective position that one of the categories to be considered when deciding on the eligibility list will be self-initiated activity." The supervisor continued: "Have any of you heard comments such as, why should I produce when I know I'm not getting a raise? Well, some people are about to find out why." The email concludes with the instruction to "[k]eep in mind, productivity (self-initiated activity) cannot decline for next year."

FPD has communicated to officers not only that they must focus on bringing in revenue, but that the department has little concern with how officers do this. FPD's weak systems of supervision, review, and accountability have sent a potent message to officers that their violations of law and policy will be tolerated, provided that officers continue to be "productive" in making arrests and writing citations. Where officers fail to meet productivity goals, supervisors have been instructed to alter officer assignments or impose discipline. In August 2012, the Captain of the Patrol Division instructed other patrol supervisors that, "[f]or those officers who are not keeping up an acceptable level of productivity and they have already been addressed at least once if not multiple times, take it to the next level." He continued: "As we have discussed already, regardless of the seniority and experience take the officer out of the cover car position and assign them to prisoner pick up and bank runs. . . . . Failure to perform *can* result in disciplinary action not just a bad evaluation." Performance evaluations also heavily emphasize productivity. A June 2013 evaluation indicates one of the "Performance-Related Areas of Improvements" as "Increase/consistent in productivity, the ability to maintain an average ticket [sic] of 28 per month."

Not all officers within FPD agree with this approach. Several officers commented on the futility of imposing mounting penalties on people who will never be able to afford them. One member of FPD's command staff quoted an old adage, asking: "How can you get blood from a turnip?" Another questioned why FPD did not allow residents to use their limited resources to fix equipment violations, such as broken headlights, rather than paying that money to the City, as fixing the equipment violation would more directly benefit public safety.[10]

However, enough officers—at all ranks—have internalized this message that a culture of reflexive enforcement action, unconcerned with whether the police action actually promotes public safety, and unconcerned with the impact the decision has on individual lives or community trust as a whole, has taken hold within FPD. One commander told us, for example, that when he admonished an officer for writing too many tickets, the officer challenged the commander, asking if the commander was telling him not to do his job. When another commander tried to discipline an officer for over-ticketing, he got the same

response from the Chief of Police: "No discipline for doing your job."

The City closely monitors whether FPD's enforcement efforts are bringing in revenue at the desired rate. Consistently over the last several years, the Police Chief has directly reported to City officials FPD's successful efforts at raising revenue through policing, and City officials have continued to encourage those efforts and request regular updates. For example, in June 2010, at the request of the City, the Chief prepared a report comparing court revenues in Ferguson to court revenues for cities of similar sizes. The Chief's email sending the report to the City Manager notes that, "of the 80 St. Louis County Municipal Courts reporting revenue, only 8, including Ferguson, have collections greater than one million dollars." In the February 2011 report referenced above, Chief Jackson discussed various obstacles to officers writing tickets in previous months, such as training, injury leave, and officer deployment to Iraq, but noted that those factors had subsided and that, as a result, revenues were increasing. The acting prosecutor echoed these statements, stating "we now have several new officers writing tickets, and as a result our overall ticket volume is increasing by 400–700 tickets per month. This increased volume will lead to larger dockets this year and should have a direct effect in increasing overall revenue to the municipal court."

Similarly, in March 2011, the Chief reported to the City Manager that court revenue in February was $179,862.50, and that the total "beat our next biggest month in the last four years by over $17,000," to which the City Manager responded: "Wonderful!" In a June 2011 email from Chief Jackson to the Finance Director and City Manager, the Chief reported that "May is the 6th straight month in which court revenue (gross) has exceeded the previous year." The City Manager again applauded the Chief's efforts, and the Finance Director added praise, noting that the Chief is "substantially in control of the outcome." The Finance Director further recommended in this email greater police and judicial enforcement to "have a profound effect on collections." Similarly, in a January 2013 email from Chief Jackson to the City Manager, the Chief reported: "Municipal Court gross revenue for calendar year 2012 passed the $2,000,000 mark for the first time in history, reaching $2,066,050 (not including red light photo enforcement)." The City Manager responded: "Awesome! Thanks!" In one March 2012 email, the Captain of the Patrol Division reported directly to the City Manager that court collections in February 2012 reached $235,000, and that this was the first month collections ever exceeded $200,000. The Captain noted that "[t]he [court clerk] girls have been swamped all day with a line of people paying off fines today. Since 9:30 this morning there hasn't been less than 5 people waiting in line and for the last three hours 10 to 15 people at all times." The

City Manager enthusiastically reported the Captain's email to the City Council and congratulated both police department and court staff on their "great work."

Even as officers have answered the call for greater revenue through code enforcement, the City continues to urge the police department to bring in more money. In a March 2013 email, the Finance Director wrote: "Court fees are anticipated to rise about 7.5%. I did ask the Chief if he thought the PD could deliver 10% increase. He indicated they could try." Even more recently, the City's Finance Director stated publicly that Ferguson intends to make up a 2014 revenue shortfall in 2015 through municipal code enforcement, stating to *Bloomberg News* that "[t]here's about a million-dollar increase in public-safety fines to make up the difference."[11] The City issued a statement to "refute[]" the *Bloomberg* article in part because it "insinuates" an "over reliance on municipal court fines as a primary source of revenues when in fact they represented less than 12% of city revenues for the last fiscal year." But there is no dispute that the City budget does, in fact, forecast an increase of nearly a million dollars in municipal code enforcement fines and fees in 2015 as reported in the *Bloomberg News* report.

The City goes so far as to direct FPD to develop enforcement strategies and initiatives, not to better protect the public, but to raise more revenue. In an April 2014 communication from the Finance Director to Chief Jackson and the City Manager, the Finance Director recommended immediate implementation of an "I-270 traffic enforcement initiative" in order to "begin to fill the revenue pipeline." The Finance Director's email attached a computation of the net revenues that would be generated by the initiative, which required paying five officers overtime for highway traffic enforcement for a four-hour shift. The Finance Director stated that "there is nothing to keep us from running this initiative 1, 2, 3, 4, 5, 6, or even 7 days a week. Admittedly at 7 days per week[] we would see diminishing returns." Indeed, in a separate email to FPD supervisors, the Patrol Captain explained that "[t]he plan behind this [initiative] is to PRODUCE traffic tickets, not provide easy OT." There is no indication that anyone considered whether community policing and public safety would be better served by devoting five overtime officers to neighborhood policing instead of a "revenue pipeline" of highway traffic enforcement. Rather, the only downsides to the program that City officials appear to have considered are that "this initiative requires 60 to 90 [days] of lead time to turn citations into cash," and that Missouri law caps the proportion of revenue that can come from municipal fines at 30%, which limits the extent to which the program can be used. *See* Mo. Rev. Stat. § 302.341.2. With regard to the statewide-cap issue, the Finance Director advised: "As the RLCs [Red Light Cameras] net revenues ramp up to whatever we believe its annualized rate will be, then we can figure out how to balance the two programs to get their total revenues as close as possible to the statutory limit of 30%."[12]

The City has made clear to the Police Chief and the Municipal Judge that revenue generation must also be a priority in court operations. The Finance Director's February 2011 report to the City Council notes that "Judge Brockmeyer was first appointed in 2003, and during this time has been successful in significantly increasing court collections over the years." The report includes a list of "what he has done to help in the areas of court efficiency and revenue." The list, drafted by Judge Brockmeyer, approvingly highlights the creation of additional fees, many of which are widely considered abusive and may be unlawful, including several that the City has repealed during the pendency of our investigation. These include a $50 fee charged each time a person has a pending municipal arrest warrant cleared, and a "failure to appear fine," which the Judge noted is "increased each time the Defendant fails to appear in court or pay a fine." The Judge also noted increasing fines for repeat offenders, "especially in regard to housing violations, [which] have increased substantially and will continue to be increased upon subsequent violations." The February 2011 report notes Judge Brockmeyer's statement that "none of these changes could have taken place without the cooperation of the Court Clerk, the Chief of Police, and the Prosecutor's Office." Indeed, the acting prosecutor noted in the report that "I have denied defendants' needless requests for continuance from the payment docket in an effort to aid in the court's efficient collection of its fines."

Court staff are keenly aware that the City considers revenue generation to be the municipal court's primary purpose. Revenue targets for court fines and fees are created in consultation not only with Chief Jackson, but also the Court Clerk. In one April 2010 exchange with Chief Jackson entitled "2011 Budget," for example, the Finance Director sought and received confirmation that the Police Chief and the Court Clerk would prepare targets for the court's fine and fee collections for subsequent years. Court staff take steps to ensure those targets are met in operating court. For example, in April 2011, the Court Clerk wrote to Judge Brockmeyer (copying Chief Jackson) that the fines the new Prosecuting Attorney was recommending were not high enough. The Clerk highlighted one case involving three Derelict Vehicle charges and a Failure to Comply charge that resulted in $76 in fines, and noted this "normally would have brought a fine of all three charges around $400." After describing another case that she believed warranted higher fines, the Clerk concluded: "We need to keep up our revenue." There is no indication that ability to pay or public safety goals were considered.

The City has been aware for years of concerns about the impact its focus on revenue has had on lawful police action and the fair administration of justice in Ferguson. It has disregarded those concerns—even concerns raised from within the City government—to avoid disturbing the court's ability to optimize revenue generation. In 2012, a Ferguson City Councilmember wrote to other City officials in opposition to Judge Brockmeyer's reappointment, stating that "[the Judge] does not listen to the testimony, does not review the reports or the criminal history of defendants, and doesn't let all the pertinent witnesses testify before rendering a verdict." The Councilmember then addressed the concern that "switching judges would/could lead to loss of revenue," arguing that even if such a switch did "lead to a slight loss, I think it's more important that cases are being handled properly and fairly." The City Manager acknowledged mixed reviews of the Judge's work but urged that the Judge be reappointed, noting that "[i]t goes without saying the City cannot afford to lose any efficiency in our Courts, nor experience any decrease in our Fines and Forfeitures."

Changes Necessary to Remedy Ferguson's Unlawful Law Enforcement Practices and Repair Community Trust

The problems identified within this letter reflect deeply entrenched practices and priorities that are incompatible with lawful and effective policing and that damage community trust. Addressing those problems and repairing the City's relationship with the community will require a fundamental redirection of Ferguson's approach to law enforcement, including the police and court practices that reflect and perpetuate this approach.

Below we set out broad recommendations for changes that Ferguson should make to its police and court practices to correct the constitutional violations our investigation identified. Ensuring meaningful, sustainable, and verifiable reform will require that these and other measures be part of a court-enforceable remedial process that includes involvement from community stakeholders as well as independent oversight. In the coming weeks, we will seek to work with the City of Ferguson toward developing and reaching agreement on an appropriate framework for reform.

Ferguson Police Practices
1. Implement a Robust System of True Community Policing

Many of the recommendations included below would require a shift from policing to raise revenue to policing in partnership with the entire Ferguson community. Developing these relationships will take time and considerable effort. FPD should:

a. Develop and put into action a policy and detailed plan for comprehensive implementation of community policing and problem-solving principles. Conduct outreach and involve the entire community in developing and implementing this plan;

b. Increase opportunities for officers to have frequent, positive interactions with people outside of an enforcement context, especially groups that have expressed high levels of distrust of police. Such opportunities may include police athletic leagues and similar informal activities;

c. Develop community partnerships to identify crime prevention priorities, with a focus on disconnected areas, such as Ferguson's apartment complexes, and disconnected groups, such as much of Ferguson's African-American youth;

d. Modify officer deployment patterns and scheduling (such as moving away from the current 12-hour shift and assigning officers to patrol the same geographic areas consistently) to facilitate participating in crime prevention projects and familiarity with areas and people;

e. Train officers on crime-prevention, officer safety, and anti-discrimination advantages of community policing. Train officers on mechanics of community policing and their role in implementing it;

f. Measure and evaluate individual, supervisory, and agency police performance on community engagement, problem-oriented-policing projects, and crime prevention, rather than on arrest and citation productivity.

2. Focus Stop, Search, Ticketing and Arrest Practices on Community Protection

FPD must fundamentally change the way it conducts stops and searches, issues citations and summonses, and makes arrests. FPD officers must be trained and required to abide by the law. In addition, FPD enforcement efforts should be reoriented so that officers are required to take enforcement action because it promotes public safety, not simply because they have legal authority to act. To do this, FPD should:

a. Prohibit the use of ticketing and arrest quotas, whether formal or informal;

b. Require that officers report in writing all stops, searches and arrests, including pedestrian stops, and that their reports articulate the legal authority for the law enforcement action and sufficient description of facts to support that authority;

c. Require documented supervisory approval prior to:

1. Issuing any citation/summons that includes more than two charges;

2. Making an arrest on any of the following charges:

   i. Failure to Comply/Obey;
   ii. Resisting Arrest;
   iii. Disorderly Conduct/Disturbing the Peace;
   iv. Obstruction of Government Operations;

3. Arresting or ticketing an individual who sought police aid, or who is cooperating with police in an investigation;

4. Arresting on a municipal warrant or wanted;

d. Revise Failure to Comply municipal code provision to bring within constitutional limits, and provide sufficient guidance so that all stops, citations, and arrests based on the provision comply with the Constitution;

e. Train officers on proper use of Failure to Comply charge, including elements of the offense and appropriateness of the charge for interference with police activity that threatens public safety;

f. Require that applicable legal standards are met before officers conduct pat-downs or vehicle searches. Prohibit searches based on consent for the foreseeable future;

g. Develop system of correctable violation, or "fix-it" tickets, and require officers to issue fix-it tickets wherever possible and absent contrary supervisory instruction;

h. Develop and implement policy and training regarding appropriate police response to activities protected by the First Amendment, including the right to observe, record, and protest police action;

i. Provide initial and regularly recurring training on Fourth Amendment constraints on police action, as well as responsibility within FPD to constrain action beyond what Fourth Amendment requires in interest of public safety and community trust;

j. Discontinue use of "wanteds" or "stop orders" and prohibit officers from conducting stops, searches, or arrests on the basis of "wanteds" or "stop orders" issued by other agencies.

3. Increase Tracking, Review, and Analysis of FPD Stop, Search, Ticketing and Arrest Practices

At the first level of supervision and as an agency, FPD must review more stringently officers' stop, search, ticketing, and arrest practices to ensure that officers are complying with the Constitution and department policy, and to evaluate the impact of officer activity on police legitimacy and community trust. FPD should:

a. Develop and implement a plan for broader collection of stop, search, ticketing, and arrest data that includes pedestrian stops, enhances vehicle stop data collection, and requires collection of data on all stop and post-stop activity, as well as location and demographic information;

b. Require supervisors to review all officer activity and review all officer reports before the supervisor leaves shift;

c. Develop and implement system for regular review of stop, search, ticketing, and arrest data at supervisory and agency level to detect problematic trends and ensure consistency with public safety and community policing goals;

d. Analyze race and other disparities shown in stop, search, ticketing, and arrest practices to determine whether disparities can be reduced consistent with public safety goals.

4. Change Force Use, Reporting, Review, and Response to Encourage De-Escalation and the Use of the Minimal Force Necessary in a Situation

FPD should reorient officers' approach to using force by ensuring that they are trained and skilled in using tools and tactics to de-escalate situations, and incentivized to avoid using force wherever possible. FPD also should implement a system of force review that ensures that improper force is detected and responded to effectively, and that policy, training, tactics, and officer safety concerns are identified. FPD should:

a. Train and require officers to use de-escalation techniques wherever possible both to avoid a situation escalating to where force becomes necessary, and to avoid unnecessary force even where it would be legally justified. Training should include tactics for slowing down a situation to increase available options;

b. Require onsite supervisory approval before deploying any canine, absent documented exigent circumstances; require and train canine officers to take into account the nature and severity of the alleged crime when deciding whether to deploy a canine to bite; require and train canine officers to avoid sending a canine to apprehend by biting a concealed suspect when the objective facts do not suggest the suspect is armed and a lower level of force reasonably can be expected to secure the suspect;

c. Place more stringent limits on use of ECWs, including limitations on multiple ECW cycles and detailed justification for using more than one cycle;

d. Retrain officers in use of ECWs to ensure they view and use ECWs as a tool of necessity, not convenience. Training should be consistent with principles set out in the *2011 ECW Guidelines;*

e. Develop and implement use-of-force reporting that requires the officer using force to complete a narrative, separate from the offense report, describing the force used with particularity, and describing with specificity the circumstances that required the level of force used, including the reason for the initial stop or other enforcement action. Some levels of force should require all officers observing the use of force to complete a separate force narrative;

f. Develop and implement supervisory review of force that requires the supervisor to conduct a complete review of each use of force, including gathering and considering evidence necessary to understand the circumstances of the force incident and determine its consistency with law and policy, including statements from individuals against whom force is used and civilian witnesses;

g. Prohibit supervisors from reviewing or investigating a use of force in which they participated or directed;

h. Ensure that complete use-of-force reporting and review/investigation files—including all offense reports, witness statements, and medical, audio/video, and other evidence—are kept together in a centralized location;

i. Develop and implement a system for higher-level, inter-disciplinary review of some types of force, such as lethal force, canine deployment, ECWs, and force resulting in any injury;

j. Improve collection, review, and response to use-of-force data, including information regarding ECW and canine use;

k. Implement system of zero tolerance for use of force as punishment or retaliation rather than as necessary, proportionate response to counter a threat;

l. Discipline officers who fail to report force and supervisors who fail to conduct adequate force investigations;

m. Identify race and other disparities in officer use of force and develop strategies to eliminate avoidable disparities;

n. Staff jail with at least two correctional officers at all times to ensure safety and minimize need for use of force in dealing with intoxicated or combative prisoners. Train correctional officers in de-escalation techniques with specific instruction and training on minimizing force when dealing with intoxicated and combative prisoners, as well as with passive resistance and noncompliance.

5. Implement Policies and Training to Improve Interactions with Vulnerable People

Providing officers with the tools and training to better respond to persons in physical or mental health crisis, and to those with intellectual disabilities, will help avoid unnecessary injuries, increase community trust, and make officers safer. FPD should:

a. Develop and implement policy and training for identifying and responding to individuals with known or suspected mental health conditions, including those observably in mental health crisis, and those with intellectual or other disabilities;

b. Provide enhanced crisis intervention training to a subset of officers to allow for ready availability of trained officers on the scenes of critical incidents involving individuals with mental illness;

c. Require that, wherever possible, at least one officer with enhanced crisis intervention training respond to any situation concerning individuals in mental health crisis or with intellectual disability, when force might be used;

d. Provide training to officers regarding how to identify and respond to more commonly occurring medical emergencies that may at first appear to reflect a failure to comply with lawful orders. Such medical emergencies may include, for example, seizures and diabetic emergencies.

6. Change Response to Students to Avoid Criminalizing Youth While Maintaining a Learning Environment

FPD has the opportunity to profoundly impact students through its SRO program. This program can be used as a way to build positive relationships with youth from a young age and to support strategies to keep students in school and learning. FPD should:

a. Work with school administrators, teachers, parents, and students to develop and implement policy and training consistent with law and best practices to more effectively address disciplinary issues in schools. This approach should be focused on SROs developing positive relationships with youth in support of maintaining a learning environment without unnecessarily treating disciplinary issues as criminal matters or resulting in the routine imposition of lengthy suspensions;

b. Provide initial and regularly recurring training to SROs, including training in mental health, counseling, and the development of the teenage brain;

c. Evaluate SRO performance on student engagement and prevention of disturbances, rather than on student arrests or removals;

d. Regularly review and evaluate incidents in which SROs are involved to ensure they meet the particular goals of the SRO program; to identify any disparate impact or treatment by race or other protected basis; and to identify any policy, training, or equipment concerns.

7. Implement Measures to Reduce Bias and Its Impact on Police Behavior

Many of the recommendations listed elsewhere have the potential to reduce the level and impact of bias on police behavior (e.g., increasing positive interactions between police and the community; increasing the collection and analysis of stop data; and increasing oversight of the exercise of police discretion). Below are additional measures that can assist in this effort. FPD should:

a. Provide initial and recurring training to all officers that sends a clear, consistent and emphatic message that bias-based profiling and other forms of discriminatory policing are prohibited. Training should include:
   1) Relevant legal and ethical standards;
   2) Information on how stereotypes and implicit bias can infect police work;
   3) The importance of procedural justice and police legitimacy on community trust, police effectiveness, and officer safety;
   4) The negative impacts of profiling on public safety and crime prevention;

b. Provide training to supervisors and commanders on detecting and responding to bias-based profiling and other forms of discriminatory policing;

c. Include community members from groups that have expressed high levels of distrust of police in officer training;

d. Take steps to eliminate all forms of workplace bias from FPD and the City.

8. Improve and Increase Training Generally

FPD officers receive far too little training as recruits and after becoming officers. Officers need a better knowledge of what law, policy, and integrity require, and concrete training on how to carry out their police responsibilities. In addition to the training specified elsewhere in these recommendations, FPD should:

a. Significantly increase the quality and amount of all types of officer training, including recruit, field training (including for officers hired from other agencies), and in-service training;

b. Require that training cover, in depth, constitutional and other legal restrictions on officer action, as well as additional factors officers should consider before taking enforcement action (such as police legitimacy and procedural justice considerations);

c. Employ scenario-based and adult-learning methods.

9. Increase Civilian Involvement in Police Decision Making

In addition to engaging with all segments of Ferguson as part of implementing community policing, FPD should develop and implement a system that incorporates civilian input into all aspects of policing, including policy development, training, use-of-force review, and investigation of misconduct complaints.

10. Improve Officer Supervision

The recommendations set out here cannot be implemented without dedicated, skilled, and well-trained supervisors who police lawfully and without bias. FPD should:

a. Provide all supervisors with specific supervisory training prior to assigning them to supervisory positions;

b. Develop and require supervisors to use an "early intervention system" to objectively detect problematic patterns of officer misconduct, assist officers who need additional attention, and identify training and equipment needs;

c. Support supervisors who encourage and guide respectful policing and implement community policing principles, and evaluate them on this basis. Remove supervisors who do not adequately review officer activity and reports or fail to support, through words or actions, unbiased policing;

d. Ensure that an adequate number of qualified first-line supervisors are deployed in the field to allow supervisors to provide close and effective supervision to each officer under the supervisor's direct command, provide officers with the direction and guidance necessary to improve and develop as officers, and to identify, correct, and prevent misconduct.

11. Recruiting, Hiring, and Promotion

There are widespread concerns about the lack of diversity, especially race and gender diversity, among FPD officers.

FPD should modify its systems for recruiting hiring and promotion to:

a. Ensure that the department's officer hiring and selection processes include an objective process for selection that employs reliable and valid selection devices that comport with best practices and federal anti-discrimination laws;

b. In the case of lateral hires, scrutinize prior training and qualification records as well as complaint and disciplinary history;

c. Implement validated pre-employment screening mechanisms to ensure temperamental and skill-set suitability for policing.

12. Develop Mechanisms to More Effectively Respond to Allegations of Officer Misconduct

Responding to allegations of officer misconduct is critical not only to correct officer behavior and identify policy, training, or tactical concerns, but also to build community confidence and police legitimacy. FPD should:

a. Modify procedures and practices for accepting complaints to make it easier and less intimidating for individuals to register formal complaints about police conduct, including providing complaint forms online and in various locations throughout the City and allowing for complaints to be submitted online and by third parties or anonymously;

b. Require that all complaints be logged and investigated;

c. Develop and implement a consistent, reliable, and fair process for investigating and responding to complaints of officer misconduct. As part of this process, FPD should:

 1) Investigate all misconduct complaints, even where the complainant indicates he or she does not want the complaint investigated, or wishes to remain anonymous;

 2) Not withdraw complaints without reaching a disposition;

d. Develop and implement a fair and consistent system for disciplining officers found to have committed misconduct;

e. Terminate officers found to have been materially untruthful in performance of their duties, including in completing reports or during internal affairs investigations;

f. Timely provide in writing to the Ferguson Prosecuting Attorney all impeachment information on officers who may testify or provide sworn reports, including findings of untruthfulness in internal affairs investigations, for disclosure to the defendant under *Brady v. Maryland,* 373 U.S. 83 (1963);

g. Document in a central location all misconduct complaints and investigations, including the nature of the complaint, the name of the officer, and the disposition of the investigation;

h. Maintain complete misconduct complaint investigative files in a central location;

i. Develop and implement a community-centered mediation program to resolve, as appropriate, allegations of officer misconduct.

13. Publically Share Information about the Nature and Impact of Police Activities

Transparency is a key component of good governance and community trust. Providing broad information to the public also facilitates constructive community engagement. FPD should:

a. Provide regular and specific public reports on police stop, search, arrest, ticketing, force, and community engagement activities, including particular problems and achievements, and describing the steps taken to address concerns;

b. Provide regular public reports on allegations of misconduct, including the nature of the complaint and its resolution;

c. Make available online and regularly update a complete set of police policies.

Ferguson Court Practices
1. Make Municipal Court Processes More Transparent

Restoring the legitimacy of the municipal justice system requires increased transparency regarding court operations to allow the public to assess whether the court is operating in a fair manner. The municipal court should:

a. Make public—through a variety of means, including prominent display on the City, police, and municipal court web pages—all court-related fines, fees, and bond amounts, and a description of the municipal court payment process, including court dates, payment options, and potential consequences for non-payment or missed court dates;

b. Create, adopt, and make public written procedures for all court operations;

c. Collect all orders currently in effect and make those orders accessible to the public, including by posting any such materials on the City, police, and municipal court web pages. Make public all new court orders and directives as they are issued;

d. Initiate a public education campaign to ensure individuals can have an accurate and complete understanding of how Ferguson's municipal court operates, including that appearance in court without ability to pay an owed fine will not result in arrest;

e. Provide broadly available information to individuals regarding low-cost or cost-free legal assistance;

f. Enhance public reporting by ensuring data provided to the Missouri Courts Administrator is accurate, and by making that and additional data available on City and court websites, including monthly reports indicating:

1) The number of warrants issued and currently outstanding;

2) The number of cases heard during the previous month;

3) The amount of fines imposed and collected, broken down by offense, including by race;

4) Data regarding the number of Missouri Department of Revenue license suspensions initiated by the court and the number of compliance letters enabling license reinstatement issued by the court.

g. Revise the municipal court website to enable these recommendations to be fully implemented.

2. Provide Complete and Accurate Information to a Person Charged with a Municipal Violation

In addition to making its processes more transparent to the public, the court should ensure that those with cases pending before the court are provided with adequate and reliable information about their case. The municipal court, in collaboration with the Patrol Division, should:

a. Ensure all FPD citations, summonses, and arrests are accompanied by sufficient, detailed information about the recipient's rights and responsibilities, including:

1) The specific municipal violation charged;

2) A person's options for addressing the charge, including whether in-person appearance is required or if alternative methods, including online payment, are available, and information regarding all pending deadlines;

3) A person's right to challenge the charge in court;

4) The exact date and time of the court session at which the person receiving the charge must or may appear;

5) Information about how to seek a continuance for a court date;

6) The specific fine imposed, if the offense has a preset fine;

7) The processes available to seek a fine reduction for financial incapacity, consistent with recommendation four set forth below;

8) The penalties for failing to meet court requirements.

b. Develop and implement a secure online system for individuals to be able to access specific details about their case, including fines owed, payments made, and pending requirements and deadlines.

3. Change Court Procedures for Tracking and Resolving Municipal Charges to Simplify Court Processes and Expand Available Payment Options

The municipal court should:

a. Strictly limit those offenses requiring in-person court appearance for resolution to those for which state law requires the defendant to make an initial appearance in court;

b. Establish a process by which a person may seek a continuance of a court date, whether or not represented by counsel;

c. Continue to implement its online payment system, and expand it to allow late payments, payment plan installments, bond payments, and other court payments to be made online;

d. Continue to develop and transition to an electronic records management system for court records to ensure all case information and events are tracked and accessible to court officials and FPD staff, as appropriate. Ensure electronic records management system has appropriate controls to limit user access and ability to alter case records;

e. Ensure that the municipal court office is consistently staffed during posted business hours to allow those appearing at the court window of the police department seeking to resolve municipal charges to do so;

f. Accept partial payments from individuals, and provide clear information to individuals about payment plan options.

4. Review Preset Fine Amounts and Implement System for Fine Reduction

The municipal court should:

a. Immediately undertake a review of current fine amounts and ensure that they are consistent not only with regional but also statewide fine averages, are not overly punitive, and take into account the income of Ferguson residents;

b. Develop and implement a process by which individuals can appear in court to seek proportioning of preset fines to their financial ability to pay.

5. Develop Effective Ability-to-Pay Assessment System and Improve Data Collection Regarding Imposed Fines

The municipal court should:

a. Develop and implement consistent written criteria for conducting an assessment of an individual's ability to pay prior to the assessment of any fine, and upon any increase in the fine or related court costs and fees. The ability-to-pay assessment should include not only a consideration of the financial resources of an individual, but also a consideration of any documented fines owed to other municipal courts;

b. Improve current procedures for collecting and tracking data regarding fine amounts imposed. Track initial fines imposed as an independent figure separate from any additional charges imposed during a case;

c. Regularly conduct internal reviews of data regarding fine assessments. This review should include an analysis of fines imposed for the same offenses, including by race of the defendant, to ensure fine assessments for like offenses are set appropriately.

6. Revise Payment Plan Procedures and Provide Alternatives to Fine Payments for Resolving Municipal Charges

The municipal court should:

a. Develop and implement a specific process by which a person can enroll in a payment plan that requires reasonable periodic payments. That process should include an assessment of a person's ability to pay to determine an appropriate periodic payment amount, although a required payment shall not exceed $100. That process should also include a means for a person to seek a reduction in their monthly payment obligation in the event of a change in their financial circumstances;

b. Provide more opportunities for a person to seek leave to pay a lower amount in a given month beyond the court's current practice of requiring appearance the first Wednesday of the month at 11:00 a.m. Adopt procedures allowing individuals to seek their first request for a one-time reduction outside of court, and to have such requests be automatically granted. Such procedures should provide that subsequent requests shall be granted liberally by the Municipal Judge, and denials of requests for extensions or reduced monthly payments shall be accompanied by a written explanation of why the request was denied;

c. Cease practice of automatically issuing a warrant when a person on a payment plan misses a payment, and adopt procedures that provide for appropriate warnings following a missed payment, consistent with recommendation eight set forth below;

d. Work with community organizations and other regional groups to develop alternative penalty options besides fines, including expanding community service options. Make all individuals eligible for community service.

7. Reform Trial Procedures to Ensure Full Compliance with Due Process Requirements

The municipal court should take all necessary steps to ensure that the court's trial procedures fully comport with due process such that defendants are provided with a fair and impartial forum to challenge the charges brought against them. As part of this effort, the court shall ensure that defendants taking their case to trial are provided with all evidence relevant to guilt determinations consistent with the requirements of *Brady v. Maryland,* 373 U.S. 83 (1963), and other applicable law.

8. Stop Using Arrest Warrants as a Means of Collecting Owed Fines and Fees

As Ferguson's own Municipal Judge has recognized, municipal code violations should result in jail in only the rarest of circumstances. To begin to address these problems, Ferguson should only jail individuals for a failure to appear on or pay a municipal code violation penalty, if at all, if the following steps have been attempted in a particular case and have failed:

a. Enforcement of fines through alternative means, including:

   1) Assessment of reasonable late fees;

   2) Expanding options for payment through community service;

   3) Modified payment plans with reasonable amounts due and payment procedures;

4) A show cause hearing on why a warrant should not issue, including an assessment of ability to pay, where requested. At this hearing the individual has a right to counsel and, if the individual is indigent, the court will assign counsel to represent the individual. *See* Mo. Sup. Ct. R. 37.65; Mo. Mun. Benchbook, Cir. Ct., Mun. Divs. § 13.8;

b. Personal service on the individual of the Order to Show Cause Motion that provides notice of the above information regarding right to counsel and the consequences of non-appearance; and

c. If the above mechanisms are unsuccessful at securing payment or otherwise resolving the case, the court should ensure that any arrest warrant issued has the instruction that it be executed only on days that the court is in session so that the individual can be brought immediately before the court to enable the above procedures to be implemented. *See* Mo. Mun. Benchbook, Cir. Ct., Mun. Divs. § 13.8 ("If a defendant fails to appear in court on the return date of the order to show cause or motion for contempt, *a warrant should be issued to get the defendant before the court for the hearing.*") (emphasis added).

9. Allow Warrants to be Recalled Without the Payment of Bond

Ferguson recently extended its warrant recall program, also called an "amnesty" program, which allows individuals to have municipal warrants recalled and to receive a new court date without paying a bond. This program should be made permanent. The municipal court should:

a. Allow all individuals to seek warrant recall in writing or via telephone, whether represented by an attorney or not;

b. Provide information to a participating individual at the time of the warrant recall, including the number of charges pending, the fine amount due if a charge has been assessed, the options available to pay assessed fines, the deadlines for doing so, and the requirements, if any, for appearing in court.

10. Modify Bond Amounts and Bond and Detention Procedures

Ferguson has two separate municipal code bond schedules and processes: one for warrantless arrests, and another for arrests pursuant to warrants issued by the municipal court. Ferguson's municipal court recently limited the number of municipal code violations for which officers can jail an individual without a warrant, and reduced the amount of time the jail may hold a

defendant who is unable to post bond from 72 to 12 hours. These changes are a positive start, but further reforms are necessary. The City and municipal court should:

a. Limit the amount of time the jail may hold a defendant unable to post bond on *all* arrests for municipal code violations or municipal arrest warrants to 12 hours;

b. Establish procedures for setting bond amounts for warrantless and warrant-based detainees that are consistent with the Equal Protection Clause's prohibition on incarcerating individuals on the basis of indigency, and that ensure bond shall in no case exceed $100 for a person arrested pursuant to a municipal warrant, regardless of the number of pending charges;

c. At the time of bond payment, provide individuals with the option of applying a bond fee to underlying fines and costs, including in the event of forfeiture;

d. Take steps necessary, including the continued development of a computerized court records management system as discussed above, to enable court staff, FPD officers, and FPD correctional officers to access case information so that a person has the option of paying the full underlying fine owed in lieu of bond upon being arrested;

e. Increase options for making a bond payment, including allowing bond payment by credit card and through the online payment system, whether by a person in jail or outside of the jail;

f. Institute closer oversight and tracking of bond payment acceptance by FPD officers and FPD correctional officers;

g. Initiate practice of issuing bond refund checks immediately upon a defendant paying their fine in full and being owed a bond refund;

h. Ensure that all court staff, FPD officers, and FPD correctional officers understand Ferguson's bond rules and procedures.

11. Consistently Provide "Compliance Letters" Necessary for Driver's License Reinstatement After a Person Makes an Appearance Following a License Suspension

Per official policy, the municipal court provides people who have had their licenses suspended pursuant to Mo. Rev. Stat. § 302.341.1 with compliance letters enabling the suspension to be lifted only once the underlying fine has been paid in full. Court staff told us, however, that in "sympathetic cases," they provide compliance letters that enable people to have their licenses reinstated. The court should adopt and implement a policy of providing individuals with compliance letters immediately upon a person appearing in court following a license suspension pursuant to this statute.

12. Close Cases that Remainon the Court's Docket Solely Because of Failure to Appear Charges or Bond Forfeitures

In September 2014, the City of Ferguson repealed Ferguson Mun. Code § 13-58, which allowed the imposition of an additional "Failure to Appear" charge, fines, and fees in response to missed appearances and payments. Nonetheless, many cases remain pending on the court's docket solely on account of charges, fines, and fees issued pursuant to this statute or because of questionable bond forfeiture practices. The City and municipal court should:

a. Close all municipal cases in which the individual has paid fines equal or greater to the amount of the fine assessed for the original municipal code violation—through Failure to Appear fines and fees or forfeited bond payments—and clear all associated warrants;

b. Remove all Failure to Appear related charges, fines, and fees from current cases, and close all cases in which only a Failure to Appear charge, fine, or fee remains pending;

c. Immediately provide compliance letters so that license suspensions are lifted for all individuals whose cases are closed pursuant to these reforms.

13. Collaborate with Other Municipalities and the State of Missouri to Implement Reforms

These recommendations should be closely evaluated and, as appropriate, implemented by other municipalities. We also recommend that the City and other municipalities work collaboratively with the state of Missouri on issues requiring statewide action, and further recommend:

a. Reform of Mo. Rev. Stat. § 302.341.1, which requires the suspension of individuals' driving licenses in certain cases where they do not appear or timely pay traffic charges involving moving violations;

b. Increased oversight of municipal courts in St. Louis County and throughout the state of Missouri to ensure that courts operate in a manner consistent with due process, equal protection, and other requirements of the Constitution and other laws.

Conclusion

Our investigation indicates that Ferguson as a City has the capacity to reform its approach to law enforcement. A small municipal department may offer greater potential for officers to form partnerships and have frequent, positive interactions with Ferguson residents, repairing and maintaining police-community relationships. *See, e.g.,* Jim Burack, *Putting the "Local" Back in Local Law Enforcement,* in *American Policing in 2022: Essays on the Future of the Profession* 79-83 (Debra R. Cohen McCullough & Deborah L. Spence, eds., 2012). These reform efforts will be well worth the considerable time and dedication they will require, as they have the potential to make Ferguson safer and more united.

Notes

1. *See 2012 Census of Governments,* U.S. Census Bureau (Sept. 2013), *available at* http://factfinder.census.gov/bkmk/table/1.0/en/COG/2012/ORG13.ST05P?slice=GEO~0400000US29 (last visited Feb. 26, 2015).

2. *See 2010 Census,* U.S. Census Bureau (2010), *available at* http://factfinder.census.gov/bkmk/table/1.0/en/DEC/10_SF1/QTP3/1600000US2923986 (last visited Feb. 26, 2015).

3. *See 1990 Census of Population General Population Characteristics Missouri,* U.S. Census Bureau (Apr. 1992), *available at* ftp://ftp2.census.gov/library/publications/1992/dec/cp-1-27.pdf (last visited Feb. 26, 2015).

4. *See Race Alone or in Combination: 2000,* U.S. Census Bureau (2000), *available at* http://factfinder.census.gov/bkmk/table/1.0/en/DEC/00_SF1/QTP5/1600000US2923986 (last visited Feb. 26, 2015).

5. *2010 Census, supra* note 2.

6. *See Poverty Status in the Past 12 Months 2009–2013 American Community Survey 5-Year Estimates,* U.S. Census Bureau (2014), *available at* http://factfinder.census.gov/bkmk/table/1.0/en/ACS/13_5YR/S1701/1600000US2923986 (last visited Feb. 26, 2015).

7. This is evidenced not only by FPD's own records, but also by Uniform Crime Reports data for Ferguson, which show a downward trend in serious crime over the last ten years. *See Uniform Crime Reports,* Federal Bureau of Investigation, http://www.fbi.gov/about-us/cjis/ucr/crime-in-the-u.s (last visited Feb. 26, 2015).

8. Each of these yearly totals excludes certain court fees that are designated for particular purposes, but that nonetheless are paid directly to the City. For example, $2 of the court fee that accompanies every citation for a municipal code violation is set aside to be used for police training. That fee is used only by the City of Ferguson and is deposited in the City's general fund; nonetheless, the City's budget does not include that fee in its totals for "municipal court" revenue. In 2012 and 2013, the police training fee brought in, respectively, another $24,724 and $22,938 in revenue.

9. FPD's financial focus has also led FPD to elevate municipal enforcement over state-law enforcement. Even where individuals commit violations of state law, if there is an

analogous municipal code provision, the police department will nearly always charge the offense under municipal law. A senior member of FPD's command told us that all Ferguson police officers understand that, when a fine is the likely punishment, municipal rather than state charges should be pursued so that Ferguson will reap the financial benefit.

10. After a recommendation we made during this investigation, Ferguson has recently begun a very limited "correctable violation" or "fix-it" ticket program, under which charges for certain violations can be dismissed if corrected within a certain period of time.

11. Katherine Smith, *Ferguson to Increase Police Ticketing to Close City's Budget Gap,* Bloomberg News (Dec. 12, 2014), http://www.bloomberg.com/news/articles/2014-12-12/ferguson-to-increase-police-ticketing-to-close-city-s- budget-gap.

12. Ferguson officials have asserted that in the last fiscal year revenue from the municipal court comprised only 12% of City revenue, but they have not made clear how they calculated this figure. It appears that 12% is the proportion of Ferguson's *total* revenue (forecasted to amount to $18.62 million in 2014) derived from fines and fees (forecasted to be $2.09 million in 2014). Guidelines issued by the Missouri State Auditor in December 2014 provide, however, that the 30% cap outlined in Mo. Rev. Stat. § 302.341.2 imposes a limit on the makeup of fines and fees in *general* use revenue, excluding any revenue designated for a particular purpose. Notably, the current 30%

state cap only applies to fines and fees derived from "traffic violations." It thus appears that, for purposes of the state cap, Ferguson must ensure that its traffic-related fines and fees do not exceed 30% of its "General Fund" revenue. In 2014, Ferguson's General Fund revenue was forecasted to be $12.33 million.

Critical Thinking

1. What are the central findings of the Department of Justice regarding policing in Ferguson?

2. What are there commendations for reform?

3. Are these findings and recommendations technical matters or do they also address deeper questions of government structure, community relations, the democratic resolution of values, and the distribution of benefits and burdens of public resources and talent?

Internet References

Discover Policing
   http://discoverpolicing.org/
National Criminal Justice Reference Service
   www.ncjrs.gov
Urban Institute
   www.urban.org

United States Department of Justice Civil Rights Division. "Investigation of the Ferguson Police Department", *United States Department of Justice Civil Rights Division,* March 2015.

Article   Prepared by: John A. Kromkowski, *The Catholic University of America*

50 Years of the Voting Rights Act

The State of Race in Politics

KHALILAH BROWN-DEAN ET AL.

Learning Outcomes

After reading this article, you will be able to:

- Explain the origin and evolution of the Voting Rights Act of 1965.

- Describe minority voter registration and turnout, polarized voting, outcomes by race, and why such information is essential to understanding democracy in America.

President's Message

This year marks the 50th anniversary of the historic "Bloody Sunday" on March 7, 1965, in Selma, Alabama, and the enactment of the Voting Rights Act on August 6, 1965.

As black voters were added to the election rolls, their ballots changed the composition of many legislatures, commissions, and councils. The Joint Center was founded five years after the Voting Rights Act of 1965 to support those newly elected officials of color.

How much progress have we made since 1965? How much more work is there to do?

These are contested questions, subject to ideology and opinion. A study published in *Perspectives on Psychological Science,* for example, shows that on average whites and African Americans differ on the amount of racial progress we have made, with whites now believing anti-white bias is more prevalent than anti-black bias. We have elected an African American president, but studies have shown that some government officials are less likely to respond to inquiries from citizens with seemingly black or Latino names. The questions are also at the core of many ongoing debates about voting rights in the U.S. Supreme Court and Congress, as well as in many states, counties, and municipalities.

Four prominent political scientists—Professors Khalilah Brown-Dean, Zoltan Hajnal, Christina Rivers, and Ismail White—provide empirical data that offer important answers in this report. I hope you enjoy it.

Regards,

Spencer Overton

President & CEO of the Joint Center for Political and Economic Studies

Executive Summary

This report examines minority voter registration and turnout, racially polarized voting, policy outcomes by race, and the number and share of minority elected officials from the enactment of the Voting Rights Act of 1965 until today. This information is essential in thinking about the future of race, politics, and voting rights.

Key findings in this study show:

- **Since 1965, the black/white racial gap in voter turnout has decreased dramatically in presidential elections.** Turnout among black Southerners exceeded that of their white counterparts in four of the twelve presidential elections since 1965, and nationwide black turnout clearly exceeded white turnout in presidential elections in 2012 and perhaps in 2008.

- **Local election turnout is lower and possibly less diverse.** Presidential general election turnout is generally 60% of the voting-age population, but local election turnout averages 27% and in some cases is less than 10%. As overall turnout declines in local elections, the electorate may become less representative of the racial diversity of the community as a whole.

- **Latino and Asian American turnout increased but remains low.** Turnout rates among both Asian Americans and Hispanic Americans in presidential elections remain 10 to 15 percentage points below black Americans and 15 to 20 points below white Americans.
- **Party politics is increasingly polarized by race.** Since 1960, the party identification and partisan voting patterns of blacks and whites have become sharply divided.
- **Race is the most significant factor in urban local elections.** In urban local elections, race is a more decisive factor than income, education, political ideology, religion, sexual orientation, age, gender, and political ideology. The 38 point racial gap exceeds even the 33 point gap between Democratic and Republican voters.
- **Based on available data from 1972 to 2010, blacks were the least advantaged group in America in terms of policy outcomes.** Blacks were policy winners only 31.9% of the time, compared with 37.6% for whites. This difference seems small, but it is ten times larger than the 0.5 point difference between high- and low-income earners.
- **Since 1965, the number of elected officials of color has grown enormously.** Over this period, African Americans went from holding fewer than 1,000 elected offices nationwide to over 10,000, Latinos from a small number of offices to over 6,000, and Asian Americans from under a hundred documented cases to almost 1,000.
- **People of color remain underrepresented in elected office.** Based on the most recent data, African Americans are 12.5% of the citizen voting age population, but they make up a smaller share of the U.S. House (10%), state legislatures (8.5%), city councils (5.7%), and the U.S. Senate (2%). Latinos make up 11% of the citizen voting age population, but they are a smaller share of the U.S. House (7%), state legislatures (5%), the U.S. Senate (4%), and city councils (3.3%). Asian Americans are 3.8% of the citizen voting age population but a smaller share of the U.S. House (2%), state legislatures (2%), the U.S. Senate (1%), and city councils (0.4%).

Introduction: The Origins and Evolution of the Voting Rights Act

In 1965, over half the population of Dallas County, Alabama, was African American, but only 156 of the county's 15,000 voting-eligible African Americans were registered. In contrast, two-thirds of the county's white population was registered. White politicians held all elected positions and maintained their

power by requiring that applicants for registration pass an oral exam about the U.S. Constitution and possess "good character."

Four years earlier, Justice Department lawyers had filed a lawsuit against the Dallas County registrars, and after thirteen months of procedural wrangling, the case came to trial. By that time, the county registrars had resigned and the trial judge refused to ban tests because the newly hired county registrars had not yet discriminated against blacks. After an appeal, federal courts finally ordered county registrars to stop requiring voters to interpret the *federal* constitution. The county registrars then added a new test that required voters to demonstrate an "understanding" of the *state* constitution. After additional legal filings by the Justice Department, federal courts finally banned the new test. Yet during the four years the lawsuit was working its way through the courts, only 383 of the 15,000 eligible black citizens registered.

Dallas County was not alone. Throughout Alabama, only 19.4% of African Americans were registered, and in Mississippi only 6.4% of African Americans were registered. Since the 1870s, white elected officials in many parts of the South had used violence, literacy tests, interpretation tests, poll taxes, and other devices to exclude African Americans. The Justice Department filed 71 voting rights lawsuits in the Deep South before 1965, but cases were typically complex, time-consuming, and expensive. When a court struck down one type of discriminatory device, local officials simply erected a different device that effectively excluded most African Americans.

In early 1965, the registration rate for African Americans was less than 20% in Alabama and less than 7% in Mississippi.

On March 7, 1965, state troopers attacked a group of peaceful demonstrators on the Edmund Pettus Bridge in Selma, Alabama (the seat of Dallas County government). Television networks broadcast images of the attack around the world, attracting widespread attention and demonstrations in support of the voting rights cause. These events—as well as the deaths of activists Jimmy Lee Jackson, Viola Liuzzo, and James Reeb in Selma—produced sufficient public pressure for Congress to pass the Voting Rights Act, which President Lyndon Johnson signed into law on August 6, 1965.

The Act suspended literacy and interpretation tests, and it allowed federal officials to register voters and monitor local elections in particular jurisdictions. The Act also had a nationwide, permanent provision that allowed private parties or the Justice Department to bring lawsuits to stop racially discriminatory election laws and electoral plans.

Further, the "preclearance" provision of the new Act required that jurisdictions with a history of discrimination submit new election rules or plans to federal officials. State and local officials could implement a proposed election rule or plan only after federal officials approved it. By shifting the burden to states and localities to prove to federal officials that changes were not discriminatory, the preclearance process avoided the delays and expenses of litigation, and it stopped discriminatory laws before they were used in elections. The preclearance provision applied to jurisdictions that had tests or devices and low turnout or registration in the 1964 presidential election (all or parts of 11 states), and it was originally scheduled to expire in five years.

Congress extended the preclearance provision and updated the Act in other ways in 1970, 1975, 1982, and 2006. In 1970, new states were added to the coverage formula, and the ban on tests and devices was expanded nationwide. During the 1975 renewal, Congress made the ban on tests and devices permanent. Congress also expanded preclearance to cover jurisdictions with large numbers of language minority groups (e.g., speakers of Spanish, Asian, American Indian/Native Alaskan languages) that had English-only voting materials and low registration or turnout. Further, the 1975 renewal required language assistance (e.g., bilingual ballots, registration forms) in jurisdictions with large numbers of language minority groups with limited proficiency in English. In 1982, Congress amended the Act to clarify that discriminatory *purpose* was not required to bring a lawsuit to invalidate election procedures that *result* in discrimination.

The Voting Rights Act's preclearance process avoided the delays and expenses of litigation, and it stopped discriminatory election rules before they were used.

In 2013, the U.S. Supreme Court struck down the coverage formula that determined which jurisdictions must preclear new election rules and plans, which effectively rolled back preclearance. Writing for five members of the Court (four justices dissented), Chief Justice John Roberts indicated that the coverage formula was outdated because flagrant discrimination no longer persisted in covered jurisdictions and the "country has changed."

Subsequently, Representatives John Lewis (D-GA) and Jim Sensenbrenner (R-WI) co-sponsored a bill to update the Act. The proposed legislation would apply preclearance to jurisdictions with a record of voting rights violations within the previous 15 years, would make it easier for courts to block discriminatory rules before they are used in elections and harm voters, and would require disclosure of voting changes nationwide.

In a comprehensive report providing evidentiary support for updating the Act, the National Commission on Voting Rights collected contemporary instances of structural dilution of minority votes in the context of at-large elections and redistricting plans. The Commission also documented the emergence of various restrictions on voting, such as proof of citizenship, voter purges, felony disenfranchisement, voter identification, voter challenges, and restrictions on registration drives. Further, the Commission's report chronicled failures to provide adequate language assistance materials, failures to provide registration at public assistance agencies, and attempts to roll back early in-person voting and same-day registration.

Others have also written on contemporary election structures that adversely affect minority voters. For example, many states disenfranchise former offenders after they have completed their sentences, and as a result, 7.7% of black adults are disenfranchised nationally, including 22% of black adults in Kentucky and 23% in Florida. By counting inmates as residents of the jurisdiction where they are incarcerated rather than as residents of their home prior to incarceration, many states inflate the voting strength of populations who live near prisons (often rural areas) and diminish the voting strength of non-incarcerated people in the prisoners' home communities. Many states have adopted restrictive identification laws, and the General Accounting Office reported that 84% of registered white voters possess a valid driver's license, compared with only 63% of registered black voters. North Carolina and other states have attempted to roll back early voting on Sunday, and data show black voters accounted for 53% of Sunday early voters in North Carolina and Georgia in the 2014 midterm election.

While analyzing contemporary election practices that diminish minority voting is critical, we also need facts about minority turnout, racially polarized voting, policy outcomes, and the number of minority elected officials to fully understand our progress since 1965 and to look toward the future.

Critical Thinking

1. Explain the values contradiction found in voter exclusion and democratic, representative government.
2. Why did various state governments pass laws that excluded persons from voting?
3. Can the courts effectively assure free and fair elections?

Internet References

American Civil Liberties Union (ACLU)
    www.aclu.org
Human Rights Web
    www.hrweb.org

KHALILAH L. BROWN-DEAN, PHD is an Associate Professor of Political Science at Quinnipiac University in Connecticut. Professor Brown-Dean's current research agenda focuses on the political dynamics surrounding the American criminal justice system. **ZOLTAN HAJNAL, PHD** is Professor of Political Science at the University of California, San Diego. A scholar of racial and ethnic politics, urban politics, immigration, and political behavior, Dr. Hajnal is the author of a number of books. **CHRISTINA RIVERS, PHD** is an Associate Professor of Political Science at DePaul University. Her areas of expertise focus on the intersection of race and law in American politics, including voting rights law and equal protection law, as well as black political thought from abolition through the civil rights movement. **ISMAIL WHITE, PHD** is an Associate Professor of Political Science at the George Washington University. He studies American politics with a focus on African American politics, public opinion, and political participation.

Brown-Dean, Khalilah et al. "50 Years of the Voting Rights Act: The State of Race in Politics", *Joint Center for Political and Economic Studies,* 2015. Copyright © 2015 by *Joint Center for Political and Economic Studies.* Reprinted by permission.

Article   Prepared by: John A. Kromkowski, *The Catholic University of America*

Obama Answers Immigration Ruling with Vow to Fight Courts and Congress

JOSEPH TANFANI AND MICHAEL A. MEMOLI

Learning Outcomes

After reading this article, you will be able to:

- Understand why immigration reform is important.

- Identify what the responsibilities of Congress and the executive branch are for the government's ability to establish and maintain the integrity of clear and fair governance of practices related to immigrants.

The Obama administration promised Tuesday to fight against opposition from both the courts and Congress to keep in place its expansive new programs to shield millions of immigrants from deportation, a key piece of the president's effort to shape his legacy in his final years in office.

A federal judge in Texas issued an order late Monday that temporarily blocked the administration from putting into effect President Obama's executive actions on immigration. The ruling touched off a day of cheering by Republicans, logistical and legal scrambling in the White House and vigorous efforts by advocates around the country to reassure potential applicants that they shouldn't give up.

The administration said it would swiftly appeal the order, which came less than 48 hours before immigration officials were scheduled to begin accepting applications for the first of the programs to defer deportation.

Despite that setback, the president predicted that courts would ultimately uphold his efforts as lawful.

"The law is on our side and history is on our side," Obama told reporters in the Oval Office. "This is not the first time where a lower court judge has blocked something, or attempted to block something, that is ultimately going to be lawful. And I'm confident that it is well within my authority."

For now, though, his administration put on hold plans to start its expansion Wednesday of the 2012 program that has shielded from deportation nearly 600,000 young people, so, called Dreamers, and a much larger effort to defer action on deportations that could apply to about 4 million adults living in the U.S. illegally.

The broader initiative had been set to begin in May, and its future is uncertain for those who hoped to qualify for it.

"We're asking people to not be fearful or be discouraged. We believe it will be overturned," said Larry Kleinman, a co-chair of a national effort by advocacy groups to prepare for the program's rollout.

Saying he was tired of waiting for Republicans to fix a broken immigration system, Obama announced in November that he would use his executive authority to protect millions of immigrants from the threat of being deported.

The largest piece of his plan would be open to immigrants who've lived here for five years, have no serious crimes on their records and are parents of legal residents.

He was sued over his executive action in a case eventually joined by 26 states, most led by Republicans.

U.S. District Judge Andrew S. Hanen issued an injunction on the grounds that the states had a strong argument that the administration had not followed correct procedures in establishing the program. A full trial would be needed to resolve the case, Hanen said, and his order was intended to preserve the status quo until that could take place.

Hanen, an appointee of President George W. Bush who has taken a hard line on enforcement in other immigration cases, said the Obama administration had overstepped its authority in establishing the program, which he says would grant "legal presence and benefits to otherwise removable aliens."

Administration lawyers have not decided whether to ask an appeals court for an emergency stay of Hanen's order, according to Cecilia Muñoz, director of the White House Domestic Policy Council.

Temporarily at least, the ruling has complicated the administration's efforts to get ready to handle millions of applications without bogging down the rest of the system.

The U.S. Citizenship and Immigration Service, which is to oversee the applications, has leased a new processing center and has begun preparing to hire hundreds of workers. The agency had already posted a list of questions and detailed answers on its website about the expansion of the Deferred Action for Childhood Arrivals program; it removed the Web page Tuesday afternoon.

Hanen said that if the government were to begin to allow immigrants to stay in the country while the court case proceeded, "the genie would be impossible to put back into the bottle." He added that he agreed with the plaintiffs that legalizing the presence of millions of people would be a "virtually irreversible" action.

Some experts in immigration law predicted Hanen's opinion would be overturned.

"The federal courts have been very deferential to the executive branch on immigration issues," said Stephen Yale-Loehr, a professor at Cornell Law School. Though the question might ultimately end up before the Supreme Court, he said he expected that the justices would wait to weigh in until lower courts had heard the constitutional issues.

Republicans in Congress said the ruling vindicated their opposition to the immigration programs, and leaders gave no indication that they might change course.

In a strategy largely pushed by conservatives who are against illegal immigration, Republicans are attempting to use Homeland Security Department funding as leverage to stop the administration's effort to protect millions from deportation.

But a House measure to fund the agency only on the condition that it not implement the programs has stalled in the Senate in the face of united Democratic opposition.

Without a resolution by Feb. 28, many department employees would be furloughed while others would be forced to work without pay.

Though some Republicans privately say they fear a shutdown of the department would be a political disaster for the party, House Speaker John A. Boehner (R-Ohio) said in an interview on "Fox News Sunday" that he was "certainly" prepared to let that happen if the Senate couldn't pass the House bill.

One Republican leadership aide, granted anonymity to discuss the situation candidly, said the court order would probably lead members of the party to feel they "are doing the right thing" by seeking to block the policy, and hoped it would force Senate Democrats to reconsider.

Senate Majority Leader Mitch McConnell (R-Ky.) has scheduled a fourth procedural vote on the House bill when the Senate returns to Washington on Monday.

The ruling could signal to Republicans that their best chances of undoing the president's actions are through the courts, giving lawmakers cover to advance a spending bill without any immigration-related provisions.

But one Republican aide noted that the Texas judge's ruling could be reversed before lawmakers return from their week-long recess this week, which would leave Republicans exactly where they started when they left.

Democrats reiterated Tuesday that they would remain firmly against the House bill, and Obama, who has said he held off on his action until it became clear that Congress could not find a way to overhaul the immigration system, urged lawmakers to try again to find a broader solution.

"With a new Congress, my hope has been that they now get serious in solving the problem," he said. "Instead what we've had is a series of votes to kick out young people who have grown up here and everybody recognizes are part of our community, and threats to defund the Department of Homeland Security."

Advocates who work with immigrants worried that the judge's decision could confuse and frighten applicants who are already nervous identifying themselves to immigration authorities.

"People just need to sit tight and remain confident that this program is something that will ultimately prevail," said Gregory Chen, director of advocacy for the American Immigration Lawyers Assn.

Across the country, immigrants who are eligible were wondering how to proceed.

"I have no idea what I'm going to do yet," said Rocio Andiola of Mesa, Ariz. "I didn't know how to react."

Andiola, 35, who came to the U.S. illegally from Mexico, is eligible for deferred action on possible deportation, as is her husband, as they have two American-born sons, ages 13 and 15. She has been gathering documents required to apply.

"We've been doing things right—paying taxes and stuff," she said. "We deserve an opportunity to live here."

Critical Thinking

1. Why is immigration reform important?

2. What are the responsibilities of Congress and the executive branch for the breakdown of public confidence in current practices of governance related to persons living in this country?

3. What do you make of the linguistic confusion over "illegal immigrants" or "undocumented persons"?

Internet References

Diversity.com
www.diversity.com

Immigration Policy Center
www.immigrationpolicy.org

U. S. Bureau of Citizenship and Immigration Services
www.uscis.gov

U.S. Census Bureau
www.census.gov

Unit 10

UNIT

Prepared by: John A. Kromkowski, *The Catholic University of America*

Overcoming Mythologies of Universalism, Recognizing the Reality of Diversity, Recovering the Value of Tolerance, and Discovering the New Horizons of Cultural Pluralism

The Detroit area has a large Polish-American population (600,000), the largest Arab-American population in the United States (300,000), a sizeable Italian-American group, and a growing Hispanic (largely Mexican-American) population anchored by a city which has an 80 percent African American population. Its universities have centers for the study of Arab and Hispanic populations and a new endowment for a Polish chair and center. The area's fifth largest ethnic group is Italian-American. The key to convergence in this metropolitan area will be to have groups reflect on their history and experience in America and the adaptation of their cultures to the American reality. This must be done with an eye for learning how to utilize that experience in shaping a generous and genuinely multicultural society and civic life. It is important to note, as a caution, that insofar as we espouse and practice multiculturalism and believe in a pluralist and open society, we are being quintessentially Western and especially American. It might even be ironically seen as one of our ethnocentricities given the fervor of our commitment. No other modern world culture has placed such a high premium on pluralism, nor developed the theoretical underpinnings of diversity as well

as we have. These are not transplanted concepts without roots in our culture. Thus, we should have greater certainty that we can succeed at them, perhaps more than any other society in the world. We need to be able to take this fact into consideration in our preparation for the work we will do.

The words race, religion, and ethnicity have been used to describe a wide and sometimes ill-defined and contradictory set of experiences and identities. The apparent confusion arises because race and ethnicity are contextual—more a social process than a primordial and fixed given of biology and origin. Their meanings change in each place with time and circumstances for each group. The discussion of race, religion, and ethnicity require attention to methodological approaches and interpretive categories that frame the current ferment in this field at the practical and theoretical levels. However, one finding is beyond doubt. Patterns of intersection of religion, race, and ethnicity are definitely specific to the locations and regimes within which they are embedded. Moreover, even the claims and efficacy of scientific knowledge and applications appear to be influenced by their history and most significantly, the privileging of certain ways of knowing and languages within respective power fields established and maintained by regimes. In certain respects, race and ethnicity are simultaneously indigenous and transplanted social inventions that have become rooted in the social experience and fostered by regime development. The search for fresh insight, conscious of the social and symbolic formation of cultures, is an important meta-descriptive challenge. The debate regarding the relationship of various ways of knowing invites us to search for understanding and particular skills, competencies, and rules for dialogue among religious, ethnic, and political traditions. Support of civilization and peaceful means of resolving differences are clearly imperative. While the situation caused by these issues is worldwide, understanding and action in this arena is nearly always local and specific.

The transmission of ethnic tradition through music, an avenue of expression with the particular capacity to mediate stirrings of the spirit, suggests linkages between religion and ethnicity. The interaction of ethnicity and religion is curiously exposed in the etymology of the Greek word ethnikos: the rural, Gentile, or pagan people of the ancient Mediterranean world. Though such philological roots no longer drive our principal understanding of ethnicity, the experience of social affinity and cultural affiliation elaborated in the following articles about ethnics deepens our awareness and understanding of ethnicity—a changing yet persistent aspect of human identity and social cohesiveness. Understanding race and ethnic relations can be pursued by considering the comparative intensities of ethnic and race identities of large immigrant-receiving countries and small countries.

The affiliation of people places and their profound senses of rootedness to a place, even to exclude the desire and prospect of ever leaving kith and kin, are clear markers of ethnic intensity. The articulations of human consciousness into patterns of explanation and shared bonds of union are ongoing human expressions. They are transmitted through socialization and in detailed, useful, and sustaining forms of knowledge about four central aspects of existence and realty. These are the self, others, nature (the world and universe), and finally (as well as initially) the mystery of being that transcends the mundane. This existential mystique invites human consciousness to participate and to cocreate our selves and our relations with others and nature in whatever ways we wish.

Thus, ethnicity emerged as a modern form of symbolization and displaced the sciences and ideologies of linear universal human development. This can be called the historical and cultural turn of the social creation of human organization and its attendant redefinition of an epoch of human development as post-modern. This shift in perspective suggests that new attention to the ways and modalities of explaining social order and its foundation in human imagination must be added to the discussion of race and ethnic relations. The relationship between personal consciousness and shared consciousness as a group are oftentimes mediated through ethnic symbolizations. These are grounded in the meaning provided by evocation of ethnicities that are derived from historical and imagined ethnic experiences and traditions.

Article   Prepared by: John A. Kromkowski, *The Catholic University of America*

More than a House: Home and Hospitality in Camden

PILAR HOGAN CLOSKEY

Learning Outcomes

After reading this article, you will be able to:

- Describe the intersection of race, ethnicity, and poverty in Camden, NJ.

- Discuss the goals of the Reinvestment Fund and community-based approaches to urban renewal and social justice.

Introduction

The topic, "*Building Community in a Mobile/Global Age: Migration and Hospitality,*" presents a daunting challenge. That challenge is multiplied many times over when applied to a city like Camden, NJ, perhaps America's poorest city and, ironically, located in one of America's richest states. That irony, with its ups and downs and pros and cons, seems to be a hallmark of globalization, urbanization and migration. The primary task of this short paper, however, will be limited in scope to a brief local case study from Camden, describing the work of the St. Joseph's Carpenter Society (SJCS), one of the ministries of St. Joseph's Pro-Cathedral Parish in East Camden. The paper will outline some grounding principles for making affordable housing available to the working poor and immigrant families. The process which emerges points to the deeper value and meaning of "home" and homeownership with significant implications for understanding person, community, migration and hospitality.

The principles, listed below, have their origin in the body of thought known as Catholic Social Teaching (CST).[1] In *Ecclesia in America,* Pope John Paul II highlighted the phenomenon of urbanization. "The frequent lack of planning in this process is a source of many evils . . . In certain cases, some urban areas are like islands where violence, juvenile delinquency, and an air

of desperation flourish . . ."[2] Camden is a graphic example of what John Paul was writing about. That warning is all the more relevant today as the globe goes all the more urban.

This paper will be developed in four parts: some background on the City of Camden; an introduction to SJCS; and a brief case study of the ongoing "Carpenter's Square" housing development. What consistently emerges is the determined spirit of Camden's people, longtime residents and new arrivals, often motivated and led by the city's various religious congregations. This core, even in the worst of circumstances, does not give up on the dignity of the human person and the search for community.

Background

Camden is a city of nine square miles and some 77,000 people, a population that has almost been cut in half in the last 40 years. Currently the population is almost equally African-American, 48 percent, and Hispanic, 47 percent. There are long-standing stable communities of African-Americans and Puerto Ricans, significant numbers of Central Americans and Dominicans, and smaller communities of Whites, Haitians, and Vietnamese. The largest contingent of new immigrants (before the recent lockdown) is from Mexico. Camden was once a proud middle and working class city that was home to RCA Victor, Campbell Soup and one of the largest shipbuilding industries in the U.S. All that changed with the unrest of 1969–71 when most of the major companies started moving out. The current unemployment rate hovers at about 20 percent but functional unemployment has been estimated as high as 30–40 percent.

Camden has also suffered dramatically from crime and drugs. Over the last few years, the city has consistently been ranked as one of the most violent in the U.S. Open drug markets flourish on many corners and the murder rate has reached new highs. Nonetheless, budget cuts have caused deep reduction in Police and Fire service and, recently, a merger of County and City Police forces. Public education has suffered dramatically. "In Camden, only slightly more than 6 percent of adults have a college degree, while over 40 percent lack even a high school diploma."[3] The high school drop-out rate is among the highest in the country. Governance problems have been made more difficult by the recent economic crisis—42 percent of the residents live below the official poverty level. Median income is about $26,000, compared to $71,000 for the rest of New Jersey. For many years, Camden has been blighted by abandoned, boarded up houses—often due to tax structures that make "running out" more sensible than selling. In spite of various past and ongoing efforts to clean-up abandoned properties, there are still about 4000 abandoned buildings out of a housing stock of about 28,358.[4] That means, approximately, one out of every seven houses is abandoned, boarded-up and often used for drugs and prostitution.

In 2002 the seemingly invincible spirit of Camden's people appeared to win a big battle. Confronted by a coalition of urban church groups, Camden Churches Organized for People (CCOP) and Concerned Black Clergy (CBC), the State of New Jersey was compelled to respond to the city government's inability to govern. The city was awarded $175 million in bonds and loans and, in return, the state took over management of the city—including police, fire and schools. However, the outcome of this effort was less than effective and left a deep sense of frustration in local communities. Referring to the state's substantial investment in the Adventure Aquarium, one reporter sarcastically remarked, "Thanks to $25 million in recovery money, America's poorest city now has hippos."[5] Nonetheless, big projects were carried out—the Camden waterfront has been rebuilt, the downtown area somewhat renovated, hospitals and universities in the city have been financed and expanded. Some jobs have come out of the "takeover" and, clearly, the hospital and university investment in the city holds potential for future growth. However, the blighted neighborhoods with abandoned buildings, whose residents and churches led the struggle, never got their fair share of the promised "bailout."[6] Nonetheless, the spirit of human dignity, search for community, hospitality, and solidarity, continue. The people, churches, public agencies, and local non-profit organizations did not give up. The organizing and projects morphed into new approaches and concentrated on local neighborhoods—the struggle goes on. The echo of Pope John Paul can still be heard in Camden:

> The exercise of solidarity within each society is valid when its members recognize one another as persons . . . positive signs in the contemporary world are the growing awareness of the solidarity of the poor among themselves, their efforts to support one another, and their public demonstrations on

the social scene which, without recourse to violence, present their own needs and rights in the face of the inefficiency or corruption of the public authorities. By virtue of her own evangelical duty, the Church feels called to take her stand beside the poor, to discern the justice of their requests, and to help satisfy them . . . in the context of the common good.[7]

St. Joseph's Carpenter Society—Overview

Abandoned buildings, crime and drugs, combined with the lack of city services provoked a new, more community-based, approach to parish work in East Camden. One of the first ministry offshoots, created by the pastor, Fr. Bob McDermott, brought St. Joseph's into urban planning, community organizing, community development, and affordable housing. The Carpenter's Society was founded in 1985 to help families improve their quality of life and create safe neighborhoods through homeownership. SJCS believes, and solid evidence indicates, that homeownership leads to a higher quality of life by encouraging stability, fostering personal pride, promoting the development of community ties, allowing families to build wealth, and attracting private capital to underinvested areas. To promote successful homeownership, the Carpenter Society performs three interrelated functions: community organizing; housing development; and homeowner education. SJCS's primary work targets abandoned homes for acquisition, rehabilitates those homes and sells them to neighborhood families.[8]

After creating housing opportunities in Camden for several years, SJCS gradually realized that if neighborhoods were to be reborn and a spirit of community rekindled, the rehabilitated houses needed more than good carpentry and masonry work. They needed to house socially and financially responsible families and informed community members. This realization, in 1994, led to the establishment of the Campbell Soup Homeowner Academy. The six week "Money Basics" and "Homebuyer Education" courses are both mandatory for all homebuyers. The first series of classes—pre-purchase—assess each applicant's status as a potential homebuyer and owner. Is this family ready to move forward or is more preparation needed? Issues dealt with include: budgeting and credit, searching for an affordable home, negotiating in making a purchase, doing the settlement; changing from tenancy to responsibility for one's own property. The second series of classes, also required pre-purchase, teaches families the basics of financial management and the mortgage process, as well as the responsibilities of being a homeowner and community member. Trained staff members lead classes, in both English and Spanish, in physical maintenance of homes, as well as the State of New

Jersey's expectations concerning state subsidies for affordable home purchase. The training is completed with discussions on growth of assets beyond house purchase. A wide range of topics is covered, with the hope of avoiding future crisis—including budget and credit, mortgage payments, predatory loans, insurance, liability, taxes, record keeping, banking tools for saving, and finally community involvement, integration and hospitality in your new neighborhood. Individual counseling in all these areas and more are readily available in English and Spanish. In 2012, 134 individuals graduated from the Homeownership Academy, while 228 people attended some classes. Over the years, some 7,000 people have attended the classes and about 3500 have graduated and been certified.[9]

A key element of the Carpenter Society's neighborhood redevelopment model is community organizing to form networks of residents and groups capable of addressing local concerns. Community organizing moves values and principles into action. Becoming involved in the community, knowing your next-door neighbors, playing an active role in the upkeep and development of the neighborhood are encouraged for all new homeowners. This is very important given the diversity in Camden's neighborhoods and the constant arrival of new immigrants. Recently, SJCS has begun a new neighborhood organizing initiative, "The East Camden Neighborhood Marketing Plan." The staff, along with community members, has worked out a three year plan, including a community steering committee and a program of local events (concerts, competitions, seminars) to promote neighborhood engagement.[10]

An additional component of this approach to community development is stabilizing the local housing market. This is, of course, extremely important in our multicultural, global, urban society fighting a deep economic recession. Too often markets make victims of the working poor and the immigrant. The recent real estate crisis was a worse-case scenario which hit the poor hardest. Nonetheless, to date, the Carpenter Society has developed more than 935 residential properties in targeted neighborhoods of Camden. Over 620 of these have resulted in homeownership. Typically, new home-buyers are African American, Hispanic or Asian. Depending on language, education and income level, more time might be needed for homeowner education. That is part of the hospitality and outreach to community members.[11]

A typical household annual income for potential homeowners is between $20,000 and $35,000. However, in spite of dismal economic times, the value of SJCS homes has risen dramatically. In 1990 rehabilitated homes sold for $20,000; today these homes sell for between $72,000 and $150,000. This constitutes a significant step forward, of growth and wealth accumulation for the working poor. Moreover, home ownership has had significant impact on family life and neighborhood stabilization. It is significant that over 90 percent of all SJCS homes sold are still owned by original buyers or their families. In addition and in spite of the recent terrible real estate crisis, SJCS foreclosure rate is only three percent. The fact that SJCS homes values are appreciating and that families are able to survive and thrive in Camden's tough social and economic environment is an endorsement of the community development and educational approach used. A *Philadelphia Inquirer* article summed up the effort:

> Since the Carpenter Society's founding in 1985, it has been chipping away at Camden's vexing housing problem. It initially worked on one house at a time—raising money, bringing in volunteers, and selling the fixed-up homes for cost of materials, less what was raised. The society soon hired and paid workers, fixing one block at a time. Now it can rebuild an entire neighborhood. . . . The results have been stunning.[12]

One other recent effort on the part of SJCS deserves mention. Since the economic downturn in 2008, Camden's situation has become even more dire. In spite of the efforts of various organizations, religious, public and private, the ranks of the poorest grew. One of the very visible outcomes of this was the increase in the number of homeless. SJCS set out to make a small contribution to dealing with this and, in 2010, in partnership with Lutheran Social Ministries, established Joseph's House, a house of hospitality and shelter for some of Camden's homeless women and men. A building has been purchased and renovations will soon begin.[13]

CST Principles: Translation and Application

The principles and approach employed at SJCS owe their inspiration to two sources. The first is the vision of Fr. Bob McDermott, who understands church as a community called to and energized by the participation and empowerment of people. Deeply influenced by Vatican II and the social mission of the church, he is committed to the "option for the poor" and is guided by the inspiration of Archbishop Oscar Romero that, "The poor tell us what the world is and what service the church can offer the world. The poor tell us what the *polis*—the city is, and what it means for the church to live in the world . . ."[14]

The second source of inspiration is the principles culled from CST. Seven themes have been articulated by the U.S. Bishops and provide a starting point and ready reference for the affordable housing program at SJCS. Basic concepts include: life and the dignity of the human person; importance of family, community and participation; rights and responsibilities;

option for and with the poor and vulnerable; dignity of work and the rights of workers; solidarity and subsidiarity; and care for God's creation and environment.[15]

The Carpenter Society program and staff emphasize the importance and respect due to all clients. Family and community are key components of every project. As to rights and responsibilities, the educational program seeks to balance and foster both autonomy and solidarity. The staff seeks to educate homebuyers for independence and self-reliance but at the same time foster a sense of interdependence, community and solidarity. The fundamental option for the poor is the key underlying principle and defines what we do. SJCS strives to protect the rights of our own workers and also to promote the dignity of work and workers' rights in Camden. Solidarity is a core principle. The Society tries to get homeowners to expand their concept of neighbor beyond family, national, racial and religious lines. In turn, we understand "solidarity" in sync with "subsidiarity." That is, we do what is needed and helpful, but not too much, allowing, even demanding, that families and homeowners take on the responsibility for their new homes and new neighborhoods. Finally, SJCS has worked hard to be environmentally responsible in our housing and neighborhood rehabilitation. The community is keenly aware that Camden, like other poor urban centers, has too often been treated as an environmental dumping ground. As *Renewing the Earth* pointed out, "it is the poor and the powerless who most directly bear the burden of current environmental carelessness. Their lands and neighborhoods are more likely to be polluted or to host toxic waste dumps, their water to be undrinkable, their children harmed."[16] In down to earth street language, SJCS tries to convey these principles and put them into action.

Nonetheless, to make the above CST principles come alive, SJCS needs to make them more concrete and translate them into redevelopment strategy, community development, planning, and housing construction language. This we attempt to do when we design and delineate project plans. Our redevelopment strategy roughly follows these steps:

- The target area is defined; we look for clear boundaries, landmarks or institutions, which might unite a neighborhood, such as a church or community center. This allows for relationships to be built and neighborhood identity to emerge.
- Geographic Information System (GIS) is used; we map the conditions of the targeted area and identify area strengths and weaknesses.
- Redevelopment planning and work begin in the areas of strength and move gradually toward the areas of weakness.
- A scattered site rehabilitation approach is used; we redevelop areas that can be stabilized, but, for example,

if abandonment exceeds 30 percent, experience indicates that rehab is not an appropriate tool and demolition might be necessary.
- Investment in an area is utilized to gradually move real estate values over a period of time; consistent and predictable reinvestment patterns will ultimately be incorporated into the pricing structure of the local market.
- Regular updates and comparisons of GIS maps help us to track neighborhood change; this feedback tells us what is working and what is not, and allows for readjustment.

Throughout this process, SJCS seeks to weave in human dignity, personal rights and responsibilities, common good, community participation, and care for the environment. Recently the Society has sought to further localize and personalize this planning approach by working, in collaboration with Cooper's Ferry Partnership (CFP) and the Regional Plan Association (RPA), to develop a resident-driven neighborhood plan—*My East Camden: Many Voices, One Vision / Muchas Voces, Una Vision.* This plan began with a walking inspection of every building in the four census tracts of East Camden, carried out by staff and student volunteers. It continued with a house-to-house survey of homeowners, administered by hired, local-residents. We surveyed 386 residences in East Camden. Initial results indicate a very positive response to this participatory research and planning model and strong support for the new efforts at neighborhood revitalization.

Case Study: Carpenter's Square

In 2008, SJCS completed 219 for-sale units in the Baldwin's Run HOPE VI project. This extensive and concentrated rehabilitation project transformed a distressed 25 acre public housing site and surrounding area into an affordable, stable community.[17] The project was instrumental in bringing about the construction of the new Cato School and the new Boys and Girls Club. SJCS sought to replicate this model in other severely distressed neighborhoods, specifically Boyd and Morse streets near Baird Boulevard, the gateway to East Camden. The Carpenter's Square project was launched in 2009–2010. The area of the project is the location of "the alley," a place notorious for drug dealing and prostitution. SJCS had worked there for over 5 years rehabilitating homes, but then began working on the most blighted streets. The project will improve the infrastructure in the immediate area, offer safe and affordable housing that is attractive and wellsuited to the existing neighborhood, provide redevelopment that increases the homeownership ratio, and, in turn, reduce crime and drug activity in the area.

There are 85 parcels located along Boyd and Morse Streets. Four units, at the intersection of Baird Boulevard, were already rehabilitated and sold. The vacancy rate for these blocks is a key indicator in terms of the overall health of the area; 24 units were vacant and boarded-up. In partnership with SJCS, the City of Camden has demolished 20 abandoned units. Working with residents of the area, the Carpenter Society designed a plan that will allow for the majority of homeowner-occupied, single family homes to remain. Redevelopment will occur mainly in the location of the duplex rental units. As part of the project, SJCS has redesigned problem alleys, updated local infrastructure, and improved streetscapes. Decorative street lighting has been installed on the main street, Baird Boulevard, as part of the gateway and renewal strategy. The combination of these elements had dramatic effect on the Baldwin's Run project and will play a crucial role in the Boyd and Morse Streets area. SJCS has partnered with Cooper's Ferry Development Association for this infrastructure work. Sewers, streets, lighting, and the problematic alley system have been renovated. Long-time alley flooding has been alleviated. Sewers, and water and gas lines, have been replaced; curbing, street paving, new sidewalks and fencing have been installed. As reporter Kevin Riordan stated:

> Consider as well the dramatic difference of Carpenter Square, where new homes rise at the former site of a notorious openair drug market. The society recently finished the first four of 42 new units in the 200 block of Morse. The three-bedroom homes sell for between $76,000 and $129,000 to graduates of the society's Homeowner academy, which helps working people qualify for private mortgages.[18]

With funding support from the New Jersey Housing and Mortgage Finance Agency (NJMFCA) Choice Program, the City of Camden's HOME Program, and construction expertise support from The Reinvestment Fund-Development Partners (TRF-DP), SJCS will build and sell 42 new homes in Carpenter's Square. The first phase is for 17 single family units; 11 units have already been sold and the other six units are under construction, with four committed buyers. This first phase is scheduled for completion by December, 2013.

Conclusion

As SJCS approaches its one thousandth renovated or new home, it has become clear that "home" is, indeed, much more than a house. It is not just the difference between the "before" and "after" photos showing the evolution from a boarded-up, abandoned building to an attractive house. Rather it is the realization that homeownership fosters a deeper sense of person and personal pride, promotes community, hospitality and

solidarity, advocates for community and educational development, attracts capital to under-invested areas, and allows families to build wealth. It is reflected in the proud faces of parents when keys are handed over and in the smiles of little girls and boys who can play in their yards, ride bikes on safe streets and welcome friends to their homes.

In sum, homeownership empowers people, strengthens families, and builds revitalized and hospitable neighborhoods. In the midst of the real estate and economic melt-down and global migration, we need to confront the culture of displacement and homelessness. On a local scale, SJCS seeks to do just that by opening a path to home ownership for the working poor and the immigrant. Owning a home is not just the "American Dream." In virtually every culture, it is a graphic sign of acceptance, roots and hospitality.

Endnotes

1. Cf. Pontifical Council for Justice and Peace, *Compendium of the Social Doctrine of the Church* (Vatican City: Libreria Vaticana, 2004); Cf. also, Charles E. Curran, *The Social Mission of the U.S. Catholic Church: A Theological Perspective* (Washington: Georgetown University Press, 2011; and Marvin L. Krier Mich, *The Challenge and Spirituality of Catholic Social Teaching,* rev. ed. (Maryknoll, NY: Orbis Press, 2011).

2. Pope John Paul II, *Ecclesia in America, no.21.*

3. Alan Mallach, *In Philadelphia's Shadow: Small Cities in the Third Federal District* (Philadelphia: Federal Reserve Bank of Philadelphia, May 2012), p. 34.

4. US Census Bureau, quickfacts.census.gov

5. Alan Mallach, *In Philadelphia's Shadow: Small Cities in the Third Federal District,* p. 59; Cf. also, Matt Katz, "Camden's Waterfront and its Woes," *Philadelphia Inquirer,* November 9 (2009).

6. Cf. Howard Gillette, Jr., *Camden after the Fall: Decline and Renewal in a Post-Industrial City* (Philadelphia; University of Pennsylvania Press, 2005); Cf. also John P. Hogan, "Taking a City off the Cross: Camden Churches Organized for People," *Credible Signs of Christ Alive: Case Studies from the Catholic Campaign for Human Development,* (Lanham, MD: Rowman and Littlefield, 2003) pp. 45–63); Cf. also "Camden's Crisis—Ungovernable?" *The Economist,* Nov. 26, 2009.

7. John Paul II, *On Social Concerns,* 1988, no. 39.

8. For background on SJCS, Cf. Sean Closkey and Pilar Hogan, "Building Houses, Educating Communities: A Praxis/Reflection Model," *Living Light,* (Summer, 1999), pp. 38–43, and Pilar Hogan Closkey and John P. Hogan, "Romero's Vision and the City Parish: Urban Ministry and Urban Planning," *Romero's Legacy: The Call to Peace and Justice,* eds. Pilar Hogan Closkey and John P. Hogan (Lanham, Md: Rowman and Littlefield, 2007), pp. 1–10.

9. SJCS is most grateful to the Campbell Soup Foundation and other foundations for the generous donations and grants that make the education program possible.

10. This initiative is being implemented, with funding and technical consulting support from *Neighbor Works America,* a congressionally chartered community development agency, comprised of a national network of more than 240 local community development and affordable housing agencies; see www.nw.org

11. For this whole effort, a special note of thanks is expressed to the SJCS staff for their excellent team-work: Felix Torres Colon, Adriana Alvarez-Cintron, Felicia Bender, Rosie Figueroa, James Roche, Tracy Bell, Tracy Dinh, Richard Kochanski, Michael Welde, James Herman, and Joseph Ramos. Gratitude is also expressed to Msgr. Robert T. McDermott, pastor of St. Joseph's and founder of SJCS, and to the dedicated members of SJCS Board of Trustees.

12. *Philadelphia Inquirer* (February 2, 2007.)

13. Thanks is expressed to the many volunteers who have helped in this endeavor, and especially to John Klein, for his dedication and leadership.

14. Oscar Romero, *A Martyr's Message: Six Homilies of Archbishop Oscar Romero* (Kansas City: Celebration Books, 1981) p. 82.

15. Papal encyclicals and Bishops' statements form the basis of modern CST. However, numerous summaries are available. Cf. for example, Thomas Massaro, SJ, *Living Justice: Catholic Social Teaching in Action* (Franklin,WI: Sheed and Ward, 2000); Cf. also Charles E. Curran, *Catholic Social Teaching, 1891–Present: A Historical, Theological and Ethical Analysis* (Washington: Georgetown University Press, 2002) and Marvin L. Krier Mich, *Challenge and Spirituality of Catholic Social Teaching,* pp. 8–13.

16. U.S. Bishops, *Renewing the Earth,* 1992, 2

17. "A Good Life: Top 10 Cottage Neighborhoods," *Cottage Living,* July/August (2008).

18. *Philadelphia Inquirer,* November 28 (2010).

Critical Thinking

1. What are the goals of The Reinvestment Fund (TRF)?

2. What is community development? Economic development? Cultural democracy?

3. What are the structural causes of poverty and its differential locational consequences?

Internet References

Habitat for Humanity
www.habitat.org

National Association of Neighborhoods
www.nanworld.org

The National Neighborhood Coalition
www.neighborhoodcoalition.org

National Neighbors
www.ncrc.org

Neighborhood Revitalization Initiative
www.whitehouse.gov/administration/eop/oua/initiatives/neighborhood-revitalization

Article   Prepared by: John A. Kromkowski, *The Catholic University of America*

The Major Demographic Shift That's Upending How We Think About Race

WILLIAM H. FREY

Learning Outcomes

After reading this article, you will be able to:

- Explain the problems with race labels generally used to document racial categories and boundaries.

- Identify the historical changes and patterns of interracial marriage.

The usual way that race labels are applied in the United States in everyday parlance and in government statistics fails to capture a phemenon poised to reshape how race is actually lived in America: the increase in multiracial marriages and births, which almost certainly will lead to more blended populations in future generations. As this trend continues, it will blur the racial fault lines of the last half of the twentieth century. The nation is not there yet. But the evidence for multiracial marriages and multiracial individual identity shows an unmistakable softening of boundaries that should lead to new ways of thinking about racial populations and race-related issues.

Sociologists have viewed multiracial marriage as a benchmark for the ultimate stage of assimilation of a particular group into society. For that to occur, members of the group will already have reached other milestones: facility with a common language, similar levels of education, regular interaction in the workplace and community, and, especially, some level of residential integration. This is what we saw with European immigrants from Italy, Poland, and Russia in the last century. After decades of being kept at arm's length by "old" European groups such as those from Britain, Germany, and Scandinavia, the newer arrivals finally began to intermarry with the more established ethnic groups as they became more upwardly mobile

and geographically dispersed. Hispanics and Asians differ from white Europeans, of course—most significantly, for these purposes, Americans tend to view them as racial groups rather than ethnic groups. And race divisions, especially between whites and blacks, have historically been far less permeable. So the blending of today's new racial minorities through multiracial marriage is breaking new ground.

Multiracial marriages have been rising dramatically. In 1960 (before federal statistics enumerated Hispanics and before the 1965 legislation that opened up immigration to more countries) multiracial marriages constituted only 0.4 percent of all U.S. marriages. That figure increased to 3.2 percent in 1980 and to 8.4 percent in 2010. More than one in seven newlywed couples are now multiracial.

Amid this overall increase, the propensity to marry out of one's racial or ethnicity varies. Among recently married whites, 17 percent were married to someone of another race, but for Hispanics and Asians, more than four in ten recent marriages are multiracial. Among minorities,blacks continues to have the lowest prevalence of multiracial marriages, a legacy of the anti-miscegenation statutes that persisted in 16 states until 1967, when the Supreme Court declared them unconstitutional in the landmark *Loving* v. *Virginia* decision. It was only after this ruling in the post–civil rights environment that black multiracial marriages began to rise noticeably, but among recent, typically younger marriages involving blacks, nearly three in ten were multiracial marriages, signaling an important breakthrough in the long history of black marital endogamy.

Especially noteworthy is the rise in white-black multiracial marriages: In 1960, white-black marriages amounted to only 1.7 percent of all black same-race marriages, but in 2010, they amounted to 12 percent. White-black relationships are even more prevalent among recent cohabiting couples.

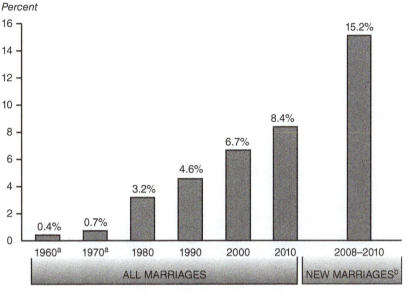

Multiracial Marriages as a Percent of All Marriages, 1960–2010

Percent

Source: 1960–2010 U.S. censuses; American Community Survey 2008–10.

[a] Multiracial marriages involving Hispanics were not included

[b] Marriages that occurred in last 12 months

Multiracial Marriages in the United States by Type, 2010

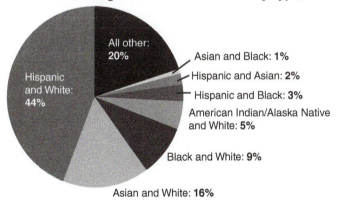

All other: 20%

Hispanic and White: 44%

Asian and Black: 1%

Hispanic and Asian: 2%

Hispanic and Black: 3%

American Indian/Alaska Native and White: 5%

Black and White: 9%

Asian and White: **16%**

Source: American Community Survey, 2008–10.

The geographic dispersion of new minority populations to the New Sun Belt states in the South and Mountain West—and into the largely white, interior Heartland states—is dispersing multiracial marriages along with it. The highest prevalence of multiracial marriages is found in Hawaii, where three in ten marriages are multiracial, followed by Alaska and Oklahoma. These states have long-standing populations of Asians, Alaska Natives, and American Indians, respectively. Just below are a mix of states where Hispanic and Asian immigrants have maintained a long-term presence, including New Mexico, California, Texas, Washington, Oregon, Arizona, Nevada, and Colorado. At least one in ten marriages in these states is multiracial. Multiracial marriages are also growing in the New Sun Belt (states such as Georgia, Utah, Idaho, and North Carolina) and even several Heartland states (Minnesota, Connecticut, Pennsylvania, and Indiana). Although many new Hispanic migrants to these regions are less assimilated than elsewhere with regard to measures such as English language proficiency and education, they are likely to have substantial interaction with their states' non-Hispanic populations, which may be leading to more multiracial marriages than might otherwise occur. For example, in Idaho and Utah, the prevalence of multiracial marriages among Hispanics is 43 and 44 percent, respectively. These rates stand in contrast to rates of 26 and 21 percent in the more mature Melting Pot states of California and Texas.

At the other end of the spectrum are 14 states where multiracial marriages account for less than 5 percent of all marriages. In West Virginia, only about 3 in 100 marriages are multiracial.

An obvious consequence of a rise in multiracial marriages would be an increase in multiracial children, which would lead to a greater share of the population claiming a mix of racial backgrounds. The marriage of individuals from various European immigrant backgrounds led to the melting pot that characterizes much of today's white population. It would

Multiracial Marriages as a Percent of All Marriages, 2010

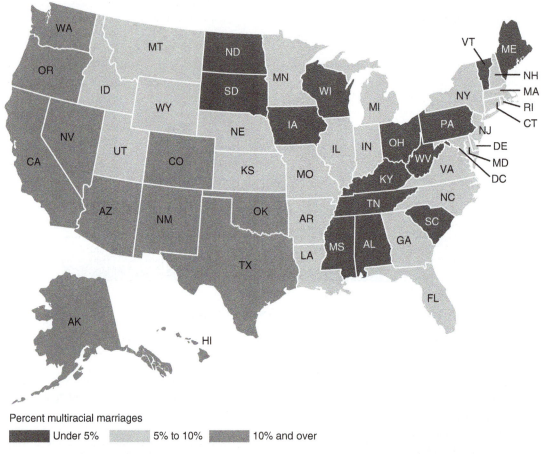

Percent multiracial marriages

Under 5%   5% to 10%   10% and over

Source: American Community Survey, 2010.

seem only natural to anticipate a similar boom of multiracial persons in the years ahead. Yet in the case of multiracial marriages, national and cultural boundaries are not the only lines being crossed. New ground is being broken, pushing back against long-standing social and even legal constraints that often subjugated multiracial persons—particularly those with white black ancestry—to second class status. In many cases, individuals who could "pass" as white tried to do so in order to become part of the mainstream.

The practice of dividing whites from blacks and other nonwhites began in the early years of nationhood, when the slave population was counted separately and the "one drop" rule stipulated that if a person had any black ancestors, they could not be classified as white. Although classifications in later censuses included Chinese, Japanese, Filipino, and Hindu, there was little attempt to think of these largely "racial" categories as subject to mixing. This stands in contrast to the collection of information on parental birthplace and ancestry or

national origin, which was widely used to study the blending of white ethnic populations. Although multiracial populations emanating from multiracial marriages certainly existed, they were not well documented in national statistics.

Beginning with the 2000 census, federal guidelines mandated that when U.S. government statistical agencies collect information on race, they must provide options for persons who identify with more than one race. The impetus for this change came from a well-organized grassroots effort by people who thought of themselves as multiracial and wanted to be officially recognized as such.

The census permits identification of combinations of up to six specific racial categories, including "some other race," a catch-all category for those races not specifically identified. In 2010, those identifying as "white and black" made up the largest single group—a population that more than doubled over the preceding decade, especially among the young. For every 100 black toddlers under age five, 15 toddlers are identified as both white and black—a sharp rise since 2000. In a handful of Western, Great Plains and New England states, the population of "white and black" persons is more than 20 percent of the black-only population.

But the more vivid evidence of the erosion of the white-black divide is found in the South, the region historically most resistant to racial change. Because of past prejudices and customs, the white-black population, as a percentage of all blacks, is still considerably lower in the South than in other parts of the country. In a slew of states from Maryland to Texas, "white and black" populations amount to less than 5 percent of the black-only populations; in Mississippi and Louisiana, "white and black" populations constitute only 1 percent. Yet the South is attracting blacks in large numbers, including multiracial blacks, from all parts of the country. And when states are ranked by the *growth* in their "white-black" multiracial populations in the first decade of the 2000s, rather than their current totals, the southern states lead all others. In that period, the Carolinas, Georgia, Mississippi, and Alabama more than tripled their white-black multiracial populations. Tennessee, Florida, Arkansas, Louisiana, and Kentucky were not far behind. In fact, southern states as a whole accounted for 41 percent of the nation's decade-long gain in the "white and black" multiracial population.

Overall, the share of the U.S. total population that categorizes itself as multiracial—2.9 percent—is surprisingly small in light of the pervasiveness of multiracial marriages. There are several reasons to believe that the official numbers markedly understate size. One is that the census does not include Hispanics in its count of multiracial persons because they are considered an ethnic rather than a racial group. After the 2010 census, the Census Bureau began to experiment with the implications of changing this policy. It allowed respondents to choose new multiracial categories such as "white and Hispanic" or "black and Hispanic." This change led, in one scenario, to a rise in the multiracial share of the population to 6.8 percent, well above the 2.9 percent in the 2010 census. Moreover, earlier projections using a similar approach by non-census researchers show the U.S. multiracial population reaching 10 percent in the year 2020 and 18 percent in the year 2050.

A second reason why the multiracial population may be going undercounted is that the single racial status of children is often determined by the adult who fills out the census form. Research suggests that in identifying the race of their children, multiracial couples often select single race identities that they believe will be more socially acceptable or will better prepare their children for success. This, of course, may change as these children come of age and begin defining themselves. President Barack Obama, the child of a multiracial marriage, announced through his spokesperson that he identified himself as "black" rather than "white and black" on his 2010 census form. It is likely, however, that younger and future generations of Americans from multiracial families will be more likely to embrace their heritage.

Critical Thinking

1. What geographic, historical, and group specific categories would most adequately measure human diversity?
2. Discuss the reasons and purposes for race and ethnic data collection.
3. Explore the implications of concepts: "ascription of identity" and "self-identification."

Internet References

Center for Comparative Studies in Race and Ethnicity
https://ccsre.stanford.edu
Center for the Study of Race and Ethnicity in America
www.brown.edu/academics/race-ethnicity

Article

Prepared by: John A. Kromkowski, *The Catholic University of America*

'Birth of a Nation' Anniversary Has a Heck of a Bookend

MICHAEL PHILLIPS

Learning Outcomes

After reading this article, you will be able to:

- Describe the thesis of "The Clansman," the novel from which the early 20th century film, "The Birth of a Nation," was derived.

- Contrast the recent screening of the film, "Selma" in the White House with President Wilson's screening of "The Birth of a Nation."

In the history of American cinema, D.W. Griffith's 1915 landmark "The Birth of a Nation" is the gift that keeps on generating misgivings.

Based on Thomas Dixon Jr.'s 1905 novel "The Clansman," and the subsequent stage version, Griffith's 12 reel Civil War epic, slightly more than three hours in length, remains a uniquely vexing achievement. It is often painful to watch, even when its techniques and ambitions command attention, even now. The film is as accomplished and sophisticated visually as it is notorious and vicious thematically. It's also readily available on YouTube and other sites.

"The Birth of a Nation" defends white Southern honor in the Civil War and depicts the postwar Reconstruction era as another kind of war, grotesque and humiliating. On one side, we have the blacks, newly freed, played mostly by white actors in blackface plus a few actual African-Americans. In the film's distorted remembrance of Reconstruction, we watch the black and biracial characters enjoying the rights the story cannot abide (equality, the vote, intermarriage). On the other side of the war: whites, the besieged majority whose salvation arrives with the creation, according to Dixon and Griffith, of the Ku Klux Klan, defender of "the Aryan birthright."

The Dixon novel, published in 1905, contains passage after passage such as this one:

"Now a negro electorate controlled the city government, and gangs of drunken negroes, its sovereign citizens, paraded the streets at night firing their muskets unchallenged and unmolested. A new mob of onion-laden breath, mixed with perspiring African odour, became the symbol of American Democracy."

Dixon, a friend of fellow Southerner Woodrow Wilson, adapted "The Clansman" for the stage as a response to the success of "Uncle Tom's Cabin," which he viewed as dangerously sympathetic to African-Americans.

"My object," Dixon wrote, was to "demonstrate to the world that the white man must and shall be supreme." Griffith's film cannot disguise this sensibility, even if Griffith's gifts lifted it to a higher poetic realm of lies.

Not all anniversary stories in mainstream journalism are created equal, or equally celebratory. This one's bittersweet. But it has a remarkable bookend.

On Feb. 18, 1915, President Wilson held a private screening of "The Birth of a Nation" in the White House. It was the first such event, if you don't count the White House lawn screening of the 1914 Italian feature "Cabiria," a film that showed Griffith and others new ways to mobilize the camera.

"Like writing history with lightning," Wilson was alleged to have said of Griffith's evocation of the Civil War and its aftermath. That was 100 years ago this month. A few weeks ago director Ava DuVernay was invited to screen her film "Selma" at the White House, at the invitation of Barack and Michelle Obama.

It was a small event as White House gatherings go. Yet DuVernay felt the significance of it and took to Instagram to mention, among other things, the "Birth of a Nation" screening a century earlier. Seeing "Selma" in the house where Wilson saw Griffith's film, DuVernay wrote, was "a moment I don't have to explain to most . . . heavy with history and light with pure, pure joy all at once."

In "Selma," we see a beautifully dramatized idea of what Martin Luther King Jr. learned about politicking, and how he took what he learned to the people. Like Steven Spielberg's "Lincoln," DuVernay's film relishes procedure and keeps a careful eye on maneuvers akin to a high-stakes chess match. In some ways "Selma" follows the contours of conventional historical fiction; in others, and those others are crucial, we're allowed closer and more revealing proximity to the guts of history.

"The Birth of a Nation" is more of a blunt instrument. In its initial engagements it gathered up a lot of anger, great swaths of covert and overt racism, and played to it, fomented it. The results made a lot of money. The film held the box-office record until 1937, when "Snow White and the Seven Dwarfs" took it away. And then, two years later, another film (like Griffith's) featuring the burning of Atlanta and a lot of racial stereotypes (title: "Gone With the Wind"), conquered the planet.

Chicago's history with "The Birth of a Nation" was like that of many big cities: protests, debate, politics, capitulation. After a New York screening, National Association for the Advancement of Colored People board member Jane Addams, founder of Chicago's Hull House, told the New York Post that the film was "a pernicious caricature of the negro race." Initially the film was refused its Chicago exhibition license. Politically the opposition did not hold, and in the summer of 1915, anyone who could afford the $2 admission price (roughly $46 today) made the trip to the now-vanished Illinois Theater downtown to see what the fuss was about.

In Lafayette, Ind., a white man killed a black teenager after seeing the movie. It's still a dangerous topic, this film; in 1995, Turner Classic Movies canceled its airing of a restored "Birth of a Nation" print, in the wake of the O.J. Simpson murder trial.

What do its defenders say? Plenty. Griffith was a pioneer of the silent era, with one foot in Victorian romanticism and the other in the medium's newfound expressive possibilities. Lillian Gish, among others in the film's ensemble, worked in a naturalistic style of performance eons away from most of the theatrics on screen at the time. The film, like Leni Riefenstahl's "The Triumph of the Will" a generation later, is the work of a front-rank director who knows exactly what he's doing, although Griffith felt blindsided by the intensity of the controversy over the racism. "Why take a romance of the civil war so seriously?" he wrote after the film's release. He made "Intolerance" following "The Birth of a Nation," as an act of defiance and atonement.

Like many, I first encountered "The Birth of a Nation" in a high school film class. I barely had the resources to process it. I couldn't, and never will, reconcile the scenes of grotesque caricature with the Mathew Brady-like pictorial beauty of its landscapes. The film contains a title card defending itself with the statement that it is "not meant to reflect on any race or people today." Yet on the screen, its calumny against a people is permanent. Funny thing is, Dixon thought the calumny was against people like him.

The film Wilson invited to the White House imagines a sinister day indeed, when "all blacks are given the ballot." But to state the obvious: A lot happens in a century. "Selma" takes up the matter of black voting rights and comes to a rather different conclusion than Griffith's infernal classic did. "The Birth of a Nation" shall not, I hope, ever be banned from public viewing or availability. We are who we are, and we must realize where we've been. If we don't defend free speech, however ashen the taste, even when it maligns millions, then we are Americans no longer.

We have endured long enough as a nation to see Griffith's film screened for one president in 1915 and DuVernay's film for another in 2015. And that's one hell of a set of bookends.

Critical Thinking

1. What meanings and understandings of the "American mind" emerge from juxtaposing White House screenings of "The Birth of a Nation" and "Selma"?

2. Discuss the impact of the film images and the role of a president in shaping the public attention.

3. Discuss the narrative that these films, The 50th Anniversary of Bloody Sunday in Selma, and President Obama's speech at that event, create of the ongoing process of intersecting the past and present to influence the "American mind."

Internet References

The Council for Research in Values and Philosophy
www.crvp.org
National Catholic Bishops Conference
www.USCCB.org
Sociosite
www.sociosite.net

Article   Prepared by: John A. Kromkowski, *The Catholic University of America*

Catholic Theologians Weigh In on Protests, Call for 'Police Reform and Racial Justice' in America

Vinnie Rotondaro

Learning Outcomes

After reading this article, you will be able to:

• Describe the theological and moral foundations for the action recommended in this statement.

• Discuss the problems and benefits of public religious appeals that challenge ingrained and institutionalized patterns of social and political order.

A statement from Catholic theologians is calling for "police reform and racial justice" in America.

The statement–penned by Tobias Winright of St. Louis University, Alex Mikulich of Loyola University New Orleans, Vincent Miller of University of Dayton, and Bryan N. Massingale of Marquette University, with help from colleagues—comes at a time of great civil unrest, with demonstrations taking place across the nation in protest of racially charged police killings.

"The killings of Black men, women and children," the statement reads, naming Rekia Boyd, Eric Garner, Michael Brown, John Crawford, Aiyana Stanley-Jones and Tamir Rice, "by White policemen, and the failures of the grand jury process to indict the police officers involved, have brought to our attention not only problems in law enforcement today, but also the deeper racial injustice in our nation, our communities, and even our churches."

In light of such injustice, Catholics and Christians should "raise [their] voices about the imperative of a just peace in [a] fragmented and violent world," the statement reads.

Referencing the Rev. Martin Luther King Jr. and Pope Francis, the statement explores what Catholics and Christians "raising" their voice might mean.

"King challenged 'white moderate' Christians for being 'more devoted to "order" than to justice,'" it reads, "and for preferring 'a negative peace which is the absence of tension to a positive peace which is the presence of justice.' This challenge to the White Christian community is as relevant today as it was over 50 years ago. Such a negative peace calls to mind the warning by the prophet Ezekiel, 'They led my people astray, saying, "Peace!" when there was no peace' (13:10)."

The statement then quotes Pope Francis from his apostolic exhortation, *Evangelii Gaudium:*

Today in many places we hear a call for greater security. But until exclusion and inequality in society and between peoples are reversed, it will be impossible to eliminate violence. The poor and the poorer peoples are accused of violence, yet without equal opportunities the different forms of aggression and conflict will find a fertile terrain for growth and eventually explode. When a society—whether local, national or global—is willing to leave a part of itself on the fringes, no political programmes or resources spent on law enforcement or surveillance systems can indefinitely guarantee tranquility. This is not the case simply because inequality provokes a violent reaction from those excluded from the system, but because the socioeconomic system is unjust at its root. Just as goodness tends to spread, the toleration of evil, which is injustice, tends to expand its baneful influence and quietly to undermine any political and social system, no matter how solid it may appear.

The authors of the statement express their "wish to go on the record in calling for a serious examination of both policing and racial injustice in the US."

"The time demands that we leave some mark that US Catholic theologians did not ignore what is happening in our midst," they write, "as the vast majority sadly did during the 1960s Civil Rights movement."

The statement then includes a list of pledges:

- To "examine within ourselves our complicity in the sin of racism and how it sustains false images of White superiority in relationship to Black inferiority."
- To "fast and to refrain from meat on Fridays during this Advent season and through the seasons of Christmas and Epiphany, as well as during Lent, as a sign of our penitence and need of conversion from the pervasive sin of racism."
- To "commit ourselves to placing our bodies and/or privilege on the line in visible, public solidarity with movements of protest to address the deep-seated racism of our nation."
- To "support our police, whose work is indeed dangerous at times," but also "call for a radical reconsideration of policing policy in our nation." Specifically, to "call for an end to the militarization of police departments in the US," and support "the proven, effective results of community policing."
- To "call for a honing of the guidelines for police use of lethal force so that they are uniform in all states within the US and so that the use of lethal force, echoing Catholic teaching on 'legitimate defense,' is justified only when an aggressor poses a grave and imminent threat to the officer's and/or other persons' lives."
- To "support those calling for better recruiting, training, and education for our police so that they may truly and justly do what they have sworn, namely, to 'serve and protect' their communities."
- To "support new efforts to promote accountability and transparency, such as body cameras for police officers."
- To "call for the establishment of publicly accountable review boards staffed with civilian attorneys from within the jurisdiction and/or for the appointment of independent special prosecutors' offices to investigate claims of police misconduct."

- To "support calling for a Truth and Reconciliation Commission to examine race in America."
- To call for "investigations of the Ferguson Police Department, the New York Police Department, and other police forces involved in the killings of unarmed Black citizens."
- To "call upon our bishops to proactively proclaim and witness to our faith's stand against racism," and to "revisit" previous pastoral statements and documents on the subject "in parishes, dioceses and seminaries" in an effort to bring the church's teaching on the subject "to the forefront of Catholic teaching and action in light of the present crisis."

"As Catholic theologians and scholars," the statement reads, "we commit ourselves to further teaching and scholarship on racial justice. Our faith teaches us that all persons are created in the image of God and have been redeemed in Christ Jesus. In short, our faith proclaims that all lives matter, and therefore, Black lives must matter, too. As part of this commitment, we pledge to continue listening to, praying for, and even joining in our streets with those struggling for justice through nonviolent protests and peaceful acts of civil disobedience."

Critical Thinking

1. Discuss the intersection of religious leadership and public affairs.

2. What type of persuasion does religious discourse bring to our assessment of correct public behavior, appropriate ways of living, and the language of morality based in sacred texts?

3. What can religious approaches bring to race and ethnic relations?

Internet References

NETWORK: A National Catholic Social Justice Lobby
www.networklobby.org

Religion, Poverty and Social Justice
www.crop.org

VINNIE ROTONDARO is *NCR* national correspondent.

Article   Prepared by: John A. Kromkowski, *The Catholic University of America*

The Local and the Global: Recovering Neighborhood Communities in the Metropolitan World

JOHN A. KROMKOWSKI

Learning Outcomes

After reading this article, you will be able to:

- Describe the dynamics and tension between the local and the global perspectives of the reality of large-scale and integrated metropolitan areas.

- Explain ethnicity and diversity as essential aspects and factors of globalization.

- Describe the elements of the local development model and the practices it fosters.

The topic and title of this seminar, *Building Community in a Mobile and Global Age,* is in certain respects an invitation to reconsider the ongoing process of human development from the compact forms of rural community to the highly differentiated forms and modes of organization created with the invention of urban settlements. Beginning with the ancient experiences of the polis and onward toward the contemporary movement of persons into urban settlements new bonds of union are required among the variety of populations for the complex relations among persons and the new modes of actions availed by larger scale human orders. It is beyond contention, however, that the development of large-scale urbanization has become a world–wide phenomenon. All countries are engaged in the formation of integrated systems of transportation and the coordination of market activities and the movement of people from village life is by far the most stunning geo-demographic of the post WWII transformation of cultures and civilizations.

The implications of globalization can be best viewed as an extension of urbanization toward mega-regional forms of human organization. Mega-regions include the regime capacity to govern large areas and populations, the economic capacity to assure stability and policies, which highlight the importance of the migration of people into market economies and metropolitan polities. The 'migration' of technology and the organization of markets and attendant new relations among places and people pose exceptional challenges, opportunities and advantages. The question of building community in a global age of metropolitan urbanization can be framed by recognizing the types of human organization and dimensions of urban communities: the economy, the polity and sociality. These differentiated yet overlapping spheres of human order can be ranked by their power capacity in the new metropolitan world of globalization: (a) the economic, built upon profit and which provides for material needs; (b) the political, built upon power which implements social engagement and decisions of collective action limited by laws in pursuit of the economic well-being and the common good; and (c) the cultural and ultimately meaning-giving and religious (in the broadest and non-sectarian sense of the word), in which the purpose and deepest levels of human diversity find their common threads. It is the third sector of human sociality that is the primary concern of the following exploration and explication. Although this sector can be measured and quantified such descriptions and data are indicative of its elemental reality. These indicators are important and valuable, but do not capture the existential and essential characteristics of human association and organization. The disparities among various places express the enormity of the human challenges related to the shattering experiences of eclipsed communities and the challenge of building new communities in the metropolitan world. The final section of this paper will address aspect of renewal that are related to the contemporary process of building communities in the current phase of globalized urbanization and the destruction of communities. The extensive urban interaction that emerged in the 19th century and its acceleration in the 20th century has propelled new forms of knowledge, including knowledge of various societies and their particular sociality grounded in their symbolizations of order. The following excerpt from Eric Voegelin's *New Science of Politics* provides a compact and yet precise expression of the core issue and central considerations of human organization and social realities. Voegelin writes:

> For man does not wait for science to have his life explained to him, and when the theorist approaches social reality he finds the field pre-empted by what may be called the self-interpretation of society. Human society is not merely a fact, or an event, in the external world to be studied by an observer like a natural phenomenon. Though it has externality as one of its important components, it is as a whole a little world, a cosmion, illuminated with meaning from within by the human beings who continuously create and bear it as the mode and condition of their self-realization. It is illuminated through an elaborate symbolism, in various degrees of compactness and differentiation—from rite, through myth, to theory—and this symbolism illuminates it with meaning in so far as the symbols make the internal structure of such a cosmion, the relations between its members and groups of members, as well as its existence as a whole, transparent for the mystery of human existence. The self-illumination of society through symbols is an integral part of social reality, and one may even say its essential part, for through such symbolization the members of a society experience it as more than an accident or a convenience; they experience it as of their human essence (p. 27).

Globalization has enormously influenced cultures. Culture defines a form of commons and culture is a popular language term related to the technical term "symbolization of order," especially to the social practices embedded in the action and behavior of persons and their institutions which are derived from the dominant and social efficacious "symbolizations of order." Symbolizations of order are essential access points into depths and heights of the mystery of existence. These realities are an especially important concern and in many respects a neglected dimension that this seminar aspires to broach in a variety of ways. The mystery of existence extends to the mystery in historical changes of order and thus to the problematic

of migration and the interaction of cultures. At this level migration and globalization are metaphors for a moment in human existence. At its extreme these metaphors are about the universal and ultimate action from birth to death—from beginning into the beyond of existence. Along that way, however, we are invited to consider additional dimensions, perspectives and modes of organization that are definitive and measure our participation in the personal and social aspects of being. However, as we seriously engage in the critical clarification of personhood and social realties we are invited to be attentive to the senior partners-in-being that are beyond the personal and social, but accessible at the depths and heights (in different ways, registers, intensities, texts, languages, levels of compactness and differentiation) of all social order. Persons and societies in an age of technological and material interdependency force us to also engage science and its relationship to nature and those manifestations of the mundane and the transcendent which are woven into the substance of the bonds of community. The task of understanding building communities, thus transcends the personal and social, but holds them central to fundamental participation in the mystery of being and existence that is only discoverable through understanding and building communities. This is not because the economic or the political are unimportant; indeed they have fully absorbed our efforts in modern times. But there is now an emerging awareness that though necessary these are insufficient. They concern how we are to live, but not what we live for; they enable, but do not inspire; they are useful means, but to unexamined ends. Hence in recent times, especially at the end of the ideologies or perhaps as the reason for this ending—attention turns to culture and awareness of the commitments of a people. But with the emerging self-awareness of ones' own culture, the intersection with others achieves new depth as well. For the enhancement and extension of human hopes require new dimensions of cultural awareness and new directions related to intercultural cooperation and the related new leadership and competencies. We need now to begin to think together so as to move beyond divisiveness and conflict.

The sciences of human affairs have deepened our ability to know of one's own society. The critical clarification of symbolizations of order and comparative analysis and interactive relationship to other symbolizations of order encountered are especially evident in immigrant receiving countries and particularly painful and distressing in regimes that oppress and conquer ethnic groups and nationalities within the reach of their power. Such contexts pose the following options: 1) to appropriate or reject symbolizations of order and ways of substantial participation in the world of meaning conveyed by symbolizations of order; 2) to refashion older symbolization and modes of participation into other bonds of union that give fresh meaning. However, interaction with other cultures may also produce alienation and isolation. Moreover, the transportation, communication and technological capacity for maintaining relationships with one's pre-immigration culture have complicated the process of assimilation and acculturation. In addition, the formation of isolated enclaves by choice or by imposition of law or economic disparity and the lack of education to pursue an economic mobility strategy poses vexing problems. Life and settlement in the metropolitan world are segmented by design, which generally form patterns measured by income, education and cost of housing. Such clusters are the context within which the task of building community through personal and social encounters occurs. The function and purpose of communities is related to the ever-human desire for meaning within larger scale forms of human settlement as well as the political, economic and social exchanges that cannot be achieved except for the existence of communities. The exploration of the worldwide power-field and its complicity in the creation of new types of cultural bonds to drive and define social action and aspiration are topics beyond the scope [of] this paper. However, my sense is to follow Simone Weil's observation that one can expect that the uprooted will uproot others and that building community is a difficult, but important process of transplanting and nurturing new growth in new contexts from which the human/divine spirit may flourish in the metropolitan world.

What seems interesting to me about the structuring of the world which we call urbanization/globalization and the processes that have now reached mega-regional extents is that this re-configuration of geography and agglomeration of peoples has consequences which are especially difficult for the cultivation of community. The pluri-formality and multiplicity of communities and the fragility for human bonds influenced by mobility pose enormous strains for person integrity and identity. The development of new competencies to build communities is the imperative of our time.

The macro-level of large-scale forms of human organization is the locus of modernity, and the contemporary re-theorization of modernity and the transmission of such findings into the re-articulation of more human practice is a worthy agenda which links the reconstruction of theory with the reconstitution of community-based practice. Urban places such as universities and institutes are the locus of the research space within which the central questions regarding reality are posed. The claim is made that persons with the leisure to ponder and thematize issues and remedies are an essential aspect of the critique and development of cultures and the recovery of sociality as a civilizational resource. Urban places are the locus of fresh searches for the attunement of human action to the imperatives of eternal realities—nature, persons, societies and gods. These primordial elements are given to human experiences and

about which the task is to find the approaches required for the re-articulation of human cultures and sociality. If human sociality is becoming eclipsed within the mega-regional urban formed by a coalition of economic and state power, then how can the retrieval of human substance be proclaimed and nurtured? Can these forces that have shaped these large-scale worlds of urbanization, i.e., a coalition of economic and state power and its domination over others be reordered to a more equitable sharing and shaping of the burdens and benefits of life and culture? Can the critique of these particular spheres as being bereft of the fuller sources of being and for its diminishment of capacities for excellence that are only accessible from participation in forms of human sociality become a pathway toward the recovery of sociality? Sociality is a fragile but grounded relationship among persons that is accessible through evocative participation in symbolizations of order. Sociality understood in this sense the source of the substance and capacity to re-attune persons to the ground of reality needed for the full flourishing of nature and persons as partners in the human–divine mysteries of existence. Sociality is the source of being-in-participation with others. The sources of sociality are found in the foundational myths, memories, rituals, music, accounts of the beginning and the beyond. Sociality is community, but its ongoing existence and presence is always uncertain. Some of its portals of being-in-participation seem to have been narrowed and even closed so that their evocative and saving power has been lost through forgetfulness and ignorance. Others have been crowded-out and clogged by the over-confidence that filled the modern mind and its action that in effect closed-off ways of knowing and made their capacity for action inefficacious even into the present moment.

Although the successes of market production and state coercion are clearly ascendant, it is more than obvious that our time is haunted by the ever so incomplete message of the era to satisfy the yearning that emerged with the *QUESTION* of meaning and the *MEANING* of fundamental questions. In fact the question posed in this seminar suggests this exact point. I am told by some cyclical determinists that the beginning of a new phase of human consciousness is emerging as another slips-away—about every 500 years in China. Vico had another calculus and time line. But in my neighborhood this form of consciousness emerges within me whenever I recall what I learned from a significant poet from my home state: he borrowed from another older poet when he wrote something like the following: there are two ways to get an education: One, to recall a sacred memory from your childhood: Two, the experiences that rush into your soul when you discover that a person who is publicly respected and honored is in fact a malicious lunatic. And three, the experience of meeting a person who set out to save the world. He soon recognized his failure, but set out to heal a country. He resigned from this project before the saving moment occurred, but then he met another person with other experiences and other aspirations. She wanted to save, organize and develop her neighborhood. Her scale of human action is an interesting beginning and a worthy perspective for understanding community and communities.

But the consequences of the changes initiated by globalization demand rethinking relationships among people and cultures at all levels of human association and organization. Communities, as the title of this seminar indicates, are neither automatic nor naturally stabile, persistent and lasting institutions. In fact, all association, organizations, communities, neighborhoods, even regimes are human inventions that may become institutions. Institutions are essentially relationship among persons that last over time which enable collected/group action and that possess some form of sharable object that expresses some level of substantive and/or procedural bond of union. Community is a type of sociality that requires leadership initiatives in the cultivation of a shared substance and in the process of interpersonal dynamics leading toward building an organization that can frame collective goals and achieve collective objectives [that] reach beyond the strategies and tactics of the past and beyond the crisis of the moment. They must include, but also dig deeper than the campaigns to energize passions that are woven into popular evocations and forms of cultures. Without neglecting goals promoted by economic and governmental institutions which generally diminish the legitimacy of sociality that is the ground of culture and people-hood, the current challenge is to discover more deeply and richly the nature of cultures. The task is to rediscover and apply the resources of the various cultural heritages, to develop new understandings of inter-cultural coalition-building and cultivate multi-culturally competent leadership, and to evolve the processes of information and agenda sharing among existing community-based organizations, institutions and networks.

This initiative would explore aspects and the bonds of union that are available and that can be nurtured as a new urban sociality based in the human and humanizing instants of the various cultures. Unlike the notion fostered by earlier eras, which typically assumed that existence of human solidarity would emerge as a consequence of economic development or as a bond of alliance to the state, the new perspective recognizes the legitimacy of the economic and governmental sectors, but posits the relevance of cultivating a community-based expression of participation that has been ignored and neglected. The new symbolization could be popularly imaged as a form of local identity that could become a new bond of affinity to economic and state action and a substantive institution of human scale and personal relations among and between persons which appears to be missing from the functional relations that predominate in the economic

and governmental arenas which drive the development of countries. The processes of organizing and developing communities at the neighbourhood level are proposed as approaches to overcoming the dominance of the economic and governmental sectors in this era of global urbanization. The consequent rebalancing of economy, polity, and, sociality would yield the added value of the transmission of substantive cultural and traditional aspects which convey the meaning bearing messages of cultural traditions.

The process of community organizing and community development must be rooted in the fresh insights and benefits of human imagination that are discoverable and discernible from the summary of findings and conclusions that follow. The community building process promotes the realization that human life and relationships are not entirely and totally physical and material, nor entirely accidental and matters of convenience, but representative of the human search for commonalities that provide transcendence and its expression in the little words of meaning found essentially in human communities. Certain aspects of this process are illustrated in the case study portion of this paper.

Case Study: Neighborhood Revitalization

Formative and guiding forces of human experience grounded in community traditions teach profound lessons. What one learns and values at the first intersection of the personal in one's family and of the public in one's neighborhood shapes one's judgment and action in the urban arena of culture, government and economy that constitute the urbanized settlements in which larger and larger numbers of people live. Periods of change often produce a conflict but more importantly they force us to define the commonweal we share. But groundless expectations for the future based in ideological images of the past eclipse honest-to-experience representations of reality, which ought to inform and guide us. Immigration to America included the experiences of persons and communities uprooting' themselves from native lands, making the arduous journey to America, trying to establish roots here, facing discrimination and privation, and attempting to adjust to a culture which was totally alien to the one they had left. They faced the threat and difficulty of detention or rejection, entrapment by unscrupulous shipping and boardinghouse agents, finding decent lodgings and employment and adjusting to a very unfamiliar life-style.

The success or failure of community and economic development activities throughout the cities and communities of the U.S. depends largely upon very localized characteristics, dynamics and developments. Federal agencies, state and local governments can provide various incentives and supportive programs, but they cannot supply directly the most critical need nor can they alone implement community and economic development ventures and processes. These public sector actors can, however, recognize needs and design programs which eliminate bottlenecks and promote the development of those factors which produce successful development.

Thus the argument begins: The neighborhood is the building block of a city and the neighborhood experiences are an important source of value found in sociality articulated from the substance of cultural traditions. However these sources of sociality are currently neglected elements of models of economic and governmental development which drive mega- cities in this era of globalized urbanization. A remedy for this imbalance can be approached by the gathering of human insight that has been synthesized in the following case for neighborhood revitalization and proposed as a pathway toward building community in an age of global urbanization. These findings are proposed and should be assessed, tested, and outcomes evaluated as a pathway toward the recovery of a flourishing community-based presence of sociality. The recovery of community in neighborhoods in the global metropolitan age created and dominated by the economic and governmental action that has transformed countries throughout the world is a global and local agenda. The mega-cities of all countries are equally in need of recovering their cultures but also ought to be engaging in the plethora of cultural manifestation that the movement of populations brings into urban life. This work of re-engaging culture ought to be more systematically and artfully brought into the process of globalization, which has largely been economic and governmental and not attentive of the forms of sociality, that are part of the human legacy of world.

In the American experience, the small-scale settlement of urban areas—the neighborhood—not only mediated the passage of immigrants toward becoming American ethnics, citizens, producers and consumers; as importantly, it mediated the person from family into the public world of common culture, politics and economics. Through such interaction and relationship a society fashions bonds of association and exchange. The neighborhood is the initial locus of an interesting set of intersections, which may be fruitfully named the public, private and community sectors of the American reality. Thus the neighborhood is a social invention whose capacity for economic and cultural well-being appears to be pivotal for social formation, economic well-being and political development. Contemporary urban neighborhoods exist in uneasy tension with large-scale governmental, cultural and economic institutions. The agenda proposed for urban neighborhoods and the endorsement of social formation influenced by immigration and ethnicity does not invoke either of these sources as merely symbolic or as romantic political totems. The neighborhood agenda emerges from experiential analysis of the relation of immigration and ethnicity to the moral universe of exchange of goods and services. Such experiences informed by pragmatic common sense suggest the ground from which preference for the neighborhood can be determined without the sleight of hand employed by either romantic nostalgia or destructive progressivism.

The factors which ensure the steady increase in potential production and consumption, as well as participation and ownership in a given community, form a complex equation. Community and economic development depend on a host of interacting processes: entrepreneurial activity, the actual basis of all production, the availability of productive processes and resources, the accessible level of technique, social institutions and attitudes, capital, and sufficient population and level of consumption. The saliency of these various contextual factors shift from time to time, and their relationships to each other change. Some of the factors are of course external and beyond the influence of a community. But, experienced neighborhood analysts and proven practitioners of neighborhood revitalization have fashioned an understanding of this complex process. They can help discern what is meaningful, effective and needed to develop a community and to promote its full economic potential.

In addition to a correct analysis of economic and market factors, it is now more than obvious that the full use of community resources, in all their variety, is important to any particular local economic development endeavor. The non-participation of any sector public, private or community puts a venture at extreme risk. Citizens groups, private businesses and other institutions can either oppose change and stifle development or be the primary impetus for development and improvement. Frequently, the difference between the adoption of one or another posture is determined by a group's self-interest and its understanding of its ability to share in the development.

It is clear then that the process by which a neighborhood economic development program is carried out requires this process of cooperative interaction. The public sector, primarily municipal government, must create the proper environment in order for business to operate effectively. The private sector, principally business people and financial institutions who indicate a desire to remain and invest in the neighborhood, must take a central position in the actual process of business development. Organized community groups must actively participate in the planning and implementation of the revitalization program, provide broad-based citizen support, relate the economic development program to the overall neighborhood revitalization process, and mediate between conflicting interests when and if the occasion arises. The three sectors should be jointly involved from the outset. The following narrative model includes a description of the public, the private and the community sectors each, and the role each must play in an effective economic revitalization program.

Public Sector

The primary responsibility of the public sector is the delivery of various types of services and actions which are essential to a healthy community environment. In many cases, adequate delivery by the public sector can be a sufficient trigger for considerable private investment in the neighborhood. Provision of certain services and/or public actions by the municipality can spell the difference between the feasibility and non-feasibility of development projects. A partial listing of those necessary services and actions include:

- Police/security
- Parking
- Sanitation and neighborhood appearance
- Transportation facilities
- Code enforcement
- Other public actions—zoning, taxing, etc.

Adequate lines of communication should be established between public agencies and the private sector. Also because they are composed of and represent, the interests of the residents of the area (who are the electorate), the community leadership must also play a vital role in this communication process.

Private Sector

In the context of the revitalization process, the private sector generally is made up of the local business and financial community. In any economic development program, this sector must carry the bulk of the development activity. The existence of a strong local merchants' association is often a precondition for an effective program. The members of such associations should be expected to contribute to the support of their organizations by both financial involvement and the contribution of in-kind services.

Experience has shown that business development must involve all or most of the following aspects of the neighborhood economy. A neighborhood commercial revitalization program, as carried out by a local public/private partnership, must be able to deliver services in all the following areas.

Improving the Competitiveness of the Existing Merchants. Local merchants forced to compete with regional shopping centers, generally are unable to do so effectively. By forming and working through active merchants' associations patterned along the lines of those regional shopping centers,

merchants can upgrade the physical appearance of their stores and the quality of merchandise, increase the scale of operations, promote the neighborhood as an interesting and convenient place to shop, institute building and equipment maintenance programs, and achieve cooperation in other programs of mutual benefit.

Providing Basic Commercial Services Lacking in the Neighborhood. Most old urban neighborhoods are underserviced in terms of availability of basic goods and services. Treating the neighborhood essentially as a shopping center or district provides a way to analyze demand patterns, identify opportunities for new commercial activities, locate potential entrepreneurs, and assist in packaging and developing new business enterprises such as supermarkets, drug stores, junior department stores, hardware stores, etc.

Quality of Life Elements. A viable neighborhood economy should have interesting and entertaining commercial establishments such as restaurants, boutiques, and other shops, drawing heavily on the ethnic or cultural foundations in the neighborhood. These quality of life elements enhance life in the neighborhood and also attract customers from outside the neighborhood.

Involvement of Financial Institutions in the Local Economy. The local banks must play a central role in the revitalization process by providing loans to the merchants and property owners for rehabilitation and physical improvement. In most cases, banks are far more receptive to loan applications if they are properly packaged and part of a larger revitalization effort. For this reason, a local development organization should assist in individual business packaging and should help structure an overall development program. Its participation in establishing effective lines of communication between the financial institutions and the overall development effort can help assure an ongoing and mutually beneficial working relationship between the financial institutions and the local business community.

Upgrading the Employment Base in the Community. Except in very rare cases, the revitalization process will be severely limited if there is no expansion of the job base provided by the industrial sector. The city's overall economic development entity and community-based organizations should develop an active program to retain what industry is already in the neighborhood and to attract new industry by acquisition and relocation. In most cases, light assembly-type plants providing 50–70 jobs each are ideal for urban neighborhoods because they generally are nonpolluting and relatively labor intensive.

Community Sector

While the bulk of revitalization activity will come from the private sector, there are several aspects of the revitalization process in which community development organizations play a critical role. As part of their involvement in the planning process, community organizations must see that the economic revitalization program relates to, and supports, the overall neighborhood development program, especially as it pertains to land and physical development (e.g., housing) as well as to stability and neighborhood cohesion. Areas in which the community development organizations might be involved include the following.

Property Maintenance. Just as maintenance of commercial property is critical to the success of a commercial revitalization program, overall neighborhood revitalization requires physical maintenance and improvement programs for residential property. By working with homeowners, the development organization can assist in arranging for property improvement loans through local banks and savings and loan associations. The confidence generated on the part of lending institutions toward the economic revitalization program should be transferable into other areas of a neighborhood revitalization program, including housing and home improvement programs. Certainly the lines of communication and working relationship established by the development organization between the financial institutions and the community should result in a closer partnership in these areas.

Development of Land and Physical Resources. Neighborhood revitalization cannot occur without reference to the land and physical resource needs of the area. These needs include living and working space (housing and building construction and rehabilitation), social services (e.g., medical and educational facilities), and recreational opportunities (places of entertainment, sport and relaxation). In each of these areas there are obvious opportunities which a community development organization can help identify and package. Keep in mind that local ownership or oversight of these resources is a primary goal and requirement for neighborhood stabilization.

Local Ownership of Commercial Real Estate. To allow for greater local participation in neighborhood land use, programs can be developed to increase the local ownership of commercial and industrial real estate. The development organization can assist in the development of investment syndicates, organize property management companies, and recommend methods for improving the attractiveness and marketability of the commercial locations. It is also felt that broad-based community ownership of commercial real estate could improve the quality of maintenance and reduce vandalism.

However, these strategies and techniques regularly are neglected by economic planners. Moreover, the impacts of investments which improve the capacity of community-based economic development are not factored into traditional approaches to unemployment, joblessness and poverty. New, yet tested, opportunity-creating approaches are needed to promote community development as an alternative to welfare dependency. Research and demonstration projects in neighborhoods which are successfully revitalizing their commercial strips suggest the validity of the following neighborhood economic revitalization (NER) approach. This approach replicates ordinary entrepreneurial processes which take into account different variables in each neighborhood. It is structured around ordinary entrepreneurial processes so that performance can be measured by profit and loss and assessed by community satisfaction.

A Neighborhood Economic Revitalization Approach

There are four major steps in such an approach: 1) identification and capacity building; 2) development; 3) implementation; and 4) wrap-up. These steps parallel those a private developer/entrepreneur would take to revitalize a commercial strip.

1. Step one begins by focusing on a troubled but still robust neighborhood which includes a neighborhood commercial area. The neighborhood residents and their institutions, along with local businesses, financial organizations and city officials are organized to shape their future through the initiatives of energized local leaders. Local leaders often are assisted by small seed grants and professional neighborhood organizers. They begin a process of meeting local needs, addressing unfairness in public and private allocation of resources, and developing neighborhood confidence. At this point, a rudimentary plan of action is clear and a series of development sites and possibilities are proposed.

2. In step two, the development process, the leaders contract for a market analysis of the existing area, hire an architect or engineer to review the physical plans and environment, expand the staff organization if necessary, and coordinate funding allocations and availability. They also work with a planner, the city, businessmen and residents to draw up a plan for their area. Step three involves implementing the plan. The final step, wrap-up, includes grand opening ceremonies and management of the commercial operation.

The revitalization of an inner city commercial strip involves the same public and private sectors which led to its decline in the first place. The major task is revitalizing the spirit of these forces to bring about a concerted, comprehensive program for the total rehabilitation of the social, economic and physical environment.

The selection criteria used in the identification process are comparable to the ordinary entrepreneur's identification of a suitable market place. The economic revitalization of a community depends on the existence of a host of preconditions which ensure the profitable rebuilding. Profits must be measured not merely in cash flow balances of the merchants or cost benefits to city coffers, but also in the sense of place, dignity and freedom from fear of the inhabitants of the neighborhood. Initial and ongoing processes of community organizing and empowerment, leadership training and recruitment, as well as fashioning indigenous institutions to meet the challenges of rebuilding community cohesion, are needed to achieve optimum improvement.

Commercial revitalization will be most successful in an area where other programs for housing, crime control, jobs and health care exist. The ills of a ten to twenty year period of disinvestment cannot be cured piecemeal or quickly, even if all the people will it to happen. The pump can be primed with grant/subsidy dollars, but the successful operating cash flow mechanism for restoration of a neighborhood's life blood requires more dollars than it is politically possible to extract from the coffers of government. With an organized community, a series of coordinated programs and an active publicity campaign for communication between all sectors, the approach can operate successfully in the overall fabric for neighborhood economic revitalization.

The neighborhood economic revitalization approach will operate with few government controls or reviews, but it requires capital input at several points to ensure the successful capture of conventional funds. A careful balance, therefore, must be maintained between effective public control mechanisms and the allocation of limited public resources. It will take hard surveys and human energy for organizing groups into productive contributors in order to rebuild neighborhoods, cities and the nation; it is, therefore, important that local government be a sensitive, helping partner rather than a bureaucratic obstacle. Although it requires only a small amount of seed funds to begin the process, an astute organizer is needed to entice the initial capital investment which, in turn, is used to leverage other investments of capital. There are a number of sources of capital and matching capital funds, i.e. public and private sector funds, foundation funds, etc. An organization can afford to call in technical assistance to further its efforts at banding the neighborhood together, identifying revitalization processes and determining goals and objectives as some of these capital sources are identified and become available.

As a tool for the reversal of disinvestment in neighborhoods, the revitalization approach includes almost all applicable steps or activities necessary to affect reinvestment. It has taken at least ten to twelve years for neighborhood organizations in the inner city to coalesce, to identify themselves and their needs, and to learn the processes of reinvestment. This approach is an outgrowth of these decade-long efforts. Continued efforts of the sort and the consequent successful rebirth of inner cities for

all peoples who live and work there can be accomplished during the next two decades.

Conventional approaches to development could be operational in inner city sites if redlining by bankers and insurance companies were not a counterproductive factor. The Home Mortgage Disclosure Act, the Community Reinvestment Act as well as some features of the tax code are rudimentary incentives for recapitalizing jobless and poor areas. The perceptions of large-scale financial institutions should be refocused so that dependency and decline may be abated. Building or restoring the participation of banks, insurance companies and other investing institutions as trusting partners is thus a key factor in this approach. The political machinery and bureaucratic process should also be refocused so that the faith of all the parties concerned and affected by the process of revitalization can be restored. Most successful efforts towards revitalization are achieved by joint efforts of community residents and merchants acting in concert with public agencies and public and private sources of investment capital.

An important difference between this and conventional approaches is the nature of the "entrepreneur." From one decisive, profit-motivated individual this approach goes to a tripartite group of various vested (and often conflicting) interests. Whereas the conventional entrepreneur works almost singlehandedly and with single purpose of mind, in the neighborhood approach the entrepreneurial team must relate to a host of negative influences and obstructions. This challenges the simple-minded notion of the individualistic entrepreneurship which neglects the effects of positive and negative external factors and fails to see that the neighborhood is a micro-market and economic multiplier. In point of fact the use of the neighborhood approach has begun the reexamination of conventional wisdom and market trends.

Reinvestment in urban neighborhoods by ordinary entrepreneurial interests will probably accelerate. However, this action for justice through development is not an automatic mechanism. It must be catalyzed and assisted by public, private and community resources. These must be targeted toward local projects that increase the flow of reinvestment and market activity in neighborhoods and encourage the development of viable establishments which will increase the range and quality of goods and services available to the community.

Projects could accomplish such goals through various program components that:

- lend support to potential businesses that will employ neighborhood residents
- encourage an increase of local ownership and involvement in new businesses
- aid in making the commercial corridors more competitive with outside markets by supporting physical

development programs that will improve the appearance of and help stabilize the district

- support the establishment of a strong and active business association to organize cooperative advertising and promotional events
- encourage the involvement of community residents supporting and developing the direction and programs of the project.

Thus the process and the project of neighborhood revitalization includes more than invocation of wholesome values and symbols. The celebrated recover of squandered practices is mostly imagery. In most respects neighborhood revitalization is a complex contemporary artifice—a contemporary social economic invention. The measures of success proposed in this agenda are articulated and exercised by the persons involved. That the large-scale mechanism of cultural, economic and social formation ought to be attentive to the presence of the social fabric that constitutes the lived experience of urban neighborhoods is as important today as it was in the early 20th century. The record of that era is as uneven as it is today. The ongoing work of social and economic justice is a task for each generation and each period of immigration. Honest-to-experience recollection of the immigrant experience, ethnic social mobility and neighborhood decline are the pathway to normative and practical prescription about multi-cultural social formation and neighborhood development.

Critical Thinking

1. Discuss the dynamics of urbanization and the movement of people from their local forms of ethnic identity into more complex relations with others.

2. Discuss the formation of new communities and new bonds of loyalty that can be created by urban life.

3. What are the human challenges and adequate human responses to new, large-scale societies, economies, and politics?

Internet References

Comparative Migration Studies
   www.comparativemigrationstudies.com
The Council for Research in Values and Philosophy
   www.crvp.org
The National Neighborhood Coalition
   www.neighborhoodcoalition.org
National Neighbors
   www.ncrc.org
